Marketing
Management

Kenneth E. Clow would like to dedicate this book to his wife, Susan,
who has been so supportive and to his sons, Dallas, Wes, Tim, and Roy.

Donald Baack would like to dedicate his efforts and contributions to this book to the
memory of his father, Rev. Edward R. Baack, to his mother, Martha Jean Baack, and to his wife, Pamela.

Marketing Management
A Customer-Oriented Approach

Kenneth E. Clow
University of Louisiana at Monroe

Donald Baack
Pittsburg State University

Los Angeles | London | New Delhi
Singapore | Washington DC

For information:

SAGE Publications, Inc.
2455 Teller Road
Thousand Oaks, California 91320
E-mail: order@sagepub.com

SAGE Publications Ltd.
1 Oliver's Yard
55 City Road
London EC1Y 1SP
United Kingdom

SAGE Publications India Pvt. Ltd.
B 1/I 1 Mohan Cooperative Industrial Area
Mathura Road, New Delhi 110 044
India

SAGE Publications Asia-Pacific Pte. Ltd.
33 Pekin Street #02-01
Far East Square
Singapore 048763

Printed in Canada

Library of Congress Cataloging-in-Publication Data

Clow, Kenneth E.
Marketing management: A customer-oriented approach/Kenneth E. Clow, Donald Baack.
    p. cm.
Includes bibliographical references and index.
ISBN 978-1-4129-6312-1 (cloth)
    1. Marketing—Management. I. Baack, Donald. II. Title.

HF5415.13.C57 2010
658.8—dc22   2009021715

Printed on acid-free paper.

09 10 11 12 13 10 9 8 7 6 5 4 3 2 1

Acquiring Editor:	Lisa Cuevas Shaw
Associate Editor:	Deya Saoud
Editorial Assistant:	MaryAnn Vail
Production Editor:	Sarah K. Quesenberry
Copy Editor:	QuADS Prepress (P) Ltd.
Proofreader:	Christina West
Typesetter:	C&M Digitals (P) Ltd.
Cover Designer:	Glenn Vogel
Marketing Manager:	Christy Guilbault

Brief Contents

Detailed Contents

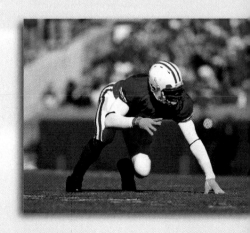

Chapter 3: Data Warehousing   57

Chapter 4: Building a Customer-Oriented Marketing Department   81

PART 2: MANAGING CUSTOMER ACQUISITION   110

Chapter 5: Customer Acquisition Strategies and Tactics   113

Chapter 6: Pricing   137

Chapter 9: Personal Selling   223

PART 3: MANAGING CUSTOMER INTERACTIONS   252

Chapter 10: Internal Communications   255

Chapter 11: External Communications   281

Chapter 12: Distribution and Supply Chain Management   309

Chapter 13: Web Site and Internet Management   339

PART IV: MANAGING CUSTOMER RETENTION   364

Chapter 14: Customer Retention and Recovery   367

Chapter 15: Marketing Control   395

Preface

"The only thing constant in life is change." This famous quote, generally attributed to the French philosopher François de la Rochefoucauld, seems custom-made for marketing. Clearly the field is changing. New technologies, economic shifts, emerging social trends, and many other forces make marketing one of the most interesting and volatile career choices possible.

We developed *Marketing Management: A Customer-Oriented Approach* because we concluded that the methods used to teach today's emerging marketing professionals should change. Further, we believe that the texts currently available do not meet the needs of the majority of students enrolled in the marketing management capstone course required for most marketing majors. Toward that end, this book features four themes that make it distinct from other books and more useful to marketing students. These are

1. strongly emphasizing customer service,
2. focusing on entry-level and first-line supervisory positions,
3. carefully integrating the disciplines of marketing and management, and
4. incorporation of statistical methodologies and approaches.

First, then, as the book title notes, we offer *a continuing focus on customer orientation* in every chapter. In today's economy, competitive forces emerge from many sectors, including alternative products, companies, industries, and even firms in other countries. One popular response, featured in many marketing textbooks, is a strong emphasis on branding. While we agree that a powerful brand helps a firm maintain a strong position in the marketplace, the interactions with the company itself, through the many contact points that exist, provide major opportunities to foster another type of loyalty; one based on quality human relationships.

One the front lines of those face-to-face and media-based communications are individual employees. Much of the time, these people are entry-level workers, supervised by recent college graduates who have just been promoted into lower-level management. Consequently, the second major difference in our approach is an emphasis on the tasks and challenges associated with those types of positions. While marketing strategies and tactics cannot be ignored in a capstone marketing management course, we have shifted the emphasis to *entry-level and first-line supervisor employment* situations. This should be helpful to college seniors about to begin their careers as well as those currently serving in such positions.

The third major novel feature of this textbook is a more powerful *integration of the fields of marketing and management*. While there are separate presentations of both fields in various places in the text, the primary emphasis is pointing out managerial applications of marketing tactics and practices throughout the entire book, both in the subject matter itself and in the end-of-chapter materials. Many textbooks do not address this type of combination of disciplines in any meaningful way. Our backgrounds as professors of marketing (Clow) and management (Baack) place us in a unique position to offer a more integrated approach.

Fourth, this textbook features numerous *statistical, mathematical, and numbers-based analytical methods* where they are relevant. Many students may find that they will be expected to use these and other formulas as part of the process of developing and assessing marketing programs. Consequently, we have included calculations of customer lifetime values, RFM scores, contribution margins, break-even points, regressions, and other formulas both in the text and in end-of-chapter assignments.

These four points of emphasis are presented using a framework that provides numerous real-world examples, applications, and learning exercises. The chapters feature firms as small as a local bookstore or an ice cream parlor and as large as Southwest Airlines and IBM. We also tried to include both well-known and unusual types of companies, including an online retail company (Zappos), a minor league baseball team (Round Rock Express), and movie distribution systems on one side, and Maybelline, LensCrafters, and Kraft on the other. The purpose is to make the book fun to read and filled with illustrative and interesting cases.

Key Features

This textbook was designed to help students learn, understand, and apply the concepts, theories, formulas, and ideas presented. A variety of methods are used to reach this goal. Each has a special purpose that addresses a component of learning.

Opening Vignettes

Each chapter begins with a lead-in vignette that in some way corresponds with the topics presented in that chapter. Almost all of them are oriented to success stories across a variety of industries. These include vignettes about Costco, Aflac (the American Family Life Assurance Company of Columbus), Smucker's, and INSIGHT, Inc. Other vignettes feature companies encountering various challenges. Thus, the recent charges against Southwest Airlines regarding the company's failure to carefully address safety issues opens Chapter 1; the difficult marketplace being approached by Vonage is found in another chapter; and the challenges associated with trying to tackle mainstays such as Gatorade are described in the vignette titled "Electrolyte Nation."

Stop and Think Features

Two Stop and Think boxes are placed in each chapter. These exercises ask students to consider the materials they have just read and apply them to a company or product. The objective is to assist in immediate learning and application. Many of the boxes also pose questions about the ethical ramifications of a given situation and action.

Visuals

To make the reading move smoothly, we use charts, tables, and figures, where relevant, to enhance materials in each part. Also, photographs and figures have been added to make the pages flow and to maintain reader interest.

YourCareer

At the conclusion of every chapter, the YourCareer feature addresses students entering marketing careers in several ways. First, some are devoted to explaining the types of jobs students may take upon graduation. Second, seven of the features highlight the careers of newly minted (most of them 7 years or less) graduates who have achieved success. Each explains the positions they currently hold, along with some of the challenges they encountered following that first promotion. The third type of YourCareer feature offers tangible tips about how to do well in a marketing career.

Chapter Terms

Every term presented in bold is defined in the place where it appears in the chapter. This helps students to both review the chapter and reexamine the terms to make sure they understand them.

Review Questions

One method students can use to quickly summarize what they have read in the chapter is to answer the review questions. These items are presented in the order in which chapter concepts have been presented. They are designed to highlight the primary points and concepts, along with some definitions, that have been offered in the chapter.

Customer Corner

Each Customer Corner presents a specific incident or circumstance requiring a response from a marketing manager. These short stories focus on customer service as it pertains to first-line supervisors and entry-level employees. These application exercises go beyond remembering materials to using them in various situations, many of which were real-life experiences of the authors or their friends.

Discussion and Critical Thinking Questions

These items can be used for individual analyses of marketing management concepts or to guide in-class conversations. Some of the questions require students to apply the mathematical and statistical models and formulas they have seen in the chapters.

Chapter Case

Each chapter concludes with a short case designed to illustrate the major concepts in the chapter. The cases cover a variety of companies and circumstances, from small, single-person operations to major corporations. Each poses a series of questions tying the case to key concepts and materials.

Comprehensive Cases

At the end of the text are eight comprehensive cases featuring a variety of companies and products. The cases are designed to challenge students' abilities. They require an in-depth analysis and synthesis of the case material with textbook materials. Students then must derive the marketing problem faced by the company and a feasible approach for the future. Prior to the cases is a section on how to prepare a case and the types of material that should be presented in each section of the analysis.

Resources for Professors

One of our goals in creating this textbook is to help professors augment what is written in each chapter with additional teaching resources. To make sure that these items seamlessly mesh with what is presented in the textbook, we have prepared the majority of them ourselves. Further, SAGE offers additional materials that give professors a rich variety of teaching resources. The total package for this book includes the following on a password-protected Web site. Go to **www.sagepub.com/clow** to access the site.

Instructor's Manual

The manual provides an in-depth outline of each chapter that can be used as a guide for lectures. Questions that can be posed to students in class regarding concepts and companies are provided in each section. Answers and suggestions for discussion are provided for each question posed in the Stop and Think boxes.

Solutions to End-of-Chapter Materials

The end-of-chapter materials include the review questions, customer corner, discussion and critical thinking exercises, and the short case. Basic answers to all the questions are provided, except in the cases where no one specific answer may be given. Questions that also would be useful for in-class discussion are highlighted.

Additional Instructor's Resources

The instructor portion of the Web site features additional resources including: chapter-specific PowerPoint slides; suggested course projects, classroom activities, and discussion questions; links to marketing-related videos; reading suggestions; and sample syllabi. A section on marketing plan creation includes samples and templates that instructors can provide to their students.

Test Bank

The test bank consists of true/false, multiple-choice, and short- and long-essay questions. Answers to these are provided along with the corresponding page numbers in text. The questions range from simple memory exercises to those requiring more sophisticated thought processes and answers. The test bank is available with Diploma computerized testing software on CD-ROM. Word files of the test bank are provided on the password-protected Web site.

Resources for Students

To maximize students' comprehension of this material, as well as to provide them with the critical-thinking skills they need to be successful in future careers in marketing, we have provided the following student resources. These are available on the open-access portion of **www.sagepub.com/clow.**

- Electronic flashcards that students can use to review key terms and concepts
- Study quizzes consisting of multiple-choice and true/false questions that students can use to practice for exams
- Internet resources and exercises, which help students delve deeper into the material and examples included in the text
- SAGE journal articles with discussion questions provide access to recent, relevant articles from leading journals, along with critical thinking questions that ask students to reflect on their reading
- Information about and directions for creating a marketing plan, along with samples and templates

Acknowledgments

There are many persons who have assisted us in the development of this textbook. We would like to thank the various editors at SAGE who have been part of the process, including Al Bruckner and Lisa Shaw, both of whom serve as executive editors. We are very grateful to Deya Saoud for her editorial work on this project. Our thanks to MaryAnn Vail, who helped us at several points along the way.

We would like to thank the following individuals who assisted in the preparation of the manuscript through their careful and thoughtful reviews:

David Arnold, Loyola Marymount University

David Aron, Dominican University

Gerard Athaide, Loyola University Maryland

Connie Bateman, University of North Dakota

Parimal Bhagat, Indiana University of Pennsylvania

Karen Burger, Pace University

Debbie Campbell, Temple University

William Carroll, St. John's University

E. Vincent Carter, California State University, Bakersfield

Patricia Clarke, Boston College

Jim Curran, University of South Florida Sarasota-Manatee

Timothy Donahue, Chadron State College

Sujay Dutta, Wayne State University

Alexander Edsel, University Texas at Dallas

Sunil Erevelles, University of North Carolina Charlotte

Gordon Flanders, University of Montana

Fred H. Fusting, Loyola University Maryland

Michael Gravier, Bryant University

Albert N. Greco, Fordham University

Joel Herche, University of the Pacific

Steven C. Huff, Brigham Young University

John Hulland, University of Pittsburgh

Kate Karniouchina, Chapman University

Dale Kehr, University of Memphis

Douglas Leister, Howard University

Avinash Malshe, University of St. Thomas

Alan Malter, University of Illinois at Chicago

David Mick, University of Virginia

Lynn Murray, Pittsburg State University

Vivek Natarajan, Lamar University

Charles Noble, University of Mississippi

Louis I. Nzegwu, Univeristy of Wisconsin—Platteville

James Oakley, University of North Carolina at Charlotte

Nikolai Ostapenko, University of the District of Columbia

Elizabeth Purinton-Johnson, Marist College

Alfred Quinton, The College of New Jersey

Sandra Rahman, Framingham State College

Adam Rapp, Clemson University

Joseph Redden, University of Minnesota

Ron Rex, Colorado Christian University

Dan Rice, Louisiana State University

Richard Rocco, DePaul University

Gaia Rubera, Michigan State University

Amit Sani, University of Nebraska - Lincoln

Daniel Sersland, Auburn University

Deb Skinner, Butler University

Prashant Srivastava, The University of Akron

Sven Tuzovic, Pacific Lutheran University

Yong Wang, Ohio University

Qiyu Zhang, Loyola University Maryland

Finally, Kenneth Clow would like to thank many individuals at the University of Louisiana at Monroe who continue to provide an exciting and accommodating work environment. He would also like to thank his sons Dallas, Wes, Tim, and Roy, who offer continuing encouragement and support.

Donald Baack would like to thank his department chair, Eric Harris, for his aid and advice. He also appreciates the help given by Paula Palmer as administrative assistant to the department, as well as the student workers who make everyday life easier. He would also like to acknowledge the support of his children, Jessica, Dan, and David.

We would like to especially thank our wives, Susan Clow and Pam Baack, for being patient and understanding during those times when the work seemed monumental. They have been enthusiastic and supportive for many, many years.

About the Authors

Kenneth E. Clow is a professor of marketing and holds the Biedenharn Endowed Chair of Business in the College of Business Administration at the University of Louisiana at Monroe. Previously, he served as dean at both the University of Louisiana at Monroe and the University of North Carolina at Pembroke. His teaching career began at Pittsburg State University, where he also served as the MBA director. He has published a total of 190 articles in academic journals and proceedings and has written 13 textbooks. He has published articles in journals such as *Journal of Services Marketing; Services Marketing Quarterly; Journal of Business Research; Marketing Management Journal; Journal of Economics and Finance Education; International Journal of Business, Marketing, and Decision Sciences; Journal of Internet Commerce; Health Marketing Quarterly;* and *Journal of Restaurant and Foodservices Marketing.* Books coauthored by him include *Integrated Advertising, Promotion, and Marketing Communications* (fourth edition), *Concise Encyclopedia of Advertising, Essentials of Marketing* (third edition), *Services Marketing* (second edition), *Concise Encyclopedia of Professional Services Marketing,* and *The IMC PlanPro Handbook.* Prior to earning his doctorate, he owned and operated a commercial cleaning service in Joplin, Missouri, and Fayetteville, Arkansas. He started as a sole employee, and the company grew to become one of the largest cleaning services in Northwest Arkansas, with 40 employees. He obtained his PhD from the University of Arkansas in 1992. He is married to Susan and has four sons, Dallas, Wes, Tim, and Roy.

Donald Baack holds the rank of University Professor of Management at Pittsburg (Kansas) State University, where he has taught since 1988. He previously held positions at Southwest Missouri State University, Missouri Southern State College, and Dana College. He is a consulting editor for the *Journal of Managerial Issues* and has published in the journal. He has also published in *Human Relations, Journal of High Technology Management Research, Journal of Ministry Marketing and Management, Journal of Management Inquiry, Journal of Customer Service in Marketing, Journal of Professional Services Marketing, Journal of Global Awareness, Journal of Business Ethics, Journal of Euromarketing, Journal of Nonprofit and Public Sector Marketing,* and *Journal of Advertising Research.* He has authored *Organizational Behavior, International Business,* and *Integrated Advertising, Promotion, and Marketing Communications* (coauthor to Kenneth D. Clow). Clow and Baack also wrote the *Concise Encyclopedia of Advertising.* Baack and his son Daniel W. Baack recently prepared a series of 10 modules titled *Ethics Across the Curriculum.* He has also published three popular press books in the area of romance/self-help. He has been active in the Southwest Academy of Management for many years, serving as its president in 1996. He was nominated for SWAM's Distinguished Educator award in 2007 and 2008. He received his PhD from the University of Nebraska in 1987. His primary area of study was organization and management theory. He is married to Pamela and has three children and eight grandchildren.

part 1

Marketing Foundation

How has Southwest Airlines been able to keep passengers happy while other carriers have struggled?

chapter 1

The Nature of Marketing Management

Southwest Airlines: Fun, Profit, Customer Satisfaction, and a Major Bump in the Road

In 2008, Southwest Airlines was charged by the Federal Aviation Administration (FAA) with "failing to follow rules that are designed to protect passengers and crew," according to Nicholas A. Sabatini, the FAA's associate administrator for aviation safety, in a written statement. The complaint documents were prepared by two FAA safety inspectors who requested whistle-blower status and legal protection.

The inspectors reported that FAA managers knew about the lapse in safety at Southwest but decided to allow the airline to conduct

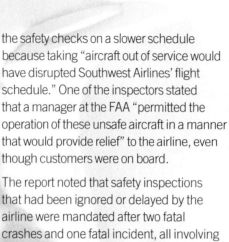

the safety checks on a slower schedule because taking "aircraft out of service would have disrupted Southwest Airlines' flight schedule." One of the inspectors stated that a manager at the FAA "permitted the operation of these unsafe aircraft in a manner that would provide relief" to the airline, even though customers were on board.

The report noted that safety inspections that had been ignored or delayed by the airline were mandated after two fatal crashes and one fatal incident, all involving Boeing's 737, the only type of airplane Southwest flies. Although the incidents were not on Southwest flights, there was reason for concern. Documents revealed that 70 Southwest jets were allowed to fly past the deadline for the mandatory rudder inspections. The complaint also stated that 47 more Southwest jets kept flying after missing deadlines for inspections for cracks in the planes' fuselage, or "skin."

An inspector discovered that dozens of planes had missed mandatory inspection deadlines. The FAA charged that Southwest operated 46 Boeing 737s on nearly 60,000 flights between June 2006 and March 2007 while failing to comply with an FAA directive that requires repeated checks of fuselage areas to detect fatigue cracking.

The FAA also initiated an action to seek a $10.2 million civil penalty against Southwest. The complaint alleged that the company operated 46 airplanes without conducting mandatory checks for fuselage cracking. These same types of cracks had been associated with airline crashes and problems in several instances.

The airline's management team prepared the following response: "Southwest Airlines discovered the missed inspection area, disclosed it to the FAA, and promptly reinspected all potentially affected aircraft in March 2007. The FAA approved our actions and considered the matter closed as of April 2007." The company's leaders also promised full cooperation with the investigation.[1]

These incidents were the first major bump in the road for a company that had

enjoyed nearly legendary status for being efficient, employee friendly, and customer oriented. In fact, in 2007, Southwest's customer satisfaction rating was at the top and had increased from the previous year's rating. This was in spite of a shifting environment, one in which the number of passengers continued to rise while customer satisfaction had been dropping at an alarming rate.

The most common customer complaints focus on flight delays, overbooked planes, and an endless variety of problems with service personnel. Baggage is lost and agents are uncaring, unsympathetic, or even rude. Flying has become, for many, an ordeal. In fact, a new term, "air rage," has become part of the vocabulary of airline travel.

How had Southwest been able to succeed at keeping people happy while other carriers struggled? "We've done as well as we have up to date by making sure our customers have a rich experience, and that's largely due to our people," said Beth Harbin, a spokeswoman for Southwest, which also is one of the few consistently profitable airlines.

The Southwest experience touches every part of the organization. Employees are recruited and selected based on characteristics such as being positive and energetic, with a genuine desire to serve. A sense of humor helps. The company hosts what are, in essence, pep rallies for the work force to improve morale and build cooperation.

At each "turnaround" (the time spent preparing a plane for its next flight after arrival), everyone from gate agents to the flight captain descends on the plane cabin to help with cleanup and prepare the plane for reloading. Team spirit is a key component.

The advertising and promotions programs at Southwest are the industry standard. Light-hearted and memorable ads feature the ongoing tagline, "You are now free to move about the country." To make this possible, the Southwest Web site is simple to understand and navigate. Purchases can be made quickly and easily for regular tickets, discounts, specials, and other flights are available through the Southwest "Ding" program. Southwest gift certificates are another new feature.

Southwest only flies one type of plane. This allows the maintenance team to specialize in repairs and upkeep. It also creates a more uniform traveling experience for customers. Southwest has long been known for its seating programs that are designed to get passengers on board quickly and efficiently. Meals are not served on flights, only a small snack and soft drink. Each step of the process appeals to the no-frills crowd. Price is one major consideration, convenience a

second, but the overriding goal is to make the travel experience as pleasant as possible. Recently, Southwest upgraded the actual seats on each plane to make them more comfortable.

For many years, the company culture of Southwest was one of the organization's major advantages. The lessons provided by its original owner, Herb Kelleher, would apply to any organization seeking to build and maintain a solid customer base. Time will tell if the customer loyalty that had been built over several decades would carry Southwest through a period of negative publicity and concerns about the carrier's commitment to customer safety.[2]

Chapter Overview

Marketing involves providing goods and services for customers at the right time, at the right place, at the best price, and with the highest possible quality. While this may sound easy, it has become increasingly difficult. Why? First, each competitor strives to do the same thing. Maintaining an edge becomes difficult. Second, buyer needs and wants change over time. This means company leaders and marketing personnel must constantly keep in touch with customers, with prospective customers, and with what occurs in the environment.

The field of marketing continues to change, as many new challenges and issues emerge each year. Along with increasing competition, the influence of technology, shifts in media preferences among consumers, growing customer uncertainty about safety in the world, frustrations with product and service quality as well as anger over defective goods, difficult financial circumstances, and a fast-paced communication network in which negative rumors about a firm can quickly drive it to ruin, the marketing department and those who lead that unit struggle to keep a company moving forward.

This textbook examines the field of marketing management. The goal is to help students prepare for careers in the field of marketing. In this first chapter, the nature of marketing management is described, along with a review of the basic principles of both marketing and management. The second section highlights *BusinessWeek's* "customer service champs." The "champs" are companies that excel at providing excellent customer service. The final section of this chapter provides a review of the materials presented in the rest of this textbook.

The Nature of Marketing Management

The term marketing management refers to two separate but related items. First, marketing management is a common name for a capstone course presented to students with either a major or a concentration in marketing. The course should be designed to help a student integrate business and marketing concepts to better prepare that individual to join the work force. These students are the main audience for this textbook.

For many, the first job following graduation will be as an entry-level manager or manager trainee in some aspect of marketing, such as in-house or business-to-business sales, advertising,

marketing research, promotions, or e-commerce. These people will be on the front lines of a firm's marketing efforts and will encounter the shifting marketing environment first hand.

Consequently, this book considers the perspectives of entry-level to midlevel marketing professionals rather than focusing primarily on top-level management concerns. The rationale for this approach is to help prepare students for marketing careers by featuring information that pertains to that first job or after a promotion to a management position within a marketing department.

Marketing management also describes a business process. In this context, marketing management is the process of managing the marketing activities in a profit-seeking or nonprofit organization at the supervisory, midlevel management, and executive levels. Marketing Management is a combination of the concepts present in the fields of marketing and management that must be truly integrated by any supervisor, leader, or executive in order to achieve success.

Both audiences (students taking the marketing management course and practicing managers in the field) should have something in common: an interest in customers. The text emphasizes customers and customer satisfaction. A business cannot exist without clients and customers. The same holds true for nonprofit organizations and government entities. It is vital, therefore, to describe managing a marketing department based on relationships with customers and to examine the potential impact each decision may have on consumers and clients.

This textbook was written to help students like Kylie prepare for entry-level marketing positions on graduation.

The Fields of Marketing and Management

As the name implies, marketing management combines the fields of marketing and management. A brief review of these fields indicates how the two can be integrated to help leaders at all levels in the company complete various tasks. To do so, the field of marketing is described first, followed by management.

Marketing

Most experts in the field would agree that a marketing program should be driven by customers, whether it is a for-profit business, a nonprofit, or a governmental organization. In each type, "customers" represents the individuals served by the organization. A company or organization must understand, reach, and satisfy customers in order to achieve the sales needed to stay in business.

In 2007, the American Marketing Association (AMA) created the following definition: "Marketing is the activity, set of institutions, and processes for creating, communicating, delivering, and exchanging offerings that have value for customers, clients, partners, and society at large." This definition suggests that the goal of marketing should be to develop relationships with an organization's customers and other publics. To do so, the many elements of a marketing program are brought together into an integrated program. A more traditional definition of marketing has been:

1. Discovering consumer needs and wants
2. Creating the goods and services that meet those needs and wants
3. Pricing, promoting, and delivering the goods and services

Using this definition, the first element of marketing is to understand consumer needs and wants. The foundation of any marketing management program consists of clearly identifying groups of consumers that share a common desire for a good or service. Only then can the goods or services be created and sold. In the field of marketing, the most common topics are those implied by the definition (see Figure 1.1). Thus, the six major subjects are

- markets,
- products,
- prices,
- places (distribution systems),
- promotion, and
- people.

Markets consist of people (or businesses) with wants and needs, financial resources, and the willingness to spend resources to satisfy those wants and needs. The most common method used to discover individual markets is to divide them into various consumer and business-to-business segments. Table 1.1 lists some of the major variables used to identify market segments.

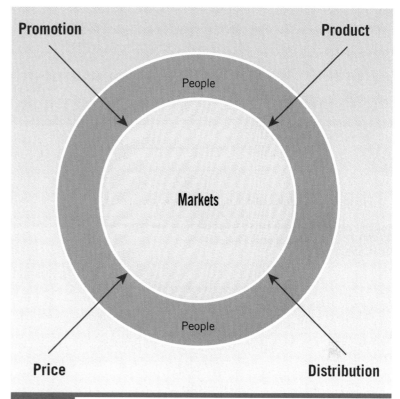

Figure 1.1 | The Field of Marketing

Products are the physical goods sold to consumers and other organizations as well as services that are offered to individual consumers, other businesses, and the government (see Figure 1.2). Physical goods include both durable goods that last more than 1 year and nondurable goods with shorter uses. Nondurable goods include convenience items, shopping goods, and specialty products. Convenience items consist of frequently purchased products that typically feature low prices. Shopping goods require some level of effort by consumers to make choices and purchases. Specialty products are sold at unique outlets and require a more concerted effort by the individual consumer to find them and purchase them.

Durable goods are sold to both consumers and businesses. Durable goods include those that are renewable, such as products created from agriculture, fishing, forestry, or other sources

Type of Market	Segmentation Variable	Examples
Consumer market	Demographic	Gender, age, income, education
	Psychographic	Lifestyles, values, activities, interests, opinions
	Geographic	City, county, state, region, country
	Behavioral	Benefit, usage rate, user status, occasion
Business-to-business market	Industry	NAICS code, type of industry, type of product
	Geographic	City, county, state, region, country
	Behavioral	Product usage, usage rate, usage occasion, order size

Table 1.1 | Common Segmentation Strategies Used in Consumer and Business Markets

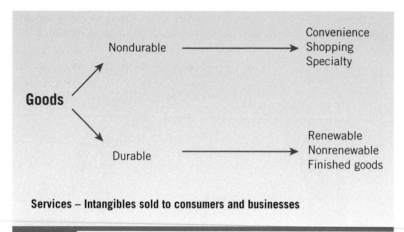

Services – Intangibles sold to consumers and businesses

Figure 1.2 Classification of Products

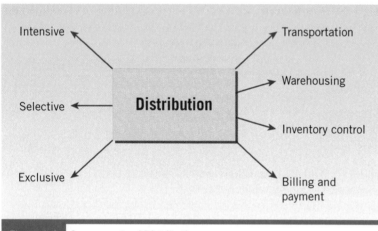

Figure 1.3 Components of Distribution

that can regenerate (solar energy). Nonrenewable durable goods are taken from the earth and cannot be replaced. Nonrenewable goods are found in mining and drilling processes. Some durable goods are the raw materials that become part of a firm's production process. Other durable goods are created to become parts of other products, such as boards, nails, and sheets of metal. A third set of durable goods includes finished products, including items such as photocopy machines for businesses and appliances for consumers.

Services consist of the intangible items that are sold to others. Typical services are associated with banking, finance, insurance, credit, transportation, leisure, travel, entertainment, and personal services such as hair styling. Services may be offered to individual consumers, to other businesses, and to the government.

Prices of goods and services are normally based on (1) costs, (2) demand and supply, (3) competition, and (4) profit goals. When a new good or service is developed, the company's leaders typically decide to use *skimming,* where the price charged is as high as possible, or *penetration* pricing, where the price is set as low as the firm can afford. Skimming helps to quickly recover product development costs. The goal of penetration pricing is to quickly capture a large market share and make the market less attractive to potential competitors. Over time, prices tend to move toward an equilibrium in which the level of quality or exclusivity offered in a good or service differentiates the competition. Pricing includes both setting prices and developing methods to discount those prices.

Place, or *distribution,* involves deciding where, how, and when products will be made available to potential customers (see Figure 1.3). It includes making a decision about the type of distribution approach to be used: intensive, selective, or exclusive. *Intensive distribution* means selling the product in every available location. It is often associated with convenience goods. *Selective distribution* means placing products in outlets that are believed to be profitable or project a certain image and not using other outlets. *Exclusive distribution* restricts the availability of the product to a highly select group of outlets, normally only one per geographic region.

The second activity associated with distribution is the physical distribution program. The tasks involved include choosing methods of transportation, types of warehouses, forms of inventory control, and methods of billing and payment.

A major component of marketing is promotion, which consists of creating the advertising programs, consumer and trade promotions programs, personal selling tactics, and supporting public relations efforts. The most recent trend in promotion involves carefully integrating all these elements into an *integrated marketing communications* plan.[3] Promotional activities have been strongly influenced by the availability of new alternative media outlets. Traditional advertising and promotional programs have been adapted in response to new technologies and new methods of making contact with customers.

Furniture is a shopping good and a durable good.

The final, and perhaps most critical, component of effective marketing is people. In a service company, the people performing the service make or break the business. To a manufacturer of goods, the people who operate the machines, deliver the products, and design the marketing program are the key. In a nonprofit operation, it is the people providing the services to the public along with the volunteers who make the organization successful. Without people, an organization cannot continue to survive.

In recent years, customer satisfaction and customer retention have received a great deal of attention. Numerous articles and books focus on what a company or organization should do to achieve customer satisfaction and customer retention, most of which can be summarized by these words: *product quality and customer service*. Without product quality, there will be no customer satisfaction and no customer retention. Without customer service, the importance of product quality quickly diminishes.

Beyond the emphasis on customers and customer satisfaction, the field of marketing has been strongly affected by three other trends (see Figure 1.4). Recently, an emphasis on the company's *brand* has emerged. Brand development, enhancement, and management receive a great deal of attention from marketing professionals at all levels of the organization.

Another trend affecting marketing is the *influence of the Internet* on all marketing activities. Company leaders are aware of not only the firm's e-commerce program but also recognize that blogging and other informal communication networks can affect perceptions of the firm and its brands. Internet and Web site management have become critical ingredients in today's marketing programs.

Finally, the *internationalization* or *global competition* aspects of marketing create powerful new challenges. The Internet and newly sophisticated distributions systems mean competition

- Emphasis on customers and customer satisfaction
- Emphasis on branding
- Influence of the Internet
- Internationalization and global competition

Figure 1.4

Current Trends Affecting Marketing

emerges not only from the company down the street but also from organizations around the world.

Marketing professionals continually adapt to a changing environment, shifting consumer tastes and preferences, and new technologies. Taking advantage of the tools from the field of management assists marketing managers in meeting these challenges.

Management

One of the frustrations present in the study of management is that there is little agreement on a precise definition of the field. One simple approach suggests that management is the process of getting things done through other people. The typical distinction to be made is between "doing" and "managing." Doing means "doing things yourself." Often, a person will be promoted into a supervisory role because she is the most technically talented individual in the department. The tendency, then, is to want to "do" everything rather than to help others succeed. Managing consists of the ability to help others get things done and to improve their skills.[4]

A standard management program includes five basic functions. Each will be performed by people at every rank, from first-line supervisors to top-level executives. As illustrated in Figure 1.5, the five functions of management are: planning, organizing, staffing, directing, and control.

Planning outlines a course of action for the future. Plans are made in three time horizons. The first, the short term, consists of plans with an impact of 1 year or less. Short term plans are often called *operational plans*. Second, medium-range tactics cover the time period of 1 to 3 years. Third, long-range strategies have an impact of 3 years or more. The plans made for each time period must mesh with and support plans made in the other two areas. Plans are made and carried out by managers at all levels of the company.

Plans are created by first assessing the company's environment, where managers seek to identify opportunities and threats that exist. Next, the management team examines internal company strengths and weaknesses. Managers also study forecasts to help make planning decisions. Forecasts are created to predict future economic conditions, company sales, and changes in technology. Third, managers make planning decisions, where they choose what to do and what not to do. Part of decision making includes eliminating options that are not best for the firm. Fourth, actual plans are written for each of the time horizons. Finally, planning becomes complete when goals and standards are established. These standards spell out success criteria.

Organizing combines people and resources to make goods and services. Organizing consists of three activities: (1) job design, (2) departmentation or departmentalization, and (3) drawing lines of authority and responsibility. Job design is the process of assigning tasks to individual jobs, making sure every activity that must take place is consigned to one specific job or another. Departmentation means placing jobs into individual departments, such as the production department, marketing department, accounting department, quality control department, and others.

When lines of authority and responsibility are drawn, the company has an *organizational chart* that specifies the rank of every position in the company, from entry-level employee to chief executive officer. Authority includes the right to direct the activities of others and to make decisions. Responsibility means being held accountable to get things done correctly and exercising authority fairly.

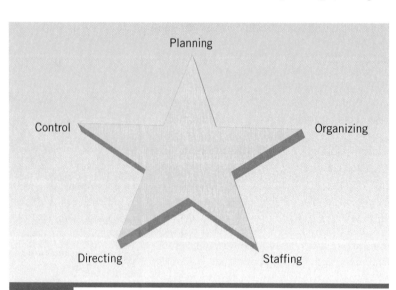

Figure 1.5   The Functions of Management

Once hired, employees require direction in order to achieve high levels of performance.

Staffing consists of attaining and preparing quality employees. Staffing often may be referred to as the human resources management department or function. It consists of everything from making plans about future personnel needs, to recruiting, selecting, training, and compensating workers. Human resources also involves conducting performance reviews, enforcing discipline systems and safety rules, helping employees manage careers, and coordinating management efforts in union-management relationships.

Directing is also called *actuating* and involves seeking to achieve the highest levels of performance. Directing includes teaching, motivating, leading, communication, and working with teams and groups. Directing reflects the people side of business.

The control process consists of comparing performance to standards, making corrections when needed, and rewarding success. Control occurs at three levels: (1) individual, or the performance appraisal process, (2) departmental, and (3) companywide performance. Two major areas are the focus of control systems. The first is identifying problem areas and finding ways to respond. The second is making sure that individuals, departments, and company leaders are rewarded when they set standards and then achieve those goals.[5]

Two of the issues that have changed the nature of marketing have also affected the field of management in profound ways. The first is the *emergence of the Internet*. Planning systems, distribution systems, organizational-design issues, and control systems have all been affected by the speed and precision the Internet offers.

The second topic is *internationalization* and *globalization*. Many large firms are no longer tied to a single country. Instead, multinational firms are a major factor in both local and global economies. Management systems should adjust to various cultures around the world. The impact of globalization reaches all of the planning, organizing, staffing, directing, and control functions.

Marketing strategies

↓

Marketing tactics

↓

Operational plans

The Marketing
Management Process

Marketing and Management Issues

When marketing ideas are combined with management tactics, several terms and ideas emerge, which are illustrated in Figure 1.6. In the area of planning, **marketing strategies** are the broad, sweeping plans based on a company's mission. They provide the most general direction for the marketing department. Marketing strategies outline the products to be sold as well as the target markets for those products. From a strategic perspective, consider the efforts associated with the Mountain Dew brand. Each product in the line reflects the goal of creating a high-energy drink aimed at younger consumers. Everything from the product itself, to advertising and promotional programs, to new product introductions revolves around the same strategic vantage point.

Marketing tactics are based on marketing strategies. **Marketing tactics** feature all the mid-range or medium-term (1 to 3 years) efforts designed to support marketing strategies. Many product design issues are tactical issues. Numerous products will be revised on a 3-year cycle. For example, shaving razors are redesigned about every 3 years. Gillette's products can be tracked from the days when a razor was a double-edged device, to disposable razors, then two-bladed, three-bladed, four-bladed, and currently five-bladed shaving instruments. Tactics include changing the product's packaging or label, revising or creating new advertising taglines, and improving the methods used to support promotional efforts. While most midlevel marketing managers will not be involved in developing marketing strategies, they are heavily engaged in creating and implementing marketing tactics.

Operational plans, or *short-term plans*, are created to carry out marketing strategies and tactics. They include plans for the day-by-day activities of the marketing department. Typical short-terms plans are departmental budgets, projects, and programs. A *budget* represents a financial map of how funds will be acquired (sales, payments, selling stocks and bonds, loans) and how funds will be spent. The budget spells out the areas in which these funds will be spent, such as for product research, advertising design, promotional programs, Web site development and maintenance, plus other, more routine, activities. *Projects* are short-term plans created for one-time activities. Projects are also called single-use plans. A project would be a plan for remodeling the interior of a store. Once the store is changed, the plan is complete. A *program* consists of a set of projects that leads to a permanent new course of action. An example of a *marketing program* is the creation of a new product. The projects associated with that program include developing the physical product, choosing a brand name, creating a package and label, and other activities.

Most students who begin their careers in marketing at the entry level will quickly become familiar with the department's operational plans. As these individuals are promoted into supervisory roles, they oversee operational plans and coordinate the department's effort to facilitate the tactics and strategies that guide the entire organization. As a career unfolds and the individual is promoted into middle-level or top management, more time and effort will be given to developing and implementing the company's marketing strategies.

In the area of organizing, the ways in which marketing functions are conducted vary from company to company and are often determined by the size of the company. The size of a company affects not only the types of plans made by company leaders but also the design of the total organization, the marketing department, and individual jobs within the department.

The number and types of specialists employed by a marketing department largely depend on the size of the firm. Larger organizations employ advertising specialists, individuals who are solely responsible for sales activities, e-commerce experts, and others who work with both consumer and trade promotions. Many companies have both a marketing department and separate public relations department. In smaller organizations, the marketing department is probably going to handle public relations efforts.

Further, in a large multiproduct corporation such as Procter & Gamble or General Foods, a vice president of marketing oversees a marketing department and has oversight of the brand managers responsible for individual brands (Colgate, Lever, etc.). In a small company, one or two individuals may not only develop marketing strategies but also be responsible for day-to-day marketing activities. This in turn affects the staffing process as well as the use of directing techniques, such as motivational programs, the use of teams and groups, and leadership efforts.

The size of an organization also influences control processes. Performance appraisals of individual salespeople, departmental goals, and companywide objectives are shaped, in part, by the company's size. The larger the firm, the more specialized and sophisticated will be both the standards set and the methods used to measure performance. Consequently, whether it is a large corporation with a large marketing department or a small business with only one marketer, marketing management includes a variety of activities that must be integrated into the overall business program.

A Customer Service Failure

Jessica Moreland had not been on an airplane since she was 4 years old. Now, at the age of 30, she was about to fly again. Her father purchased Jessica a ticket from Dallas to Denver so that she could visit her brother and his wife, who just had their first baby. Jessica was excited about making the trip, but she was also nervous. She worried about getting through security, finding the right gate, obtaining a boarding pass, and other things that regular passengers would not even notice.

With a great deal of coaching from family and friends, Jessica navigated through the airport without any problems. Her dad had carefully reserved a seat near the front of the plane, because he knew was slightly claustrophobic and thought it might help. He also arranged a window seat, so that she could see the mountains as she flew over Colorado.

As the flight began, a male attendant approached Jessica and demanded that she move to the back of the plane. Jessica was bewildered and asked why. The attendant caustically replied that it was for safety reasons. Jessica had no idea that she could refuse, so she quietly complied.

What went wrong? Why did Jessica have such a bad travel experience?

Her new seat was on the aisle. Jessica had brought along a small overnight case with a few items. She set the case on the floor and pushed it under the seat in front of her. Soon, the same attendant approached her and started yelling, "That bag is not properly stowed. Take care of it, now!" Shocked, Jessica asked what she had done wrong. The attendant stormed off. The attendant glared at Jessica through the rest of the trip and did not serve her the soft drinks and snacks that the other passengers received.

When the flight was over, Jessica's brother Daniel was greeted by a sobbing sister. He asked what happened. She told him how scared she was and how intimidating the attendant had been. He looked around for the attendant to confront him, but could not find the man. Daniel then went to the Customer Service desk, only to discover that it was closed.

After hearing the story, Jessica's father angrily called the airline. He was soon extremely frustrated, as the phone system would not connect him with a live customer service agent. Instead, he heard an automated message telling him that the only way to reach the company to file a complaint was by using the firm's Web site. At the Web site, the father discovered he was limited to only 200 words to describe his complaint. He received an automated reply stating that someone would contact him within a few days, by e-mail.

One week later, the father received a personalized e-mail conveying the company's apology and offering a $100.00 voucher for a future flight. He then wrote a second message, noting that this "apology" meant he would have to spend money in order to receive any compensation, since airline tickets rarely cost less than $100.00. He also complained that passengers who give up seats on overbooked flights routinely receive vouchers of $200.00 or more, and that this incident was far more harmful than the inconvenience of taking a later flight. Finally, he pointed out that the apology should have been directed to his daughter, not to him.

One week later, a second message arrived stating that the company would be willing to send a letter to Jessica, but that the $100.00 would not change. The father e-mailed back saying he was fed up with the entire issue. He also made it a point to tell everyone he knew about the incident and how this airline had attempted to resolve the problem. The father resolved to never use the airline again. On his next trip to the airport, he went to the Customer Service desk and tore up the voucher in front of a service employee.[6]

STOP AND THINK

1. From the perspective of marketing, what types of customer service failures took place in this story?

2. What can the airline do to keep these types of customer service failures from occurring in the future?

3. From a management perspective, what should the flight attendant's supervisor do?

4. Which of the management functions can be used to describe the company's failure to effectively serve its customers?

5. Does this story result from a strategic, tactical, or operational failure on the part of the airline?

6. Do you believe that the airline's response was ethically or morally correct?

Customer Service Champions

Contrast the previous experience with that of Bob Omig, who was flying home to St. Louis on a Southwest Airlines flight. It was December. After backing away from the gate, the passengers were informed the plane would have to be de-iced before they could depart. Two and one half hours later, when the plane was ready for takeoff, the passengers were informed that the pilot had passed the hours-in-the-cockpit limit set by the FAA and could not fly. A new pilot was summoned. When the pilot arrived, the aircraft had to go through another de-icing. Five hours after the scheduled departure time, the flight finally took off for St. Louis.

For most people, such a scenario would have been totally frustrating, but not for Bob Omig. Why? First, the Southwest Airlines pilot walked up and down the aircraft aisles answering questions and offering constant updates on their status during the entire delay. The flight attendants showed genuine concern rather than a token attitude. They kept informing the passengers about the status of connecting flights out of St. Louis. Finally, within a week after the incident, Bob received a letter of apology from Southwest Airlines with two free round-trip ticket vouchers enclosed. He was amazed that the office acknowledged the 5-hour wait and provided two free tickets for the inconvenience.

STOP AND THINK

1. Southwest's approach to this incident is called "service recovery." Name the ingredients in the service recovery used in this case.

2. What management programs described in the vignette at the start of this chapter regarding Southwest airlines created an impact on the employees in this story?

3. What supervisory skills are necessary to maintain the type of customer-oriented environment that is found at Southwest?

Southwest Airlines' response to Bob's situation is an example of how the organization became the only airline to make *BusinessWeek*'s list of the top 25 elite customer service companies. Displaying such care for customers is no accident for Southwest Airlines; it is standard procedure. In 2001, Fred Taylor was selected by the president of Southwest Airlines, Colleen C. Barrett, to oversee all proactive communications with customers. He has the responsibility of sending out letters to customers who are caught in major storms, air traffic snarls, or other travel mishaps. In many instances, the letter of explanation or apology includes a travel voucher. According to Fred Taylor, being proactive in communicating with customers is "not something we have to do, but it's just something we feel our customers deserve."[7]

Table 1.2 lists *BusinessWeek*'s top 10 "Customer Service" elite companies. The rankings were based on a survey of over 3,000 *BusinessWeek* customers. The companies that made the

Rank	Company	Process Grade	People Grade	Service Index
1	USAA	A+	A+	992.6
2	Four Seasons Hotel	A+	A+	991.3
3	Cadillac	A+	A+	985.4
4	Nordstrom	A	A–	947.1
5	Wegmans Food Markets	A–	A	938.9
6	Edward Jones	A–	A	938.2
7	Lexus	A+	A+	932.5
8	UPS	A	B+	931.5
9	Enterprise Rent-a-Car	A–	A–	926.8
10	Starbucks	B+	B+	920.3

Table 1.2   *BusinessWeek*'s Top 10 Customer Service Elite Companies

- Establish customer empathy.
- Connect pay to service.
- Consider a chief customer officer.
- Involve the very top.

Figure 1.7

Best-Practice Ideas to Consistently Provide Quality Customer Service

list provided extraordinary service and displayed consideration and compassion. In every company, the caring attitude started at the top. Top executives in these companies often mingle with customers and front-line employees. Many spend time answering phone calls and letters. The emphasis is as much on employee loyalty as it is on customer loyalty. These executives recognize that building award-winning customer service requires satisfied and committed employees.

Based on an analysis of the top 25 companies in *BusinessWeek*'s list, the magazine listed several common themes, which were termed "best-practice ideas,"[8] the concepts presented in Figure 1.7. Creating a positive customer experience requires employees to have an empathetic, caring outlook toward customers. In order to do so, the company should hire the right people, provide the proper training, and, most important, connect quality service to the organization's reward system. When quality service is rewarded (especially as part of an employee's financial package), the individual has a strong incentive to emphasize customer well-being. At the same time, unless the entire management team displays the same approach to both customers and employees, it will not happen.

These customer service champions employ managers who understand the critical role that employees play in a firm's long term success. This means that many key management activities become part of the process. Positive customer experiences result from using quality management principles while developing compassionate, professional employees. Notice that each of these companies also has a powerful level of brand awareness and customer loyalty. Marketing and management go hand in hand in creating a successful customer-based company and environment.

The Design of This Book

A customer-oriented marketing management program consists of building a strong foundation, creating effective methods to acquire customers, refining the systems used to interact with consumers, and developing programs that emphasize customer retention. Figure 1.8 displays this approach to marketing management as it is presented in this book.

The Marketing Management Foundation

The bottom layer in the chart is the marketing management foundation. This foundation begins with understanding the basic marketing management activities and conducting an effective marketing analysis. These issues are described in Chapter 2.

The importance of developing an effective data warehouse to store information about consumers and markets will be noted in Chapter 3. Information is the lifeblood of any successful marketing program. A data warehouse contains sales data, customer data, and an effective protocol for data mining.

Chapter 4 outlines many of the managerial aspects of building an effective marketing management program. The goal is to develop a solid, customer-oriented marketing department by implementing the management functions at all levels. When the foundation is built, the marketing management team has a strong basis from which customers can be contacted and acquired.

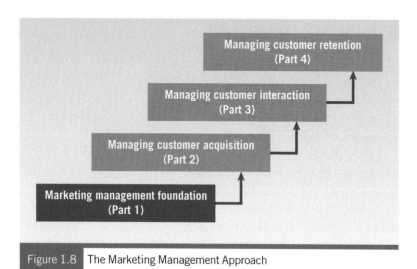

Managing customer retention (Part 4)

Managing customer interaction (Part 3)

Managing customer acquisition (Part 2)

Marketing management foundation (Part 1)

Figure 1.8 The Marketing Management Approach

Customer Acquisition

The second part of this book focuses on customer acquisition. The issues in that section include the methods a marketing team will use to reach out and contact potential customers. These customers may be acquired as first-time buyers, by taking them away from competitors, or by finding new and untapped markets.

Chapter 5 reviews many of the factors that help attract customers. Developing quality products is part of the equation. Customer acquisition includes understanding the product life cycle, identifying markets, improving and updating products, and developing strong brands.

Pricing programs are described in Chapter 6. Pricing begins with preparing a sound strategy. The strategy will be implemented through price-setting programs, discounting tactics, and making certain the prices meet all legal and ethical requirements.

Advertising programs are featured in Chapter 7. The development of persuasive and action-inducing advertisements help companies attract and retain customers. Using other tactics, including traditional approaches such as pricing and distribution, also assists in attaining new customers. Recently, newer, less traditional techniques including guerrilla, lifestyle, and Internet marketing have emerged.

In Chapter 8, consumer and trade promotions programs are discussed. Consumer promotions consist of the coupons, premiums, refunds, samples, and other items that are designed to attract buyers and pull the product through the channel. Trade promotions rely on allowances, incentives, contests, and trade shows to push products from the manufacturer through the marketing channel.

The most direct method for acquiring customers is through the efforts of a sales representative. In Chapter 9, the relationship between personal selling and customer acquisition is explained. The managerial processes of recruiting, selecting, training, compensating, and motivating the sales force are described.

Customer Interaction

The third component of a quality marketing management program is the element emphasizing customer interaction. These are the two-way streets of marketing management, in which the company contacts the customer but the customer can also contact the company.

Chapter 10 emphasizes the importance of internal communications. Employees must be kept "in the loop" in order for any marketing program to succeed. Quality internal communications are an absolute necessity in today's marketing departments. It is disastrous for a customer to hear about a special promotion through a television advertisement only to find out the local employees know nothing about it and, therefore, will not honor it.

Changes in technology play a major role in the discussion of external communication presented in Chapter 11. Many new methods of communication make it possible for customers to interact with both the company and each other. Members of the marketing department and its leaders should be aware of the myriad of messages that reach the organization and find ways to effectively respond to both positive and negative communications.

In Chapter 12, the discussion moves beyond communication to other methods by which customer interactions take place. In a company's supply chain and distribution systems, many types of information move back and forth. Solid relationships with people in these organizations provide a vital level of support for any company vending products.

In the final chapter of the part featuring customer interaction (Chapter 13), Web site management is the focus. Web design, communication programs, and personalization efforts are vital to success in the world of business, which is so strongly affected by what takes place online.

Customer Retention

The culmination of an effective marketing management program occurs when customers are retained. Part 4 of this text emphasizes methods for keeping satisfied customers. Doing so allows the management team to make plans for the next generation of goods, services, and customers.

The nature of customer retention and recovery is described in Chapter 14. Employing marketing tactics such as frequency and loyalty programs makes it possible to create strong bonds

Some
Experiences
in Life are
Breathtaking...

BASS
Masters
Classic®
B.A.S.S.
OFFICIAL SPONSOR

YAMAHA

...Owning a Skeeter is One of Them.

The joy of owning a truly great boat is the close bond you form with it... how it creates a sense of harmony between boat, fisherman and water. When you're hauling in a big northern pike from the cold, heavy waters of a glacier fed lake, this bond is crucial. One boat rises to the task. The Skeeter Deep V.

It's no surprise that the company that built the first bass boat in 1948 is now leading the way in multi-species hull design. The Deep V's long, deep fiberglass hull is hydrodynamically engineered to spray water down and away for a dry ride and excellent stability in big swells. Its transom is uniquely designed to accommodate the

25" shaft of Yamaha's quiet, powerful four stroke engine.

Of course, the ZX Deepwater series also offers features that Skeeter owners expect – spacious interior, walk-through console with full electronic instrumentation, aerated livewells, huge tackle and storage boxes, up to 52-gallon fuel system – all in a layout specifically designed to fit the special needs encountered by the angler in search of northern species. It's enough to overload the senses. But don't take our word for it – try out your own Skeeter Deep V. It will leave you breathless.

Eat. Sleep. Fish.

YAMAHA   www.skeeterboats.com   Call 1-800-SKEETER to order a catalog, or visit your local Skeeter dealer.

SKEETER®
PERFORMANCE FISHING BOATS

Advertising is a critical component of marketing because it can attract and retain customers.

with ongoing customers. When a customer becomes disenchanted with the firm, customer recovery programs can be used. Customer recovery means finding ways to restore confidence in the company's products, services, and employees.

Chapter 15 is devoted to control systems. Customer retention and recovery are facilitated by effective use of performance feedback and corrections to current problems. Marketing Management programs rely on each of the management functions to succeed. Control represents the beginning and the ending of this process. The control function ends the planning cycle by identifying things that have gone wrong with previously made plans. This also begins the next cycle by spelling out ideas for ways in which a firm can be improved.

YOURCAREER

Tarah Wilson graduated in 2002. Her current position is with Advance Mortgage Corporation. The company was founded in 1989 by her father, James Wilson, and business partner Bruce Howard. Currently, the company operates in 23 states, and its corporate offices are located in Overland Park, Kansas.

Advance Mortgage Corporation offers a diverse product line. Tarah reports, "We provide all types of home loans: conventional, jumbo—loans over $417,000, FHA [Federal Housing Administration]—government-insured loans, VA [Department of Veterans Affairs]—loans for U.S. veterans. We also work with contractors to finalize the end loan on construction loans for those building homes. This is a benefit for the contractor, who knows that the client has financing in place when the home is complete."

Tarah serves two roles. The first is as a loan officer. "I help people obtain financing, to purchase a new home or refinance a current home. The part I enjoy the most is getting to listen and converse with the borrowers. Every borrower

is of utmost importance and each has their own story and history. I work to personalize each loan to the lifestyle and needs of the borrower."

The most difficult part of this role is dealing with customers who have credit problems. Tarah believes there is an important educational experience in dealing with these individuals. "Clients don't always qualify for loans, and this is disappointing for them. They can't always afford what they want, or their current credit status is insufficient. Disgruntled applicants are an opportunity for the loan officer to grow. The last thing the loan officer wants is for a client to be disappointed. So, as a loan officer I will counsel the client on what changes need to be made in their personal finances or credit to help them achieve financing in the future. It is important for the borrower to be informed and understand the home loan process."

Tarah's second role involves helping coordinate the wholesale division of Advance Mortgage Corporation, where she markets the company's products to mortgage brokers nationally. "I create a product e-flyer weekly to send to thousands of brokers all over the nation. These brokers use our products and guideline information to market to their potential clients. I often conduct financing information seminars for our broker network and visit their offices to answer any questions and train their loan officers on matters regarding our product line. Once a broker has a complete application loan file, he/she submits the loan information to me for review and eligibility for closing at Advance Mortgage."

When asked what part of her college experience was most helpful, Tarah replied, "In-class speeches plus individual and group presentations. These experiences prepared me immensely for my frequent public speaking occasions. The management classes definitely helped in my supervising role. When I visit broker offices for presentations, both my marketing and management skills really come into play. I have two agendas at these seminars: to educate and to market. I am informing the brokers about the ever-changing industry and superior products we offer. My goal is to represent myself and Advance Mortgage as a great loan resource."

The future of Advance Mortgage is bright, even after the wave of foreclosures that took place in many real estate markets. "We are successful because of the extremely knowledgeable staff we employ, the multiple resources we have available, our contacts with various business professionals, and the relationships we have formed within the real estate community. A person comes to Advance Mortgage Corporation because other places offer less excellence and less service. Employing educated and talented people helps keep us at the top. A career path is about doing what you like and then blending in a little natural aptitude. I like the financials—there are lots of dimensions to it—and mortgage is probably the biggest piece of that for most families, and I am here to help."[9]

Chapter Summary

Marketing management is the process of managing the marketing activities in a profit-seeking or nonprofit organization, at the supervisory, midlevel management, and executive levels. The process may be used by practicing managers and by those about to enter the field of marketing. Marketing management combines the concepts present in the fields of marketing and management and integrates them into a plan of action for every level of the organization.

Marketing programs consist of the analysis of markets, products, prices, places or distribution points, promotions, and people. Management functions include planning,

organizing, staffing, directing, and control. These ideas must be combined to create an effective marketing management program.

Customer acquisition and retention are key components of any marketing management effort. There are many advantages to retaining current customers. At the same time, the goal of acquiring new customers cannot be ignored. This book is designed to build a foundation for a marketing management program and then to offer ideas about customer acquisition, interactions with those customers, and methods to retain clients in the long term.

Chapter Terms

Consumer and business-to-business segments   (p. 7)
Control   (p. 11)
Directing (also called actuating)   (p. 11)
Management   (p. 10)
Marketing   (p. 6)
Marketing management (1)   (p. 5)
Marketing management (2)   (p. 6)
Marketing strategies   (p. 12)
Marketing tactics   (p. 12)
Markets   (p. 7)

Operational plans (or short-term plans)   (p. 12)
Organizing   (p. 10)
People   (p. 9)
Place (or distribution)   (p. 8)
Planning   (p. 10)
Prices   (p. 8)
Products   (p. 7)
Promotion   (p. 8)
Staffing (p. 11)

Review Questions

1. Define marketing management. Explain how the term applies to a college course and to the business world.

2. Define marketing. Name the six major components that are part of a marketing program.

3. Name the two major forms of market segments.

4. How are prices determined?

5. What types of distribution can a company use?

6. Define management. Describe the difference between "doing" and "managing."

7. What are the five functions of management?

8. Define marketing strategies, marketing tactics, and operational plans.

9. According to *Business Week*, what common principles were found among the customer service champions?

10. What are the four parts of a marketing management program?

11. What activities are present in building a marketing management foundation?

12. What issues are associated with customer acquisition? Customer interaction?

13. Name the activities associated with customer retention.

CUSTOMER CORNER

As Brandon and Jena were enjoying a tasty meal at one of the local chain restaurants, they noticed a placard on the table advertising a $25 gift card and a $5-off coupon with the purchase of a dessert. The couple had just been discussing what to give their hairdresser for a wedding gift. A meal for the two of them and some cash would be a perfect gift.

When the waiter appeared, they ordered a dessert to share and handed him the placard asking him to add it to the bill. When he returned with the dessert, he informed Brandon and Jena that the discount was no longer available. The company's central office had discontinued the promotion the previous week. Setting the placard back down on the table, the waiter asked if they still wanted to purchase the gift card.

1. What type of message did this incident send to the customers, Brandon and Jena?

2. If the promotion had been discontinued, why do you think the placard was still on the table and why would the waiter put the placard back? How does this affect the customer's image of the restaurant?

3. If you were the manager of this restaurant, how would you now handle this situation?

What type of impact might this incident have on Jena and Brandon's future patronage of the restaurant?

Discussion and Critical Thinking Questions

1. Explain the relationships between these topics:

   - Top management, middle managers, first-line supervisors
   - Marketing strategies, marketing tactics, operational plans
   - Short term, medium range, long range
   - Markets, products, prices, distribution systems, promotions, people

   How have the Internet and globalization affected the interactions between these topics?

2. Think about a company that has demonstrated great customer care. What did the employees do to make the company stand out in your mind? Think about an incident in which you became highly dissatisfied with a company. Could the people in that organization do anything to regain your trust? If so, what?

3. The emphasis of this book is on effectively combining marketing and management activities, focusing on entry-level supervisory positions and emphasizing customer care. Based on these three concepts, create a list of the talents, skills, and characteristics you believe are crucial to success in a supervisory job and in terms of being promoted to higher-level positions later in your career. Are the skills needed to succeed as a supervisor exactly the same as those needed to be promoted?

4. Choose a fast-food restaurant, such as Taco Bell, McDonald's, SUBWAY, or Burger King. Find the company's Web site. Discuss each of the following briefly in relation to the information on the Web site.

   - What is the target market of the Web site?
   - What products are being promoted? Do the products fit the target market?
   - What prices are being promoted? How does this fit with the last two items?
   - Does the Web site provide any information about locations (i.e., distribution)?
   - Discuss the various types of promotions on the Web site, such as advertising, coupons, specials, and contests. Do these fit with the previous sections?
   - What information is provided about the people behind the company? Is there information about careers in the company? If so, what information?

5. Pick one of the companies listed in Table 1.2. Using the Internet, locate information about the company in terms of its customer service and customer interaction. Write a short paper featuring the company and how its employees interact with customers.

6. Interview five people who are not in your class. Ask about their experiences with various companies. Ask them to identify companies that they feel are great and companies they would never visit again. Compare the responses. What common themes did you find?

Chapter 1 Case

iPhone Madness

On June 29, 2007, Apple introduced a new product: the iPhone. The amount of buzz created by the company in the media was so outstanding that lines formed at retail stores, in some places 2 or 3 days in advance of the release, throughout the United States. In every city, the iPhone went on sale at exactly 6:00 P.M. in each time zone. Several major television networks featured stories about the phenomenon. Numerous talk shows and comics mentioned the product in the days leading up to the product going public. Many major magazines and newspapers carried feature stories about the iPhone and all the excitement it created.

An iPhone advances cell phone technology to include the ability to play full-length videos, replay music, take pictures, send e-mails, and surf the Internet. These functions are performed using a touch screen. Part of the appeal of this new technology may be based on a "first on the block" mentality, the rest on its unique features.

The first iPhones were expensive, costing as much as $600. At the same time, some of the people in the waiting lines were able to sell their spots for amounts up to $1,000. Others bought the new product and quickly resold it on eBay. Clearly, price and cost were not the driving factors in the desire to own one from the first batch.

The Apple company's leaders carefully selected retail locations for the new product. Stores were chosen based on strong relationships with Apple. Each also featured employees with a solid understanding of how to operate the new product.

Among the criticisms of the iPhone was its slow loading time for Internet transmissions. Also, the product's

How did the iPhone become so popular so quickly?

incompatibility with many corporate e-mail services was an issue for some customers. Others were concerned that the touch screen technology was different enough that it might cause problems for customers who were used to touching buttons to text message and perform other functions. Also, after a short period of time, the price of the iPhone dropped by more than $100.00. This led some of the initial purchasers to believe they had been overcharged, resulting in some negative publicity for the product.

The iPhone was expected to make slower inroads into other markets around the world. Many other technical problems must be solved to help the product succeed in Europe and other major global markets. In the media,

many note that the iPhone is as much a handheld computer as a cell phone, suggesting the name may be confusing in both domestic and foreign markets.

Once the initial surge of energy and interest has passed, several other challenges remain. One is to continue to expand sales into more households over time. Also, upgrades and maintenance issues must be solved. Customers with lower levels of knowledge about the product must be served as effectively as the enthusiastic first adopters. And finally, it is likely that other companies will develop similar technologies or products with fewer uses but also lower prices.

The world of technological innovation remains fast paced, global, and driven at least in part by fads and trends. In this environment, Apple will look to find new innovations and adaptations of older products to stay on top in this marketplace.[10]

1. Describe the issues surrounding the marketing concepts of markets, products, prices, distribution, promotion, and people present at the time of the iPhone release.
2. Describe the issues related to marketing strategies, tactics, and operational plans that should have been addressed as the iPhone was developed and released.
3. As the manager of a retail store selling the iPhone, what do you believe are the keys to success for this product and others? What types of assistance would you seek out from Apple Corporation?
4. As an individual salesperson, what are the keys to success in selling the iPhone and other related products? What types of assistance would you want from your supervisor?

Go to **www.sagepub.com/clow** for additional exercises and study resources. Select **Chapter 1, The Nature of Marketing Management** for chapter-specific activities.

Can Pickle Juice Sport and enlyten SportsStrip gain market share in the National Football League, even though Gatorade is an official sponsor?

chapter 2
Market Analysis

Electrolyte Nation

Any athlete or hardcore personal trainer knows that maintaining sufficient levels of electrolytes is one key to a successful workout. If the level drops too low, fatigue kicks in, and the person tires more quickly. Electrolyte replacement gives a boost of energy, greater stamina, and recovery from an exercise regimen.

For many years, Gatorade held the dominant position in the electrolyte replacement marketplace. The company's products held the advantages of being first, the most visible, and the most closely connected with athletic programs at all levels. The ritual of pouring Gatorade on the winning coach of a major football game places the product at the level of being practically a cultural symbol of success.

Such a lucrative market was bound to attract competitors. At first, similar products reached the market. One of the more notable, POWERADE, was developed

by the Coca-Cola company. The product is designed to offer more nutrients than Gatorade, in a wide variety of flavors.

Recently, however, two new forms of electrolyte delivery have been made available. The first is simple pickle juice. Pickle Juice Sport advertises that golden pickle juice contains 30 times the amount of electrolytes as POWERADE and 15 times more than Gatorade. Of course, the primary drawback is taste. Even with this disadvantage, however, the company's sales continue to climb.

Another new option is enlyten™ Electrolyte SportStrips™. The company's marketing materials claim that the strips "are a fast, easy and effective way to replace lost electrolytes during athletic performance!" Enlyten SportsStrips replace the electrolytes bodies lose while exercising through buccal (cheek to gum) absorption. The company's Web site notes that this mode of absorption is vastly different from all other electrolyte delivery predecessors. Gastric absorption is bypassed, and the electrolytes are directly absorbed into the body. The company also claims that using Electrolyte SportsStrips helps avoid the

overhydration that often accompanies the excessive consumption of sports drinks.

What could be simpler? Just pop a strip in your mouth, let it dissolve, and enjoy the different flavors (the original was orange). No more feeling full from excessive amounts of sports drinks that are much slower to provide the performance enhancement that any athlete needs immediately. Naturally, Gatorade's marketing team had to respond. Since Gatorade is the official sports drink of the National Football League, the company quickly managed to get a league memo sent out stating that no other form of electrolyte replacement could be endorsed by any team. Still, at least 10 teams quietly note that players do use SportsStrips.

Will Pickle Juice Sport and enlyten SportsStrips succeed in a marketplace in which every high school, college, and professional coach and trainer already knows about Gatorade and POWERADE? The owners of both companies clearly believe they can. It will take time combined with a great deal of consumer information and marketing programs to gain a foothold in this inviting marketplace.

Chapter Overview

Understanding the market in which a good or service will be offered is a key ingredient in marketing success. Such an understanding will be largely derived from a market analysis. A market analysis program includes examining environmental factors, the competition, the position the firm's products occupy in the marketplace, and the customers who purchase the product. This chapter studies each of these factors.

This chapter also reviews the ways in which the marketing department helps a company's leaders estimate demand for a product as well as for the industry in which the firm operates. Finally, the chapter closes with a presentation of how to estimate contribution margins and break-even points, which are used to evaluate marketing programs and to help make decisions about future marketing efforts.

Market Analysis

A **market analysis** involves studying a company's customers and competitors along with the overall industry and environment. From these analyses, the marketing team can identify who to target, what products to market, and the best promotional approach to influence the attitudes and purchase behaviors of potential customers. Typically, a market analysis program consists of the following:

- Environmental analysis
- Competitive/industry analysis
- Analysis of product positioning
- Market segment analysis
- Customer analysis

An examination of the past reveals the ways in which market analyses changed the landscape for various products and had an impact on the ways people live. A market analysis encouraged Starbucks's owner to capitalize on the changing consumer behaviors and attitudes and helped the company find a niche in the highly competitive coffee market. JCPenney moved into the private labeling of jeans when a market analysis revealed changing consumer attitudes toward store brands just as national brands such as Levi's were losing their luster. A market analysis may have saved Harley-Davidson. Facing financial ruin and bankruptcy, Harley-Davidson's leadership used governmental assistance to complete a market analysis to better understand the motorcycle market and how to compete effectively against foreign motorcycle manufacturers.[1]

Environmental Analysis

An effective market analysis begins with an environmental analysis. This includes monitoring all of the external variables that have an impact on a particular industry. An environmental analysis is a key component in the strategic management process as well. Both include assessment of many factors, including

- political forces,
- social forces,
- economic forces,
- technological forces, and
- semicontrollable forces.

Many political forces come from laws, regulations, and regulatory agencies, such as the Occupational Safety and Health Administration (OSHA), the Environmental Protection Agency (EPA), laws regarding discrimination, and the many laws and agencies that oversee marketing activities, including the Federal Trade Commission (FTC). Courts often influence marketing and business through decisions regarding product safety and reliability and fair advertising and promotion tactics and in protecting the interests of various groups. Political forces also include the ways in which government influences an economy; taxes companies, products, and individuals; and provides subsidies and loans to various organizations. At times, the government even competes with private enterprise (U.S. Postal Service vs. FedEx and UPS).

The social forces that have an impact on business include changing demographics or population characteristics, shifting cultural and subcultural trends, and rising educational levels. Demographic trends include the aging of the population as the baby boomer generation retires as well as shifting locations of populations away from core parts of cities to the suburbs and from the northern and eastern United States to more southern and western states. Other demographics that influence marketing are the size and composition of family units, including single-parent households and mixed families. Also, the racial distribution in an area affects marketing patterns, such as when Hispanic families move into new regions, towns, and cities. A wide variety of cultural trends affect marketing and business.

Economic forces are all the factors that have an impact on a product's market in a given region. This would include levels of economic growth, employment, unemployment, and inflation as well as the cost of living in an area.

Baby boomers are an important market segment that requires an understanding of attitudes, opinions, interests, and lifestyles.

The prices and availability of raw materials needed to produce a good or a service are also economic forces. For example, an increase in fuel costs triggers increases in transportation costs and an increase in raw material costs for a number of chemicals, plastics, and other products that are made from petroleum. When the costs are passed on to other members of the channel of distribution, then each succeeding level in the channel is affected. Company leaders consider the impact of a price change on a finished product as well as price elasticity. The greater the elasticity, the more managers are concerned about increasing the price of the product. In the short term, consumers may turn to competitor products with a lower price; in the long run, buyers may search for suitable substitutes.

Technological forces include new products created by technology as well as product improvements and improvement in production methods. Technology also has an impact on the ways in which marketing materials can be delivered and on marketing jobs and occupations. Consider, for example, the ways in which technology has changed the methods for creating interesting and attention-getting Internet and television commercials.

Semicontrollable forces create an impact on a company; however, the company's leaders are able to respond and exert some influence in return. Semicontrollable forces include the local community, suppliers, financial institutions, stockholders, and unions. The community can be influenced through fair and reasonable management practices, such as hiring, firing, promotion, and pay programs. The local community may also be influenced by marketing tactics and public relations activities. Suppliers and unions are both influenced through bargaining methods and tactics. Financial institutions and stockholders may be influenced by effective record keeping and "clean" company finances. Table 2.1 summarizes the various forces examined in an environmental analysis.

Looking Fit Tanning Salon

An effective market analysis examines the various forces operating within a particular company's environment. Consider the environmental analysis conducted by Looking Fit in the tanning salon industry.[2] Statistics indicate that over the past 10 years the tanning industry has more than doubled, with 60% of the growth coming from current salon owners expanding or opening new outlets. The average salon has approximately 2,400 customers and a minimum of 10 pieces of tanning equipment. Typically, salons provide three to five levels of tanning with six basic tanning beds, two premium units, and one upgrade or stand-up unit.

In conducting this environmental analysis, it is important to consider any *political* or *legal* factors that may have an impact. For the indoor tanning industry, California is considering a law that would make it illegal for anyone under the age of 18 to tan without a doctor's or surgeon's prescription. Currently, California prohibits 14- to 18-year-olds from using indoor tanning salons without parental consent. Michigan, New Hampshire, North Carolina, and other states are also proposing legislation that would require parental consent for anyone 18 or under to tan in a salon.

In terms of *social forces,* tanning has become a lifestyle for a large segment of people in the United States. Many of these individuals go to indoor tanning salons because they provide a controlled and relaxed atmosphere. They expect salon operators to provide professional

Political Forces	Social Forces
Laws and regulations	Changing demographics
Courts and judgments	Cultural trends and changes
Taxes and subsidies	Rising educational levels
Governmental competition	

Economic Forces	Technological Forces
Economic conditions (inflation)	New products
Price and availability of raw materials	Product improvements
	Improvements in product methods

Semicontrollable Forces	
Local community	Suppliers
Financial institutions	Stockholders
Labor unions	Retailers or channel members

Table 2.1 Environmental Forces

advice on tanning as well as skin care products that will enhance their tans and personal appearance.

Demographically, the majority of individuals using indoor tanning are between 18 and 49 years of age, with 70% being females. Within this group, 53% are women between the ages of 20 and 39. Industry analysis indicates, however, that there has also been a steady growth in the number of women from 40 to 49 years of age who tan. The fastest-growing segment is younger females, ages 16 to 19. While men account for only 30% of the tanning market, they have shown an increasing interest in professional skin care products in addition to tanning.

Tanning involves spending disposable income that is not used for necessities, such as food, clothing, and shelter. Therefore, local *economic conditions* would create an impact. An easy service to stop using in hard economic times would be personal tanning.

A new *technological* trend in the industry is sunless products that provide an immediate cosmetic, tanned look without any ultraviolet (UV) exposure. Sunless products have become important to salon owners because they offer salons a new way to build business and increase profits. Sunless products are especially attractive to a specific market segment that in the past had not used tanning salons. These are individuals who have difficulty in getting a tan or an even tan, whether through indoor tanning beds or outside in the sun.

Finally, salon owners would consider any *semicontrollable* forces that may affect companies. These include local communities and zoning ordinances, suppliers of tanning products, and banks and financial institutions that may offer funding and other services to salon owners.

What caused the tanning salon industry to expand in the past decade?

STOP AND THINK

1. Besides limiting tanning to young people, what other laws or regulatory agencies would be concerned with tanning salons?
2. Is having a rich, dark tan as socially desirable as it was 20 years ago? Why or why not?
3. How could court judgments regarding skin cancer affect the industry and the Looking Fit Tanning Salon?
4. How has technology changed the nature of the tanning business?
5. When a tanning salon is located next to a massage or tattoo parlor, does the location affect perception in the local community? Why or why not?

Competitive/Industry Analysis

While they vary in terms of economic structure, companies in all industries engage in competition, unless the company is authorized by a government entity to be a monopoly. When the marketing team does not closely watch industry trends, it can fail to recognize opportunities and may lose customers to competitors who are more in tune with what is going on in the marketplace and with changes in customer preferences. This means that a competitive analysis involves constant surveillance of ongoing and anticipated industry trends. Such an analysis is critical to maintaining a strong, competitive position.

Levels of Competition

Marketing managers must spend a great deal of time considering all the forms of competition that affect a market, a product, and individual consumers. A competitive analysis begins with identifying the various levels of competition.

Consider Figure 2.1 and the competitors that sell clothing from the viewpoint of Target stores. The most direct competitors are the discount stores offering clothes similar to Target, such as Kmart and Wal-Mart. At the next level are department stores. These retailers sell clothes, but typically, they are higher priced and of higher quality. As shown, competitors at this level include Dillard's, JCPenney, Belk, and Sears. The third level consists of clothing specialty retailers that focus on one or more brand name lines or types of clothing, such as Rave, Talbots, Banana Republic, Abercrombie & Fitch, Lane Bryant, and Old Navy. The fourth layer would be all the other retail stores competing for the consumer's dollars. Instead of purchasing clothes, for instance, an individual could purchase something from Best Buy, Office Depot, or Bass Pro Shops.

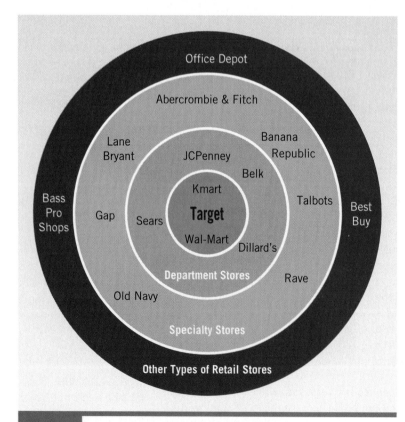

Figure 2.1   Levels of Competition for Clothing at Target

What stores carry clothes that are similar to those at Target?

Investigation of Competitors

Once competitors have been identified, some questions that should be investigated include:

- What are the competition's strengths and weaknesses?
- What product-positioning strategies do the competitors use?
- What is the target market for each competitor?
- Who are the customers in each market?
- Why do individuals buy from a competitor? What makes a competitor's product unique or attractive?
- What types of marketing programs do the competitors use?
- How does the competition promote and/or advertise products?
- What competitive advantage do they seem to possess or promote?

Considerable information can be gathered about competitors without hiring a spy or using espionage. Figure 2.2 lists some of the typical available sources. It helps to learn everything possible in order to accurately predict or quickly react to actions by other competing companies.

Each competitor's *Web site* reveals a tremendous amount of information about the company and its products, personnel, marketing approach, and positioning strategy. Many marketing teams find it useful to monitor these Web sites for new information and marketplace trends.

Another source is the competition's *advertisements.* Most marketing departments maintain files of competitor print ads and ads from other media. While Web site materials and advertisements are designed to present the competitor in its best light, remember that this is the same information that a company's customers and others see.

- Web sites
- Advertisements
- News articles
- Trade and professional associations
- Online forums and blogs
- Competing products and locations
- Customers
- Salespeople

Figure 2.2

Sources of Competitive Information

Additional sources of information include *media articles, trade and professional journals, and online forums and blogs.* These sources help the marketing team to view the competition as others see them. While some of these sources strive to remain neutral, others provide information based on personal opinions and experiences.

Some company leaders believe it is important to purchase a competitor's product and reverse engineer it in order to see how the item is made. Also, when a competitor has a retail outlet, many marketing managers send someone to *visit the store* on a regular basis. The goal is to understand how the competitor displays merchandise and to find out what in-store marketing techniques are being used. In-store visits also provide information about how the competitor's salespeople deal with customers.

The other two sources of information are from internal sources: *customers* and *salespeople.* When a marketing leader deploys a field sales force or uses other types of salespeople, they meet customers and prospects on a regular basis. Salespeople can learn a great deal about the competition while dealing with customers. A salesperson may be the first to discover a competitor's new product, new marketing campaign, or new promotion. Customers are often willing to talk about how they view competing brands. Those who have actually purchased competing brands may offer even more helpful comparisons.

In conducting a competitive analysis, Table 2.2 can be a useful tabulating form. You will need to modify the factors in the left column to fit the product being sold. The column headings can also be altered to fit the circumstances, and the competitors should be identified by name.

Analyzing the competition helps a company's leaders comprehend how the organization is perceived by customers. The analysis assists the marketing team in understanding how a firm's brand and products are viewed and may reveal any unique benefits the company can provide to customers. It can also identify areas in which the company might be able to outperform the competition.

Factor	Competitor A	Competitor B	Competitor C	Our Position Relative to Competition	Our Brand Relative to Competition	Relative Importance to Customers
Product benefits						
Product quality						
Price						
Selection						
Customer service						
Reliability						
Expertise						
Reputation/image						
Locations						
Appearance						
Sales methods						
Advertising						
Marketing						

Table 2.2   Analysis of Competitors

A competitive rivalry can bring out the best in a company. Without competition to drive excellence and continuous improvement, company employees may become complacent. There may not be a driving need to improve or develop new products. As long as customers can choose from among at least two brands, however, competition and rivalry exist. Competition can also help educate customers about a product category. Although each competitor emphasizes its particular brand's attributes and benefits, such a process may actually simultaneously present the benefits that are available from other brands in the industry.[3]

Analysis of Product Positioning

Consumers and businesses normally have several brands from which to choose in a product category. Most products are in the mature stage of the product life cycle, which means competition is intense. Brands are often perceived as being highly similar, which in marketing terms is called brand parity. When brand parity is present, no distinctive attributes make any brand stand out. The opposite of brand parity is brand equity, which is a situation in which a company's goods and services are perceived to be different and better.

To survive a competitive environment and to achieve brand equity, marketing professionals examine the position each product holds in the marketplace. Doing so makes it possible to find out if a product holds a unique place in the minds of consumers. Then, the marketing team can change, refine, or accentuate the position. Two methods are used to develop a positioning strategy. The first is product differentiation, and the second is through market segmentation.

In the wine industry, which would be most likely, brand parity or brand equity?

The Nature of Product Positioning

Product positioning involves the place a good or service occupies (1) in the minds of consumers and (2) relative to the competition. Although what people in the company think of its products is important, it is what consumers think that determines purchase behaviors. In developing the positioning statement, four components should be considered:[4]

1. The target audience
2. The good or service
3. The frame of reference or category
4. The point of differentiation or uniqueness

Since positioning involves the mental location of a product in the minds of consumers, positioning begins by defining the target audience. The good or service is then placed in a frame of reference or category, such as beverages, compact cars, designer clothes, or breakfast foods. The third component involves determining whether or not a product is generally perceived as being different or unique in the reference or category. This may be achieved by the product being viewed, for example, as the uncola among beverages (7 Up) or the nonmeat item among breakfast foods.

Positioning Strategies

Unless the product is completely new, it is beneficial to understand the current place a product holds in the minds of customers before developing a product-positioning strategy. This can be accomplished through market surveys and other data collection methods. There are seven primary positioning positions, as listed in Figure 2.3.[5]

When positioning by *attribute,* the brand will be marketed as having a unique and superior feature. In the automotive industry, BMW stresses engineering and handling, while Volvo stresses safety.

Positioning by *use or application* is similar to attribute positioning. Instead of emphasizing a particular attribute, however, the ways to use the product are stressed. When a significant decline in home baking began to take place, ARM & HAMMER repositioned its baking soda as a deodorizer to be used in a refrigerator, in carpet-cleaning products, and even in dental care.

Occasionally, a brand may be positioned relative to *competitors.* This positioning strategy works best when a lesser known brand can be compared with a strong, well-known brand. Many years ago, the rental car company Avis was not often recognized. The company's advertising agency developed a campaign to reposition the brand against the industry leader, Hertz. In a series of advertisements, Avis was compared to Hertz. The ads admitted the company was not the industry leader but instead stated, "We try harder." A similar campaign was used by Chrysler when it faced potential bankruptcy. The company admitted it was not the industry leader, but because it was not, the focus turned to other aspects, such as quality.

Two closely related positioning strategies are by product user or by product class. The goal of a *product user strategy* is to position the product as being superior for a given product user. For instance, Johnson & Johnson touted its famous baby shampoo for individuals who washed their hair frequently and, as a result, needed something mild. When Apple first developed computers, the products were positioned as being best suited for educational institutions, which were the product's users.

When marketing efforts feature a *product class,* the brand is positioned as being best or superior in that particular set, or class, of products. For instance, Morningstar Farms has developed an entire range of meatless products for breakfast meals. The Morningstar Farms brand is promoted as the best meatless breakfast food for vegetarians as well as for individuals who are concerned about cholesterol in traditional breakfast meats, such as bacon and sausage. Several years ago, the leaders of the orange juice industry attempted to change orange juice from being

- Attributes
- Use or application
- Competitors
- Product user
- Product class
- Price/quality relationship
- Cultural symbol

Figure 2.3

Product-Positioning Strategies

viewed as only a breakfast drink to an anytime beverage, moving the product into a wider product class that included soft drinks and energy drinks.

Price/quality positioning involves convincing consumers they are getting more for their money. Wal-Mart has achieved success using the price-quality positioning strategy, featuring the "everyday low price" motto for years. Recently, however, when sales at Wal-Mart slowed, the company began offering better-quality products and higher-reputation brand names to appeal to higher-income individuals. The challenge will be to maintain the "everyday low price" position even as more expensive items fill the shelves.

The final product-positioning strategy is probably the most difficult to attain. It is difficult to incorporate a *cultural symbol* within a positioning strategy. Chevrolet has, for years, attempted to achieve the position of being as American as baseball, hot dogs, and apple pie. As a new generation matures, however, new cultural symbols are rare. McDonald's may have had its status as a cultural symbol reinforced when characters on the popular television program *Grey's Anatomy* used the nicknames McDreamy and McSteamy.

In summary, the key to successful product positioning is finding a position a brand can occupy that is either unique or superior. It is better to be viewed as "the best" in a small pond than be viewed as "just another brand" in a large pond. A brand will be purchased when consumers feel that it offers some advantage or differentiation from the others.

STOP AND THINK

Consider the following positioning statement by Highland Financial Services: "To working women with incomes over $75,000, Highland Financial Services is the life insurance company with 125 years of experience providing AAA, insured life insurance investments."[6]

1. What is the target market in this statement?
2. What is the basic product for the company?
3. What product category or frame of reference is mentioned in this statement?
4. What unique feature is being described?
5. Which positioning strategy best fits Highland Financial Services? Defend your choice.

Perceptual Mapping

Perceptual mapping can be used to investigate and determine the optimal product-positioning strategy for a product. A perceptual map typically uses two axes that are key variables regarding how a product or company is viewed. Perceptual mapping may include more axes; however, the most common approach is to use two or three. It is almost impossible to visualize more than three components.

Figure 2.4 is a perceptual map for the new Starbucks Frappuccino blended beverage before it was introduced. In this case, the two critical purchase criteria for a drink are price and perceived quality. Starbucks believed the new Frappuccino drink would compete most directly with Jamba Juice. Company research indicated that the Frappuccino drink was perceived as having slightly higher quality with a slightly lower price.

Perceptual mapping provides a useful tool for assessing product positioning because it identifies important purchase criteria and provides a visualization of where a brand stands in relation to competitors. Remember that if the perceptual map is to be beneficial, it must be based on the views that consumers have of the various brands within a product industry. It also must be based on the decision criteria that are used to determine the brand to be purchased.

Perceptual maps assist a marketing team in determining how to proceed in strengthening or changing a product's position. The team may choose to emphasize price, quality, or the price/quality relationship.

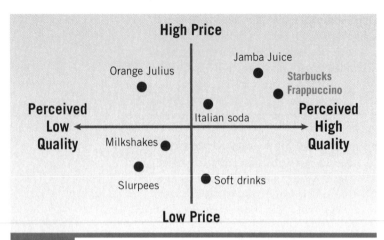

Figure 2.4   Positioning of Starbucks Frappuccino Blended Beverage

Product Differentiation

As noted earlier, the opposite of brand parity is brand equity. Product differentiation attempts to create this difference in perception. When brand parity exists, marketing departments are often forced to compete based on price. When a high level of brand equity exists, the marketing team can focus on unique differences and advantages. Price may or may not play a role. Product differentiation can be created in two ways: (1) through an actual difference or (2) by creating the perception that there is a difference.

The airline industry, where a great deal of brand parity exists, serves as an example. Midwest Airlines has developed a new strategy in which the company emphasizes that it offers more direct flights combined with a more luxurious travel experience—complete with wider leather seats (two per side rather than three) and freshly baked cookies, with an aroma that fills the entire cabin, near the end of the journey.

Product differentiation is also important in business-to-business markets. Manufacturers of aluminum sheets used for cans have recently created growth opportunities through product differentiation. With the rising number of specialty drinks on the market, can manufacturers have developed containers in various sizes to meet this market niche. Another form of product differentiation that is now developing is in aluminum bottles, which were designed to compete with other types of containers. Aluminum bottles have been widely accepted in Japan, where they were first offered, and are now being introduced in other parts of the world.[7]

Market Segment Analysis

Every product and company has a specific customer base from which to draw. **Market segmentation** involves categorizing customers into groups and identifying the characteristics of each of these groups. Using this information, a firm's management team can design product features and benefits that will be most attractive to the particular market segment and develop marketing materials that are more likely to resonate with them.

Figure 2.5 identifies the typical methods used to segment the consumer market. Most marketers understand demographics, and as a result, demographics are often used as segmentation strategies. There are many viable categories of segments solely based on age, gender, ethnic background, and so forth. Many marketers stop at that point. They go no further in understanding the various segments. As a result, the marketing plan is based on a demographic profile and not on a segment's psychographic, behavioral, or geographic profile.

Psychographic segmentation examines mental characteristics and predispositions that are connected to purchasing habits. For example, the personality of someone who sees himself as being "macho" or "manly" may be connected to sales of products such as clothing, cologne, and other personal grooming items. The lifestyle of long-distance runners as a group ties them to purchases of sports equipment, energy drinks, and so forth, regardless of gender. A commonly used marketing technique known as AIO (activities, interests, opinions) identifies sets of consumers with common psychological characteristics that may in turn be used as target markets. A market segment is viable when

- a distinct group can be identified,
- members of the group have money to spend, and
- members of the group are willing to spend money on a specific good or service.

Behavioral segmentation identifies segments by how consumers use a product, the benefits they derive from that product, and how often the product is purchased or used. A simple product such as chewing gum may be targeted at people who chew gum to help them quit smoking or people who chew gum because it calms them or tastes good, and its consumers may be categorized as heavy, moderate, or light users.

Geographic segmentation targets the location of a company or the locations of potential buyers. Geographic segmentation strategies are often used in conjunction with other methods of identifying target markets. For example, geodemographic segmentation seeks out groups of consumers with identifiable demographic characteristics within a specific geographic region, such as male hunters in Deep South states.

Segmentation in the Exercise Industry

Often the marketing team is tempted to focus on *who* purchases a particular product rather than *why*. Answering the "why" question, however, may lead to a better understanding of the "who," that is, the various segments. To illustrate, consider the fitness industry and the question "Why do individuals exercise?" The typical responses are likely to be

- to lose weight,
- to maintain a healthy body,
- to build muscle mass,
- to prevent or counter a medical problem,
- for enjoyment, and
- to meet people.

Once the question "why" has been answered, the marketing group can proceed to describe each segment in terms of its demographic profile, psychographic composition, behavior, and possibly geographic location.

Consider the first group, individuals who exercise to lose weight. *Demographically,* the segment consists primarily of females, the middle-aged, and the middle-income group. In terms of *psychographics,* these individuals typically have sedentary lifestyles and do not participate in any type of sports or athletic activities. They tend to be socially oriented and as a result are concerned about physical appearance. They may be fashion conscious and want to lose weight

- **Demographics** – gender, age, income, ethnicity, generational cohorts
- **Psychographics** – personality, lifestyles, activities, interests, opinions
- **Behavioral** – benefit, usage rate, occasion
- **Geographic** – city, county, state, region, country

Figure 2.5

Consumer Segmentation

Asking the question "why" provides a better understanding of the reasons women prefer group experiences rather than individual exercises.

to look good in the newest fashions. They often enjoy shopping and especially like to shop for clothes and other personal items.

Notice that when the question "why" was answered, it resulted in a *behavioral* segmentation approach. The benefit this segment desires is loss of weight. In terms of occasion, the desire to lose weight is often the result of a New Year's resolution and due to overeating and lack of physical activity over the holidays. Most of these individuals are light to medium users of a fitness center. Their goal is to lose weight. Most are not regular users and never will be. They have a specific weight loss goal and, as a result, a time frame for usage.

The same approach can be used for each of the six segments identified through answers to the question "why." The composition of each segment varies considerably. For instance, while there are some women who exercise to build muscle mass or tone muscles, most tend to be men. Individuals who exercise to prevent or counter a medical problem tend to be older and exercise only because they have been told to do so by a physician. They see exercise as a means of prolonging life, preventing a medical problem, or as a response to a medical problem. Someone who has experienced a heart attack may decide to start working out on a regular basis to prevent future attacks. Therefore, it helps to describe each segment using all four segmentation categories. Creating effective marketing plans requires a richer understanding of each market segment than demographic variables alone will yield.

Business-to-business segmentation is performed in a similar fashion. *Demographic* or *firmographic* factors would include such variables as the number of employees, sales volume, and the number of locations. Firm *psychographics* include a business's "personality," the way the company conducts business, how decisions are made as well as the firm's culture, growth orientation, and customer focus. *Behavioral* variables consist of the benefits a company derives from a product, the quantity purchased, the frequency of purchases, the timing of purchases, and the occasions for which the product is purchased. *Geographic segmentation* refers to the geographic location of the business. Businesses often cluster around customers and suppliers. When an automobile factory is built, a number of businesses will locate in close proximity to provide the parts needed by the automobile manufacturer. Likewise, a large number of companies have located offices in Bentonville, Arkansas, to sell to Wal-Mart.

Identifying the Most Profitable Segments

Once the marketing segmentation is complete, the firm's marketing managers must decide which segment or segments to pursue. Figure 2.6 provides a list of the major criteria. While all of the factors are important, the first factor is critical. The product being sold must match well with the benefits sought by the particular market segment being targeted (*product/market match*).

International House of Pancakes (IHOP) offers affordable meals in a family-oriented atmosphere. As such, the company serves three primary market segments. The first consists of low- to middle-income families with little or no education beyond high school. The secondary market is single adults, area employers that surround each IHOP restaurant, truck drivers, and transit travelers with similar income and educational levels as the first target. The third market is made up of individuals who work night hours or late evening hours and have the desire or need to eat meals during the night.

Once it is clear that the benefits offered by a company's product match the needs and wants of a particular market segment or segments, it becomes essential to examine the *size of the market segment,* its sales potential, and its *growth potential.* The market segment must be large enough for the company to earn a sufficient profit. The larger the target segment, the higher the *sales potential,* and the higher the future growth rate, the more attractive the market segment.

If the market segment is viable from the standpoint of size and growth, then the analysis turns to the company's ability to effectively *reach the target segment.* The marketing team normally seeks to find out whether the company can reach the segment effectively with marketing messages and how *responsive* the members will be. Not all segments are reachable. For instance, a competitor may control the channel or be so large in a particular region that it is not economically feasible for any new entrant. A competitor's customer base may be so loyal that they will not listen to a new company's marketing message.

- Product/market match
- Segment size
- Sales potential
- Growth potential
- Reachability
- Responsiveness
- Retention potential
- Level of competition

Figure 2.6

Identifying the Most Profitable Segments

Company leaders also examine the *retention potential* and the lifetime value of potential customers. Reaching customers with a message and persuading them to make an initial purchase is only part of the battle. The cost of acquiring a new customer is much higher than the cost of retaining a current customer. This makes it absolutely essential to retain customers whenever possible. It is hard to survive when a company must continually acquire new customers.

The final factor to be considered is the *degree of competition*. The more intense the competition within a segment, the less attractive it is. Most markets are now in the mature stage of the product life cycle. Consequently, a company cannot afford to give up customers and market share. Most competitors fight vigorously to prevent the loss of customers.

Customer Analysis

A customer analysis should be designed to provide companies with an in-depth understanding of customers. The more a company's marketing team knows about the firm's customers, the better it can serve them. Again, collecting demographic information about customers may not be enough. Marketing professionals try to understand customers from psychological, sociological, and behavioral viewpoints.

Types of Customers

To begin the customer analysis process, the marketing team thinks about the various types of customers that the firm can reach. The most common type of customer is the *consumer*. Even manufacturers that do not sell directly to consumers need to understand them. Products must be designed to meet consumer needs. Most manufacturers prepare some marketing materials for end users in order to pull the product through the channel, and most retailers expect manufacturers to help promote products.

In addition to consumers, many companies also sell to *other businesses*. This is not a function of the distribution channel. Instead, this market consists of the other businesses that consume the good or service. If the business simply resells the product, then it is the channel of distribution. The final type of customer group to be considered is *nonprofit organizations*. Nonprofits include various levels of government. Schools, hospitals, and charitable organizations such as the Red Cross are nonprofits.

Managers in every business organization make decisions about how to handle the Internet and whether the company will sell products directly. While offering merchandise from the Internet provides direct access to customers and increases profit potential, it also has potential pitfalls. A product being sold by other channel members causes the marketing team to give careful consideration to the impact Internet selling may have on those wholesalers and retailers. Purchases made over the Internet mean lost sales for channel members. This may create an adverse situation where the channel members reduce efforts to sell the company's products. To keep this from happening, some companies offer product information over the Internet but then refer potential customers to a channel member for the purchase.

The Ws of Customer Analysis

The goal of a customer analysis is to collect detailed information about customers in order to develop effective marketing plans. Typically, a customer analysis involves answering the questions "who," "where," "when," "what," and "how." Finding out "who" provides a demographic and psychographic profile of customers. Sometimes one target market is served, while in others, the goal is to reach multiple target markets. The marketing team will develop a profile for each type of customer that requires a different marketing approach. For example, when demographics are used, it may be that the product benefits sought by the 18- to 30-year-old female target market are substantially different from the benefits sought by females 31 to 45 years of age. In that case, the two segments should be described separately.

Where are consumers likely to go to purchase carpeting for their homes?

The "where" question identifies the location or locations in which products are purchased. For an item purchased in a retail store, which types of retail stores? Is it primarily purchased at discount stores or department stores? In addition, what other products typically are purchased with it? The answers can be especially helpful in the placement of the product in the store, in various geographic areas, and in creating tie-in promotions with various retailers.

Serious consideration must also be given to the Internet. Are online sales feasible? If so, what other sites does a person visit before and after purchasing or examining the product? The purpose of asking "where" is to determine not only where the product is purchased but also what other types of products are purchased or examined with it.

"When" involves determining the most likely times a product is purchased. This information can be extremely valuable in the timing of a marketing campaign. While a product such as candy may be purchased all year, there are spikes in sales at Halloween, Christmas, and Easter. The question of when is often closely tied to the question of where. For instance, if a product is placed in a point-of-purchase (POP) display at the end of a retail aisle during a holiday, sales may be greater than if the POP display is used during nonholidays.

The "what" is a crucial issue. What are customers purchasing? In most cases, rather than the product's attributes, it is the benefits those attributes deliver. Most people have no idea what chemicals are used in cosmetics; however, they do know how a particular brand of cosmetic makes them feel and how it enhances beauty. Few people can tell you how automobiles run, yet they can tell you how it makes them feel to be seen in a sleek red convertible. Ford's leadership understood this concept when the company offered the "retro" Mustang in 2005, which looked like the first Mustangs built in the 1960s. While young people purchased the car, the target market for the retro Mustang was baby boomers, who were teenagers in the 1960s. Many owned Mustangs or idealized those who did. The car immediately resonated with this target market because it brought back their "youth" and gave them an opportunity to feel like a teenager again. To this market, the purchase was not a car but rather reliving of their teenage years.

Consumer Buying Decision Making

The "how" of a customer analysis involves examining how purchases are made. It is not just the method of payment: cash or credit. It is the entire process. Figure 2.7 identifies the steps in the consumer buying decision-making process. The purpose of a customer analysis is to examine each step with the goal of understanding how consumers arrive at purchasing decisions.

Problem Recognition

In the first step, the problem recognition stage, the question of "what," as noted previously, helps describe what triggers the problem or need. A need may emerge from something as simple as running out of a product, such as toothpaste, or it may be more complex. Someone might see that a neighbor has just purchased a new stereo system. To keep pace or to maintain the impression that the person is successful, she may wish to purchase a similar or better stereo system.

Internal Information Search

When a problem or desire is triggered, the consumer first conducts an internal search in which he examines personal internal knowledge structures while seeking a solution. If the person was satisfied with his last purchase of a brand, then the search process will typically be very short. If the same person was dissatisfied with the last brand or desires something new, then he will give more thought to possible solutions and brands. If a consumer feels neutral about the last purchase, then the individual is likely to spend at least some time thinking about other brands.

When considering an internal search for information, two concepts are important: share of mind and share of heart. Share of mind deals with brand recall and whether or not the brand is typically located in customers' minds. Share of heart reflects attitudes or feelings toward a company's brands and the consumer's willingness to purchase the brand. A brand may create a high share of mind so it is readily recalled but still have a low share of heart because the brand creates a neutral or negative reaction so that the product is not considered as a viable alternative.

Share of mind can be measured by asking consumers to name the first two or three brands that come to mind when a product category is suggested, such as toothpaste. Share of heart is measured by asking consumers which brand they would prefer. The idea is to be high in both share of mind and share of heart. Usually only one or two firms per industry achieve such

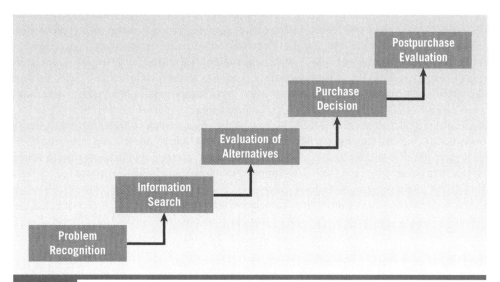

Figure 2.7   Consumer Decision-Making Process

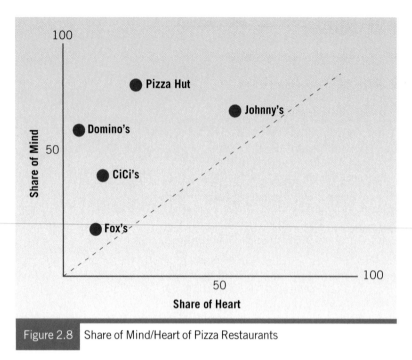

Figure 2.8   Share of Mind/Heart of Pizza Restaurants

a status. It is more common for a brand to score considerably higher in share of mind than in share of heart. As greater brand parity creeps into product industries, however, less distance separates brands in terms of share of heart.

Figure 2.8 displays the results of a marketing analysis of pizza restaurants in a Midwestern city. Respondents were asked to name the first two pizza restaurants that came to mind. They were then asked to identify their top choice. Notice that Pizza Hut had the highest share of mind, with a score around 80%; Johnny's was second, and Domino's third. All three had share of mind scores of 50% or higher. Much lower were Fox's and Cici's.

Before interpreting the concept of share of heart, notice the dotted line. It represents the point where share of mind equals share of heart. If a brand was located on the line that would mean that every person who mentioned it as one of the top of mind brands also chose it as their top choice. The local pizza restaurant, Johnny's, is almost in this position. Of the individuals who named it as top of mind, most (236 of the 280) also said it was their top choice. Notice Fox's has a very low share of mind, cited by only 15% of the sample. Most people do not think about it in their list of top two. If they did, however, it was almost always their top choice since about 11% of the sample said it was their preferred restaurant. Of the brands mentioned for this particular location, Domino's has the weakest position. The company has a relatively high share of mind, but an extremely low share of heart.

A perceptual map presents a wealth of information about the position a brand occupies in the minds and hearts of consumers. Figure 2.8 suggests that Domino's marketing team may need to develop a plan aimed at increasing loyalty since less than 5% said it was their top choice, yet over 50% cited it as one of their two top of mind brands. Fox's Pizza, however, should create a plan to increase awareness.

The concept of share of mind continues to be important when investigating business-to-business markets and the company's distribution channel. A few years ago, Mazda's marketing group concluded that share of mind was crucial for its branding rebirth campaign. Mazda had few stand-alone dealerships. Most of the time, the cars were featured in dual or multiple dealerships, with Mazda being the No. 2 player or lower. To increase emphasis of the Mazda brand name at these dealerships, Mazda offered dealerships three different but closely tied incentives. Dealerships could earn up to 3% of the sticker price for each vehicle sold if the dealership (1) improved sales, (2) improved customer service, and (3) improved facility design. If the dealership only met one or two of the three, then the incentive was reduced accordingly to 1% or 2%, respectively. That meant a dealership selling 500 Mazda vehicles a year with an average sticker price of $20,000 could earn an extra $300,000 per year if the company met all three incentives.[8]

Customer service plays a crucial role in share of heart. In many instances, entry-level workers and their supervisors have the greatest impact on these feelings. A customer evaluating Pizza Hut is most likely going to consider the closest local outlet rather than the entire chain when expressing positive or negative feelings. Someone who is treated well by the local unit on a consistent basis is most likely to have a positive share of heart response.

External Information Search

When a consumer cannot satisfy a need with a good or service identified in an internal search, the individual conducts an external search for additional information. External sources typically include

- family and friends, or word-of-mouth information;
- magazine and newspaper articles;
- visits to stores;
- surfing the Internet; and
- examining advertisements and other marketing materials.

Each of these may be given a different weight in the mind of the shopper. Some have more credibility and have more impact than others.

For your community, which pizza places would have the highest scores for share of mind? What about share of heart?

Evaluation of Alternatives

The next step in the decision-making process is the evaluation of the alternatives. This includes alternative products as well as alternative brands within a product category. Understanding how consumers conduct the evaluation helps in developing an effective marketing campaign. Consumers often use one of three methods or combinations of the three methods. The methods are (1) affect referral, (2) the evoked set, and (3) the multi-attribute method.

In the *affect referral* method, consumers choose the brand (or product) that they like or about which they hold the most positive feelings. The term *affect* refers to the affective component of an attitude, which is the feeling or emotional component. Consumers choose the brands for which they have the highest positive emotions.

The second method is the *evoked set* method. This method models circumstances in which a consumer chooses a brand from a set of brands that are viewed as acceptable. The acceptable brands constitute the evoked set. In many product categories, consumers have two or three brands that are viewed as up to standard and often as being of comparable quality. For certain products, such as restaurants, being part of the evoked set is important, because only brands in the evoked set are considered.

Two other sets of products or brands exist, the inept set and the inert set. The *inept set* holds the brands the consumer will not purchase. Normally, this occurs because of a bad personal experience. The *inert set* contains the brands the consumer knows little or nothing about. Consumers have neither positive nor negative attitudes about the brand, because they know little about it.

The final method of evaluation, the *multi-attribute* approach, is the most complex. The approach matches high-involvement purchases and socially visible products. In this method, the consumer's attitude toward the product is determined by[9]

- the brand's performance on product or brand attributes and
- the importance of each attribute to the consumer.

The concept is that an individual evaluates alternatives based on several key attributes, knowing that it is highly unlikely that one brand will score the highest on all attributes. Thus, the person considers how important each attribute is, how well each brand scores on each attribute, and which brand performs the best overall.

Understanding the information search process helps in two primary ways. First, by examining the internal search process, marketers can discover the mental processes that occur when individuals search for solutions to problems they have just recognized. Second, by studying the external search process, marketers have better knowledge about where consumers search for additional information.

The Purchase Decision

The fourth step is the purchase decision. It is useful to understand that many factors may influence the final decision. In-store signage, promotions, and other factors may alter the final decision. Knowing about them may help prevent the competition from winning a brand's customers.

Postpurchase Evaluation

Postpurchase evaluations are the final key step. In a nutshell, if a customer is satisfied, then retention becomes easier. If she is not, then a firm's marketing department may make use of customer recovery programs or damage control measures. Understanding how consumers evaluate a product after it is purchased is critical in providing goods and services that yield higher levels of customer satisfaction.

When someone chooses a place to eat, why is it important for a restaurant to be in the consumer's evoked set?

Demand and Market Potential

Thus far, this chapter has focused on the *behavioral* side of market analysis. This section is devoted to the *numerical* side. Many times, the marketing department may be asked to provide demand estimates and contribution margin projections. The most common methods used to calculate these estimates are described next.

Understanding Demand

Three terms are commonly used when discussing demand: (1) market potential, (2) market demand, and (3) company or brand demand. *Market potential* consists of the total number of individuals (or businesses) that could potentially purchase a particular product. It is the maximum number of potential customers. *Market demand* is the total current existing demand for a product, which is the sum of all brands sold within a product industry. *Company or brand demand* is the demand for a particular company's brand, and it is often referred to as *market share*.

To illustrate the differences in these terms, consider the demand for personal computers in China. The following statistics apply to Chinese households, based on per capita income, national wealth, and other factors:

Market potential = 101 million households that might want personal computers.

Market demand = 27 million households that have purchased personal computers.

Company demand = *Demand for one brand* (e.g., Apple in China) (or *market share*)

$$= \frac{10 \text{ million}}{27 \text{ million (Apple's Market Share)}}$$

$$= 37\% \text{ of the Chinese market.}$$

One additional factor may also be considered, called the penetration rate. It is calculated as follows:

$$\text{Penetration rate} = \frac{\text{Market demand}}{\text{Market potential}} = \frac{27 \text{ million}}{101 \text{ million}} = 27\%.$$

Many factors can influence the penetration rate for a product and how quickly market demand grows (see Figure 2.9). Market research can be used to identify how strongly each factor is influencing market potential and increasing market demand. This type of analysis can be used to develop a marketing approach that will increase the number of users of the product or the primary demand for the product with the goal of increasing the current market demand until it reaches the full market potential point.

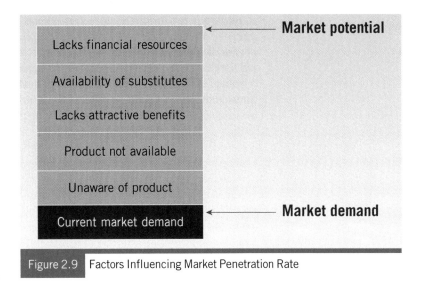

Figure 2.9   Factors Influencing Market Penetration Rate

Market Potential Factors

Figure 2.9 suggests that market penetration is affected by the number of individuals or households that are *aware (or unaware) of a product*. The greater the level of awareness for a product, normally the higher the penetration rate will be.

Product availability often becomes an issue early in the release of a new product. Consumers may be aware of a product but do not buy one because it is not available. This can also be the case in international expansion, especially when distribution channels in the new country are not fully developed.

The third factor that influences market penetration is the *lack of attractive benefits*. If individuals do not understand a product's benefits or do not see them as more attractive than the benefits of what they currently use, then it is unlikely they will purchase the new product. Closely tied to the lack of attractive benefits is the *availability of substitutes*. As an example, consider the unique, tangible benefits that cell phones offer when compared with landline phones (mobility, low long-distance charges). At the same time, consumers who are homebound and those who do not make long-distance calls may not see any real new benefits from cell phones and probably will not buy them.

The final factor influencing market penetration is the *availability of resources*. In some countries, available resources are a major factor for high-tech products such as personal computers and cell phones. While consumers in poorer countries may wish to buy cell phones or personal computers, their incomes may not be high enough to purchase both. Thus, while personal computers may be desirable, many individuals who live in poverty can only afford to purchase cell phones, because of the lower price, especially when a cell phone can be a substitute for a landline phone.

Estimating Demand

- Customer surveys
- Sales force estimates
- Executive opinions
- Quantitative methods
  - Trend projections
  - Moving averages
  - Exponential smoothing
  - Regression analysis

Figure 2.10

Methods of Estimating Demand

Few marketing managers are asked to calculate market potential, market demand, and rate of market penetration. The information is normally provided by trade associations, marketing research companies, and research institutions. Most marketing departments will, however, be asked to calculate company or brand demand.

Brand demand is used for a wide variety of purposes, such as for developing budgets, production levels, staffing levels, and stocking units. Figure 2.10 lists the primary methods of estimating the demand for a particular brand.

Customer surveys are used in industries where the number of buyers is relatively small. For instance, Boeing often uses customer surveys to evaluate the demand for jet aircraft. Producing each airplane is expensive and time-consuming. Boeing's marketing team obtains estimates about how many aircraft are required, which sizes, and when the various buyers anticipate placing orders. The same type of survey can be used by companies that build jet engines or other components of an aircraft. These types of surveys are relatively accurate in business-to-business markets, where there are a limited number of customers and projections of future needs are relatively stable.

For consumer good companies and other types of high-volume sales situations, a *sales force estimate* is often used. The sales force estimates future sales when this method is employed. Normally, a 1- or 2-year prediction is made. When asking members of the sales force for estimates, researchers must be careful about how the information is gathered and how it is used to avoid a bias in the estimates. When the estimates are used to set sales quotas, salespeople tend to provide lower numbers so that the quotas are less difficult to reach. When the estimates are not used for quotas, then salespeople might be more optimistic and suggest higher numbers. Many companies use the latter method and then adjust the sales estimates with a set reduction percentage, knowing that salespeople tend to inflate what they believe they will sell. That is, a salesperson who sold 3,000 units this year may project that he can sell 4,000 next year.

A third approach is *executive opinion*. This method avoids some of the pitfalls of the sales force estimate since experts and/or executives are asked their opinion. Typically, this method employs the Delphi technique to arrive at the final demand estimate. The Delphi method involves receiving an initial estimate from each executive. The first batch is then sent back to the group. Members are asked to reevaluate their initial estimate and send in a new one based on a review of what the other executives submitted. This iterative process continues until all the executives agree on a specific number or range for the forecast. The advantage of the executive opinion approach is that company leaders often have the most specific knowledge about the market. It may, however, be hard to recruit executives to participate, especially because the Delphi method may be viewed as being time-consuming.

Quantitative Methods

For current products on the market, quantitative methods can be used. These base future projection on past sales histories. They work well for relatively stable markets. They are not as effective when markets experience high levels of fluctuation or when they are not stable. Quantitative methods are also less accurate when significant changes in sales are related to extraneous environmental events.

Trend projections take past sales figures and use them to predict the future. If there is a steady rise in sales over time, then a clear trend exists and future predictions should be relatively accurate. For instance, if over the past 10 years of sales, data show a steady increase of about 1.35% per year, then it can be assumed that sales for the next year will also rise by 1.35%. The more past demand has fluctuated, the less reliable using a trend projection becomes.

Which of the quantitative methods of projecting sales would be appropriate for forecasting sales of children's shoes?

The *moving average* method makes a prediction based on average sales over past periods. The researcher can set the number of periods to use, such as over the past 3 years. If sales in the past 3 years have been $1.5 million, $1.7 million, and $1.2 million, the moving average would be the total of these three sales figures divided by 3, resulting in a prediction of $1.46 million for the upcoming year. This method works better than the trend projection if sales have fluctuated some during the past years but the fluctuations are not great. The number of periods in the moving average can be adjusted to allow for normal business or economic cycles.

Exponential smoothing is used when the past years' data indicate little variation and no identifiable trends. It involves adjusting the prediction by a calculation that accounts for any variance in the last period's forecast. Exponential smoothing works well in situations where demand remains stable over time.

The final quantitative method is *regression analysis*. Regression analysis may be used to identify variables that have an impact on demand. The types of variables vary depending on the product being sold. The list of variables may include national statistics such as the inflation rate or the consumer price index (CPI), state variables such as per capita income or the number of housing starts, and company statistics such as the size of the advertising budget, the number of sales calls by the sales staff, and the price of the product. Other variables may be competitive factors such as the price the primary competitors charge for the product, the number of retail outlets where the product is sold, and the size of the shelf space allotted by retailers. The purpose of a regression analysis is to incorporate all of the variables that the researcher believes may have an impact on the demand for a product. It is a much more sophisticated form of forecasting and is often more accurate than the other quantitative methods.

Contribution Margin and Break-Even Point

Two other calculations marketing managers are often asked to make are contribution margin and break-even. These two numbers have many different applications but involve the same basic concepts. The *contribution margin* is a number that represents the additional revenue that money spent on a marketing program adds to the company's financial position as compared with the costs of the program. For example, if a company spends $10,000 on a booth at a trade show and the projections are that the booth generated $15,000 in new business revenues, then the following calculation would result:

Contribution margin = Additional revenues − Costs

= $15,000 − $10,000

= $5,000.

Contribution margins may also be calculated for individual products or units. For example, if a restaurant owner adds French fries to the menu and calculates that each serving of fries costs 75 cents to produce and is sold at a price of $1.25 per serving, the contribution margin is as follows:

Contribution margin = Additional revenue per unit − Cost per unit

= $1.25 − $0.75

= $0.50 per serving.

A *break-even point* is the number of units that must be sold to cover both the fixed and the variable costs involved in producing a product or the number of additional units that must be sold to cover the costs of a marketing program. In the French fries example above, the fixed costs are those associated with buying the frying machine. If the machine cost $1,600, that is the fixed cost number. The variable costs are those associated with the ingredients (sliced potatoes, cooking oil). The break-even point is calculated as follows:

$$\text{Break-even point} = \frac{\text{Fixed cost}}{\text{Contribution margin (Price per unit − Variable cost per unit)}}$$

$$= \frac{\$1,600}{\$0.50}$$

= 3,200 units of French fries must be sold to break even.

In introducing new products, marketing managers often calculate break-even points. These help in determining whether a particular product should be offered. The same is true for adding marketing programs. In such situations, a company's leadership examines how many additional units must be sold in order to cover the costs of the proposed marketing program.

Contribution margin calculations and break-even point analyses are tools designed to assist the marketing team in spending dollars wisely. While the numbers are valuable, they must always be considered within the context of other marketing activities.

YOURCAREER

Careers in Marketing

Careers in marketing vary widely. The primary categories include advertising, marketing research, product or brand management, public relations, sales, and sales promotions. Within each of the categories are a number of different types of jobs.

Advertising

Advertising consists of a broad field with individuals employed in an array of industries. Most jobs in advertising are with advertising agencies. Some firms employ advertising experts to oversee in-house responsibilities, while others completely manage all advertising efforts. Some of the most common jobs in advertising include the following:

- Account executive—handles all aspects of an account and represents the advertising firm with clients. Responsibilities include coordinating the planning, creating, production, and implementation of an advertising campaign. Most account executives are also required to make new contacts and solicit new accounts. This job involves a variety of management skills, because the executive directs the activities of most of the other individuals in the agency.
- Media planner—determines the best mix of traditional and nontraditional media to use for advertising campaigns, matching media with the company's target market.

- Media buyer—is responsible for purchasing media space and time.
- Copywriter, creative illustrator—are responsible for the creative aspect of advertising. They design ads and write copy.
- Traffic manager—is responsible for coordinating the in-house activities of an advertising agency for the various campaigns and creative work being done. The traffic manager oversees the selection of personnel to work on various accounts and monitors all the work being done to ensure deadlines are met, which requires a number of managerial skills.

To prepare for careers in these areas, standard marketing courses are the starting point. A media planner and buyer may also take courses in communication to better understand the media. Copywriters and creatives often receive training in creative writing, art, music, and even theater or drama. A traffic manager will employ skills learned in accounting courses and will also have a marketing degree.

Marketing Research

Marketing researchers work with marketing managers or in independent research firms to conduct various types of research on consumer and business-to-business buyer behaviors. They design research projects, collect data, analyze data, and report findings to marketing managers. Researchers also collect data on market activities on an ongoing basis, such as the Nielsen media-rating reports. Marketing researchers may work for advertising agencies, marketing research firms, or corporations. In addition to marketing knowledge, these positions require solid statistical skills as well as training in the various types of research methods.

Product or Brand Management

Product or brand managers are responsible for managing a particular product category, such as the beverage category for a particular company, or managing a particular brand, such as Nabisco. They are responsible for the oversight of all aspects of brand or product management, including product modifications, package design, advertising, and sales promotions. The success or failure of a brand or product category rests on the shoulders of this individual.

Larger companies, such as Kraft, Procter & Gamble, and 3M, normally have a number of positions under the product or brand manager. These include market analysts, assistant managers, and individuals in charge of specific brands within a product category. Such companies also employ individuals who are responsible for managing a specific brand for a specific client, such as managing the Oscar Mayer brand for the Wal-Mart or Target account.

Brand and product managers usually need a number of years of marketing experience as well as a broad knowledge of both marketing and management.

Public Relations

The standard jobs in public relations are with specialized companies that provide public relations services. Many organizations and companies also have a public relations officer or staff. The responsibilities of the public relations department are to interact with the various constituencies of the organization, deal with the media, and promote the organization in a positive way. Public relations individuals work closely with any sponsorships or cause- or event-related marketing efforts. Most jobs in public relations require a degree in journalism or communications, although some individuals with marketing degrees work in the public relations field.

Sales

There are more career opportunities in sales for individuals with marketing degrees than in any other area of marketing. Sales positions vary widely from retail sales to corporate sales. Most sales positions are in the business-to-business and channels sectors. Salespeople call on large retail accounts, such as Wal-Mart, Best Buy, or JCPenney. They also call on manufacturers, such as General Electric and Sony, to sell raw materials and component parts. Salespeople are seen in almost every industry, including nonprofit organizations. The responsibilities of salespeople vary depending on the size of the accounts. For all salespeople, the primary goal is to encourage someone to make a purchase. Salespeople are on the revenue-generating side of a business. This means the income potential is normally higher than for other marketing types of jobs. This is especially true if commissions are paid on sales. Sales training consists of marketing courses, training in effective human interaction, and product- or company-specific knowledge.

Sales Promotions

Sales promotions include both consumer promotions and trade promotions. In large companies, these responsibilities are divided. In smaller companies, they are often combined. The sales promotion manager selects the proper sales promotions to accomplish specific brand, product, or corporate objectives. This individual is responsible for overseeing the creation of the promotion, the advertising of the promotion, and its implementation. Most sales promotions efforts are geared to specific targets, and because results are usually measurable, sales promotions jobs have a high degree of accountability. Sales promotion positions involve managerial activities such as planning and control processes and require marketing knowledge.

International Careers

As companies become more global, the need for marketers who can assist in international marketing will continue to rise. All the careers presented here are available in international firms and advertising agencies. In addition, the position of cultural assimilator, the primary person responsible for making sure every marketing activity matches the cultural and language specifics of a particular country, is present in a variety of international companies. Training for careers in international marketing includes marketing courses, foreign language classes, plus country-specific knowledge regarding cultural issues and cultural sensitivity.

Chapter Summary

Market analysis involves studying company customers and competitors along with the overall industry and environment. The average market analysis program consists of analyses of the environment, competition, product positioning, market segments, and customers.

An environmental analysis is normally composed of studies of political, social, economic, technological, and semicontrollable forces. Each must be understood to help assess the potential impact on current and future activities.

A competitive analysis begins with understanding all the levels of competition that a product and a company face. Then, an investigation of competitors reveals more specific information to which the marketing team can form a response.

Product positioning helps the marketing team understand the place a good or service holds in the minds of consumers and relative to the competition. Four components should be considered: (1) the target audience, (2) the good or service, (3) the frame of reference or category, and (4) the point of differentiation or uniqueness. Then, a positioning strategy can be employed based on the product's attributes, uses or applications, competitors, product users, product class, the price/quality relationship, or through a cultural symbol approach. Perceptual mapping is helpful in understanding product positioning.

Market segments can be identified through the demographic, psychographic, behavioral, and geographic characteristics of consumer markets. The most profitable segments are identified using variables such as the product-market match, segment size, sales potential, growth potential, reachability, responsiveness, retention potential, and levels of competition. It is also crucial to identify viable business-to-business segments.

Customers may be analyzed by type, where three categories exist: (1) consumers, (2) other businesses, and (3) nonprofit organizations. Applying the steps of the buying decision-making process can help the marketing team identify key opportunities to present and promote goods and services. Share of mind and share of heart are desired brand characteristics.

Many times the marketing team will be asked to estimate demand. This may be accomplished by studying market potential, market demand, and company or brand demand. It is helpful to identify the factors that will influence the market penetration rate of a company and its products. Demand is estimated using customer surveys, sales force estimates, executive opinions, and various quantitative methods.

Contribution margin and break-even analyses are designed to help the marketing team understand the values of various marketing activities. These techniques point to times when a marketing program has been successful and when it has not; however, the simple figures must always be used in the context of evaluation of the entire short- and long-term marketing program.

Chapter Terms

Brand equity   (p. 33)
Brand parity   (p. 33)
Economic forces   (p. 27)
Market analysis   (p. 26)
Market segmentation   (p. 36)
Political forces   (p. 27)
Product differentiation   (p. 36)

Product positioning   (p. 34)
Semicontrollable forces   (p. 28)
Share of heart   (p. 41)
Share of mind   (p. 41)
Social forces   (p. 27)
Technological forces   (p. 28)

Review Questions

1. Define market analysis. What analyses are a part of a market analysis program?
2. What forces are identified as part of an analysis of the company's environment?
3. Describe the levels of competition various products and companies face.
4. Define product positioning and brand parity. How are the concepts related?
5. What types of product-positioning strategies are used by marketing managers?
6. Explain the nature of perceptual mapping.
7. Name the factors that are used to identify consumer market segments.
8. Name the factors that are used to identify profitable market segments.
9. Describe the Ws of customer analysis.

10. Name the steps of the consumer buying decision-making process and the marketing challenges associated with each one.

11. Define share of mind and share of heart, and explain why they are crucial to marketing success.

12. Explain the factors that influence the market penetration rate for a good or service.

13. Name and explain the methods available to estimate demand for a good, service, or company.

14. Describe a break-even analysis and the concept of contribution margin.

CUSTOMER CORNER

Over the past two decades, the demand for and use of cell phones has exploded, both domestically and in international markets. A number of firms have entered the industry, offering a wide variety of options. Connections and contracts between companies that manufacture cell phones and telecommunications companies make the marketplace complex, volatile, and increasingly difficult to enter.

One organization that has attempted to enter the cell phone derby is Jitterbug. The approach used by the marketing team in conjunction with the manufacturing department is to match the nature of the product with the characteristics of individuals in various market segments.

One segment that Jitterbug attempts to reach is seniors. The company introduced a no-frills cell phone. It features large buttons, a large print display, 24-hour customer service, and flexible plans for low-usage customers. Presumably, this means the company's market analysis indicates that seniors are lower users and tend to have problems with vision and hand-eye coordination.

In contrast, a second product offered by Jitterbug is the Kajeet. It is a cell phone aimed at tweens and their parents. The kids get a grown-up phone with age-appropriate games, wallpapers, ring tones, and instant

What cell phone features would be the most important to older consumers?

messaging. Parents can turn the phone off at certain times of the day and control who pays for what.

For wealthier individuals who are pressed for time, Jitterbug offers the Voce. This phone costs $200 a month and is a leather or gold-plated Motorola cell phone. The fee includes annual upgrades and access to a virtual personal assistant that is available 24 hours a day to schedule appointments, make reservations, and handle other tasks.[10]

1. Using the information from this chapter, describe the market segments Jitterbug is attempting to reach as well as those it is not.

2. Explain the concepts of market potential, market demand, and company demand as they apply to cell phones and to the various brands mentioned in this Customer Corner.

3. Develop a set of talking points for supervisors working with individual salespeople who will explain the various products to customers.

4. Create a set of ideas about advertisements and promotions that would be sent along to creatives and those in the promotions department to help them develop specific marketing materials for each product and each market segment.

Discussion and Critical Thinking Questions

1. Describe an environmental analysis on these three levels, for these three types of companies:
   - A local radio station
   - A regional chain of radio stations operating in four western states
   - A national radio network

2. You are a member of the marketing department for a manufacturer of recliners and other closely related furniture products, such as living room chairs that do not recline. You have been assigned by your supervisor to gather competitive information on all your company's relevant competitors. Describe how you will go about completing this task in terms of identifying the levels of competition and how exactly you will gather competitive information.

3. The Roughneck Well Drilling Company is in the business of drilling for water, oil, and natural gas. Identify the consumer markets that are available to the company. Identify the business-to-business market segments for the company. Are there any nonprofit organizations that also may be reached? If so, which ones?

4. Walk through the steps of the consumer buying decision-making process for a company's line of lipstick products. Draw a perceptual map that explains the lipstick's position in the industry and as part of an external information search by an individual consumer. Apply the following concepts to the analysis:
   - Share of mind
   - Share of heart
   - Affect referral
   - Evoked set
   - Inept set
   - Inert set

5. Explain the following concepts:
   - Market potential
   - Market demand
   - Company or brand demand

   Apply the concepts to the following products:

   - MP3 players for automobiles
   - Global positioning systems (GPS) for combination cell phone/personal computer products
   - Long-term care insurance (nursing home cost coverage) for the elderly
   - Diet centers for women

6. Table 2.3 provides sales data for Thomas Enterprises from 2000 to 2008. Using the quantitative forecasting methods of trend analysis, moving averages, and exponential smoothing, forecast sales for 2009.
   a. For trend analysis, run a simple regression analysis with sales as the Y or dependent variable and the year as the X or independent variable. The beta coefficient for the X variable will be the trend of the sales data. To predict sales in 2009, add the beta coefficient to the 2008 sales figure.
   b. For moving averages, use a 4-year moving average. Add the sales for 2005 through 2008, and divide by 4. The answer will be the forecast for 2009.
   c. For exponential smoothing, use a smoothing coefficient of 0.3. The sales prediction for the 2008 year using exponential smoothing was $879,235. To forecast sales for 2009, use the following formula:

   2009 Sales = (2008 Actual sales × 0.7) +
                (2008 Forecast × 0.3).

Year	Sales $
2000	669,374
2001	737,705
2002	673,616
2003	783,310
2004	766,068
2005	823,036
2006	917,730
2007	877,246
2008	901,488

Table 2.3 Sales for Thomas Enterprises

7. The marketing manager for Thomas Enterprises believes a number of factors affect the company's sales. These include the company's price compared with the industry average, the money spent on promotions and advertising, the number of sales calls and sales demonstrations, the inflation rate, and the CPI. Use the data below and multiple regression analysis to forecast sales for Thomas Enterprises for 2009. The estimates for 2009 are as follows:

   Price index average = 95.0
   Promotional expenditures = $44,000
   Ad budget = $50,000
   Sales calls = 900
   Sales demonstrations = 170
   Inflation rate = 5%
   CPI = 220

Year	Sales $	Price Index Average	Promotions $	Ad Budget $	Sales Calls	Sales Demos	Inflation Rate (%)	Consumer Price Index
2000	669,374	102.0	31,432	36,120	660	123	2.74%	169.8
2001	737,705	95.4	34,721	40,210	740	135	3.73%	175.1
2002	673,616	106.3	31,000	36,800	684	124	1.14%	177.1
2003	783,310	99.3	37,241	42,500	781	146	2.60%	181.7
2004	766,068	102.1	36,433	41,832	766	143	1.93%	185.2
2005	823,036	96.3	38,500	44,905	822	154	2.97%	190.7
2006	917,730	91.2	42,715	50,250	911	173	3.99%	198.3
2007	877,246	94.5	40,116	47,700	876	164	2.08%	202.4
2008	901,488	93.2	43,121	49,512	890	168	4.28%	211.1

Table 2.4 Regression Data for Thomas Enterprises

8. The 2008 sales for Thomas Enterprises was $901,488. Cost of goods sold was $522,863, cost of consumer and trade promotions was $43,121, and advertising costs were $49,512. What was the contribution margin in dollars and as a percentage of revenue?

9. One of the products sold by Thomas is priced at $32.89. Variable costs are $19.65 each, and fixed costs were $56,000. What is the contribution margin per unit, and what is the break-even point to cover the fixed costs?

Chapter 2 Case

Scooping Up Success?

Everyone loves ice cream. At least that is what Kraig Andersen always believed. For more than 20 years, he and his wife operated the Andersen's Ice Cream Shop in Destin, Florida. The relatively warm climate of the area, an active tourist trade, and an excellent location near the beach all contributed to the success of the store.

Ice cream takes many forms. Originally, the two main types were soft serve and hard ice cream. Over time, products evolved to include fat-free versions and "lite" versions of ice cream along with hard and soft frozen yogurt and sherbet. Kraig had held his ground in his store, serving hard ice cream and its many variations, most notably sundaes, banana splits, and cones.

How important is an area's climate and location to the success of an ice cream shop?

In 2005, Destin experienced a glancing blow from a major hurricane. The Andersen's Ice Cream Shop endured major water damage, and the building's roof was completely destroyed. Although his insurance settlement did not fully cover the damages, Kraig repaired his building and reopened the business, only to suffer a major heart attack 1 year later. He concluded it was time to sell the business.

Several prospective buyers were shown the store. Many asked if they could keep the same name or if they would need to find a new brand. Others asked for statistics on sales and profits over the past 10 years, but especially before and after the hurricane. Some wondered if most of the business came from the locals or if tourists provided the major source of revenue. They also asked about ages: Were most of the customers families with children, or did a wider variety of people visit the shop?

One prospect noted that an ice cream shop in the Hilton Head area of South Carolina, offered hard ice cream with a twist: each person was able to "customize" his or her ice cream with a wide variety of toppings that were set out in a smorgasbord-type arrangement. Everything was available, from nuts to sprinkles to jelly beans, along with all types of toppings (strawberry, chocolate, pineapple, and 10 others) and whipped cream and cherries to top things off. This buyer wondered if a similar addition to Andersen's Ice Cream Shop would create greater revenues.

Kraig responded that his business was based on more than just the products. It was the entire ice-cream-buying experience that kept people coming back. The store was brightly lit and clean, with music from the 1950s and 1960s playing softly in the background. People sat in booths similar to ice cream parlors from the past. He believed that nostalgia played a major role in his return business and that word of mouth brought in new customers.

Many prospective buyers noted that ice cream was available in grocery stores, fast-food outlets such as McDonald's and Wendy's, and convenience stores with soft serve dispensers and that recently a Braum's Dairy Store had just opened down the street. The Braum's chain offered all varieties of ice cream plus meals, such as hamburgers and other fast-food-type items. These buyers wondered if the shop would be able to compete with all these other outlets.

Kraig noted his longstanding ties in the community of Destin. His store sponsored many local sports teams, including Little League Baseball, basketball, and soccer youth programs; bowling teams; and an adult coed softball team. He had made a point of distributing discount and free sample coupons for people to use following Wednesday night church services by giving the coupons to the local clergy. His store also provided cakes and ice cream for birthday parties and to local businesses when special events took place.

The final buyer to visit, and the one that made an offer, said his decision was based not on speculation but on market analysis. The buyer noted that some things would be left the same while others would need to be updated and changed. Reluctantly, Kraig handed over the keys to the building and began his retirement.

1. Assess the environment surrounding the Andersen's Ice Cream Shop.

2. Assess the industry and competitors that the new buyer of the Andersen's Ice Cream Shop probably considered.

3. Explain the role that customer service may have played in the past success of the store using the following terms: brand parity, brand equity, product positioning, perceptual mapping, and product differentiation.

4. Outline the market segments Andersen's Ice Cream currently served as well as potential new segments if they exist. If not, explain why there are no new segments to be tapped.

5. Which model of buying behavior best suits an analysis of Andersen's Ice Cream Shop: affect referral, evoked set, or multi-attribute?

6. Explain how the concepts of market potential, market demand, and company demand would enter into the decision to buy the Andersen's Ice Cream Shop.

Go to **www.sagepub.com/clow** for additional exercises and study resources. Select **Chapter 2, Market Analysis** for chapter-specific activities.

Customers at warehouse stores such as Costco earn annual incomes that average over $75,000.

Data Warehousing

Costco: Data-Driven, Employee-Centered Marketing

The average retail grocery store carries 40,000 different products. Similar merchants, such as Wal-Mart, Sam's Club, and Target, feature even more units on the shelves. Tracking and stocking such a wide variety of products becomes a massive undertaking. Making decisions with regard to which products to add, which to delete, and which ones deserve special attention (end-of-the-aisle placement, eye-level shelf placement), requires a great deal of investigation.

Enter Costco, with a new marketing model. Costco was founded as a single store in Seattle in 1983 using a simple idea that has been repeated ever since. The typical Costco retail store stocks only 4,000 products, many in high-volume containers. Instead of a 16-ounce jar of peanuts, the Costco version is

more likely to weigh 3 pounds. Costco loyalists know that they will pay lower prices for higher quantities of the products they choose.

Costco stores carry more than groceries. Furniture, clothing, and other items are sold at the best possible prices. Many of the products featured are both low priced but also high quality. The standard markup for any item sold in the store is 14%. No private-label item is marked up by more than 15%. In contrast, supermarkets generally mark up merchandise by 25% and department stores by 50% or more.

Customers have responded. In order to enter Costco and take advantage of the great prices, each household purchases a membership card with an annual fee. Costco has nearly 50 million members. Households pay about $50 per year for a membership, and small businesses pay $100. The membership cards allow Costco's marketing department access to a great deal of customer information to be used in marketing programs. The company's marketing team carefully tracks product purchases to identify which items are the most viable. Successes are reordered and those that do not move are replaced.

The marketing team recognizes that Costco's members are not just low-income bargain hunters. The average annual household income of Costco customers is over $75,000, with 31% of the regular customers earning over $100,000 per year.

Costco's marketing department makes sure that the company does not drift too far into offering only low-cost merchandise, even at the warehouse stores. The company

routinely offers what is called a "treasure hunt," which is an occasional, temporary special for items such as exotic cheeses, plasma screen televisions, Waterford crystal, French wine, and $5,000 necklaces. The gems are scattered among staples such as toilet paper by the case and institutional-size jars of mayonnaise. The treasure hunts create a sense of excitement and generate customer loyalty.

Customers are not the only ones who are happy with Costco. The company pays much higher wages than any of its competitors in the same category. Eighty-five percent of Costco's workers have health insurance, as compared with fewer than half at Wal-Mart and Target. Part-time workers become eligible for health insurance after just 6 months on the job, as compared with 2 years at Wal-Mart. The company also covers many dental expenses. Costco contributes generously to its workers' 401(k) plans, starting with 3% of salary the second year and rising to 9% after 25 years. It is not surprising that many Costco workers have long-time records of committed service.

The results have been dramatic. In 2005, in the United States, Costco stores averaged $121 million in sales annually, far more than the $70 million for Sam's Club. Currently, the company has nearly 500 retail store locations, mostly in the United States. Some stores are also in Canada, Britain, South Korea, Taiwan, and Japan. The company's track record of success continues, as new customers discover the benefits of this unique type of shopping experience.[1]

Chapter Overview

Today's marketing managers cope with the impact of two major innovations. The first, improvements in computer technology, creates many new possibilities in the areas of storing information and analyzing the data being stored. The second, increasing competition, results from Internet usage and the expanding worldwide marketplace. Responding to these challenges means that the development of a quality database program has become essential for businesses in the 21st century. The cornerstone of a database program is the data warehouse, which holds all customer data and can be accessed by any employee who deals with customers in any capacity.[2]

This chapter examines the role of the data warehouse in an overall marketing management program. A quality data warehouse is now an irreplaceable tool for a marketing program. The marketing team uses data to identify individual consumers and market segments. Data can be collected and analyzed to facilitate numerous marketing functions, beginning with effective customer service.

In the first section of this chapter, the basic nature of a data warehouse and the functions it provides are discussed. The next section features analytical data, noting two key methods of using data: a lifetime value analysis approach and the recency, frequency, and monetary (RFM)–analysis technique. Data-driven marketing programs are then described, followed by a presentation of the importance of testing data-based marketing tactics.

Customer data assist the efforts of every member of the marketing department beginning with entry-level salespeople and inbound telemarketing operators. The same data program becomes invaluable to supervisors seeking to improve departmental outcomes, such as increasing sales and customer satisfaction. Marketing managers employ data analysis techniques to assist with strategic marketing efforts such as adding or eliminating products as well as selecting methods to effectively reach target markets.

The Data Warehouse

As the world becomes increasingly impersonal and technology driven, many marketing managers have reached the conclusion that two key ingredients in marketing success are knowing your customers and having them know you. An effective data warehouse facilitates both of these objectives.

In building a data warehouse, the first distinction to be made is between an operational database and the marketing database. The *operational database* contains the transactions customers have with the firm. It follows generally accepted accounting principles. The *marketing database* holds information about current customers, former customers, and prospects, as well as transactional data. A marketing database also carries records of every interaction between the customer and the company, regardless of which employee the customer spoke with, and includes any other form of contact.

Data Warehouse Functions

Cutting-edge data warehouses are designed to be much more than repositories of names, addresses, and past purchases. These warehouses have many uses. The most common functions are listed in Figure 3.1.

Customer communication emerges as the most vital function served by a data warehouse. Information stored in a database can be used to improve contacts between the company and its customers. Building customer loyalty along with strengthening perceptions of brand equity over time are key goals. The Internet and e-mail offer the lowest cost methods of communicating with customers. Both are accessible 24 hours per day, 7 days per week.

One method to improve communication is building greater levels of personalization, in which a consumer receives distinct marketing offers and other advantages tailored to his individual identity and needs. This enhances that perception that the customer is valued and known by those in the company. A data warehouse that fails to facilitate quality communication has little real value.

A strong company presence on the Internet remains crucial. Just being on the Internet is not enough. A *Web site operation* includes database technology that allows for

- Customer communication
- Web site operations
- Data-driven marketing programs
- Customer service operations
- Customer information
- Sales staff operations
- Market planning

Figure 3.1

Functions of a Data Warehouse

Why is personalization of a Web site helpful when selling products online?

personalization of Web content. It also provides product information that is easy to access along with convenience and financial incentives for those who visit the site and make purchases. In addition, the Web site should gather pertinent information about and from customers that can be used for future communications, marketing programs, and interactions.

Numerous *data-driven marketing programs* may be developed using the data warehouse. The database analytics discussed later in this chapter allow marketing experts to locate the customers who are the most likely to respond to particular marketing programs. Rather than sending the same marketing piece to every customer and/or business prospect on a list, specific individuals and companies can be targeted. Then, the content presented in the marketing piece or sales presentation is modified based on information obtained from the database. This creates cost savings and improves response rates at the same time.

The data warehouse provides valuable assistance for *customer service operations*. When a customer contacts the company, the employee who answers already has access to a great deal of information about the person. Today's databases relay the information instantly and allow a trained customer service representative to provide better quality assistance. This creates the potential to enhance the relationship between the customer and the company.

Another key feature of a database program is offering quality *customer information*. The costs associated with running customer service operation centers are high. Consequently, most marketing teams place a great deal of information on the company's Web site. Some take the form of a FAQ (frequently asked questions) file. Other information may be provided through an indexed menu. The text explains how to operate or use a product. It can also offer troubleshooting advice or help a customer find a brick-and-mortar location for the company. The site can be used to update shipping information on an order that has been placed or on the status of a back order. Posting information in this way allows customers to gather information without needing to call a store or visit in person.

For business-to-business operations, a data warehouse equips field salespeople with instantaneous information about customers. Salespeople review information about clients or prospects immediately before making sales calls. When orders are requested, the salesperson immediately places the order online. Access to information about past orders and shipping information are provided on the spot. A salesperson may even check the company's inventory level to make sure sufficient merchandise remains in stock to fill the customer's order.

The data warehouse supplies important product sales information to be used in preparing marketing plans. Most databases have the capability of analyzing when products were sold, where they were sold, and to whom. Building profiles of customers of a particular product through sales data takes the guesswork out of identifying target customers. Wise marketing decisions are made when the correct data are stored and the best analytical tools are used to extract the needed information.

Members of the information technology (IT) department should be made aware of the functions a data warehouse will serve. The functions dictate the type of data to be collected and how to format and store the data.

An effective data warehouse program *facilitates customer service*. In the current marketing environment, many times a consumer does not have a face-to-face interaction with a salesperson or other company personnel. These new technologies help ensure that a consumer feels that she is receiving unique, personalized service.

The Data in the Data Warehouse

A data warehouse can only be as good as the data it holds. Figure 3.2 identifies the four primary types of data contained in a marketing data warehouse. Customer and transaction data are collected internally. Appended data are purchased from external sources. Analytical data are the outcome of data analysis procedures and manipulations of the data.

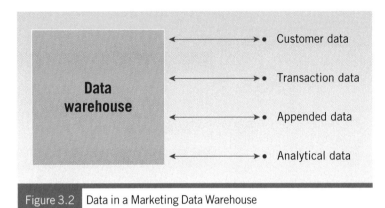

Figure 3.2   Data in a Marketing Data Warehouse

Customer Data

Data warehousing begins with collecting customer names, addresses, and contact information, including phone numbers and e-mail addresses. For business-to-business companies, this information should be easy to gather because the type of information will be exchanged as part of the ordering or purchasing process. For retail consumers, it can be more challenging. Information must be gathered without violating the customer's privacy. Consequently, the best situation occurs when the customer volunteers the information. One common method used with consumers is through membership cards, such as the ones sold by Costco, or by offering a frequency or loyalty club. These programs request customer information in exchange for discounts and other rewards.

The basic rule of thumb in collecting customer data remains "the more the better." Companies rarely collect too much information. Often, too little is collected. At the same time, when the marketing team solicits customer information, the team should only ask for information related to the products being sold or the benefits of joining the club or incentive program. For instance, a retail-clothing clerk may ask for a customer's birth date knowing that the marketing department plans to send the individual a birthday card containing a gift or special offer.

Approximately 20% of Americans move each year. Consequently, contact information must be constantly updated. When individuals fill out a change-of-address form with the U.S. Postal Service, the information is sent to all the service bureaus authorized to sell the information to businesses. A company that sends database names to one of these service bureaus receives address updates for only a few cents per hit, or per individual who moves. Updating mailing addresses normally occurs at least once each year or prior to any mass mailing or when any marketing program is undertaken using contact information from the database.

A strong marketing database includes customer profiles with specific information regarding each customer's personal preferences. The manner in which these profiles and any personal preference information are collected varies by company. Some obtain it from customer surveys. Others gather the information from visits to a retail store or the firm's Web site.

Transaction Data

Customer purchases, communications, and interactions with the company are tracked as transaction data. Details regarding every purchase must be entered into the database. Doing so is simple and routine as long as individuals identify themselves. When they do not, there is no way of knowing who made the purchase. This leads marketing professionals to offer incentives that encourage self-identification. Effective incentives provide real benefits to customers and give them a compelling reason to self-identify.

How can cookie information be used to personalize greetings and Web content?

Information about every interaction a customer has with the company will be stored as transaction data. If the customer sends an e-mail to tech support for assistance, the information should be placed in the database. When a customer returns a product or calls customer service with a complaint, the information is documented. Every interaction, regardless of mode, can be recorded. This information assists customer service representatives as they handle future interactions. A customer service rep who sees a customer called about a problem 2 months ago and is calling again about the same problem will be better equipped to handle the problem. When a customer makes contact for a different reason, the customer service rep recognizes a problem occurred 2 months ago and should ask if the problem has been resolved.

The same methodology can be used to provide reassurance about previous purchases. Thus, a salesperson might ask the customer if he enjoys the suit he purchased 3 weeks ago. When the customer expresses concern about its fit or some other problem, the salesperson suggests remedies.

Transaction data may also be used to generate follow-up e-mails after a period of time has elapsed since the purchase. For example, 30 days after a purchase, an e-mail can be sent thanking the customer for the purchase. The e-mail typically provides contact information if for any reason the customer becomes dissatisfied. Cross-selling of compatible or related items might also be included in the e-mail. The marketing team should be careful, however, and remember that the main focus of the e-mail is thanking the customer and not trying to initiate new sales.

Another aspect of a customer's data history is often considered. Many times, someone from the company initiates contact with customers. This information should also be placed in the database, along with the customer's response.

Most data warehouse programs also track visits to the organization's Web site. Through cookies, information about what products the customer viewed and even how long she stayed on a particular page can be gathered. This information can be helpful; however, what is more valuable is the ability to personalize the firm's Web site for each customer. When a customer logs onto the site, a greeting such as "Welcome back Hannah" can appear. The cookie technology makes it possible for the system to recognize that Hannah, or at least someone using her computer, is accessing the Web site. If Hannah has purchased products or browsed the catalog in the past, then the content of the Web pages may be further personalized to contain the products she might have an interest in purchasing.

Information obtained from cookies can also be used to target specific customers with specific marketing offers. To illustrate the power of the Web site and database technology, Williams-Sonoma, a cookware and tableware retailer, tracks every visitor to its Web site. An e-mail offer sent to customers who had browsed for a particular item on the Web site led to a response rate that was 9 times higher than an indiscriminate mass e-mail. The Pottery Barn's marketing team targeted an e-mail for the Chesapeake furniture collection to only those buyers who had previously made purchases from the company. Responses were 18 times higher than responses for untargeted e-mails.[3]

One important concept for any marketing manager to remember is that useful transaction data collection programs include much more than simply recording what has happened in the past. When used correctly, these data can be a major force in creating a customer-oriented marketing program. The net results may be improved customer loyalty and the potential for greater sales and profits.

Appended Data

Customer information is extremely valuable but may not always be enough. This will be especially true for a business that has difficulty collecting personal information. In such situations, additional demographic and even psychographic information may be obtained through a number of independent marketing or database research firms that specialize in collecting customer data. KnowledgeBase Marketing, Donnelly, Dialog, and Nielsen Claritas are four of the many companies that sell this type of information.

These firms collect data about individuals such as income, age, family members, lifestyle, and purchase behaviors. For example, KnowledgeBase Marketing maintains a database consisting of 236 million U.S. consumers. The data include demographic information such as exact age, income, type of home, lifestyle information, and transaction data. These data are updated monthly from about 20 different sources, including the U.S. Census Bureau.[4] A company can send its customer data file to one of these research firms, which will append the customer's current information. With such data available, almost any type of business will be able to develop an in-depth database.

A valuable appended procedure for nationwide companies is geocoding, the process of adding geographic codes to each customer record so that the addresses of customers can be plotted on a map. Geocodes are used for targeting direct mail campaigns and choosing a location for a retail outlet. Geocoding also allows for combining demographic information with lifestyle data. This assists the marketing manager in selecting media where ads are most likely to be noticed.

One version of geocoding software is named *CACI Coder/Plus*. The software identifies a cluster in which an address belongs. A group such as Enterprising Young Singles in the CACI system contains certain characteristics, such as enjoying dining, spending money on videos and personal computers, and reading certain magazines. A business could then target this group with mailings and special offers.

Geocoding software such as CACI Coder/Plus allows company marketers to identify characteristics of a market segment, such as the magazines they tend to read.

Analytical Data

The final component of a data warehouse is the analytical data. It consists of the data and codes generated through the analysis of the data. While many types of analysis can be performed, the two most common are lifetime value analysis and RFM analysis. These two methods are helpful in a variety of marketing efforts.

Lifetime Value Analysis

The first form of analysis is the calculation of the lifetime value of a customer or market segment. Lifetime value is a monetary figure that represents the profit stream that a customer generates over his lifetime. Remember that 20% of Americans move every year. Therefore, the typical lifetime of a consumer will be calculated as lasting 5 to 6 years, because the term *lifetime* refers to the time that a customer can make purchases from a particular firm before moving to a new address, not the literal life span of an individual. For business-to-business customers, a lifetime may be longer because businesses continue in existence even when there are changes in management.

Some companies calculate the lifetime values of individual customers, while others calculate it for market segments. Many marketing experts believe the latter is more accurate because it aggregates revenues and costs across the entire segment. Using a market segment provides information that aids the marketing manager in developing programs aimed at the entire consumer group. Individual lifetime value calculations result in figures for individual customers and therefore are less useful when considering the overall population of customers and potential customers.

The key figures in calculating the lifetime value of a customer or set of customers are revenues, costs, retention rates, and visits or purchases per time period, normally 1 year. Revenue and costs are normally easy to obtain, since companies record these numbers for accounting purposes.

The cost of acquiring a new customer is a key figure. It is calculated by dividing the total marketing and advertising expenditures in dollars by the number of new customers obtained. As an example, if $200,000 dollars are spent and the company acquires 2,000 new customers as a result, then the acquisition cost will be $100 per customer.

Another key figure is the cost of maintaining a database. This amount represents the cost of maintaining the marketing database and populating it with data on a daily or regular basis.

Retention rates and *purchases per year* are more challenging. Both require an accurate marketing database system and are based on the principle that individuals within the database are identified each time a purchase is made. If this is done, then it becomes easier to calculate the average number of purchases made per year. It is a little more difficult to determine the retention rate, which specifies how many customers were kept and how many were lost during the year. In some cases, a customer may not have defected but for some reason has not made a recent purchase. The problem becomes less severe when analyzing an entire market segment consisting of several thousands or millions of customers.

Lifetime Value Calculations

One method for calculating lifetime value is shown in Table 3.1. The table presents a lifetime value calculation of The Hot Spot Fashions customers holding membership cards. The Hot Spot is a small retailing chain whose primary target market is 15- to 30-year-old females.

At the time the calculation was performed, The Hot Spot had approximately 5,000 customers in its database. Approximately 50% of the customers provided information for the retailer's database by signing up for a membership card in the first year. In the second year following the sign up, 60% were expected to continue with the club. By the third year approximately 70% were expected to stay with the club.

	Year 1	Year 2	Year 3
Customers	5,000	2,500	1,500
Retention rate (%)	50	60	70
Visits/year	2.9	4.3	8.6
Sales/visit ($)	63.25	95.30	114.60
Total revenue ($)	917,125	1,024,475	1,478,340
Variable costs (%)	65	65	65
Variable costs ($)	596,131	665,909	960,921
Acquisition costs ($52)	260,000		
Database costs ($3)	15,000	7,500	4,500
Total costs ($)	871,131	673,409	965,421
Gross profit ($)	45,994	351,066	512,919
Cumulative gross profit ($)	45,994	397,060	909,979
Lifetime value ($)	9.20	79.41	182.00

Table 3.1   Lifetime Value for The Hot Spot Fashions

The Hot Spot calculation of a customer's lifetime value was for a period of 3 years. There is nothing magic about the figure. The marketing team can use any number of years, but the longer the period, the more difficult it becomes to estimate future behavior. If only 1 or 2 years are used, then the period is too short to accurately project behavior and determine purchase habits.

Notice that the calculations for Year 2 and Year 3 are for the Year 1 cohort only. Each year, this fashion retailer will add new members. It is best if each year, the lifetime value for that year is kept separately because of the cost of acquiring customers during that first year.

The total revenue is calculated for just the 5,000 customers who signed up during Year 1. As long as members identify themselves, the revenue record remains accurate. If members do not, then the purchases they make are not included in these calculations. That is why it is important to have an incentive that encourages the person to show the membership card. Employees can also be trained to ask for membership cards at each sale. If the customer does not have the card with her, it should be available through a telephone number or other easy-to-use method.

Three cost figures are needed to determine the lifetime value: variable costs, acquisition costs, and database costs. While variable costs do fluctuate for each item of clothing that is sold, the retailer can estimate an overall variable cost for the merchandise sold in the store. The acquisition cost is the total marketing and advertising budget for that year, which in this case was $260,000. The Hot Spot just barely breaks even in Year 1. It is not unusual for a business to actually lose money in acquiring new customers. The database costs are an estimate of how much it costs per person to maintain and update the information in the database.

The lifetime value of this original set of customers over a 3-year period is $182.00 per customer. This is the average amount of profit each of the customers who joins the fashion club generates. The figure gives the marketing manager at The Hot Spot an idea of how much can be spent seeking to maintain customer loyalty.

Applications of the Lifetime Value Concept

When spending marketing dollars, standard goals include increasing revenues and lifetime values. A marketing program that does not increase the overall lifetime value of a market segment has a questionable value.[5] As an example, consider how the marketing team at The Hot

Brianna returned to The Hot Spot Fashions to shop for clothes after receiving a $25 coupon on her birthday.

Spot might evaluate offering a $25 coupon to each customer on his birthday. The objective could be to encourage the patron to join the club, to use the membership card on purchases, or simply to remain as an active member. The cost of the coupon reduces the lifetime value of each member by $16.25 ($25 × 0.65, the variable cost of the clothing sold). The decision to be made by the marketing manager will be whether the coupon vouchers increase the number or monetary value of future purchases to the point where they exceed the additional costs.

The average lifetime value for each customer ($182.00) provides valuable information when dealing with her. For instance one customer, Renee, brings back a dress that she purchased because she is dissatisfied with the way it fit. In looking up Renee's account, the salesclerk notices that Renee's personal lifetime value is $400, based on a higher frequency of purchases. Also, in the past 3 years Renee has only returned one other item. Knowing this, the clerk cheerfully takes the dress back and offers her credit toward her next purchase.

In contrast, a second customer, who only makes an average of two purchases per year, has a lifetime value of $33. This person has returned items three times in the past year. Unless the item is defective, as stated in the store's return policy, the clerk may refuse to accept the return. The salesclerk may conclude that a loyal customer such as Renee deserves extra-special treatment, whereas the other customer does not.

Finally, as shown in Table 3.1, loyal customers make more purchases and also increase the amounts they spend on each visit. Retaining them is clearly more efficient and cost-effective than constantly seeking to acquire new customers. This, once again, points to the value of maintaining a strong customer-oriented approach in managing a business.

STOP AND THINK

1. Name some events or changes that could affect the lifetime value calculation for an individual consumer (*Hint:* Think in terms of personal events, such as marriage, divorce, etc.).

2. In the example featuring Renee returning an item and receiving credit while another customer was refused, do you think it is wise to treat customers differently based solely on a lifetime value figure? Defend your answer.

3. As a supervisor in a sales department, what kinds of benefits and problems might emerge from your sales force having access to the lifetime value calculation of each customer?

4. Can you think of companies that would be likely to assign you a high lifetime value number? Do they make decisions based on your value to them?

5. Which is more valuable to the advertising department, the lifetime value of an individual customer or the lifetime value of a segment of customers? Would your answer be the same for the sales manager?

RFM Analysis

RFM stands for recency, frequency, and monetary. *Recency* represents the date of the last purchase. *Frequency* is the number of purchases within a specific time period, normally 1 year. *Monetary* refers to the level of monetary expenditures with a firm and is usually expressed as total expenditures per year.

Each individual customer receives a code number based on the RFM analysis procedure. First, recency is coded based on when a customer's last purchase was made. The database is divided into five approximately equal groups based on the date of each individual's last purchase. The groups are then coded. The standard values are 5, 4, 3, 2, and 1. A code of "5" is assigned to the group that has made the most recent purchases, "4" for the second most recent group, and so forth, with those making the least recent purchases coded "1."

The same procedure will be used for the frequency. The database is resorted by frequency of purchase and divided into five approximately equal groups. The group that made the highest number of purchases receives the highest number. Thus, a "5" is selected for those who have made the most frequent purchases, a "4" for the next group, down to a "1" for those who made the least frequent purchases.

Table 3.2 displays the frequency values assigned to The Hot Spot's database of customers. As shown, 913 shoppers are coded "5," and 1,340 are coded "1." While the ideal would be to have five equal groups, data do not always lend themselves to such a concise analysis.

The same procedure is used to code the total amount of money spent during the year by each individual. Those who purchased the most are coded "5," and those who spent the least are coded "1."

When the three codes have been assigned, each customer is represented by a three-digit code that corresponds to the person's recency, frequency, and monetary expenditures. Codes range from 555 to 111. A person with a score of 235, for instance, has not recently made a purchase, has made an average number of purchases in terms of frequency, but has spent a large amount of money during the year.

Applications of an RFM Analysis

In an RFM analysis, the codes can be aggregated to provide excellent information as a whole and may also be used for each customer individually. Clearly, customers with values of 555 hold the highest importance to the company, and customers with a 111 are the least significant. The marketing department typically looks for common characteristics for both types of groups. For example, when the manager discovers that most customers having values of 444 or higher are likely to be female professionals with higher incomes and with college degrees, the information can be used in choosing television programs for commercials as well as the themes presented in those advertisements. If the manager finds out that most customers with values of 222 or lower are males and have not attended college, certain advertising venues and messages should be eliminated.

Number of Visits	Quantity	Code
5+	913	5
4	657	4
3	922	3
2	1,146	2
1	1,340	1

Table 3.2   Frequency Groups for The Hot Spot Fashions

Typically, the recency value has the most significant impact on future purchases. Individuals who have purchased recently (those with a score of "5" as the first number in the code) are more inclined to purchase again. The longer the time since the last purchase, the less likely it becomes that the customer will make a purchase or respond to a marketing initiative.

The same holds true for frequency, although frequency is not as precise in predicting future behaviors as is recency. The more frequently an individual makes a purchase (with a score of "5" as the second number in the code), the more likely the person is to make another purchase.

The least predictive figure in the RFM analysis is monetary, the third number in the code. The amount of money a person spent does not necessarily predict that the person will make a purchase in the near future. Consequently, it offers a less clear indication of how valuable that customer may be.

In summary, analytical data are used to perform calculations of lifetime values and RFM values. The results can be used at top levels to make strategic choices such as product modifications, brand extension programs, and other marketing programs. The same information, when passed along effectively to first-line employees and supervisors, can assist in customizing interactions with individual customers. Both programs highlight the value of customer service in building loyalty, especially with a firm's best customers.

Data Mining

Two additional methods are available to analyze data in order to identify meaningful patterns and relationships. One primary technique is data mining. Data mining includes two activities: (1) building profiles of customer segments and (2) preparing models that predict future purchase behaviors based on past purchases.

Profiles of Customer Segments

Data mining may be used to develop a profile of the company's best customers. The profile, in turn, can help to identify prospective new customers or locate current customers who can be upgraded through marketing endeavors to the "best" customer category. For example, The Hot Spot's marketing team may develop a profile of the customers who average five or more purchases per year. Using this profile allows the marketing department to identify customers in the firm's database who fit the profile but are not making five or more purchases per year. A marketing manager can then develop a special marketing effort designed to tie these customers closer to the company and encourage additional purchases. It may be a premium offer, or an offer to a special fashion show sponsored by The Hot Spot.

AutoNation's marketing department systematically collects information from its customers and appends it to purchase information from third party sources. Both in-house and external data sources allow the marketing team to collect demographic information such as age, income, family situation, and current vehicle. Lifestyle information such as travel records, magazine subscriptions, and memberships in organizations is then attached to each customer's record. In-market data, including vehicle repair records, the age of the vehicle, and Internet keyword searches, are added to the database. Finally, loan balances, especially on automobiles, are added along with credit scores.

This type of profile information assists in locating the individuals who are most likely to be in the market for a new or used car. To illustrate the power of this type of data mining program approach, consider the following statistics: An AutoNation mailing that was sent to 103,000 people indiscriminately, not using the database, resulted in 94 sales. Each sale cost $998 to generate. When the marketing department used data mining to build a profile of individuals likely to be in the market for a vehicle, a second AutoNation mailing was sent out to 245,000 potential customers. It resulted in 1,008 vehicles sold at a marketing cost of only $228 per sale.[6]

Predicting Future Purchase Behaviors

The second data mining method involves developing models that predict future sales based on past purchasing activities. This information may be used in a number of ways. It can be helpful for cross-selling, development of special marketing programs, or creating specific communications. For instance, suppose that through data mining a marketing manager at The Hot Spot learns that 40% of the customers who purchase a particular skirt also purchase one of three tops. To encourage additional purchases of the two products together, the salesclerk points out how well the top matches the skirt. Also, the items can be displayed together to encourage joint purchases.

The marketing team at Goody's family clothing store used data mining when analyzing baskets of merchandise purchased by individual shoppers. The data mining analysis revealed the types of items customers tended to purchase together.[7] This information assisted in the development of advertising and consumer promotions programs, point-of-purchase displays, and store layouts.

Data mining provides a marketing manager with information that may be used in many ways. By basing marketing decisions on analysis of purchase data, particular products might be emphasized or de-emphasized, sales tactics may be modified, and specific marketing offers can be sent to the people who are most likely to take advantage of them.

Through data mining, AutoNation's advertising team was able to reduce direct-mail marketing costs from $998 per sale to $228 per sale.

Data-Driven Marketing Programs

There are a number of data-driven marketing programs available to be used in conjunction with a data warehouse. Figure 3.3 identifies the most common one. Most of these are described in greater detail in future chapters of this textbook. The programs are often used as tactics associated with customer interactions and customer retention.

- Trawling
- Direct marketing
- Permission marketing
- Frequency or loyalty programs
- Viral marketing
- Customization

Figure 3.3

Data-Driven Marketing Programs

How can database technology be used to reach the individuals who are most likely to buy through direct mail?

Trawling

One form of data-driven marketing that has grown in popularity is known as trawling, a process of searching the database for a specific piece of information for marketing purposes. For example, The Home Depot and Lowe's marketing programs include trawling to locate individuals who have recently moved or listed their homes to sell. These potential customers often make expenditures associated with fixing up a home for sale and making changes in the new home that has just been purchased.

Other marketers trawl a database to identify anniversary dates with the company. Thus, a letter with a free gift or special offer may be sent to individuals on the 5th or 10th anniversary with the company. Some car dealerships send correspondence on each year's anniversary of a car purchase to see if the customer remains satisfied or might be interested in trading for a new vehicle. Trawling includes finding ways to offer marketing incentives to specific individuals who meet a certain criterion.

Trawling also helps identify individuals in the database who have not made a purchase recently. As noted earlier, recency is a prime indicator of future purchases. Consequently, identifying individuals who have not made a recent purchase can lead to programs designed to regain those customers. A special "we missed you" communication with some type of incentive to make another purchase may be sent. Such communication lets customers know that they have been missed and the company would like to have them back. If, by chance, the customer was dissatisfied, it also provides an opportunity for that person to lodge a complaint. The marketing team then responds to fix the problem and build loyalty for the future.

Direct Marketing

Direct marketing occurs when a company sells items directly to end users. Common forms of direct marketing include standard mail, inbound telemarketing, television infomercial offers, catalog orders, and purchases over the Internet. Direct marketing provides a rapid and low-cost connection with consumers wishing to place orders.

Through database technology, direct marketing today is efficient and cost-effective. Instead of sending a direct-mail piece to everyone, data analysis can be used to select the individuals, or businesses, that are the most likely to respond. This not only increases the response rate, it also decreases total costs. Instead of mailing out 1 million offers at a cost of 70 cents each, only 400,000 may be mailed out, which reduces the total cost. The savings may be used to increase the quality of the pieces that are mailed.

Permission Marketing

Permission marketing involves sending marketing offers to individuals who have given the company permission to do so. Response rates will certainly be higher. The key, however, is to make sure the person has truly given permission and wants to receive the offers. Some companies have obtained names for permission marketing programs without the person realizing he gave permission. Such strategies do not lead to favorable attitudes toward the company and can often be more detrimental than beneficial. The most common way this occurs is with an online order and a box checked that says they want e-mails or offers in the future. Unless the person unchecks the box, she has automatically been enrolled in the company's permission marketing program.

Frequency and Loyalty Programs

Marketing experts have long known that keeping customers is more cost-effective than finding new ones. Frequency and loyalty programs offer points or other incentives to individuals who make repeat purchases. Such programs are highly popular in the travel industry (airlines), in the hospitality industry (hotel stays, meals in restaurants), and in credit card programs. Database technology makes it possible to track individual purchases and manage these programs efficiently.

Viral Marketing

Viral marketing involves attaching or including an advertisement or marketing offer in an e-mail or other customer correspondence, such as a blog. If an individual recommends a brand to someone else, the chance of that second person making a purchase becomes much greater. To be successful, such efforts need to be honest and often include something unique or special.

Customization

Customization and personalization are not the same. Personalization means that communications are sent to specific individuals by name. Customization is the ability to modify marketing programs or offers to different groups of individuals within a database.

Northwest Federal Credit Union in Virginia used a customization approach in an auto loan promotion. First, individuals who were in the latter stages of paying on a current auto loan with Northwest or another financial institution were identified. Then, customized preapproved auto loan offers were created. Individuals with credit scores between 681 and 720 were preapproved for auto loans up to $25,000. Individuals with scores between 721 and 760 were preapproved for loans up to $30,000, those with scores between 761 and 790 were preapproved for $35,000, and individuals with credit scores above 790 were preapproved for $40,000. This information was placed as a banner ad across a monthly statement sent by mail or across the top of the Web site if the customer banked online. By customizing the auto loan offer, Northwest's response rate was much higher. It also prevented the problem that would occur with a mass offer to all its customers, alienating customers who were turned down for an auto loan because of their credit history or credit score. Such individuals did not receive the offer.[8]

Unisys Corporation, which markets financial and information security services to various industries, created a highly personalized targeted mailing campaign to its top customers. An analysis of Unisys sales data revealed that 80% of the company's business came from 50 clients. To reach these and other business executives with a targeted, personalized mailing, the company sent each executive an issue of *Fortune* magazine with a faux cover wrap featuring the executive's own picture. A personalized headline appeared on each cover declaring how selecting Unisys had helped the manager's company become successful.[9]

STOP AND THINK

1. Which of these data-driven marketing programs have you experienced?
2. Would programs such as trawling and customization have an impact on advertising clutter? If so, is the impact negative or positive?
3. Could programs such as trawling, viral marketing, and customization be viewed as being unnecessary invasions of privacy and therefore unethical?
4. Which of these data-driven marketing programs is most likely to enhance customer loyalty? Which is least likely? Why? Does the type of good or service being sold make a difference?
5. The benefits of frequency or loyalty programs include the possibility of enhancing customer loyalty and increasing sales. What might be the potential costs?

Testing Database-Driven Initiatives

A well-constructed database provides the opportunity to test a wide array of marketing offers. Testing an offer before it is launched companywide can increase its response rate, efficiency, and cost-effectiveness.

To illustrate a test using RFM information, consider a buy-two-get-one-free offer for The Hot Spot's summer fashions, such as tops, blouses, shorts, and skirts. The offer is only made to database customers. To test the response, the marketing team could first send the offer to 10% of the database rather than all 5,000 customers. The offer is extended to customers from all five codes for recency. The results of the test are provided in Table 3.3.

Table 3.3 indicates that the offer was most attractive to customers in Codes 3 and 4. Individuals from the Code 5 group had purchased most recently, which made the offer less attractive to them. Individuals in Groups 1 and 2 had not shopped at The Hot Spot recently, and the offer did not draw them in.

Based on analysis of the test data, the marketing team at The Hot Spot may decide to send the offer to only those customers who were coded a 3 or 4 for recency in the database. The average of the response rates for these two groups was 10.2% as shown in Table 3.3. The average purchase made by these two groups was $98.78.

After the trial run, the marketing manager at The Hot Spot was able to project gross revenues to be $14,314. This assumes that the response rate for the entire Groups 3 and 4 would be the same (10.2%) as the test market group and the average purchase ($98.78) would be the same. Consequently, instead of mailing out 5,000 total offers, The Hot Spot only sends a total of 1,918 (1,422 plus test market of 496). The projected revenue would be close to $16,800.

The testing process created several benefits. First, it provided for a smaller mailing with a much higher response rate, which in turn should lead to increased revenues while reducing costs. It also provided incentives for customers in Groups 3 and 4 to increase their purchases. This may move these customers toward Group 5 by creating higher levels of loyalty among them. Since Group 5 already purchases frequently, they are not being bothered with a less attractive offer. Finally, the marketing team gains evidence that this type of offer is not likely to change the buying habits of individuals who have not purchased recently (Groups 1 and 2).

A similar testing procedure can be used by marketers in national or international firms using the three-digit RFM code. Table 3.4 indicates the results of a test for a company with approximately 1.2 million names in its database. To test a direct e-mail offer, the marketing

Code	Sample	Responses	Response Rate (%)	Total Purchases ($)	Average Purchase ($)
5	91	6	6.6	534.57	89.10
4	65	8	12.3	802.54	100.32
3	92	8	8.7	777.87	97.23
2	114	4	3.5	264.32	66.08
1	134	2	1.5	123.42	61.71
Total	496	28	5.6	2,502.72	89.38
Total (3 and 4)	157	16	10.2	1,580.41	98.78
Database (3 and 4)	1,422	145	10.2	14,314.29	98.78

Table 3.3   Direct Mail Test for The Hot Spot

RFM Code	Number of Responses	Response Rate (%)	Percentage of Total
542	43	4.3	
543	42	4.2	
532	41	4.1	
521	41	4.1	
544	39	3.9	
452	38	3.8	
455	36	3.6	
545	35	3.5	
424	34	3.4	
532	32	3.2	
Top 10	381	3.8	29.0
Top 20	611	3.1	46.4
Top 30	738	2.5	56.1
Top 40	802	2.0	60.9
Overall	1,316	1.1	

Table 3.4   Top 10 RFM Codes From Test E-mail Offer

team randomly selects 1,000 individuals from each of the 125 RFM codes ($5 \times 5 \times 5 = 125$ codes). Thus, a total of 125,000 e-mail offers would be sent.

As shown, the highest response rate was for the RFM code 542. The second highest was for code 543, and so forth. When the top 10 response codes are examined, they all come from either Group 4 or 5 in terms of recency, which means they have made a rather recent purchase. Notice the second digit, frequency, varies from 2 to 5. It is not as accurate a predictor by itself. The last digit ranges from 1 to 5, which is even less accurate.

The summary figures displayed at the bottom of Table 3.4 are what a marketing manager examines. Then a decision will be made regarding whom to send the e-mail offer to. The average response rate for the top 10 RFM categories listed is 3.8%. The last column in Table 3.4, labeled "Percentage of Total," indicates the percentage of the total number of responses that a particular category contributes. The top 10 RFM codes accounted for 29% of the total in the test market that responded. The remaining 115 codes account for the rest of the responses, or 71%.

This type of analysis provides the marketing team with key information regarding which codes to include in the launch of the e-mail direct-mail offer. Sending the offer to all 1.2 million customers in the database would not be cost-effective. If the marketing manager sends the offer to the top 40 RFM codes, the expected response rate would be roughly 2%. If the offer is sent to only the top 20 codes, the response rate would be 3.1%. The exact number of groups to include remains a judgment call. The test analysis provides information about which customers are most likely to respond. Sending it to these people only increases the response rate and decreases costs, producing greater marketing efficiency.

The standard test market size used by most companies is 10%. It does not have to be this figure; however, the test market should be large enough to yield accurate results yet small enough to allow for cost savings. If 50% of the database is used in the test market, then very little cost savings occurs. If less than 10% of the customers are tested, the results may not be an accurate predictor of behaviors of the remaining individuals, or businesses, in the database.

YOURCAREER

This book is considered an introductory textbook, a relatively new area of focus for SAGE. The company has long served the needs of academics and others by providing a variety of professional journals and various works aimed primarily at researchers, as well as texts for upper-level undergraduate and graduate courses. The company's recent expansion into textbooks for lower-level undergraduate courses poses several challenges and opportunities for SAGE.

Jennifer Reed Banando serves as the senior marketing manager in charge of seeing that this book makes it into your hands. She has been employed by SAGE for nearly 4 years. She had worked in a few other positions, including stints in merchandising, public relations, and business development, prior to graduating with an MBA in marketing in the early 2000s. Many of the marketing efforts designed to support this text come from SAGE's extensive database program. "We have a substantial customer database that we have developed over time through our books, encyclopedias, and journals publishing," Jennifer reports.

In contrast to some of the other major publishing companies, such as Pearson/Prentice Hall and McGraw-Hill, SAGE does not currently employ an "on the ground" sales force; rather, they rely on an in-house sales team. While the competition tends to focus on visits by sales representatives to professors on various campuses, SAGE supplements the efforts of the telesales team with targeted direct and email marketing.

The database has been built from a variety of "leads," Jennifer notes. This includes collecting names, addresses, and business cards from professors attending national conferences, such as the ones held by the American Marketing Association each winter and summer. Other names are garnered from subscription lists to SAGE's journals. Book authors, purchasers, and textbook adopters also provide names to the company. Students working in SAGE's intern program gather additional names by examining Web sites of various colleges and universities. The interns look up the classes to be taught, the names of the professors, and other data that help SAGE target the right professors for any new textbook the company is publishing.

These leads are then added to a database in which professors can be categorized by their relationships to SAGE, such as book or journal writers, editors of journals, reviewers or adopters of textbooks and journal articles, or teachers of specific courses, with cross references to their areas of interest in terms of research or other teaching assignments. Jennifer commented, "We have developed a sophisticated Web technology, which means I can tell if I've e-mailed you about a particular textbook and what your response was. Then, I can personalize a marketing communication to you based on that response."

Without as much person-to-person contact as the competition, SAGE relies on an extensive e-mail, direct-mail, and telemarketing program. "We start about 1 to 1 and a half years ahead of the publication of a book for our high priority projects," Jennifer said. "We enlist the help of reviewers of the book to give us feedback on various chapters. This gives us information about how the market perceives the book and hopefully helps us to secure some adoptions before publication." An "adoption" means that a given professor or college has decided to use the book in a class. Someone who has reviewed the book before it is published is more likely to become an adopter, especially when the review was positive.

Direct mail and e-mail are part of a book's launch. "I strategize all elements of a book's marketing plan, including but not limited to email and direct mail," Jennifer reports. "I plan for a book brochure or a brochure for a set of related books which are then designed and executed by our art and marketing communication specialists." Then, the database is used to send targeted professors direct-mail pieces and even review copies of the text. The professors who ask for complimentary review copies receive follow-up contacts. Of note, any professor receiving a book may first receive a marketing communication from SAGE that asks him or her to simply open the book to explore key features. The professor will be directed to key pages that demonstrate the book's strengths and differences from the books sold by other companies.

The telemarketing team handles inbound calls with requests for information or complimentary copies. SAGE also engages in outbound telemarketing calls to professors to replace in-office sales visits.

Jennifer enjoys the challenges of her position and this new effort at SAGE. When asked to name the college courses that support her profession, she pointed out that her undergraduate degree was in psychology. She said her first public speaking course helped to build her confidence, that a course in logic was helpful to her thinking process, and that social psychology helped her understand "motivation, groups, and group dynamics."

In her MBA program, Jennifer took a marketing management course that became highly useful for this job. She learned the value of quantitative methods and research as tools to be more effective. A course in branding helped her see how various advertising and marketing campaigns create synergies. A course in consumer behavior taught her about how customers perceive products, brands, and prices.

Jennifer quickly moved into a supervisory role early in her career while working at the headquarters for Circuit City. The primary challenge was being promoted "two steps" above her peers. Some tried to take advantage and "bulldoze" her on various decisions. Jennifer said, "I always tried to turn it around and ask for their advice. I would try to involve my subordinates in as much decision making as possible." She reported that it quickly worked, and her new rank "became less of an issue."

How does SAGE measure success? Naturally, it begins with sales in units of books and sales in dollars. These figures are calculated for territories across the country as well as by specific books, although sales at times are hard to track because books are often sold by wholesalers, which makes the information more difficult to collect. The marketing team's goal is to identify the total size of the market and then to reach market share targets.

Time will tell if this marketing management textbook finds a niche in the marketplace. As you can imagine, two guys named "Clow" and "Baack" are cheering hard for Jennifer to succeed.

Chapter Summary

A data warehouse holds all the customer data that can be accessed by any employee who deals with customers in any capacity. A primary reason for building a database, coding the information, and data mining is to use the output to establish effective lines of communication with customers. Personalized communication builds relationships and leads to both repeat business and customer loyalty. Other functions served by a data warehouse include guiding the operation of a firm's Web site, developing marketing programs, improving customer service, assisting the sales staff, and market planning for the future.

The data in a marketing data warehouse include customer data, transaction data, appended data, and analytical data. Two forms of analysis for data that are commonly used by marketing managers are lifetime value analysis and RFM analysis. Information from both programs can be used to enhance the efforts of employees at all ranks in the company.

Data mining programs are used to analyze data to identify meaningful patterns and relationships. Data mining includes building profiles of customer segments and preparing models that predict future purchase behaviors

based on past purchases. Both help the marketing team better understand the tendencies of persons who buy company products and create programs and offers to reach those individuals.

Data-driven marketing programs result from the analysis of data. Some of the more commonly featured programs include trawling, direct marketing, permission marketing, frequency or loyalty programs, viral marketing, and customization efforts. Each program is designed to improve customer loyalty while increasing sales.

Any data-driven marketing effort can first be tested. A sample of potential customers taken from a database can be given a marketing offer to see if sales warrant extending the offer to the entire group or targeted segments of consumers present in the database.

One goal of a data warehouse program is to move the company and its product from a brand parity situation to a higher level of brand equity. Understanding the consumers represented in a database allows for personalization and customization of marketing efforts. This, in turn, can lead them to view what might have been perceived to be an impersonal company in a more personal and connected fashion.

Chapter Terms

Customization (p. 71)
Data mining (p. 68)
Data warehouse (p. 58)
Direct marketing (p. 70)
Geocoding (p. 63)
Lifetime value (p. 64)

Permission marketing (p. 70)
Personalization (p. 59)
RFM (recency, frequency, and monetary) (p. 67)
Trawling (p. 70)
Viral marketing (p. 71)

Review Questions

1. What is a data warehouse?
2. How is an operational database different from a marketing database?
3. Name the main functions provided by a data warehouse.
4. What four kinds of data are found in a marketing data warehouse?
5. Describe the nature of customer data.
6. What are transaction data?
7. What are appended data, and how are they collected?
8. Explain the nature of analytical data.
9. What does the lifetime value of a customer describe?
10. What do the initials RFM stand for? Explain each term.
11. What two activities take place in a data mining program?
12. What are the major forms of data-driven marketing?
13. What is trawling?
14. What is the difference between permission marketing and viral marketing?
15. What is customization and how is it different from personalization?
16. Describe the kinds of results that can emerge from testing a data-driven marketing program.

CUSTOMER CORNER

Clothing remains an important purchase for most consumers because of its social visibility. Clothes project a specific image to others that may have an impact on social interactions and the corresponding acceptance and rejection by other people that follows. As a result, a large number of consumers want to purchase the most recent, trendy fashions but are limited by the amount of much discretionary income that they generate along with other financial obligations that they face. These dynamics have produced a market segment called "trendy labels for less." The goal of this market segment is to purchase trendy labels but at a lower price.

An online retailer has developed a database of 135,000 names of individuals who have purchased clothes, both male and female, that fit this particular profile. The company now wants to develop a lifetime value table. Table 3.5 has the data needed for the calculation. Complete the table by calculating total revenue, dollar value of variable costs,

total costs, gross profit, cumulative gross profit, and lifetime value.

To create effective marketing communications and marketing programs from database information, it is critical to view them from the customer's viewpoint. Assume you are a member of the "trendy labels for less" market segment that has purchased from this online retailer. Discuss how this online clothing retailer could use each of the following to better communicate with you and develop marketing programs to meet your needs. Be specific. What would you want from them?

1. Your personal customer's lifetime value score compared to the segment average.

2. Your personal RFM score.

3. A profile of the retailer's "best" customers.

	Year 1	Year 2	Year 3
Customers	135,000	64,800	40,176
Retention rate (%)	48	62	73%
Visits/year	2.7	4.1	5.9
Sales/visit ($)	58.25	93.15	111.67
Total revenue ($)			
Variable costs (%)	70	70	70
Variable costs ($)			
Acquisition costs ($)	2,300,000		
Database costs ($5)	675,000	324,000	200,880
Total costs ($)			
Gross profit ($)			
Cumulative gross profit ($)			
Lifetime value ($)			

Table 3.5   Lifetime Value for Online Clothing Retailer

Discussion and Critical Thinking Questions

1. You have been hired as the new marketing director for a shoe store chain with 34 outlets. Your first task is to develop a data warehouse. The vice president does not see the benefit of a warehouse and balks at the idea of spending $50,000 to build it. Using Figure 3.1,

explain the various functions of the data warehouse and how it can benefit the shoe store chain.

2. Referring back to Question 1, assume you have been granted permission to build the data warehouse. For

each of the following types of data, explain why they are important, how they will be collected, and how they will be used.

- Customer data
- Transaction data
- Appended data
- Analytical data

3. You are employed by a national airline and have been assigned to collect and interpret data using a lifetime value analysis procedure. Using information collected from a loyalty program, the average lifetime value of business people who sign up for the frequency program is $5,000. After a further analysis, three categories emerged: (1) light users with lifetime values of $3,000 or less (33%), (2) moderate users with lifetime values of $3,000 to $5,500 (57%), and (3) heavy users with lifetime values of $5,500 or more (10%).

   a. Which group of users deserves the most attention from the marketing department? Why does it have more potential than the others?

   b. What type of marketing or communication programs would you design for each of the three lifetime value groups?

4. When using RFM data, recency tends to be the best predictor of future purchases, followed by frequency, and monetary is last. Can you explain why? Discuss each of the RFM components as they would relate to each of the following goods or services:

- Clothing
- Jewelry
- Tanning salon
- Theme park
- Automobile service center

5. An effective data mining program relies on customer profiles and other information about customer preferences to design marketing programs. The Hot Spot and online retailers such as Bluefly.com, send e-mails about new fashions that have arrived to those in the data file. These messages are not mailed to every person in the database. They only go to those individuals who have indicated a desire to receive such information or have indicated they have an interest in fashion news. The goal is to make these customers feel they are receiving special "inside" information. Is this a logical approach? Given that e-mail has practically no cost, why wouldn't these companies send the message to every person in the database? Identify three other types of retailers or businesses that could use the same concept to send regular "news" items to individuals who have granted permission.

6. Personalization is a concept that is important to data warehouse programs. Explain how this concept would (or would not) apply to

- trawling,
- direct marketing,
- permission marketing,
- frequency or loyalty programs,
- viral marketing, and
- customization.

7. A well-constructed database provides the opportunity to test a wide array of marketing offers. Who benefits the most from the results, whether they are positive or negative—front-line employees, supervisors, middle managers, or top managers in the marketing department? Who benefits the least?

Chapter 3 Case

Majestic Mountain Ski Resort

John Mulvaney had served as the marketing director for Majestic Mountain Ski Resort for nearly 10 years. During that time, annual visits to the lodge had increased by nearly 100%. John believed that this level of success was achieved due to a carefully designed data warehouse program that focused on three basic goals.

The first goal was for the marketing team to develop a strong understanding of the types of visitors who came to Majestic Mountain. After years of research, four categories became the most visible: (1) families with children on vacation, (2) singles looking to meet singles, (3) dating couples, and (4) ski enthusiasts who enjoyed "destination" trips. Each of these groups had vastly different characteristics and

dramatically different needs. Families were interested in vacation package deals that lowered the overall cost, skiing lessons, kid's meals in the restaurant, and other activities such as video games. Those involved in the dating scene were more likely to be drawn to the bar or the hot tub and were much less inclined to take lessons. In fact, many never made it onto the slopes. They preferred romantic dinners served in relative seclusion. Ski enthusiasts looked for last-minute deals and wanted access to the best equipment. This group watched the weather closely, looking for ideal conditions, and then made quick trips to the resort.

The second goal was achieved by developing customized marketing programs for each of the four groups. The three groups easiest to identify and gather information from were families, singles, and dating

How should the marketing message change among the four skiing categories?

couples. All of them quickly signed up for the lodge's reward program based on the number of stays and the number of nights per stay. The ski enthusiast group was least loyal to any given resort, because weather was a more important consideration. John and his team discovered that they could get information from enthusiasts by offering deeper last-minute discounts in exchange for providing the data. Then it was possible to try out and test various offers, such as a free extra-night stay program, romance packages with champagne and flowers, "kids stay free" nights, and others.

The third goal was to build loyalty and return visits over time. John knew that it was much easier to retain a customer than acquire a new one. Consequently, his staff took seriously the challenge to provide the most positive experience possible. He hired one expert to deal exclusively with children. He hired another to specialize in fine dining and wine. The marketing team constantly collected information regarding positive reports of customer stays along with files about complaints and problems.

In 2008, John feared that a new threat was about to hit the lodge. During the early part of the year, gasoline prices were around $2.25 per gallon. By the time the summer tourist season peaked, gas was over $4.00 per gallon. The economy also appeared to be headed toward a recession. John had watched the news and noted that many tourism destinations were suffering with low attendance. Many people stayed home. Others only traveled short distances during the Memorial Day and Labor Day weekends. John knew it was time to examine the data warehouse of the resort to see if his team could identify the types of enticements that would ensure a successful winter season.

1. What types of data would be most valuable for the Majestic Mountain Ski Resort to respond to these new circumstances?

2. How might rising gas prices affect the lifetime value calculation for each of the four key groups that visit Majestic Mountain?

3. How might a recession or declining economy affect an RFM analysis and the numbers it provides to the marketing team at Majestic Mountain?

4. How might a data mining program assist the marketing team in preparing for the next skiing season?

5. Which data-driven marketing program might be most useful for the Majestic Mountain Ski Resort marketing department? Why?

Go to **www.sagepub.com/clow** for additional exercises and study resources. Select **Chapter 3, Data Warehousing** for chapter-specific activities.

Aflac was rated by *Fortune* as one the 50 best companies for minority workers.

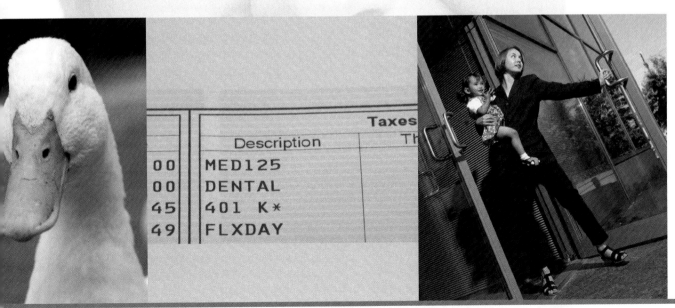

Building a Customer-Oriented Marketing Department

Aflac: Employee-Centered Customer Care

Numerous management practices have come under a great deal of scrutiny in recent years. One key criticism focuses on the excessive amount of pay doled out to CEOs.

Never before has the differential between top management salaries and pay for first-line workers been so dramatic. Buy-out packages and other "golden parachutes" were offered to executives who, by all evidence available, simply failed.

Against this backdrop, Aflac CEO Dan Amos took a unique stance. He displayed his new compensation package front and center to everyone within and outside the company. In addition, the company's stockholders cast votes on whether his upcoming contract was reasonable. The proposed level of pay was far below that of his peers. Amos received $1.2 million in salary, $2.5 million as a bonus, and an additional $2.5 million in stock bonuses in 2005, as compared with Home Depot CEO Bob Nardelli, who collected a $210 million exit check after being fired for poor performance in the same year.

Amos believed that the key to success at Aflac was the link between pay and performance. He noted that no one would be in a position to fail in the company and still walk away with a great deal of compensation. Even though the stockholder vote was to be a nonbinding directive, Amos agreed to abide by the decision. The vote also applied to four other top executives in the company.

Aflac received a great deal of praise for the program, which now also goes by the name of an *advisory vote.* Simply having stockholders cast ballots on executive pay, however, is not the entire key to success in the company. Aflac offers a generous and far-reaching benefits program to all employees, covering everything from health insurance to 401(k) investment plans and more. Employees clearly see the linkage between their efforts and subsequent compensation.

Further, the company, with its home office in Georgia, hosts the state's largest on-site child-care facility, which goes by the name of "Imagination Station." *Working Mother* magazine has, more than once, recognized Aflac as one of the top 100 family-friendly companies in the United States.

The Aflac management team reaches out to other employees and groups as well. *Fortune* magazine consistently rates Aflac as one of the 50 best companies for minority workers in the United States. *Hispanic Magazine* included the company in its list of top 100 firms for Hispanic workers for more than 10 years—a streak that continues.

Dan Amos sees quality programs for employees as much more than just an altruistic instinct. As is the case with other employee-centered companies, the Aflac philosophy is that the courtesy and care extended to workers quickly turns into positive relationships with clients and customers. Company leaders are proud of the firm's customer satisfaction ratings. Aflac is more than a successful domestic company. The firm holds a major market share in Japan, where one in four households is insured by Aflac. Additional growth is expected in the next decade. The simple lesson for marketing management that Aflac teaches is that a customer-oriented marketing department undoubtedly begins at the top. The entire culture or the organization will be based on managerial attitudes, the treatment of employees, as well as fair and reasonable motivational and compensation practices.[1]

Chapter Overview

Any racecar driver knows that one of the most important components of any car is its tires. The ability to start, steer, maneuver, and stop all begin where "the rubber meets the road." Without quality tires, a driver cannot compete as effectively. In the business world, the marketing department holds the same status. Customer contacts are often generated by the materials sent out by marketing—from flyers to advertisements, to coupons, and contest offers. Customers respond with phone calls, Web site visits, and personal trips to a retail store. Creating and maintaining quality customer relationships is one of the most vital elements of a customer-oriented marketing management program.

This chapter focuses on management issues as they relate to effectively directing a customer-oriented marketing department. The chief issues facing top management, middle managers, and first-line supervisors within the marketing division include

- developing a successful management style,
- providing effective leadership,
- making quality decisions,
- building a customer-oriented culture,
- motivating employees,
- inspiring creativity, and
- handling personal and employee stress.

The goal in describing these topics is both to provide an overall understanding of the general nature of a management program as well as to offer specific ideas about how to effectively manage the people under one's direct supervision.

Developing a Successful Management Style ————

The managerial style exhibited by the CEO and other top executives in an organization affects the activities and demeanor of managers and employees who serve at lower levels. Legendary individuals such as Sam Walton, the founder and CEO of Wal-Mart, exhibited styles that influenced organizational members at all ranks, including entry-level employees. Walton's approach was very open, including his insistence that employees are *associates,* not subordinates. His willingness to chip in on even the most menial tasks within the company created a highly favorable organizational environment. Other successful leaders such as Ray Kroc, the driving force in the early McDonald's empire, may have been more directive as they led their companies to the top.

No one style works best. Four styles of management, as shown in Figure 4.1, are found in organizations. Each carries specific advantages and disadvantages for organizational members.

Authoritarian Management

It may seem as if an authoritarian management style would never be appropriate in today's world. The reality is, however, that when an organization is challenged due to poor sales; declining demand; or a crisis, such as a natural catastrophe or a major lawsuit, employees may actually prefer a strong, hands-on, directive managerial style. Some employees may favor an authoritarian approach because they desire direction and become unsure when granted autonomy. Some leaders are more comfortable in situations where their authority goes unchallenged.

The authoritarian style of management offers the benefit of granting organizational members a sense of direction. Many military and other similar types of organizations emphasize a strong chain of command in which disagreements are handled privately. This style may be useful when new personnel are placed in a marketing department that has become dysfunctional or when a company is facing a potential marketing disaster.

Conversely, an authoritarian style tends to stifle creativity and individual initiative. Individuals who believe they are primarily order followers can easily become overreliant on management, never going beyond taking orders and even exhibiting attitudes of laziness. Conflicts can take place behind the scenes, and often, key organizational members feel as though they are operating in the dark.

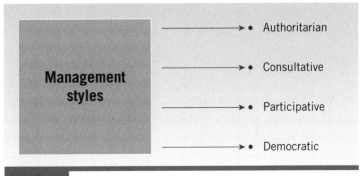

Figure 4.1   Management Styles

Can a consultative
management style
create confusion among
employees?

Consultative Management

A consultative style is one in which managers assume a great deal of authority and discretion but at the same time will ask for advice, input, and help. In essence, management directs activities with a strong hand but not an iron fist. Consultative management gives employees a voice, at least at some level, because the leader knows they have the skills, tools, and knowledge that will assist in keeping the company healthy and on the cutting edge.

The problems with consultative management are largely the same as in authoritarian companies. This style may also stifle creativity and individual initiative. Often, those who are kept out of the loop when consultations take place probably have a sense of alienation or believe that the top managers are playing favorites.

The circumstances in which this style works best are similar to those surrounding authoritarian organizations. Although the threats to the firm may be less severe, it may be advisable to exhibit this type of style when the marketing department faces some type of crisis because the marketing manager may exert stronger leadership while still seeking input from the various employees.

Participative Management

For many years, a participative style has been recommended by a wide variety of management experts, specialists, and consultants. An *open door* policy, by which any employee has access to management, creates an environment of trust, initiative, and ingenuity. Instead of a directive approach, managers submit ideas to employees regarding plans to be made, decisions to be rendered, and control systems to be used.

In a participative style of management, marketing managers maintain what is essentially veto power over the direction of the marketing department. At the same time, employees tend to hold a strong sense of empowerment and a stake in the outcome, since in many instances

Can a participative style help build a positive atmosphere within the marketing department?

their work directs the company's actions. On an organization-wide level, delegation of decision making and authority is called **decentralization**. Decentralized companies tend to be more participative in decision-making processes.[2]

Among the primary advantages of participative leadership are strong levels of employee involvement, satisfaction with the company, and organizational commitment. The indicators of *satisfaction* with the organization include lower levels of absenteeism, tardiness, turnover, accidents, grievances, and vandalism. The indicators of *organizational commitment* include positive statements about the company made by employees to both coworkers and people outside the company; considerable effort being given to the firm, especially in crisis situations; and a willingness to work without supervision.

The problems associated with a participative style of management begin with the potential for conflict when subordinates have differing points of view on an issue. Those who do not get their way when an action is taken may feel out of the loop or disrespected in some way. It takes a skillful manager to balance the desires of all stakeholders in a participative organization.

Most marketing departments are composed of individuals with a wide variety of skills. It is not unusual for a marketing department to consist of creatives with art backgrounds, media production individuals with mass communication backgrounds, marketing research people with statistical backgrounds, and salespeople with marketing backgrounds. In addition, there may be individuals with highly specialized skills, such as photographers, artists, and database specialists. Due to the differing backgrounds and skills of these individuals, most marketing departments are well served by a participative leadership style. In such departments, the marketing manager walks a fine line balancing the need for employee participation while at the same time providing direction and control.

Democratic Management

Very few business organizations are truly or completely democratic. Such an approach remains unlikely since management is essentially surrendering all decisions to the will of the group.

A democratic form of management might be found in an employee-owned company or in a nonprofit organization.

Democratic management may be more decision or action specific. In other words, there may be instances in which the will of the group is the only factor considered. Clearly this is the case when members vote on creating a union, which is called a *certification election*. There may be marketing situations as well, such as deciding which advertisement should be presented to a client or the company's management. The rest of the time, however, it is likely that managers will seek to maintain some level of control.

Some writers suggest that the more democracy, the better. Having a strong voice in day-to-day matters as well as the strategic direction of the organization offers the same benefits as those found in a participative style of management. The same holds true for the potential problems.[3]

Providing Effective Leadership

A difference exists between managing and leading. Managing involves all the classic principles related to planning, organizing, staffing, directing, and controlling, as described in Chapter 1. Leading, or leadership, is a more specific concept. *Leaders* influence behaviors in organizations. Leadership takes two forms in organizations:

1. Formal leadership

2. Informal leadership

A formal leader has been authorized to direct activities in an organization. Typically, formal leaders are elected, appointed, or promoted into their roles. A formal leader would be the vice president of marketing, the head of a task force or committee, or a project manager. In the marketing department, formal leaders are normally designated by rank. Other individuals lead when asked to head specific projects, such as creating a sponsorship program or a direct-mail program.

Informal leaders are also known as *emergent leaders* because they move into the role due to circumstances or because of a personal trait or characteristic, such as expertise or charisma. Thus, a person who is artistically gifted may find that she often leads brainstorming sessions or focus groups designing new advertising campaigns, not due to rank but rather because of her artistic insights. As a result, others may begin to rely on the individual for creative ideas, direction, and other forms of support.[4]

The theories regarding formal leadership can be placed into three main categories, as shown in Figure 4.2. Each category offers useful ideas for marketing managers.

Traits and Characteristics Theories

The basic premise of the first approach is that effective leadership results from specific traits and characteristics. Individuals who possess them are more likely to be effective. The primary flaw in this thinking is that a personality characteristic that might work very well in one marketing department may become a major liability in another. Consider, for instance, the difference between trying to lead a marketing department for a major retail chain versus having the responsibility of leadership for an outbound telemarketing operation.

While no specific trait or characteristic can guarantee success as a marketing manager, certain characteristics may have more universal advantages. The ones that are most likely to bode well for an organization include the characteristics displayed in Figure 4.3.

Task maturity involves a full understanding of the nature of the job. For a sales manager, this means understanding how to prospect, make sales calls, handle objections, and close sales. For an advertising executive, task maturity includes knowledge of how to develop effective ads, select the correct media, and support the advertising message through other marketing materials.

- Traits and characteristics theories
- People and production theories
- Recent theories

Figure 4.2

Categories of Formal Leadership Theories

Emotional maturity is the ability to adjust to changing circumstances, challenging situations, and other moments when calm leadership can accomplish more than panic, screaming, or some other emotional response. Emotions often rise when creative personnel face deadlines and are forced to be innovative as an advertisement or some other type of marketing piece is due soon or when a client rejects an advertisement that the creative staff spent 3 weeks preparing. In these stressful situations, successful leaders display emotional maturity.

A *human relations orientation* means that the leader focuses on relationships with subordinates and customers because of an inner desire to be helpful and build quality bonds with others. Employees respond better to management that displays a caring attitude and understands the challenges in being creative, especially under pressure and when faced with the constraints imposed by a client. Leaders who are harsh and critical may have employees who do not respond as well.

A human relations orientation also helps in customer service and sales situations. If a supervisor wants employees to display a desire to be helpful to customers, then it is essential for the manager to model the same behaviors for employees.

Intelligence serves any leader in any circumstance. The ability to step back and assess a developing crisis or problem and find quality alternatives is a major advantage for a leader or supervisor. Intelligence helps a marketing manager recognize when a particular ad or marketing material is creative and will be effective.[5]

- Task maturity
- Emotional maturity
- Human relations orientation
- Intelligence

Figure 4.3

Traits of a Successful Marketing Manager

People Versus Production Theories

Many of the leadership theories that evolved in the time period between 1940 and 1975 note that some leaders primarily focus on subordinates and personal relationships (people), while others center attention on outputs, productivity, correcting errors, and other tangible measures of performance (production). Neither style is necessarily good or bad.

The primary lesson for a marketing department manager is that both people and production are important and that they are related to each other. Many of the companies cited in this textbook as examples of success achieved that status because the leaders in those firms emphasize quality relationships with employees that lead to workers creating positive relationships with customers and producing quality work.

In terms of day-by-day operations, managers and supervisors working in the marketing department must balance the emotional and interpersonal needs of employees with the need to finish tasks and meet deadlines. Much of the work of a marketing department is not repetitive, which means both production and people issues constantly arise. Managers seek to motivate employees to be productive, to be creative, and to meet deadlines. They must, however, do this in a manner that considers individual feelings and emotions.

Recent Theories of Leadership

Since 1975, several new theories regarding leadership have been proposed. Of these, three offer some direction for marketing department leaders:

1. Leader-member exchange theory (LMX)
2. Substitutes for leadership
3. Path-goal theory

The *leader-member exchange theory (LMX)* suggests the importance of building in-group relationships with employees. An in-group relationship consists of persons who have close ties to the leader, which results in better communication, more trust, and a bond that extends beyond the leader and the follower to concerns about the well-being of the group or department.

Hunter is an audio editor and does not require a high level of supervision to perform his tasks.

The *substitutes for leadership* approach recognizes that various items often substitute for the presence of a leader. When these are present, the leader feels free to work on other goals and projects and can rely more heavily on employees to work independently and effectively. A sales manager with an experienced sales team knows the benefits of these characteristics. The same holds true for an art director managing experienced creatives and artists.

The primary lesson that the substitutes for leadership theory offers is that the manager should be well acquainted with her situation and the employees in the department. Then, orders, directions, and other forms of supervision can be oriented to subordinates and jobs where they will be the most helpful.[6]

Path-Goal Theory

Path-goal theory suggests that leaders succeed when they are able to create a style of leadership or forms of leader behavior that include two items: (1) the follower's personal characteristics and (2) the characteristics of the situation. Figure 4.4 identifies four basic forms of leader behavior.

Each style matches different situations and types of followers. Leaders may be more likely to be directive when the situation is unclear and with subordinates who prefer such an approach. Leaders are more likely to be successful with a supportive style when the task is clear and subordinates prefer autonomy to direction. An achievement-oriented style of leadership works best when the leader has clear access to rewards for both individuals and groups. Unrewarded performance does not bode well for an achievement-oriented leader.

A marketing department leader should assess each individual within the group to make sure that the behaviors the leader exhibits mesh with the preferences of those in the department. The behaviors also should not contradict the nature of the job. An achievement-oriented style is best suited to marketing tasks that are easily measured, such as the number of sales calls made, changes in unit or dollar sales, and other tangible outcomes. Remember, however, that the style only succeeds if the manager has access to some type of reward based on performance.[7]

- *Directive*, a style in which the leader sets clear task instructions, deadlines, and schedules while closely following subordinate activities
- *Supportive*, displaying friendliness and concern for subordinates
- *Participative*, actively seeking out employee opinions and ideas
- *Achievement oriented*, a focus on goal setting, coaching and helping, and rewarding those who reach their performance targets

Figure 4.4

Forms of Leader Behavior Outlined by Path-Goal Theory

STOP AND THINK

Consider the opening vignette regarding CEO Dan Amos from Aflac.

1. Which management style is being used in his organization?

2. Is there an ethical component to the decision made by Dan Amos to let his subordinates vote on his level of pay?

3. Do you think Aflac is more likely to have people-oriented or production-oriented leaders throughout the company? Would this be true in every department?

4. Which style would you expect from a supervisor at Aflac—directive, supportive, participative, or achievement oriented? Would more than one style apply?

5. What type of individual would be best suited to work at Aflac?

6. What do you think would be the benefits of working at Aflac? What would be the challenges you would face?

Making Quality Decisions

Many of the characteristics found in an overall style of management become manifest in decision making. Managers in authoritarian companies make decisions in ways much different from the consultative, participative, or democratic organizations. Three activities influence the quality of decisions made by marketing departments.

1. Creating an ethical decision-making climate

2. A focus on customer-oriented decisions

3. Open versus secretive decision making

The first is *creating an ethical decision-making climate.* Among the major challenges faced by corporations in the past decade have been an increasing number of scandals involving top-level managers. Most scholars agree that ethical and responsible companies are more likely to survive in the long term and face fewer problems with governments and unhappy consumers in the short run. Therefore, an organization's management team should provide a clear example of ethical behavior and reward individuals for acting in the firm's best interests by identifying and responding to legal and ethical violations.

A second element in quality decision making is *maintaining a customer orientation.* Effective decision making in a marketing department begins with keeping customers in mind as each decision is made. This includes every aspect of the marketing program. Hopefully, the same mindset also influences decisions and activities throughout the organization. If it does not, then it will be difficult for the marketing department to maintain a high level of customer orientation.

The third aspect of decision making is whether the process is *open or secretive.* At the departmental level, a supervisor may discover that he is forced to keep secrets due to the wishes of higher-level managers. At the same time, an overly secretive organization invites suspicion and intrigue. Most of the time, keeping subordinates informed is a better choice.

Figure 4.5 lists other factors that can lead to poor-quality decisions and ways to overcome those problems. Managers in marketing departments should be aware of these behavioral concerns in decision making and respond appropriately. This can be accomplished by reviewing what decisions have been made and looking for the reasons why they were made.[8]

Behavioral Factor	Tactics to Respond

Expectations of others
  – Supervisor
 	
  – Peers (peer pressure)
  – Subordinates
	Be aware when your supervisor is forcing you into a bad choice.
	Do not let peers unduly affect your thinking or judgment. Avoid making bad decisions because they might affect your popularity or standing with your subordinates.

Emotions
  – Anger
  – Depression
	Do not make decisions when you think these emotions may affect your reasoning.

Organizational politics	Think about company politics; make decisions that are right for your department or the company, not to gain power or influence.
Personal attitudes and biases	Withdraw when you know you cannot make an unbiased decision.
Mismatch between the decision maker and the decision	Let others know if you believe you are not qualified to make a quality decision; explain the reasons why.

Figure 4.5   Behavioral Factors That Cause Poor Decisions

Building a Customer-Oriented Culture

Creating a customer-oriented culture includes emphasizing the customer service legends, stories, and folklore that are all part of an organization's environment. For example, a legend associated with the Frito-Lay company that routinely circulates is a story about a small, remote retail store calling the company and asking for a shipment of a single bag of Fritos. Even though it was an inconvenient time and clearly not a cost-effective response, a manager at Frito-Lay delivered the bag. The lesson in customer service was far more valuable than the cost of the trip.

Working With the Human Resource Department

Human resource management is the process of attaining and preparing quality workers to serve in an organization. The functions performed include human resource planning, recruiting, selection, orientation, employee training, performance appraisal, manager training, compensation management, discipline and rules, workplace safety, and working with unions. Nearly every one of these functions may in some way be used to help build a customer-oriented culture in both the marketing department and other parts of the company.

Human resource planning processes should incorporate the goal of identifying and actively seeking out individuals who enjoy working with the public, who feel challenged by solving problems that assist customers, and who are team players. Recruiting can then build on these goals by choosing the right places to meet potential new employees. Selection criteria should emphasize giving an edge to such individuals in order to make sure the right person gets the job. For example, one of the major car rental companies, Enterprise, has de-emphasized the role that academic grades play in recruiting and selection. Instead, the company looks for college graduates who have been involved in social or academic organizations, such as fraternities, sororities, sports teams, and student government. The idea is that students who were active in such groups are better suited to jobs that involve constant interaction with the public.

Customer service techniques and their importance must be stressed both during orientation sessions and throughout the employee-training processes, even for non-marketing-department workers.

Customer service must also play an active role in performance appraisal criteria. Individuals who expect to be included in manager-training programs should have demonstrated a keen interest in serving customers and helping coworkers. Another major key is to make certain that some part of an employee's compensation, pay raises, and other rewards will be connected to how well the employee works with customers. Consequently, the management team in the marketing department should expect to work closely with those in the human resource department.[9]

Techniques for Building Customer-Oriented Programs

Managing a marketing department at any level (supervisor to vice president) involves creating and maintaining a customer-oriented culture. This culture should permeate activities from top-level strategy making to individual actions by people on the sales floor—making external sales calls, answering the phone, or responding to e-mails. Three techniques that assist in building a customer-oriented workforce are

In hiring someone for a marketing department, what types of questions should the interviewer ask?

1. goal-setting programs,
2. reward systems, and
3. peer approval through role modeling and coaching.

Successful customer-oriented *goal-setting* programs should be based on two concepts: (1) the goal-setting process and (2) the goals themselves. The goal-setting process starts with reminders about the importance of customer service quality. The goals themselves should be designed to reflect that commitment. Both supervisors and employees may contribute quality ideas regarding how to better serve constituents that can be built into various goals.

Remember that goal setting only works if employees are rewarded when the goals are achieved. *Reward systems* can incorporate pay raises, bonuses, prizes, and perks, such as an employee-of-the-month designation, complete with its own parking space, in the system.[10]

Finally, do not underestimate the importance and power of *peer pressure*. Successful employees often become role models and coaches for others. As a supervisor, it is critical to be keenly aware of what is being modeled and what is being coached. If it appears to others that high-performing members of the organization have achieved that status by focusing on concepts regarding quality customer service, others will quickly get the message.

The Benefits of a Customer-Oriented Culture

The concepts of quality goal setting, effective reward systems, and peer approval, as they pertain to building and maintaining a customer-oriented business, apply to both individuals and groups or teams. Many marketing programs involve teams working with customers or preparing marketing materials. Applying the proper incentives helps build an environment in which team members

- share information,
- encourage one another,
- help out during crisis periods or with difficult problems, and
- work together to build quality relationships with customers.

A customer-oriented culture can lead to a positive corporate image, brand loyalty, repeat business, increased sales, fewer complaints, more compassion or understanding when a company does make a mistake with a customer, positive word-of-mouth endorsements, higher profits, and the ability to expand a product line or brand more easily.

Motivating Employees

Motivation consists of what starts behaviors, what maintains behaviors, and what stops behaviors. In a marketing department, there are many behaviors that supervisors would love to get started and then maintain. There are also behaviors managers would like to stop. Figure 4.6 lists some of the more obvious. Motivation theories can be placed in three categories:

1.   Need based

2.   Operant process

3.   Cognitive process[11]

Need-Based Theories

Employee needs often drive their actions and activities. *Maslow's hierarchy of needs* suggests a path by which a person moves from basic physiological needs (food, clothing, and shelter) to needs for safety and security, to needs for belongingness and love, to the need for esteem, and finally to the need for self-actualization.

This simple approach suggests some commonsense ideas for both workers and managers. First, someone who is just trying to survive by getting and keeping a good job will probably be far less concerned with things such as esteem and self-actualization. Indeed, a sense of self-esteem can be derived by feeling you are performing "honest work."

Second, the hierarchy notes the importance of positive social relationships, opportunities to succeed and receiving recognition for those successes, and the job itself being part of a motivational drive. These ideas apply to basic entry-level positions in a marketing department as well as more specialized positions.[12]

Start and Maintain	Stop
• Attendance (show up)	• Absenteeism
• Punctuality (on time)	• Tardiness
• Effort or productivity	• Gossip
• Support coworkers with praise and advice	• Unprofessional dress/appearance
• Good citizenship	• Wasting time or lack of effort
– Keep work area clean	• Unethical behaviors
– Pitch in when needed	– Discrimination
– Make quality suggestions	– Harassment
	– Theft
	– Lying

Figure 4.6   Employee Behaviors to Start, Maintain, and Stop

Manifest Needs Theory

A second approach based on individual needs is found in David McClelland's *manifest needs theory* or *motivational needs theory*. McClelland identifies three needs that drive an individual's participation at work:

1. Need for achievement
2. Need for affiliation
3. Need for power

The *need for achievement* plays a unique role in marketing and especially in sales. Essentially, the issue is how people "keep score." Many winning salespeople are most impressed by money, status, and an ostentatious lifestyle. They view achievements as the tangible rewards associated with success. A supervisor should try to understand how the need for achievement exists in first-line employees.

The *need for affiliation* contributes to a person's sense of well-being, as well as the individual's level of motivation. Those who crave intimate personal relationships with coworkers and customers respond to managerial tactics that emphasize such connections. Individuals who are less social should try to find positions where interactions with customers and others are minimized.

The *need for power* may create a major advantage or disadvantage for a marketing department. A leader who is "into power" may drive away talented individuals who seek autonomy and control over how best to perform a job. Many management experts believe a difference exists between wishing to exercise authority and seeking to help subordinates. An individual who is driven to rise through the ranks often possesses motives that are less useful for subordinates and others in the department.

The bottom line to motivation from a needs-based perspective is that both supervisors and rank-and-file workers should be aware of which needs they feel are important and how those needs may be met on the job.[13] In summary,

1. Supervisors should note that the motives and needs of an entry-level employee who is under the age of 35 may be far different from the motives and needs of someone of the same rank who is over 50 (think in terms of health care, retirement packages, vacation time, family orientation, and simple "respect").

2. Supervisors should realize that needs vary by individual. The supervisor or marketing manager should become acquainted with each employee to discover what motivates each employee and then adjust the techniques used to match the individuals within the department.

3. Supervisors should also be aware of their own personal needs. How do you keep score? Are you most impressed when you develop and inspire your employees, or are you more concerned about your own personal accomplishments?

Operant Process Models

Operant process models focus on what happens following a behavior as emitted by a person. In other words, individual behaviors are connected to four responses: (1) positive reinforcement, (2) negative reinforcement, (3) punishment, or (4) extinction. The first two increase the likelihood that a person will repeat a behavior. The final two are related to decreases in repetition of a behavior.

Increases in Behaviors

Positive reinforcement is a pleasant or pleasing consequence. A multitude of behaviors meet with favorable outcomes. At work, positive reinforcement takes the form of pay, praise, favorable performance appraisals, promotions, benefits, statements of approval by peers, and so forth. B. F. Skinner, who created the original operant process framework, strongly

Type of Schedule	Example
Fixed ratio	
Reward on a fixed number of behaviors (e.g., 1:1, 3:1, or 5:1; every time, every third time, or every fifth time a behavior occurs)	Commission (reward for every sale)
Variable ratio	
Reward on a random timetable of desired behaviors	Praise (for any act: helping a customer, responding to a complaint, making a sales call, developing a quality advertisement, etc.)
Fixed interval	
Reward for maintaining a behavior over a fixed interval of time (minutes, hours, days, weeks, months)	Weekly paycheck, monthly paycheck
Variable interval	
Reward on a random timetable for maintaining a behavior over time	Promotion based on excellent work

Figure 4.7   Positive Reinforcement Schedules

believed in the power of positive reinforcement as a method to shape behaviors for the future. Figure 4.7 indicates four positive reinforcement schedules and how they would apply to a marketing department. The presence of positive reinforcement increases the odds that a behavior will be repeated.

Negative reinforcement can occur in only one circumstance, which is known as an *aversive situation*. This means that something bad is happening and the individual performs a behavior that stops the aversive situation. In other words, the bad thing stops happening. Taking an aspirin to relieve a headache is an example of a negatively reinforced behavior. Remember, negative reinforcement *increases* the likelihood that a behavior will be repeated. Beating a deadline and feeling good about it is a form of negative reinforcement.

Decreases in Behaviors

Punishment is a consequence that *follows* an act and is *related* to that behavior. A person who eats a strawberry, not knowing that she is allergic, will soon experience a punishing consequence in the form of a rash or some other physiological reaction. Skinner has written that while punishment is appropriate in some circumstances, it is often overused. Punishment should be saved for the most egregious actions.

Extinction means that behaviors that are not associated with any kind of consequence, favorable or unfavorable, eventually disappear. Removing a reward often leads to extinction, because the favorable consequence is gone. Stopping punishment can also be associated with extinction; that is, if a manager stops punishing a behavior that has a rewarding aspect to it, the behavior will very likely return. For example, if a marketing manager stops punishing employees for chewing gum while dealing with the public, eventually gum chewing will resume.[14]

For a supervisor in the marketing department, applications of operant conditioning may be as follows:

1. Use positive reinforcement whenever possible. Connect rewards to actual actions, such as making sales calls on potential new clients; following up with a phone call, letter, or e-mail after a sale has been completed; successfully responding to a customer's complaint; completing a marketing project on time; and so forth. Anything from praise to buying someone lunch, to an e-mail to those of higher rank lauding the efforts of a subordinate constitutes positive reinforcement.

How can Donna use operant conditioning to motivate Reid to produce higher-quality work?

2. Save punishment for dire circumstances, such as when a customer service rep treats a client in an unprofessional manner or materially misrepresents a product in a way that places the company in jeopardy.

3. Recognize the value of negative reinforcement. A person who has not quite hit a quota will feel a great deal of relief when that quota is reached.

4. Be aware that you will not need to provide all the reinforcers to every person. Employees also learn by watching what happens to others (*vicarious reinforcement*), and they will also reward and punish themselves (*self-reinforcement*) for various actions.

Cognitive Process Models of Motivation

Cognitive process models of motivation focus on the thought processes associated with various behaviors and activities. Two of the most prominent theories are (1) Adams's equity theory and (2) Vroom's expectancy theory.

Equity Theory

Adams's equity theory can best be described as follows:

1. People at work exchange inputs for outputs. Inputs are the items employees trade to an organization, including their time, level of effort, degree of productivity, knowledge, and skills. Outputs are the items companies trade in return, including pay, praise, the opportunity to be promoted, benefits, and prizes or awards.

2. People at work have a natural tendency to make social comparisons, most notably with someone who is the worker's *referent other*. A referent other is a person who is singled out for one reason or another and viewed to be similar in some way.

3. The nature of the comparison is

$$\frac{\text{Employee input}}{\text{Employee output}} = \frac{\text{Referent other input}}{\text{Referent other output}}$$

4. If this comparison is in balance, or *equity* exists, behavior is maintained.

5. If this comparison is out of balance, or *inequity* exists, there is a strong motivational force to restore equilibrium, by giving more or less effort, asking for a raise, reevaluating or rationalizing, influencing the referent other, or participating in dysfunctional behaviors.

The primary concept to remember regarding equity theory is that people in the marketing department are comparing themselves with one another and with individuals in other departments. If an individual believes he is not being treated fairly or is being given unequal treatment, that employee will be dissatisfied and will seek to make things right, either by changing the situation on-the-job or by looking for a new position elsewhere. Consequently, managers in marketing departments are advised to make sure that a company's top employees feel they are being given the best possible treatment. This theory also helps a manager understand why someone may not be giving his best effort—because the person feels his work is not being recognized or rewarded.[15]

Expectancy Theory

The second cognitive process approach is called expectancy theory. The theory consists of three key components:

How can expectancy theory explain why Janelle has reduced her job effort?

1. Expectancy

2. Instrumentality

3. Valence

Expectancy is a term that links effort to performance: in simple words, how strongly a person believes she can successfully complete a task, or "If I try hard, can I do this?" *Instrumentality* is the link between succeeding or completing a task and access to rewards—in other words, "If I succeed, will I get the reward?" *Valence* is the value of the reward. There are two elements to valence: One is the value associated with knowing you have successfully completed the task, and the second is the value attached to the reward received. In essence, *motivation occurs when a person believes he can successfully complete a task and that, when he does, his performance will be rewarded with something he values.*[16]

In summary, the cognitive theories of motivation offer these concepts to marketing department managers:

1. Get to know your employees, and find out what they value. Tie valued rewards to performance.

2. Provide clear task instructions and visible, tangible goals.

3. Follow through and reward performance. The least successful supervisors are those who promise rewards and then fail to deliver them.

4. Remember that motivation comes from two sources: (1) the outside world and (2) internal thoughts and responses. Many valences are essentially personal feelings of pride or accomplishment.

5. Treat employees fairly. Playing favorites limits your ability to manage effectively.

Empowering and Engaging Employees

Employee empowerment can take many forms, from delegating decisions to participative programs related to planning, performance appraisal, and control systems. The benefits include more satisfied, committed, and loyal employees, which leads to extra effort.

Engaging employees can be tied to motivational processes through well-designed goal-setting programs. For many years, management literature has suggested that goal setting is tied to higher levels of performance. Quality goal-setting programs, such as *Management by Objectives,* provide what is called *role clarity,* whereby the employee has a clear idea of the most important aspects of his or her job or, in essence, is able to say, "I know what I'm supposed to be doing." This is because goals are set regarding the key parts of the employee's job. When the employee participates in the goal-setting process, a sense of empowerment is also built.[17]

STOP AND THINK

1. Operant process models of motivation focus on reinforcing various employee behaviors. Name some employee behaviors that would be important in retail sales, creating advertising materials, and operating a direct marketing program.

2. Cognitive process models focus on thought processes that lead to various behaviors. What kinds of motives would new employees think about the most? Are the motives the same for supervisors?

3. Which do you think is the more powerful motive in a marketing department, having a behavior rewarded or thinking about a situation and then responding?

4. What role does money play in an operant process model? What role does money play in equity theory? Is there a major difference in how money is used based on the motivational model? Why or why not?

5. Is there an ethical component to treating employees equitably? If so, what is it?

Inspiring Creativity

Creativity comes from three sources in a company. The first is through methods used to recruit and select employees. The second is the firm's environment. The third source is the use of creativity techniques to assist employees.

Recruiting and Selection

The marketing department's manager should make sure she has input into the criteria used to screen and select employees. An emphasis should be placed on finding new workers who have displayed an interest in creative activities in the past. This includes any creative writing the person has produced; artistic pieces of art or photography; an interest in theater, debate, or speech; and any other activity in which the individual displays creative thinking and behaviors. These indicate that the individual has a creative side.

A Creative Environment

Many companies stifle employee creativity in subtle ways, from the design of the office to restrictions on work apparel, to an insistence on formal titles. Offices featuring closed doors and

To encourage employee creativity, a marketing manager balances the need for innovation, freedom, and creativity with maintaining order.

other physical restrictions to access send the message that there are formal channels and chains of command to be followed at all times. Companies that insist on suits and ties most likely are seeking to create and maintain a certain image to both the public and those inside the firm. The same is true when rank and title are emphasized in the organization.

Developing a creative environment means balancing the need for innovation and freedom of expression with the need for order. Clearly, chaos cannot rule, but the most creative individuals tend not to mirror mainstream society. They think differently and look at the world differently. It is this different outlook on the world around them that allows them to be creative. In managing a marketing department, it is important to provide employees with freedom of expression, which often means they will look, act, and talk differently than individuals in other departments. Marketing managers must provide a supportive and relaxed environment, yet also provide some level of leadership and control.

An important element in a creative environment is allowing for the absurd and even for failure. To come up with the marketing gem or the golden advertising campaign requires innovative thinking. It may require suggesting and trying absurd or seemingly ridiculous ideas. The light bulb was not invented on the first try. In fact, Thomas Edison's failures far outnumber his successes. It is the same in marketing and advertising. Marketing employees must believe they have the freedom to fail. If not, then the next marketing campaign or next advertisement will only be a slight variation of the current one. It will not be revolutionary or different. The idea of using a duck to sell insurance makes about as much sense as using cows to sell energy drinks. Yet Aflac is known today because of the wild, creative idea of using a talking duck. Red Bull is well-known today partly based on its logo of two cows madly rushing toward each other.

Creativity Techniques

The most popular creativity technique used in business is undoubtedly some form of brainstorming. Brainstorming is a verbal technique in which a diverse group of people is assembled, a problem is read, and then the members of the group are asked to shout new and innovative potential solutions. The goal is to generate as many ideas as possible, to combine ideas, and to think up the most off-the-wall solutions possible. One key to a successful brainstorming session is to make sure that no one passes judgment on ideas until after the session is complete.

In some companies, individuals are more reserved. In those instances, nominal groups or the *nominal group technique* may be used. It functions in basically the same way as brainstorming, with one key difference: Instead of shouting out ideas, group members simply write them down and present them in a more orderly fashion, a round-robin approach.

The third creativity technique involves using some type of *analogy* to describe a problem, hoping this will lead to new ways to fix the situation. For example, trying to identify new customers can be compared with "finding a needle in a haystack." Slow sales are analogous to being "stuck in the mud," and so forth. The goal is to let the simile or metaphor guide the discussion to new and creative responses.

A fourth approach is to try to break a problem down into smaller components. This method is sometimes called *seeking the lowest common denominator.* For instance, a retail store with low sales may seem like a massive problem; however, if the major issue is as simple as enticing more people to visit the store, then the rest would take care of itself and solutions would be much easier to identify.

The fifth method used to discover ingenious new approaches to solving problems is to simply *talk to an outsider* or someone with a different point of view. A coworker from a different discipline or even an individual who is not part of the company may have a unique perspective on how to address an issue.

The use of creativity techniques ties back to the concept of developing and maintaining a creative environment. Employees who participate and are rewarded when they come up with quality ideas and suggestions are likely to feel better about their jobs and empowered to be creative over time.[18]

Handling Personal and Employee Stress

One of the factors that can quickly harm a person's career, a marketing department, or an entire business is stress. One portrayal of the nature of stress and of the research that has been generated looks like this:

$$\text{Events} \rightarrow \text{Stress} \rightarrow \text{Events}$$

The events that cause stress are called the antecedents of stress, and the events that are the result are known as stress outcomes.

Antecedents or Causes of Stress

The primary factors that predict potential problems with stress are displayed in Figure 4.8. As shown, some of the elements arise from circumstances at work. A second group occurs with life in general. And finally, some individuals are more prone to stress than others due to certain personality traits.

The Nature of Stress

One view of stress, as displayed in Figure 4.9, poses a model in which individuals encounter stimuli or issues on a regular basis. Some stimuli are pleasant and positive. For instance, at work, closing a major sale, being given a pay raise, and completing major assignments are all events that are stimulating but positive at the same time. Other stimuli are essentially neutral, such as when a person hears a knock at the door or is told that he or she is about to receive a phone call. A third set of stimuli encompasses all the negative, challenging, or problematic events a person encounters, from problems at home to getting a traffic ticket on the way to work, to worries that a marketing piece that has been created will be rejected by management or the client. It is the accumulation of all these events that eventually can lead to what some call *distress* or *strain.* Typically, the events associated with distress are those that create personal problems, troubles at work, and other difficulties.

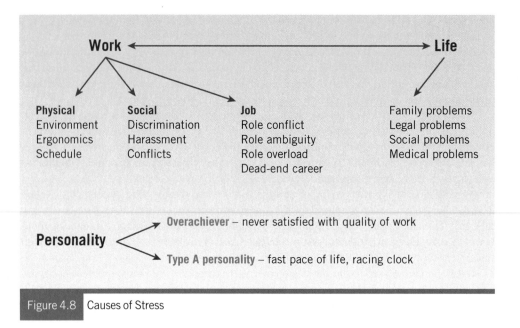

Figure 4.8   Causes of Stress

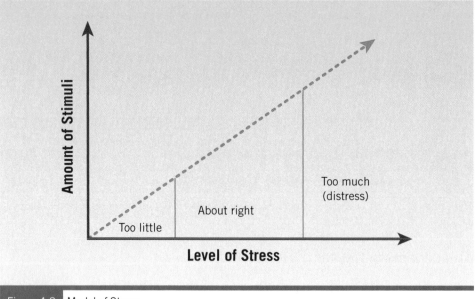

Figure 4.9   Model of Stress

Outcomes of Distress or Strain

Figure 4.10 displays the most prevalent outcomes of distress or strain. As shown, the outcomes appear as physical, psychological, or social symptoms. One of the complications of stress is that these symptoms may become additive, meaning that mental fatigue or pressure often exacerbates physical symptoms or problems. The reverse is also true. Someone experiencing chronic pain or discomfort often becomes despondent or depressed as a result. This, in turn, can affect the individual's social life, which creates an entire new cycle of distress.

Stress can exact a toll on members of a marketing department. It can affect entry-level and first-line employees and supervisors or managers. The potential for distress exists for entry-level employees due to a combination of the potential causes noted above. Any young person beginning a career probably feels pressures beyond those on the job due to less financial stability,

Physical Symptoms	Psychological Symptoms	Social Symptoms
• Heart attack	• Insomnia	• Inappropriate behaviors
• High blood pressure	• Mood swings	• Creating conflicts
• Stomach ulcers/gastritis	• Depression	
• Skin hives/acne/dermatitis	• Nervous breakdown	
• Nervous cough/ hyperventilation		

Figure 4.10 Signs of Distress

developing interpersonal relationships (including dating, marrying, cohabitation, and having children), living alone for the first time, and other factors.

Stress can affect supervisors and managers. The demands of a supervisory position include both those associated with completing various marketing tasks as well as the challenges of maintaining a functioning department. The supervisor often serves as a referee or go-between when conflicts arise within the department, between departments, and with persons or groups outside the organization. Supervisors face more deadlines and may feel that their performance is being evaluated based on things that are somewhat outside their control. For example, a department experiencing a decline in sales could simply be dealing with the effects of an economic downturn in the region, or it could be because a new company has created additional but unexpected competition, rather than something the company has done. Still, the supervisor often receives the brunt of the criticism when sales do not meet expectations.

Responses to Stress

In both instances (entry level and supervisory), reduction of stress occurs through both individual responses as well as the methods used in the department and company. For individuals, the best approach to managing stress is a combination of all the factors shown in Figure 4.11. Combinations of physical coping strategies, psychological strategies, and social contacts can provide the greatest relief from a stressful work environment and other life events.

Companies can also take measures to reduce stress, and marketing managers can be instrumental in reducing stress for themselves as well as the individuals in their departments. Company responses should take place in four basic areas:

1. Reduce the sources of stress on the job.
2. Place people in the right job.
3. Identify people with stress-related symptoms, and provide help.
4. Teach stress management techniques to all employees.

Psychological	Physical	Social
• Time away to relax	• Diet	• Support from family
• Prioritizing activities/goals	• Exercise	• Support from friends
• Relaxing hobbies	• Sufficient rest	
• Biofeedback programs		
• Daily quiet time		

Figure 4.11 Coping With Stress

An organization has many opportunities to *reduce the sources* of stress. Careful employee training combined with specific and clear job descriptions create greater role clarity and job understanding, which makes the job less stressful, especially for new and uncertain entry-level workers. Quality goal-setting programs combined with fair, transparent, and objective feedback and performance appraisal programs may improve both employee effectiveness and employee feelings toward the company. Constant monitoring of issues such as discrimination and harassment (of both women and new employees or minority group members) helps ensure a more positive work environment. Conflict resolution plans help members work well with each other both within the department and with other members of the firm. Management is also charged with making certain that employee contacts with persons outside the organization are balanced in the sense that while customer service remains the highest priority, the employee should not feel as if he has become a "whipping boy" or must tolerate any and all abuse that takes place.

Placing people in the right job means making certain that a new employee has the talent, skills, and temperament needed to perform the job to which he is assigned. Being overqualified or under qualified increases the likelihood that the person will fail on the job and experience distress at the same time. Further, a quality placement program should be able, at some level, to gauge a person's ability to handle stressful situations. Some people work more efficiently than others, for instance, with deadlines for creating marketing materials or generating ideas for a new ad campaign. The goal is to try to assign a new employee to the job that "fits" the best.

There are many checklists and "signs to watch for" to assist supervisors in *identifying people with stress-related problems*. Helping an employee deal successfully with stress is not only helpful to the individual, but it is also beneficial to the company, since the employee is more productive and less prone to illness and absenteeism.

Many companies offer *stress management programs*. These range from items as simple as hiring a professional masseuse to massage necks and backs to fitness and wellness programs, and beyond.[19] Employee training often includes sessions on how to handle the pressures of the job and in one's personal life.

Time Management and Stress Management

Closely related to stress management is time management. One of the sources of stress is the feeling of being constantly behind or overwhelmed. As the typical workweek continues to expand and as employers have access to employees via e-mail, global positioning satellite systems, and cell phones on more of a 24/7 basis, it is not surprising that a great deal of employees believe they never get free time or time away from work.

Time management involves a series of tactics designed to complete work more efficiently. They include goal setting, setting daily priorities for which tasks to finish first, and eliminating unnecessary activities that distract the worker or cause the individual to use time inefficiently.

One two-edged sword in the world of time management is *multitasking*, or working on more than one thing at the same time. On the one hand, it may feel as though the individual is getting more done during the time period. On the other, the person may be working less efficiently on both tasks due to being unfocused or distracted. Also, experiencing a continual need to multitask may play into the feeling of being overworked or overloaded.

In today's world, effective time management involves two concepts. The first is to work efficiently and complete tasks as expeditiously as possible. The second, and perhaps more important, is to insist on downtime; this includes time for rest and play and for time with family and friends. Within the marketing department, downtime is needed to rejuvenate the mind and to energize the creative juices. Ideas that can't seem to emerge during a work session may be sparked by something at lunch or while tossing a Nerf ball to associates. Experts on stress management agree that one key to success is a balanced life. Reaching that point may involve adjusting one's personal attitude, trading time for money, and within the work environment trading some time on the task for rejuvenation time.[20]

YOURCAREER

Getting Promoted

In practically every type of organization, there are four components that help a person become noticed and move up the organization hierarchy. Your goal should be to carefully consider how to build these four ingredients of your personal portfolio.

Education

An educational track record consists of four key parts:

1. *Degrees*—beyond a bachelor's degree, other items managers consider are
    *   the quality of the institution,
    *   the student's major and minor, and
    *   enrollment in postgraduate programs.

2. *Grades*—even with grade inflation, a GPA matters. It doesn't have to be a 4.00, but it must be good. It indicates you took your education seriously.

3. *Courses taken*—managers will look to see if the employee or applicant has taken classes that are related to a specific job or department where he or she is seeking a promotion.

4. *Activities*—students who participate in clubs, sports, or additional outside activities seem more well-rounded and potentially better candidates for a promotion, especially if they held leadership roles in those organizations.

Experience

When it comes to experience, three items are useful:

1. *Types of experience*—sales, advertising design, customer service, management, and so on.

2. *Length of the experience*—just doing a job for weeks or a few months is not ordinarily considered a quality experience.

3. *What you learned*—the person who can articulate why an experience was helpful and how it relates to the new position has an edge in interviewing for a promotion.

Skills

Three skills are especially important:

1. *Analytical, critical thinking*—You need to be able to demonstrate that you can think logically and apply your body of knowledge to unique new circumstances.

2. *Communication*—The ability to write in a clear and concise manner, make oral presentations, and communicate effectively with other employees is vital.

3. *Desire to continually learn*—Someone who takes the extra step to learn more about computers, or a foreign language, or some other new type of information will have an edge when promotions are granted.

Contacts

Two types of contacts are vital:

1. *A get-you-started contact*—someone who will write a reference or give a heads-up that a job is going to be available. Many jobs go to insiders and are never posted.

2. *Your mentor*—someone higher up in the organization or profession who is willing to spend time helping you navigate through the early stages of a career. In business and marketing, one common truism is "It's not what you know, it's *who* you know."

Chapter Summary

Building a customer-oriented marketing department means taking advantage of various management concepts, theories, and ideas. First, the overall management style exhibited in the company affects all other levels of activity and leadership. The four primary styles include authoritarian, consultative, participative, and democratic management.

Effective leadership is the result of understanding and applying leadership theories to the marketing department. Traits and characteristics theories point to task maturity, emotional maturity, a human relations orientation, and intelligence as factors related to a successful leadership style. The people and production theories note the important balance between treating customers and employees well but at the same time setting realistic and achievable standards in sales, production, and other areas. LMX notes the value of positive in-group relationships with employees. The substitutes for leadership approach points out situations in which the leader can rely on other factors such as subordinate experience, expertise, and professionalism to complete marketing tasks. Path-goal theory recommends matching leader style to subordinate characteristics and the nature of the task in order to succeed.

Effective marketing managers make quality decisions. They do so by knowing when to delegate authority and how to focus decisions on customers and by making certain decisions are made in an open environment.

The human resource department can help in the process of creating a customer-oriented culture through recruiting, selection, performance appraisal, and reward processes. Goal-setting programs and peer approval will also assist in building a strong customer orientation.

Motivational theories may be used by leaders and managers in marketing departments to achieve tangible goals such as sales and also to reach intangible outcomes such as positive, customer-oriented attitudes. The need-based theories point to the importance of knowing both subordinate and customer needs in the marketing program. The operant process models suggest ways to motivate employees through positive and negative reinforcement as well as ways to slow down or stop undesirable behaviors using punishment or extinction. Equity theory states the importance of treating employees fairly. Expectancy theory shows the manager how to motivate subordinates by understanding employee valences, clarifying tasks, and rewarding successful performance.

A key component in marketing success is creativity. Higher levels of creativity may be generated by recruiting and selecting the right kinds of employees, developing and maintaining a creative environment, and employing various creativity techniques when issues and challenges arise.

Customers and employees are best served when company leaders work to reduce stress on the job. Both supervisors and entry-level employees are subject to a wide variety of stressors. Therefore, it is important to know how to manage personal stress and create a lower-stress environment for others. One tactic that can be used is effective time management.

Chapter Terms

Antecedents of stress   (p. 99)
Brainstorming   (p. 98)
Decentralization   (p. 85)
Extinction   (p. 94)
Formal leader   (p. 86)
Human resource management   (p. 90)

Informal leader (emergent leader)   (p. 86)
Negative reinforcement   (p. 94)
Nominal groups (nominal group technique)   (p. 99)
Positive reinforcement   (p. 93)
Punishment   (p. 94)
Stress outcomes   (p. 99)

Review Questions

1. What are the four basic management styles that have an impact on the marketing department?

2. Define formal leadership and informal leadership.

3. Name four leadership traits that may help make an individual a successful marketing manager.

4. What type of relationship should be developed with subordinates from the perspective of the LMX model?

5. Which three factors may influence the quality of decisions made in marketing departments?

6. Name three techniques that will help build customer-oriented marketing programs.

7. Define motivation.

8. From the perspective of the manifest needs theory, which three types of need play a role in worker behaviors??

9. Describe positive and negative reinforcement along with punishment and extinction.

10. Describe Adams's equity theory. How would it be useful to a marketing manager?

11. Describe expectancy theory. How would it be useful to a marketing manager?

12. What three things can help inspire creativity in a marketing department and overall in a company?

13. Name the forms or types of antecedents or causes of stress.

14. Name the three categories of signs of distress.

15. What is multitasking? How is it related to time management and stress-related issues?

CUSTOMER CORNER

Irene Freitas had never yelled at a client or customer—until today. As a sales representative for a major freight-carrying company, Irene sold and wrote shipping contracts for domestic and international transport for nearly 20 years. She encountered a wide variety of problems, challenges, petulant customers, and mistakes by people in her firm without ever losing her cool.

What made today different? The problem presented by the client was not unusual—a shipment had been delayed by customs and did not arrive on time. The difference was the company's demands on Irene. She had been issued a cell phone and instructed to keep the cell phone turned on at all times. Her laptop tracked her location at every moment of the day. She no longer felt free to even stop to buy lunch without the company knowing her every move. The company, which was in financial trouble, imposed increasing and unrealistic sales goals that were followed by threats of termination for those who did not reach them.

Recently, Irene had been experiencing episodes where her blood pressure rose quickly. She had chest pains and shortness of breath on several occasions, even though she had been a lifelong runner and exercise junkie. She was terse with friends both on and off the job. Her physician advised her to either take a different job or find better ways to cope with the one she held.

1. What are the sources of stress affecting Irene?

2. What symptoms of distress is Irene exhibiting?

3. How should Irene and the company change in order to lessen these types of problems?

How likely will Irene's job performance be affected by the stress she now experiences?

Discussion and Critical Thinking Questions

1. The four main management styles are authoritarian, consultative, participative, and democratic. Do any of these styles seem more likely to create in-group relationships between first-line supervisors and their employees? Do any of these styles seem more likely to create company-wide feelings of equity, that the organization is fair with its employees? Which style would be best suited to developing a creative environment? Which style would be best suited to applying the expectancy theory approach to marketing jobs, or could all four styles be adapted to such an approach? Why or why not?

2. Create a list of specific behaviors a company's management team would be interested in starting, maintaining, or stopping for the following occupations:
   - Advertising creative
   - Outbound telemarketing phone caller
   - Retail sales clerk
   - Market researcher, data collection
   - Media buyer

3. Explain how the following terms may be connected:
   - Fulfilling needs
   - Positive reinforcement
   - Valences
   - Sense of equity or fairness

4. Many dot.com companies in the 1990s and early 2000s attempted to create work environments that were far different from typical organizations. They included open office spaces with no walls; entertainment venues, such as pinball machines and ping-pong tables; freedom for each employee to decorate his or her own area; on-site snow cone machines and popcorn makers; and the freedom to come and go without the permission of a supervisor. While most of these organizations no longer exist, several notable companies still use these ideas. Explain how such a work environment might affect
   - perceptions of the managerial style exhibited by top management,
   - leadership approaches,

- levels of creativity,
- motivational programs, and
- stress levels and responses to stress.

5. Assume you are the marketing manager of a small marketing department. You have eight employees working under your direction. In interacting with the employees, you notice Dominic has a strong need for power, Layla has a strong need for achievement, and Isabel has a strong need for affiliation (based on McClelland's manifest needs theory). Discuss how you would manage each of these individuals to motivate each one to perform at his or her highest level of capability.

6. You supervise a telemarketing call center of 25 employees who handle incoming calls from customers and prospects. You have one employee, Kyle, who is habitually late for work, sometimes coming in as much as 45 minutes late. When he takes breaks or goes to lunch, he is almost always late in returning, anywhere from just a few minutes to as much as 30 minutes. You have talked to him a couple of times, but the behavior continues to persist and has even gotten worse. You are afraid other employees may start displaying similar behaviors. You do not want to fire Kyle because he is one of your top internal salespeople and is well liked by clients. Discuss possible courses of action you can use with Kyle based on the theory of operant conditioning.

7. Tristan has just barged into your office and complained that a fellow employee was given a nice pay raise. Tristan feels he is just as good as the employee who received the pay raise, works just as hard, and deserves the same pay raise. Explain Tristan's feelings based on Adams's equity theory. As his supervisor, how can you deal with Tristan if you believe the quality of work he produces is inferior to that of the employee who received the raise?

8. You are the assistant manager of a retail store and notice one of your employees, Nicole, who you believe has considerable potential to be an assistant manager. You notice, however, that she puts in the minimal amount effort at work and has sometimes demonstrated curt behavior with customers. You have mentioned to her before that she has the potential to manage a store, but she shrugs you off with the comment "They will never promote me." Explain Nicole's attitude and behaviors in terms of expectancy theory. Using the same theory, how could you motivate Nicole to change her attitude and behaviors?

9. Look through the list of causes of stress identified in Figure 4.8. List and discuss the stress you experience in your life and the causes of the stress. Examine the signs of distress in Figure 4.10. Which of the symptoms have you displayed? Finally, look at Figure 4.11. Discuss ways you currently deal with stress. What other methods from the list in Figure 4.11 could you use to reduce stress in your life?

Chapter 4 Case

The New Boss

Jim Logan could hardly contain his excitement. He graduated from college 3 years earlier, joined the company AdSmart as an entry-level advertising creative, and now was being given his first chance to direct an entire advertising program. This included making the pitch to the client company, meeting with the client's personnel, finalizing the contract, and creating the ads. Jim would also be in charge of oversight of relations between AdSmart and the client through the entire process. This presented a clear opportunity to move into an entry-level management position and enhanced his career prospects for the immediate future.

Jim's team consisted of four people. The first, an experienced media buyer who was several years older than Jim, had been friendly and served as a kind of mentor

regarding media purchasing issues. He had been with the company for 10 years. The second, a young woman who joined AdSmart the same month as Jim, served as a consumer promotions liaison. She would develop any coupons, premiums, sweepstakes, contests, and bonus packs that would be part of the campaign. The third member was an older woman who primarily performed clerical tasks. Her role would be to finalize all the paperwork, including the actual paper document to accompany any proposal, the contract, and other similar matters. She had a great deal of experience and was often asked to perform the same types of tasks on other projects.

The fourth member, Dirk, troubled Jim. Dirk's assigned role was to be the advertising creative. Jim had seen Dirk's work previously and had not been impressed. Further, Jim found Dirk to be a prima donna who often displayed disrespect to other members of the company.

Jim Logan realized his greatest challenge would be how to handle Dirk.

Whether real or just imagined, Jim felt additional pressure because AdSmart's founder, Blake Bard, began his career as a creative. Blake's free-spirited nature led him to manage the firm with a highly decentralized, participative style. One of Blake's favorite expressions was "If you want your people to succeed, you have to set them free." Blake had a great deal of disdain for what he called "micromanaging types."

On the other hand, Jim's only experiences with teams and leadership had been in college, on class projects, and during his time as president of the Marketing Club. What he found in that realm was that if he wanted something done, he needed to do it himself. Trusting and relying on others had never worked out very well. Jim knew that the first three members of his team would make it easier for him to let go and delegate. On the other hand, he worried about using the same approach with Dirk, who had an ego that was already too big.

The prospective client was a small local Mexican restaurant with a limited advertising and promotional budget. Jim believed this meant his team would have to be innovative and creative in order to create an effective campaign while spending a small number of dollars.

One of the first tasks Jim directed was to create an integrated message that could be presented on billboards, in local newspaper ads, and for 4 weeks on local television. He wanted to make sure that his consumer promotion tactics fit with the theme of the advertisements and the restaurant's primary message before making the pitch presentation.

The next decision was to identify the members of the team who would accompany Jim to make the pitch in person. He knew that only one or two people should go along. He didn't want to offend any member of the team in making the selection. Jim was confident he would win the contract due to AdSmart's track record of success in restaurant marketing in the area.

Jim's final worry as the project began was what would happen if Dirk designed advertisements that Jim thought were substandard. He considered secretly preparing an alternate set in advance so that he would be ready if Dirk's ads were rejected. After all, this was his first big shot, and he didn't want anything to go wrong.

1. Role conflicts occur in companies when a manager's expectations are different from the follower's experiences and methods of completing tasks. Describe the role conflicts that Jim is experiencing in this case.

2. What motivational theory would best fit Jim's task? Does the same theory apply equally well to every member of the team?

3. Which leadership theory do you think Jim should apply to this project? Explain how it would work, and defend your choice of theory.

4. In designing the advertising and promotional approach, which creativity technique should Jim use?

5. How should Jim handle Dirk? Which theories of motivation would be the best to follow?

 Go to **www.sagepub.com/clow** for additional exercises and study resources. Select **Chapter 4, Building a Customer-Oriented Marketing Department** for chapter-specific activities.

part 2

Managing Customer Acquisition

How was Sony able to build a strong brand name and reputation?

Customer Acquisition Strategies and Tactics

Sony: From Humble Beginnings to a Worldwide Brand

Today's college students may not recall that, for many years, Japanese products were considered to be low-cost, inferior intrusions into the marketplace. "Made in Japan" became the punch line for a variety of jokes. It took many years and major changes in attitudes for American customers to trust and respect what are now powerful worldwide brands. Among them, Sony has achieved a great deal of stature in the world of technology.

In 1946, the Tokyo Tsushin Kogyo K.K., or Tokyo Telecommunications Engineering Corporation, was formed. The Japanese

company, which was also known as Totsuko, began researching and manufacturing telecommunications and measuring equipment. Early success led to innovations in tape-recording equipment and in transistors, the cutting-edge technology of the time.

Eventually in 1955, a new brand name, Sony, was assigned to Totsuko's products, which included Japan's first transistor radio. The company expanded its operations into the United States in 1960, at a time when Japanese goods were not viewed favorably. Still, new televisions, stereos, and tape recorders were added to the product line.

Among the more noticeable innovations that led to respect for Sony's products was the introduction of Trinitron technology, which added depth and quality to the company's color television picture in 1968. Sony became the first Japanese company to be awarded an Emmy Award for technological achievement for Trinitron. Two years earlier, the company had also begun producing and selling one of the first color video cassette players. At that point, Sony's scope of operations reached Spain, France, and Germany, and soon after, Great Britain.

Some of Sony's product names remain part of the technology lingo of today. Betamax, the ½-inch-tape VCR product, was one of two major competing technologies in the late 1970s. In 1979, the "Walkman" was introduced. Three years later, the world's first CD player reached the marketplace carrying the Sony brand.

The Sony Corporation expanded into the music-recording industry as Sony Music Entertainment. The company moved into the life insurance marketplace through a coordinated effort with Prudential Insurance.

Most of the corporation's operations remain focused on technological innovations. The company was among the first competitors in the camcorder marketplace as well as high-definition television (HDTV) design.

A division of Sony opened in China in 1996. At the same time, the company expanded into digital technologies that are now commonplace. Flat-screen televisions soon followed.

Today, Sony exists as a multinational corporation that continues to reinvent itself on a regular basis. The range of products now offered includes banking services, semiconductors, and numerous others.

The power of the Sony brand rests on quality products, innovation, superior service, effective marketing communications, and successful management techniques. Changing consumer perceptions took time. At one point, the company's advertising tagline was "Sony, No Baloney." Such modesty is no longer necessary. What was once an unknown but innovative technology company is now a recognizable brand around the world.[1]

Chapter Overview

The first part of this textbook was devoted to building a solid marketing foundation focused on developing a customer-oriented company. In Part 2, various methods of acquiring new customers are described. This chapter examines the nature of customer acquisition beginning with the distinction between existing products and new goods and services. Markets, products, and brands are examined with the goal of customer acquisition in mind.

The remainder of Part 2 considers additional elements of customer acquisition. Chapter 6 addresses pricing. Chapter 7 reviews the role of advertising, including the use of nontraditional promotional programs. Chapter 8 examines the roles that consumer and trade promotions play in developing a strong customer base. Chapter 9 analyzes personal selling tactics. Each of these ingredients is a vital part of a marketing management approach that emphasizes a customer orientation in the process of building a loyal base of consumers.

From there, techniques to create positive interactions with them may be developed, and customer retention can be enhanced (see Figure 5.1).

The first portion of this chapter provides a brief review of the product life cycle concept, focusing on the industry level. An analysis of the product life cycle reveals the importance of and difficulties associated with customer acquisition. Next, various approaches to customer acquisition are described, focusing on markets, products, and branding approaches. This chapter concludes with a review of the implications for customer service in developing quality customer acquisition programs.

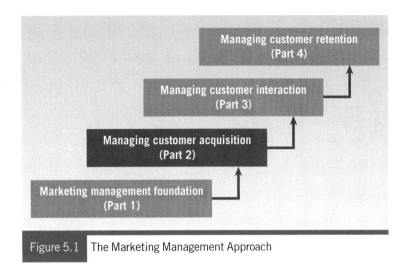

Figure 5.1 The Marketing Management Approach

The Product Life Cycle

The product life cycle models how sales of an item move over the lifetime of the item. A typical life cycle model consists of the introductory growth, maturity or saturation, and decline stages. Each presents new challenges for marketing managers.

When a marketing expert considers the product life cycle, it is helpful to first think in macro terms, or an assessment of the entire industry. Figure 5.2 illustrates the typical life cycle of a product in an industry (the camera industry) in terms of total sales revenues and industry profits.

A new product or innovation begins the *introduction stage*. In 1888, George Eastman created the first photographic film, and as a result, modern photography was born. In the 1890s, the first cameras were produced and sold by Eastman Kodak. Picture quality was poor and demand was low. Sales were limited to the few individuals willing to make purchases and those who knew how to operate the cameras. The early companies in the camera industry tended to experience losses, even though prices were high, as firms tried to recover development costs.

The basic marketing goals during the introductory stage are to increase consumer awareness of the product, incite interest in the generic product, and encourage customers to make trial purchases. The more radically different a product, the more difficult and lengthy the introductory stage will be, because it takes time for many consumers to accept a change. Still, some customers may purchase the product because of its uniqueness. If is too similar to other products already on the market, then consumers will continue purchasing the former product rather than something new.

In 1913, the 35-mm still camera was created. The flash bulb was introduced in 1935. Advances in technology continued, competition increased, and prices were driven down. At that point, many families could afford a camera. Cameras had entered the *growth stage* of the life cycle.

During the growth stage, marketing managers emphasize differentiating the company's brand and highlighting the superiority of the brand. Marketing tactics tend to focus on building brand preference and, ultimately, brand loyalty. Customer acquisition becomes

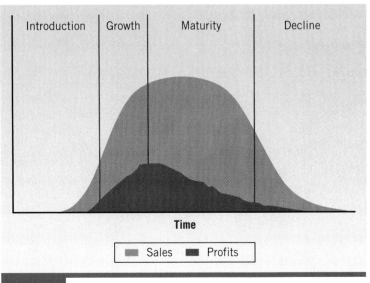

Figure 5.2 The Product Life Cycle

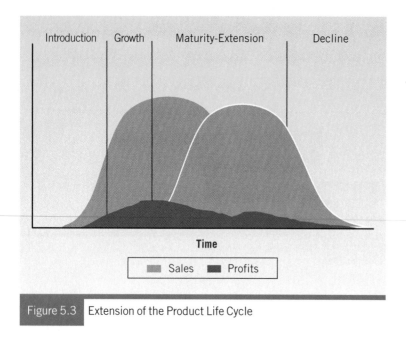

| Introduction | Growth | Maturity-Extension | Decline |

Time

■ Sales   ■ Profits

Figure 5.3   Extension of the Product Life Cycle

increasingly important. The total market expands rapidly, which provides the opportunity for a company to capture market share by acquiring new customers. As a result, money is invested in a variety of customer acquisition methods.

Next, *market saturation* or the *maturity stage* occurs. By the middle of the 20th century, most Americans owned one or more cameras. Sales and prices tend to level off in the maturity stage. Competition becomes intense, because in most cases too many companies have entered the industry with a version of the product. To grow, companies must take customers and sales away from competitors. To prevent a loss of market share, competitors often retaliate by using tactics such as cutting prices, offering coupons, or developing unique versions of the product that appeal to smaller, individual market segments. As the maturity stage continues, some companies are shaken out, or go out of business. The remaining competitors tend to find the equilibrium in which prices and marketing programs start to stabilize.

During the maturity stage, managers of the marketing department focus on long-term strategies for the company, including an emphasis on research and development to create product improvements or completely new products. Tactics used during the maturity stage include finding ways to maintain a competitive edge. Since there is no influx of new buyers into the market, the focus shifts to existing markets or to modifying the current product to meet the needs of specific target markets.

Most products today are in the maturity stage of the life cycle, which means intense competition exits. To survive, a company must continually modify its marketing approach to meet changes in competitor tactics and changes in consumer preferences. Company leaders also look for new products or modifications of current products in order to extend the life cycle or create a mini burst in the maturity stage of the life cycle. Figure 5.3 illustrates this process. In the camera industry, it took place when Kodak started marketing Kodachrome film in 1935. The maturity stage continues until a substitute product is invented or consumer tastes change. Cameras that use film remained in the maturity stage until digital cameras were invented.

How has the digital camera changed the photography industry?

The first digital camera was introduced in 1981 by Sony for the commercial market, because the price was too high for consumers. Then in 1991, Kodak took the technology one step further and developed a digital camera for photography professionals and journalists. As competitors entered the digital camera market with new versions, prices quickly declined until consumers could afford the new format. When this occurred, the film camera industry moved into the *decline stage*. Seeing the advantages of digital cameras, consumers are quickly changing over, and the demand for film cameras is plummeting. This change in the market, in turn, causes leaders of marketing departments to revise the company's strategies and tactics to address the change from film cameras to digital cameras. The introduction and growth stages for digital cameras occurred more quickly because consumers were already familiar with cameras and photography.

The characteristics of each stage of the product life cycle are unique. Therefore, the marketing strategies companies use will also change. Table 5.1 provides greater detail about the characteristics and marketing strategies used in each stage of the life cycle.

Stage of PLC	Characteristics	Marketing Strategies
Introduction	1. Market is small. 2. Growth rate is slow. 3. Often only the company is the pioneer. 4. Companies experience losses.	1. Build primary demand for the product. 2. Establish a distribution channel.
Growth	1. Market grows rapidly. 2. Competitors enter the market. 3. Profits are high.	1. Differentiate the brand. 2. Promote competitive advantage or product differentiation. 3. Build distribution channel.
Maturity	1. Growth slows and then flattens. 2. Competition is most intense. 3. Profits decline. 4. Some firms drop out due to competition. 5. Price becomes more important. 6. Large amounts are spent on marketing.	1. Segment market and focus on one or more segments. 2. Promote brand and product differentiation. 3. Focus on customer service, customer satisfaction, and customer retention. 4. Expand product or market opportunities.
Decline	1. Market declines. 2. Profits decline. 3. Substitute product is found.	1. Decide whether to leave market or be a niche player. 2. Promote the niche to those who still want the product.

Table 5.1   Characteristics of and Marketing Tactics for the Product Life Cycle (PLC)

The Importance of Customer Acquisition

As noted, many firms operate in the intensely competitive environment of the maturity stage of the life cycle. In that stage, the marketing team knows that in order to maintain current sales levels, new customers are needed to replace those who are lost or who have migrated to competing firms. The team can never reach the point where they can relax, believing the company has enough customers. Consequently, companies face a continuing struggle on two fronts: (1) keeping current customers and (2) finding new customers.

The number of new customers required to maintain the status quo or to grow depends on how well a firm retains its current customers. A firm that loses 5% of its customers every year needs to gain at least that many new ones during the year. It is clear that long-term marketing success is based, in part, on acquiring new customers. To do so, a progression of marketing goals must be met, starting with making consumers aware that a company or brand exists. Next, potential customers must be moved from awareness to more positive emotions, such as liking and preference, and eventually to the point of making the purchase. Then, postpurchase feelings are addressed, including offering reassurance and support by suggesting that the customer has made a wise choice and should consider repeating that choice in the future.

Acquiring new customers is difficult in the maturity stage of the product life cycle because each of the firm's competitors also tries to acquire new customers. When industry sales have stabilized, a firm acquires a new customer by enticing that person away from a competitor. In general, there are three basic forms of customer acquisition:

1. Developing existing or new markets
2. Developing existing or new products
3. Branding

At the same time, when developing marketing programs to acquire new customers, marketing managers should not lose sight of ways to retain current customers. The temptation exists to spend more time and money on acquiring new customers as current customers drift away. Such an approach ultimately creates problems for the company. Fortunately, many of the methods used to acquire customers may also help to keep them.

Customer Acquisition: Identifying Markets ————

- Existing markets
  - Brand switching
  - New needs
  - Product differentiation
- New markets
  - Discover or create new segments
  - Adapt current products
  - Geographic expansion
    - Domestic
    - International

Figure 5.4

Customer Acquisition Strategies: Markets

Marketing managers seeking to acquire new customers through identifying new markets can examine two primary areas: (1) existing markets and (2) potential new markets (see Figure 5.4). The goal is to find customer segments that can be approached through various marketing programs.

Existing Markets

Many times, new customers are located in existing markets. Any industry, from products such as clothes, medicines, and automobiles to services such as travel, life insurance, and banking, contains segments of individuals who may be enticed to change brands or who have not purchased the product for the first time yet. One approach to customer acquisition is to focus on *brand switching* within existing market segments. Thus, a consumer in the yogurt-as-health-food segment may be enticed to move from Dannon to Yoplait because one offers different features, ingredients, or taste as compared with the other.

Also, there are times when customers may be discovered because *new needs arise in existing markets,* due primarily to changing situations or cultural trends. For example, in 2009, all television stations in the United States moved from analog transmission to digital signals, known as HDTV. The existing market, television set owners, had fragmented into those owning old analog sets, those who purchased analog sets with the ability to receive an HD signal, and customers owning HDTV receivers. One market segment, owners of analog-only televisions, created a market opportunity for companies to produce and sell the adapters needed to translate the HD signal into an analog format. A similar situation emerged when the city of New York passed an ordinance outlawing the use of trans-fats in food preparation in any restaurant in the city.

A third approach is to create the perception that an existing product or brand is different and better, which is *product differentiation*. Brand equity and product differentiation are closely related. In both instances, the difference can be real or created in the consumer's mind through various marketing practices.

New Markets

New markets are discovered using a variety of tactics. Products may be used in new ways, new markets may be created, or a market may expand or evolve on its own. One common customer acquisition approach is to *discover or create new segments based on changing needs.* The past contains several examples. In personal grooming, past generations of males went to barber shops and females visited beauty salons. Currently, both genders go to style salons and receive more than just hair care. Many also offer manicures and pedicures along with other services. One group of physicians has expanded from traditional doctor's office formats to spa-based cosmetology, massage therapy, and other forms of care that may or may not be considered medically necessary. Avon's Skin So Soft lotion has evolved into an insect repellant product as well, thereby reaching a much wider and dramatically different market (think of hunters and fishermen).

Finding new market segments may be the result of *creatively adapting products to new markets* by thinking about what a good or service has to offer. Thus, the traditional segments of demographics, psychographics, geographic areas, product usage, user type, and others should continually be reexamined to see if a new group can be reached by creating a new product, modifying an existing product, or changing the ways in which an existing product is marketed.

Not all these efforts to find, define, or redefine existing and new markets are the result of strategic decisions made by top managers. In more than one instance, a first-level employee had made a suggestion that was passed along to a supervisor, and eventually the idea was implemented. The Starbucks top management team actively solicits ideas from *baristas* and even customers. Several items sold at Starbucks were introduced based on suggestions from these sources. Entry-level employees often believe that discovering such innovations may be a pathway to quicker promotion and/or a bigger pay raise.

Geographic Expansion: Domestic Markets

Geographic expansion can take place through domestic expansion or by seeking out international markets. Customers may be acquired by expanding to a geographic area in which a good or service is not offered or where a particular brand is not being sold. Geographic expansion often creates a new set of obstacles, such as having to increase the number of units, offices, and employees. These become more complicated in any international program.

Many companies find the best route to growth is simply by adding new locations or finding new geographic markets to enter. This can be done by entering a new territory. There was a time in which Coors beer was only sold in Kansas, Colorado, and California. Part of the success achieved by the company resulted from entering other states.

Many times, a product has a regional base, which offers the possibility of moving into nearby territories. Other times, a firm many identify geographic areas with specific characteristics. For example, the Costco chain added locations in major metropolitan areas. The same was true for many years in the Krispy Kreme company.

One common strategy used for domestic expansion is *franchising*. The dramatic growth of many fast-food chains, including McDonald's and SUBWAY, is based on selling franchises in new locations.

Past generations of males used barbershops for haircuts; in recent years, beauty shops have targeted services to both genders.

Geographic Expansion: International Markets

As has been noted, many company leaders, even in small firms, view a firm's marketplace as the entire globe. Assisted by new technologies and more sophisticated delivery systems, smaller companies can identify customers and sell products around the world.

The standard methods for entering international markets begin with simple exporting but also include the other modes of entry shown in Figure 5.5. The problems associated with entering foreign markets are as well documented as the potential benefits. Company leaders carefully consider not only the method to be used in expanding but also how the various obstacles may be overcome.

In the summer of 2008, the Oreo cookie was being marketed for the first time in Great Britain. Many of the logistical issues were quickly and easily resolved. Culturally speaking, the challenge was much larger. It turns out that many British citizens are fiercely loyal to their "biscuits." Changing minds and attitudes toward an "American" product may prove to be difficult.[2]

Market research plays a key role in international expansion. Company leaders should be able to present solid evidence that expansion will succeed before attempting to export goods or beginning operations in a new country.

• **Indirect exporting**	One company handles exported goods for another company.
• **Direct exporting**	A company exports it own goods and services.
• **Turnkey project**	A company designs, builds, and starts up a business in another country and then sells the operation to a local client company.
• **Licensing**	A company transfers the rights and grants permission to produce and sell its products overseas to a foreign firm.
• **Franchising**	The license to sell applies only to a single good or service or to a single unit of operation.
• **Joint venture**	Two companies work together making and selling a product or operation.
• **Strategic alliance**	Cooperative agreements between potential competitors in a foreign country.
• **Wholly owned subsidiary**	A multinational corporation owns a company in another country.

Figure 5.5   Modes of Entry

Customer Acquisition: Developing Products

Acquisition of new customers often results from the implementation of a product strategy. Products attract new customers by offering new features, eliminating old problems, and solving different needs. The three most common product development strategies are displayed in Figure 5.6. Products are only developed when they can be matched with a viable market segment or when they can be differentiated from competing brands in the marketplace.

Product Development

Product development is a marketing strategy in which new goods and services are developed and then added to current lines and marketed to existing customers. Product diversification occurs when new goods and services are created for new market segments not currently being served by the company. Many firms spend large sums of money developing new products. When company leaders believe a viable market exists that can be tapped by offering a completely new product, funds will be authorized to turn the idea into a reality.

Before beginning the physical development of an item, various forms of testing take place. One of the more common is the use of focus groups. A focus group consists of a set of individuals who are prompted to discuss an item or topic. In 2007, Amazon.com began to offer a new product, the Kindle, which is a method of carrying a series of books and other reading materials in a portable device that offers a variety of features, including a dictionary that can be accessed while reading something else and the ability to load books, magazine articles, and even blogs from any location. In the past, focus groups had pointed out the problems with other methods of downloading books. The Kindle was developed to solve those problems.[3]

Cultural trends and other changes may also lead to development and diversification strategies. McDonald's added products such as fruit cups, yogurt, and salads to its standard menu. The products were developed to entice more health-conscious customers into the restaurant. Pizza Hut added several pasta products to its menu in an attempt to widen its customer base.

The strategy of developing a new product only succeeds through proper *implementation*. The product and its advantages must first be understood by internal employees. Then, these employees should be motivated to emphasize the new item to existing customers and potential new customers. The role of the first-line supervisor is to follow through and be certain that those at the entry level support the new product.

Sidebar (Figure 5.6):

- Product development
  - Development
  - Diversification
- Product improvements
  - Based on customer needs
  - Based on technology
- Product line extensions

Figure 5.6

Customer Acquisition Strategies: Products

Product Improvements

Products are often improved in order to solve small, specific problems based on *customer needs*. For example, standard luggage in the past century was often quite large and only had a handle to be used for carrying the suitcase. One product improvement resulted from the frustrations many passengers had with baggage handlers, and the carry-on bag was developed. A second product improvement emerged when the concept of adding rollers to the suitcase was developed.

Products may also be improved when *new technologies* become available. Battery technology, for example, has evolved a great deal over the years. Alkaline-based batteries are now only one form. Competition comes from both nickel metal hydride and lithium batteries.

Product improvements often are marketed as the "better mousetrap." The advantages of the improvement become the key selling point. The improvements should match the needs of a viable market segment or create brand equity in the total market.

It is important to explain the advantages of a new version of a product to everyone in the company. Those holding first-line positions will be the ones to explain these features to potential customers. Supervisors should be able to reward those who make the effort to pass the information on to the public.

Product Line Extensions

Customers can be acquired through product line extensions. Many food and beverage producers use product line extension tactics. Recently, Bud Light was extended to include a Bud Light Lime product. Campbell's Soups added a series of lower-sodium "sea salt" products. The producers of Kool-Aid constantly add (and delete) versions of the product, as do the makers of Lipton Tea (caffeine-free, sweetened, unsweetened, lemon flavored, raspberry flavored, and peach flavored).

Extending product lines often involves customizing products to more specific tastes and individual preferences. In the eyeglass industry, some customers prefer tinted lenses while others want clear lenses. Extending product lines increases the chances that a set of customers will switch brands, because the new version more closely meets their needs.

In summary, the definition of marketing offered in Chapter 1 suggested that it is "discovering consumer wants and needs, *creating the products and services that meet those needs*, pricing, promoting, and delivering the products and services." One clear route to acquiring new customers is creating or adapting products that meet the needs of a set of consumers.

STOP AND THINK

Consider this statement:

Nearly 40,000 new products are brought to the marketplace each year. *Most fail to survive.*

Using the information you have read thus far, answer the following questions:

1. What market-based factors might explain this failure rate?
2. What product-based factors might explain this failure rate?
3. What market-based factors explain why one product succeeds while others fail?
4. What product-based factors might explain why one item succeeds and others fail?
5. Explain the connections between products and markets that explain success and failure.
6. Is it harder to create and sell a new good or a new service? Why?

How have Gillette and Schick developed strong brand names?

Branding

In the world of marketing management, creating a powerful brand has emerged as a key ingredient in the long-term success of a company. When a woman decides she needs a new perfume, one of her first thoughts is probably about the names of different perfumes she knows or has heard about. When a man thinks about buying cologne, various names probably may come to mind. In both instances, the name is the product's brand, whether it is for a specific item such as Cool Water, L'air du Temps, or Polo or a house name, such as Ralph Lauren, Yves Saint Laurent, or Paul Sebastian.

Strong brands can contribute to customer acquisition. For example, as a young man begins to discover the need to shave, he is likely to first consider well-known brands, such as Gillette or Schick. Major brands have the benefit of being the first considered for new shoppers as well as those who are in new situations. For instance, someone traveling in Europe for the first time may be enticed to stay at the Holiday Inn simply because the consumer remembers the brand name.

Types of Brands

Brands are assigned to individual products, such as an iPod; to lines of products, including all the Green Giant vegetables and juices; to companies offering products (Golden Corral, SUBWAY); to individual services; and to companies that offer services. MasterCuts is a brand assigned to a hairstyling service. The name MasterCard applies to both the service, a credit card, and to the company that offers the service. Visa uses the same name to identify the corporation and individual services such as the Visa Check Card.

There are several ways in which names and brands appear. The term used to identify an entire company is the corporate name, which may or may not be a brand. Procter & Gamble (P&G) is a corporate name that is not assigned to any product. The corporate name Campbell's is added to every product the company offers. In that situation, the name Campbell's is considered to be a house mark form of brand. A brand is the name given to a product and, in some instances, to the company. The primary forms of brands include

- family brands,
- flanker brands,
- brand extensions,
- private brands (or private labels),
- cobrands, and
- global brands.

Family Brands

A family brand is the name used when a company offers a series or group of products under one brand. For instance, the Black & Decker brand is used for a series of power tools. It is very similar to a house mark. The difference is that one company may feature several family brands. For instance, the Masco Corporation sells faucet and plumbing supplies using three family brands—Delta, Peerless, and Brizo.

The primary advantage of a family brand is that consumers usually transfer the image associated with the brand name to any new products added to current lines. When Black & Decker offers a new power tool, the new item automatically carries the reputation associated with the Black & Decker name. These transfer associations occur as long as the new product remains in the same product category. When additional products are not related to the brand's core merchandise, the transfer of loyalty may not occur as easily.

Flanker Brands

A flanker brand is the development of a new brand by a company in a good or service category in which the company currently has a brand offering. Flanker brands may be used to expand a portfolio of products by adding higher- or lower-priced versions or versions aimed at particular markets. They are also featured when concerns arise that using the family brand name will confuse consumers and dilute the brand equity that has developed over the years.

Procter & Gamble's primary laundry detergent brand names are Cheer and Tide. Over the years, additional flanker brands, such as Ivory Snow were introduced. In total, Procter & Gamble offers 11 different brands of detergents in North America; 16 in Latin America; 12 in Asia; and 17 in Europe, the Middle East, and Africa. The company's marketing team introduced these flanker brands to appeal to target markets that they believed its main brand was not reaching.

Sometimes a flanker brand is introduced when company leaders conclude that offering the product under the current brand name will adversely affect the overall marketing program. Hallmark created a flanker brand known as Shoebox Greetings. The cards sell in discount stores as well as Hallmark outlets; however, the Hallmark brand sells only in its named retail stores. Shoebox Greetings cards are lower priced and allow Hallmark to attract a larger percentage of the market. Firms often use this type of strategy in high-end markets that want to compete in low-end markets. Doing so makes it possible to acquire a new set of customers for the company.

Flanker brands may also be part of an international operation. As noted, Procter & Gamble sells Ariel laundry detergent in Latin America, Asia, Europe, the Middle East, and Africa but not in North America. Offering different brands for specific markets continues to be a common flanker brand strategy in international markets.

Black & Decker's strong brand name allows the company's marketing team to introduce new products with immediate brand equity.

Challenges of Brand Extensions and Multiple Brands

A brand extension is the use of the firm's current brand name on new products and new versions of current products. Due to its complexity, managing brand extensions and multiple brands is one of the most challenging tasks facing the marketing manager. Successful brands continuously evolve to meet the changing needs of a diverse marketplace.

Cannibalization

While multiple brands and brand extensions provide benefits as already mentioned, they can also create problems. The first is cannibalization. When a new product's sales take away from sales of the rest of the company's line, the new product does not contribute significantly to income or company profit.

To ensure that cannibalization does not occur, the target market for the new product or brand must be clearly different from the target market for current brands. The goal is to gain market share from competitors and new customers, not by diluting sales of current brands. Recently Jeep

	Quarterly Sales ($)		Change in Sales	
	1st Quarter	2nd Quarter	Dollars	Percent
Total of all oatmeal products	734,207	755,213	21,006	2.86
Sales of new oatmeal flavor		112,528		
Sales of oatmeal Flavor A	324,675	327,549	2,874	0.89
Sales of oatmeal Flavor B	123,763	96,543	–27,220	–21.99
Sales of oatmeal Flavor C	285,769	218,593	–67,176	–23.51

Measuring cannibalization effect	Change in Sales ($)	Percent Sales
Sales of new oatmeal flavor	112,528	
Sales of oatmeal Flavor B	–27,220	24.19
Sales of oatmeal Flavor C	–67,176	59.70
New sales generated by new flavor	18,132	16.11

Table 5.2   Cannibalization Effects

- Lighter manufacturer Bic spent $20 million to launch a line of perfume.
- Pond's, a face cream manufacturer, launched a toothpaste.
- Levi's in the 1980s introduced tailored suits.
- Victoria's Secret launched a new line of athletic wear.

Figure 5.7

Questionable Brand Extensions

introduced four additional models to accompany current lines. For years, Jeep only sold three models. Now there are seven. Jeep's marketing team defended the brand extension, stating that the new models appeal to different target markets. If they do, Jeep has succeeded with the extension. If they cannibalize sales of current models, then it will have been a mistake.[4]

A simplified example of the cannibalization effect is illustrated in Table 5.2. The first-quarter sales of a company that offers three flavors of breakfast oatmeal is $734,207. A new flavor was introduced that generated sales of $112,528 for the second quarter. An examination of sales for the company and for individual flavors indicates a serious problem of cannibalization. Although revenues for the new flavor were over $112,000, the company only experienced a sales increase of 2.8%, or $21,006. Only 16.11% of the sales of the new flavor came from new customers trying the flavor, or perhaps from individuals who would have purchased Flavor A. Sales of Flavor A did increase, which means it is unlikely that there was much of a cannibalization effect. The decline in purchases of Flavors B and C indicates that most of the individuals who tried the new flavor switched from these two flavors to the new one. Almost 60% of the sales of the new brand came from decline in the sales of Flavor C, and almost 24% of the income resulted from individuals who switched from Flavor B.

A Poor Fit

The second possible obstacle to an effective expansion occurs when a company moves into product categories that are not a good match. While sales may not cannibalize current products, the failure of the new product brand can damage the company's reputation and possibly adversely affect the brand equity associated with current products. Figure 5.7 highlights some of the brand extensions that have not achieved a great deal of success. Most of these companies entered markets that did not align well with the original core business. Therefore, when considering brand extensions, it is helpful to assess the impact the new brand will have on the company's current image and products currently on the market.

Private Brands

Closely related to brand extensions are private brands or private labels. In the past decade, private label brands have become increasingly popular. The trend resulted from changing consumer views of private labels. Where they were once viewed as being low-cost, low-quality alternatives, many now believe quality levels are similar to manufacturers' brands.

In addition, the methods retailers use to market and display private brands in retail stores lead to a situation in which many consumers do not know if they are purchasing a private label brand or a manufacturer's brand. For instance, 45% of JCPenney's clothing revenue comes from its private labels such as Arizona Jeans, a.n.a., and American Living. The American Living brand was recently created by Ralph Lauren and added as a higher-end fashion line priced slightly higher than some national brands.[5] Wal-Mart offers eight different private brands of clothing, such as No Boundaries, Simply Basic, Metro 7, and Kid Connection. Unless consumers are knowledgeable about specific brands, many times they do not know if it is a private label or a manufacturer's brand.

The rise in the sales of private labels has led to many manufacturers producing private label brands in addition to the firm's primary brands. Others may consider this type of approach. Producing private label merchandise becomes viable when the manufacturer has excess plant capacity and a significant increase in sales of its brand does not seem likely. The manufacturer's management team also considers whether producing a private label might damage the reputation or hurt the sales of the company's brand. These issues were undoubtedly considered by Whirlpool's leaders when the company began to manufacture the Kenmore brand of appliances for Sears. Private labeling allows a manufacturer to increase sales without inviting the complications and marketing costs of flanker branding.

Retail marketing managers consider the private label option when the power of the store's name can be extended to individual products or when the store has a large customer base that is not highly loyal to manufacturers' brands. This allows alternative brands to be offered alongside manufacturers' brands, thereby increasing consumer choices. It also allows the retailer to earn larger margins on store brands. The presence of additional choices may be what it takes to expand a retail store's customer base by attracting new customers.

Private labels tend to experience higher sales during recessionary periods. Customers seeking lower-priced options may turn to them, both in big box stores such as Wal-Mart as well as in higher-end retail outlets.

What caused the rise in the sales of private labels?

Cobranding and Ingredient Branding

For some producers, cobranding and ingredient branding are vital elements in the company's marketing program. Cobranding occurs when two firms work together to market a good or service. Any credit card that carries both the card name (Discover, MasterCard) and another company's name (American Airlines, Sears) is part of a cobranding program. Ingredient branding takes place when a product is featured as a key ingredient or component of another product. A simple example is NutraSweet, which is used in over 5,000 products and is featured on many of the labels of those products. The Dolby sound system is another example of an ingredient brand.

The goal for both cobranding and ingredient branding is to take advantage of the two brands in order to reach a wider audience. Both programs allow for cooperative advertising, sharing data files regarding customers, and cross-selling of additional products once a purchase has been made. The stronger the power of the two brands, the more likely it becomes that these strategies will attract new customers.

Cobranding becomes a disadvantage when one brand in the relationship endures negative publicity or some other brand- or image-damaging event. The power of the NutraSweet brand may have been diminished in the past few years when some raised concerns about the possibility of injury to consumers' health. If so, there may be carryover effects to products containing the ingredient, even when the concerns are not legitimate.

- Brand continuously delivers benefits that meet or exceed expectations
- Ongoing relevance to defined audiences
- Price captures customers' perception of value
- Flexibility in communication with consistency
- Employees understand brand promise
- Brand is managed as a long-term asset

Figure 5.8

Characteristics of Top Global Brands

Global Brands

A global brand is one that is used by a multinational corporation. The same remains consistent across national boundaries. The name Sony is a global brand. Brands that achieve recognition in more than one country create a natural advantage in acquiring new customers and new markets.

Recently, Interbrand's Jeff Swystun discovered several common characteristics among the top 100 global brands, as shown in Figure 5.8.[6] Many of these items reflect the concept of brand equity.

Developing strong global brands requires the same types of marketing efforts as those dedicated to domestic brands. These efforts must permeate the entire organization. First-line employees should be as devoted to the success of the brand as the brand manager and CEO.

Developing Powerful Brands

A strong brand creates major opportunities for a company's marketing professionals. Developing successful brands, however, often takes time and money. Typically, a winning brand development strategy involves three components:

1. Brand awareness
2. Brand equity
3. Brand loyalty

Brand Awareness

The starting point in generating a strong brand is awareness. Two levels of awareness should be developed. The first is simple general knowledge that a brand exists. This includes knowing the brand name and what the brand offers—the good or service's characteristics and selling points. The second level emerges when members of specific target markets go beyond the most basic understanding that a brand is available and begin to gather more extensive information about the product.

Consider the introduction of a new product such as the Nintendo Wii. The primary goal in marketing such an innovation would be to raise general awareness about the product, including its differences from currently available products. Next, potential first-time buyers, or members of the primary target market, are provided with additional information. In this instance, the Nintendo's previous success in the video game marketplace gives the brand an advantage, as does the use of the house name Nintendo, because many gamers are aware of it.

In the simplest of terms, consumers do not purchase goods and services until they are aware that those items exist, which makes brand awareness the first step in acquiring customers. It is the responsibility of the marketing department to create brand awareness across the widest possible spectrum of potential customers, using all means available, including advertising, promotions, sales force activities, and public relations efforts.

Brand Equity

As has been noted in previous chapters, *brand equity* is the general perception by consumers that a good or service with a given brand name is different and better. The five pillars that build brand equity are displayed in Figure 5.9.[7] *Differentiation* means the product carries a unique, different, or superior attribute as compared with competing brands. *Relevance* is the personal appropriateness of the brand to consumers. The item fits into a lifestyle and resonates with the consumer. *Esteem* refers to the perceived popularity, public acceptance, and perceived quality of the brand. *Knowledge* involves the customer understanding the brand and believing the

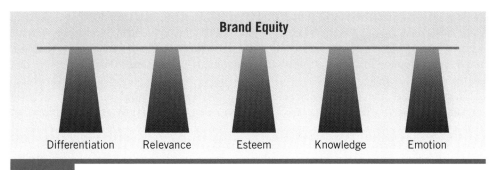

Figure 5.9 | The Pillars of Brand Equity

brand is superior to other brands within the product category. *Emotion* contains the level of feelings the consumer has toward the brand, including the attributes of trust, confidence, image, and perceived value.

Brand equity not only creates a guarantee of quality, it can also alter the ways a customer perceives that quality. In a recent survey of satisfaction with mobile phone networks, consumers reported that Virgin Mobile's performance was superior to that of T-Mobile. The surprising aspect of this outcome is that Virgin Mobile does not actually operate its own network; it rents from T-Mobile. Thus, the evaluation involved the same product but different brand names. The result was a perceived difference in service performance. Since T-Mobile operated both networks, no actual differences in service actually existed.[8]

Harris Interactive, Inc. measured the level of brand equity of 1,170 brands. Over 20,000 individuals participated in the study and ranked a random sample of brands on six factors: familiarity, quality, purchase consideration, brand expectations, distinction, and trust. Figure 5.10 identifies the top 10 brands from this study.

Brand equity improves the odds that a particular brand will be selected when a consumer buys an item. Consumers and businesses are most likely to trust and buy brands that they are familiar with and have an affinity for. Therefore, a strong brand can be a major advantage in acquiring new customers and in encouraging current customers to purchase again.

Brand Loyalty

Brand loyalty occurs when a consumer makes a concerted effort to find and purchase a specific brand, because the consumer has developed a mental affinity with that brand. Brand loyalty can exist between a consumer and a retail operation, such as when a child begs to go to McDonald's

Rank	Brand	Overall EquiTrend Score
1.	Heinz Ketchup	79.27
2.	M&M's Plain Chocolate Candy	77.79
3.	HERSHEY'S Milk Chocolate Candy Bar	77.51
4.	HERSHEY'S KISSES Chocolate Candy	77.20
5.	Duracell Batteries	76.75
6.	Cheerios Cereal	76.53
7.	Discovery Channel	76.17
8.	Kraft Foods, Inc.	75.93
9.	Kleenex Facial Tissues	75.57
10.	NEOSPORIN Ointment	75.54

Figure 5.10 | Top 10 Brand Equity Score Winners

and nowhere else. Loyalty may be found in allegiance to a specific brand, such as Coke or Pepsi. It also takes the form of loyalty to a line of products. This may be found in purchases of various products, from simple items such as food products to expensive goods including automobiles and designer clothing. Brand loyalty leads to repeat purchases, even in the face of evidence that another brand may be just as good.[9]

In terms of customer acquisition, brand loyalty leads to word-of-mouth endorsements. Loyal customers become *advocates* who are likely to encourage others to try and use a brand. In essence, a loyal customer can become a valuable tool in the marketing program's efforts to attract new customers.

Brand loyalty may be based on the product's features. It may also be related to the customer's experience with the company. A loyal restaurant patron may like the food but is loyal due to positive interactions with the wait staff. Customer service is often a key ingredient in the levels of loyalty expressed by customers.

The Brand Parity Problem

Brand parity exists when consumers believe there are few tangible distinctions between competing brands. This is often the case for products in mature markets. It tends to produce three adverse situations.

First, consumers become price sensitive and buy the brand featuring the lowest price, believing that all brands offer the same basic benefit. Second, brand parity tends to be inversely related to brand loyalty. The greater the brand parity, the less loyal consumers are to any particular brand. Third, when brand parity exists, consumers do not use price as a cue regarding quality. When brands are viewed as being almost identical, consumers do *not* believe the higher-priced brands carry greater levels of quality.[10]

In the past, one response to brand parity was to rely on advertising to create perceptions of higher levels of quality. This approach may not be effective. It only works when levels of brand parity are relatively low or when actual differences can be emphasized.

What can the marketing management team do when brand parity exists? There are three potential approaches. First, the product can be redesigned to develop an actual difference. A second method is to create a perceived difference among the brands. The third approach is to accept the fact that brand parity exists. The marketing department adjusts to the idea that parity is a natural consequence of the maturity stage of the product life cycle and that brand equity may no longer be possible. In these circumstances, advertising focuses on price or another decision variable rather than a product attribute or product difference.[11]

STOP AND THINK

Consider the various stages of the product life cycle in conjunction with the concepts of brand equity and brand parity.

1. What stage in the product life cycle best explains airline travel? Are there any airlines that have achieved brand equity in this marketplace?

2. What stage in the product life cycle best explains fax machines? Are there any companies that have achieved brand equity in this marketplace?

3. What stage in the product life cycle best explains the iPod? Have any companies been able to achieve brand equity in this market besides Apple?

4. What stage in the product life cycle best explains the printed newspaper industry? Can brand equity be achieved in such a way as to prolong the life cycle of any given newspaper?

The Role of Customer Service

Brand awareness, brand equity, and brand loyalty grow as the result of coordinated efforts by many individuals in a company. Perceptions of excellence are based on tangible product features but also emerge from intangibles. When attempting to attract and acquire new customers, quality service plays a role in each of the four activities described in this chapter.

Regarding markets, any company seeking to move into a new market will be well served by the reputation of offering the best service. Discovering new market segments may be the result of a successful market research effort. Winning that market will be based, at least in part, on how the consumers perceive the company. Quality service adds an intangible element to the image of the company, which makes attracting new customers more likely.

Manufacturing

In creating and delivering products, manufacturing operations gain market power and recognition by providing superior products; however, brand loyalty and equity only emerge when those products are delivered on time, in accurate amounts, with correct billing procedures, and with quality service after the sale. When items are damaged in shipping or other service failures take place, the importance of quality customer service becomes immediately clear. A manufacturer with a reputation for poor customer service to wholesalers and retailers may soon be placed in great jeopardy.

Retail

Retail operations encounter the same scenario as manufacturers. A store offering the best-value merchandise only succeeds when salespeople, delivery teams, repair departments, and anyone

What role does customer service play in attracting new customers and retaining current customers?

else associated with the operation work diligently to ensure quality service. In an era of mega stores, a small local merchant should be aware that the brands being sold in the store are only a small portion of the brand power of the store itself. Restaurants, dry-cleaning stores, and other local companies are most likely to succeed when the firm's name is recognized and customers are loyal based on a series of positive experiences.

Services

The importance of a brand reaches a premium when a company offers services. Services are intangible, which makes the name or brand the primary means by which the company is identified. Insurers such as Prudential and Allstate enjoy an advantage in the marketplace due to powerful brands. When State Farm faced accusations of poor or unfair customer service following the Hurricane Katrina tragedy, the brand may have suffered as well.[12] Success in many service industries, including banking, insurance, personal services (hair care, financial planning), travel, and entertainment, is largely based on the quality of service offered. This, in turn, is reflected as brand loyalty and consumer perceptions of brand equity.

Brands can be powerful tools in both acquiring and keeping customers in service industries. The responsibility for building a strong brand spreads from the top marketing manager through the entire organization, including first-line employees both within and outside the marketing department.

Pricing

Finally, a connection exists between pricing and customer service. For openers, customers paying higher prices expect the best customer service. This is true for both tangible goods and intangible services. Someone who pays a few extra dollars for tires expects them to be installed quickly and properly by a courteous service staff. A customer who pays more for a hairstyle expects the best possible look and the best possible treatment by the stylist.

In general, any time a customer considers a new company, new product, or new service, several factors will influence the final choice. The one common denominator for markets, products, brands, and prices is the connection to customer service. The company that delivers memorable, quality service automatically has an advantage.

YOURCAREER

Sometimes the path to success in a people-centered career does not take a direct route. Jerry Ross is on a journey that has already taken a series of dramatic twists and turns. At this point, the stopping place is as senior vice president for the First State Bank in Joplin, Missouri.

In college, Jerry Ross was a walk-on football player who earned a scholarship. He was eventually rated as a top-10 tight end by the NFL analyst Mel Kiper. Even though he was not drafted, Jerry signed a contract and was on the practice roster of the Buffalo Bills for a full season. The next year, Jerry was drafted by Amsterdam in the NFL Europe league and played a season there. He was then signed by the Jacksonville Jaguars, where he injured his knee in the pre-season and was eventually cut from the squad. Jerry returned to college and finished his degree. At the same time, he began working as a mortgage loan officer in Pittsburg, Kansas. Soon after, an offer came from First State Bank.

First State Bank is the last remaining local bank in Joplin, Missouri. "We offer the full array of banking services; we have an investment arm, wealth management, individual brokers, account managers, and we offer life insurance policies," Jerry reports. "We also carry mortgages and the full array of commercial and industry services. We are a full stop shop, plus we're getting further into online products, such as deposit capture and all of the other services that our competitors offer."

When asked to describe the differences with mega banks in town, Jerry offered, "It's easier to have personal service at a smaller bank. I worked in a large bank. In the large bank, you have to understand the way they want it done. You become an in-between person. You have to understand your customers and their needs, and then you have to understand how the mega bank looks at things—then you take what they need and make it fit the mega bank. You can't fight the system."

He adds, "The difference is that in a smaller bank we are less rigid in our policies. When it comes to employees, you start with good employees and manage them to be empowered. A policy here is 10 pages. Over there it was three volumes full. Here, I can go across the hall to the owner and say, 'We need to restructure this loan in this way,' and he will either agree or disagree. I don't have to rewrite the whole policy."

There are also differences in management style. "We're basically committee driven when it comes to management style," he notes. Decisions are by consensus. "We do a really good job of working until we all agree. We all have the same goal, return on assets; as long as we make decisions with that in mind, we're in good shape."

Brand management is another key area of difference between First State Bank and the mega banks located in town. Jerry stated it this way: "Our brand carries us. When you're going to a customer, it's a local individual working with someone with local ties. We are Joplin, and the customer is very important to us. The money stays here in town. We're taking your dollars and reinvesting them here. We are able to help customers more when things don't go so well. Your name still means something to us. Your standing in the community means something to us." All of this is summarized in the bank's advertising tagline: "People you know, people you trust."

There is a downside. Jerry said, "Where it can be a hindrance is with larger corporate customers. They don't care as much about local ties, because their headquarters are somewhere else. So the larger mega banks are more likely to have the market on that. We struggle with this. We have to work harder and faster to change to stay up with the big banks."

As for personal success, Jerry was modest. "I'm still on a learning curve when it comes to dealing with retail customers. To me, customer service means that the biggest thing I face is taking the time to understand what that customer is really looking for and providing the service that matches. The bank is just my tool. My business is me and the relationships I have with customers. We all sell the same products. The technology has made it that way. Being able to sell something is based on that relationship."

As for his college experience, Jerry was straightforward. "I went to school to play football, and I succeeded. That was my goal. A lot of life experiences brought me to this point. When I came back to school after football, the classes I took made me more focused. Of course, the accounting classes were most important to what I do today. Mostly, the rest to me was about discipline. That is what college really did for me. Work ethic and discipline."

Chapter Summary

Customer acquisition programs are built to market existing products and new products. Finding customers in both areas helps the company grow and succeed over time. In this chapter, the acquisition strategies devoted to markets, products, brands, and prices are examined.

The types of tactics used in the area of markets include identifying market segments within existing markets and in potential new markets. Geographic expansion of markets can take place domestically as well as in the international arena.

New customers may be attracted by a company's products. Through the use of product development and diversification, products may be added to reach new or existing customers. Product improvements based on either customer needs or improvements in technology may also reach a new group of customers. Product line extensions are another method by which customers may be acquired, because they meet a unique set of needs.

Brands take many forms. Regarding brands, the most common goals are brand awareness, brand equity, and brand loyalty. Each can increase the number of customers a company serves. The marketing team will also seek to reduce perceptions of brand parity. Strong brands are a major force in both domestic and international markets.

Branding programs go beyond one name. Brand extensions are made through family brands and flanker brands. Companies may also increase sales and market coverage using private brands as well as cobranding and ingredient branding agreements. Quality customer service plays an invaluable role in developing a powerful brand.

The secret to effective utilization of markets, products, brands, and prices is customer service. Quality service plays a role in creating customer perceptions of the firm and in determining how they respond to other marketing efforts.

Chapter Terms

Brand   (p. 122)

Brand extension   (p. 123)

Brand loyalty   (p. 127)

Cobranding   (p. 125)

Corporate name   (p. 122)

Family brand   (p. 122)

Flanker brand   (p. 123)

Focus group   (p. 120)

Global brand   (p. 126)

House mark   (p. 122)

Ingredient branding   (p. 125)

Product development   (p. 120)

Product diversification   (p. 120)

Product life cycle   (p. 115)

Review Questions

1. What are the four stages of the product life cycle, and how do they affect customer acquisition?

2. Name three ways in which customers may be acquired in existing markets.

3. When studying potential new markets, which two approaches can be used to acquire new customers?

4. What is product development and product diversification?

5. What role does a focus group play in developing a product diversification strategy?

6. Product improvements can be made in two ways to assist in customer acquisition. What are they?

7. Define the term corporate brand.

8. What advantage does a family brand have in customer acquisition?

9. How can flanker brands help a company expand its customer base?

10. What is cannibalization?

11. What are the three components of developing a winning brand strategy?

12. Identify and describe the pillars of brand equity.

13. Name and describe four methods for creating advertising budgets.

14. What is the relationship between brand parity and brand equity?

15. How can brand loyalty help a company acquire new customers?

CUSTOMER CORNER

While many companies think of marketing children's products to parents, few have noticed the potential of marketing to grandparents. Here are some facts about today's grandparents as they relate to grandchildren:[13]

- About one third of American adults are grandparents (70 million).
- The average age of the first-time grandparent is 47.
- Today's grandparents have a higher level of education and a higher level of income.
- Grandparents are actively involved in grandchildren's education and cultural enrichment.
- Grandparents spend more than $30 billion a year on grandchildren.
- Grandparents account for 17% of all toy sales in the United States.
- Grandparents traveling with grandchildren account for 20% of all trips taken with children. (Six million Americans vacationed with grandchildren in a typical month).

Given this information, it is clear that grandparents represent a viable new target market.

1. Can you identify any market segments among grandparents?
2. What types of products are best suited to grandparents seeking to buy gifts for grandchildren?
3. What types of brands are the most well known to grandparents? Do you believe they are more or less likely to be loyal to those brands?
4. What types of discounts can be successfully offered to grandparents?

When marketing to children, grandparents are an excellent target for products.

Discussion and Critical Thinking Questions

1. For each stage of the product life cycle, identify at least one product that is in that stage. Discuss the marketing strategies that are being used. (Remember, the life cycle concept applies to a product category, not to specific companies.)

2. Two new products that were introduced in 2008 include Bud Light Lime and a new line of pastas sold at Pizza Hut. What are the primary market segments served by these products, in the hope of acquiring new customers? Do you think it would be wise for the two products to be sold internationally? Why or why not?

3. Suppose you were the manager of a pizza restaurant close to your campus. Based on your knowledge of pizza restaurants in your area, what type of customer acquisition strategy would you pursue? Would you seek new markets or new products, or would you develop a branding campaign? Justify your answer.

(Before you make a decision, you will need to look carefully at the competition.)

4. An argument can be made that certain motion pictures have become brand franchises. Examples include *Indiana Jones, Bourne,* and *Shrek.* When a sequel of these films comes out, what branding strategy is being employed? When action figures of the characters in the films are sold, what product strategy is being used?

5. The following product categories may be used as examples of brand parity. Explain how you would proceed to develop stronger perceptions of brand equity in each one.
   - Soft drinks
   - Milk
   - Toothpaste
   - Aspirin

6. Explain the linkages between the three topics presented in this chapter: markets, products, and brands. Think in the following terms:
   - Customers needs
   - Changes in technology
   - Customer service
   - Changes in economic conditions
   - Social trends

7. Use the information given in Table 5.3 to calculate the cannibalization effect of introducing a new lawn mower model. Was the new model a success? Justify your answer.

Quarterly Sales	2008	2009
Total company sales	$1,979,312	$2,251,055
Sales of the new AZ24 model		$354,276
Sales of Model AZ 18	$532,876	$427,689
Sales of Model AZ 9	$248,764	$231,356
Sales of Model AW 11	$328,438	$354,478
Sales of Model AW 14	$869,234	$883,256

Table 5.3   Cannibalization Data for New Lawn Mower

Chapter 5 Case

LensCrafters

Many times, an innovation helps a company gain a major advantage in the marketplace. Over time, competitors copy that innovation. In order to continue to succeed, other elements such as a strong brand name and effective advertising are required.

The original LensCrafters store opened in 1983. Two innovations were featured. The first was that the company offered to deliver quality eyewear in "about an hour." The message that "we are fast" fit nicely with the busy lifestyles of consumers.

The second innovation was to bring the eye doctor, the optical laboratory, and a retail store featuring a variety of frames to the same place. This form of "one-stop shopping" represented a level of convenience that was not otherwise present in the marketplace.

Over time, LensCrafters expanded into numerous locations, most notably in shopping malls and other convenient-access places. A strong national advertising campaign highlighted the stores' key features in television, radio, magazine, and local newspaper advertisements and commercials.

As would be expected, competitors, such as Pearle Vision, duplicated or provided similar services. In order to respond, the marketing and management teams for LensCrafters decided it was time to move to a new positioning strategy, one that emphasized the emotional side of eyewear rather than the rational side. Consumer research indicated that many people view their glasses less as medical devices and more as fashion statements.

In response, LensCrafters began to rely on other brands. The stores feature frames by Prada, Versace,

Bvlgari, Chanel, Ray-Ban, Vogue, and Dolce & Gabbana. This led to cooperative advertising possibilities and the ability to take advantage of consumer loyalty to these popular fashion brands.

The marketing team at LensCrafters also developed advertising campaigns focused on eyewear as a fashion accessory. The messages encouraged people to think about eyeglasses just as they would think about purchasing a pair of jeans or shoes, or some other personal fashion statement. The ads were placed in print and on television.

The company's Web site was also revamped to make it more user-friendly and to convey the new message. A new feature of the Web site is an interactive "face shape selector," which allows individuals to upload their photos on the site. The software analyzes the person's face shape and then provides suggestions on which eyeglasses would look the best. At the same time, LensCrafters remodeled company stores to convey the same fashion message.[14]

Consistency across advertisements and across advertising campaigns is important to ensure that the target audience is receiving the same message. This means watching the visual, the tagline, and the product positioning. It does not mean that all ads must be identical. What it does mean is that there needs to be a common thread through all advertisements. If the positioning strategy is that of "fashion," as was indicated by LensCrafters, then that same message needs to be seen in all the firm's advertising. If ads that emphasized 1-hour service were thrown into the mix, then it would not be consistent with the message that LensCrafters wants to attain.

1. What markets are currently served by LensCrafters? Can you identify any new markets that might help the company acquire new customers?

2. Can you think of any other products that could be added to a line of eyewear (product line extensions)?

Why would LensCrafters use an advertising campaign to convince consumers that eyeglasses make a personal fashion statement?

3. Evaluate LensCrafters in terms of brand name, brand equity, and brand parity. Is it operating in a product industry with a high or low level of brand parity? Discuss the branding strategy that LensCrafters is using. Evaluate the strategy in terms of pros and cons.

4. When LensCrafters markets a new line of eyewear, what type of branding campaign should it use?

5. When other eyewear companies also begin to emphasize the fashion side of products, what should be the next move for LensCrafters?

Go to **www.sagepub.com/clow** for additional exercises and study resources. Select **Chapter 5, Customer Acquisition Strategies and Tactics** for chapter-specific activities.

Will Priceline.com achieve long-term success?

chapter 6
Pricing

Priceline.com: Reverse-Auction Pricing Continues to Survive

In 1997, entrepreneur Jay Walker started a new business focusing on a new method for setting prices: the reverse auction. In the standard pricing model, the business sets the price for customers, and negotiations begin from there. The business may lower the price or offer additional incentives to complete the sale.

In contrast, the original Priceline.com model starts with customers, who are

encouraged to "name your own price." Consumer-driven pricing seemed well suited to the travel industry, most notably airline travel and hotel accommodations. Both routinely experience unsold inventory. In the case of airlines, Walker estimated that each day nearly 500,000 seats were not filled on flights around the country. Hotel rooms that go unrented represent unrealized revenues.

The Priceline system allows the customer to bid a price for a flight or room. The retailer (hotel/airline) can then either accept or reject the bid. In exchange, the customer understands that the flight time might not be ideal and may involve more changes of planes during the trip. Priceline receives a fee for tickets and stays that are sold.

One of the enticements for Priceline's business customers is that they are selling unused space without offering a formal discount to the general public. Convincing most of the airlines that it was a good idea took time. Originally, only two small airlines were willing to give the system a try. It took nearly a decade to get the other airline companies on board.

One major shift arrived when actor William Shatner became Priceline's key spokesperson. Shatner agreed to appear in television commercials without monetary compensation, instead receiving shares of Priceline stock. The campy, Shatner as

singer-poet ads received both attention and acclaim. More recently, his highly visible presence as The Negotiator has served the company well.

Even with a very public face out front, the ride for Priceline has been turbulent. The stock price for the company soared as high as $165 per share and dropped as low as $1.10 per share. The firm has earned respectable revenues for years; however, profitability has been more difficult to achieve. After a few profitable seasons in the early 2000s, the company hit hard times following the September 11, 2001, attacks.

As the first decade of the new millennium comes to a close, the economy has moved toward recession. Ironically, this may bode favorably for companies such as Priceline, as customers look for lower-priced methods to travel. The question remains as to whether this unique pricing system will succeed in the long term.

Chapter Overview

Of all the variables considered by a marketing manager, prices may have the most direct and immediate impact. Product and service prices tend to reflect the image and position the company's marketing team seeks to achieve. When compared to the product's quality, price becomes an expression of an item's value. Further, changes in price can result in instantaneous changes in sales, in both directions.

Prices can play a major role in both attracting customers and keeping them. Marketing managers consider several issues and options when setting prices and changing them. A quality pricing program builds the foundation for profitable operations.

In this chapter, the nature of prices as a marketing tool is described first. Next, the factors that affect the company's general pricing strategy are investigated. Then, methods for setting prices, including the prices of new items as well as ongoing goods and services, are described. Also, methods of discounting are noted as methods for leading some customers to make purchases, to keep others loyal to a brand, and to entice others to engage in brand switching. Further, other forms of price changes, including price increases, are discussed. Finally, the ethical and legal considerations associated with pricing are analyzed along with the implications for customer service.

Price Considerations

An item's *price* is the amount charged for a good or service. Setting prices reflects a complicated set of circumstances. The marketing team tries to identify how various factors are related to a company and its merchandise. This may be difficult because the factors may shift or change over time. Pricing involves continual monitoring of the impact prices have on a company's relationships with its customers because as a customer makes a purchase decision her view of the item's price may be affected by emotional and situational factors.

Emotional Factors

Many products and services contain emotional components. As a simple example, consider expenditures on weddings, funerals, and prom nights. Families and individuals who would normally be highly conservative with money often pay high prices for dresses, tuxedos, meals, and caskets. With regard to services, marketers know that families with low incomes may be willing to spend considerable amounts of money on tickets to rock concerts or to see a local sports team in person. Emotional components are present in hair care, personal fitness, and other service items including insurance, fashion, transportation, and entertainment.

Situational Factors

Price also reflects the immediate circumstance in which a customer is located. *Impulse buys* are made on the spot. Often, price is not the primary decision factor when an impulse purchase is made. For example, at many college football bowl games, vendors stand outside the stadium selling T-shirts specific to the event for $10.00 to $20.00. When the game is over, those same T-shirts can be purchased for substantially less.

Consequently, a marketing manager considers a range of ingredients when developing a pricing program. One helpful tool in understanding a company's current pricing situation is a perceptual map.

Price Perceptual Map

A price perceptual map helps the marketing team examine brand image and brand market position relative to competing brands along the variables of image (or quality) and price. Consider the perceptual map of janitorial services in a Midwestern town shown in Figure 6.1.

The map depicts a relationship between image and price. The lower the price, the lower the image, and the higher the price of the service, the higher the image tends to be. The marketing director for a new janitorial service makes a decision regarding where the firm should be located. As shown, the top three firms in terms of image are Fuqua, Servicemaster, and then Morris. In terms of price, the ranking is Servicemaster, Fuqua, and Morris, which means these three companies represent the top tier of janitor firms in the area.

In the second tier of firms, note that the prices charged by Morris are only slightly higher than those charged by Beltway, even though Morris enjoys a much stronger reputation. One reason for this may be that Morris is a local owner-managed operation. The owner of the company, Chip Morris, works on or personally supervises every account. Beltway is owned by an out-of-state individual and is managed by an employee who does not provide a level of service that is commensurate with the prices charged. Unless quality improves in the future, this company is headed for a downward spiral in accounts and revenue and may eventually go out of business. The strongest second-tier firms are All Clean and Spring River. Both are moderately priced and have relatively good images based on pricing structures. The bottom tier firms offer businesses low-cost options but provide lower levels of service.

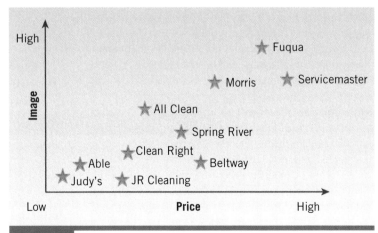

Figure 6.1   Pricing Perceptual Map

In choosing a pricing strategy for a new service, one approach would be to price services just below Fuqua. The main competitor would be Morris because Beltway does not offer any significant competition. The higher price charged by the new service should allow the firm to compete with All Clean and Spring River in quality of service and image reputation. The owner of Morris personally manages all his accounts, which means his number of clients would be limited. That leaves Fuqua and Servicemaster as the major competitors. If the new company can charge a slightly lower price and offer service that is comparable to Morris, the company has a good chance of doing well in the market.

The perceptual map provides a visual portrayal of the relationships between brand image, brand market position, and competition. It allows a new firm's marketing manager to develop a pricing approach and also provides current firms with information regarding possible pricing modifications. For example, consider All Clean. The company's reputation and strong image allow it to charge more, possibly to the price level of Beltway. Such a move puts a great deal of pressure on Beltway, because customers might soon wonder why they would want to pay the same amount of money for inferior quality. Spring River would also have a hard time competing. Consequently, All Clean would be in the best position in the second-tier market.

To illustrate the impact on profit margins, assume that All Clean generates revenues of $1.3 million with expenses totaling $1.18 million. As Table 6.1 shows, a profit of $120,000 would be generated. If All Clean increased prices by 5% and all expenses remained the same, the profit would increase by 54% to $185,000, if all other things remained constant.

Remember, however, that other factors could affect perceptions of the various companies and the prices they charge. As a result, pricing often takes on an "ebb and flow," as various competitors seek to gain an advantage.

How can a price perceptual map help the marketing team develop a pricing strategy?

Customer Value

Another tool that can be used to examine pricing decisions is the evaluation of customer value. As shown in Figure 6.2, customer value is based on a number of primary and secondary factors. The primary factors are quality, brand image, price, and competitive comparisons. Secondary factors include perceived substitutes, uniqueness, switching costs, and availability.

When a customer determines the value of a particular brand, the person compares quality, image, and price with other competitive options. A trade-off exists between the first three (quality, image, and price), but it is based on comparisons with what other brands offer. A brand that

All Current	Current	With 5% Increase
Income ($)	1,300,000	1,365,000
Expenses ($)	1,180,000	1,180,000
Profit ($)	120,000	185,000
Change in profit (%)		54.17

Table 6.1   Impact of 5% Price Increase

has a strong image, such as Kraft, can charge more for its products than a local company that produces the same products or a private-label brand.

The reverse is also true, but in a slightly different way. Advertising a brand that is priced lower does not suggest that the product is inferior in quality. Instead, the focus shifts to the value of the purchase. The consumer may assume that while the quality is not quite as high, the price makes purchasing the item a bargain. Many times, advertisements for less well-known brands imply that customers are paying more money just for the name. Take the name away, and the lower-priced product is equally good.

In general, a customer's rationale for purchasing a low-priced brand may vary but often centers on a brand that "suffices." Buying more expensive versions may be viewed as a waste of money or extravagant when the lower-priced (and lower quality) item will work. It is not unusual for these individuals to convince themselves that they have found a bargain and brag about how much they have saved. The low-priced versions are especially attractive to price-conscious consumers and businesses.

In addition to the primary factors, secondary factors may have an impact on the perception of customer value. These include perceived substitutes, uniqueness, switching costs, and availability. If no or few *substitutes* are available for a particular product, then the value becomes greater. The same holds true for *uniqueness*. A brand that is viewed as being unique carries a higher customer value. *Switching costs* follow the same pattern. The greater the costs of switching to another brand, the more value the current brand holds and the greater the value of the new brand that has just been purchased. *Availability* works in reverse. The more difficult a product is to find, or the less it is available to consumers, the more valuable it becomes. By controlling these secondary factors, a firm's marketing department can increase the perceived customer value of its brands.

- Primary factors
  - Quality
  - Brand image
  - Price
  - Competitive comparisons
- Secondary factors
  - Perceived substitutes
  - Uniqueness
  - Switching costs
  - Availability (distribution)

Figure 6.2

Customer Value

STOP AND THINK

Many marketing teams continue to engage in what is known as *odd pricing,* in which an item sells for 99 cents rather than $1.00. A car with a list price of $29,995 is supposed to cause the consumer to think of the price as below $30,000.

1. Which aspect of a price is odd pricing designed to affect—practical, emotional, or situational?
2. What types of products are best suited to odd pricing? What types are not?
3. Is it ethical to attempt to "trick" consumers into thinking something costs less than it does?
4. Do you believe odd prices work, or are they simply a relic from the past?

Pricing Strategies and Objectives

A **pricing strategy** is the basic direction the company's marketing and management teams take when setting prices. Typically, a pricing strategy expresses the relationship between the level of quality a company seeks to provide and the prices it will charge. While some companies stress quality, others stress price. The starting point for a pricing strategy is a decision regarding the pricing objective.

Pricing Objectives

Pricing objectives reflect the overall pricing strategy. Four common pricing objectives are listed in Figure 6.3. Each may be reached in various ways. The objectives reflect the marketing team's primary focus and desired outcome when prices are combined with other marketing efforts.

- Sales maximization
- Profit maximization
- Market share maximization
- Competitive parity

Figure 6.3

Pricing Objectives

The goal of *sales maximization* may be achieved in a variety of ways. A marketing manager could conclude that sales will be highest when the lowest possible price is charged. This leads to less revenue per unit but higher total sales due to increased volume. A second manager may believe that a higher price may result in fewer units being sold, but total dollar sales will be highest because of the revenue per unit.

To achieve *profit maximization,* the price is considered along with the cost of the item. The objective is to select a price that optimizes profits. Typically, that will mean a slightly higher price because a higher price generates a greater gross margin.

When the objective is *market share maximization,* the company's marketing team attempts to build market share that they believe leads to long-term success. To do so, prices are lowered to lure customers away from the competition, or quality may be increased while keeping price constant in order to attract them. In both instances, profits are lower, but over time the company believes it will gain a competitive advantage and a larger market share.

The *competitive parity objective* typically means the price will be in the middle of the pack of competitors or near the company's primary competitors. With this objective, the strategy is to compete on other variables, such as service, product features, or brand name, believing that these items, rather than price, are the keys to success in terms of total sales and profits.

As a general rule, marketing experts agree that *consistency* in pricing is as important as consistency in product quality, in promotional programs, and every other aspect of a company's operations. Customers rely on consistent prices to help them make purchasing decisions, both in terms of making the decision to purchase something and in terms of which supplier or product to choose. Therefore, no matter which objective is chosen, the company's best option is to maintain some consistency in pricing practices.

Setting Prices

It is normally the role of the marketing manager to help set the actual prices for products. The four basic approaches for setting prices are

1.   cost-oriented approach,
2.   demand-oriented approach,
3.   competition-oriented approach, and
4.   profit-oriented approach.

Typically, more than one approach is used. One is given priority, and the others are taken into consideration.

Cost-Oriented Approach

Normally, the costs associated with producing a good or service serve as the price floor, or the absolute minimum to be charged. Firms must earn enough to cover fixed and variable costs in order to stay in business. There may be instances when a product would be sold below costs, but this will be a temporary measure. Many companies base the selling price of a product on the costs associated with producing each unit. The two most common methods are

1.   cost-plus pricing and
2.   markup pricing.

The **cost-plus pricing** method bases the price of a product on its fixed costs, its variable costs, and a desired contribution margin (see Table 6.2). A manufacturer of wood furniture may use cost-plus pricing to set the price of a new office desk. First, the fixed costs are identified. In this instance, $70,000 is allocated to the desk. Next, the variable costs associated with producing the desk are calculated. The variable cost is $140.00 per unit. A company seeking to earn $125,000 in total contribution margin from the desks may project that 5,000 units can be sold. Table 6.2 displays the calculation of the price of the desk, which would then be set at $179.00 (895,000/5,000) in order to achieve the desired contribution margin.

Units produced	5,000
Variable cost/unit ($)	140.00
Fixed costs ($)	70,000
Desired contribution margin ($)	125,000
Variable cost for 5,000 ($)	700,000
Total costs ($)	895,000
Price per desk ($)	179.00

Table 6.2 Cost-Plus Pricing

The second method of setting the price, using a **markup**, reflects the difference between the price of an item and the cost to produce that item. In most cases, no fixed costs are allocated to the item. This method works well for retailers that may stock as many as 50,000 items. It also works well for a manufacturer that produces hundreds of items. The price of each item is marked up based on a certain percentage of the item's variable costs. Table 6.3 provides examples of three markups, using differing percentages.

As shown, the variable cost per product is $23.17. If a 20% markup is used, then the retailer sells the product for $28.96. This price is calculated by dividing the costs (23.17) by 1 minus the markup price (1 − 0.20 = 0.80). If the retailer used a 25% markup, the item would be priced at $30.89 per unit (23.17/[1 − 0.25]). A 30% markup would result in a price of $33.10 (23.17/0.70).

	Markup A	Markup B	Markup C
Variable costs ($)	23.17	23.17	23.17
Markup percentage	20	25	30
Value of 1 − markup	0.80	0.75	0.70
Price of product ($)	28.96	30.89	33.10

Table 6.3 Markup Pricing

Demand-Oriented Approach

A second variable that marketing professionals may consider when setting prices is demand. Typically, as the price of a product goes up, demand goes down, and vice versa. The equilibrium point may be found when there is a balance between the amount available (supply) and what people are willing to pay (demand). Any type of shortage normally drives up the price, and excess supply pushes the price down.

Calculating the exact impact of pricing on supply and demand may be difficult. The marketing team examines the relationships between price, supply, and demand. Table 6.4 provides an illustration of these relationships. As shown, the variable costs incurred at a car wash for labor and materials are $10.00 per vehicle. Thus, the price floor that the firm could charge per car wash is $10.00, and at the $10.00 price, the company could wash 11,000 cars per month, the maximum number it could handle based on its capacity. Further, assume that for each $1.00 increase in price the demand would fall by 1,000 vehicles. Variable costs would remain the same.

If the contribution margin for each price were drawn on a graph, it would take the shape of an inverted U. At the $10.00 price, demand is 11,000, but the contribution margin is 0 since it costs $10.00 per vehicle to wash and clean it. At the $21.00 price, demand has fallen to 0, thus no contribution margin. The highest contribution margin is between $15.00 and $16.00 per vehicle. At both these prices, the contribution margin is $30,000.

Price ($)	Demand	Income ($)	Variable Costs ($)	Contribution Margin ($)
10.00	11,000	110,000	110,000	0
11.00	10,000	110,000	100,000	10,000
12.00	9,000	108,000	90,000	18,000
13.00	8,000	104,000	80,000	24,000
14.00	7,000	98,000	70,000	28,000
15.00	6,000	90,000	60,000	30,000
16.00	5,000	80,000	50,000	30,000
17.00	4,000	68,000	40,000	28,000
18.00	3,000	54,000	30,000	24,000
19.00	2,000	38,000	20,000	18,000
20.00	1,000	20,000	10,000	10,000
21.00	0	0	0	0

Table 6.4   Impact of Supply and Demand

The challenge of producing a supply/demand table is estimating or deciphering demand at each price. Test markets may be used to obtain these estimates. Also, company leaders can modify the price of a product and measure the subsequent impact on demand. In both cases, extraneous factors can interfere with the demand, such as competitive actions. Fortunately, calculating the exact impact of the price on demand is not usually necessary. Understanding the interrelationship between price and demand remains the key.

A related concept is the price elasticity of demand, which is the change in demand relative to a change in price. Elasticity is calculated by dividing the percent change in demand by the percent change in price. The elasticity of a product changes as the price of a product changes.

To illustrate, consider Table 6.4 and demand at the various prices. When the price increased from $10.00 to $11.00, demand decreased from 11,000 to 10,000 cars, a change in demand of 9.09% ([10,000 – 11,000]/11,000). The change in price was 10% ([$11.00 – $10.00]/$10.00). When the percent change in demand is divided by the percent change in price, the elasticity value is 0.91 (see Table 6.5). The value of 1 is called *unitary* elasticity of demand because the change in demand is equal to the change in price. If the value is below 1, it is *inelastic,* indicating that the change in demand is lower than the change in price. Values greater than 1 are *elastic,* which means the change in demand is greater than the change in price.

A change from $15.00 to a $16.00 price is optimal in terms of gross margin because the price elasticity of demand is between 2.0 and 2.5. This means that for every 1% change in price, demand changes 2% to 2.5%. Most goods and services have an elastic-price demand curve because as price increases, consumers either do without the product or look for other alternatives. As illustrated by this car wash example, as the price of the car wash increases above the $16.00 price, the price elasticity of demand climbs more dramatically. Customers now become less willing to pay the higher price and either wash the car themselves or go to a self-service car wash. When the price moves from $19.00 to $20.00, the price increase is only about 5%, but demand falls by 50%.

The advantage of understanding price elasticity is that it provides the marketing team with a relatively good idea of what will happen to demand when considering a price change. By keeping an accurate record of demand and price changes, a marketing manager can maintain an elasticity estimate. Remember that extraneous factors can also affect demand. Actions of competitors, advertising, sales promotions, the economy, and even the weather can change levels of demand.

Price ($)	Demand	Percent Change		Elasticity
		Price	Demand	
10.00	11,000			
11.00	10,000	10.00	−9.09	0.91
12.00	9,000	9.09	−10.00	1.10
13.00	8,000	8.33	−11.11	1.33
14.00	7,000	7.69	−12.50	1.63
15.00	6,000	7.14	−14.29	2.00
16.00	5,000	6.67	−16.67	2.50
17.00	4,000	6.25	−20.00	3.20
18.00	3,000	5.88	−25.00	4.25
19.00	2,000	5.56	−33.33	6.00
20.00	1,000	5.26	−50.00	9.50
21.00	0	5.00	−100.00	20.00

Table 6.5　Price Elasticity of Demand

When considering a price increase, marketers prefer to see a low-price elasticity value. An inelastic price curve would be ideal, because it means that even though the price of the product is increased, the change in demand will be low. Conversely, when reducing price to stimulate sales, a high-elastic price curve is best. This would generate a large increase in demand relative to the price decrease.

Competition-Oriented Approach

The competitive approach is often used by firms selling products that are in the mature stage of the product life cycle. The market tends to be highly competitive due to the large number of firms. Customers have a large array of brands from which to choose, and in many cases, substitute products can be purchased. As a result, prices tend to be highly elastic.

The marketing team can respond to the competition in one of three ways. The three basic approaches to competition-oriented pricing are

1. below the industry average,
2. at the industry average, and
3. above the industry average.

Pricing *below the industry average* means that a lower price is the primary tactic being used by the marketing department. Wal-Mart enjoys considerable success as the "low-price leader" in the discount store industry. At the same time, a company's marketing department must make sure consumers do not associate the brand with being "cheap." One way Wal-Mart does this is to use the slogan "Save money, live better."

Pricing *at the industry average* is present in oligopolistic situations and other circumstances where brand parity exists. The guiding philosophy is to make price a less relevant feature and to emphasize other elements instead, such as service quality or convenience. The advertising claim "We will not be undersold" suggests a company seeking to meet any competitor's price and then attempting to gain advantage through some other element, such as selection or service after the sale.

Other companies use price as a method to distinguish themselves from the competition by emphasizing exclusivity, quality, or superiority. Marketers in these firms deliberately set prices *above the industry average* to convey the message that the brand is superior to others. Marketers using this approach carefully consider demand elasticity. When the price curve is highly elastic, a price that is much higher than the industry average results in a sharp decline in sales.

In all instances, competition-oriented pricing is used in highly competitive markets where price elasticity is high, brand parity is prevalent, and customers have a large array of options.

Profit-Oriented Approach

Another approach is to maximize profits by setting the price at the highest level possible. The underlying concept is "Why sell the product for $40 if customers are willing to pay $100, $150, or even more?" The profit-oriented approach examines pricing from the perspective of what consumers are willing to pay, not the cost of the item.

Bill Gates understood this principle when he first priced the Windows operating system for computer manufacturers. Rather than sell Windows systems for a flat fee, he charged a small fee for each computer installation. The cost of the software had been incurred during its development. The cost of the disk that actually contained the program was miniscule compared with the installation price. The result of this pricing approach was the creation of the Microsoft empire.

Airlines also use the concept for pricing of business and first-class seats. A person who desires luxury pays a premium. Those who purchase a ticket just days before departure pay even more. As a result, the airline is able to charge a business passenger $1,000 for a seat that would only cost a leisure traveler $300.

Many music artists and concert planners use profit-oriented pricing. The goal is to increase the price until demand falls to match the capacity of the facility of the concert. If the venue holds 30,000 people and 60,000 people try to purchase tickets, then the price was set too low. Through computer databases and accurate records of requests, concert planners can increase the price of tickets until demand falls to 30,000. Instead of the ticket price being $50, it may be $90 because 30,000 people are willing to pay the higher amount. Selling 30,000 tickets at $90 generates $2.7 million in revenue compared with $1.5 million at the $50 price. There are also 30,000 fans who are not upset because they could not purchase tickets for a sold-out concert.

An additional issue in profit-oriented pricing is the concept of prestige, or "snob appeal." Some consumers are willing to pay high prices for brands carrying higher levels of prestige. Restaurants, hotels, and resorts often use this approach. High-quality products and services are being delivered, but they do not correlate with the increase in price.

Pricing Within Comparable Brand Sets

When consumers and businesses make purchase decisions, they compare prices of the various brands within consideration or evoked parity sets. A **consideration or evoked parity set** is the set of brands the consumer views as being approximately equal in all aspects of the customer value, such as in the ingredients mentioned in Figure 6.2. Within each group, consumers expect to pay approximately the same price for each brand.

Figure 6.4 illustrates an evoked parity set of a consumer for personal radios. Sony, Coby, and Audiovox are in the first-consideration set. These three brands are perceived as being approximately equal and in the top tier. The second set of brands (jWIN, Kaito, Sangean, and Emerson) are very close to the first set in terms of consideration. The third and fourth sets are more distant and are part of the consumer's inert consideration set. He has seen the brands but knows very little about them, and therefore they are not being considered.

Figure 6.4 represents the view of only one consumer. What if, instead, the figure resulted from a survey of 1,000 consumers or 2,000 consumers? It would then become a *brand comparison perceptual map*. Such a mapping procedure can be developed by asking consumers to identify brands they believe are equal. For instance, consumers would be asked to identify brands that they consider to be equal to Sony, jWIN, Kaito, and the other products. The brands would be randomly selected, and each consumer is asked to group the brands in equal sets or identify brands they view as equal. Note that if this was an actual brand comparison perceptual map, it would not contain the term *inert parity sets* as shown in Figure 6.4.

The brand comparison perceptual map may provide valuable information for pricing. The prices of Sony, Coby, and Audiovox are likely to be the highest in the market but approximately equal to each other. Slightly lower prices may be featured by jWIN, Kaito, Sangean, and Emerson. The prices of Tivoli, Eton, Panasonic, and RCA are probably going to be considerably lower, and at the bottom of the price scale should be Princess and Zadro.

In summary, marketing professionals consider numerous factors when setting prices. Pricing is not an exact science. Instead, prices fluctuate as market conditions and company circumstances evolve over time.

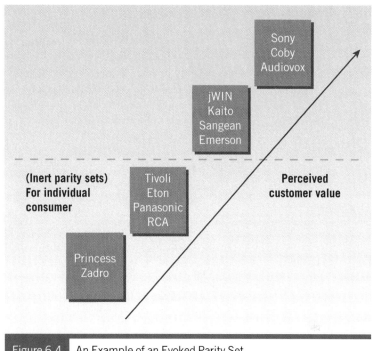

Figure 6.4   An Example of an Evoked Parity Set

Pricing New Products

Introducing a new product creates a unique pricing situation. The product has not been sold before, which means the company's leaders have some latitude in setting the price. When considering the price of the new product, the marketing manager often identifies two thresholds: the price ceiling and the price floor.[1] The ceiling is the highest possible price. The ceiling will be determined by the product's benefits, the product's unique advantages, and competitive intensity. The more unique the product, the stronger and more defined the benefits, and the less the competitive intensity, the higher the price ceiling becomes. The price floor is determined by the product's costs. The first task in pricing a new product consists of identifying levels of demand at various price points between the price ceiling and the price floor. The marketing team can then make a decision regarding the best pricing point. The two extremes (ceiling and floor) are associated with pricing strategies known as skimming and penetration pricing.

Skimming

A price set as high as the market will bear reflects a **skimming price strategy**. This method works best when the product is difficult to copy, when a level of prestige might be associated with owning the item, when copyright or patent protections exit, or when a "first on the block" mentality can be created. For example, people who stood in line to buy iPhones paid substantially more than those who waited just a few months for the price to drop.

Skimming is often used in *dual-channel marketing*. The procedure is to charge a high price first in the business-to-business market. Businesses tend to be less price sensitive, especially when a new product offers benefits that cannot be found elsewhere. It is not surprising that the cordless telephones, fax machines, and digital cameras were introduced in business-to-business markets with much higher prices than consumers eventually paid. Part of the reason for the higher prices is that the lower demand does not allow for any economies of scale that accompany higher levels of production as items reach consumer markets. In other words, producing 100,000 units normally has a lower cost per unit than producing only 1,000 units of the same item, because raw materials are purchased in bulk and assembly methods become more efficient.

- Advantage or uniqueness
- Similarity to substitutes
- Risk
- Switching costs
- Corporate image/reputation
- Copyright/patent protection
- Ease of market entry

Figure 6.5

Factors in Pricing New Products

Penetration Pricing

The extreme opposite of skimming, penetration pricing, means the price will be set as low as possible, especially as the product is being introduced. From the customer's viewpoint, penetration pricing reduces the psychological impact of trying something new by keeping the purchase risk low. The lower price normally stimulates demand. The goal is to recoup development costs through a higher sales volume rather than through per unit gross margins. The low price also discourages entrants into the market and helps the company that introduced the product to build a larger market share.

Figure 6.5 identifies factors that are considered in pricing a new product. If a new product offers specific *advantages* not available in other products or it provides some type of *uniqueness,* a higher price or skimming approach can be used. On the other hand, if *substitutes* can be purchased that are similar to the new product, then it will tend to be priced closer to the substitute products or consumers will just purchase the substitute.

Risk and *switching costs* are often related. A new product carrying a high-risk purchase makes it difficult to charge a high price. The same is true when switching costs are high. To persuade consumers (or businesses) to purchase a new product for a high price requires low risk and low switching costs.

A company or brand's *reputation* and *image* also influence the price that can be charged. A company that is known for its innovations and is well respected by consumers can charge more for a new product than a company that is not well known or that has a lower image. For example, when Black & Decker introduces a new product, consumers are normally willing to pay more because of the Black & Decker name.

As has already been mentioned, *copyrights* or *patent protections* allow a company to charge a skimming price. Still, competitors can develop technologies or products that use a similar technology to circumvent the copyright or patent. While these products are not identical, they can closely resemble the new product and be considered by consumers as viable substitutes. The easier the new product can be copied, the riskier it becomes to use a skimming pricing strategy. The skimming strategy often reduces demand for the product and, at the same time, encourages competitors to develop viable alternatives.

The final factor to consider is *ease of entry* into the market, or the ease of a competitor developing a similar product. When competitors can easily or quickly copy a new product, the original producer tends to offer a lower introductory price.

The Incremental Approach

The initial price of a new product is important because it sets the reference price. The reference price is the price customers identify with the new product. It conveys what the company thinks the product is worth. When the price of a new product is set too low, the company loses potential revenue.

Consequently, when setting a price, the marketing manager can use an incremental approach, which prices a new product based on the incremental costs of producing the new product over the costs of producing an existing product. For example, if a new product costs 20% more to produce than the existing product, then the new item will be priced 20% higher.

Unfortunately, the incremental approach does not account for consumer benefits and value of the product to customers. For example, the first makers of the portable bar code readers estimated the amount of time the portable reader would save customers and then priced the product accordingly. These company leaders failed to consider other benefits, such as improved logistics planning, viable just-in-time inventory levels, and the ability to use real-time inventory control. The portable device saved customers much more than just hours reading inventory. By pricing the new product too low, these first makers lost at least $1 billion as potential profit.[2]

Price Discounts

The most common pricing tactic available for attracting new customers is offering some type of discount. Lowering the list price might make an item seem more attractive and less of a purchase risk. A sense of time pressure can be created by offering the discount for a limited time. Figure 6.6 lists some of the more common types of price discounts. Most are capable of attracting new customers, as well as helping to retain current customers, when used correctly.

Some discounts focus on customers or end users. They may be granted by manufacturers or by retail outlets. The second group of discounts is offered to businesses. An important consideration with any form of discount is to increase the volume of sales enough to offset the cost or lost revenue from lower per-unit margins.

A *sale price* can take on one of three forms: (1) loss leader, (2) promotional, or (3) introductory. A loss-leader price means the product is sold below costs in order to attract the customer into the retail store or entice a business to try the product. The belief is that the customer will buy additional products. For instance, at Thanksgiving, turkeys are often priced as loss leaders. In almost all cases, consumers purchase additional items that cover the loss on the turkey. A business may sell a photocopier as a loss leader with a contract to supply the firm's paper and toner, which is used to capture profits.

For Consumers	For Businesses
• Sale price	• Sale price
– Loss-leader price	– Loss-leader price
– Promotional price	– Promotional price
– Introductory price	– Introductory price
• Seasonal discount	• Volume discount
• Quantity discount	• Early-payment discount
• Bundle discount	

Figure 6.6 Forms of Price Discounts

A *promotional price* is a short-term price reduction. It may be printed on signage within the store or in company advertisements. It can be a markdown from the standard retail price. It may take the form of a percentage discount given on a per-item basis or placed on every purchase in a retail outlet. Sales are often associated with holidays (pre-Christmas, after Christmas, Labor Day, etc.) and sometimes with off-seasons, where the name might be "white sale."

An *introductory price* may be offered with the introduction of a new product. It may just be a brand extension, such as a new flavor of snack crackers. When this is done, the introductory price encourages consumers to try the product. The danger becomes that consumers may be willing to purchase the product at the reduced price but not at the regular price. The same occurs in the business-to-business sector.

Seasonal discounts are used to drum up business during slow periods. The price of a lawn mower may be at its lowest when the summer mowing season is about to end. The same is true for vacation spots and resorts that experience peaks and valleys in attendance. Cutting the price may entice a customer to try and purchase the product.

Quantity discounts offer the buyer more for their money. A single bar of soap may be sold for $1.00, two bars packaged together are priced at $1.79, but six bars in a package sell for $3.29. The price per unit goes down with the larger quantity. This may or may not attract new customers, since most will want to try a small amount before making the leap to a larger quantity. In the business-to-business sector, quantity discounts are known as *volume discounts*. The principle is the same, although the quantity is much higher. While a consumer purchases 6 bars of soap, a retailer may purchase 6,000 bars.

Another type of consumer discount, a *bundle discount,* means that a consumer receives a discount on one item with the purchase of another item or set of items. These bundles often become standard, such as in the fast-food industry. Hamburgers, fries, and drinks can all be purchased separately, or they can be purchased together as combo meals at a lower price. Bundle pricing does not have to be permanent. It may be a special sale that is valid for a limited time. For example, a retailer may offer a package of six batteries for a special price with the purchase of a flashlight.

Business-to-business discounts include *early-payment discounts,* which are part of the credit-granting process. The payment schedule "2/10 net 30" means that an invoice that is paid within 10 days receives a 2% discount. The total invoice must be paid in 30 days. The more generous the first figure (3/10 vs. 2/10), the bigger the discount and enticement to pay early.

A Discount Break-Even Analysis

When seeking to boost sales or attract new customers, often the first thought will be to offer a price discount or price reduction. The danger, however, is that while sales increase, profits often decline. To illustrate, examine Table 6.6.

Calculation	Formula	Result
Current weekly sales are 7,000 units at $7.98	(7000×7.98)	$55,860
Cost of goods sold for 7,000 units ($5.80)	(7000×5.80)	$40,600
Contribution margin from weekly sales		$15,260
Contribution margin/unit for $1.00 price discount	$(7.98 - 5.80 - 1.00)$	$1.18
Units needed to generate $15,260 contribution margin	$(15260/1.18)$	12,932
Percent increase in sales needed	$(12932 - 7000)/7000$	85%

Table 6.6   Break-Even Analysis for Price Discount

In the example, currently weekly sales of the product are 7,000 units at the retail price of $7.98 each. The production costs are $5.80 per unit. The contribution margin per week is $15,260 ($55,860 − $40,600). If the retailer offers a $1 price discount and sells the product for $6.98, each unit generates a contribution margin of $1.18 per unit instead of $2.18. To equal the same contribution margin of $15,260, the retailer must sell 12,932 units instead of 7,000. This represents an 85% increase in sales. The $1.00 price discount equates to a 12.5% price reduction. To offset the 12.5% price discount, sales must increase by 85%. This type of ratio is common.

When considering price discounts, marketing managers should be aware of the impact on contribution margin and the type of increase in demand necessary to offset the lower price. This does not mean, however, that the price discount should not be offered unless the same amount of profit can be earned. The marketing manager may be trying to capture market share or match a competitor's offer. Sometimes it is a good decision to offer the discount even though the profits are lower.

- Reaction of consumers (or businesses)
- Reaction of competitors
- Industry leader versus industry follower
- Impact on brand image
- Impact on gross margin

Figure 6.7

Factors to Consider When Changing the Prices of Existing Products

Changing Prices of Existing Products

Changing the price of an existing product requires careful consideration, whether it is a price increase or a price decrease. Figure 6.7 highlights the factors involved. Decreasing the price of a product certainly is easier than increasing the price. Firms often decrease prices during the growth and maturity stages of a product's life cycle and when new technologies reduce the costs of producing a product.

Before making the decision to modify a price, marketing managers evaluate the potential *reactions of buyers* and *competitors*. Consideration also must be given to the impact the change may have on the brand's *image* and *gross margin*. Also, company leaders decide whether the goal is to become the *industry leader* and be the first to modify the price or if it would be better to wait and be a follower.

It is to a company's advantage to be the first to reduce prices. Other companies are forced to either follow or take the chance of losing market share. For price increases, being a follower is usually a better approach. The idea is to let another company take the heat and possible decline in sales from the price increase. There is also the danger that none of the other companies will follow with a corresponding price increase. When that occurs, the price increase becomes even more noticeable to customers.

Another principle to consider comes from Weber's law. Weber was a German physiologist, and Weber's law addresses the link between a physical stimulus and a desired response. This concept may be applied to pricing. Regardless of the product category, consumers have been conditioned that for a price change (a stimulus) to be noticed, it must be greater than 10% before it generates a response. A price change of less than 10% is too low to be noticed.[3] If a price of a pair of jeans is $80, consumers will not notice the price has changed until it is raised above $88 or lowered to less than $72. Based on this principle, a marketer seeking to increase prices may wish to do so by less than 10%; otherwise the increase in price will be noticed, and shoppers may look for new alternatives. Conversely, a price reduction should be more than 10% for it to be noticed by consumers.

Price Reductions

A price reduction is different from a price discount. A discount is temporary; a price reduction is permanent. The marketing manager normally only reduces the price of a product under one or more of the following conditions:

- Lower production costs
- Increased competition
- To meet a competitor's price reduction
- Decline in demand

If the *costs of producing* a product decrease, the manager considers whether the company should pocket the difference or pass some or all of the savings along to the customer. One critical variable that affects this decision is predicting the reaction of the competition. The manager will want to know if production costs have become lower for competitors as well. If so, the question becomes "Will the competition lower prices, and if so, by how much?" Also, as mentioned earlier, tied to these issues is the decision whether to be the first to reduce prices or be a follower.

Increased competition can trigger a price reduction decision, especially when a company begins to lose market share to competitors. A marketing manager, however, carefully considers such a decision because if competitors match the price reduction, then nothing is gained. In fact, the company is worse off unless production costs are also lower. The company receives a lower margin on each item sold and therefore loses profits. Before reducing prices, the marketing manager examines other elements of the marketing mix, including possible product modifications, to see if alternative tactics can be developed that make the brand stand out from among the competition without reducing prices.

When a *competitor reduces prices,* then careful consideration should be given to matching the price reduction. This is especially important if the two brands are in the same consideration parity set. When other competitors in the consideration set follow with price reductions, it is almost impossible not to reduce the price. Again, as with increased competition, the marketing manager may look for ways to increase customer value for the brand without reducing the price.

When *demand for a product declines,* a quick fix marketing managers often use to meet sales quotas is a price reduction. Such a strategy may stimulate sales in the short run but may prove to be more damaging in the long term. Before reducing the price, research may be conducted to find out why the demand declined. If the decline is due to a new substitute product being introduced, then a more serious problem may exist. The product might be entering the decline stage of the product life cycle. Reducing prices may not stimulate demand. It may even be time for the marketing manager to consider divestiture of the product.

Price Increases

The number one reason for increasing a price is a rise in production costs. Deciding how and when is the biggest challenge. In most industries, an industry leader is usually the first to make a price increase. When that particular company or brand makes the move, others in the industry normally follow. Occasionally, prices go up due to an increase in demand or a reduction in supply. For instance, when a particular toy suddenly becomes a fad, demand may spike quickly. With the rush by consumers to purchase the new toy, the price often rises.

Making the decision to increase prices often depends on predictions of the reactions of competitors and customers. When competitors raise prices, it becomes relatively easy to do the same. For the industry leader, the challenge becomes predicting whether competitors will follow suit. When they do not, the company's marketing leader faces a tough decision. The company can drop the price back down or stay with the price increase. Dropping prices back down may create the impression that the company was just trying to gouge its customers. When the company does not lower the price, the risk of losing market share increases.

Methods for Increasing Prices

Another decision is the method to be used. One approach is to increase the price at once. A second would be to raise the price in small increments. Also the marketing team will decide if customers should be notified of the price increase or if instead it is best kept quiet in the hope that customers do not notice the change.

In consumer goods and services, prices are often raised incrementally, and customers are not usually notified. The rationale for the incremental approach is that customers often do not notice small changes in prices (remember Weber's law). Also, if competitors do not follow with an increase, it is easier to drop the price back down when only a small change was made. Most companies try to avoid negative publicity. Explaining why a price was increased invites media and customer scrutiny and increases the potential for negative publicity.

When increasing the price of consumer goods, such as clothing, why are prices increased in small increments? Should customers be informed about the price increase?

An exception to the incremental approach occurs when costs of other items increase, and the public is aware of these additional costs. For instance, during the spike in gasoline prices in 2008, food prices also increased. Although consumers complained about the increase in food prices, they knew it was the result of the increased cost of fuel and transportation. They knew it would happen even before it occurred, and the food companies were not blamed as much as the fuel companies.

In business-to-business pricing, company leaders normally notify customers of price increases and explain the reasons. Typically, the price is increased all at once rather than incrementally. If at all possible, however, the price increase will be kept below the 10% threshold level. By keeping it below 10%, business customers are not as likely to consider alternatives since it is not viewed as a significant change.

The marketing manager also attempts to discover what will be the reaction of competitors and how difficult it is for a customer to switch to another company. Lower switching costs make it easier for a customer to change to a competitor, especially if the competitor did not increase prices. The relationship with the customer contributes another factor to be considered. The stronger the relationship and the more trust the company has with customers, it becomes less likely that the customer will look for an alternative source.

A Price Increase Analysis

When making a price increase, the key decision is in regard to maintaining the same gross margin in dollars or as a percentage. Table 6.7 displays the difference. First, the current situation is shown. The next column shows a 10% increase in production costs of a product. At the same selling price, a decline in the gross margin of $2.33 per item (the change expressed in dollars) will occur, representing a reduction in gross margin from 28.46% to 21.31% (the change expressed as a percentage of the current price).

	Current	10% Cost Increase	Same Gross Margin ($)	Same Gross Margin (%)
Selling price ($)	32.50	32.50	34.83	35.75
Product costs ($)	23.25	25.58	25.58	25.58
Gross margin ($)	9.25	6.93	9.25	10.17
Gross margin (%)	28.46	21.31	26.56	28.45
Increase in costs ($)		2.33	2.33	2.33
Increase in price ($)			2.33	3.25
Increase in price (%)			7.2	10.0

Table 6.7 Price Increase Analysis

A marketing manager seeking to regain the gross margin in dollars, due to the increased costs, must increase the selling price by $2.33. This results in a change in gross margin of 26.56%, instead of the original 28.46%, and requires only a 7.2% increase in price. This approach allows for a smaller price increase. This will be possible when the increased costs are all absorbed in producing the product. It is also a good approach when the manager believes that competitors may not increase their prices the full 10%. It may also be used when the manager believes that the company's customers are price sensitive and will switch to substitute products.

In some instances, increases in production costs result in a corresponding increase in overhead costs. In that situation, the manager may decide to increase the selling price by the full 10%. Notice the last column, which displays the increase in the selling price to $35.75. This increase restores the gross margin to 28.45% and results in a gross margin dollar value of $10.17.

When looking at gross margins per item, the real impact of a change may not be as evident until results for an entire year are considered. Table 6.8 shows the impact for a company

	Before Cost Increase	10% Cost Increase	Same Gross Margin ($)	Same Gross Margin (%)
Revenue (300,000 units) ($)	9,750,000	9,750,000	10,449,000	10,725,000
Costs ($)	6,975,000	7,672,500	7,674,000	7,674,000
Gross margin ($)	2,775,000	2,077,500	2,775,000	3,051,000
Gross margin (%)	28.46	21.31	26.56	28.45
Change in gross margin ($)		(697,500)	697,500	276,000
Change in gross margin (%)		−25.1	0.0	9.9

Table 6.8   Price Increase Impact for the Year

that sells an average of 300,000 units per year. If the 10% increase in cost is absorbed with no increase in the selling price, the result is a gross margin decline of almost $700,000, which equates to a 25.1% loss of gross profits. If the same gross margin in dollars is obtained by increasing the selling price by $2.33 per unit, the gross margin for the year increases to the original $2.77 million, but the overall gross margin is 26.56% instead of 28.46%. This is based on the 7.2% increase in the price. If the selling price is increased the full 10% to match the increase in costs, the gross margin is $3.051 million, which is a 9.9% increase in gross margin and restores it to the 28.45% level, where it was before the cost increases occurred. When examining the impact for the entire year, it becomes more apparent that the company will be likely to increase its selling price to offset increases in production costs. How much depends on how the cost increase affects overhead and fixed costs, what the competitors do, and how customers will react.

Keep in mind that the $2.775 million gross margin shown in the fourth column only restores the company's overall gross margin, which is used for overhead operations. A company that does not increase prices would experience a decline in gross dollars of about $700,000. This would have an impact on other company operations and probably result in a net loss for the year. Consequently, a 7.2% increase in price is needed to maintain the same amount for the operation. To maintain the same gross percentage, the price would increase by 10% and earn a $3.051 million increase in gross margin.

Company leaders have one other alternative. Rather than increasing the price, the product can be altered so that the production costs per unit remain the same. Cereal manufacturers and candy manufacturers have used this tactic. Rather than increase the price of the cereal or candy bar, the content size is reduced. Thus, a cereal manufacturer can offer a box holding 15 ounces of cereal rather than 16 ounces. The candy bar manufacturer may reduce the size of the candy bar by a certain percentage. This allows the company to hold its cost per unit at the same level and keep the same price. Often, customers do not notice that this tactic has been used.

STOP AND THINK

In the early 2000s, one pricing tactic that came under a great deal of scrutiny was the practice of routinely raising interest rates on credit card purchases, using a variety of excuses such as a late payment, a balance higher than the credit line, the use of more than one card, and others. The same companies also charged numerous fees for various actions, such as late payment fees and fees for payment checks that bounced.

1. What justification might a credit card company use for increasing the interest rate?
2. What justification might a credit card company use for charging extra fees?
3. Are these tactics ethical? Are they even noticed by consumers?
4. What can consumers do when interest rates are raised?

Legal and Ethical Pricing Issues

Figure 6.8

Legal Issues in Pricing

In order to safeguard the public's interests, a number of pieces of legislation have been passed to protect consumers and businesses from unfair pricing tactics. In addition, the Federal Trade Commission (FTC) and other agencies closely monitor the pricing practices of firms. Figure 6.8 highlights the most common legal and ethical issues in pricing.

Price discrimination involves selling merchandise to different buyers at different prices. This unethical practice became illegal in 1936 with the passage of the Robinson-Patman Act. Consumers and businesses now are guaranteed they will not be charged a different price based on race, gender, size of business, or any other possible factor. Companies can modify the price only if the product has been modified or the service that accompanies the product is modified. Any modification then must be made available to all customers who want it.

This law does not apply to differential pricing—that is, if the price modification is based on a legitimate factor and the same price is charged to all consumers (or businesses). For instance, at a baseball park, a team's ticket office can charge different prices for bleacher seats, box seats, and first-, second-, or third-tier seats. A zoo can offer a lower admission price to children under 12. A movie theater can charge a different price for the afternoon matinee than it does for the evening shows. In all these instances, the different price is legal because it does not discriminate against any particular individual.

Price fixing is an agreement between competitors to charge the same price for a good or service. The pricing fixing does not have to be a formal agreement among the firms. It can occur when one company charges a price and all other companies immediately change prices to match the first company. The FTC carefully monitors industries to ensure that companies are not engaging in any type of price fixing.

As noted in the discussion of price increases, it is common for companies to follow an industry leader that increases prices. When the FTC examines such an occurrence, the agency looks for substantiation of or a justification for the price increase. A change in price due to increased costs of raw materials affects all the companies in the industry. In such a situation, the FTC is not likely to investigate any further. When there is no apparent reason for a price increase, then a more thorough investigation occurs. Remember that price fixing can occur without companies ever talking to each other or agreeing jointly to increase prices or charge a certain price.

Deceptive pricing is any pricing practice that misleads consumers. This is a major pricing issue for many companies, and it is the most difficult for the FTC to monitor. When looking for deceptive pricing, the FTC uses the same test as it does for deceptive advertising:

- Did a substantial number of people or is the "typical person" left with a false impression or misrepresentation that relates to the product?
- Did the misrepresentation induce people or the "typical person" to make a purchase?

The vagueness of those two statements makes deceptive pricing difficult to monitor. Note that *intent* is not part of the language. It does not matter whether the company's marketers intentionally priced a product to deceive customers. It becomes illegal when and if customers are deceived and if they were induced to make purchases.

One practice that has been used by retailers and is illegal is bait and switch. The retailer may advertise a particular printer for only $99. When customers arrive at the store, however, they find out that the retailer is out of the "sale printers" but has other printers that can be purchased. Another scenario that may occur is that the salesperson tells the customers about the deficiencies of the "sale printer" and attempts to talk them into purchasing a more expensive model. Both practices are considered bait and switch and are unethical as well as illegal.

When investigating bait-and-switch allegations, the FTC uses three primary factors to determine whether the retailer engaged in illegal activity. First, the inventory level of the advertised printer may be examined to determine whether the retailer ordered additional and sufficient inventory to handle the demand created by the advertised price. If not, then the retailer has engaged in a bait-and-switch tactic. Second, the investigator tries to determine whether undue pressure was exerted by retail personnel on customers to purchase a more expensive model.

This is more difficult to prove and relies on the testimony of customers and store personnel. Third, the agency finds out whether customers were offered "rain checks" for the advertised printer when the retailer had sold all its models and if the company indeed did order for these customers the advertised printer at the price that was advertised. This must take place in a reasonable amount of time based on current order and shipping data for the advertised printer and like models. A retailer can't offer a "rain check" and then take 6 months to acquire the printer for the customer if it normally takes 4 days to obtain shipments of like orders.

The final area of concern is predatory pricing, which is pricing designed to eliminate competition. As with deceptive pricing, predatory pricing is difficult to prove. In fact, it is even more difficult to prove because in predatory pricing the FTC has to discover the intent to eliminate competition. Reducing prices to gain sales and to gain market share is acceptable and legal, but reducing prices with the sole intent of restricting free trade by destroying competitors is not.

In determining intent, one of the factors the FTC investigator considers is costs. A firm that is selling a product below cost may be engaging in predatory pricing, but not always. The company's intent may be legitimate, such as to attract customers, build market share, or boost sales. This practice, known as loss-leader pricing, is a common practice. In most situations, the business wants to attract customers in the hope that they will purchase other products that will offset the loss on the advertised item. The practice becomes illegal when the intent is to destroy or run a competitor out of business. In the early part of the 20th century, large chains of gas stations would reduce the price of fuel below costs until they ran competitors out of business and then increase the price to a higher level.

The Role of Customer Service

A strong connection exists between prices and customer service. Simply stated, customers paying higher prices expect greater customer service. This is true for both tangible goods and intangible services. Someone who pays a few extra dollars for tires expects them to last longer and be installed quickly and properly by a courteous service staff. A customer who pays more for a hairstyle expects the best possible look and the best possible treatment by the stylist. A college student attending a high-tuition institution expects a better educational experience than would be received at a school with lower tuition.

In general, any time a customer considers a new company, new product, or new service, several factors will influence the final choice. The one common denominator for markets, products, brands, and prices is the connection to customer service. The company that delivers memorable, quality service automatically has an advantage.

YOURCAREER

Negotiation Skills

Among the skills needed to further your career in marketing, negotiation and bargaining abilities may have a major impact. These abilities are valuable in at least four circumstances:

1. Finalizing sales
2. Making personal purchases
3. Negotiating your salary package, benefits, and pay increases
4. Bargaining for job or task assignments

An effective negotiator knows how to handle five processes, known as the "Four Cs and one I."

Common Interests

The ability to identify what you have in common with the person at the other end of the negotiation is crucial, finding common interests and building trust and a sense of partnership.

Conflicting Interests

A negotiation is not necessary when the two sides share the same opinion. An effective negotiator knows which items are "on the table" and which are not. Seeking to understand the other party's perspective (empathy) makes it easier to look for proposed solutions when conflicts arise.

Criteria

To make a case that your position is better or more viable, ground rules must be in place. In many sales, money is the primary criterion, but it interacts with others, such as delivery time, quality, and the potential to build a relationship for the future.

Compromise

An effective negotiator knows the difference between a "go to the wall" issue and one where give and take is possible. He or she also knows how to "give ground" without appearing to be weak or desperate. Remember that your degree of leverage, or *bargaining power,* depends on whether you can achieve your goals in the negotiation without compromise. The weaker your position, the more compromise you will need to offer.

International Skills

In a global economy, it is vital to know how negotiations are different, depending on the culture and customs of your bargaining partner. This includes understanding items such as the importance of punctuality, the use of eye contact, the degree of directness in language, who speaks first (and who does not), effective methods of expressing disagreement, and the importance of "honor" or "saving face" in a given country or culture.

Building a successful marketing career involves knowing when and how to negotiate for pay raises, promotions, and other career-advancing opportunities. It is important to be confident, yet not arrogant. It is important to be bold, yet not abrasive. Timing and tact are important elements of the personal career negotiation process.

Chapter Summary

A price is the amount charged for a good or service. In the eyes of consumers, prices often contain practical considerations, emotional factors, and situational factors. A pricing perceptual map can be used to examine brand image and brand market position relative to competing brands along the variables of image and price.

A pricing strategy reflects the basic direction that a company's marketing and management teams take when setting prices. Some of the more common pricing objectives based on these strategies include sales maximization, profit maximization, market share maximization, and competitive parity.

Pricing programs begin with the choice of method used to set the price, based on costs, demand and supply, or the competition. Typically, all three factors are taken into consideration as prices are set.

Setting prices for new products can take the extreme step of a skimming price strategy, which reflects the highest amount a company may charge for the item. At the other extreme, penetration pricing involves setting the price as low as possible. Over time, prices move toward an equilibrium based on other factors in the marketplace.

Prices are then often discounted to both consumers and other businesses. Also, prices may be increased and decreased as a new situation emerges, such as a drop or rise in production costs.

The legal and ethical issues that accompany pricing include price discrimination, price fixing, resale price maintenance, deceptive pricing, and predatory pricing. The Federal Trade Commission is largely responsible for making sure pricing programs meet legal requirements.

The secret to effective utilization of markets, products, brands, and prices is customer service. Quality service plays a role in creating customer perceptions of the firm and how they will respond to other marketing efforts.

Chapter Terms

Consideration/evoked parity   (p. 146)
Cost-plus pricing   (p. 142)
Deceptive pricing   (p. 155)
Incremental approach   (p. 148)
Markup   (p. 143)
Penetration pricing   (p. 148)
Predatory pricing   (p. 156)

Price discrimination   (p. 155)
Price elasticity of demand   (p. 144)
Price fixing   (p. 155)
Price perceptual map   (p. 139)
Pricing strategy   (p. 141)
Reference price   (p. 148)
Skimming price strategy   (p. 147)

Review Questions

1. Define price.

2. In terms of consumer perceptions, what are the two major factors?

3. Which two factors are used to create a pricing perceptual map?

4. Name the primary and secondary factors associated with customer value and pricing.

5. What are the four standard pricing objectives described in this chapter?

6. Which four methods are used to set prices?

7. Explain the methods used to set prices using cost-plus pricing and markups.

8. What are the three ways to set price based on the competition?

9. What is a consideration or evoked parity set?

10. Describe a skimming pricing strategy and penetration pricing.

11. How is the incremental approach used when setting prices for new products?

12. Name the types of discounts that can be granted to consumers and to other businesses.

13. What factors affect the changing prices of existing products?

14. What are the main ethical and legal issues associated with pricing?

15. Describe the relationship between pricing and customer service.

CUSTOMER CORNER

Doris Moeller had never taken the time to complain at a retail store, even when she thought someone had done something wrong, until today. She was shopping at a high-end department store, looking for bargains after Christmas. In the children's section, Doris found several items for her grandchildren marked 60% off. She took them to the cash register in that section. The cashier asked, "Do you have our coupon for an additional 15% off?"

"No, I sure don't," Doris replied.

"That's okay," the clerk replied, "I'll get you one." She then took out a newspaper page and quickly added the additional discount. Doris was pleased and thanked the cashier profusely for her service.

Believing that she could get the same result anywhere in the store, Doris began looking at more expensive women's clothes. She had a formal reception to attend in the upcoming week and wanted something "new" and "nice" to wear. She finally found a dress that had been marked down from $120.00 to $70.00. Doris figured that with 15% more off the price, it would be around $60.00, a figure she could justify to her husband when she got home. She took the dress to the closest cashier. The cashier said nothing about a discount, rang up the dress, and said, "That will be $74.42," which was the price including sales tax.

Doris told the clerk, "When I was in the children's section, they gave me 15% off with a newspaper coupon."

The cashier glared at her and said, "Well then, someone screwed up."

Doris replied, "You mean I have to walk all the way back to the children's section just to get the discount?"

The cashier answered, "You could, but she really shouldn't give it to you."

Annoyed, Doris set the dress down on the counter and said, "Let's just forget the whole thing."

"Whatever," came the response.

Doris immediately began looking for the customer service office.

What went wrong? Why did one clerk offer Doris a discount while the other didn't?

1. Which aspect of pricing affected Doris most when she went to purchase the dress?

2. The customer service manager told Doris that the cashier for the dress had actually done the correct thing in terms of not giving her the discount, even though she was not happy with the tone used by the clerk. Should the salesperson in the children's department receive a reprimand?

3. The cashier in the children's department told the customer service manager that she recognized Doris as a regular in the store and thought that giving her the extra discount would "make her happy and keep her coming back." How should the customer service manager respond?

Discussion and Critical Thinking Questions

1. A pricing perceptual map reflects the relationship between image (or quality) and price. Develop such a map for an industry in your area. Suggested industries might be fast-food restaurants, dine-in restaurants, tanning salons, bookstores, clothing stores, sporting goods stores, or nightclubs. Pick an industry with which you are familiar and that has a number of companies.

2. How would cost-plus pricing apply to the sale of insurance policies? What are the fixed costs? The variable costs?

3. For each of the following products discuss the importance of costs, demand, and competition and how it affects the setting of prices. Discuss how the price would be different depending on the management team's objective.
   - Pizza
   - Doughnuts
   - Coffee
   - RV motor homes
   - Sporting events, such as football, basketball, or baseball

4. Figure 6.5 lists the factors that affect the pricing of new products. Explain how each factor would apply to the original release of the iPhone.

5. Use the Cost-Plus Pricing Table below to calculate the selling price for each of the following products based on the given financial information.

6. Use the markup approach to calculate the selling price for each of the following products, based on the markup percentages recommended in the Markup Pricing Table.

7. A retailer plans to offer a $2.00 price discount on an item that sells for $19.98. Using the following data, calculate how many units the retailer would have to sell to offset the price reduction. What is the percent change in price? What is the percent change in sales volume needed to earn the same weekly income?
   - Current weekly sales—20,000 units
   - Cost of goods sold—$14.32/unit

8. Suppose a commercial hand vacuum, used by janitorial services, currently costs $48.60 to manufacture and is sold to distributors for $93.25. Suppose costs increase by $4.86 (10%) to $53.46 per unit. How much would the manufacturer need to increase the selling price, in dollars and percentage, to maintain the same gross margin in dollars per unit? What would be the new contribution margin percentage? To maintain

Cost-Plus Pricing

	Product A	Product B	Product C
Units produced	7,000	11,000	18,000
Variable cost/unit ($)	23.00	19.00	15.00
Fixed costs ($)	50,000	50,000	50,000
Desired contribution margin ($)	75,000	75,000	75,000
Total variable costs ($)			
Total costs ($)			
Selling price ($)			

Markup Pricing

	Product A	Product B	Product C
Variable costs ($)	4.55	6.13	7.11
Markup percentage (%)	50	45	40
Value of 1 – markup			
Price of product ($)			

the same contribution margin percentage, what selling price and what percent increase in price will be necessary?

9. Using the data from Question 8, what is the impact on yearly sales if the manufacturer currently sells 180,000 vacuums a year? Answer the following questions:
   a. What was the yearly gross margin in dollars and percentage before the cost increase?

b. If the selling price was left at $93.25, how much gross profit would the firm lose, and what percent decline is this?

c. To maintain the same overall gross margin in dollars, what would be the sales revenue?

d. If the selling price of the vacuum was increased by 10% to $102.58, what is the impact on annual sales revenue, costs, and contribution margin in both dollars and percentage?

Chapter 6 Case

Pricing: That's How the Cookie Crumbles

Susan Roberts loves baking. After years of working in a job she did not enjoy, Susan finally found a place where she could make a living doing something fun, when she became the assistant manager of the bakery in a local grocery store. After her basic training, Susan began making and selling the store's recipes.

One day, Susan asked Roy, the bakery manager, if she could show him how to make better chocolate chip cookies than what was currently being offered. Roy agreed. After sampling the batch, he gave her an assignment. Susan was to teach her recipe to the other two employees in the department, who worked mostly the night and weekend shifts. To make it a little more interesting, Roy said, "I also want you to set the price. How much per cookie, how much per dozen, and how much for large orders, such as 10 dozen or more?"

Susan loved the idea that her cookies would become the store's in-house brand. She was a little daunted by the idea of setting the price. When one of the bakery's vendors stopped for a visit, she cornered him and asked how his company set prices for the baguettes and sourdough loaves that he brought each week. The vendor said, "Well, it's pretty simple. We take into account our costs, what the competition is doing, and the amount the store buys per visit."

Based on this information, Susan decided to undertake some in-store marketing research. First, she went to the store's packaged cookie department. She found five primary brands on the shelves, Keebler, Mrs. Fields, Pepperidge Farms, Chips Ahoy!, Famous Amos, and the grocery store's generic, called Chips A'Plenty. There were also packages of Always Save cookies available. The prices ranged from $1.00 per package to $4.79 for the most expensive version. The number of cookies in each package ranged from about 30 in the lower-priced package to 24 in the most expensive. Susan calculated that the

Susan was excited about her cookies becoming the store's in-house brand but was worried about how they should be priced.

top brand, which was a 24-pack priced at $4.79, had a price of 20 cents per cookie. She knew that the cost per cookie for her version was far less than that ($1.20 per dozen for ingredients and estimated labor), which gave her a great deal of latitude.

Susan gathered a group of friends, telling them they were invited to a cookie-tasting party. She asked them

In setting the price of the in-store cookies, is it helpful to compare the proposed price with that of others?

to rate each of the brands and give explanations for why each one was better or worse than the others. She also asked them about how much they were willing to pay for the cookies.

The primary features of the cookies seemed to be freshness, softness, and the number of chips in each. Harder, dryer, few-chipped cookies rated the lowest. Not surprisingly, these were the generic brands. The brand that rated the best among her sample of 12 friends was also the highest priced. In between, however, there was less consistency. Some of her guests thought softness was the most important feature; others said that the number of chips made the difference in their quality ratings.

Susan gave each guest a giant glass of milk and asked them to wait for half an hour. They all played card games until the time had passed. Susan then brought out a batch of her freshly baked cookies. She asked them to compare her cookies with all the packaged brands. They all agreed that the quality of her cookies was much higher and said they would be willing to pay more for a dozen. Figure 6.9 is a perceptual map of her findings.

The next step was to set the price. Susan had to take into account several additional factors. First, any remaining cookies that did not sell within 48 hours had to be either sold at a dramatic discount or thrown away. This added to any calculation of cost per cookie. Second, Susan knew that shoppers had to make a special effort to

visit the bakery, which was at the far end of the store. It didn't seem likely that there would be any impulse buys. Third, she had no advertising budget. She did convince the store manager to give her some space in the weekly newspaper ad for the entire store, but this was nothing compared with the advertising budgets of her corporate competitors. Fourth, Susan expected that shoppers would purchase her cookies in smaller quantities.

To her advantage, Susan gained permission to give free samples of the cookies (in pieces) to those who passed by the bakery. She even managed to set up a small sampling area near the cash register on two consecutive Saturdays. She also had the advantage of smell. When the cookies were baking, the aroma would permeate a section of the store near the bakery. Armed with all this information, Susan was ready to set her prices, for singles, dozens, and more. She knows the initial price is very important because it will set the reference price for the cookies.

1. Describe the emotional and situational factors associated with the price of a cookie.
2. Would your answer to Question 1 be the same if you knew that there was an independent bakery within two blocks of the grocery store?
3. Has Susan completed all the needed research to set prices? If not, what other research would you suggest?
4. Based on the price perceptual map (Figure 6.9), what price would you suggest per cookie, per dozen, and for large orders of 10 or more dozen?
5. Since the initial price will serve as the reference price, if an error is made, is it better for the initial price to be too low or too high? Explain why.
6. As Susan passed out samples, she asked customers what they would pay for a dozen cookies and how many they would purchase at different price levels. She learned that when the price was 20 cents per cookie ($2.40) or lower, the estimated sales would be 200 dozen a week. Going lower than $2.40 would not increase sales. She estimated that the demand would decline 10 dozen a week for each 12 cent increase in price until she reached $3.00. The demand then seemed to decline more rapidly, at 20 dozen per week. Complete Table 6.9. What did you learn from the analysis? What price would she charge per dozen if the objective was market share maximization? For sales maximization? For profit maximization?

Figure 6.9 Susan's Perceptual Map

Price/Dozen ($)	Demand/Week (dozens)	Gross Income ($)	Total Variable Costs ($)	Contribution Margin ($)
2.16	200		240.00	
2.28	200		240.00	
2.40	200		240.00	
2.52	190		228.00	
2.64	180		216.00	
2.76	170		204.00	
2.88	160		192.00	
3.00	150		180.00	
3.12	130		156.00	
3.24	110		132.00	

Table 6.9 Estimated Demand at Different Prices

Go to **www.sagepub.com/clow** for additional exercises and study resources. Select **Chapter 6, Pricing** for chapter-specific activities.

What has made the Smucker's brand successful?

chapter 7

Advertising, Alternative and Direct Marketing

Smucker's: It Has to Be Good

Many of today's products originated with historical events. For example, M&M's candies were an invention that arose out of the Civil War. Another well-known name arose from historical roots: Smucker's. In the 19th century, the person who became known as Johnny Appleseed made his way through the state of Ohio, planting trees as he went. Many years later, an enterprising gentleman named Jerome Monroe Smucker took the fruits of those trees, began making apple cider in 1897, and later apple butter. It didn't take long for the J.M. Smucker brand to become associated with quality fruit products.

A little more than a 100 years later, the Smucker's brand remains attached to jams, jellies, and preserves that are sold across the United States. Over 40 varieties and

flavors are available. Children of all ages can enjoy not only the basics, apple, strawberry, blackberry, and red raspberry, but also the more exotic versions, such as mint apple and currant. The various versions of the products come in organic and low-sugar forms. Smucker's also features fruit butter, a set of products called Simply Fruit, and another known as Squeeze.

For many years, the tagline used in company advertising has been "With a name like Smucker's, it has to be good." This approach, in advertising lingo, is known as turning a disadvantage (a somewhat awkward name) into an advantage (a statement about quality). The image of the firm is that it provides high-quality, reasonably priced fruit products for the whole family, especially children.

Beyond traditional advertising, Smucker's promotes products through its Stars on Ice program, in cooking and recipe contests, and through endorsements, including a recent

award by the Parents Television Council. Recently, the company initiated a contest with the prize being a free personal fitness consultation with expert Denise Austin.

The company has not rested on its laurels. Through the years, the J.M. Smucker Company has moved into several closely related markets, starting with peanut butter (goes with jelly) with the brands Smucker's All Natural and Jif. Ice cream toppings include both the classic Smucker brand and Magic Shell. The corporation also merchandises other products using the brands PET, Pillsbury, Eagle, Borden, Milnot, Martha White, and Hungry Jack, among others.

While the organization now has an international reach, the home office remains in Orrville, Ohio. It continues to be a family-owned enterprise. A fourth generation of the original family now manages the corporation. With its broad reach of products, markets, and customers, the future of the J.M. Smucker brand looks sweet.[1]

Chapter Overview

A strong argument can be made that, in the past decade, the world of advertising has changed more rapidly and dramatically than any other element of marketing, and it continues to evolve. New forms of technology, such as the DVR (Digital Video Recorder) and iPod, have lessened the impact of traditional advertising venues, such as television and radio. These same technologies create a variety of ways to reach customers with messages.

This dynamic environment affects everyone involved, from the highest-ranking marketing official in a company to those charged with buying advertising space and creating the ads themselves. Advertising agency managers continually adapt to these new circumstances, while at the same time they face increasing pressures to demonstrate that the agency produces tangible results for clients.

This chapter opens with a brief discussion of advertising management. The presentation contains a more general view of the advertising management processes, along with more specific information about the role advertising plays in customer acquisition efforts. Major topics include establishing advertising objectives, creating a budget, choosing an agency, overseeing the advertising program, and assessing effectiveness. The chapter concludes with descriptions of nontraditional methods for acquiring new customers, including guerrilla marketing, lifestyle marketing, buzz marketing, and direct marketing programs.

Advertising Management

Some view advertising as the "glamor" part of marketing, and it can be exciting and challenging. The role of the marketing manager in an advertising program begins with not getting caught up in the hype. Instead, the manager carefully focuses on each element of the program to make certain the company spends dollars wisely to achieve tangible goals. **Advertising management** is the process of developing and overseeing a company's advertising program. In doing so, the marketing manager will

- establish advertising objectives,
- create an advertising budget,
- choose an advertising agency,
- oversee the advertising program, and
- assess advertising effectiveness.

Establishing Advertising Objectives

A crucial starting point in advertising management is establishing clear objectives. These goals are based on the nature of the product, the stage in the product life cycle, the activities of the competition, the target audience, and other considerations. Figure 7.1 lists some of the most common advertising objectives.

The first objective, creating *brand and product awareness,* is a vital part of advertising new products or when a product is being introduced to a new market or a new market segment. These advertising objectives often work together in key ways. *Image* and *information* are part of *persuasion.* When Barnes & Noble announces an Internet sales program, customer perceptions of the firm's image are combined with information about the new service. This helps persuade online book buyers to consider Barnes & Noble rather than competitors such as Amazon.com. The goal of *encouraging action* is often part of supporting other marketing tactics. The key in managing the various advertising objectives is emphasizing a goal without neglecting the others.

- Create brand and product awareness.
- Build brand image.
- Provide information.
- Use persuasion.
- Support marketing efforts.
- Encourage action.

Figure 7.1

Advertising Objectives

Creating an Advertising Budget

The advertising objectives that have been established must then be funded. Priorities are set based on the dollars that are available. The marketing manager makes certain that enough money can be allocated to reach the goals. The primary forms of advertising budget creation include these methods:

- Percentage of sales
- Meet the competition
- Arbitrary allocation
- Objective and task

The **percentage of sales** method allocates funds to advertising and promotion based on either a percentage of the previous year's revenues or a projection of the upcoming year's sales. The **meet the competition** approach means establishing a budget for advertising that matches estimates of competitor spending. An **arbitrary allocation** occurs when company leaders set the budget at a level they think should be spent or believe the firm can afford. The **objective and task** approach begins with the company's marketing objectives. The budget is based on estimates of how much must be spent in order to achieve those objectives. Each budgeting method features various advantages and disadvantages. The marketing manager selects the one that best matches the company's situation.

The actual amount to be spent per objective raises concerns. How much is enough? Most marketing managers believe they need more at any given time. To make the case for increased funds, one approach is to examine the industry to see what the average expenditure is. Table 7.1 lists several prominent industries and the average advertising budget as a percentage of sales.

Industry	Advertising as Percentage of Sales (%)
Apparel and accessory stores	3.7
Beverages	7.5
Computer and office equipment	1.2
Household appliances	1.6
Perfume and cosmetics	7.9
Restaurants	2.0
Women's clothing stores	3.7

Table 7.1   Advertising as a Percentage of Sales for Selected Industries

Spending the average amount on advertising does not guarantee a favorable outcome. Instead, advertising success depends on the content of the advertisements, the quality of the ads, the media selected, and other factors. Advertising new products or products being introduced in new markets may not immediately yield results. It may take some time before consumers are persuaded to give something new a try. An effective marketing manager carefully reviews not only how much has been spent but also how well the money has been used given these constraints.

Choosing an Advertising Agency

Handling the company's advertising program is a key challenge for marketing managers. Once the objectives and budget for an advertising program are known, the first choice is whether the advertising can be developed internally or if an agency should be selected.

In-House Advertising

A marketing manager may believe he can handle the advertising function, especially when the person has a marketing degree. Two justifications may be offered for this approach. The first is cost. It is cheaper to create and manage the advertising program in-house rather than through an agency. Second, by handling the function in-house, the marketing manager maintains greater control.

The success of an internally directed advertising program depends on the skills of the marketing manager who handles the creative staff and manages the preparation of the actual advertisements. In many smaller companies, members of the marketing department are expected to conduct the entire advertising program. This means even employees from lower ranks may be involved in creating commercials, buying media time, and assessing the effectiveness of the advertising program. While conducting the advertising program in-house sounds exciting, in reality, very few firms and marketing managers have the expertise to do so.

Outside Advertising Agencies

In most companies, the advertising function, or at least part of the advertising function, is handled by an external agency or even multiple agencies. Learning to manage external agencies is critical for marketing managers. A consistent message must be maintained across campaigns and over time. While choosing a full-service advertising agency or a boutique does not guarantee results, it may increase the chances of a positive outcome. Outside agencies have two primary advantages: objectivity and creativity.

Skyjacker is one company that does all its advertising production in-house. What are the advantages for Skyjacker?

External personnel can be *objective* because they are not tied to a particular product or influenced by individuals in an organization. They do not have biases developed from knowing the history of the product. They see the product from an external point of view and, as a result, can develop the campaign from a customer's perspective.

Closely tied to objectivity is the concept of *creativity*. While many companies employ talented and innovative people, as a rule, individuals who work for an agency tend to be more creative. They often have experiences with a number of different products and different target markets, which gives them a broader base of knowledge. It is not unusual for a creative to get ideas for a product from another product that may be totally unrelated. In addition, agency creatives tend to spend all their working time creating, while in-house personnel often have other duties in addition to their creative work. As a result, agency creatives develop higher levels of expertise.

Selecting an Outside Advertising Agency

- Size of agency
- Relevant experience of agency
- Conflicts of interest
- Creative ability
- Services available

Figure 7.2

Criteria for Evaluating
Advertising Agencies

Before contacting prospective advertising agencies, the marketing manager consults with other marketing personnel and administrators to establish the selection process and selection criteria. The objective is to reduce biases that may enter into the decision process. Figure 7.2 lists some of the major issues to be considered as part of the selection process.

When a large firm hires a small agency, the agency may be overwhelmed by the account. A small firm hiring a large agency may find that the company's account gets lost or is treated as insignificant. In general, the *size* of the company should be large enough so that the agency will deem it to be an important account but small enough so that if the account is lost, the agency would not be badly affected.

Relevant experience and *conflicts of interest* go hand in hand. An agency with experience in a given industry better understands the product, the customers, and the structure of the marketing channel. Still, the agency should not have any conflict of interest created by representing a direct competitor. Thus, a weight loss program such as Weight Watchers might be considering various agencies. The advertising agency Bozell's client list indicates that the company has considerable experience, some of which might be relevant to a client such as Weight Watchers, because Bozell has created ads for Slenderizing Secrets and Complete Nutrition.[2] Bozell also works with several medical facilities and medical programs. These experiences might also carry over knowledge to Weight Watchers. If Bozell does not represent a direct competitor, the agency would become a company to consider.

An agency's *creative reputation* and *capabilities* are also relevant. They may be difficult to judge. One method is to ask for a list of advertising awards the agency has won. Awards do not always translate into effective advertisements; however, there is often a positive relationship between winning them and future success. Most creative awards are given by peers. As a result, these awards are often good indicators of what others think of the agency's creative efforts.

Another way to evaluate creativity is for each agency under consideration to prepare and present a *creative pitch*. This is a formal proposal where the agency explains how it would handle a specific situation or problem. For instance, the agencies may be asked to design a new branding campaign. This process, often called a *shootout,* involves advertising agencies competing for a contract. The goal is to understand what kind of message each agency would create in the advertising campaign and how that message would be delivered. It takes considerable time and money for an advertising agency to prepare a creative pitch. Consequently, they are normally only requested after the prospective list has been narrowed down to two or three agencies.

The final selection criterion is the *services available*. Firms range from full-service agencies that provide every type of advertising and marketing activity to highly specialized boutiques offering only one or a very limited number of services. Many agencies subcontract specific services to boutique firms or media firms. It is not especially critical that an agency provide every option as long as the agency has subsidiaries or relationships with other firms that do offer them. For instance, many advertising agencies use other firms to develop broadcast ads and to buy media. These types of services require higher levels of expertise and capital equipment. Some agency executives want to concentrate on the creative aspect of advertising and let other firms perform the actual production function.

STOP AND THINK

Reread the opening vignette about Smucker's and then answer these questions:

1. What should be the primary objective for the Smucker's brand?

2. Should the company use an in-house or external agency? If an external agency is chosen, what types of criteria should be used to make the selection?

3. Imagine leading a focus group and asking the participants to say the first thing that comes to mind when you say the term *Smucker's.* What if the most common responses are "old people," "grandma and grandpa," or "old fashioned?" How can advertising address this issue?

4. Can you name any of Smucker's main competitors? How are they differentiated from Smucker's?

Overseeing an Advertising Program

The role of marketing managers in advertising is to oversee the advertising process, including the methods used to design various ads. The actual commercials or advertising pieces are prepared by in-house creatives, freelance creatives, or advertising agencies. Effective oversight of an advertising program consists of (1) reviewing the advertising design and (2) confirming media selection choices made by the agency and media planner.

Reviewing the Advertising Design

After the selection process, an in-house or advertising agency's creative needs a general idea of the nature of an upcoming campaign. This information is summarized in the **creative brief,** which is an outline of the major elements of an advertising campaign. Figure 7.3 displays the components of a standard creative brief.

The marketing manager works to make certain that the advertisements being developed match with the company's image and position in the marketplace as well as with the established advertising objectives. The advertisements are being created for specific media. Therefore, the marketing manager's task is to make certain that all the ingredients come together, including a match between the messages, media, and target audience. This requires constant and consistent communication between the advertising creative or agency and the client company.

Media Selection

Media selection represents a crucial component of advertising. The goal is to match the company's target market with the audience profile of the media that is selected. Research may be conducted to understand the media habits of the company's target. Once this information has been gathered, media choices are made. Typically, a *primary medium* is selected as well as logically connected to *secondary media.* The traditional list of media includes

- television,
- radio,
- magazines,
- newspapers,
- outdoor/billboards,
- direct mail, and
- the Yellow Pages.

- Objective of advertisement or advertising campaign
- Target audience
- Message theme that is to be conveyed
- Support for message theme
- Constraints that must be considered by the creative

Figure 7.3

Elements of a Creative Brief

The individuals who work together to make the picks include the company's representative (marketing manager), who works with the media buyer, media planner, creative, and advertising agency account executive. The choice must fit the company's budget, advertising objectives, and all other considerations.

Nontraditional Media

At the same time, the marketing team also considers nontraditional media (see Figure 7.4). Each year, more money is spent on nontraditional media. Expenditures on these forms continue to grow at a much more rapid rate than money spent on traditional media.[3]

Advertising on the Internet, while not totally new, is normally considered as a more nontraditional form. Ads may be placed on company or product Web sites, on sites linked with other companies, and on sites dedicated to news (cnn.com), entertainment (people.com), or sports (sportsillustrated.com). Advertising may also be found on social networking sites, such as MySpace. Finally, advertising is placed on Internet search engines, such as Yahoo! and Netscape.

Recently, Maxwell House, which normally used only print and broadcast ads for its coffee, broke with tradition. To reach a target market featuring the positioning strategy as a coffee for "optimistic, hard-working, early-rising people," a new campaign was developed by the Ogilvy & Mather advertising agency, as follows.

- Video games
- Cinema movies
- Subway tunnels
- In-flight magazines
- Parking lots, park benches
- Escalators
- Carry-home menus and bags
- Clothing
- Mall signs and kiosks

Figure 7.4

Examples of Nontraditional Media

- On the Wednesday before Thanksgiving, Maxwell House paid the toll for an estimated 100,000 drivers passing through toll booths. They were greeted with "Your toll is on the House." Each received a sample package of Maxwell House coffee, made with Arabica beans.
- On the same day, from 7 a.m. to 9 a.m., Maxwell House handed out free Metro cards, samples, and brochures at five New York City subway stations.
- A new Internet microsite (www.brewsomegood.com) was launched. The site permitted consumers to upload photos, post videos, and smile into a Web camera after receiving coupons from Maxwell House. They were encouraged to share uplifting stories.
- During the Christmas season, Maxwell House handed out more than 1 million cups of coffee to shoppers in 14 different cities.
- To promote and reinforce these nontraditional efforts, Maxwell House launched both print and television ads with the "Brew some good" tagline.

Such promotional efforts are being used more frequently by companies as marketing professionals begin to more fully understand the power of the Internet and nontraditional media. Figure 7.5 breaks down current spending patterns for various media. Notice that alternative media now account for 17.4% of total ad spending. Figure 7.6 displays spending on the some of the alternative media.

Today's marketing managers look for combinations of traditional and nontraditional media that will achieve the greatest impact. Once this has been accomplished, evaluating the results becomes the next task.

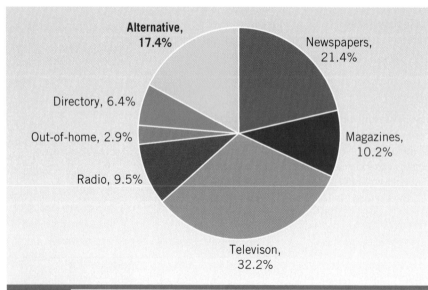

Figure 7.5 | Ad Spending by Media Category

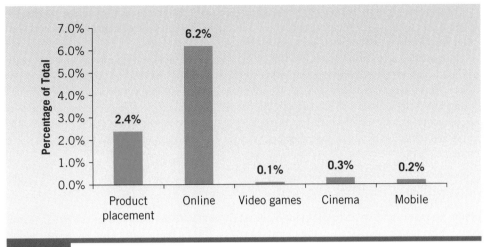

Figure 7.6 | Ad Spending for Primary Nontraditional Media

Assessing Advertising Effectiveness

The final component of advertising management, assessment, requires several tools, careful judgment, and a variety of inputs. Clear-cut, decisive results from an advertising and promotional campaign do not often or always become available, especially when longer-term goals such as brand loyalty and brand equity have been established. Typically, advertising success should be assessed on at least three levels, immediate results from an advertising campaign, analysis of annual programs, and progress toward long-term, strategic outcomes. Only after all three levels have been examined can the overall advertising program be fully evaluated in the proper context.

A typical advertising campaign lasts between 4 weeks and 3 months. Various methods may be used to schedule advertisements. In the first, a *continuous format,* advertising runs uniformly throughout the year. A *pulsating format* features advertisements throughout the year, with a spurt of additional advertising during major seasons. Many retail chains take this approach, with bursts during key seasons, such as Christmas, Easter, and others. A *discontinuous format* includes periods when there are no advertisements and others when advertisements are heavily used. Diet and exercise programs may place numerous ads during the New Year's resolution season and again at the start of summer, with no ads during off-seasons. The same may be true for resorts and other forms of entertainment in which there are on- and off-seasons. Each approach makes use of campaigns. The typical variables used to measure the success of an advertising campaign can be found in two realms: (1) attitudinal effects and (2) behavioral effects.

Attitudinal Effects

Attitudinal effects are typically measured using interviews or surveys by phone, via the Internet, through mail, in person, or through focus groups. The focus is on the cognitive and affective components of attitude. The most common evaluations include increases or decreases in:

- Recall of the advertisement or brand
- Recognition of the advertisement or brand
- Attitudes or feelings toward the brand
- Brand positioning
- Brand attitudes and level of loyalty, equity, and parity

The first two assess brand awareness. The next three examine degrees of liking and preference for a brand. Brand attitudes reveal how a brand is viewed and its standing compared with other brands in the marketplace.

Attitudes or changes in attitudes may or may not result in immediate sales. Instead, sales normally lag behind advertising. Individuals exposed to an advertising campaign may experience increases in brand awareness. The commercials might even heighten levels of brand equity. Still, sales do not typically occur immediately. Sometimes this is because the consumer is not in the market for the product. For example, when an advertising campaign features durable goods such as televisions or dishwashers, consumers see the messages but normally do not immediately buy the items.

Behavioral Effects

Many company leaders insist on identifiable and immediate results from an advertising campaign. Advertising agencies and their employees feel this increasing pressure, as do marketing managers and brand managers in companies. Some of the more standard behavior measures include increases or decreases in:

- Store traffic
- Inquiries by telephone, mail, or Internet
- Web site visits
- Direct marketing responses
- Redemption rates of sales promotions, including coupons, premiums, and entries to contests or sweepstakes
- Sales by units or total sales volume

These more tangible numbers represent a kind of "bottom line" regarding the effectiveness of an advertising campaign, which may not be a valid conclusion. Several factors may influence the results of an advertising campaign. These include political forces, social forces, economic forces, and technological forces. A recession can affect the sales of luxury goods and negate advertising efforts. An economic boom can spur sales of products even if no advertisements have been used. Political activities, social trends or changes, and technological innovations could lead to similar results. While some of these forces can be monitored and their impact on sales predicted, others occur randomly.

Competitive actions can also affect the effectiveness of an ad campaign. A competitor that runs a sale or another promotional offer may partially negate the impact of an advertising campaign. When a competitor offers a superior brand at a lower price, it becomes difficult or impossible to overcome this disadvantage with advertising. It is often necessary to spend about the same amount as the competition in order to keep up and maintain a market share. Indirect competitors also can influence the outcome. For instance, heavy advertising by a dine-in restaurant might affect the sales of a fast-food chain even though they are not direct competitors.

A variety of additional random events can affect sales and lead to misconceptions about the impact of an advertising campaign. For instance, an extremely cold spell in an area with a moderate climate may increase the demand for coats, gloves, and other winter clothing items. A movie star wearing a particular brand or style of clothing can create an immediate fad. On the reverse side, food poisoning at one restaurant can adversely affect the demand at all the chain's restaurants. Bad weather can also keep people home and out of stores. A celebrity endorser for a product being arrested or charged with a crime or inappropriate behavior may create a backlash against the products he endorses.

In general, the primary error associated with assessing advertising campaigns occurs when marketing professionals make the unrealistic assumption that there is a direct relationship between expenditures on advertising and subsequent sales revenues or market share. Seldom does it work that way. Increasing advertising expenditures by 25%, for instance, does not guarantee a 25% increase in sales. Advertising typically does not create such an immediate and direct impact on customer decision making. Only when advertising is tied to some other marketing promotion will quick results occur.

In measuring the impact of this ad campaign for Marion State Bank, what other factors may influence the results?

This makes assessing the effectiveness of a specific advertising campaign difficult. The marketing team should consider numerous factors before drawing any concrete conclusions. There are additional complications to consider.

Relationship Between Sales and Advertising Expenditures

To understand more specifically the relationship of sales to advertising expenditures, a marketing manager may find it helpful to use a typical response curve resulting from advertising, as shown in Figure 7.7, which displays sales over time. Notice that sales build slowly, rise rapidly, and then begin to decline. This curve illustrates several factors that explain the relationship between expenditures on advertising and sales, including

- lag effects,
- threshold effects,
- carryover effects, and
- decay effects.

The first part of the sales curve illustrates the *lag effect* of advertising. At some point, sales begin to increase at a more rapid pace; however, they lag behind advertising expenditures.

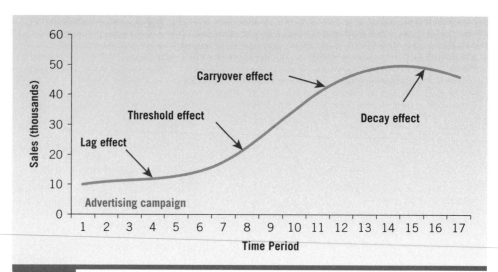

Figure 7.7   Advertising Expenditures and Sales

When sales catch up with expenditures, it demonstrates the *threshold effect*. Unfortunately, when this occurs is almost impossible to predict. As consumers become more aware of the product, or a particular brand, the desire to purchase it may increase. This results in initial purchases. When a positive consumer experience takes place, additional purchases are made. Also, word-of-mouth endorsements begin to produce additional sales.

When a company stops advertising or a campaign ends, the sales curve tends to continue to rise, but the growth rate begins to slow. This illustrates *carryover effects*. These occur due to the positive impact of the ad being remembered even though the campaign has ended.

Over time, when advertising expenditures have ended, sales will level off and eventually begin to decline. This is the *decay effect*. It occurs when the impact of the advertising has worn off or decayed.

The point at which each of these effects occurs is virtually impossible to predict. Advertisers know there will be a time lag before the impact of advertising takes effect. For most advertising campaigns, there will be a threshold effect point where sales begin to rise more rapidly. After the campaign ends, there will be a period during which sales will continue to increase but at a slower rate. As time continues, a decay effect will occur, resulting in declining sales. At that point, it is time to develop a new campaign.

The marketing team may be tempted to continue advertising, believing that, as a result, sales will continue to rise. This does not occur, however, because of *wear-out effects*. When a new ad or a new campaign is launched, it normally garners greater attention. People are more likely to notice the advertisement. The more they like the ad or ad campaign, the more attention they give to it. Over time, that interest wanes. New ads from other companies and maybe even from competitors appear and capture attention. Also, once an ad has been seen several times, the consumer knows what to expect. There is no longer a need to watch. Thus, even if the ad campaign continues, there will be a leveling-off of its impact and a decline in sales because the campaign (or commercial) is worn out and no longer effective. This is illustrated by the shape of the response curve in Figure 7.7. It may take longer to reach this point, but it will happen. That is why marketing teams continually design new ads or produce variations of current ads.

The task the marketing manager faces is estimating when the threshold effects for individual campaigns will take place. This helps the production department stay ready for the sales bump. Then, the manager will be interested in estimates of when the wear-out and decay effects will begin. The manager should contact the ad agency far enough in advance to make sure that a new ad campaign will be ready to go. The time periods for these changes cannot always be accurately predicted. The challenge is to run commercials long enough to allow the maximum benefit to occur but not so long that wear-out and decay effects arise.

STOP AND THINK

Consider all the Aflac Duck commercials that you have seen over the years and then answer the following questions:

1. How soon after the Duck commercials began running do you think it took to achieve the threshold effects?

2. Most advertisements for supplemental health insurance are serious, often focusing on emotions such as fear of financial ruin or pride in taking care of one's family. How would this influence lag effects and threshold effects for Aflac's advertising?

3. Estimate the time it takes for an updated Duck commercial to start to experience decay effects.

4. Will a time come when the Duck commercials go beyond decay effects and begin to experience wear-out effects?

5. What should Aflac do if the Duck commercials clearly no longer work?

Alternative Marketing Programs

In today's marketplace, traditional and nontraditional advertising programs may not be sufficient. Consequently, several new approaches for reaching potential customers have emerged. These include guerrilla marketing, lifestyle marketing, and buzz marketing. Savvy customers have become very efficient at tuning out many advertising messages, which makes these new programs attractive to marketing managers.

Guerrilla Marketing

Guerrilla marketing was first described by Jay Conrad Levinson as a method to obtain instant results with limited resources using tactics that rely on creativity, quality relationships with customers, and the willingness to try unusual approaches. Since its introduction, the program has been used by numerous companies. It is viewed as a creative, off-the-wall, unconventional method of reaching customers. Figure 7.8 provides a list of rules for effective guerrilla marketing campaigns.

Effective guerrilla marketing campaigns begin with employees thinking and talking about unique ways to reach the target consumers. Including target consumers in *brainstorming sessions* increases the probability that a distinctive and attractive campaign can be developed.

The approach, no matter how innovative, must be *relevant to the target audience*. In other words, it must relate to potential consumers in a personal way. For example, the release of the film *Sex and the City* featured numerous guerrilla marketing tie-in events for women, sponsored by spas, fashionable-clothing stores, nightclubs, and women's health clinics. The typical theme was "Women's Night Out."

Guerrilla marketing is designed to *reinforce the brand's image*. A cosmetics event should be designed to focus on the corresponding image, whether it is glamor, style, sexiness, or reducing the effects of aging. Cosmetics for women under the age of 30 feature a different image than those for women over 60 years old.

Planning is essential. A poorly designed program can result in negative publicity. Therefore, the marketing team carefully thinks through every detail. They chart every contact point between the company and its products and customers. Research will be conducted to fully understand the target audience and reach them with the correct message.

Guerrilla marketing emphasizes *quality* rather than *quantity*. It is not concerned with how many people hear or see the guerrilla marketing campaign but the quality of people who see it. If a million people are exposed to a guerrilla marketing effort but only 50,000 are target

- Brainstorm for ideas.
- Make it relevant to the target audience.
- Make it reinforce the brand's image.
- Plan the campaign thoroughly.
- Go for quality, not quantity.
- Use good timing.
- Be sure it is legal and ethical.

Figure 7.8

Rules for Effective Guerrilla Marketing Campaigns

The movie *Sex and the City* generated a number of guerrilla marketing campaigns by various companies using the primary theme "Women's Night Out."

customers, then the campaign will not be nearly as cost-effective as a campaign that reaches only 75,000 people of which 40,000 are target consumers.

Good timing means the program should be launched at a time when the target audience is receptive to the message. When the timing is correct, the message can influence a purchase decision or change attitudes toward the brand. The program must be timed to synchronize with the other marketing efforts.

Finally, a guerrilla campaign must be *legal* and *ethical.* Failing to do so has resulted in jail time for some of the promoters and created difficult situations for their companies. Paramount realized this too late after its guerrilla campaign for the motion picture *Mission Impossible III* had been launched. The program was designed to have *Los Angeles Times* newspaper racks blare out the theme song for the motion picture when it opened. Some people mistook the device for bombs, which caused the evacuation of a nearby medical center and the destruction of several newspaper racks by the Los Angeles police's bomb squad.[4]

Conversely, a well-designed guerrilla marketing program can create a great deal of publicity and excitement. To promote the motion picture *Blades of Glory,* Paramount/DreamWorks supplemented advertising with a guerrilla marketing campaign. The advertising agency hired by the studio sent out 16 leotard-clad skating couples to bars, quads, and other hangouts near 50 universities and colleges. The couples waited until individuals approached them and asked them about their sparkly spandex unitards. They then proceeded to show off skating moves, asking the audience to rate them. The campaign lasted 1 month and involved visiting 1,700 locations. The couples distributed 200,000 headshots of the movie characters, 150,000 fliers, and 100,000 postcards. It is estimated that nearly 9 million people met one of the skating imposters; saw one of the fliers, headshots, or postcards; or received information about the movie and/or imposters from a friend. The movie captured the highest box office revenues for several weeks following the premier.

Guerrilla marketing can be used in the business-to-business and channel sectors. When Milliken faced the challenge of attracting visitors to a trade show booth, it turned to guerrilla marketing. Milliken manufactures various chemicals and textiles. The company's marketing team identified 30 highly qualified prospects from a trade show attendees list. Milliken reps developed circular self-adhesive wallpaper swatches and convinced bellhops to let them place the swatches on the prospects' hotel room televisions. The swatch carried the message "To see something revolutionary, don't look here. Go to Booth No. 2616." The outcome was that 20 of the 30 prospects visited the booth. This compared with only a 10% return using other methods of attracting attendees to the booth.[5]

Guerrilla marketing requires entry-level employees and their supervisors to be enthusiastic and willing to think about creative approaches. The program encourages participation of people of all ranks, which can lead to innovative new ideas about how to reach a target audience.

Lifestyle Marketing

Closely related to the concept of guerrilla marketing is lifestyle marketing. **Lifestyle marketing** involves tapping into a target audience's core lifestyle, music, culture, and fashion. It involves pinpointing the passions and interests of the target market and then developing marketing methods to reach them through these venues. Lifestyle marketing includes engaging with consumers at places such as farmer's markets, bluegrass festivals, citywide garage sales, flea markets, craft shows, stock car races, and other places where there are large concentrations of potential customers. A lifestyle marketing program aligns with the company's advertising and in-store messages.

A | X Armani Exchange is a 94-unit retail outlet that sells Giorgio Armani merchandise at lower prices. The primary target market is the 18- to 24-year-old consumer, which includes

What are the key
ingredients of a
successful lifestyle
marketing campaign?

both professional and fashion-conscious students. To reach these target markets, A|X Armani Exchange used lifestyle marketing to supplement a traditional advertising program. One lifestyle marketing effort focused on the young, urban, and hip 18- to 24-year-old by sponsoring a series of events at the grassroots level, including music festivals and fashion shows in college towns throughout California, Texas, and Florida. The company sponsored the Ultra Music Festival in Miami, which included dance and club music events. In fact, A|X Armani sponsors so many music and dance events that the company employs its own DJs to travel from club to club.

Many types of companies can take advantage of event marketing. For example, firms vending fertilizers and pesticides can establish lifestyle marketing events at county and state fairs. Lifestyle marketing's key goal is to identify a venue where the target market goes for relaxation, excitement, socialization, or enjoyment. An opera or symphonic performance creates a venue for music lovers. Those attending the performance may be reached with marketing materials unique to their interests and passions.

Buzz Marketing

Buzz marketing is also known as *word-of-mouth marketing*. It is an approach that involves consumers passing along information about a product and is one of the fastest-growing areas in alternative-media marketing. The annual estimated expenditures of all companies that use buzz marketing now exceed $1 billion. Buzz, or word of mouth, can be generated by

- consumers who truly like a brand and tell others;
- consumers who like a brand and are sponsored by a company to tell others; and
- company or agency employees posing as customers of the company, telling others about the brand.

The first situation is the most ideal. A recommendation by another person who *likes the brand* carries a higher level of credibility than does an advertisement. It is also more powerful than the words of a paid spokesperson or endorser.

When and where does
buzz marketing work
the best?

Many companies *sponsor individuals* as agents or advocates to introduce new products. *Brand ambassadors* or *customer evangelists* are typically individuals who like the products that they sponsor. They are often offered incentives and rewards in exchange for advocacy. Selection of ambassadors is based on devotion to the brand. Once recruited, these individuals deliver messages to social circles, families, friends, reference groups, and work associates. They often promote the brand through blogs or on social networks such as MySpace.

The final group of advocates, *employees posing as customers*, has been used by some companies. Doing so is risky. According to the Word of Mouth Marketing Association, it is dishonest and unethical, unless the person is upfront and clearly identifies himself as being with the company. The Word of Mouth Marketing Association provides guidelines for companies that want to generate word-of-mouth communications through employees, agency employees, or even sponsors or agents. The association encourages:

- *Honesty of relationship:* Be honest about the relationship between consumers, advocates, and marketers.
- *Honesty of opinion:* Be honest in presenting opinions about the brand, both good and bad.
- *Honesty of identity:* Identify honestly who you are.[6]

Buzz marketing works for two primary reasons. First, people trust someone else's opinion more than paid advertising. Second, people like to give their opinions. They like to share their thoughts because as human beings there is an innate desire for social interaction and a concern for the welfare of others. Also, a person's ego and sense of self-worth may be elevated by sharing an opinion with others. This is especially true when a word-of-mouth recommendation leads to a friend, peer, or relative being satisfied with the product.

Buzz moves through many channels of communication, including the media, the Internet, personal conversations, discussions at parties and in social gatherings, and even snail mail. Any time a marketing team can create positive buzz about a product or marketing program, the chances for success increase.

An alternative form of buzz marketing that has become popular and will be discussed later in this textbook is online social networks. Facebook and MySpace are the largest, but numerous smaller niche sites have risen. Companies including Calvin Klein, Adidas, Victoria's Secret, and Ralph Lauren, not only advertise on these sites but also create company-sponsored profile pages to spread word about the various brands.

One of the fastest-growing areas of online social networking is Twitter, which is a free social networking and microblogging service that allows its members to send and read other user's messages, more commonly known at *tweets*. Users can post messages on their profile pages that will be delivered to every user in their friend list.

Direct Marketing

Direct marketing occurs when a company makes direct contact with customers without the use of a middleman. Direct marketing remains a popular method for acquiring new customers. It also helps to retain current customers. According to the Direct Marketing Association, about 60% of a typical direct marketing budget is used for prospecting for new customers while the other 40% will be used to retain current customers.[7]

Figure 7.9 identifies the various forms of direct marketing and the percentages of companies that use it for prospecting for new customers. Direct mail continues to be the most common method. Direct response TV and direct response radio are the least used. In any case, many companies employ multiple forms of direct marketing to increase response rates.

Acquiring customers through direct marketing requires careful planning. Figure 7.10 identifies eight tips for developing an effective direct marketing campaign. Even if a direct marketing agency is hired to conduct the campaign, the marketing manager should be familiar with how a direct marketing campaign is put together and what it takes to make the program successful.

The key to an efficient direct marketing campaign is a *good-prospect list* based on a clear profile of the company's target audience for the product or products being sold. The marketing team should understand the *target audience* of the product being promoted. Demographic, psychographic, and behavioral information are all critical.

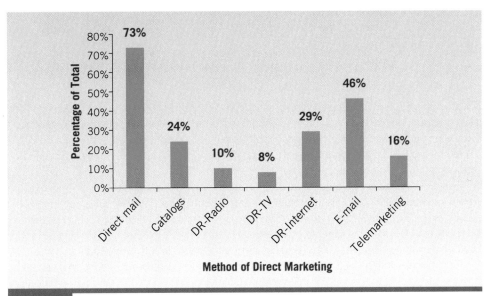

Figure 7.9   Methods of Direct Marketing Used to Acquire New Customers

> - Develop a good-prospect list.
> - Create a target customer profile.
> - Personalize direct marketing materials.
> - Design attention-getting materials.
> - Make clear promises to customers.
> - Use repetition and remain consistent.
> - View it as an investment, not expense.
> - Track results.

Figure 7.10

Tips for Effective Direct Marketing Campaigns

Direct marketing messages that are *personalized* achieve the highest response rates. The marketing piece should also *capture the person's attention*. Anything that looks like junk will be thrown away. The message should provide a *clear customer promise*. Customers should be able to see and understand the advantages and benefits of the offer.

Some marketers believe that prospects must see something 3 times before they will recognize it. They must see a message 7 times before they can tie the customer promise to the product and brand being sold. They normally encounter a message 27 times before they are willing to consider making a purchase. While these numbers are probably not exact, the point is that *repetition and consistency* are important in converting prospects to customers.[8]

The marketing team views the program as an *investment rather than an expense*. A customer who purchases once and has a satisfactory experience is likely to return. This makes the initial expenditures allocated to attracting the customer an investment.

The marketing team *tracks results* to ensure that the program has been both efficient and effective. Through the use of special phone numbers, e-mail addresses, and URL Web links, it is easy to trace how many individuals responded and how they responded. This information becomes invaluable as future direct marketing campaigns are developed. A direct marketing program should be meshed with the company's overall marketing communications program.

Direct Mail

As noted, mail remains the most common form of direct marketing. It may be sent to both individual consumers and business-to-business customers. Direct mail can target the individuals or businesses that are most likely to respond. Tracking results using direct mail is relatively simple.

In developing a direct mail piece, one key ingredient is a clear and concise method of response. "Stop in at one of our convenient locations" is not an appropriate cue. Instead, an application, tear-off coupon, postage-paid return-mail piece, Web site address, or telephone number should be provided. Ease of response is critical.[9]

Direct mail makes it possible for marketing managers to test various versions and offers. This includes the type of offer, copy in the letter, graphics used, color, and size of the mail packet. Direct mail can be used to supplement e-mail, and vice versa. Direct mail may also be used to promote a firm's Web site. Direct mail opens the line of communication between a company and a customer. A study by Pitney Bowes revealed that direct mail was an effective tool for promoting the company's Web site, with 43% of its annual sales prompted by direct mail offers.[10]

Not all direct mailings are successful. A marketing manager should be aware that extraneous events can alter the response rate. What appears to be a successful campaign or unsuccessful campaign may have little to do with the direct offer itself but more with some other event, such as an economic downturn or the release of a competitor product that has advantages over what the company is offering.

Catalogs

Many consumers enjoy catalog shopping. They can view items at their leisure. Catalogs provide a low-pressure direct marketing method that allows people time to consider goods and prices. They can place orders when they want. Catalogs can be kept and shared. A recent study conducted by the U.S. Postal Service revealed that while consumers tend to purchase online, they still want a catalog to be mailed to them.[11]

The most significant change in the area of catalog marketing is the use of a targeted database for mailing catalogs. This approach requires an enhanced database. Many catalog companies, such as L.L. Bean, Spiegel, and JCPenney, also create smaller specialty catalogs that are geared to specific market segments. The catalogs have a lower cost and produce a higher yield, because they target segments of individuals who are the most likely to respond.

Catalogs are essential selling tools for many business-to-business marketing programs. The benefits are similar to those for consumers. Catalogs can be kept, filed, and passed along to other members of the organization. Often, they provide an easier reference to use than does the online catalog. Ordering takes place by phone, online, or through a mail-in form.

E-mail

E-mail has become a common method of direct marketing for customer acquisition. The primary advantage is cost. Sending 10,000 e-mails costs virtually no more than sending 100 e-mails. E-mail makes it possible to target specific customers, personalize information and offers, and precisely measure the impact.

When using e-mail, it is important to begin with a quality prospect list. The best prospect lists are those built from the company's own Web site and database. The trap to avoid is mass e-mailing, believing the cost differential is small. Mass e-mails can damage a brand and the company's image. The marketing team prunes the prospect list down to potential customers with the same demographic, psychographic, and behavioral profiles. This increases response rates without spamming.

A key advantage of e-mail is the ability to precisely measure the impact. Figure 7.11 identifies the various metrics that can be used.[12]

The e-mail should clearly spell out how to respond in order to be successful. E-mail may direct the potential buyer to a Web site or a phone number or allow for a direct e-mail response.

- Delivery rate
- Opened rate
- Read rate
- Unsubscribe rate
- Forward rate
- Click-through rate
- Goal conversion rate
- Return rate

Figure 7.11

Methods of Measuring E-mail Direct Marketing Results

Internet

Numerous companies guide prospective consumers to the Internet as the place to respond to direct marketing offers. Many companies, including Amazon.com and Target, have highly successful direct marketing programs on the Internet.

In addition to a company's main Web site, microsites, which are specialized Web sites, can be designed by the marketing team for specific purposes, such as to highlight a single product, event, or offer. Oftentimes, microsites are used because of their many potential advantages (see Figure 7.12).

Microsites are *efficient* because they are relatively simple to construct and inexpensive. Material can be borrowed from the company's regular Web site, and links to components of the company's normal Web site can be included. The marketing team can design a direct marketing program promoting a specific product with a specific promotional offer, at a low *cost*.

Microsites make *tracking* simpler. By *customizing* each URL to match specific marketing programs, it is easy to review the results. It is also much easier to *control* what customers see. This means customers do not have to wade through other pages of a Web site looking for a specific direct marketing offer.

CircuitAlert.com launched a new hand tool, the Circuit Alert wire stripper, with a microsite. Every advertisement, public relations effort, and marketing material directed individuals to the site to see a video demonstration of the tool. The target audience of the marketing campaign was electrical contractors and distributors. The marketing effort resulted in 25,000 visitors to the microsite. Almost 45% of them watched the 60-second video.[13] The microsite created a much higher response rate than any other response mechanism used by CircuitAlert.com.

Volkswagen created a microsite featuring the new model of the Golf GT in virtual 3D. Consumers could go online and choose their own specifications for the car. The site was promoted through both direct mail and e-mail. It targeted the individuals who were already in the Volkswagen database.[14]

- Efficiency
- Tracking
- Customized URLs
- Control
- Cost

Figure 7.12

Advantages of Using Microsites

Telephone

The rise of the Internet and e-mail has reduced the use of the telephone for direct marketing; however, it has not been completely eliminated. Even the National Do Not Call Registry did little to diminish the use of telemarketing. While some consumers find it annoying, telemarketing remains a successful technique for customer acquisition. Outbound telemarketing continues to be a primary component of many business-to-business customer acquisition programs.

Cold calls in either consumer markets or business-to-business markets are not likely to be successful. They tend to create more ill will than results. Therefore, the marketing team should conduct a thorough marketing research study to locate prospects before starting a calling program.

Why is telemarketing more successful in the business-to-business sector than in consumer markets?

Direct marketing calls should be relevant and timely. Using database information, each call should be customized for the individual recipient. While this method of telemarketing is more expensive, it yields better results. The caller should take the time to gather information about the prospect in advance, especially in the business-to-business sector. In many situations, a personal telephone call to the buyer is an effective medium that can be used to solidify a relationship with the customer.

Mass Media

The mass media that are used in direct response marketing include television, radio, magazines, and newspapers. Television ads can be targeted to specific audiences through cable channels or satellite television channels. Infomercials may also be designed to entice consumers to make a response. Radio does not have the reach of television, but it can be targeted by the type of station format. Radio direct marketing ads must repeat the response telephone number or Web site URL frequently so that consumers can remember it. Consumers normally do not have a pencil handy to write down information. Consequently, the address or telephone number should be something easy to remember, such as www.greenlawn.net. Print media can also be targeted to specific market segments. Print normally offers the opportunity to provide more information as well as multiple types of response mechanisms, such as a mail-in card, a telephone number, or a Web address.[15]

In summary, the goals of guerrilla marketing, lifestyle marketing, buzz marketing, and direct marketing are to reach customers in new and interesting ways, to create personal or personalized interactions, and to build relationships with them over time. When combined with more traditional advertising methods, the company stands a better chance of finding and acquiring new customers.

Financial Analysis of Direct Marketing Programs

Most direct marketing programs have the advantage of allowing the marketing manager to perform a financial analysis. This is possible because of the use of code numbers and microsites. It is relatively easy to track individuals who made a purchase or inquiry from a direct marketing campaign.

Item		Total
Printing costs ($)		151,200
Total mailed	240,000	
Database costs (per thousand) ($)	35.00	8,400
Mailing costs ($)	0.65 each	156,000
Number of responses	5,231	
Response rate (%)	2.18	
Revenue ($)		591,835
Cost of goods sold ($)	52%	307,754
Shipping ($/order)	6.24	32,641
Contribution margin ($)		−64,160

Table 7.2 Financial Analysis of a Direct Mail Campaign

Table 7.2 provides the analysis from a direct mail campaign. A total of 240,000 pieces were mailed to a highly targeted list through a commercial database firm. The cost of printing the materials was $151,200, the cost of the commercial database service was $35.00 per thousand names, and the mailing cost was 65 cents each. The commercial database company selected individuals who had recently made direct mail purchases, which resulted in a higher response rate. Typical response rates for direct mail are under 1%. The response rate for this mailing was 2.18%. The revenue generated from the direct mail campaign was $591,835. When printing costs, database charges, mailing costs, shipping costs, and cost of goods sold were subtracted, the company's loss was $64,160 on the campaign.

Was the campaign a failure? Likely not, but it depends on the makeup of the 5,231 individuals who responded and the objective of the direct mail campaign. If the direct mail offer was sent to prospects and all 5,231 are new customers, it was an overwhelming success because the firm now has 5,231 new customers. Many will purchase again if they are satisfied with the products they received. If all the responses came from current customers, then the only positive benefit may be the extra half million in revenue. Even in the latter situation, the campaign may be considered successful if those who responded were borderline customers or individuals who had not purchased recently.

When analyzing a direct marketing campaign, the manager first looks at the objective and then the contribution margin. In most cases, companies lose money on direct marketing programs. The programs are justified in other ways, as has already been suggested.

Analyzing the other forms of direct marketing would be similar to analysis of direct mail. Total costs are calculated and subtracted from total revenue to obtain a contribution margin. Then, the manager examines the profile and future expenditures of the individuals (or companies) who responded.

Implications for Entry-Level Employees

Most of the interactions that take place in guerrilla marketing, lifestyle marketing, and buzz marketing programs are between customers and entry-level employees along with supervisors. Consequently, employee training regarding effective and positive ways to meet and greet potential customers in these venues is crucial. Even before the training, the recruiting and selection process should identify potential employees who enjoy unusual events and face-to-face contact with the public. Supervisors carefully monitor events to make sure those involved have positive interactions with company employees.

YOURCAREER

Lee McGuire has an undergraduate degree in marketing and an MBA. She now serves as the marketing director at Skyjacker Suspensions. Her responsibilities include leading the part of the marketing department that handles

national television, print, radio, online, and event marketing. Managing the creative team, developing ad campaigns and promotions, and event planning are the major functions Lee performs. Along with all contract negotiations for ad buys, event sponsorships, and driver sponsorships, she oversees a line of corporate apparel and promotional items.

Lee uses many of the skills and much of the knowledge she acquired in college. She notes, "My advertising classes played a huge role in how I manage the creative process here. The consumer behavior course was essential in understanding our customers and what their motivations to buy are. Skyjacker sells strictly business to business but spends a large share of ad dollars on consumer marketing. Understanding the consumer side of the business is critical when it comes to where to place ads and the message you are using to reach those consumers. With an ad budget, you only have so much reach, and a huge role I play is determining where those ad dollars are spent. Advertising buys are very expensive, so sharp negotiating skills are a must so that I ensure we get the most bang for our buck. Another class that had real-world applications was marketing research because in the complex automotive aftermarket I had a lot to learn about the male 18–34 demographic and methods. What I was taught in marketing research applied to learning about this important demographic. My position at Skyjacker is a wonderful learning experience, and the management role that I have assumed was helped along by principles I learned in marketing management."

McGuire's college education provided a solid foundation to start her position at Skyjacker. There were still things to learn. When asked what may have prepared her better, she replied, "Learning more in-depth about the creative process and how to actually create ads in sophisticated software would have been a huge plus and would have reduced the learning curve for terminology and dealing with magazine companies. A large part of the principles taught in class focused on the sales aspect of marketing, and in my position the other aspect of marketing is used much more."

Lee's BBA and then MBA indicate her continuing desire to attain new knowledge and use that knowledge to be an asset to Skyjacker. She also pursues other avenues to learn more about the ever-changing and complex world of marketing in order to ensure that Skyjacker's marketing stays on the cutting edge.

Chapter Summary

Advertising management includes five major tasks. First, advertising objectives must be established. The most common objectives are to create brand and product awareness, build a brand's image, provide information, persuade consumers to make purchases, support other marketing efforts, and encourage action.

The second task in advertising management is to create an advertising budget. The methods include percentage of sales approach, meeting the competition, making an arbitrary allocation, or the objective and task technique.

Making a choice between an in-house advertising program and using one or more advertising agencies is the third task of advertising management. Outside agencies are selected based on criteria including the agency's size, relevant experience, potential conflicts of interest, creative abilities, and services offered.

Overseeing the advertising program is the fourth advertising management activity. The two primary tasks are reviewing the advertising design and selecting from a wide variety of traditional and nontraditional media. The marketing manager works closely with the advertising agency's executive to ensure that the advertisements speak with a clear voice.

The final element of advertising management is assessing the impact of a campaign or program. Three levels of analysis include immediate results, annual results, and progress toward long-term, strategic outcomes.

Beyond traditional advertising, various programs may be added to help attract and acquire new customers. Guerrilla marketing emphasizes instant results with limited resources using tactics that rely on creativity, quality relationships with customers, and the willingness to try unusual approaches. Lifestyle marketing focuses on the target audience's core forms of entertainment and activity, including music, culture, and fashion. Buzz marketing, or word-of-mouth marketing, seeks to enhance the potency of personal endorsements of products. Direct marketing programs are designed to make contacts and create lines of communication between the selling company and individual customers.

Response rates of direct marketing campaigns can be tracked. This allows marketing managers to assess the financial impact of each direct marketing campaign. In addition to examining the contribution margin, other factors should be considered, including the objective of the campaign and the composition of those who responded.

Entry-level employees and first-line supervisors play major roles in completing the tasks of advertising managers. The employees who make contact with the public must be aware of any special offers or advertising features for the campaign to succeed. The supervisors who hire, train, and reward entry-level workers should themselves be rewarded for facilitating the movement from being attracted by an advertising message to making the actual purchase. The same holds true for the nontraditional programs. The people on the "front lines" will make or break any guerrilla marketing, lifestyle marketing, buzz marketing, or direct marketing program. High-quality customer service remains the key to acquiring new customers using these methods.

Chapter Terms

Advertising management (p. 167)
Arbitrary allocation (p. 167)
Buzz marketing (or word of mouth) (p. 179)
Creative brief (p. 171)
Guerrilla marketing (p. 177)

Lifestyle marketing (p. 178)
Meet the competition (p. 167)
Objective and task (p. 167)
Percentage of sales (p. 167)

Review Questions

1. Define advertising management.
2. What are the five main tasks associated with advertising management?
3. Name the most common objectives associated with advertising programs.
4. Name and briefly describe the four methods used to create advertising budgets.

5. What is the first issue to consider when choosing an advertising agency?

6. What are the steps involved in selecting an advertising agency?

7. What is a creative brief?

8. Name the three levels of assessment of advertising effectiveness.

9. Describe lag effects, threshold effects, carryover effects, and decay effects as they relate to advertising campaigns.

10. What is guerrilla marketing?

11. What is lifestyle marketing?

12. What is buzz marketing?

13. Define direct marketing.

14. What venues may be used to reach customers in direct marketing programs?

15. Explain how a direct marketing campaign should be evaluated.

CUSTOMER CORNER

GEICO insurance has been available for several decades. In the past few years, the company has drawn considerable attention for its various forms of advertising and advertising campaigns. Three of the most well known are the "Cave Man" series, the "Celebrity" series, and the GEICO "Gecko." The Cave Man features phony advertising suggesting that using GEICO is so simple that even a caveman can figure it out. The cavemen who see the ads are modern, miffed, and mortified. The ads became so popular that at one point a television series spun off from the ads. Celebrities are used as stand-in spokespersons for real GEICO customers. Little Richard, Peter Frampton, James Lipton, Michael Winslow, and Gladys Knight's Pips have all spoken on behalf of real people getting "Real

Service, Real Savings." The Gecko, speaking with an Australian accent, provides an animated spokesperson for the firm. The ads have created a great deal of buzz and notoriety in the advertising world.

1. Do you think having the three vastly different forms of advertising is confusing to customers or targeted to different segments?

2. What target markets is each form of advertising designed to reach?

3. Should advertising results be tracked through the three different forms or aggregated into overall results? What kinds of complications might arise when trying to assess the success of each form?

Discussion and Critical Thinking Questions

1. Many advertising taglines are very basic and general statements. For each of the following, identify the primary advertising objective. Examine Figure 7.7. Where would you place the impact of the tagline on the sales response curve? Also consider the "wear-out effect."

   - Verizon—"Can you hear me now?"
   - De Beers—"A diamond is forever."
   - BMW—"The ultimate driving machine."
   - Nike—"Just do it."
   - Hallmark—"When you care enough to send the very best."
   - GoDaddy—"The Web is your domain."

2. You have just been hired by the shrimping industry to create advertisements for shrimp as a food choice. The industry leaders point out the success of the milk ("Got Milk?"), beef ("It's what's for dinner"), and Florida oranges ("Deliciously sweet. Naturally juicy") campaigns. Using the selection criteria listed in Figure 7.2, describe the type of advertising agency that might win the account.

3. Most advertising agencies now blend traditional and nontraditional media when creating advertising campaigns. For each of the products listed, identify what you believe would be the top three traditional media to use and the top three nontraditional media to

employ in the item's next advertising campaign. Justify your choices.

- High-definition television
- Medical spa
- New breakfast food
- National fast-food restaurant
- Singles introductions—statewide
- Rock group's upcoming concert tour

4. Think about the advertisements that have recently been shown for the following companies. Make a list of the top one or two attitude effects the commercial was designed to create and the top one or two behaviors the ad was designed to incite.

- Miller Lite
- Allstate Insurance
- Tide to Go Instant Stain Remover
- SUBWAY Sandwich Shop
- Hanes Underwear for Men

5. Describe a guerrilla marketing, lifestyle marketing, or buzz marketing program that you believe would suit the needs of the following products or companies.

- New stomach antacid
- Women's fitness workout gym
- New product carrying Mountain Dew brand
- Hannah Montana movie
- Gasoline additive to increase miles per gallon

6. Look up the HeadBlade company online (headblade.com). Explain the forms of direct marketing that this company employs. Would it be possible to expand the marketing program by adding new direct marketing methods? If so, which ones, and how would they work?

7. Use the following data to calculate the contribution margin for a direct e-mail campaign that was sent to a firm's customers who had purchased a product within the previous 3 months. Evaluate the campaign.

- Total e-mails sent—850,000
- Database costs per e-mail—1.2 cents
- E-mail ad design cost—$5,000
- Cost of microsite—$18,000
- Number of responses—6,205
- Revenue—$416,728
- Cost of goods sold—72%
- Processing costs per order—$6.52

8. BMG Music has decided to run a direct TV campaign on a special anniversary album that sells for $35.00 plus $7.00 for shipping and handling. Using the data provided, calculate the contribution margin of the campaign. Evaluate the campaign.

- TV ad design—$72,000
- TV ad time—$600,000
- Number of responses—72,651
- Commercial call center to handle incoming calls—$2.35 per order
- Revenue per response (including the shipping and handling)—$42.00
- Cost of goods sold—55%
- Process shipping and handling costs per order—$7.53

Chapter 7 Case

Wild West Rodeo

Ashley Bowers grew up on a horse ranch. She loved the rodeo since childhood. In the past year, she obtained her dream job as marketing director for the Wild West Rodeo circuit. The circuit is held in the Southwest and West. Some of the major cities that hold Wild West Rodeos include Lubbock and Amarillo, Texas; Albuquerque and Taos, New Mexico; Phoenix and Flagstaff, Arizona; San Diego and Los Angeles, California; and Reno and Las Vegas, Nevada.

Each rodeo contains the main events, steer roping, team roping, tie-down roping, barrel racing, bull riding, bareback riding, and saddle bronc riding. Cowboys pay entry fees to participate in events either by themselves or through sponsors. Winners receive cash prizes. Audience members are eligible for drawings and other prizes. Beyond being entertained by the events themselves, rodeo clowns and country music performers help to enliven the events.

Ashley is acutely aware of the opportunities and challenges present. On the plus side, the people who attend events are extremely loyal. Rodeo attendance and participation constitute an early and ongoing form of social networking. Many parents take their children to the rodeo, using it as a gateway to earlier times when life was less complicated and families went to events together. Surprisingly, the Internet has created new opportunities. Participants can film spectacular rides and spectacular tumbles and post them on MySpace and other places.

Ashley Bowers had her dream job as marketing director for the Wild West Rodeo circuit.

Lines of communication between rodeo devotees remain open year-round. Sponsors continue to be loyal, as many products such as cowboy boots, belts, and hats have highly concentrated target audiences at the events.

The challenges begin with a declining farm and ranch population. Many in the rodeo community are growing older, with fewer potential new enthusiasts to take their places. This problem extends not only to people in the grandstand, the customers, but also to the number of cowboys wishing to participate.

Further, the variety of ways to be entertained continues to grow, just as the amount of free time to enjoy them has diminished. The forms of rodeo have also changed. Besides the standard types of outdoor events, some are held indoors. Other entertainment venues offer similar experiences, such as the Dixie Stampede in Branson, which threatens to expand into Wild West's territories.

Rodeo events have also received some negative press. Most of it takes the form of complaints by the People for the Ethical Treatment of Animals (PETA), who maintain that rodeo is cruel to horses and cattle. There have been minor protests at some of the venues.

Another challenge is the cost of operating the circuit. Fuel prices have risen, and minimum wages continue to increase. The additional costs associated with feeding the animals and tending to medical needs also have gone up.

Ashley believed her main tasks would be to identify potential new customers who might attend a rodeo for the first time while keeping the long-time, loyal attendees. She had been encouraged to find ways to add some "sparkle" to the events, such as through fireworks and laser light shows at the end of the meets. Others thought it would help to find ways to turn young children into more than just spectators by letting them get closer to the cowboys and the animals. Ashley worried that anything that seemed like a "gimmick" might drive away rodeo traditionalists.

Ashley decided to work in two areas. The first was to design an advertising campaign for the upcoming year. The second was to develop a marketing program and advertising that would be measured over time, with the key metric that would measure success being the growth in attendance. Ashley knew it wouldn't be easy but relished the chance to help the sport and lifestyle she loved.

1. Should Ashley use an in-house or external advertising agency? Why?

2. If Ashley chooses an external advertising agency, what selection criteria would be most important?

3. What attitude and behavioral effects should be the criteria for success in the next year's campaign?

4. Suppose Ashley wants to run ads on the local television stations, local radio stations, and local newspapers before entering a city for a rodeo. Describe the television and radio ads that Ashley should use. Design the newspaper ad.

5. Can you think of ways to incorporate guerrilla marketing, lifestyle marketing, buzz marketing, or direct marketing into the Wild West tour without upsetting the most traditional and loyal customers?

What challenges did Ashley Bowers face in marketing the Wild West Rodeo circuit?

Go to **www.sagepub.com/clow** for additional exercises and study resources. Select **Chapter 7, Advertising, Alternative and Direct Marketing** for chapter-specific activities.

Although Kraft is synonymous with cheese, the company carries a variety of well-known brands.

chapter 8
Sales Promotions

Kraft: Eat and Live Better

Numerous multinational corporate giants operate in today's global marketplace. Many have essentially the same story: An entrepreneurial individual starts a business with one product and a dream. Over time, the dream becomes reality. In the world of cheese, one such entrepreneur was J.L. Kraft, who sold his first product in 1903 from a horse-drawn carriage. By 1914, Kraft had opened a cheese production facility in Chicago. In 1928, the company acquired the Phoenix Cheese Company and later introduced a new brand, Philadelphia Cream Cheese. Another product, Kraft Macaroni and Cheese, was introduced in 1937. In 1989, Kraft and General Foods merged to become Kraft General Foods. The name has now evolved to Kraft Foods, Inc.

Over the years, Kraft acquired and developed a variety of powerful brands.

The list includes Oscar Mayer, Planters, Oreo, Nabisco, Maxwell House, Jell-O, Tang, Crystal Light, Ritz, Grey Poupon, Chips Ahoy!, Milka Chocolates, and LU Biscuits, among others. The company is headquartered in Northfield, Illinois. Kraft operates in 70 countries and sells products in over 150 nations. Profit centers are located in North America, in the European Union, and in developing markets.

Even with such a massive international operation, Kraft relies on a variety of promotional tactics aimed at individual consumers. These include the use of coupons of many varieties, price-off deals, bonus packs, and cross-ruff offers. The competitive nature of the food industry makes it necessary to continually compete in all categories, from simple processed cheese (Velveeta) to entire lines of health and wellness brands (Sensible Solutions and Golden Harvest).

Kraft deals with a variety of distribution systems. Each country has its own method of food distribution. Where many sales in the United States are made in mass merchandise stores such as Target and Wal-Mart along with larger grocery wholesale and retail chains, other systems involve mostly small, independent retailers. There are also legal complications in international operations. In 2008, the company was forced to divest some of its trademarks in Spain and Hungary to meet regulatory requirements in those nations.

The corporate leaders at Kraft emphasize the importance of being good global citizens. The company's statement of corporate responsibility identifies product quality and food safety as key areas of concentration. Kraft's managers stress community involvement for each employee and division as well as legal compliance and company integrity, and the company's executives have recently highlighted the importance of sustainability in various operations.

Kraft's most recent strategic efforts have been in the areas of "rewiring" the corporation to sustain growth, reframing product categories, taking advantages of its sales capabilities, and driving down costs without forfeiting quality. Given the long history of success and growth, it seems most likely the corporation will continue to thrive.[1]

Chapter Overview

Many marketing budgets allocate substantial amounts of money to promotions. In some instances, the promotions receive more dollars than advertising. This is because they are often instrumental in helping the marketing department reach its goals. Promotions consist of two types: consumer promotions and trade promotions. Consumer promotions are incentives directed toward end users of a product with the goal of "pulling" that product through the channel. In other words, when customers ask for items, they pull them from the manufacturer's warehouse through to the retail store's shelves.

Trade promotions are used by channel members and directed to other channel members to "push" the product through the channel. Manufacturers offer them to wholesalers, and wholesalers offer them to retailers to entice them to purchase the items and stock them.

This chapter examines promotions by first reviewing the most common objectives associated with such programs. Consumer promotions programs are then presented in detail. The analysis includes an overview of the various types of consumers and how they respond to promotions programs. Trade promotions are then presented. Finally, the implications for marketing managers, most notably in the area of customer service, are explored.

Objectives of Promotions

In larger companies, the task of managing promotions typically is assigned to a specific individual who has no other responsibilities. This person communicates with members of the marketing department to make sure all efforts are carefully coordinated. As is the case in every department, managing an activity begins with making plans and setting goals. Consumer and trade promotions are routinely designed to accomplish four primary objectives, as listed in Figure 8.1.

Stimulating sales (or demand) normally serves as the primary objective of promotional programs. Compared to advertising and other marketing tactics, consumer and trade promotions tend to yield quicker results. Not only are the results more immediate, but in most cases the impact can be measured.

Consumer promotions can be used to *acquire new customers* and to *encourage repeat purchases* by current customers. Trade promotions targeted to retailers and other channel members only have an indirect impact on customer acquisition and retention. At the same time, an effective trade promotions program results in retailers and channel members purchasing and stocking items, which in turn stimulates sales to both new and repeat customers.

Promotions are used to *counter competitive actions.* When Pizza Hut sends out a flyer containing a $1.00-off coupon, other pizza chains will likely respond with competing offers.

From a marketing management perspective, note that the first three objectives are more *proactive,* which means they are designed to create a response or action among consumers. The fourth objective, countering the competition, places the company in a more *reactive* stance, in which the action only responds to what other companies have done. The marketing manager chooses an approach when considering various consumer promotions offers.

- Stimulate sales (or demand)
- Acquire new customers
- Encourage repeat purchases by current customers
- Counter competitive actions

Figure 8.1

Objectives of Consumer and Trade Promotions

Managing Consumer Promotions

Advertising often creates awareness, sparks interest, and produces excitement about a product. The final step, enticing the consumer to make the purchase, may be spurred by the use of consumer promotions. Consumer promotions can encourage consumers to switch brands, sample a new brand, and keep current customers from considering competitive brands. In the retail industry, consumer promotions help to generate customer traffic and increase store sales.

In designing the consumer promotions program, marketing managers examine several factors, as shown in Figure 8.2. First, the *objective* should be restated. Then, the marketing manager selects the best *promotional approach.* Understanding the pros and cons of each type of consumer and trade promotion assists in making the best choices. Once the decision regarding which promotions will be used has been made, a *method of distribution* is selected.

Next, choices are made regarding all *accompanying advertising or communications.* The retailer selects from the traditional and nontraditional advertising media described in the previous chapter. For example, when a hardware store's marketing team decides to employ a contest to attract customers to see spring garden plants, flowers, and tools, information about the contest will be sent out. Advertisements on the radio, in newspapers, and on local billboards may be accompanied by lifestyle events at county fairs and messages to gardening clubs by e-mail or telephone.

Before launching a promotion, a *break-even analysis* may be performed. The analysis identifies the response rate needed to break even on a promotional effort. For instance, offering a 25% discount on merchandise should only occur when a significant boost in sales can be reasonably expected. The purpose of a break-even analysis is to identify the amount of sales needed to offset the price tag of the promotion based on the contribution margin for each product. If the additional sales do not cover the costs of the promotion, it may be abandoned unless the marketing team believes that there will be a longer-term impact.

- Objective
- Promotional approach
- Distribution method
- Accompanying advertising or communications
- Break-even response rate
- Potential non–sales benefits

Figure 8.2

Factors to Consider When Choosing a Consumer Promotion

The final factor to be considered is the potential long-term, *non–sales benefits* of a promotion. These include brand awareness, brand equity, brand loyalty, and positive word-of-mouth recommendations. Sometimes the marketing team decides that it is worthwhile to lose money on a promotion in order to increase awareness or generate customer traffic. A new hardware store might use a sweepstakes as part of a grand opening program with the goal of attracting consumers to the store. The sweepstakes may result in a financial loss in the short term but may be deemed beneficial because of the large number of individuals who visited the store to enter the sweepstakes and then later became customers.

Types of Consumer Promotions

Several methods are available to marketing managers to attract new customers and retain current customers. Among the tactics are the product and brand strategies, pricing approaches, and the advertising programs described in previous chapters. In this section, the promotional efforts aimed at consumers are reviewed. They include

- coupons,
- premiums,
- contests and sweepstakes,
- bonus packs,
- price-offs,
- refunds and rebates, and
- sampling.

This section concludes with a look at how various types of customers respond to these methods along with the impact each might have on acquiring new customers.

Coupons

A coupon is a price reduction offer to a consumer or end user. The coupon may state a percentage off the retail price such as 25% or an absolute amount (75 cents). In the United States, 323 billion coupons are distributed annually, and approximately 3 billion are redeemed. The current redemption rate is less than 1% (0.93%) but represents approximately $3.47 billion in savings for consumers.[2] Approximately 80% of all U.S. households use coupons and nearly two thirds are willing to switch brands with coupons.

Coupons can be distributed in various ways (see Figure 8.3). About 80% of all coupons are issued by manufacturers, with the remaining 20% distributed by retailers. The majority of all coupons are sent using print media, such as freestanding inserts, direct mail, and magazines. Of the coupons delivered by print media, the majority are distributed through freestanding inserts (FSIs), which consist of sheets of coupons placed in newspapers or sent by mail.[3]

Marketing teams often prefer distributing coupons through *print media*, because consumers must make a conscious effort to clip the coupon. The process of cutting the coupon for future use enhances brand recall. Even when it is not redeemed, the consumer has seen the brand name and the coupon offer. This causes the consumer to consciously take the coupon to the retail outlet to purchase the product.

Coupons may be distributed in retail stores and placed *on, near,* or *in packages* where the consumer can redeem the coupon on site. This approach, known as using *instant redemption coupons*, often leads to trial purchases of products. Many grocers allow a manufacturer's representative to cook a new food product and offer *free samples* along with a coupon giveaway in the store. Placing coupons in dispensers near various products provides convenient access for customers. All of these are forms of instant redemption coupons.

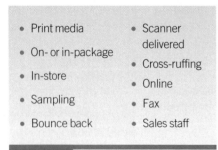

- Print media
- On- or in-package
- In-store
- Sampling
- Bounce back
- Scanner delivered
- Cross-ruffing
- Online
- Fax
- Sales staff

Figure 8.3

Methods of Distributing Coupons

Bounce-back coupons are placed inside packages so that customers cannot redeem them as quickly. This approach encourages repeat purchases, because the customer has to purchase the product again to use the coupon.

Some companies issue coupons at the cash register. These are called *scanner-delivered coupons,* because they are triggered by the item being scanned. The coupon often is for a competitor's product. This approach encourages brand switching the next time a consumer makes a purchase. The effectiveness of acquiring new customers depends on how loyal the customer is to the brand being purchased as compared with the one triggered by the scanner.

Cross-ruffing coupon is the placement of a coupon on one product for another product. A coupon for a French onion dip placed on a package of potato chips is a cross-ruffing coupon. A manufacturer may use cross-ruffing to encourage consumers to purchase another one of its products. For instance, Kellogg's might place a coupon on a Rice Krispies box for another cereal, such as Frosted Flakes or an oatmeal product.

Coupons can be distributed through the Internet, by fax, or through salespeople. Providing coupons *online* offers convenience to consumers, but the company has no control over who downloads and uses the coupon. *Fax coupons* are mostly used in the business-to-business sector. Office supply companies and other vendors use them to entice business customers to make purchases or place orders.

Some firms distribute coupons through *sales representatives*. This creates instant results, because the salesperson also takes the order. Both fax and sales force distribution allow companies to carefully select who gets coupons, which makes it easier to place them into the hands of the individuals and businesses that are not current customers.

Advantages and Disadvantages of Coupons

From a marketing management perspective, coupons offer several advantages. First, coupons are typically an effective method for stimulating sales. They can be used to match a competitor's offer, which can prevent the loss of sales and customers to the competition. Coupons also encourage current customers to make additional purchases.

What are the primary advantages of distributing coupons?

Coupons can be misredeemed, which means the manufacturer paid for a coupon for another company or one for the wrong size of its own product. Coupons may be counterfeited and sent to manufacturers for redemption without ever having been used in a retail store. And finally, coupons are not the best method of acquiring new customers. Most coupons tend to be redeemed by current customers.

A Coupon Contribution Margin Analysis

The marketing team should study the impact of a coupon program on a company's contribution margin. Consider a coupon distribution by a hardware store. Prior to the distribution of the coupons, the break-even analysis shown in Table 8.1 may be calculated. The cost of printing and distributing 150,000 coupons is $35 per thousand, for a total of $5,250. The selling price of the items listed on the flyer averaged $11.22. The cost of goods sold for the items averages 60%, which means the store gains a 40% contribution margin per item. The coupon offers $2.00 off of the purchase price. The cost to process the coupons is $1.12 each. Consequently, instead of averaging a contribution margin of $4.49 per item, the store nets $1.37 after the coupon. To cover the cost of the FSI distribution would require 3,838 coupons, or a 2.56% response rate. Recall that the average national response rate is currently 0.93%.

In this example, the marketing manager decided to go ahead with the FSI coupon distribution. It resulted in redemption of 1,642 coupons, a 1.09% response rate, which was lower than needed to break even. The gross sales resulting from the coupons and after $2.00 was taken off of each item was $15,139. As displayed in Table 8.2, the cost of goods sold was $11,053, the cost

Calculation	Formula	Result
Cost of 150,000 FSIs ($)	(150 × 35)	5,250
Contribution margin per item ($)	(11.22 × 0.40)	4.49
Redemption processing costs ($)		1.12
Coupon face value ($)		2.00
Contribution margin after $2-off coupon ($)	(4.49 − 2.00 − 0.85)	1.37
Items to break even	(5,250/2.49)	3,838
Response rate needed (%)	(3,838/150,000)	2.56

Table 8.1   Break-Even Analysis for a Coupon Promotion

Note: FSIs = freestanding inserts.

Calculation	Formula	Result
Coupons redeemed		1,642
Response rate (%)	(1,642/150,000)	1.09
Gross sales after $2-off coupons ($)	(9.22 × 1,642)	15,139.24
Cost of goods sold ($)	(11.22 × 0.6 × 1,642)	−11,053.94
Redemption processing costs ($)	(1.12 × 1,642)	−1,839.04
Cost of coupon distribution ($)	(150 × 35)	−5,250.00
Contribution margin of promotion ($)	(Sales − Costs)	−3,003.74

Table 8.2   Contribution Analysis for a Coupon Promotion

to process the coupons was $1,839.40, and the cost of the coupon distribution was $5,250. This resulted in a loss of $3,003.74.

In terms of a break-even analysis, the coupon distribution lost money; however, the marketing manager may decide that the program was worthwhile. The added benefits of the program include the following:

- It brought new customers into the store.
- Regular customers purchased additional items, making the "basket" purchase larger.
- Some customers commented that they didn't plan to make a purchase until the coupon was offered.
- The coupons kept customers from shopping at a competitor's store.
- There was a potential impact on brand awareness and brand knowledge.

It might be difficult to identify a dollar figure to represent these benefits. The marketing manager could use them to provide justification for a coupon promotion that, on the surface, cost the company money.

STOP AND THINK

Kraft Foods, Inc. houses numerous brands, nine that average over $1 billion in sales annually, including Kraft, Oscar Mayer, Philadelphia, Maxwell House, Nabisco, Oreo, Jacobs, Milka, and LU.

1. How many of these brands have you or someone in your family purchased?

2. What types of coupons would best match with these brands?

3. Are there opportunities to acquire new customers with these brands? Why or why not?

4. Which of the other consumer promotions programs do you think Kraft should use?

5. The Kraft Web site notes that the company has become actively involved in listing any ingredients that might create allergic reactions on product labels. What are the legal and ethical implications of this decision, domestically and internationally?

Premiums

Premiums are the prizes, gifts, or other special offers consumers receive when purchasing products. One premium might be a free set of barbecue tools with the purchase of a grill. Another could be a second bag of charcoal at half price with the purchase of a regular bag. Premiums are often used by fast-food restaurants that offer prizes or toys as part of a children's meal. Prizes are found in boxes of cereal as well as the most famous place, Cracker Jack boxes. Premiums are a widely used consumer promotions tool. Over $4.5 billion is spent on premiums each year in the United States.[4]

Advantages and Disadvantages of Premiums

The primary advantage of premiums is that consumers pay full price for the goods or services, in contrast to coupons, which grant price reductions. Premiums can boost sales and acquire new customers. The right kind of premium, such as a highly desired toy, can create a great deal of buzz.

The main disadvantage of premiums is that they usually are not as successful as coupons or other promotions in stimulating sales or attracting new customers. There are additional costs associated with producing a gift or prize. Additional marketing dollars must be allocated to advertising the promotion, which also increases its cost.

Calculation	Formula	Result
Income from premium ($)	$48 + (48 \times 0.50\%)$	72.00
Cost of two bags of fertilizer at 60% ($)	$(48 \times 70\% \times 2)$	67.20
Contribution margin of promotion ($)		4.80
Contribution margin on first bag ($)	(48×0.30)	14.40
Contribution margin on second bag ($)	$24 - (48 \times 0.7)$	−9.60

Table 8.3   Contribution Analysis for 50%-Off Premium Promotion

Analysis of a Premium Program

Many premiums are offered in retail outlets, normally at the location in the store where a consumer makes a purchase decision. Thus, a premium promotional offer for lawn fertilizer will be placed near other lawn care items in a hardware store. In this analysis, the offer is a second bag of Scott's fertilizer at 50% off the retail price of $48.00. Consequently, someone who was going to purchase one bag may decide to buy the second bag. Table 8.3 displays the financial calculation for this promotion.

The retail income from the two bags will be $72.00, because the second bag is sold at half price ($48.00 + 24.00). Each bag has a 70% cost of goods sold. This means the two bags cost the retailer $67.20. The total revenue received minus the cost of goods sold results in a contribution margin of $4.80 ($72.00 – $67.20). The retailer actually lost $9.60 on the second bag, because the revenue received was less than the cost, but a net profit was made because the sale of the first bag resulted in a gain of $14.40 ($48.00 × 30%).

A more in-depth analysis of Table 8.3 reveals an additional item, which is the opportunity cost. An opportunity cost represents monies not received from one activity because they were spent or forgone on another. The opportunity cost in this example consists of the profits that were not realized because of the promotion. If the retailer had sold two bags of fertilizer at the retail price without the premium, the store would generate a profit of $28.80 on the sale of two bags ($14.40 × 2). With the premium, the retailer only nets $4.80 on the two bags. The opportunity cost becomes $24.00 per sale ($28.80 – $4.80). The figure represents the amount of profit the retailer is losing in order to offer the premium.

Why would a hardware store offer a premium that results in such a loss? The answer may be found in the promotional objective. For example, if the retailer down the block offers a coupon for Scotts fertilizer, the retailer may be using the premium to prevent loss of sales to that competitor. Alternatively, a retailer might use the same promotion to attract customers to the store in the early spring with the hope that those customers will return in the summer to purchase additional merchandise. A third possible explanation is that customers who were only planning on purchasing one bag of fertilizer may purchase an additional bag.

When marketing managers consider premiums and other promotions, they examine the potential nonsales benefits along with the primary objective of the promotion. A certain amount of judgment and instinct is required to make the decision.

Contests and Sweepstakes

Contests and sweepstakes are popular promotions. Approximately $1.8 billion is spent on them each year.[5] While the words *contest* and *sweepstakes* tend to be used interchangeably, some legal distinctions between the two remain. Contests normally require the participant to perform some type of activity. The winner is selected based on who performs best or provides the most correct answers. Often, contests require participants to make purchases to enter. In some states, however, it is illegal to force a consumer to make a purchase to enter a contest. The marketing manager investigates any potential legal restrictions before creating a contest.

In a sweepstakes, no purchase is required. Individuals can enter as many times as they wish, although it is permissible for firms to restrict customers to one entry per visit. The chances of winning a sweepstakes are based on a probability factor that must be publicly available. The probability of winning each of the prizes offered must be stated on all point-of-purchase (POP) displays and advertising materials.

One major goal associated with many contests or sweepstakes is to capture names and contact information to be kept in the company's database. McDonald's used its Monopoly sweepstakes to attract patrons to retail stores as well as to the company's Web site. In one monopoly game, over 500,000 names were collected. McDonald's sent e-mails to the individuals in the database to encourage them to play the game online. During the 7-week promotion, McDonald's sent 5.7 million e-mail messages. In 1 week of the promotion, 71% of those receiving an e-mail opened it and 29.2% immediately clicked through to the Web site to play the game.[6]

The prize list often determines the success or failure of contests and sweepstakes. The game or contest itself is also important. The perceived value of a contest or sweepstakes includes two components: (1) extrinsic value and (2) intrinsic value. The *extrinsic value* represents the actual attractiveness of the prize (a Caribbean vacation vs. a free sandwich). The greater the perceived value, the more likely it is that people will participate. One tactic that can be used is to increase the extrinsic value as long as the individual keeps playing.

Intrinsic values are those associated with playing or participating. A contest requiring the use of a skill, such as choosing the final four teams in the NCAA basketball tournament or an essay contest, entices entry by individuals who enjoy demonstrating a skill. Winning combines the intrinsic value of participating with the extrinsic value of the prize.

Instant reward prizes, such as scratch-and-win cards, are also effective. Recently, a mobile phone promotion was developed by HipCricket, a mobile marketing and event company. The event provided instant notification of winning via text messaging. HipCricket developed the sweepstakes for Miller Brewing Company's Icehouse brand. The sweepstakes was the first to be conducted live, during a rock concert. Music fans 21 years or older could enter by text messaging the words "Pick Me" during the concert. At 10:00 p.m., one concertgoer, Melissa Hasty, received word via text message that she had won the grand prize, a 5-day, 4-night Caribbean cruise on the "Rock Boat." Other concert fans won secondary prizes throughout the night. They were also notified on their cell phones' instant messaging system. Winning is always fun. For Melissa and others at the concert, winning instantly made it even more exciting.[7]

What made the contest offered by HipCricket successful?

Why is the redemption rate higher for products valued at $50 or more?

Advantages and Disadvantages

The main advantages of contests and sweepstakes are that they create interest, excitement, and buzz. An attention-getting prize adds to the value of the event. When Sen. Barack Obama ran for president in 2008, two contests were created by the campaign staff during the primary season. In Indiana, young people who provided evidence that they had registered to vote were entered into a contest in which the prize was getting to play in a three-on-three basketball game with Obama. A second contest entered everyone who made a contribution to the campaign, no matter what the amount, into a drawing to have lunch with the candidate.

In addition, it is becoming evident to marketers that contests and sweepstakes may also increase brand awareness and brand loyalty and also create a positive company image through multiple exposures over time, such as when McDonald's ran its Monopoly contest over a series of years.

The disadvantages include the actual results. Many times, the stated objectives of contests and sweepstakes are to encourage customer traffic and stimulate sales. While they may result in additional traffic, the question remains as to whether they actually boost sales. Some do, others do not.

Refunds and Rebates

Refunds and rebates are cash returns offered to consumers or businesses following product purchases. Consumers pay full price and then mail in a proof of purchase. The manufacturer then refunds a portion of the purchase price. A refund is a cash return on "soft goods" such as food or clothing, and rebates are cash returns on "hard goods" such as automobiles and appliances. Normally, refunds are smaller and rebates are larger. For example, the typical refund offered on a food item may be $1; the typical rebate on a car is $1,000 or more.

Only about 30% of all rebates are ever claimed. For rebates valued at $50 or more, the percentage of claims rises to about 65%. The major reason for the low response rate is the inconvenience associated with obtaining the rebate. Too many steps or long waiting times because of "snail mail" are common complaints about rebates. It is not unusual for consumers to wait for up to 6 months to receive a rebate check.[8]

Advantages and Disadvantages

The advantages of rebates to manufacturers include creating interest in brands that otherwise may not be considered. They can be used to blunt competitive efforts and maintain a customer base without lowering the "list" price. Rebates are normally offered to incite action, causing the buyer to move forward and make the actual purchase. Manufacturers can offer a larger rebate dollar value while knowing that not everyone who purchases the product will send it in.

Rebates are attractive to retailers because the amount is paid by the manufacturer. The retailer can still sell the brand at the regular retail price. Rebates sometimes draw customers into a retail store who might not otherwise visit.

Rebates also offer the advantage of creating cooperation between manufacturers and retail outlets. The programs create a natural connection for developing cooperative advertising campaigns. Also, a retailer may offer to grant the rebate on the spot and bill the manufacturer for the amount later. This may lead to a quicker purchase decision by the consumer. Both the retailer and the manufacturer win when this happens, because the sale has been made.

Refunds granted by manufacturers can create more immediate sales, moving customers more quickly to purchase decisions. The same holds true for retail outlets that offer refunds. Refunds may also lead to point-of-purchase brand switching, especially in situations where a great deal of brand parity exists.

The disadvantages of refunds and rebates begin with the costs of lost revenues combined with the record keeping and mailing that takes place. In some industries, especially automotive, many customers have become so sensitized to rebates that they will not buy a car until a rebate is offered.

Analysis of a Rebate Program

SkeeterVac offers an electric mosquito killer product. Table 8.4 provides financial data on a rebate program for the company for the SV3100 series mosquito killer. The SV3100 retails for $299. SkeeterVac sells it to retail stores for $210. Variable costs are $123.00 per unit. During the 60-day rebate program, SkeeterVac sold 13,200 units with 62% of the customers mailing in the $75.00 rebate. After the rebate processing costs and co-op advertising costs, the contribution to profits for SkeeterVac was $292,002.

To measure the success of the rebate program, the marketing manager compared the rebate sales with the previous year when no rebate was offered. The demand with the rebate increased by 41.6%; from 9,320 units to 13,200 units. Other factors could have affected the sales of the SkeeterVac in addition to the rebate, such as advertising, the weather, in-store location, or in-store signage. It seems likely, however, that the program did contribute to increased sales.

Assuming that the increase of 41.6% was due to the rebate, the marketing manager's next step is to calculate the opportunity costs of the rebate. If the increase was due entirely to the rebate, then it could be assumed that only 9,320 would have been sold. Sales of 9,320 units without the rebate would have generated a contribution profit of $594,840. The co-op advertising program was in place both years, which means its cost must be added to the calculation. Notice that the opportunity cost, or lost profit, is $302,838. Even with a 41.6% increase in demand, the $75-off rebate generated approximately half of the contribution margin.

How much would demand have to increase to earn the same amount of money? Table 8.5 displays the calculation for a break-even analysis using the 62% redemption rate. SkeeterVac earns $87.00 per unit with no rebate but only $8.75 per unit with the rebate. To earn the same amount of contribution profit with the rebate as was earned on the sale of 9,320 units the previous year, SkeeterVac would have to sell 21,060 units. This would be a 126% increase in demand, which seems highly unlikely.

It is clear that the rebate promotion will generate fewer funds. Why would SkeeterVac use it? Several possible explanations exist. First, the 8,184 rebates mailed in provide SkeeterVac with names and contact information for its database. These can be used for cross-selling additional

Calculation	Formula	Result
Gross income on 13,200 units sold ($)	(13,200 × 210)	2,772,000
Cost of goods sold—13,200 units ($)	(13,200 × 123)	1,623,600
Cost of 62% redemption rate ($75 off) ($)	(13,200 × 0.62 × $75)	613,800
Processing costs ($)	(13,200 × 0.62 × $3.25)	26,598
Co-op advertising costs ($)		216,000
Contribution profit on 13,200 ($)		292,002
Increase in demand over 9,320 (%)	(13,200 – 9,320)/9,320	41.6
Contribution income on 9,320 ($)	9,320 × (210 – 123)	810,840
Co-op advertising costs ($)		216,000
Contribution profit on 9,320 ($)		594,840
Opportunity costs ($)	(594,840 – 292,002)	302,838

Table 8.4 Contribution Analysis for Rebate Promotion

Calculation	Formula	Result
Selling price to retailers/unit ($)		210.00
Contribution margin/unit – No rebate ($)	(210 – 123)	87.00
Total costs of rebate ($)	(75.00 + 3.25)	78.25
Contribution margin/unit – $75 rebate ($)	(87.00 – 78.25)	8.75
Units needed to generate $810,840	$810,840 = (8.75 \times 0.62 \times X) + (87.00 \times 0.38 \times X)$	21,060
Increase in demand for break even (%)	(21,060 – 9,320)/9,320	126

Table 8.5   Break-Even Analysis for Rebate Promotion

merchandise. Second, individuals who purchased the SV3100 model may purchase other cheaper models for other outside locations around the home or for camping needs. Third, the rebate may have provided reasons for individuals to buy the SkeeterVac rather than a competing brand.

Refunds tend to be valued by current customers but are not as likely to attract new customers. Rebates that have a large dollar value, however, can be attractive to current as well as prospective customers. It can make the difference in a particular brand being chosen if the rebate is large enough to compensate for the time it takes to complete the paperwork, mail it in, and wait for the check. Retailers can simplify the process and increase the response rate by including all relevant information on the receipt, making it easier and quicker for the customer.

Sampling

Sampling is the delivery of a good or service for a trial use. Sampling offers target both consumers and businesses with goods as well as services. Samples are provided free of charge. A coupon or price-off incentive may be provided with the sample to further entice the consumer to purchase the product.

Various methods of sampling are available. A food manufacturer may distribute the samples in retail grocery stores, where someone cooks the food and entices customers to taste it. Coupons are then offered to encourage the customer to purchase the product. For non–food items, samples can be distributed in retail outlets, through the mail, or at special events, such as concerts or state fairs. In recent years, marketers have increased usage of FSIs for the distribution of consumer product samples. A variety of products have been distributed in FSIs placed in newspapers, such as breakfast bars, coffee, shampoo, snacks, tea, and automotive cleaners.

Sampling may be used in the business-to-business sector by field salespeople. It is the primary method used by pharmaceutical companies to acquaint physicians with new drugs. Clients or customers receive samples of the product and are encouraged to use it and to compare it with their current brands.

Advantages and Disadvantages of Sampling

The benefits of sampling begin with the basic premise that trying an item for free may lead the customer or business to make a purchase. Targeting the sampling program to individuals or businesses that have not made purchases becomes the key. Sampling is also an excellent method for new product introductions. Being able to try a product without having to pay reduces the purchase risk for the customer.

In terms of disadvantages, sampling is one of the most expensive forms of consumer promotions, because free samples are distributed with no or little immediate return. To reduce the cost of sampling, marketing teams turn to more targeted approaches instead of mass sampling. The goal should be to get the sample in the hands of individuals who are most likely to make future purchases.

Recently, an England-based company, Green & Black's, launched a sampling campaign for organic chocolates at 21 outdoor concerts. Each audience member was given a bar of

Green & Black's organic chocolate at the entrance. More than 80% of the audience, a total of 105,000 people, accepted the sample bars. A tasting marquee was also set up in the concert area to allow concert attendees to try other flavors. The goal was to build a brand experience between concert attendees and the Green & Black's brand name and, in the long run, to boost sales. The program was a success. Sales of the organic chocolate bar increased 79% in the months immediately following the concerts.[9]

Bonus Packs

Bonus packs offer an additional or extra number of items in a special package. Two cans of bug spray packaged together at a special price is a bonus pack. Typically, the bonus or additional product offered ranges from 20% to 100% of the normal number of units in a package. A 30% bonus is the most common.

Advantages and Disadvantages of Bonus Packs

Bonus packs can create advantages. First, they may attract consumers who are not loyal to any particular brand who will buy any version of the product. They may try the brand because they are buying additional product at a lower cost per unit. Someone who uses bug spray, for instance, may be willing to buy the new brand because a two-can bonus pack is cheaper than buying two cans of a competing brand. Bonus packs also encourage greater use of a product. When a consumer has a second can of bug spray on hand, she is less likely to worry about running out. It may also pre-empt the consumer from buying a competing brand. Bonus packs may attract individuals who are price sensitive, if the bonus is large enough and the consumer feels she can save money.

How can the marketing team for a fitness gym use sampling to gain new customers?

Bonus packs have several disadvantages. The first is the cost of creating a new package. The second is lost revenue per item. Third, brand-loyal customers may stockpile the product when it is in a bonus pack, meaning the next purchase is further away. This means the bonus pack might delay the next purchase, because the customer has extra product to use. Further, bonus packs are not the best way to acquire new customers. Someone who has not purchased a particular brand is not likely to purchase a bonus pack, because it will cost more than a single item and includes additional product. The risk is higher. Many consumers may conclude that if they do not like the product, not only have they paid more money but they have more of the product that will not be used.

Analysis of a Bonus Pack Program

Monitoring sales during a bonus pack promotion provides information about who is taking advantage of the promotion. The graph shown in Figure 8.4 displays three possible outcomes of a bonus pack promotion, depending on who makes purchases. When current customers purchase the bonus pack, sales following the bonus pack promotion may actually decline, because they simply stockpiled the product and delayed the next purchase (Line A). When the bonus pack promotion attracts new customers, a spike in sales occurs with the offer and then sales reach a higher level after the program ends. This indicates that the new customers continue to purchase the product (Line B). If the bonus pack was purchased by price-sensitive individuals

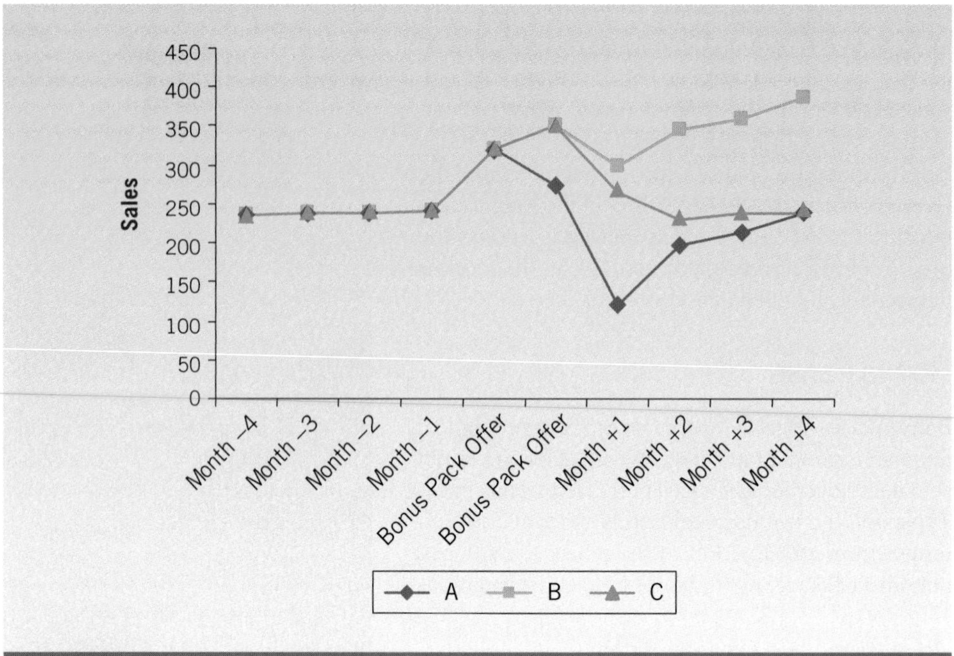

Figure 8.4   Financial Impact Scenarios of a Bonus Pack Promotion

or individuals who purchase whatever brand is being promoted, then sales would spike during the promotion and then drop back down to the level they held before the promotion (Line C).

Price-Offs

A price-off is a temporary reduction in the price of a product to the consumer. A price-off can be physically marked on the product, such as when a can of insect repellant shows the regular retail price marked out and replaced by a special retail price (e.g., $5.99 marked out and replaced by $4.99). When the manufacturer produces a label with the price reduction premarked, it forces the retailer to sell the item at the reduced price. This ensures that the price-off incentive will be passed on to the consumer. At other times, the price-off is not on the actual item but on a POP display, sign, or shelf.

Price-offs have been successful in business-to-business marketing. Reducing the introductory price may cause a business buying team to feel more inclined to try the product. This would especially be true during difficult economic times or when a new company begins operations and looks to cut costs in every way possible.

Advantages and Disadvantages of a Price-Off

The advantages of price-offs include the ability to attract new customers because the lower price reduces the financial risk of making a first purchase. Price-offs can also stimulate sales of an existing product. They might encourage a customer to switch brands when he does not have strong brand loyalty for another brand. A well-marked price-off can be a powerful enticement at the point of purchase. Just as the consumer is about to pick up an item and place it in a cart, the product a lower price may jump out and be chosen instead. Also, in cases where consumers have brand preferences, the price-off on a favorite brand encourages stockpiling of the product and possibly increased consumption.[10] A consumer who purchases additional breakfast bars because of a price-off tends to consume more. This would not be true for other products, such as deodorant or toothpaste. Stockpiling for those types of products merely delays the next purchase.

The first disadvantage of a price-off program is lost revenue per item. As with any other price discount, the marketing team considers the potential rise in sales of total units in relation to the loss per unit before offering the price-off. They will also want to be sure the price-off actually increases consumption. If not, dollars are being lost with no other gain. One danger with a price-off program is that the customer may want the company to continue selling the product at its introductory or reduced price. This holds true in both consumer markets and business-to-business markets. The problem typically occurs when price-offs are used too frequently. Then the business or consumer expects the lower price or waits until the price is reduced again to make the purchase.

What are the primary advantages and disadvantages of a price-off promotion?

Analysis of a Price-Off Program

Price-offs are easy to create and can have an immediate impact on sales. They can also substantially reduce profits. Table 8.6 displays a break-even analysis for a $1.00-off promotion on a bottle of Enforcer Flea and Tick spray. The bottle sells at the retail store for $6.99. Enforcer sells it to retailers for $5.10. Variable manufacturing costs are $3.55. To ensure the $1.00 price-off is passed along to consumers, Enforcer printed the new price on the bottle and absorbed the total cost of the price-off promotion. With weekly sales of approximately 12,000 units, Enforcer is earning a contribution profit of $18,600. To match that contribution margin, sales would need to jump from the current 12,000 to 33,818 units. That is a 182% increase in sales. The $1.00-off offer represents about a 20% reduction in selling price for Enforcer. To compensate for this 20% price reduction, demand must increase by 182%. This scenario is commonplace in price-off programs. While it seems enticing to reduce the price to stimulate demand, such actions almost always have detrimental effects on profits. Most of the time, the increase in demand does not offset the lower per-unit contribution margin.

Calculation	Formula	Result
Current weekly sales—12,000 units at $5.10 ($)	(12,000 × 5.10)	61,200
Cost of goods sold for 12,000 units ($)	(12,000 × 3.55)	42,600
Contribution profit from weekly sales ($)		18,600
Contribution margin/unit for $1.00 price off ($)	(5.10 – 3.55 – 1.00)	0.55
Units needed to generate $18,600 profit	(18,600/0.55)	33,818
Percentage of increase in sales	(33,818 – 12,000)/12,000	182

Table 8.6　Break-Even Analysis for Price-Off Promotion

In summary, successful promotions programs require meticulous planning prior to launch. There should also be a careful analysis of results. By comparing the prelaunch analysis to the postlaunch results, a marketing manager can continually refine the ability to make effective decisions about when, how, and where to use promotions.

Types of Consumers

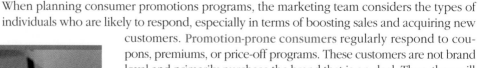

What is a preferred-brand consumer?

When planning consumer promotions programs, the marketing team considers the types of individuals who are likely to respond, especially in terms of boosting sales and acquiring new customers. Promotion-prone consumers regularly respond to coupons, premiums, or price-off programs. These customers are not brand loyal and primarily purchase the brand that is on-deal. Thus, they will respond to a consumer promotion when it is offered but then quickly move to a competing brand when it is on-deal. These consumers do not stay with one brand. Acquiring them using promotions is not an ideal tactic.

A second group consists of price-sensitive consumers. For them, price remains the primary, if not the only, criterion used in making a purchase decision. Brands are not important to these individuals, which means they will not pay more for a brand-name product. These customers take advantage of any type of promotion that reduces the price. They are even more fickle than the promotion-prone consumers. They only purchase the cheapest brand.

At the other end of the spectrum is the brand-loyal consumer, who purchases only one particular brand and does not substitute regardless of any deal being offered. The use of promotions for this group mostly consists of trying to increase the volume of purchases.

Few consumers are completely promotion prone, price sensitive, or brand loyal; most are somewhere in between. These individuals often fall into a category called preferred-brand consumers. They have certain brands they prefer, but are not completely loyal to them. Often, it is not even one particular brand, but two, three, or four brands. These customers typically purchase from their preferred list. If a brand from their preferred list features a promotion, they do not hesitate to use it. If a brand that is not part of their preferred set is offering a promotion, then they will switch only if the promotion is deemed to be an exceptional deal. Thus, it takes a stronger promotion to move them from their list of preferred brands.

Further, most consumers are seldom in a particular category for all purchases. They may be brand loyal to a life insurance company but promotion prone for potato chips. They may be preferred-brand conscious for watches, having only two or three brands from which they will purchase, but price sensitive when it comes to convenience goods such as soft drinks and snacks.

When developing consumer promotions programs that are targeted at new customers, the most attractive type to pursue is the preferred-brand consumer. These consumers respond to a promotion when it is for one of their preferred brands. If it is not for one of their preferred brands, the promotion might encourage them to at least try the brand; if they like it, then it may become part of their preferred set. Brand-loyal consumers will purchase the brand anyway, so they do not need a promotion to encourage them. Price-sensitive consumers are the least attractive because they buy whichever brand is the cheapest. Promotion-prone consumers are not attractive because they will switch to another brand as soon as a promotion is offered by another company.

International Considerations

Every marketing manager knows, or should know, that various promotions are perceived and used in different ways, depending on the country involved. For example, in some cultures, using coupons creates the perception that the person is poor rather than prudent. In those circumstances, coupon programs are not well received. There are also legal considerations. Many deal with the nature of discounts and how they may be offered.

Shipping becomes a concern when bonus packs are used. The extra shipping costs associated with larger packages should be considered as part of the program. A refund or rebate program can be difficult to implement due to legal restrictions or to less-efficient postal systems. Printing price-offs on labels creates complications when foreign currencies are being used.

In any international operation, the marketing team is likely to include a *cultural assimilator*. This person's job is to make sure that any promotional program is legal, culturally acceptable, and feasible within the constraints of a foreign country.

Trade Promotions

As noted at the beginning of this chapter, trade promotions are the incentives members of the trade channel use to push products through the channel from the manufacturer to the retail outlet. Trade promotions can be issued by any member in the channel. They may be offered to retailers, distributors, wholesalers, brokers, or agents.

The most common trade promotions are offered to retailers by manufacturers. Until about 1985, trade promotions typically accounted for about 25% of a manufacturer's marketing budget. Today, the figure approaches 70%. Trade promotions are the second largest expense for a manufacturer, after the cost of goods sold, accounting for 17.4% of gross sales.[11] Trade promotions can be divided into three primary categories:

1. Trade allowances

2. Trade incentives

3. Trade shows

Why do companies use
trade promotions?

Trade Allowances

Trade allowances provide financial incentives to other channel members to motivate them to purchase products for resale. The most common trade allowance is the off-invoice allowance, a financial discount given to a channel member per item, case, or pallet ordered. The allowances normally consist of percentage reductions in price. In almost all offers, both a minimum order such as 10,000 cases, and a specified time period, such as 60 days, are required. Approximately 35% of all trade dollars are spent on off-invoice allowances, making them the largest expenditure among trade promotions tools.[12]

Trade allowances are extremely popular with retailers and other channel members because they are able to purchase products at a lower cost. This allows the retailer to reduce the price charged to consumers. Other retailers keep the retail price the same and pocket the difference as a way of boosting profits. In most situations, the latter occurs. The savings are pocketed by the retailer or channel member and are not passed on to consumers.

Many retailers take advantage of price allowances by creating a situation in which customers are continually offered discounts. Through careful planning, the retailer will have one brand on sale almost all the time. Thus, a grocery store will offer Pepsi at a reduced price one week and Coke the next. The two products are rarely promoted *on-deal* (passing along trade allowance discounts) at the same time. By offering only one on-deal at a time, the retailer always has a brand on sale for price-sensitive consumers.

In an effort to increase profit margins, retailers often engage in two activities: forward buying and diversion. Forward buying occurs when a retailer purchases extra amounts of a product while it is on-deal from the manufacturer. The retailer then sells the on-deal merchandise after the deal period ends, saving the cost of purchasing the product at the manufacturer's full price.

Diversion occurs when a retailer purchases a product on-deal in one location and ships it to another location where it is off-deal. For example, a manufacturer may offer an off-invoice allowance of $5 per pallet for lawn fertilizer in Texas. Diversion tactics mean the retailer purchases an excess quantity in Texas and has it shipped to stores in other states. To do so, retailers first examine the potential profits to be earned, less the cost of shipping the product to other locations. Shipping costs tend to be relatively high as compared with trade allowances. Consequently, retailers do not use diversion nearly as much as forward buying.

The most controversial form of trade allowance is a slotting fee. Slotting fees are funds charged by retailers to stock new products. Figure 8.5 lists the various reasons retailers give for charging these fees.[13]

First, the introduction of a new product requires the retailer to add the item to its inventory list and then purchase enough to stock for all the company's stores. A typical supermarket carries 35,000 SKUs (stock-keeping units) and must evaluate at least 10,000 to 15,000 new products per year. Most will fail. Consequently, retailers believe that charging slotting fees forces manufacturers to weed out poor product introductions. The average total cost in slotting fees for a nationally introduced product ranges from $1.5 million to $2 million.[14]

Slotting fees also add to the bottom line for retailers. Many products have low margins or markups. Slotting fees provide additional monies to support retail operations. It has been estimated that between 14% and 27% of trade promotion monies given to retailers go directly to the retailer's bottom line.[15]

- Retailers spend money to add new products to their inventory and to stock the product.
- Adding a new product requires reducing shelf space for other brands or eliminating a current brand.
- It becomes easy for retailers to decide which new products to stock.
- Slotting fees provide funds to support retail operations.

Figure 8.5

Reasons for Charging Slotting Fees

STOP AND THINK

1. Are slotting fees ethical?

2. Do slotting fees hurt small companies or large manufacturers the most?

3. Some retailers charge "exit fees" for taking failed products off shelves rather than slotting fees. Is this a better approach?

4. What do you think the effects of slotting fees are on prices charged by manufacturers (wholesale prices)?

5. What is the impact of charging slotting fees on retailer relationships with manufacturers?

Trade Incentives

Trade incentives are similar to trade allowances, except that with trade incentives, retailers must perform some type of marketing function in order to receive the funds. The purpose is the same—to push the product through the channel and increase the amount of product purchased by the retailer. The three primary trade incentives are

1.   cooperative merchandising agreement,

2.   premium or bonus pack programs, and

3.   cooperative (co-op) advertising.

A cooperative merchandising agreement (CMA) takes the form of a formal agreement between the retailer and manufacturer to undertake a two-way marketing effort. The CMA can be for a wide variety of marketing tasks. For instance, a CMA can feature the manufacturer's brand as a price leader in an advertisement. A cooperative agreement can be made to emphasize the manufacturer's brand as part of an in-house offer made by the retail store or by using a special shelf display featuring a price incentive.

CMAs are popular with manufacturers because the retailer performs a marketing function in order to receive the allowance or incentive, in contrast to the trade allowance. CMAs provide benefits to retailers. For instance, they allow retailers to develop calendar promotions. Calendar promotions are promotional campaigns the retailer plans for customers through manufacturer trade

What benefits do CMAs
offer to retailers?

incentives. By signing a CMA, a retailer can schedule the weeks a particular brand will be on sale and offset the other weeks with other brands. By using calendar promotions, the retailer can arrange it in such a way that there will always be one brand on sale while the others are off-deal.

Although CMAs provide some benefits to retailers, most retailers prefer trade allowances. Trade allowances mean that the retailer receives practically the same financial benefit but does not have to perform a marketing function. To make CMAs attractive to retailers, manufacturers provide incentives beyond what the retailer would receive through the trade allowance. These may be in the form of a POP display, national or regional advertising, or a manufacturer's coupon that can be used in the retail store for consumers.

The second major type of trade incentive is a program to offer a *premium or bonus pack* to the retailer. Instead of offering the retailer a price discount, the manufacturer offers free merchandise as a premium. The trade incentive may also take the form of a bonus case or pack for each 20 that are purchased within the next 30 days. The bonus packs are free to the retailer and are awarded for placing the order by a certain date and for placing at minimum-size order.

The most common trade incentive is cooperative or co-op advertising. In a cooperative advertising (co-op) promotion, the manufacturer agrees to reimburse the retailer a certain percentage of the advertising costs associated with advertising the manufacturer's products in the retailer's ad. To receive the reimbursement, the retailer follows specific guidelines concerning the placement of the ad and its content. In almost all cases, no competing products can be advertised. Normally, the manufacturer's product must be displayed prominently. There may be other restrictions on how the product is advertised as well as specific photos or copy to be used.

In most cooperative advertising programs, retailers accrue co-op monies based on purchases. This is normally a certain percentage of sales. For example, Scotts may offer co-op dollars for all ads that feature the Scotts brand name and promote Scotts lawn fertilizer and other products. Manufacturers typically pay between 50% and 70% of the cost of the ad as long as the brand is prominently featured and no competing brands are in the ad. In many cases, the ads must be approved in advance by the manufacturer.

Co-op advertising programs allow retailers to use the manufacturer's dollars to produce additional advertising at minimal cost. Retailers also benefit from the image of a national brand, which can attract new or additional customers to the store. From the retailer's perspective, there is little to lose in co-op programs.

Manufacturers also benefit from co-op ads. By sharing advertising costs with retailers, the manufacturer gains additional exposure at a reduced cost. More important, almost all co-op advertising programs are tied to sales. The retailer accrues co-op advertising dollars based on a certain percentage of sales. Thus, to get the co-op money, the retailer must not only promote the brand prominently but also purchase the product for resale. As a result, it is not surprising to see the wide variety of cooperative advertisements appearing regularly in every medium.

Trade Shows

Trade shows are gatherings of buyers and sellers for the purposes of making contacts, inducing sales, and building relationships. Typically, the sellers are manufacturers and the buyers are retailers. Some shows house entire industries, such as high technology products. Others are limited to a few major companies, such as automotive shows. Another version of a trade show is one that features numerous sellers for a limited range of products. An example of this type of show would be one featuring all companies that sell romance novels.

Trade shows are used extensively in business-to-business marketing programs. The trade show provides the opportunity to discover potential customers and display new products. Relationships with current customers can be strengthened. A trade show makes it possible to find out what the competition is doing. Many times, trade shows present a situation in which a sales team can meet directly with decision makers and buyers from prospective clients. A trade show can also be used to strengthen the brand name of a product as well as the company's image.

In the United States, few deals are finalized during trade shows. Buyers and sellers meet, discuss, and maybe even negotiate; but seldom are buys completed. Instead, attendees collect business cards as leads to be followed up later. Despite the buyers and sellers' not making deals at trade shows, the shows are an excellent method of acquiring new customers, especially in the business-to-business arena.

For trade shows attended by consumers, the reverse is often true. Sales not made at the trade show seldom come to fruition. As a result, salespeople are more likely to press potential customers to make some type of commitment.

It is different for international trade shows and for attendees from other countries. International attendees tend to be senior executives with the authority to make purchases. Marketers in U. S. firms know that the international attendee often wishes to conduct business during the trade show, not afterward. The international attendees also spend more time at each manufacturer's booth. They stay longer in order to gather and study information in greater detail. The international guest, who pays more for travel expenses, wants more in-depth information than an American counterpart usually requires.

Implications for Marketing Managers

In most companies, employee pay structures encourage the use of trade promotions irrespective of the impact on profit margins. Sales managers face quotas, and when sales fall behind, the easiest way to boost them is to offer retailers a trade deal. Further, brand managers are

often evaluated based on the sales growth of a brand. The easiest way to ensure continuing growth is to offer trade deals. The pattern of using trade deals to reach short-term quotas rather than to build up a long-term image and theme will not change until top management adopts a new approach.

The best weapon a manufacturer can use to reduce trade promotions expenditures is to develop a strong brand name. Retailers stock strong brands even when fewer trade deals are offered, because a strong brand can help pull customers into retail stores. The challenge many companies face today is that strong brands are becoming more difficult to build. Consumers often see two, three, or more potential brands. In an effort to help a product receive a prominent space on the retail shelf, the sales representative will want to be able to offer trade incentives and allowances. To remain competitive, other sales reps for competing brands do the same. The result is a spiraling cycle in which companies continue to invest in trade promotions and no one can quit.

Manufacturers spend billions of dollars each year on trade promotions. These costs are often passed on to consumers in the form of higher prices. It is estimated that 11 cents out of every dollar spent for a consumer product can be attributed to the cost of trade promotions. In the grocery industry, an estimated 70% to 90% of all purchases made by retailers are on-deal with some type of trade incentive in place. The constant use of deals has trimmed manufacturer margins on products and created competitive pressures to conform. Consequently, managing trade promotions programs remains a challenging task for marketing managers. There are no easy solutions.

What are the primary implications of consumer and trade promotions for marketing managers?

Customer Service and Promotions Programs

Many of the consumer promotions described in this chapter are handled by entry-level employees. Cashiers are the ones who redeem most coupons. Any premium discount must be identified at the cash register. A salesperson on the retail floor is able to direct the customer to the premium being offered. Many contests and sweepstakes offer small prizes to be presented on the spot. First-line employees are the ones to verify the winner and present the prize, whether it is a free bottle of a soft drink or a sandwich in a restaurant. Entry-level workers are often in charge of giving out free samples.

Consequently, the crucial role played by quality customer service once again becomes clear. Friendly, knowledgeable, efficient employees improve the value of any promotional item. When customer service is poor, the value of the promotion in the customer's eyes quickly drops.

Supervisors should make sure that any promotion being offered is thoroughly understood by those who come in contact with the public. Part of an employee's performance appraisal score and subsequent pay raise or promotion should be based on the individual's willingness to give great customer service, including the delivery of consumer promotions that do not involve earning a commission.

The same holds true for trade promotions. Any sales representative who is authorized to give a trade discount or trade allowance should be able to clearly explain the benefits of the promotion. Those who run the booth at a trade show are the "face" of the company. Once again, cordial and professional behavior strengthens the impact of any deal being presented to a prospective client. In short, customer service plays an integral part in ensuring the success of every promotions program.

YOURCAREER

Trade Shows

Many new employees are asked to participate in trade shows. The phrase "manning the booth" is used to describe this activity. As a new marketing professional, you can use this time to develop several skills.

Observational Skills

People who visit your booth can be placed into five categories:

1. *Education seekers,* who browse and look, but do not buy
2. *Reinforcement seekers,* who want reassurance about past purchases
3. *Solution seekers,* who are looking to solve specific problems and are willing to buy
4. *Buying teams,* or a group of people from one company that may be ready to make purchases
5. *Power buyers,* top managers ready to buy

See if you can identify each type as people visit your booth. Develop personal strategies for responding to each category.

Sales and Presentational Skills

Practice and learn the following:

- Greet a customer in a way that makes him want to visit you again.
- Listen carefully and make mental notes about the prospect and the company.
- Ask intelligent questions about the customer and the customer's company.
- Display "booth etiquette," which includes proper dress, keeping the booth clean, and maintaining good posture.
- Make sure you obtain contact information from the prospect for future contacts.

You are being provided the opportunity to make pitches to bona fide prospects. Make the most of this time.

Networking Skills

Introduce yourself to people at other booths.

Let others know the type of work you perform and your background. Find out what they do and about their backgrounds as well.

Compliment others about their wardrobes, booths, companies, and other things that stand out. Make sure your compliments cannot be construed as sexist.

Remember that opportunities become available to those who pay attention and seize the moment.

Chapter Summary

Consumer promotions are incentives that are directed toward end users of products. Trade promotions are used by channel members and are directed to other channel members. The four most common objectives of consumer and trade promotions programs are (1) to stimulate sales, (2) to acquire new customers, (3) to encourage repeat purchases by current customers, and (4) to match competitor offers. When choosing from all the potential forms of consumer promotions, the objective, promotional approach, distribution method, accompanying advertising or communications, break-even response rate, and potential nonsales benefits should be considered. Consumer promotions include coupons, premiums, contests and sweepstakes, bonus packs, price-offs, refunds and rebates, and sampling.

A coupon is a price reduction offer to a consumer or end user. Forms of coupons include print media on- or in-package, in-store, sampling, scanner delivered, cross-ruffing, online, fax, and those delivered by a sales representative. The majority of coupons are offered through freestanding inserts.

Premiums are the prizes, gifts, or other special offers consumers receive when purchasing products. Consumers pay full price for goods or services and then receive the premium.

A contest is an event where participants perform some type of activity in the attempt to win prizes. A sweepstakes allows anyone to participate without performing an activity or even making a purchase. Prizes offered in contests and sweepstakes have both intrinsic and extrinsic values. Intrinsic value comes from participating. Extrinsic value is the worth of the prize itself.

A refund is a cash return of soft goods such as food or clothing. A rebate is a cash return on hard goods, such as appliances and automobiles. Both are designed to lead to quicker sales decisions.

Sampling is the delivery of a good or service for a trial use. It is popular in both consumer markets and business-to-business selling approaches. Bonus packs offer an additional or extra number of items in a special package. A price-off is a temporary reduction in the price of a product to either consumers or other businesses.

The best consumer promotions for acquiring new customers are price-offs and samples. Refunds and rebates often achieve success, as do contests and sweepstakes. The least likely consumer promotions for attracting new customers are coupons, premiums, and bonus packs, which are better approaches for retaining customers and building loyalty.

The four categories of consumers with regard to promotions are (1) promotion prone, (2) price sensitive, (3) brand loyal, and (4) brand preferred. Of these, the best results are achieved when a promotion attracts brand-preferred customers. It is also crucial to make certain that any promotion offered meets the legal and cultural requirements of any region or country in which it is offered.

Trade promotions are presented in many ways. The most common are the ones offered to retailers by manufacturers. Three categories of trade promotions are (1) trade allowances, (2) trade incentives, and (3) trade shows.

Trade allowances provide financial incentives to other channel members to motivate them to purchase products for resale. Some merchants may choose to engage in forward buying to stockpile products while they are on-deal. Others may use diversion to purchase on-deal merchandise and ship it to other locations. Slotting fees are those charged by retailers to stock new products.

Trade incentives are funds provided to others in the channel in exchange for performing some type of marketing function. Three types of trade incentives include cooperative merchandising agreements, premiums or bonus packs, and cooperative or co-op advertising. Calendar promotions are campaigns planned out by retailers to make sure merchandise is continually offered on-deal.

Trade shows are gatherings of buyers. They take many forms. Domestic trade shows are less likely to be places where deals are completed, in contrast to international trade shows.

Before implementing a consumer or trade promotions program, marketing managers first examine the financial impact the promotion will have on the company's contribution margin. The opportunity cost, which is monies not received from one activity because they were spent or forgone on another, should also be considered. Each promotional campaign is tracked so that the marketing team will have additional information to aid in making future decisions. Circumstances are constantly changing. Promotions that were successful in the past may not always be successful in the future. Competition and environmental factors can alter the results.

Promotions should do more than simply provide a tool to respond to the competition. Effective promotions programs build a strong company image and promote bonds with consumers and other businesses. Customer service plays an integral part in taking full advantage of a promotions program.

Chapter Terms

Bonus pack (p. 205)
Brand-loyal consumers (p. 208)
Calendar promotions (p. 211)
Consumer promotions (p. 194)
Contests (p. 200)
Cooperative advertising promotion (p. 212)
Cooperative merchandising agreement (CMA) (p. 211)
Coupon (p. 196)
Cross-ruffing coupons (p. 197)
Diversion (p. 210)
Forward buying (p. 210)
Freestanding inserts (FSIs) (p. 196)
Opportunity cost (p. 200)
Preferred-brand consumers (p. 208)

Premiums (p. 199)
Price-off (p. 206)
Price-sensitive consumers (p. 208)
Promotion-prone consumers (p. 208)
Rebate (p. 202)
Refund (p. 202)
Sampling (p. 204)
Slotting fees (p. 211)
Sweepstakes (p. 200)
Trade allowances (p. 210)
Trade incentives (p. 211)
Trade promotions (p. 194)
Trade shows (p. 213)

Review Questions

1. What are consumer promotions?

2. What are trade promotions?

3. Name four of the most common objectives associated with promotions programs.

4. What types of coupons can marketing teams offer?

5. What are the primary advantages and disadvantages of coupon programs?

6. What are premiums?

7. Name the advantages and disadvantages of premium programs offered to consumers.

8. What is the difference between a contest and a sweepstakes?

9. Describe the concept of intrinsic and extrinsic values as they apply to contests.

10. What is the difference between a refund and a rebate?

11. What are the advantages and disadvantages of rebate programs?

12. Name the advantages and disadvantages associated with giving free samples to customers.

13. What are the advantages and disadvantages of bonus packs?

14. What is a price-off?

15. What are the advantages and disadvantages of price-off programs?

16. Describe the relative ability of each type of consumer promotions program to acquire new customers.

17. Describe the differences between promotion-prone customers, price-sensitive customers, brand-loyal customers, and preferred-brand customers.

18. What are trade allowances?

19. What is a slotting fee?

20. What are the advantages and disadvantages of trade allowance programs?

21. Name three forms of trade incentives. Why do retailers prefer trade allowance programs to trade incentive programs?

22. What are the most common differences between trade shows in the United States and those in other countries?

CUSTOMER CORNER

Andy Kuo is a supervisor of the cashiers in a retail store. Recently, Andy has received memos from upper management asking him to warn his employees about being inattentive when redeeming coupons. Too many customers have been given credit for coupons for similar products (e.g., a Post Toasties coupon being redeemed for Kellogg's Corn Flakes) or for the wrong size (a coupon for 50 cents off on a 20-ounce can being redeemed for a 16-ounce can). The store has been told by several manufacturers that they are sending "mystery shoppers" in to see how coupons are being handled, to find out if they are being handled correctly. If the mystery shoppers find problems, the manufacturers may start to challenge payments back to the retail store for the coupons. Andy has two concerns. The first is offending customers by refusing to take their coupons. The second is that carefully checking every coupon may slow down check-out times and cause longer lines.

1. Should Andy consider a punishment-type approach by creating fines for coupons that are misredeemed? If so, how should he monitor the problem?

2. Should Andy consider a reward-type system for accurate redemptions? If so, how can he monitor success?

3. What should Andy do if a customer becomes angry after having a coupon refused, even when the cashier was correct in doing so?

As a supervisor of the cashiers, Andy has the difficult task of deciding how to handle a recent memo from upper management.

Discussion and Critical Thinking Questions

1. The product life cycle consists of an introduction stage, a take-off or growth stage, the maturity stage, and the decline stage. Which consumer promotions are best suited to each stage in the cycle? Justify your answer.

2. The various types of consumers in the market include innovators, early adopters, the early majority, the late majority, and laggards. Which consumer promotions are best suited to each type of consumer? Justify your answer.

3. Can each form of consumer promotion be used for services? For each promotion, explain how it would or would not be possible. Give an example of each.

4. Which of these products or companies are most likely and least likely to have brand-loyal, promotion-prone, price-sensitive, and brand-preferred customers? Why?
   - Automobile tires
   - Wine and beer
   - Life insurance
   - Airline travel
   - Fast-food restaurants, such as McDonald's and Burger King
   - Home repair stores, such as Lowe's and The Home Depot

5. The product life cycle consists of an introduction stage, a take-off or growth stage, the maturity stage, and the decline stage. Which trade promotions are best suited to each stage in the cycle? Justify your answer.

6. A buying center consists of users, influencers, gatekeepers, decision makers, and buyers. Users are the ones who actually will use the product. Influencers are those who offer information and advice. Gatekeepers decide who will or will not have access to the company. Decision makers have the final word on the purchase. Buyers are those who facilitate the actual purchase. Which trade promotions will have the biggest impact on each of these members? Why?

7. Should a sales representative give the same effort to making presentations to companies that she knows use calendar promotions or spend more time seeking out potential new clients? Defend your answer.

8. Use the following data to construct a break-even analysis table for a coupon promotion. How many items need to be sold to break even, and what response rate is needed?
   a. A total of 300,000 coupons are distributed at a cost of $42 per 1,000.
   b. A coupon is for $3.00 off the retail price of $14.95.
   c. The contribution margin per item is 35%.
   d. Redemption processing costs are $1.04 per coupon.

9. What if, in Question 8, the actual number of coupons returned was 3,205? Calculate the actual response rate and the contribution margin of the coupon promotion. Discuss the merits of the coupon distribution in light of the contribution margin answer you obtained.

10. A local hardware store is offering a 50%-off premium on the purchase of a regular bag of horse and pasture seed. The cost for a 50-pound bag is $72.00. If customers purchase one bag, they can purchase a second bag for half price, or $36.00. The cost of goods sold on the grass seed is 60%. Calculate a contribution margin for the promotion, for the original bag of seed, and for the second bag that sells for $36.00.

11. Perform a contribution analysis for a rebate program based on the following information. Calculate the contribution margin from the rebate program and the opportunity costs that resulted.
    a. The selling price for a canopy swing was $228.00.
    b. The cost of goods sold on the canopy swing was $157.00.
    c. The rebate was for $50.00 off the retail price. During the rebate program, a total of 8,500 swings were sold and 54% of purchasers mailed in the rebate offer.
    d. The processing costs for the rebates were $2.90 per rebate.
    e. The original demand for the swing was 6,000 units, so the rebate resulted in an increase in sales of 2,500 swings.
    f. The cost of co-op advertising was $125,000.

12. Using the data from Question 11, conduct a break-even analysis for the rebate promotion. How many units would have to be sold to contribute the same contribution margin without the rebate?

13. A farm supply store has Wrangler women's jeans priced at $31.96. The store has decided to mark them down to $24.98. The retailer is currently selling approximately 30,000 pairs per week. The cost of goods sold on the jeans is 64%. Conduct a break-even analysis.

Chapter 8 Case

Barney's Bookstore

Randy Barnes loved books. He enjoyed reading them and loved discussing them with others. He knew that at some point his career would be involved in the publishing industry. When a local bookstore was offered for sale, he took the leap. His first decision was to change the name, which had been The Book Center, to Barney's Bookstore, believing it had a nice ring to it. Barney was the nickname given to him by his friends.

When assessing the decision to purchase the outlet, Randy listed several advantages and disadvantages. One primary advantage was location. The site was not only in a major downtown metropolitan area but was also close to a major college campus. Randy believed that both regular readers and college students might drift into the store, especially after he built a reading room complete with a coffee shop featuring pastries and other snacks. Second, the store already had a stream of regulars who Randy believed he could keep.

The biggest obstacle was competition. About 10 blocks away was a Barnes & Noble retail outlet. The city also contained a Books-A-Million and a Hastings.

One of Randy's major concerns was that the major chain bookstores received better prices and trade promotions from major publishing houses. He worried that he would not be able to even visit with sales representatives, much less receive any kind of support. He would either have to cut his margin per book to match the big store prices or risk charging higher prices and losing customers.

What challenges did Randy Barnes face with the purchase of the bookstore?

There were also concerns about clashes between college students, who might be a little more boisterous while in the store, and regular readers, who essentially wanted more of a library-type environment.

Randy also knew that many readers simply purchase books online, through Amazon.com and other Web sites. It was clear that Barney's Bookstore would need to provide something unique in the marketplace in order to stand out enough to entice people to shop there.

The final challenges were in the area of technology. He would have to decide if he wanted to set up any Internet access. Looking at the long term, Randy wanted to be sure that the publishing industry in general would continue to deliver paper, rather than electronic books.

In spite of the challenges, Randy believed hard work, innovative marketing ideas, and high-quality customer service would help him succeed. It was time to get to work.

1. What types of consumer promotions should Barney's Bookstore offer, with regard to books?

2. What types of consumer promotions should Barney's Bookstore offer, with regard to the coffee shop?

3. If Randy is able to visit with salespeople from the major book wholesalers and/or publishing houses, what types of trade promotions should he seek? Which ones do you think he is likely to receive?

4. Besides price, what other features could Barney's Bookstore emphasize in order to provide a unique shopping and buying experience?

 Go to **www.sagepub.com/clow** for additional exercises and study resources. Select **Chapter 8, Sales Promotions** for chapter-specific activities.

What has made IBM successful?

chapter 9
Personal Selling

IBM: A Corporate Legend Continues to Grow

Most people probably believe International Business Machines (IBM) is a relatively new company. In fact, the history of the firm spans nearly a century. In 1911, the C-T-R or Computing-Tabulating-Recording Company was founded. The initial business consisted of assisting the U.S. Census Bureau in finding new and better ways to count and tabulate population characteristics.

Over the years, the original company has sold products ranging from time recorders and punch card machines to cheese slicers. In the 1930s, the legendary corporate executive Thomas Watson Sr. guided the firm. Among the accomplishments in this era were the creations of life insurance, survivor benefits, and paid vacations for employees and the completion of

a contract with the Social Security Administration to maintain employment records of 26 million people.

During World War II, IBM focused on efforts to support the U.S. government. Some of the proceeds earned during this time were dedicated to widows and orphans of IBM employees who died in battle. Following the end of the war, IBM launched the Automatic Sequence Controlled Calculator, the forbearer of the computing age. In 1952, the company launched the first vacuum tube form of computer.

Effective sales techniques have long been a part of IBM's success story. In 1993, with the arrival of Louis V. Gerstner Jr. began a time period in which what he termed *customer-oriented sensibility* was the driving force. At the time, the company was experiencing dramatic losses rather than profits. The problem seemed to be that computer components were being sold individually. The new strategic effort was to provide fully integrated solutions rather than individual products to business customers. This included incorporating the sales of services, products, and technologies into one system.

As the new millennium began to unfold, IBM business-to-business sales concentrated on support of e-commerce operations. In 2000, the company received the prestigious U.S. National Medal of Technology for innovations in the area of storage technologies. The company has long held a reputation for its superior management-training program. It has constantly been the target of other firms seeking to "raid" its ranks and hire away talented and well-trained executives.

IBM serves as an example of a company that has been able to focus on the needs of customers, employees, and the government. A rich corporate history combined with a passion for innovation means that Big Blue will continue to succeed in the fast-moving world of information technology.

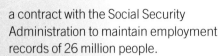

Chapter Overview

The essence of customer service is personal selling. For many customers, the salesperson is the primary, if not the only, contact with the company. An effective salesperson may hold the key to acquiring new customers as well as keeping long-time clients. A high-pressure, intense sales presentation may alienate the new customer a company wishes to acquire or the ongoing client the company needs to keep.

Customer service begins before a sales call is ever made. A well-trained sales force screens potential clients and only makes calls to the most viable of them. This means the salesperson does not waste his time or the time of the customer.

Customer service can become a major selling point for many companies. The salesperson's job is to make sure the customer becomes aware of the quality of service and convinced that it is real. Then, the salesperson follows up to make sure quality service has indeed been delivered.

An effective salesperson may at times be a counselor, advisor, consultant, and even an advocate for the customers she serves. When the company fails in any way, whether it is a defective product or a missed delivery deadline, the salesperson will be on the front lines trying to smooth things over and continue the relationship.

Any person entering the field of marketing should have a solid understanding of the role that the sales force plays in achieving success. This chapter first explains the natures of retail and business-to-business sales positions. Then, the process of business-to-business selling, especially as it relates to customer acquisition, is examined. The complications associated with making international sales calls are briefly described. Finally, this chapter concludes with an analysis of the role of management in the personal selling function.

Retail Selling

Retail sales jobs range from simple cashier-type positions to much more intricate and personal contacts with customers. The primary forms of retail sales are

- order taker,
- commission sales, and
- service salesperson.

An order taker primarily works near the cash register. These types of retail clerks may also stock shelves, answer questions, take orders, and process sales. They are not paid commissions. Many order-taking functions are now being replaced with technologies that allow for self-service checkouts in grocery stores and some of the larger big box retailers, such as Wal-Mart. The same holds true for purchasing airline tickets and making hotel reservations using the Internet rather than any personal contact with the company.

Commission sales are normally jobs in which employees sell bigger ticket items, such as appliances, automobiles, and more expensive clothing items and receive a percentage of the sale as compensation. Many times, the salesperson receives a base salary plus commissions.

A service salesperson sells the services offered by a company. These include insurance sales, stockbrokers, and other financial services. Most service salespeople are paid commissions. Many also render the service, such as a hair stylist.

Varying degrees of emphasis are placed on customer acquisition in these jobs. For example, it is unlikely that order takers focus on new customers, instead emphasizing customer service as the primary task. Order takers can help to acquire customers when a retail store develops a reputation for being a friendly, high-quality service outlet.

Renee is a salesclerk at a bridal shop and receives commissions on the sales of wedding dresses.

The Business-to-Business Selling Function

There are several forms of business-to-business selling. Field salespeople call on businesses. Time and travel costs make field selling the most expensive form of personal selling. Missionary salespeople make contacts with businesses to deliver samples, leave information, check to make sure things are in order, and build relationships. Telemarketers either make calls to potential new customers by phone (outbound) or receive calls from prospective customers (inbound). The two types of salespersons who create contacts with customers are field salespeople and telemarketers. Each follows a fairly standard set of steps involved in acquiring new customers and selling additional goods to ongoing clients.

- Generating leads
- Qualifying prospects
- Knowledge acquisition
- Sales presentation
- Overcoming objections
- Closing the sale
- Follow-up

Figure 9.1

Steps in the Selling Process

Business-to-Business Customer Acquisition

The process of acquiring new business customers revolves around following the standard steps in the selling process, which are identified in Figure 9.1. The marketing manager should try to

From Sales Staff	From Marketing
• Customer referrals	• Database
• Vendor referrals	• Inquiries
• Channel referrals	– Advertising
• Networking	– Web site
• Directories	• Sales promotions
	• Trade shows

Figure 9.2   Generating Sales Leads

What are the best methods of generating leads for Eric, a salesperson for Weymouth Industries?

understand the selling process, even in organizations where the sales function is a separate entity from other marketing elements, such as advertising, promotions, database management, and public relations. She also is likely to be involved in the selling function with the goal of making sure that the message being sent through marketing is the same as the message being conveyed by salespeople.

Generating Leads

The first task in business-to-business selling and customer acquisition is producing leads. The marketing department often helps identify prospects in conjunction with the sales staff. Some of the methods used are displayed in Figure 9.2. Finding quality leads is the goal.

Customer referrals are ideal because a satisfied person makes the recommendation, which gives the salesperson a head start. The sales rep can use the name of the person who gave the referral when she introduces herself. *Vendor* and *channel* leads are advantageous because of the established relationship with each of these entities. Salespeople can also gather leads by *networking* in civic and professional organizations, which allow for personal contacts. The least desirable method for salespeople to generate leads is using a *directory,* which may be obtained from the federal government or a professional organization. The primary problems are that names from directories are less targeted and no personal contact or introduction point exists.

On the marketing side, leads can be generated through a *database*. An effective marketing data warehouse contains three types of names: current customers, prospective customers, and former customers. *Advertising* typically features a toll-free number or Web address for interested individuals. Names can be generated from individuals who visit a company's *Web site*. A *microsite* Web address allows for tracking leads and provides valuable information for development of future marketing plans. Although cookie technology collects information about who visits a site, even if the person does not register, entering that information into the database without consent is a questionable practice. Many marketers consider this unethical. It may also alienate some potential customers. A better and more ethical approach is to only add names of leads from a Web site when the person requests additional information or provides contact information. Leads provided by advertising and the Internet are useful because the person making contact has some interest.

Individuals or companies that respond to *sales promotions* may or may not be good leads. A person may enter a contest or sweepstakes with the hope of winning and not have any interest in the product. A company may take advantage of an off-invoice allowance but not make any commitment to stock the brand on a regular basis or feature it prominently. Some individuals and companies may respond to a promotion because they are interested in trying the brand. Future success depends on how satisfied they become.

Trade shows are excellent for gathering names because attendees are potential buyers who are already interested in the product.[1] In many cases, they attend trade shows to gather more information about products on the market and to make contacts with prospective vendors.

Qualifying Prospects

Not every name or lead produces a new customer. Also, not all new customers are of equal value. With this in mind, qualifying prospects means evaluating leads on two dimensions: (1) the potential income the lead can generate and (2) the probability of acquiring the prospect as a customer. Based on the outcomes of these evaluations, a determination can be made as to the best method of contact and what happens with the lead. The high cost of making personal sales calls means that only the best leads warrant personal visits. Some prospects receive telephone calls or e-mails from an inside salesperson, while others are sent marketing materials by mail or e-mail and are not contacted directly by a salesperson.

Effectively qualifying prospects is a vital step for any company that relies on personal selling to generate the major portion of its income. Each lead will be carefully analyzed using the two categories, sales potential and probability of acquisition. There are several methods of classifying prospects. The most common approach uses the five categories illustrated in Figure 9.3.

High-income potential, Good acquisition probability	A
High-income potential, Poor acquisition probability	B
Low-income potential, Good acquisition probability	C
Low-income potential, Poor acquisition probability	D
	Not a match

Figure 9.3 | Classification of Prospects

The "A" category prospects have the best income potential. They purchase high quantities of an item and a good probability of acquisition exists. Purchase quantities can be evaluated based on company size and sales figures. The probability of acquiring the customer requires a more subjective evaluation. The marketing manager or salesperson conducting the evaluation makes a judgment call regarding the probability that the potential customer can be acquired. When the odds are promising, a field salesperson makes a personal sales call on the prospect.

The "B" category contains prospects that buy larger quantities, but, for various reasons, the probability of acquiring them is lower. It may be that the company is extremely satisfied with a current supplier or other factors may come into play. The best approach for this type of company will be to make contact by telephone, mail, or e-mail and keep it on the radar. The sales team continually looks for an opportunity to get in the door and entice the company to try the brand.

Categories "C" and "D" are less attractive. They typically buy in smaller quantities. As a result, less costly methods of contact are used rather than personal sales calls. The "C" category may be reached by telephone or e-mail. The "D" category would normally be contacted by e-mail only, if at all. These companies normally receive marketing materials only when they request them.

The final category is "not a match." These companies do not fit. The prospect does not routinely purchase the product. Or when the product is purchased, a major retooling to meet specifications is required.

Knowledge Acquisition

Knowledge acquisition begins with gathering the information needed to make an effective sales presentation. The salesperson assumes that the sales volume potential and likelihood of obtaining the prospect as a customer have already been determined through the qualifying process. Figure 9.4 identifies the types of information that should be gathered.

Understanding the prospect's *business, customers,* and *needs* is crucial. Dr. Roger Levin is a dentist. He notes that dental practices require goods and services that increase office efficiency, reduce costs, generate additional revenues, and enhance the quality of patient care. In selling to dental practices, Dr. Levin suggests that the sales representatives who know their products and are prepared to make well-informed presentations are more successful. Also, the sales reps who understand the needs of individual dental practices are better able to make sales. A practice moving toward less reliance on dental insurance to generate revenues becomes a good prospect for cosmetic services, such as veneers, whitening products, and implants. A successful sales rep also knows the demographic makeup of the dentist's patients. Pediatric dentistry has different needs than a practice catering to adults.[2] In simple terms, proper acquisition knowledge leads to better sales calls.

Purchase criteria information is important to gather. It consists of (1) the criteria that the buyer will use in making the purchase decision and (2) the importance of promotions to the

- Prospect's business
- Prospect's customers
- Prospect's needs
- Purchase criteria
- Importance of promotions
- Current vendor(s) and level of satisfaction
- Risk factors and switching costs
- Names of decision makers and influencers

Figure 9.4

Knowledge Acquisition Information

How is the marketing team involved in sales presentations?

buyer. This information guides the salesperson, who then knows what to stress in the presentation. A buyer who expresses interest in delivery times or the quality of merchandise will be handled differently than one focusing primarily on price. The salesperson also wants to know whether *promotions* are important and, if so, which type. Some prospects prefer price-off offers, while others want different incentives, such as cooperative advertising dollars.

Evaluating *current vendors* and *levels of satisfaction* with those vendors assists in making the sales call at the right time. Prospects that are satisfied with a current vendor are unlikely to change. Dissatisfied prospects and those not completely satisfied provide an opening for a new business to make a sales call. Part of this appraisal includes an analysis of *risk factors* and *switching costs*. When a high risk is associated with switching vendors, the buyer must be highly dissatisfied with a current vendor before a change will be made.

The final pieces of information to be gathered are the *names of the decision makers and influencers*. Often, the purchasing agent does not make the final decision. The purchasing agent may rely on others within the organization for advice or recommendations. Talking to these influencers is critical. Identifying and reaching decision makers may be more difficult but is often worth the effort.

Sales Presentation

A sales call serves several purposes. The sales call can be used to gather information, discuss bid specifications, answer questions, or to close the deal with a final pitch or offer.[3] The salesperson should know the primary intent of the call in advance.

The marketing department normally helps develop the sales presentation. The messages salespeople convey to prospects and customers must mesh with the messages sent in various marketing materials. The safest way to ensure that this occurs is for the marketing department to prepare all the sales literature and sales presentation kits. While this may be more difficult when the two are housed in different departments, it produces a stronger sales message that matches with the marketing message.

Many types of sales presentations are possible. The various methods that can be placed into one of the four categories are (1) stimulus-response, (2) need-satisfaction, (3) problem-solution, and (4) mission-sharing.[4]

A **stimulus-response** sales approach uses specific statements (stimuli) to elicit specific responses from customers, similar to what is called a "canned" sales pitch. Typically, the salesperson memorizes the stimulus statement (the pitch). Telemarketers, retail salesclerks, and new field sales reps often rely on this method. Marketing may be actively involved in preparing scripts for telemarketers or e-mail responders.

The **need-satisfaction** sales approach places emphasis on discovering a customer's needs and then providing solutions that meet those needs. The salesperson should be skillful at asking the right questions. Quality relationships with customers make it easier to discover their needs. Providing marketing materials for this approach may be more difficult, especially when buyer needs vary. Fortunately, in most industries an overlap of needs can be found. The marketing team can meet with the sales staff to discover the most common needs and then appropriate marketing and sales brochures or other materials are prepared.

The **problem-solution** sales approach requires employees from the selling organization to analyze the buyer's operations. A team, including engineers, salespeople, and other experts, investigates a potential customer's operations and problems and then offers feasible solutions.

This approach matches well with complex buying situations. Members of the marketing department may be asked to help prepare the final sales presentation, whether in printed form or in some other visual form, such as PowerPoint or multimedia.

In a mission-sharing sales approach, two organizations develop a common mission. They then share resources to accomplish that mission. This partnership resembles a joint venture as much as a selling relationship. With this type of approach, other members of the marketing department will be assigned to the sales team.

Each of these approaches helps the salesperson develop stronger bonds with customers. While making a sale is important, building a longer-term relationship should be another important goal when making a presentation.

Overcoming Objections

Salespeople respond to objections in a number of ways, as shown in Figure 9.5.[5] The *head-on approach* means that the salesperson handles the objection directly. Doing so indicates that the customer or prospect is wrong; consequently, tact must be exhibited by the salesperson. No one likes being told that he is wrong. The direct approach must be used in such a way that it does not offend the customer. The *indirect approach* allows the salesperson to never really tell the customer that he is wrong. Instead, the salesperson sympathizes with the customer's viewpoint and then provides the correct information.

The *compensation method* is often used when the customer raises an objection that is partially true. The salesperson can then reply "yes, but . . ." and then explain the product's benefits or features that will overcome the customer's objection.

For anxious and worried customers, the *"feel, felt, found"* method, in which the salesperson allows the customers to talk about their fears or worries about the product, may be used. The salesperson then relates an experience of another customer who had the same fears and how the customer felt. The salesperson then explains how her product calmed those fears and how the customer felt afterward.

With the *boomerang approach,* the salesperson answers the customer's objection by using it as the very reason to make the purchase. For this method to work, the objection needs to be partially true. For instance, if a prospect says "I can't afford life insurance right now" the boomerang approach by the insurance salesperson would be, "You can't really afford right now not to have life insurance." The salesperson could add, "Suppose something happened to you tomorrow. Where would your spouse and children be? Would they be able to maintain this same quality of life that you have provided for them?"

Closing the Sale

The most important part of the sales call is the closing, yet it may be the most difficult part of the sales presentation. Feeling rejected when a prospect or customer says "no" represents the primary fear. To be successful, a salesperson must overcome that fear and master the closing. She must be willing to ask for a sale. Customers rarely take the initiative themselves to close the sale with an offer to purchase the product.

Figure 9.6 provides a list of some of the more common closing methods. The one that should be used depends on the personality of the salesperson, the characteristics of the customer or prospect, and the situation around the sales call. Salespeople tend to have favorite closing methods but vary their approaches as situations change.

With the *trial method,* the salesperson solicits feedback that provides information regarding what will be the customer's reaction, without asking him directly for the sale. If the reaction is positive, then the salesperson can move on to a *direct closing,* which is an outright request for an order. Another alternative is to *summarize* the product's benefits and how it meets the customer's needs prior to asking for the order.

Sometimes a salesperson asks a series of questions along the way, ensuring that the customer will *continuously* respond "yes." By answering "yes" to smaller questions about the benefits of a product, when it is time to ask for the order, the customer will be more likely to respond with a "yes." Another way of closing is to *assume* that the customer will say "yes," so

- Head-on method
- Indirect denial
- Compensation method
- "Feel, felt, found"
- Boomerang method

Figure 9.5

Handling Objections

- Trial close
- Direct close
- Summarization close
- Continuous-yes close
- Assumptive close

Figure 9.6

Closing Methods

the salesperson will ask something, such as "How many cases do you want?" or "How would you like this to be shipped?"

Follow-Up

The follow-up is the final crucial element of an effective sales presentation. Keeping a customer happy after the purchase may result in repeat business and customer loyalty. It is much more cost-effective to retain customers than to continually find new ones. Unfortunately, following up may be neglected by the salesperson, especially when he receives commission on new sales and not on follow-up activities.

The critical importance of following up sales calls, even those in which a sale is not made, means that a follow-up plan must be developed. It can be developed by the marketing department or can be a joint effort of the marketing and sales departments. Several outcomes should be considered.

First, many sales calls do not generate orders. A decision must be made as to when, who, and how to follow up on the lead. The salesperson should record the outcome of the sales call in the database and then file a follow-up cue. The cue may read as follows:

- Have inside salesperson follow-up on this lead in 2 weeks to discuss the sending of a sample product to the business. Contact should be made by telephone.
- Marketing should send a brochure in 1 week on the new RC77 model to the attention of Mr. Danny McCarthy.

In other instances, a cue may say to make contact in 3 or 6 months. It may say downgrade to a "B" or "C" category. A follow-up is crucial after an order has been placed. The standard sequence is as follows:

- Send a thank you for the order with an estimated date of shipment.
- Send an e-mail announcing the order has been pulled and placed on a truck. A shipping number would be included for the buyer to check during shipment.
- Make a follow-up phone call or personal visit or send an e-mail to see if the merchandise has arrived and is in good working order. (The follow-up method depends on the size of the order and the customer's potential for additional orders.)
- Make a contact after a specified period of time to measure the customer's satisfaction level.

Motivating salespeople to follow up on a lead can be difficult. Some marketing managers are resigned to this problem and look for other solutions. One approach consists of making the follow-up one of the duties of the marketing department or a specific individual from the sales staff. Either way, proper follow-ups enhance the effectiveness of sales calls, including those focused on customer acquisition.

STOP AND THINK

Consider a company that sells kitchen appliances, equipment, and supplies for restaurants ranging from computer-controlled ovens and cookers to the pots and pans needed to prepare food. Although this company caters to large restaurant chains, they also strive to sell merchandise to small chains and independent restaurant operations.

1. Where should a salesperson look for prospects?
2. How should prospects be qualified?
3. Which of the four types of sales presentations is the best? Does the size of the restaurant chain affect which presentation is used?
4. What type of follow-up should the company require from its salespeople? Why is a follow-up important?

Relationship Selling

Personal selling remains a primary method of acquiring new customers. It can also result in increasing levels of purchases by current customers. The goal of a sales call, however, should not be simply to make a sale. An additional objective should be to develop longer-term relationships with customers. A stronger, more strategic partnership results from buyers and sellers working together. Reaching that point requires cooperation.

Relationship selling is the process of turning initial transactions into stronger partnerships over time. A trial purchase made by the customer does not lead to a great deal of commitment from either party. A positive experience for both sides, however, can lead to an expanded relationship through growing commitments made by the parties. This may or may not involve an actual contract. It takes time to evolve into a truly trusting relationship. Eventually, buyers and sellers who develop strong relationships may enter into data interchanges to facilitate purchases and reorders. Moving to this level can lead to a shared mission that is designed to direct the strategic activities of both companies.[6]

Personal Selling: An International Perspective

As the global marketplace continues to shrink, an increasing number of sales representatives find themselves traveling to foreign countries. International selling presents a series of complications and challenges that are not present in other contexts. The issues to confront include

- language and slang;
- culture and subculture;
- methods of introduction;
- eye contact;
- body language, gestures, and physical distance;
- giving and receiving gifts;
- use of business cards;
- table manners and foods; and
- directness in tone.

Why is relationship selling important?

To overcome language and slang issues, either the salesperson will attempt to learn the language or will be assisted by a translator. Cultural and subcultural nuances are often explained by a *cultural assimilator* who is familiar with the religions, folkways, mores, local holidays, and other differences.

One aspect of culture that affects the goals, performance levels, and performance evaluations of members of the sales force is an emphasis on the individual versus the group and the subsequent orientation toward task completion. In most Western countries, such as the United States, emphasis is placed on making deals, then closing them. Individuals are more important than the group. Asian countries, Latin America, and Eastern Europe have relationship-oriented cultures. Emphasis is placed on developing long-term relationships. Closing deals is not as important as developing strong relationships with customers. Also, groups are viewed as being more important than individuals. In such countries, salespeople spend considerable time in getting to know clients, developing relationships, and working for the benefit of the entire sales force. Individual sales are not as crucial.

Methods of introduction can be quickly learned, from bowing to handshakes and other forms of greeting. Eye contact in some cultures is to be avoided, as it appears to be challenging and aggressive. Not making eye contact may make a person seem devious or suspicious in others. Body language includes items as simple as crossing one's legs, showing the soles of one's feet or shoes, and posture. An effective salesperson knows about any gestures that are harmless in one culture but offensive in another.

Physical distance is the space between the salesperson and the client. In some countries, people stand practically nose to nose. In the United States, a much bigger distance is comfortable. There are cultures in which holding hands signifies trust and is an important part of a sales contact.

Knowing the type of gift to give is an important feature of selling internationally. Also, being aware that in some cultures a gift is not opened when received but rather later in a private setting can fend off an embarrassing *faux pas*.

In some countries, the presentation of a business card becomes a significant moment, because officials are guarded about who receives them. There are noticeable variances in what are considered to be appropriate table manners across cultures. For example, in some countries, it is rude to move your hands to where they cannot be seen below the table. Not only foods but also methods of food preparation may require some adaptation.

Directness in language and tone may be considered aggressive and inappropriate in some international selling situations. In others, it is expected and doing less indicates weakness.

Managing an international sales force presents additional difficulties. While money may be a primary motivator for some salespersons, being considered a valuable part of the team will be far more important to others. A sales manager who sends a sales force abroad must expect a period of adjustment and pay attention to obstacles, such as whether a spouse will accompany the salesperson, especially when the employee will be gone for an extended period of time.

Managing a Sales Force

Managing a sales force has been the subject of numerous books, research reports, and magazine articles. The advice ranges from savvy and sophisticated to simple and almost silly. Managing a sales department requires a unique combination of activities and relationships with other departments in the company. In this section, five key aspects of sales force management are described:

1. Recruiting and selection

2. Training

3. Compensation

4. Motivational programs

5. Performance evaluation

Recruiting and Selection

Recruiting a successful sales force requires the cooperation of the marketing department, the sales manager, the sales force, and the human resource office. Recruiting of a sales team (or any type of employee) should be ongoing and systematic.

chapter 9 | Personal Selling 233

The human resource department and the company's sales team should constantly look for people who can be encouraged to send in applications and résumés. The idea is to always have a strong pool of applicants available.

Recruiting should be *systematic* and tap all internal and external sources. Internal sources include referrals by current and even past employees. A traveling sales force can become an excellent source of information and encouragement for those thinking about joining the company.

External sources for recruiting include all the standard places listed in Figure 9.7. Each may yield sets of applicants for various positions in the company. The person in charge of recruiting should make sure that the organizations that are contacted know the primary selection criteria. The goal is to ensure that the people who apply are qualified for the positions they seek.

Cooperation between the human resource and marketing departments is crucial to an effective selection process. Most of the time, applicants are screened across four criteria:

1. Level of education
2. Degree of experience
3. Personality and personal characteristics
4. Legal compliance

- Classified ads in newspapers
- Internet job placement sites, such as Monster.com
- High school and college campus visits
- Independent recruiting companies (also called private employment agencies and headhunters)
- Government (public) employment agencies
- Job and career fairs
- Professional sales organizations
- Unsolicited applications

Figure 9.7 | External Recruiting

The first two, education and experience, are often ascertained by reviewing the employment application or résumé. Personality characteristics will be revealed in the interview process, which may be conducted by someone from the human resource department, by the marketing or sales department employee who will supervise the new hire, or by both. Legal compliance should result from the methods used to choose employees.[7]

The selection process helps the sales manager learn about the applicant's aptitudes, skill levels, and attitudes. **Aptitude** refers to a person's natural ability, including a person's verbal intelligence, mathematical ability, and reasoning skills. No consensus exists regarding which aptitudes lead to the best performance; however, verbal and math ability are important as is the cognitive ability to think logically and to solve problems.[8] Cognitive ability is especially important for the higher-order sales approaches, such as problem solving and mission sharing. Both of these approaches require the use of problem-solving cognitive skills.

How important are personal characteristics in selecting salespeople?

Skill level suggests a person's learned proficiencies, such as product knowledge, interpersonal communication skills, and presentation skills. Product and customer knowledge are essential. Salespeople need to thoroughly understand the products they sell. More important, they need to understand the customer's business in order to see how the product will meet specific needs. Sales presentation formats, closing techniques, and ways to handle objections are skills that can be acquired through training and refresher courses.

Personal characteristics include a variety of traits that make an individual unique. It helps if a salesperson is extroverted, has a strong self-esteem, is sociable, and has a strong drive to succeed. An outgoing and confident individual will be more comfortable talking to customers and prospects than an introvert. Salespeople face continual rejection, which makes self-esteem important. They must be able to continue calling on customers despite "no" responses.

The human resource manager works closely with the sales manager and other executives to create a fair selection process that identifies the candidate with the best chance of success. Selection is time-consuming and expensive. Everyone involved has a strong incentive to make the right choice the first time.

Training

Training salespeople takes place both on-the-job and off-the job. The main on-the-job methods include demonstration and sink-or-swim methods.

Often, new salespeople are trained by current, experienced salespeople, which is the demonstration method. It is important to pick the seasoned salesperson carefully. The person will have a major impact on the ways the new employee perceives the company and performs on the job. A salesperson who enjoys the teaching process is more likely to stress professionalism and emphasize acting ethically.

The sink-or-swim method involves a rudimentary training process and then the salesperson is on his own and is expected to learn by doing. Many times, this results in a great deal of turnover. For some products and some companies, however, investing in long-term training may not seem viable. In those circumstances, sink-or-swim becomes the choice.

Off-the-job training takes place using films and classroom, simulations, and interactions with trainers. Films and classrooms can focus on two elements. The first is to explain the company and its products. The second concentrates on teaching selling tactics.

Simulations are most viable for order-taker types of positions. The individual can practice closing a sale, ringing up the item, making suggestions regarding additional merchandise, offering a credit card application, making change, and bagging or wrapping the product. Many company leaders prefer some off-the-floor training before sending these new employees out to work with the public.

Sales trainers come in two major categories. The first type teaches better selling tactics. The second offers motivational speeches designed to "fire up" the new salesperson or the entire sales force. Many large companies employ internal sales trainers. Others retain external specialists to visit and make presentations.

The first-line supervisor plays a key role in reinforcing what has been taught in sales training. One of the major responsibilities of a supervisor is to carefully train and socialize new salespeople to help them fit into the company.

Compensation

The sales force will be strongly affected by the compensation system that is in place. Compensation packages vary by organization. The marketing manager, in conjunction with top management and the human resource department, analyzes the type of sales force needed and then determines the best combination of compensation and rewards (see Figure 9.8). The first choice is between paying a salary and offering commissions, or a combination of both.

Salary

A salary is a fixed amount of pay for a given time period. Typically, a salary covers a period of 1 year. Usually, paying a salary means the employee will sign an employment contract. The primary advantages of a salary are as follows:

- It frequently leads to a greater focus on customer service and meeting customer needs.
- The sales manager can emphasize nonselling activities, such as follow-up.
- Rewards are equal even when there are differences in sales territory potential.
- The system can be structured to reward experience and competence.
- The pay system reduces the inclination to use high-pressure selling techniques.

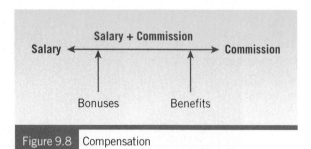

Figure 9.8 Compensation

Paying a straight salary may create disadvantages. The primary problem is that there is little incentive to push a sale. The salesperson receives the same amount of pay regardless of total sales. Also, in some instances, the salesperson may end up spending more time on nonselling activities than on selling. In general, the concern that a salary-only pay system creates is that employees may become complacent, leaving the sales manager to find new ways to inspire them.

Commissions

A second form of pay is a straight commission. Commissions are payments for sales, by the unit or by sales volume over a period of time, typically 1 month. Commissions are viewed as a better motivational tool, because they directly link pay to performance. This means the top salespeople receive the greatest rewards. Commissions are typically paid to salespeople representing bigger ticket items, including durable goods such as cars and appliances. In business-to-business sales, commissions may be based on the sales volume for a period of time, such as for 1 month.

Some companies tie sales expenses to commissions, paying expenses as a percentage of total sales. This approach reduces the amount of time a salesperson spends turning in expense vouchers and receipts and lessens the amount of time the accounting department spends on reimbursing expenses.

Straight commissions can create problems. These tend to be the opposite of the advantages of paying someone a straight salary. For example,

- The salesperson may focus less on customer service.
- There will be less effort given to nonselling activities, such as follow-up.
- There is no incentive to work with a team, the support staff, or other salespeople.
- The system can produce high-pressure sales techniques.
- The system encourages a single-transaction mentality.

In general, someone who is paid a straight commission is likely to spend less time on anything not directly related to selling. While customer relationships are important, they become significant to the salesperson only when additional purchases result. This means that a straight commission system may lead to an extremely short-term focus, and the sales manager can do little to change that mindset.

Salary Plus Commission

Most companies use a salary plus commission combination. The mix of the two depends on the products being sold and the sales manager's goals. When the objective is to stress customer service and higher-quality relationships with customers, a greater part of the pay will be derived from salary. When the primary goal is to boost sales, add new customers, and increase market share, a greater amount of compensation comes from commissions.

Bonuses

Bonuses can be used in the place of commissions or in conjunction with commissions. Bonuses may be paid for the completion of a single project or given out on an annual basis based on overall company performance. They are offered as either individual or

In choosing employee bonuses, which is the best, a group bonus or individual bonuses?

group incentives. Bonuses granted on a quarterly or semi-annual basis serve as more constant incentives. Bonus programs are developed with various goals in mind. Group bonuses encourage teamwork. Individual bonuses emphasize personal accomplishments. It is not unusual for a company to use both, depending on the project. When a sales team makes a presentation to a client, group incentives are a better fit. When sales are made by individual employees, bonuses tend to be paid on a personal basis.

Sales managers know that when bonuses are expected, such as an annual Christmas payment, they often lose value as incentives. Further, when the bonus is not paid, a negative impact on morale becomes the result.

Benefits

Managing the benefit package has become a major challenge for many human resource managers. Benefits have a major impact on three key organizational outcomes:

1. Recruiting
2. Retention
3. Cost management

In terms of *recruiting,* the sales manager clearly wants to be able to offer the best possible package, in order to entice the best people to join the company. Salespeople and other employees are interested in paid vacation days, health insurance, purchase discounts, in-house day care, life insurance, personal use of a company car, and others. Highly sought-after recruits compare benefit packages as well the other forms of pay (salary and commission).

Retention is a second critical issue. Keeping the best salespeople possible creates a major advantage for the sales manager. Experienced and quality employees know customers better, develop longer-term relationships with clients, and may have knowledge about what competitors are doing and other news from the market channel. Retention may be most affected by the cost and availability of health insurance and by the pension plan. A company that charges for health insurance will be at a disadvantage if other firms grant it for free. Pension plans are known as the "golden fetters" that help retain employees. A salesperson who has built up time in a pension program is often less inclined to start over somewhere else.

The human resource department is often charged with trying to hold down the *costs* of benefit packages. This can place the human resource manager at odds with the sales manager. The goal for both should be to develop the best possible program for the company at a reasonable cost.[9]

STOP AND THINK

Consider a marketing department that is divided into four main sections: advertising and promotion, database activities, public relations, and sales (business to business). In the first three, employees are paid salaries and only receive bonuses for companywide performance at the end of the year. The sales force receives commissions and bonuses for closing major deals as well as the end-of-the-year bonus.

1. Should the managers of each department disclose how all the employees are compensated (an open pay system)?
2. Can you see any potential effects on morale if the advertising and promotions, database activities, and public relations employees discover the differences in compensation?
3. Does this situation create any potential conflicts?
4. How should pay raises be given in this situation?

Managing Pay Systems

The ultimate objective of a pay system is to balance short-term and long-term goals. In the short term, the sales force should have sufficient incentives to work hard at both selling and non-selling activities. In the long term, the pay system should be perceived as being fair, creating opportunities to succeed, and being helpful in retaining successful employees.

A compensation package becomes more complex when an organization employs different kinds of salespeople. A firm with both field salespeople and an inside sales staff that handles inbound telephone calls and Internet inquiries is more complicated. The sales manager must decide whether the inside sales staff should be paid a commission or a salary. This becomes challenging when the inside sales staff is encouraged to cross-sell products. This may lead to the addition of some form of bonus or commission. The situation becomes even more complex when a lead that was initiated by the telephone salesperson is followed up by the field salesperson. The sales manager and human resource manager should set up a system that divides the commission or compensates both individuals.

Another complicated situation occurs when a company employs missionary salespeople, individuals who handle major accounts, and outbound telemarketing employees. Many times there are also individuals who qualify leads. Higher levels of success are likely to occur when the sales manager coordinates the efforts of all these salespeople with the efforts of the support staff. Developing a pay system that is equitable to each type of employee can become a major challenge.

Motivational Programs

Motivating a sales force means discovering the types of incentives with the best impact. An experienced sales manager knows that incentives and motives vary by individual. One person may be driven solely by financial rewards. Another may value money but also craves attention, praise, and other nonmonetary rewards. As a result, typical motivation programs designed by sales managers in conjunction with the human resource manager contain combinations of financial and nonfinancial rewards and incentives.

Financial Incentives

Beyond the pay system established by the sales department, additional money will be allocated to incentives for higher performance. The best programs recognize that these funds create both intrinsic and extrinsic rewards. An *intrinsic* reward comes from participating in the program and the feelings that accompany success. More than one sports figure has noted that winning does result in a monetary award, such as the first prize in a golf tournament or a World Series share for a baseball player, but that the winning itself is "something they can never take away." The same holds true for winning a sales contest. The *extrinsic* part of the reward is the money or prize, or what the money can buy. The most common financial incentives used in a sales department are promotions, pay raises, and contests (see Figure 9.9).

Promotions and Pay Raises

Promotions and advancements present tangible rewards for success. A promotion may be based on being the most technically skilled or showing the potential to lead and manage others. Promotions may be especially important to new and younger salespeople. These individuals have personal goals involving advancing in the organization.

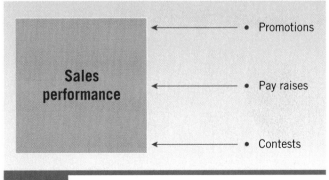

Figure 9.9 | Financial Incentives

Not every top seller makes a good sales manager. Selling skills are not the same skills needed to manage people. For this reason, many organizations create two promotional tracks. One involves moving into management as a supervisor or shift lead, district manager, and then into a role such as vice president of sales or marketing. The other track features promotions or advancements within sales. It may be a move to a larger territory or to a major account. The person is still involved in selling but with greater responsibility and, in most cases, larger and more lucrative accounts.

Pay raises accompany both promotions and meritorious performance appraisals. When pay raises are granted *across-the-board,* the motivation value is lower. When a company grants *merit raises,* and the system is perceived as being fair, a greater impact on motivation occurs.

Contests

A second financial incentive program is a sales contest. Contests can be geared to individual or group performance. They can be based on sales, on new customers obtained, or on generating qualified leads.

Contests and incentive programs that involve merchandise often generate more buzz and achieve better results than cash prizes. Jimmy Beyer, a national sales manager with Sony Electronics, notes that "choosing a product for an incentive program has a special impact because you're allowing people to win something that they might not go out and buy on their own. If you give them a big-screen HDTV, they're going to be very excited about that. If you give them a cash reward of the same amount, there's a good chance they will spend the money on something else" and have nothing to show for it.[10]

For sales contests, why are prizes, such as a HDTV, a better incentive than cash?

The impact of a sales contest varies by employee. The most competitive and those who think that they have the best chances of winning will take the event most seriously.

Someone who believes that he doesn't stand a chance of winning will probably not be affected by the contest unless the employee believes a visible lack of effort will make him look bad.

Group contests can create positive and negative outcomes. When the contest succeeds, the group cooperates and encourages each member to contribute. When the contest has a negative result, it is probably because the members of the losing team started to blame each other for the failure.

A contest only motivates the sales force when it appears to be fair. If one person has the most favorable sales territory, leading her to routinely win every contest, it will make the others in the team envious of her and dissatisfied with the sales manager. The same holds true for group contests. The criteria for winning should be established to give every participant a fair chance.

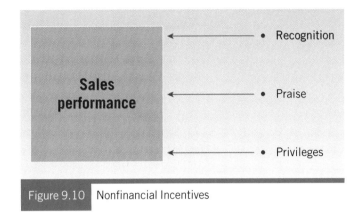

Figure 9.10 Nonfinancial Incentives

Nonfinancial Incentives

While financial incentives are the most visible motivators, the sales manager can supplement them with nonfinancial rewards. Given at the right time and in the proper context, nonfinancial awards can be powerful motivators, especially to those who value the opinions of others. Figure 9.10 identifies the primary types of nonfinancial rewards that can be used with salespeople.

Sales performance can be enhanced through *recognition*. For it to work as a motivator, recognition should be (1) presented in public and (2) difficult to achieve. When a salesperson is recognized for an accomplishment, it should be announced at public meetings, in company newsletters, or even in the local newspaper.

Recognition must be achievable for all, but it must also be meaningful. Some common examples might include "Salesperson of the Year" or public notice that a salesperson obtained the most new accounts during a specified period. Recognition can also be targeted to match specific elements of a firm's goals. When a sales manager wants to encourage salespeople to spend more time with current accounts and increase the amount these companies spend, the manager can create an award for the top person or persons based on the percent increase in orders from current customers.

Praise includes general expressions of appreciation such as "Good job!" and also commendations for specific accomplishments. A supervisor can also praise an employee when he puts in a great deal of effort, even if that effort does not succeed. For example, a salesperson might have done everything in her power to capture a new account but lost out due to favoritism by the buyer or a lower price. It still does not hurt to praise her effort. Praise can also be given for a positive attitude and spirit of collaboration. A statement such as "You're being a great team player" may yield additional effort and cooperation.

Recognition and praise are the opposite of *condemnation,* which often lowers morale. Instead of making a salesperson feel wanted and appreciated, the employee is called on the carpet for not reaching a quota. Another may be taken to task for an error that was made. Praise and recognition are far more helpful than insults and intimidation.

Special privileges are the perks that let an employee know he is appreciated. A "Salesperson of the Month" might also receive a reserved parking spot near the entrance door for the next month. A "Salesperson of the Quarter" can be given a free 1-year membership at the local golf course. The number and types of privileges a firm can offer are limitless. Making them meaningful and something of value to every employee is the key.

Are recognition and praise important motivators for salespeople?

Performance Evaluation

One of the more challenging tasks of sales management is the responsibility of evaluating sales-people. Figure 9.11 identifies the three primary categories of methods used in sales performance evaluations. Most firms employ multiple measures in evaluations and often include measures from each of the three categories. The degree of emphasis placed on each measure depends on the firm's goals as well as what an individual manager wants salespeople to accomplish.

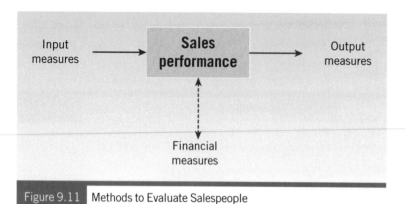

Figure 9.11   Methods to Evaluate Salespeople

- Presales activities
  - Amount of time in presales activities
  - Number of precontacts (e-mail, phone calls)
  - Number of proposals prepared
  - Number of prospects evaluated
- Selling activities
  - Number of sales calls made
  - Number of sales presentations made
  - Time spent in sales presentations
  - Number of prospects contacted
  - Number of prospects converted
- Postselling activities
  - Number of follow-up contacts
- Nonselling activities
  - Number of samples distributed
  - Number of team sales meetings
  - Number of team sales contacts

Figure 9.12   Input Measures

Input Measures

Figure 9.12 identifies various input measures used in the evaluation. The premise that guides input measures is that when salespeople spend time performing the various activities involved in selling, results will follow. An activity such as making sales calls should result in a certain percentage of orders. Time spent on follow-up calls should lead to better perceptions of customer service. This, in turn, is reflected in higher levels of customer retention and repeat business.

Input measures work best when salespeople are paid a salary or the majority of their income is generated from salary. They also work well for new salespeople who are just learning the industry.

Presales activities are measured in order to encourage salespeople to carefully prepare for sales calls. They are especially important when high dollar contract proposals and complex selling situations are present. For a member of the sales staff who qualifies prospects, a record of the number evaluated would be an important measure of the person's productivity.

In evaluating *selling activities,* the assumption is that if a salesperson carries out these activities, sales will result. The emphasis remains on carrying out the activities rather than on actual sales. This reduces the pressure on salespeople to close a sale and allows them more time to build relationships and to provide customer service.

In terms of *postselling activities,* many sales departments maintain records of how many follow-up contacts were made, the method used to make contacts, and the amount of time spent. Remember, it is not only purchase orders that require a follow-up. Unsuccessful visits should also be considered with the goal of capturing the account at a later time.

Input measures that are useful in evaluating the efforts of missionary salespeople include *nonselling activities.* Often, a sales team consists of a number of people, and making a sale can take a considerable amount of time. It is not unusual for a team to spend several months working with a client and in developing a proposal. Credit for these activities should be given as part of a quality performance appraisal program.

Output Measures

Using output measures to evaluate salespeople places greater emphasis on actual results. As a result, they work best with compensation systems that pay commissions and bonuses and grant other rewards for producing results. Figure 9.13 highlights various output measures that can be used.

The *accounts* part of output measures emphasize account activity more than the size of the order. The goal is to serve current accounts and develop new accounts. Increasing the number of accounts by placing orders is important as is reducing the number of lost accounts. When salespeople are evaluated based on account activity, management is stressing customer service and customer retention.

The *orders* part of output measures places the emphasis on sales. These measures are often used to encourage salespeople to increase both the number of orders and the size of orders. Obtaining new orders and the quantity of particular items sold should also be noted.

Financial Measures

For some marketing managers, vice presidents, and CEOs, the most important criterion for evaluating salespeople is the impact on the bottom line. A salesperson's primary task is to sell and to generate a profit for the firm. Measuring the impact of a salesperson's efforts includes analysis of

- sales volume,
- gross margin on the sales volume, and
- the contribution margin produced by each salesperson.

These figures are important regardless of other measures that are used.

The contribution margin figure becomes the most important when the salesperson can adjust the selling price and offer consumer or trade promotions to customers. Lowering the price and offering promotional incentives can not only induce sales but also may create a situation where a company has a high volume of sales but is losing money overall. As was shown regarding promotions, to offer a customer a 5% or 10% reduction in price requires a considerable increase in demand to offset the lower contribution margin that is generated.

An Example

To understand the importance of financial measures, consider Table 9.1. It displays the financial measures for four salespeople and the overall company financial status for one quarter.

- Accounts
  - Number of new accounts
  - Number of accounts placing orders
  - Number of active accounts
  - Number of lost accounts
- Orders
  - Number of orders
  - Average size of orders
  - Number of new orders
  - Quantity of each product sold

Figure 9.13

Output Measures

	Company	Salesperson A	Salesperson B	Salesperson C	Salesperson D
Sales ($)	1,787,560	436,703	511,487	451,045	388,325
Price incentives ($)	104,476	26,202	33,247	33,377	11,650
Promotional incentives ($)	47,343	5,240	21,994	18,944	1,165
Cost of goods sold ($)	1,090,412	266,389	312,007	275,137	236,878
Gross margin ($)	545,329	138,872	144,239	123,586	138,632
Direct selling expenses					
Salary ($)	39,960	10,322	10,212	11,212	8,214
Commission (3%) ($)	53,627	13,101	15,345	13,531	11,650
Travel ($)	13,564	3,243	3,143	3,723	3,455
Bonuses ($)	3,618	628	1,824	966	200
Benefits ($)	22,357	5,532	6,298	5,913	4,615
Total selling expenses ($)	133,126	32,826	36,821	35,346	28,133
Contribution margin ($)	412,203	106,046	107,418	88,241	110,499
Contribution margin (%)	23.06	24.28	21.00	19.56	28.46
Salesperson's gross pay ($)		24,051	27,381	25,709	20,064

Table 9.1　Quarterly Sales Report

As shown in Table 9.1, sales were $1.787 million. The contribution margin was 23.06%, resulting in $412,203 that could be used for operating and direct expenses.

When the four salespeople are evaluated, considerable differences exist. The contribution margin as a percent is the highest for Salesperson D, 28.46%. It is the lowest for Salesperson C, 19.56%. Thus, when it comes to generating profits for the firm, Salesperson D appears to be the best and Salesperson C the worst.

When the issue of generating sales volume is examined, Salesperson B has the highest at $511,487. Salesperson D has the lowest at $388,045. An analysis of price incentives and promotional incentives offered by each salesperson, however, is very telling regarding how each obtains sales. Consider Table 9.2.

	Company	Salesperson A	Salesperson B	Salesperson C	Salesperson D
Gross sales ($)	1,787,560	436,703	511,487	451,045	388,325
Price incentives (%)	5.8	6.0	6.5	7.4	3.0
Promotion incentives (%)	2.6	1.2	4.3	4.2	0.3
Total incentives (%)	8.5	7.2	10.8	11.6	3.3
Net sales ($)	1,635,741	405,260	456,246	398,724	375,510

Table 9.2   Price/Promotion Analysis

As shown in Table 9.2, Salesperson C is offering on the average price reductions of about 7.4%. In addition, promotional offers being given to the buyer are costing an average of 4.2% of sales. Thus, of the $451,045 in gross sales generated by Salesperson C, a total of 11.6% should be subtracted. This is due to incentives being offered by the salesperson. The calculation results in net sales of $398,724.

Compare the results of Salesperson C and Salesperson D. Gross sales for Salesperson D were only $388,325; however, this person did not give many promotional incentives and only reduced the price of the products by an average of 3%. This produces net sales of $375,510.

Each salesperson receives a commission of 3% on the gross sales generated. This rewards salespeople pushing the total volume of sales dollars. What would happen if commissions were paid on *gross margin* instead, after the incentives and cost of goods are subtracted? Table 9.3 shows the analysis. For the salespeople to get the same amount of commission, the commission rate on the gross margin would be approximately 9.83%. Compare the commissions for the four salespeople. Notice that Salesperson D will earn almost $2,000 more in commissions while Salesperson C will earn almost $1,400 less in commission. If the commission is paid on gross margins, then salespeople tend to reduce the financial incentives offered to customers, which can generate greater profit for the company.

The greatest portion of each salesperson's income is generated from commissions and bonuses rather than from a salary. This leads salespeople to push sales. It is likely that Salesperson D will start using more price and promotional incentives if the commissions are paid based on gross sales. If the commission is paid on gross margins, then it is likely that Salespersons B and C will reduce the amount of incentives and price reductions they offer customers.

Trevor Wasney, CEO of Artic Spas Oakville Group, Inc., made a similar discovery with his sales staff. He initially paid his salespeople commission on revenues generated or gross sales. To encourage customers to make a purchase, salespeople were slashing prices and throwing in free merchandise. Sales were high, but profits were low. Wasney switched to a profit-based commission based on gross margins. The more profit the company earned, the higher the commission the salespeople earned. The result was a decrease in gross sales but an increase in net profit.[11]

	Company	Salesperson A	Salesperson B	Salesperson C	Salesperson D
Gross sales ($)	1,787,560	436,703	511,487	451,045	388,325
Price incentives (%)	5.8	6.0	6.5	7.4	3.0
Promotion incentives (%)	2.6	1.2	4.3	4.2	0.3
Total incentives (%)	8.5	7.2	10.8	11.6	3.3
Net sales ($)	1,635,741	405,260	456,246	398,724	375,510
Cost of goods sold ($)	1,090,412	266,389	312,007	275,137	236,878
Gross margin ($)	545,329	138,872	144,239	123,586	138,632
Commission based on gross sales (3%) ($)	53,627	13,101	15,345	13,531	11,650
Commission based on gross margin (9.83%) ($)	53,606	13,651	14,179	12,149	13,628
Difference in commission ($)	—	550	−1,166	−1,383	1,978

Table 9.3 Comparison of Commission Methods

The results of any financial analysis should be tied into the input and output analysis. A comprehensive employee performance review considers individual contributions and accomplishments as well as all the measures as a group. The results should be tied into the compensation and reward system used in the company. This includes the selection process for promotions.

Warnings

There are several notes of caution to consider when conducting a performance appraisal program. First, the sales manager should remember that additional factors can have a major impact on sales performance at any given time. Two of these factors include (1) organizational and (2) environmental factors.

In terms of *organizational factors,* the culture of an organization affects not only a salesperson's perceived role but also his performance. When a company atmosphere is cutthroat and every person looks out for himself, then the salesperson tends to act in that fashion. A culture that reflects caring and concern for employees as well as customers yields a different result.

Other organizational factors that can influence sales performance are more directly related to marketing, such as the advertising budget, sales promotions offered, and pricing of the products. A firm that spends on advertising helps salespeople by making prospects familiar with the product and its benefits prior to sales call. A quality database marketing program yields higher-quality leads for salespeople to contact. Thus, organizations that regard marketing as a vital partner with the selling function normally experience better performance from salespeople.

Numerous *environmental factors* have an impact on sales performance. They range from actions by competitors to natural disasters, such as a hurricane. Most of these environmental factors cannot be controlled. They must still be addressed by management. When extenuating circumstances have an adverse impact on sales, the performance criteria for that time period should be adjusted to more realistic levels. For instance, should a terrorist attack disrupt a company's operations for several weeks and depress sales as a result, the sales objectives should be modified to reflect these new circumstances.

The Performance Appraisal Meeting

The final element in any performance evaluation is the actual performance appraisal meeting. Remember that any time an employee's performance is being assessed, a natural degree of tension exists. The goal of any performance appraisal program should be to create better results in the future. This does not mean deficiencies should be ignored but the intent should be to suggest methods of improvement. The following are the standard steps of a performance appraisal meeting:

1.   Give notice of the meeting well in advance.

2.   Suggest a comfortable place to hold the meeting.

3.   Begin with a list of the employee's accomplishments and strong points.

4.   Continue with a discussion of weaknesses and problem areas.

5.   Set goals for the next period of evaluation.

The salesperson should have time to prepare for the meeting, both emotionally and with any facts and figures she wishes to present. Many times, appraisals are held in break rooms or conference rooms rather than in a supervisor's office, to help keep the employee at ease. The discussion of strengths and weaknesses should guide the goal-setting process.

Some management teams add a sixth step, which is to discuss the employee's raise at the conclusion of the meeting. Others believe that the raise should be contingent on reaching the new goals that have just been established. The most important point to remember is that a performance appraisal process should focus as much or more on the future than simply on past results.

YOURCAREER

Tim Clow recently graduated with a dual major in marketing and finance. He is currently a business analyst with 3M Corporation focusing on its Wal-Mart account. His responsibilities include analyzing sales trends in Wal-Mart stores and

providing detailed recommendations to 3M's management team. He also offers advice to Wal-Mart's buyers regarding activities, such as purchase order size, point-of-purchase or in-store displays, in-store promotions, national advertising programs, and new products. He is also responsible for

studying the market performance of competing retail stores in order to make recommendations to Wal-Mart's marketing team about how the company can increase its market share.

When asked about his marketing courses in college and how he currently uses that information, Tim replied, "I use concepts on a daily basis that I learned in my consumer behavior class and marketing research class. While Wal-Mart has millions of customers, it concentrates on selling to each individual, so understanding the consumer decision-making process, and basic purchasing behaviors helps to make sure that 3M offers the right products in the right Wal-Mart stores. Business analytics in retail are not just about gathering and reporting vast amounts of information but interpreting the data to understand the reason for the trends and how to capture additional opportunities based on the information within the data. My customer, Wal-Mart, wants me to tell them what products to put on their stores' shelves, how much of that product they should order, and who is going to buy it. Answers to those questions come from understanding how to conduct marketing research analysis and what drives that consumer consumption. For me, marketing research and consumer behavior were the most critical classes in terms of my current job. But, in saying that, I must add that through marketing management, I learned how to apply that knowledge to real-world situations and that is what I am now doing every single day."

As with any job, Tim had a lot to learn when he arrived at 3M Corporation. While 3M spends considerable time and money on training, the company relies on the knowledge a new employee gained while in college. When asked what he wished he would have learned in college, Tim replied, "Until I arrived at 3M, I did not understand that sales are much more about the numbers and dollars than it is about persuading a buyer to purchase X number of your products. Both 3M and Wal-Mart focus on providing the right products to the right customers but only if it makes financial sense to do so. Understanding how to calculate potential profit, on current products as well as new products, is one of the most critical elements in selling. The buyer, which in my case is Wal-Mart, wants to know if they purchase this new product or adopt this new in-store display we are offering, what will it mean in terms of profit? How much money will they earn?"

Tim's college education and degree in marketing provided the foundation he needed to obtain a job with 3M Corporation. His need to learn, however, did not stop at graduation. The degree was just the foundation. He continually strives to seek out new knowledge and new applications that will allow him to push 3M sales to a higher level.

Chapter Summary

Personal selling is often called *the last three feet of marketing*. The salesperson on a retail floor and the salesperson making a business-to-business sales call both stand approximately 3 feet from the prospective customer. Personal selling plays a major part in both customer acquisition and customer service.

Retail selling positions include order takers, commission sales, service selling, being a service provider who also sells, and telemarketing. The degree of focus on customer acquisition depends on the job being performed.

Business-to-business personal selling consists of the field salespeople, missionary salespeople, and telemarketers who make up the sales force. In terms of acquiring customers, the standard steps are to generate leads, qualify prospects, acquire knowledge, create a sales presentation, and follow-up. International sales calls involve additional complications associated with language, culture, religion, and other customs.

Managing a sales force includes tending to recruiting, selection, training, compensation, motivational programs, and performance evaluation. Recruiting should be ongoing, systematic, and geared to the company's needs. Selection is typically based on criteria that include educational level, degree of experience, personality characteristics, and legal compliance. Training takes place both on- and off-the-job.

Compensation programs include salary only, commissions, or both. Bonuses may be paid to inspire additional effort. Benefit packages are created based on contributions to recruiting, retention, and cost management. Motivational programs add the financial incentives of promotions and pay raises as well as prizes in contests. Nonfinancial incentives include recognition, praise, and special privileges.

Performance appraisals will be based on input measures, output measures, and financial measures. At all times, the salesperson and the supervisor should use performance evaluation as a tool to prepare for the future.

Chapter Terms

Aptitude   (p. 233)
Bonuses   (p. 235)
Commission sales   (p. 225)
Commissions   (p. 235)
Field salespeople   (p. 225)
Missionary salespeople   (p. 225)
Mission-sharing   (p. 229)
Need-satisfaction   (p. 228)
Order taker   (p. 225)

Personal characteristics   (p. 233)
Problem-solution   (p. 228)
Relationship selling   (p. 231)
Salary   (p. 234)
Service salesperson   (p. 225)
Skill level   (p. 233)
Stimulus-response   (p. 228)
Telemarketers   (p. 225)

Review Questions

1. What are the main types of retail sales jobs?
2. What are the three main types of business-to-business sales positions?
3. What are the six steps of the selling process?
4. What types of sales leads are generated by the sales staff?
5. What types of sales leads are generated by the marketing department?
6. Describe a standard format for qualifying sales prospects.
7. What types of information are collected during the knowledge acquisition stage of selling?
8. Briefly describe the four types of sales presentations that can be made.
9. What is relationship selling?
10. Outline the special challenges associated with making international sales calls.
11. What four criteria are normally associated with the selection process?
12. Describe the methods used to train new salespeople.

13. What are the benefits of a straight salary form of compensation for a sales force?

14. Why do many companies use a salary plus commission form of compensation for the sales force?

15. Name the three primary issues associated with benefit programs.

16. What are the most common types of financial incentives offered to the sales staff?

17. What types of nonfinancial incentives can be provided to the sales force?

18. Name the three types of measures used to evaluate a salesperson's performance.

19. What factors that can have an impact on sales performance should also be considered in a performance evaluation?

CUSTOMER
CORNER

Susan Hanlon was startled by a new complication. Susan was the sales manager for Federal Freight, which packaged and sold space on barges, ships, and smaller vessels for shipping large durable goods. Two members of her sales force had closed major shipping deals at the same time. Unfortunately, both had checked and found available space on a barge and closed the deal, which meant the barge was overbooked. The first salesperson, George, had sold the space to a long-established customer with a history of prompt payment and the willingness to cooperate with Federal Freight. The second salesperson, Theresa, had just received a major award based on her

What should Susan Hanlon do?

ability to generate new clients and new business. She had sold the space to an up-and-coming client that had the potential to use Federal Freight for years to come. Both George and Theresa would receive large commissions for this sale. Susan looked at her options. She could ask the long-standing customer to wait for a few days for the next barge and give a discount for waiting. She could offer the same deal to the new client, hoping that doing so would not make the customer feel slighted. Her third option was to find another barge departing the same day and pay the additional costs of booking with another company, thereby costing Federal Freight the revenues from one of the two customers but not risking the possibility of upsetting either one.

1. Which of the three choices should Susan take?

2. Are there any other numbers or figures she should ask for before making her decision?

3. If Susan is forced to pick one customer over another, because no other barge is available, how should she handle the situation with her salesperson? With the client who will be forced to wait?

Discussion and Critical Thinking Questions

1. For each of the following, indicate what type of pay structure would be the best (salary, commission, or salary plus commission). Also indicate whether you should use a group or individual bonus.
   - Employees in a sporting goods store
   - Loan officers at a bank (commercial and consumer loans)
   - Employees at a travel agency
   - Call center employees handling incoming calls resulting from advertisements
   - Students at college campuses selling spring break vacation packages for a Florida resort

2. In this chapter, a method of analysis is shown for the evaluation of potential new customers. Those with the highest potential and the best chances for being acquired receive the highest priority and are the first to be visited by the sales force. As a manager of a sales team, would there be value in evaluating existing customers across the dimensions of potential for continuing future sales and potential to be taken away by a competitor? If so, what should be the classification system? Who should be the first to receive personal visits from salespeople: clients who generate the biggest revenues or those who might be lost to other companies? Why?

3. There is a common claim in the business world: "A good salesperson can sell anything. A good salesperson can sell refrigerators and freezers in Alaska." Is this statement true? If it is, how would it affect the processes of recruiting, selection, and training described in this chapter? If it is not true, what characteristics do you think are the most crucial when selecting a salesperson? Are the characteristics the same, regardless of the type of selling job? Are they the same regardless of the type of the product or service being sold?

4. Some companies think of salespeople in the following ways: *Prospectors* are people who are good at generating new business. They can find new accounts and make that first sale. Once the sale is made, however, they lose interest and want to move on to new challenges. *Wine-ers and diners* are good at customer relationships. Their strengths include the ability to keep customers happy. They don't particularly enjoy trying to develop new clients. *Fence menders* are good at restoring damaged relationships. They are skilled at conflict management and crisis management. They are seldom asked to find new customers. *Rejuvenators* are best at taking a stale territory and making it fresh again. They enjoy both wining and dining old customers and lost customers to generate extra sales and prospect for new customers. As a sales manager, which of the four types would you prefer to hire? Does each type serve a purpose? If so, what kinds of questions should you ask during an interview to find out which type of rep the applicant will become?

5. It is not unusual for someone who has been with the company a few years to say, "I know management told you that you should make 10 cold calls a week, but you don't really need to. They only care about sales. As long as you meet your quota, you are okay. And also, I should tell you that if you exceed your quota, it will go up next year. So my recommendation to you is when you make the quota for the week, go golfing the rest of

the week." As a sales manager, what can you do about this type of attitude? Which of the incentives described in this chapter would be your best tools?

6. You are the manager of an international sales force. It is your job to make sure that your reps are ready when they travel to various countries. Prepare a briefing for salespeople regarding the following issues:
   - Use of deferent language in Japan, China, and India
   - Crossing your legs, revealing the sole of your shoe in Saudi Arabia
   - Making eye contact while negotiating in Mexico, France, and Malaysia
   - Holding hands while conducting business in Syria (male to male)
   - Passing out business cards in Korea
   - Bringing gifts, receiving them, and opening them in an Asian country

   Investigate other cultural differences mentioned in this chapter. Make a report to the class on those you think are the most unusual.

7. Table 9.4 is a quarterly sales report for a district with five salespeople. Construct a price/promotion analysis similar to Table 9.2 and a comparison of commission methods similar to Table 9.3. The salespeople are currently being paid a commission of 3% on gross sales. What percentage would the sales commission be if it was paid on gross margin, for the total commission paid by the company to be the same? Evaluate each of the five salespeople with the current sales compensation structure. What would be the difference if the salespeople were paid on gross margins? Which should the company do? Justify your answer.

8. In addition to the financial information provided in Question 6, the company also collects some input and output data for each of the salespeople. These are listed in Table 9.5. Reevaluate each of the salespeople on four measures: input measures, output measures, gross sales, and gross margin. You may also want to examine how well each salesperson is doing at developing new accounts through contacting prospects and how well they do at following up with current clients. Assume that you have $2,000 to distribute among the five salespeople as a bonus for the quarter. How would you distribute the money? Justify your allocation. If you had to choose one of the salespeople as the most outstanding, which would you choose? Why?

	Company	Salesperson A	Salesperson B	Salesperson C	Salesperson D	Salesperson E
Sales	2,310,292	321,658	396,210	624,176	521,870	446,378
Price incentives ($)	171,165	22,325	18,325	48,345	50,512	31,658
Promotional incentives ($)	29,071	4,326	7,321	4,328	7,453	5,643
Cost of goods sold ($)	1,339,969	186,562	229,802	362,022	302,685	258,899
Gross margin ($)	770,087	108,445	140,762	209,481	161,220	150,178
Direct selling expenses						
Salary ($)	43,400	8,400	8,300	9,000	8,700	9,000
Commission (3%) ($)	69,309	9,650	11,886	18,725	15,656	13,391
Travel ($)	34,037	6,432	6,865	7,203	6,326	7,211
Bonuses ($)	2,850	300	300	1,000	750	500
Benefits (23%) ($)	26,579	4,220	4,712	6,607	5,774	5,265
Total selling expenses ($)	176,174	29,002	32,063	42,535	37,207	35,367
Contribution margin ($)	593,912	79,443	108,699	166,946	124,014	114,810
Contribution margin (%)	25.71	24.70	27.43	26.75	23.76	25.72
Salesperson's gross pay ($)		18,350	20,486	28,725	25,106	22,891

Table 9.4 Quarterly Sales Report

	Company	Salesperson A	Salesperson B	Salesperson C	Salesperson D	Salesperson E
Number of precontacts	279	60	54	75	32	58
Number of sales calls	1,051	213	186	243	211	198
Number of prospects contacted	134	23	17	54	15	25
Number of follow-up contacts	335	43	32	112	98	50
Number of new accounts	35	5	3	18	2	7
Number of active accounts	118	21	26	19	24	28
Number of orders	343	54	52	75	97	65
Average size of orders ($)	6,829	5,957	7,619	8,322	5,380	6,867

Table 9.5   Quarterly Activity Report

Chapter 9 Case

Hamming It Up

Kretschmar enjoys a proud tradition of providing quality meat and deli products for over 100 years. The company was founded in 1887, first by selling meat products in Europe and later in the United States. The company's headquarters currently are in Don Mills, Ontario. The main divisions are Kretschmar, Kretschmar Private Label Meat Products, Rhein Valley, and J-Kwinter Hot Dogs.

The primary customers for Kretschmar's products are supermarkets, restaurants, fast-food chains, and other food retailers. The company's products meet all requirements established by the Canadian Food Inspection Agency and are widely distributed in the United States.

Selling products to the various types of retailers that feature Kretschmar's products requires numerous skills. Supermarket managers normally look for brands that are well known to consumers. They often feature consumer promotions, such as coupons, contests and sweepstakes, price-offs, free samples, bonus packs, and refunds. There are also opportunities to build relationships with grocers through trade incentives and trade allowances.

Restaurants are far less likely to feature the brand name of a product that is served. The use of consumer promotions will be limited and different. Trade promotions of all sorts, including trade shows, are ways to contact potential new customers and build relationships with existing customers.

Fast-food chain buyers often are most concerned with price. Delivery services will be important. The salesperson may also offer trade credit and provide other functions, such as inventory maintenance.

Other food retailers, including chains such as Costco and Wal-Mart, plus specialty shops create additional sales challenges. The large discount stores seek price discounts and timely deliveries, and may be interested in other services. Specialty shops have a totally different set of needs and typically buy in much smaller quantities.

The Kretschmar Private Label Division serves the needs of a unique type of clientele. The brand does not appear on the products. At the same time, the goal remains to provide quality products with first-class service.

Among Kretschmar's primary selling points are quality and service. Quality comes from both traditional European and cutting-edge new butchering and processing technologies. The quality assurance department has a carefully designed raw materials management system, cost control procedures, and quality control protocols. The company's food technicians monitor products from the time they reach the loading dock, through the processing system, to inspections of finished goods. Kretschmar's reputation for service is based on carefully coordinated efforts to provide products in a timely fashion.

The worldwide reach of Kretschmar offers the possibilities of continued expansion. As the global marketplace continues to evolve, the company's prospects for a bright future continue.[12]

Will Kretschmar use different sales approaches for its four markets: restaurants, fast-food chains, supermarkets, and other food retailers?

1. What types of salespeople best fit the needs of a company such as Kretschmar?

2. Should different types of salespeople be chosen based on the type of customer served? Why or why not?

3. When recruiting and selecting individuals for Kretschmar's sales force, what criteria should be used, including aptitudes, skill levels, and personal characteristics?

4. What type of compensation structure would you recommend? Would it vary for the different types of clients?

5. What types of motives and incentives would best fit the sales force at Kretschmar?

6. Which input and output measures would be best suited to performance evaluation for salespeople at Kretschmar?

Go to **www.sagepub.com/clow** for additional exercises and study resources. Select **Chapter 9, Personal Selling** for chapter-specific activities.

part 3

Managing Customer Interactions

How does Zappos.com recruit and train call center employees?

chapter 10
Internal Communications

Zappos: To Live and Deliver WOW

One out of every three shoe sales is lost in brick-and-mortar shoe stores because the customer's size isn't in stock. This attention-getting statistic partly explains the success and growth of online shoe sales. In 2008, the market size had reached $3 billion, and Zappos, an adaptation of the Spanish word for "shoe," had captured a 20% share. The secret? A big inventory and an even bigger emphasis on customer service.

Zappos.com was founded in 1999 by Nick Swinmurn, who had just spent a day walking the mall looking for a pair of shoes. He was

frustrated by not being able to find the pair he wanted. His first business concept was to create an inventory so large that the odds of the customer finding exactly the right pair would be very high. Currently, the Zappos warehouse and order-fulfillment area carries 4 million pairs of shoes in its inventory.

High-quality customer service is the most important ingredient. And, as is the case with many successful customer-oriented companies, the quality of the service begins with the company's culture and an emphasis on a positive work environment for each employee.

The current CEO, Tony Hsieh, who had already made a fortune with another Internet company, receives compensation from Zappos of about $36,000 per year. He works in a small cubicle at the center of the plant, surrounded by the cubicles of coworkers. Each can be individualized and personalized to suit the temperament and preferences of its occupant. An abundant amount of free food is available every day. Employees are encouraged to be spontaneous and excited and to have fun. In contrast to the free-flowing and short-lived dot.coms of the 1990s, however, company workers are well trained and constantly reminded of the importance of each customer.

New employees are required to enroll in a 4-week training session that prepares them to work in the call center. During the course of the training, Hsieh personally offers to "buy them out" with a cash payment (of up to $2,000) that leaves the individual free to quit the company with money in his or her pocket. Those who remain—the majority of employees—learn the importance of excellent customer service. Many will be placed in nonphone-related jobs, such as

order fulfillment, inventory control, or in the finance or some other department. A graduation ceremony finalizes the training process, complete with recitation of Zappos's 10 core values, which includes phrases such as "Deliver WOW," "Create fun," "A little weirdness," "Pursue growth," "Be passionate," and "Be humble."

The majority of Zappos's sales come from online purchases. Each order is shipped free in both directions. A customer can order a pair of shoes and will receive them within a few days. If the shoe doesn't fit, it can be returned for full credit, with shipping paid, up to 1 year later.

Key customer contacts are also made via the phone center. If a customer cannot locate the exact pair of shoes she wants, the center's service representative will direct the person to two or three other companies that might have the item. Each phone operator consistently exhibits a friendly, upbeat, and helpful demeanor.

Employees who remain at Zappos receive excellent compensation, full health insurance, and dental benefits. Why not relocate the call center to somewhere cheaper? "We don't think you're going to give great customer service by outsourcing it," Hsieh calmly states.

Currently, Zappos is expanding. New product lines include clothing, electronics, and accessories. Every aspect of the Zappos experience applies to these items. Why don't other companies follow this model? Tony Hsieh speculates, "You don't really see the payoff right away." Building a business in this way takes time. On the other hand, 75% of Zappos's buyers are repeat customers. Most would agree that Zappos fulfills its mission: To Live and Deliver WOW.[1]

Chapter Overview

Acquiring customers can be difficult. Keeping them is imperative. In today's highly competitive marketing environment, the temptation to try another company's goods and services is always high. A quality marketing management program includes provisions for making sure that all the contacts between the company and its customers are of the highest quality, so that they will be less tempted to look for new purchasing alternatives.

The third part of this textbook deals with customer interactions in the overall marketing management program (see Figure 10.1). The first critical component of developing quality interactions with customers is effective communication. This chapter examines the basic nature of communication and then focuses on internal company processes. Chapter 11 describes external communications between the company and its customers. Chapter 12 explains how a company's distribution system affects the quality of its interactions with consumers. Finally, Chapter 13 pays special attention to managing a firm's Web site and Internet operations in order to sustain quality relationships with customers and other publics.

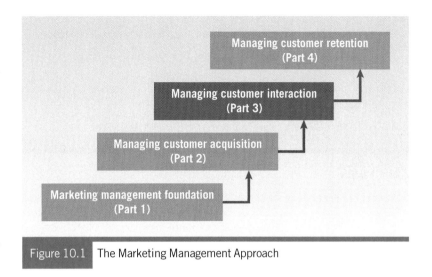

Figure 10.1   The Marketing Management Approach

Internal communication is critically important. Successful firms provide superior customer service and produce quality products. They rely on well-designed and well-maintained internal communications programs. The first topic in this chapter is a simple description of the nature of individual communication, along with the barriers that disrupt messages. Then, methods for overcoming those barriers are described. Next, the natures of organizational communication processes, both in terms of formal and informal channels, are examined. Factors that can disrupt formal communication are noted, along with methods to overcome those barriers. The chapter closes with a discussion of the relationship between internal communications and customer service. Suggestions are made regarding the best ways to build and improve a firm's communication environment, including when that environment also has international operations.

The Nature of Communication

Communication may be described in a variety of ways. Some writers compare it to glue or mortar, suggesting that communication holds an organization together. Others see it as oil, making communication the organizational feature that keeps things running smoothly. A third point of view relates communication to gasoline and other forms of energy, as the power that drives a company or, when used improperly, something that feeds the flames of conflict and discontent. No matter which of these analogies a person favors, one thing becomes clear: Communication continues to be a vital part of organizational life. Effective communication can facilitate success; poor communication may be a major factor in a company's demise.

At the most basic level, communication is the process of transmitting, receiving, and processing information. Typically, *business communication* takes two forms: (1) individual communication and (2) communication systems. When examining both types of communication, the importance of customer service should continue to be emphasized.

Individual Communication

Individual communication occurs when one person addresses another person or a group of people. A sales manager speaking with an individual salesperson in a conference room is an individual communication situation, as would be that same sales manager giving a "pep talk" to

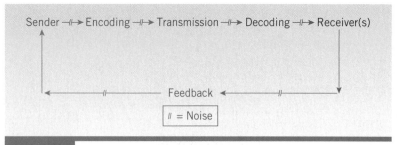

Figure 10.2 A Model of Individual Communication

a group of salespeople in the same room. Any public speaking format can be represented in the same way as one-on-one conversations. Individual communication also takes place in personal selling, when the sales rep visits with a customer or client or when a phone operator receives an inbound call. Figure 10.2 models individual communication.

A great deal of internal communication takes the form of individual communication. In the model shown, the **sender** is the person sending the message or idea. It is not unusual for the sender to be represented by the term *ideation*. **Encoding** is forming verbal and nonverbal cues. The sender transmits verbal cues by speaking, by writing, and with the assistance of other devices such as a text message or a PowerPoint presentation. Nonverbal cues are things not spoken that convey messages, such as gestures, facial expression, posture, and the actual distance between the sender and receiver. Anything that carries the message becomes the **transmission device**, including light waves, sound waves, cell phone signals, a piece of paper, and the screen of a computer. **Decoding** occurs when the receiver attempts to understand the message through the use of the five senses, hearing, sight, smell, touch, and taste. Normally a message is decoded through hearing and sight; however, when someone grabs another person's arm to emphasize a point, the message is also being felt. The **receiver** is the person for whom a message was intended. **Feedback** is the message the sender receives in return. The receiver transmits feedback in many ways, including looking bored, distracted, intense, angry, amused, confused, in agreement, and so forth. Figure 10.2 indicates that anywhere in this process the message may be blocked by **noise** or the *barriers to communication.*

The potential for noise to be present in any conversation is great. It has been suggested that in face-to-face communication body language accounts for 55% of the message received, tone of voice another 36%, and the words only 7%. In contrast, during a telephone conversation, the tone of voice accounts for 86% of what is received compared with only 14% for the words spoken.[2]

How much of individual communication is body language and tone of voice?

Consider a conversation between a marketing manager and one of her employees. The manager faces a deadline and needs the employee to finish a project by the end of the week. The manager can say, "Can you please finish this by the end of the week?" The tone of her voice and body language convey more than the words. When the words are spoken caustically or in anger, they convey a far different meaning than if they are spoken with a sigh and a shake or tilt of the head. It may be that the manager is suggesting that she has become frustrated with the deadline and is politely asking for the employee's help in meeting it. Consequently, effective marketing managers are those who understand the potential barriers to communication and find ways to overcome them.

Barriers to Individual Communication

Figure 10.3 displays a standard list of barriers to individual communication. Individual differences are those between the sender and the receiver. When speaking to someone of a different *age* group, a person's frame of reference may get in the way. Today's youth tend to rely heavily on verbal hedges and pause points, such as using the words *like* and *so* to the extreme. Many older managers (and human resource managers making hiring decisions) find these tendencies to be unprofessional and far too casual.

It has been long established that *gender differences* can lead to miscommunication. Males tend to frame business orders as statements; females may be more likely to use a question, such as "Would you mind calling this customer back to find out what went wrong?" Both want the call to be made, but the request may be framed in different ways.

Differences in status may make a talk between a top company officer and a new employee stilted and uncomfortable. *Differences in culture or subculture* are often present when persons from different regions of the country converse or when people from different countries interact. *Personality differences* come into play when a clash exists, such as when an overaggressive employee bullies or intimidates someone who is shy and avoids conflict at all costs.

Two situational factors disrupt quality communication. The first, a *setting,* means that certain circumstances disrupt messages. For example, following the announcement that a popular employee or customer has just died, very little else will be heard. The same is true when a company announces layoffs. In marketing and sales, *emotions* play a vital role in communication. When someone is angry, he may not wish to interact with coworkers or customers. For instance, if the salesperson has just lost a high-commission sale due to what he considers to be unfair tactics by a competitor, he should take some time to cool off before talking to his supervisor or the customer who did not make the purchase, lest something is said that cannot be taken back. Depression also disrupts communication. Someone experiencing a negative or bad mood may be better assigned to writing routine reports or arranging shelves than interacting with other employees or customers.

Many problems in communication occur due to mechanical issues. *Language and slang* create problems when one is speaking with employees from other countries or those for whom English is a second language. *Transmission device* problems occur when a cell phone battery is dying or the person is out of range and in any other circumstances in which the actual device carrying the message fails. One primary problem in many one-on-one communications is *nonverbal contradiction of a verbal message.* A supervisor who looks distracted while speaking with an employee sends the message that he doesn't care. Anyone who slouches, fails to make eye contact, gives a weak handshake, or "keeps his distance" may be taking away from the intended verbal message.

Individual Differences	Situational Factors	Mechanical Problems
Age	Settings	Language
Gender	Emotions	Slang
Status		Transmission device
Culture/subculture		Contradiction by nonverbal cues
Personality type		

Figure 10.3 Barriers to Individual Communications

Overcoming the Barriers to Individual Communication

In any conversation, both the sender and the receiver are responsible for effective communication. A failure by either can lead to a message not being correctly understood, to conflicts, and to other problems. The sender's duties in any conversation include

- understanding potential barriers,
- empathy,
- awareness of nonverbal cues, and
- seeking confirmation of the message.

Any new supervisor may be confronted by the barriers of age, gender, personality, and others. Simply acknowledging them is the first step toward being a more effective communicator. Several of the individuals featured in the YourCareer segments of this book have noted the challenges of dealing with older employees who are subordinates as well as with people in the organization and customers from different backgrounds.

Empathy for the audience means understanding that the frame of reference of a public relations expert with 20 years of experience will be far different from that of someone in her first year. *Awareness of nonverbal cues* plays a crucial role in a person being selected for the job. The applicant should be on time, appear well dressed, stand straight, shake hands firmly, and make eye contact to present the best impression. After being selected, the employee should continue to be aware that nonverbal cues affect conversations with coworkers, supervisors, subordinates, and the general public. *Seeking confirmation* means finding out if the message that was sent was accurately received. The question "Do you understand?" is always helpful.

Receivers are responsible for two things. First, *active listening* means paying careful attention to the conversation and not allowing oneself to be distracted. Multitasking often causes messages to be missed or misunderstood. Second, *seeking clarification* involves making sure a message is being interpreted correctly. Saying "I don't understand" can be very helpful in making sure decisions, orders, requests for information about products, and other messages are correctly construed.[3]

The Value of Individual Communication

The importance of effective individual communication cannot be underestimated. This is because the nature of communication affects nearly every aspect of business. Among the areas most directly affected by individual communication are

- interactions with coworkers within the department,
- interactions with other departments,
- internal marketing programs,
- interactions with clients and customers, and
- personal career success.

Within the Department

Individual communication plays a vital role in every aspect of managing the marketing department. Advertising programs, promotions programs, sponsorships, consumer research, public relations, and many other activities are normally collaborative efforts. For example, when preparing an advertising program, a creative brief is the form of communication that guides the efforts of those preparing the ad, the media planners and buyers, and others associated with the campaign. This means supervisors must make sure that coworkers effectively interact with one another.

How can quality
communication
strengthen the
marketing department?

With Other Departments

Communications can either unite or divide companies. Terms such as *turf war* and *empire building* describe the conflicts that emerge between departments, especially when poor lines of communication exist. An effective marketing program is not possible unless the key message and theme presented by the company speak with one clear voice. That voice must be heard, understood, and passed along by all internal departments.

Internal Marketing Programs

Internal marketing combines communications to individuals both within and between departments. Internal marketing is an ongoing process through which company leaders can align, motivate, and empower employees at all functions and levels to consistently deliver a positive customer experience. Every company's marketing leaders should recognize the unique features the firm offers to its customers. This includes all products and services. An internal marketing program continually reminds everyone in the company of those benefits and reinforces the idea that customer service leads to success. At SAGE Publications, employees receive constant messages reinforcing the concept that creating and sustaining quality relationships with both authors and those who purchase their works are key to success. Internal marketing programs may be designed for companies that manufacture and sell physical products as well as those that deliver services.

With Customers and Clients

Internal marketing then extends outward to customers. All the comments made regarding the barriers to communication and how to overcome them apply equally well to both conversations with coworkers and visits to customers. Customer service begins with effective listening.

It continues with giving clear and helpful suggestions about how a company's goods and services can solve the customer's problems. Successful interactions with customers result from well-established lines of communication.

Personal Career Success

Communication skills affect the trajectories of many careers. Those who are able to present themselves effectively during the application process are more likely to get the jobs they desire. Employees who make high-quality written and verbal proposals and presentations will be the first chosen for promotion and manager training programs. Effective communicators establish better relationships with prospects, clients, customers, members of the marketing channel, and others inside and outside the company. Any person who is about to join the workforce should carefully assess her ability to write and make verbal presentations. Those who perceive weaknesses in their communication skills are advised to take more courses in writing and public speaking and closely related subjects such as interpersonal relations and conflict resolution.

STOP AND THINK

1. Based on what you have read thus far, is individual communication more like glue, mortar, oil, gasoline, or something else?

2. How many of the barriers to individual communication exist between professors and students? Between students and their parents? Between students and other students?

3. How would the barriers to individual communication relate to poor customer service?

4. As a supervisor, how can you teach your employees to be better communicators with each other and with the general public?

Communication Systems in Organizations

Communication in organizations takes many forms. It flows in several directions. Communication can create a major advantage for one company just as poor communication can become a major liability for another. Successful marketing managers make certain the information flows smoothly and is delivered in a timely fashion to every member of the department, to the company, and to external publics.

Typically, organizational communication is portrayed as moving through two channels. Formal communication travels through the channels that are chosen or designated by the organization. Informal communication emerges in the form of gossip, rumors, and what travels through the grapevine. Figure 10.4 displays a standard list of formal communication channels. Currently, the distinction between formal and informal channels has greatly diminished. This is due to the blurring of messages that move through the same channel. For example, an e-mail may be a formal message sent in bulk from the company's president notifying every employee of a change in policy. The same channel can be used by others to pass along the gossip that someone is about to be fired. Other e-mail messages contain a formal element, such as an when a sales manager grants permission to a sales rep to offer a trade allowance discount and the message is combined with informal chitchat about the last time the sales manager played a round of golf with the salesperson.

Traditional Channels	New Channels
Direct address (supervisor to employee)	Cell phones
	Satellite transmission
Meetings	Teleconference call
Memos	E-mail
Letters	Web site
Company manual or handbook	Fax
Bulletin board	Intranet
Company magazine or newsletter	

Figure 10.4 Formal Communication Channels

Traditional Channels

Some of the traditional formal communication channels shown in Figure 10.4 are still fre-quently used. A *direct address,* or an *in-person conversation,* represents the most standard form of traditional communication. *Meetings* also continue to be a commonplace approach. These types of face-to-face interactions with employees are valuable tools for encouraging employee input and participation in decision making and creating plans, which in turn builds trust and cooperation. This can lead to increased productivity. One recent study suggests that the trust built from a participative environment can be a major contributor to improved busi-ness success, using measures such as profit margins. Participation keeps lines of communica-tion open, which leads to innovation, creativity, and better problem solving. These, in turn, lead to longer-term success.[4]

Fewer *memos* are now sent. Most companies have shifted to electronic media and have moved toward paperless operations.

There are occasions when *letters* are sent, such as when a CEO sends one to all employees about the "state of the company." Other correspondences may include invitations to special events, such as a company picnic or a press conference introducing a new product. Typically, letters sent to employees' residences are infrequent.

The information contained in a *company manual or handbook* is now more likely to be carried on a firm's intranet or internal Web site. Bulletin boards continue to have both formal and informal messages posted on them. A bulletin board is equally likely to display a reminder about an upcoming meeting, a note that someone is trying to sell a car, or a memo about orga-nizing a company softball team.

A *company newsletter* can be a valuable tool for enhancing a customer-oriented culture and the company's climate. Typically, newsletters contain a great deal of "soft" information, such as notices about company-sponsored events. Also, most people like to see their names in print, and a newsletter offers an ideal venue. Many employees enjoy reading about the three "Bs"— brides, babies, and bowling scores. The editor should try to make the newsletter attractive, fun to read, and make sure that it features numerous photographs. The goal is to make the newslet-ter something employees look forward to reading.[5]

Newly Developed Channels

The use of newer technologies to facilitate internal communications has exploded. *Cell phones,* BlackBerries, and other portable devices make it possible for a salesperson to access informa-tion from the home office, to transmit photos and other information, and to be reached while traveling. In essence, the level of access provided is higher than ever before.

Satellite transmissions allow meetings to be held over great distances. With both visual access and support from other media, it is possible to cut down on travel expenses and hold quick, emergency meetings when needed. Satellites may also be used for special occasions. For example, when the former Andersen Consulting revealed its new name, Accenture, employees around the globe were all connected by satellite to hear and see the announcement as it was made by the company's CEO.

Teleconferencing, while not as dramatic as a satellite linkage, offers the ability to bring together people from remote locations. Again, meetings can be quickly arranged, and travel costs are reduced. Both teleconferencing and satellite linkages present the opportunity to talk casually, to get to know coworkers better, and to hear them and see how they act or react interpersonally. This can, when managed properly, lead to improved morale and fewer internal conflicts.

Web sites and *e-mail* can be used to supplement the company's internal communication sys-tem. The key is to make certain that messages sent externally, through advertising, on the Web, and by other media, mesh with what has been transmitted internally.

The *fax* machine, while still widely used, may be a declining format for internal communi-cations. The ability to attach documents to e-mail has reduced the need for fax transmissions. Many times the fax machine is a fallback, when a document has not been placed into an elec-tronic format.

Are cell phones useful in creating effective business communications?

- Human resource records
- Corporate policies
- Payroll records
- Internal job postings
- Employee recognition
- Employee events
- Employee/corporate-supported causes

Figure 10.5

Ways to Use the Company Intranet

One of the newer forms of formal communication is the *intranet*. The intranet can be used in a number of ways (see Figure 10.5). One part of the intranet allows employees access to personal records. The intranet is a good place to feature corporate policies, job descriptions, and other materials that formerly were contained in a company manual or handbook. Payroll records can be posted. This is especially valuable to salespeople or employees who are paid commissions or bonuses. The amount they receive and how it is calculated should be clearly shown on a personal intranet page.

It is not unusual for a job opening to be posted on the intranet. This gives employees the first opportunity to apply. Others may provide the information to friends, who will be first in line when interviews begin. The intranet can be used to build employee morale by posting success stories and other forms of employee recognition. When other employees see the story, the value is enhanced because the individual is being recognized in a public forum. Many companies use the intranet to notify employees about company events. Information about bowling teams, softball teams, holiday parties, and other company-sponsored events can be posted. The section is likely to be loaded with pictures. This part of an intranet should be a fun place to explore.

The intranet is an excellent place to deliver information regarding corporate and employee causes, including how to get involved. This conveys the sentiment that the company cares about people and society.

Yahoo!, Google, and other online companies have changed employee preferences regarding the ways they want to communicate within the company. Employees often expect the same level of personalization, flexibility, and ease of use that they find with Google and other Internet sites.

In sum, the number of channels through which formal information can travel continues to expand. Marketing managers evaluate which are the best for a given company and its methods of conducting business. Even with such oversight, however, problems can appear.

Barriers to Formal Communication

Just as noise can distort or disrupt individual communication, many barriers to formal communication systems exist. Among the most common problems associated with formal systems are

- system overload,
- selective filtering,
- use of the wrong channel,
- transmission failures,
- informal contradiction of the formal message, and
- all the barriers to individual communication.

System Overload

Possibly the most common problem in marketing and business is the sheer volume of messages that must be processed each day. **System overload** means that the formal channel is so swamped that messages become lost. Consider e-mail as an example. E-mail is quick and easy to use and has become a primary means of communicating for employees. In the past decade, the volume of e-mails has risen drastically. The average company receives 18 MB of e-mails and attachments every day. By 2011, it is expected to be 28 MB per day.[6] Employees spend hours writing and answering e-mails.

In response to this trend, the management team at Capital One decided something had to be done. The typical Capital One employee receives 40 to 50 incoming e-mails a day. To reduce the time spent with them, 3,000 employees attended workshops to address the problem. The trainers stressed that one of the most important components of an e-mail is the subject line. The employees were taught how to write concise, descriptive subject lines summarizing the content of the e-mail. This also made the e-mail easier to find. For example, instead of putting "Answering your question" in the subject line, a more appropriate text would be "Feedback on RS 1000 Copier Price." The employees also learned how to sculpt the body of the text using bullet points, underlining, and bold text to make the presentation easier to follow. Company leaders estimated that the training and changes in e-mail correspondence saved the equivalent of 11 workdays per employee per year.[7]

How does information overload create a barrier to formal communication?

Selective Filtering

Any message passed from one person to another before reaching the final recipient runs the risk of being altered by any of the intermediaries, which is **selective filtering**. This problem occurs in many marketing situations, such as in negotiations with other companies, in the development of advertising campaigns, and in public relations programs. When a go-between exists, the person may be tempted to change the message to gain personal advantage, to "look good," or to add a personal preference. For instance, a marketing manager who strongly prefers television advertising may tell the media buyer to look for network time first, even though the product may be better served by an ad in a magazine or by a microsite. Selective filtering is often associated with employees playing politics at work.

Use of the Wrong Channel

Messages are often lost when the wrong medium is chosen. The marketing manager may find, for instance, that preparing a nice, glossy brochure spelling out the company's approach to advertising, selling, and delivering a new service may be a waste of resources. The reason would be that busy coworkers and managers in other departments do not want to take the time to read the materials. As a result, the brochure is either discarded or covered by other letters and materials in an inbox.

Transmission Failures

Internal messages are quickly lost when a company's Web site, intranet, or phone system breaks down. Transmission failures can take the form of something as simple as a secretary failing to notify a supervisor that someone has called with an important message. Power outages, viruses and worms, and other intrusions can affect a company's ability to transmit messages to employees.

Informal Contradiction of the Formal Message

Another name for this problem is *persistent rumors*. Once a rumor has been started that a company is about to experience layoffs, that a product is being pulled from the shelves due to inadequate sales, or that someone is about to be fired, the gossip often takes on a life of its own. Stopping rumors is nearly impossible, and refuting false rumors is equally difficult.

The Individual Barriers

Every barrier to individual communication also represents a potential barrier to formal communication. When coworkers deal with one another or with supervisors, there is the possibility that individual differences, situational factors, and mechanical problems will come into play. Internal communications move through formal systems, but the senders and receivers are people.[8]

Overcoming the Barriers to Formal Communication

Building an internal communications system requires two processes. The first is to establish an efficient and effective management information system. The second activity is to identify and eliminate the barriers to formal communication whenever possible.

Management Information Systems

A **management information system** consists of the people and machinery used to collect and process organizational information. An effective management information system is based on three pillars:

- Effective people
- Effective machinery
- Effective information

Effective People

Effective people include all the individuals who collect information. Marketing programs are based on the collection of information. Advertisers seek information regarding reachable target markets, media costs, and response rates. The sales force gathers information from customers about preferences, purchases, actions by competitors, complaints, and other relevant facts and figures. The public relations department looks for opportunities to present positive publicity and responds to incidents in which negative press is present.

Once the information has been collected, it must be collated. This means that another set of people must effectively *process* the information. The Web master, the person in charge of the database program, and any other individual or department that tracks and records information must perform effectively.

Effective Machinery

Effective machinery consists of phone systems, computer software and hardware, Web sites, mail systems, and any other equipment that moves information. This machinery must facilitate both internal communications and external operations. Communication systems should be constantly upgraded to keep pace with changes in technology and with what competitors and partners use.

In building a management information system, employees should carefully gather the right information from customers.

Effective Information

A management information system will not be complete or useful unless it provides effective information. The characteristics of quality information include

- timeliness,
- accuracy,
- relevance,
- conciseness, and
- proper storage.

The importance of *timely* information is mentioned in several places throughout this textbook. A salesperson making a call needs the most up-to-date information possible about the client he is about to meet. A call center operator should be able to quickly access a customer's account to assist in a purchase or in resolving a problem. In the fast-paced world of global commerce, timely information is a must.

Information must be *accurate* to have value. The many calculations related to lifetime value and break-even analyses rely on correct information in order to be useful in the decision-making processes. The same holds true for reports regarding competitor actions, changes in governmental policies or laws, and numerous other kinds of information.

Relevance means breaking through what is essentially internal "clutter." The problem of system overload becomes worse when unimportant information floods the system. Relevance is tied to *concise* reporting of facts. Most reports delivered in larger organizations begin with an "executive summary" citing the most important findings. A similar mindset should be part of all internal communications.

Proper storage means that data are placed where they can be retrieved for future use. The company's data warehouse contains a great deal of marketing information. The human resource department also maintains files regarding the history of each employee, including facts about raises, promotions, or any disciplinary actions. Accounting maintains sales records, cost information, and budget reports.

Eliminating Barriers

The second method to overcome the barriers to formal communication is finding ways to eliminate them. Management communication experts recommend several ideas. First, *choose the proper channel.* A savvy manager knows when a face-to-face conversation is in order and when a simple e-mail will suffice. Marketing managers should be aware of the best ways to reach internal employees as well as external publics.

Second, important messages should be sent through *multiple channels.* One vital element in all marketing is the "follow-up," from the follow-up on a sales call to a follow-up memo after a key meeting, to a follow-up advertisement reminding consumers about a contest or some other promotional event. When a message is sent twice, two benefits result. First the odds double that the right recipient will hear the message. Second, any message that is received twice almost immediately seems more important.

Another part of overcoming the barriers to formal communication is *managing informational communication.* This includes

- understanding the communication,
- tapping in, and
- using the channel to pass along messages.

The marketing manager should *understand* that gossip travels quickly, is accurate or partly accurate about two thirds of the time, and tends to center on things that are important to employees. This means that the manager should always hear gossip with some skepticism, because one third of all rumors are completely false. The manager should also be aware that employees tend to talk about issues such as pay, promotion decisions, termination decisions, romances, and other similar topics.[9]

Tapping in means making sure you know what rumors are circulating. Some communications experts call this *having a pipeline.* It is important to know what formal and informal issues are capturing the attention of the workforce.

Marketing managers may at times use informal communication to *pass along messages.* A compliment may be easily transmitted to a group of coworkers in an informal setting. It may have a stronger impact because it seems unprompted and not part of the formal reward system. Some managers enjoy sharing *trial balloons,* or experimental ideas, with peers and subordinates to get their reactions. This gives the manager the chance to discuss the concept in a more relaxed setting.

Finally, communications specialists recommend a periodic *communication audit.* The goal of an audit is to make sure the lines of communication remain open in every direction. Supervisors should be certain that the downward lines facilitate the transmission of decisions, orders, and inquiries. First-line supervisors should be confident that questions, requests, and other comments are taken up the chain of command. Individual department managers should feel comfortable that they can interact with other managers to exchange information, ideas, and opinions.[10]

Why does gossip travel faster than communication through formal company channels?

STOP AND THINK

When conducting a communications audit, what kinds of questions would you ask of the following individuals?

1. The company's CEO
2. The head of each major function or department, such as accounting, marketing, production, quality control, research and development, and human resources
3. First-line employees, including salespeople, those in the repair department, the order fulfillment department, the credit department, and the call center
4. Satisfied customers
5. Dissatisfied customers
6. Prospects

Internal Communication and Customer Service

A customer-oriented company does not happen by accident. For every Zappos that is managed by someone committed to high-quality customer service, there are several other firms without the same emphasis. In today's business climate, most marketing experts agree that consumers typically believe products and services are largely comparable (brand parity). To gain an edge, customer service offers a clear avenue to differentiate a company from its competition.

While a strong case can be made that a satisfied workforce will produce satisfied customers, a question remains: Is the reverse true? Do satisfied, loyal customers have any impact on the employees? Recent research suggests that they do. In essence, employees who interact with satisfied, loyal customers develop higher levels of job satisfaction, experience increased job loyalty and productivity, and are less likely to quit or be fired. Further, a company that has satisfied and loyal customers tends to attract better employees. This is especially true for highly competitive industries.[11] In essence, creating a customer-centric culture yields positive benefits with customers and produces long-term employee benefits as well.

A customer-centric culture takes time and effort to create. It involves the following internal communication actions:

- Reinforcing the company's vision and mission
- Understanding and adapting to the company's culture
- Creating a positive climate
- Engaging employees
- Encouraging open and honest communication
- Providing rewards and recognition

> Do satisfied customers have an impact on employees of a company?

Reinforcing the Company's Mission and Vision

A mission statement states the overall, most general purpose that an organization serves. It essentially answers the question "Why do we exist?" or "Why are we in business?" Most corporate mission statements are relatively short, as small as a single paragraph. A firm's *vision* explains how the mission is to be achieved. A vision statement provides a sense of direction. The corporate mission for Zappos, as noted at the start of this chapter, is "To Live and Deliver WOW." To achieve this mission, the company's leaders stress high-quality customer service, friendliness, excitement, and other aspects of the firm's 10 core values and apply them to every product and every activity.

Vision and mission statements are often reflected in advertising taglines. When the advertising for Avis concludes with "We try harder," the emphasis is on finding employees who will try hard to take care of customers and meet their needs. "You're in good hands with Allstate" implies that Allstate will take care of you and provide help when needed. RadioShack's tagline is "You've got questions. We've got answers." Managers and subordinates working at RadioShack know the goal is to offer a place where a customer can get questions answered and receive additional assistance.

When a company's mission and vision statement clearly articulate an emphasis on customer service, everyone in the organization, from first-line workers to the CEO, knows something about the type of experience the company seeks to provide. Explaining and restating the company's vision and mission should be part of the recruiting and selection process and should also be emphasized in employee training. The mission should be restated at regular intervals, during employee meetings and annual meetings and in face-to-face conversations between top managers and all publics. As noted earlier, an internal marketing program passes along this vision and mission. SAGE Publications President and CEO Blaise R. Simqu makes a consistent point that the organization was established to be an "author-friendly" company, where contributors are to be treated with the highest levels of respect and consideration. Such a vision permeates the activities of the entire company.

A Customer Service Test

To assess whether a company does indeed stress customer service, one simple method would be to ask people inside and outside the organization whether they think it has the following prerequisites of a customer-oriented company. (Each answer of "yes" receives 2 points, each "maybe some or unsure" scores 1 point, and each "no" gets 0 point.)

1. A vision for customer service, with all employees, from top to bottom, being aware of it
2. A plan for creating a customer service culture that has been followed
3. Customer contact personnel who receive training in how to deal with various customer behaviors
4. Managers who model the customer service behaviors in their daily activities with employees
5. Managers who interact and deal with customers on a regular basis
6. Frontline customer contact personnel who are among the lowest paid in the company (reverse score this item: *yes* = 0, *maybe* = 1, and *no* = 2)
7. Mystery shoppers to assess the customer service on the sales floor, in the call center, on the Web site, and at other customer contact points
8. Employees who are recognized for exceptional customer service through recognition and rewards
9. A compensation system and reward system that is closely tied to the quality of service that is provided to customers
10. Team, unit, or department bonuses that are based, in part, on the level of customer satisfaction
11. Surveys for gauging customer satisfaction on a regular basis
12. Employees who are empowered to make customer-related decisions
13. Employees, including managers, at all levels who are held accountable for the quality of customer care they demonstrate and provide
14. Employees and managers who regularly listen to customers and provide feedback to management
15. Customer service quality circles or teams that meet regularly to assess customer service and discuss ways of improving it

This list provides a valuable approach for evaluating how well the company is doing. Use the scale below to grade the company on its customer service orientation:

- Score of 27 to 30 is an "A"—The company has a strong customer service culture.
- Score of 24 to 26 is a "B"—The company provides good customer service but could make improvements.
- Score of 20 to 23 is a "C"—This company is average and in a brand parity situation. It will have to compete using price or work hard at improving customer service.
- Score of 15 to 19 is a "D"—This company is in trouble. Even competing on price will not be enough. The company must devote people and resources into changing its environment.
- Score of 0 to 14 is an "F"—Time is ticking for this firm. Unless drastic changes are made, poor service will destroy this company. It doesn't matter how low the price it offers is; customers will not tolerate poor service.

Understanding and Adapting to the Company's Culture

Having a vision and articulating it does not guarantee that it will be carried out in the way customers are treated. Working toward a customer-centric environment requires strong internal communications. The marketing team should be a prominent, if not leading, force behind those communications.

A company's culture consists of the symbols, rituals, language, myths, stories, and jargon present in an organization. Most of the time, a founder story establishes the first elements of culture. Legendary stories about James Cash Penney, Sam Walton, Henry Ford, and others set the tone for what takes place within their companies. For example, when Ray Kroc purchased the McDonald's Brothers restaurants and renamed them McDonald's, he directed the company's operations using three principles: quality, service, and cleanliness, which were shortened to QSC. The Golden Arches logo of McDonald's remains the same, as do the rituals of manager training at Hamburger University and many other parts of the company's operations.

Contrast the culture of McDonald's with that of an upcoming organization such as Mark Ecko Enterprises, directed by owner and CEO Marc Ecko. Where words such as *old fashioned* and *family oriented* would be associated with McDonald's, terms such as *hip hop, cutting edge,* or possibly even *gangsta* might apply to Ecko. Undoubtedly, the culture of Ecko is dramatically different, from the types of people who are hired to the terminology used in meetings, to product lines that are developed, to the reward system, and to the methods of conducting business.

A manager in the marketing department must first seek to understand the culture of the organization. She must remember that a culture evolves over many years and often becomes difficult to challenge or change. As an example, consider the cultures of the major automobile manufacturers in the United States. General Motors and Ford were among the slowest to react to rising oil prices and consumer demands for more fuel-efficient cars. Both companies experienced a dramatic drop in sales, especially in 2008, due to an overreliance on sport utility vehicles and pickup trucks. Changing the mindset from "power" vehicles to "fuel-efficient" vehicles takes time.

At first, a manager can only work within the parameters of the culture that exists. A culture tends to be modified slowly. Only when there is a major shift in the organization, due to a crisis, major growth, or a change in leadership will a culture change more rapidly. Building a customer-oriented culture where one does not exist requires a great deal of time and energy.

Creating a Positive Climate

Most managers find it is easier to have a more immediate impact on a firm's climate. An organization's climate is the prevailing atmosphere or environment within a company. A company's climate will be strongly affected by the organization's external environment, its internal strengths and weaknesses, and the preferences and activities of top managers. The climate in a growing and successful company, such as Zappos, will be far different from the climate of a firm in crisis or decline. Marketing managers do have tools at their disposal to influence climate. The tools include engaging employees through empowerment and building relationships through open and honest communication.

How can engaging employees help to build a more effective marketing department?

Engaging Employees

Creating a customer service orientation requires employees to "buy in." They must be engaged in the entire process. This means they understand and believe in the company's mission and vision. Then they believe they play a key part in the organization.

Employee engagement contributes to employee empowerment. To create a customer-centric environment, employees should have the authority to make customer-related decisions on the spot. Empowerment creates a more positive work situation, leads to increases in employee productivity, and results in improved customer satisfaction.[12]

The challenge company leaders often face is in getting employees involved and making them feel free to speak out. A recent study by two Harvard University professors revealed that half of the employees in an organization did not believe it was safe to speak up or challenge traditional ways of thinking. The employees were most reticent about suggesting creative ideas about how to improve customer service processes, products, or performance. They thought that speaking out would be perceived as an indictment of upper management and of their immediate supervisors. They also tended to believe that employees who spoke up would eventually find themselves working elsewhere.[13]

It takes a concerted effort to engage employees and to make them feel comfortable in being part of a customer-oriented company. The effort is necessary, however, if the management team truly wants to stress excellent customer service. When employees feel comfortable enough to contribute ideas, they will also believe in the company and want it to succeed. It is no longer a company they work for, it is *their company*.[14]

Encouraging Open and Honest Communication

One of the more natural tendencies in the workplace is called obfuscation, which means someone will try to obscure, disguise, or confuse a message. Many times, it is used to explain poor performance or some other failure on the job, taking the form of subtly implying the problem was someone else's fault or trying to find some other way to place the blame elsewhere. Obfuscation occurs when a salesperson fudges sales figures or inaccurately reports on the success of a missionary sales call. It also takes place when a poorly designed advertisement results in a less than ideal outcome and the creative tries to explain it away by saying it was due to poor slots on television or was in some other way the fault of the media buyer.

A second problem, **inclusive/exclusive language** occurs when an "in crowd" develops its own lingo and patterns of conversation. Those within the circle participate in "inside jokes" and other rituals that exclude others. Inclusive/exclusive language is used to discriminate and to make coworkers feel unwelcome. For example, men often use sports metaphors when talking about business practices. Many women are less interested in certain sports and therefore do not exactly understand what a male manager means when he suggests that the female employee "take one for the team," or "push the pile forward." Sports metaphors can be a form of exclusive language.

Internal communication can also be part of attempts to discriminate, harass, intimidate, or hurt another person in some way. While some claim that the principle of *political correctness* goes too far in attempting to protect those who may be harmed by callous remarks, others ask why people feel it is important to allow objectionable language. When words are demeaning because of racial or sexual connotations or imply that an employee is in some way handicapped or physically or mentally challenged, it is likely that there will be a negative impact on the company's environment. There is no doubt that words can hurt.

The goal of the marketing manager should be to overcome problems such as obfuscation, exclusive language, and objectionable language. Doing so involves two key processes: role modeling and coaching.

A manager as a **role model** provides a clear example of how to act within the company. To reduce problems such as obfuscation, the manager should be willing to publicly admit that he made a mistake. The manager should also respond positively when an employee becomes the first person to be willing to step up and take the blame for a mistake or error. Seeking to fix the problem and/or making sure it does not occur again creates an environment that is less punitive and more supportive. An effective manager gives credit when someone succeeds and does not try to steal the spotlight during that moment.

Coaching includes teaching and training others. For instance, when a male salesperson comments, "This sales call is just going to be a Hail Mary," the supervisor can explain to everyone present, especially females who may not watch football, that "what he means is that this is going to be a real long shot." If someone else makes a racial slur or uses some other negative stereotype, the supervisor must be the first to step in and say, "We don't use that kind of language in this company."

Open communication takes time to be established and can be easily damaged. Achieving success means continually and carefully observing how employees communicate with one another as well as with managers and customers.

Providing Rewards and Recognition

Employees who are rewarded and recognized when they succeed normally report much higher degrees of satisfaction with the supervisor, with the company, and with the job itself. Any type of worker gains confidence when he is recognized for making good decisions on behalf of the organization. Nearly everyone enjoys the feeling of being appreciated.

When employees believe that the only time they will be noticed is when they make bad decisions or do something wrong, morale declines. This wears on employees, as well as managers, and over time leads to

Why are rewards and recognition an important part of internal communications?

problems such as absenteeism and turnover. Consequently, the marketing manager should carefully guard against overemphasizing problems and instead look for examples of what employees are doing well.

Showing appreciation is easy and has no cost. When consistent positive feedback is given, employees respond. Remember that a strong connection exists between employee satisfaction and customer satisfaction. Engaging and empowering employees, opening lines of honest communication, and providing positive reinforcement and rewards give the marketing manager the best chance of working with satisfied employees and creating a customer-centric climate.

International Internal Communications

The proliferation of international conglomerates and expansion of even small businesses into foreign locations creates many opportunities and challenges for internal communication systems.

The opportunities include nearly instantaneous contact with employees and partners around the world. This provides the marketing team with the chance to quickly seize on favorable market conditions. A sales rep can quickly gain authorization to change or improve an offer to a prospect when it appears that a competitor has a chance of taking away a deal.

The challenges include standard concerns such as *language* and *slang*. Further, often employees from the same company come from different countries. The challenge of ethnocentrism must be overcome. When a person from a different country believes her local culture is better or superior, many times that attitude affects how the individual communicates with coworkers from other countries. Company leaders are advised to be aware of the potential for these attitudes to cause disharmony. Training in cultural sensitivity helps. Also, during the recruiting and selection process, applicants who do not seem to be aware of cultural differences or who exhibit negative attitudes may be screened out, while those who seem to embrace and enjoy other cultures are better candidates.

It is likely that some gaffes will still occur. For instance, an unknowing employee might ask a coworker, "What day is Ramadan?" (Ramadan is a monthlong ritual.) When a company has international partners, meet-and-greet sessions combined with training about cultural differences should reduce some of these problems.

Technical problems also must be resolved. For example, those in the home office must constantly be aware of time differences. When it is noon in Washington, D.C., it is 2:00 a.m. in Taipei, Taiwan. Also, whenever technology is involved, the possibility exists that it will fail. Creating backup plans for such contingencies should be part of the internal communication planning process.

Implications for Marketing Managers

Three activities summarize the impact of communication on entry-level employees and first-line supervisors in the marketing department. First, take care of your own house. This means it will be worthwhile to conduct a personal communications audit. Each person seeking to enter the marketing profession should assess her ability to write effectively, to engage in conversations with others, and to speak in public. If any of the three is lacking, it deserves immediate attention. Using video to record a conversation or public presentation can help an individual discover the "uhs," "likes," and "ya-knows" that make a person sound less polished.

Second, assess your listening skills. Does your mind wander during conversations? How can you be a better audience? Learn tactics that help you ask effective follow-up questions.

Third, understand how communication works in any given organization. Patterns of interaction differ, from formal to informal. In some organizations small talk is a fact of life, in others it will be strongly discouraged. Various organizations rely on differing formats, from e-mail to written documents. In essence, to get a jump on the competition when entering an organization requires finding out what "language" the organization uses and then becoming fluent in that language.

YOURCAREER

Communication Skills

Your career path will be largely influenced by the ability to communicate. Fortunately, developing these skills is usually a lifelong process. During your time in college and the first job after college, it is important to work on the following skills, so that they become second nature.

Greeting Skills

1. This may sound silly, but practice your handshake. Grasp the other person's hand firmly but not so strongly that it would hurt, in case the person has arthritis or some other problem.

2. Practice making eye contact. People who look away seem shifty.

Dining Skills

1. Learn quality table manners. Practice eating an entire meal without once talking with food in your mouth. Have a friend monitor.

2. Practice ordering food that would be easy to handle during an interview or meal with a client. It should be easy to cut, with little chance to spill. It should not cause you to need a napkin too many times during the meal.

Working-the-Room Skills

1. Learn how to make small talk. The first rule is to always ask the person about himself or herself. Let the other person guide the conversation to what she thinks is interesting. Remember what the person says, so you have a starting point for the conversation the next time you see him or her.

2. Learn how to remember names. Some suggest repeating the person's name during the conversation several times; others say the best way is to associate the name with a characteristic the person has, such as "Suzie with the long red hair" or "Pete with the comb-over."

3. Practice giving compliments. Across gender, make sure the compliment is not sexist or does not seem like you are making a romantic advance. Guys, get help from lady friends. Ladies, ask your friends how you come across in a public setting.

Formal Presentation Skills

1. If you have trouble getting up in front of an audience, volunteer to do so every chance you get.

2. Make eye contact with the entire audience. Move gradually across the room as you speak. Make sure you talk to someone in the front row and someone in the back.

3. Learn how to speak without a script. Use note cards or PowerPoint, but practice until you don't need them very often during the speech. If you use PowerPoint, make sure you are talking to the audience and not the screen where the images appear.

4. Tape yourself. Do you need verbal hedges? Can you get through an entire sentence without the words *like, ya know,* or *I mean?* If not, work very hard to eliminate these bad habits.

Written Presentations

1. Practice writing clear and concise memos and reports. Make sure your grammar and spelling are correct.

2. Learn your audience. If someone likes humor, it may work. Most of the time, however, the best rule of thumb is to be as professional as possible, especially early in a new job.

International Skills

Adapt all these skills to the cultures of other countries.

Chapter Summary

Communication is the process of transmitting, receiving, and processing information. Business communication takes the forms of individual communication and communication systems. An individual communication model explains how the sender encodes messages, which then move through a transmission device to be decoded by the receiver. The sender receives feedback in return. Noise, or the barriers to communication, consists of all the factors that can distort or disrupt communications between individuals.

The barriers to communication include individual differences such as age, gender, status, culture, subculture, and personality types. Situational factors that disrupt communication include settings and emotions. The mechanical problems that can distort individual communication consist of language, slang, problems with the transmission device, and nonverbal contradiction of a verbal message.

Overcoming the barriers to individual communication includes several sender duties, such as understanding what potential barriers exist, displaying empathy, being aware of nonverbal cues, and seeking confirmation of the message. The receiver should actively listen to the message and seek clarification when confused.

Overcoming the barriers to individual communication improves the situation within the marketing department, in its relationships with other departments and interactions with clients and customers. Effective communication skills are a major asset to an individual employee as she pursues a career.

The two main communication systems in business organizations are the formal and informal systems. Formal communication travels through the channels that are chosen or designated by the organization. Informal communication emerges in the form of gossip, rumors, and what travels through the grapevine.

The traditional formal communication channels include a direct address, meetings, memos, letters, the company manual or handbook, the bulletin board, and any company magazine or newspaper. Some of the newly developed formal channels are cell phones and other portable devices, satellite transmissions, teleconferences, e-mail, the firm's Web site, the fax machine, and the company's intranet.

The barriers to formal communication include system overload, selective filtering of messages, use of the wrong channel, transmission failures, informal contradiction of the formal message, and all the barriers to individual communication. To overcome these barriers, the marketing manager should establish an effective management information system, including the right people, machinery, and forms of information. Eliminating the barriers to formal communication also includes choosing the proper channels for messages, using multiple channels for important messages (or following up), managing informal communication, and conducting periodic communication audits.

A strong relationship exists between effective internal communications and quality customer interactions. To make certain the company enjoys the advantages of a quality communication system, the marketing manager must first reinforce the company's vision and mission, which serves as an overall guide to its activities. Also, the marketing manager should try to understand and adapt to the company's culture. An effective marketing supervisor creates a positive environment by engaging employees and developing honest and open communications. Finally, every effort should be made to provide rewards and recognition when employees succeed.

Chapter Terms

Climate   (p. 271)
Coaching   (p. 273)
Communication   (p. 257)
Company culture   (p. 271)
Decoding   (p. 258)
Encoding   (p. 258)
Ethnocentrism   (p. 274)
Feedback   (p. 258)
Formal communication   (p. 262)
Inclusive/exclusive language   (p. 273)
Informal communication   (p. 262)

Internal marketing   (p. 261)
Management information system   (p. 266)
Mission statement   (p. 269)
Noise (or barriers to communication)   (p. 258)
Obfuscation   (p. 272)
Receiver   (p. 258)
Role model   (p. 273)
Selective filtering   (p. 265)
Sender   (p. 258)
System overload   (p. 265)
Transmission device   (p. 258)

Review Questions

1. Define communication.
2. What are the two main levels of business communication?
3. Name and define each part of an individual communication model.
4. What individual differences can disrupt individual communication?
5. What situational factors can disrupt individual communication?
6. What mechanical problems can disrupt individual communication?
7. What can a sender do to overcome the barriers to individual communication?
8. What can a receiver do to overcome the barriers to individual communication?
9. Explain the value of quality individual communication to both the company and the individual employees in the company.
10. Define formal communication and informal communication.
11. What traditional formal communication channels are available to marketing managers?
12. What newly developed formal communication channels are available to marketing managers?
13. What are the barriers to formal communication?
14. What is a management information system? Which three characteristics are part of an effective management information system?
15. How can a marketing manager effectively use informal communication?
16. Beyond the use of informal communication, what other activities lead to the reduction or elimination of barriers to formal communication?
17. What international concerns are there in internal communications systems?

CUSTOMER CORNER

The use of e-mail as a formal communication channel is a relatively recent development. At the same time, some believe that channel is being replaced by even faster methods of communication, such as text messaging. Consider Figure 10.6 when answering the following questions:

1. Does this list of rules apply equally well to writing text messages?
2. Which is a better channel, e-mailing or text messaging, with coworkers? With supervisors? With the CEO and top management team? With clients and customers?
3. Can you think of additional rules that should apply to text messages? If so, what are they?
4. Which is more likely to be used for gossip and rumors, e-mails or text messages?

- Organize your thoughts prior to writing the e-mail.
- Use good rules of grammar.
- Use bullet points, underlining, and bold to clarify your message.
- Reread your e-mail before sending it.
- Use a relevant subject line.
- Send the e-mail to the employees affected; avoid mass broadcasts.
- Be sure that e-mail is the most appropriate channel.
- Be careful of content!

Figure 10.6 Rules for Writing Effective E-mails

Discussion and Critical Thinking Questions

1. Describe a breakdown in communication that you have experienced at work in each of the following areas: encoding, transmission device, decoding, and feedback. Could the problem have been avoided? If so, how?

2. More than once, the process of getting a job has been compared to going on a first date. Using the duties of both senders and receivers in creating quality communication, compare how each duty would apply to dating, getting a job, and convincing a customer to try a new product or service.

3. The management team at Union Bank of California, which employs more than 10,000 people, discovered a problem. They found that information was going out several times each day to every employee. For the most part, the information was irrelevant. To reduce the unwanted e-mails, Union Bank switched to targeted RSS Web feeds. Now, only the employees who need certain information receive it. This change in communication protocol is estimated to save the bank 30 minutes per week per employee, a cost savings of $750,000 per year (see Note 6). Describe this scenario in terms of
   - the barrier to formal communication that existed and
   - the methods of overcoming the barriers to communication described in this chapter.

4. Many companies employ the following technologies:
   - Company-owned cell phone
   - Fax machine
   - E-mail work address
   - iPhone
   - BlackBerry
   - Take-home laptop computer

   Rank these technologies, from highest to lowest, in terms of

   a. the likelihood that a message will be unintentionally misinterpreted, leading to embarrassments and conflicts;
   b. their use to spread rumors and gossip without being detected;
   c. the ability of the company to "spy" on employees, both at work and during time off; and
   d. the potential to create stress for employees, because they can never "get away" from the technology.

5. Explain how the following advertising tag lines reflect the vision and mission of the company involved.
   - "Fly the friendly skies"—United Airlines
   - "The happiest place on earth"—Disneyland
   - "Just do it"—Nike
   - "Milk: It does a body good"—Milk Industry

6. Your company faces major budget problems. Just after being promoted to manager of the marketing department, you notice that the environment seems to be cynical and lethargic, with little creativity or spontaneity. Explain how you can use the concepts present in this chapter, without spending a great deal of money, to improve the climate within your department.

Chapter 10 Case

The Zen Master

Jacque Kline's rise to the level of business-to-business sales manager in her insurance agency was unprecedented. She was the first female to hold the title, and she had been promoted after only 5 years with Bedrock Insurance. Top management was impressed with her willingness to work long hours and close sales and her ability to garner the respect of coworkers and customers. They also liked her "can do" attitude.

Unfortunately, a lack of "can do" spirit seemed to permeate the Bedrock agency. Sales to individual customers had reached a plateau, and business-to-business sales (the "big-ticket" accounts) had declined by an average of 4% per year for the past 3 years. Jacque's immediate supervisor, Director of Marketing Ryan Jacobs, had conducted an intensive strengths, weaknesses, opportunities, and threats (SWOT) analysis of Bedrock's marketing department. His conclusions were that the strengths of Bedrock were financial stability and a solid mix of insurance products. The weaknesses included a lack of diversity in the sales force and what he termed "complacency." The opportunities available to Bedrock came from a growing and increasingly affluent local community in one of the main suburbs of Spokane, Washington, combined with the influx of many service industry employers. The threats resulted from increasing local competition from both national providers, such as Allstate, State Farm, and Prudential, plus a new local agency that was started by a local football hero who had just retired from the NFL.

Jacque conducted her own research. She concluded that there was poor communication throughout the organization. Leads discovered by the database department were not being passed along to business-to-business sales reps. Complaints by individual policy holders were being ignored. When a satisfied customer made a comment or sent a letter of thanks, the information never seemed to make it to the sales rep who provided the excellent service.

Jacque convinced Ryan to hire a local consultant, who by his reputation for success was known in Spokane as the Zen Master. His real name was Tim Peterson. At their first meeting, Tim explained two main issues that he would address.

"First," he stated, "we need to tap into the goals your reps use when they talk to each other and to customers. There are three possibilities: instrumental goals, self-presentation goals, and relational goals. If they are focusing on instrumental goals, then they are spending most of their energy on accomplishing objectives, like making the sale or winning an argument with a boss or colleague. If they work most on self-presentation goals, then they are most worried about making a good impression. They probably do quite a bit of acclaiming, or taking credit for things, even when they didn't make much of a contribution. If they pay attention to relational goals, they use conversation to build relationships and socialize."

Jacque asked, "Well, which is best?"

Tim, ever the Zen Master, replied, "Which do you think you need more of in your department?" He smiled, "That's one of the things we'll work on."

Ryan asked, "Okay, so what's the other area?"

Tim responded, "This is more in your bailiwick. You need to know how information moves through Bedrock. Again, there are three possibilities: chain, wheel, and all-channel. If Bedrock uses a chain, it means you guys strictly follow the chain of command. People talk only directly to those above or below them on the organizational chart. If you use a wheel, then the manager is a focal point and all of the spokes are the employees. That means the manager has to be up on everything to keep things moving smoothly. Or if you have an all-channel network, everyone feels free to communicate with everyone else. When that happens, the manager may or may not know exactly what is going on."

Forgetting himself, Ryan asked, "Okay, so which is best?"

How could Jacque Kline improve internal communication and morale among her employees?

The Zen Master's answer was to be expected: "Which do you think would work best for your marketing department?"

Ryan liked his answer. He authorized Jacque to retain the Zen Master and to get to work on building better internal lines of communication at Bedrock.[14]

1. Which communication goal should be the primary one for Bedrock's insurance sales force—instrumental, self-presentation, or relational? If there is a mix, what percentage should each one receive?

2. Which formal channel should be used at Bedrock—the chain, wheel, or all-channel model?

3. Do you think Jacque should focus on communication only or a larger topic such as the company's culture or climate?

4. Can you make a case that the poor communication within the organization has somehow affected the sales trends present? If so, explain how it is taking place.

Go to **www.sagepub.com/clow** for additional exercises and study resources. Select **Chapter 10, Internal Communications** for chapter-specific activities.

What are the secrets to success for the Round Rock Express?

chapter 11

External Communications

Round Rock Express: Making Memories One Game at a Time

Over the past decade, a baseball phenomenon has surfaced in Round Rock, Texas. That is when the Express moved to town. The team, which is the AAA affiliate of the Houston Astros, now draws the second highest attendance in minor league baseball each year. It has been featured in *Sports Illustrated* as a prime example of how to build and maintain a successful franchise.

What is the secret to success? CEO Reid Ryan enthusiastically emphasizes,

"Awesome customer service. We want to be in the market for a long time," he reports. "We want to be a top of mind entertainment experience. Coming to one of our games should be a rite of passage."

Round Rock's management team emphasizes three groups that must be effectively served: fans, sponsors, and players. Constant communication with each group has created long-lasting bonds. As one former player put it, "The pay is better

in the majors, but it's more fun playing in Round Rock."

Communication with fans is at the core. Jay Miller, Chief Operating Officer of the Express, states it this way: "When you come to our ballpark, we are going to know your name." Employees are carefully chosen. "We don't entrust this business with just anybody," Miller notes. People are hired because they match the fan-first attitude. Many have been with the team since it was formed. Consequently, someone coming to the stadium is likely to be greeted by long-time parking lot attendant Oscar, who works hard at learning as many names as possible. The same is true for employees at the ticket windows, those who take tickets and sell concessions, as well as the ushers.

Why is it important for the players to interact with the fans, especially with children?

Employees are empowered to provide the highest-quality service. Reid Ryan noted a time in which an obviously angry patron pulled in to the ballpark and Oscar immediately decided to give the man free parking. Both Miller and Ryan routinely walk the entire stadium, talking with fans and doing what they can to make people feel comfortable. One of their favorite tactics is to find a family in the cheapest seats and move them to their own box seats next to the field.

Fans routinely interact with players. The players enter the ballpark by going through sections of fans. At each game, Little League players and those who have special needs are taken onto the field to stand for the national anthem with an Express player. Young people are invited to play catch with some of the players after games. Autographs are freely signed. "You don't have to be a baseball fan to have fun at our ballpark," Miller points out with pride.

Every Express game is designed to be a family-friendly experience. Dell Stadium is one of the most modern in Texas, complete with comfortable seats with cup holders, a large video scoreboard, and dozens of fun events, from the "kiss cam" to races on the field, to special events. Each night has a feature: fireworks, souvenir giveaways, dollar hot dogs and sodas, half-price-beer night, group rates, and fan appreciation days.

Miller and Ryan move quickly when a patron is dissatisfied. "We do whatever is needed to make them happy," Ryan said, "whether it's a refund, free merchandise, or tickets for another game." When someone is injured by a foul ball, employees quickly react to do whatever they can to help.

Each year the Express surveys fans at the end of the season. They ask for ways to improve the experience. One year, several fans complained about the long walk around the stadium to get to bleacher seats. In response, the team spent over $250,000 on a new entryway to make them easier to reach.

Ryan and Miller work hard to establish the same lines of communication and positive relationships with sponsors, the local community, and players. The approach continues to work. Jay Miller, who has received several "Executive of the Year" awards, summarizes his work this way: "Our ballpark is Round Rock's front porch."[1]

Chapter Overview

The distinction between internal and external communication may be largely artificial. Most company messages reach both company employees and external groups. For example, advertisements are viewed by both. Press releases are read or are seen by both. At the same time, it is helpful to understand the primary audience for any marketing communication.

This chapter focuses on the interactions between members of a company and those outside the company. External communications are transmitted in various ways using a variety of readily visible and some more subtle media. External communications take place with two primary groups: (1) customers and potential customers and (2) other individuals and groups. The majority of the chapter is devoted to external communications with customers and potential customers.

This chapter opens with a quick review of communications with non-customers. Then, the emphasis shifts to the many ways companies communicate with customers using less obvious and more direct cues. Topics included in this discussion are communications through institutional statements, product appearance, the business facility, personal contacts, marketing tactics, and public relations programs. The chapter concludes with a discussion of the impact of external communications on the marketing manager and the relationship between such communications and high-quality customer service.

Communications With Non-Customers

A great deal of communication takes place between members of an organization and various publics that are not customers or potential customers. Successful marketing managers know that these relationships affect the welfare of the entire organization. Most do not directly contact the marketing department. Still, members of the marketing team will find out about most of these interactions, directly or indirectly. These publics include

- suppliers,
- governmental agencies and employees,
- members of the local community,
- labor unions,
- competing businesses,
- special interest groups, and
- people in mass media (reporters, bloggers, program hosts).

Of these, the marketing team is most likely to have contact with members of the local community, the media, and, to some extent, competing businesses.

The two primary channels of communications with these publics are (1) messages and statements made by the management team and (2) messages transmitted through the public relations department. Of the two, the group most directly connected with the marketing department is public relations, although there should be ongoing interactions between publicity and other members of the company. A firm's marketing activities also affect these contact points. In other words, marketing tactics such as advertising have an effect on the local community, suppliers, special interest groups, and the other publics. The importance of contacts with non-customers cannot be overemphasized, even though they are not the focus of this textbook.

Communications With Customers and Potential Customers

The external communications that are most under the control of the marketing department are those made with members of the target market. Customer contact points are the interactions

What makes customer contact points one of the keys to customer satisfaction?

between a company, its customers, and its prospective customers. Nearly all the material presented in this textbook has an element of customer contact connected to it. A case can be made that the essence of marketing is communicating with customers in one way or another. While each marketing activity takes a different form, the goal remains to find customers to buy goods and services and convince them that a particular brand is the best choice. Sometimes, the message is transmitted from the company to the customer. At other times, the customer makes the first contact with the company. Most of the time, the quality of the interaction between members of the company and these individuals and groups determines the future of the relationship.

Members of the marketing team try to identify every potential contact point and consider each one from the viewpoint of the customer. The objective is to understand how messages are transmitted and received at those contact points. The list of contact points typically begins with members of the sales force and other marketing department employees. Additional contacts are made, some personal (face-to-face, telephone conversations) and some using impersonal methods (advertisements, letters sent to potential customers). Additional contact points include interactions with the

- product's delivery team,
- repair department,
- credit department,
- company's Web site,
- complaint department,
- company's managers and others making public appearances, and
- company's public relations team.

Interactions with individuals in one or more of these groups shape the customer's opinion and reactions to the company. For instance, a person wishing to buy a car from a used-car lot who has his credit application turned down by a member of the credit department is most likely to see that car lot through the context of the conversation. Another customer who brings a car back because the brakes failed one day after the purchase may form a completely different opinion if the brakes are quickly repaired at no charge with sincere apologies made by the salesperson and the mechanic in the repair department.

Everything Communicates

Today's marketing experts often note that in the current business environment, everything about a company communicates something. Many of these features are the direct responsibility of the marketing department. Others are tangentially related to marketing. Successful company leaders strive to manage every aspect of what is being communicated to customers and potential customers as well as to non-customers. In this section, the methods of external communication shown in Figure 11.1 are examined.

- Institutional statements
- Product appearance
- Business facility
- Personal contacts
- Marketing communication tactics
- Public relations efforts
- Image-building events

Figure 11.1

Methods of External Communication

Institutional Statements

Both customers and non-customers can learn a great deal about a company from its institutional statements, including those found in the company's mission statement and its reports to stockholders. The mission statement expresses the firm's core values and its primary reason for being. A highly visible mission statement explains the purpose and nature of the organization to employees, customers, and other publics. Mission statements are rarely revised, which means they communicate a consistent message. They are not as likely to facilitate interactions with customers.

Reports to stockholders indicate how the company intends to pursue its mission, along with any revisions or changes to that mission. These messages accompany financial information. These statements provide regular updates about the firm's well-being, making them important instruments for interacting with various constituencies. Mission statements and comments in shareholder reports tend to be general and vague, but they do provide a backdrop for other company communications.

At times, a company may also communicate through statements about a strategic vision or strategic activities. For example, when a major company such as MTV announces plans to offer programming in a new country, the media will be contacted in the new country as well as in others that MTV serves.

The same holds true for other tactics. Recently, when the Starbucks management team decided to close every unit for part of a day so that discussions about quality and service could be held, the media were notified. When the same company disclosed that several hundred stores were to be closed, a press release was sent out. These types of reports keep the public updated on a firm, making them important elements in the customer interaction processes.

Product Appearance and Package Design

Many customers consider a product's appearance when evaluating and selecting items. The appearance influences a consumer's first impression as well as subsequent purchases. It can lead to further exploration of the product or cause it to be quickly rejected. Consumers make quick judgments about product attributes, such as quality, based on appearance. This is true for consumer goods as well as in the business-to-business sector. Figure 11.2 identifies some roles that product appearance plays in the decision-making process.[2]

- Aesthetic value
- Symbolic value
- Functional value
- Attention-drawing value

Figure 11.2

Roles of Product Appearance

In evaluating garden tools, what role does functional value play in the decision?

Aesthetic Value

One of the primary features of a product or brand's appearance is its aesthetic value. Aesthetic value comes from anything that is pleasing or that the consumer likes. This includes something that is pretty or soft or that has a pleasant scent or an attractive design. It can create an emotional reaction to a product. What is pleasant to one person may not be to another. For example, some people prefer floral scents, while others prefer fruit scents. In brand parity situations, where several brands are viewed as being equal in quality and in other attributes, the aesthetic value derived from the product's appearance might become the determining criterion in the purchase decision. Aesthetic value can carry over from one purchase to the next. A customer who likes red or a particular design may continue to be enticed by the aesthetic value of that color or design.

Symbolic Value

Product appearance can provide symbolic value. A product has symbolic value when its appearance matches a person's self-image or in some other way is emblematic of something a person desires or values. Symbolic meanings are often enhanced or developed through advertising and marketing messages. For instance, the design of a toothbrush may enhance its odds of being chosen by a child when it features a colorful cartoon character on the package or toothbrush itself. The appearance of a sleek convertible sports car often conveys considerable symbolic meaning to others about the person who owns it.

Functional Value

A product's appearance also suggests that the item will or will not be functional. Functional value means the product looks like it will work properly. A product featuring a sturdy handle suggests that the item is both durable and of high quality. A product that appears to be cheap often conveys that it will not function well. Consumers can use their other senses to judge the functionality of a product. Smelling a perfume sample gives insight into the quality of the fragrance. Listening to an MP3 player allows the customer to test the sound quality of the music being delivered.

Attention-Drawing Value

A product may also have attention-drawing value, which means that consumers notice the product because it stands out from the competing brands. An item that is noticed invites a closer examination, which in turn increases the probability of it being purchased. Featuring bright colors, increasing the size of the product, and using outlandish graphics are some of the tactics manufacturers use to capture attention. When the actual product cannot be modified to attract attention, packaging can be used to create something that is eye-catching.

Consumer research indicates that roughly 30% of purchases are planned prior to reaching a store. This means that more than two thirds of all purchasing decisions are made while inside the store. Other research indicates that when consumers walk within 10 to 15 feet of a product, the brand has three seconds to make contact with the consumer.[3] The product and the package design make the first impression and may determine whether the customer stops and looks at the item or continues moving down the aisle.

Effective packaging entices the consumer to look no further. Millions of dollars may be spent on advertising to create brand awareness only to lose the sale in the retail store because of dull or boring packaging. This suggests that packaging and labels are key elements in communicating with new and ongoing customers. In the grocery industry, packaging is crucial. A consumer who purchases an item only to discover that it has inferior packaging will be more likely to switch brands the next time.[4]

Consumers are attracted to packages that are unusual and contemporary. When Nestlé created a new line of products called Nescafé Original, one primary consideration was packaging. The goal was to create a container that would both protect the contents and stand out. The result was a package with a unique geometrical set of shapes designed to appeal to younger consumers. The approach was successful.[5]

In the past, packages for private label products tended to be plain and, as a result, conveyed the message that "we are cheap" and "not as good as the national brands." Retailers also began to discover that price was not always the guiding factor in making a purchase decision. They realized that looking "cheap" did not always resonate with consumers. To change this image, some retailers began designing private labels and packaging that looked more like national brands. This also was not always well received, because many consumers viewed the private brands as "knockoffs" of national brands.

In response, the retailers began to look for creative and new package designs. According to Tim Cox of Publix Super Markets, Inc., "Creative packaging helps enhance the value of store brands significantly. When consumers see a unique or clever packaging execution on a private label product, they're more likely to realize it is not just a national brand knockoff."[6] For private labels, uniqueness and differentiation are essential to persuade consumers to make the switch from national brands. Once the switch has been made, the product may move into top-choice status the next time a purchase is being considered.

The Business Facility

Company leaders face difficult decisions when designing business facilities. A building has an impact on customers, employees, and the bottom line. If customers never visit the facility, then it is likely to have been designed quite differently than retail stores or businesses frequented by customers. Many different designs are possible. Most tend to stress a combination of cost

Figure 11.3 | Facility Design Options

efficiency, customization, and quality. These three goals can be viewed as points on a triangle, as illustrated in Figure 11.3. Seldom would a business facility have only one of the three attributes. Instead, buildings tend to be designed to emphasize one of the options while containing elements of all three.

Customization

The customization approach features a facility designed to focus on customers. In a four-star restaurant, this includes comfortable chairs for the customers while dining. It probably means subdued lighting and an upscale décor. The tableware would be fine china. Distances between tables will be greater to allow customers more privacy and greater comfort. The restaurant would be unique, and the interior would be different from that found in other local restaurants.

Cost Efficiency

The cost-efficiency approach accommodates a firm's operational needs. The objective would be to increase the staff's efficiency and productivity. Thus, the physical setting allows the firm to maximize the number of customers it can serve or the number of products it produces. The focus is high production at a low cost. A fast-food restaurant may use hard seats, bright lights, and a simple décor. These factors encourage customers to eat more quickly. Some fast-food units even pipe in fast-paced music to speed customers up.

Quality

The quality approach creates facilities that enhance either product or service quality. *Product quality* centers on the needs of employees and leads to higher-quality items. *Service quality* focuses on customer needs. Consider the layout and design of a bakery. If product quality is the focus, then the goal will be to hire the best baker in town. The interior design may not be as critical. The quality of the pastries becomes paramount, which means the baker will have the best equipment and materials available.

In contrast, when customer service is the focus, someone greets customers as they enter and serves them their orders. Comfortable tables and chairs are provided. The idea would be to ensure that customers are happy with the quality of service they receive.

Business designs do not last forever. Competition and changing consumer tastes and preferences lead company leaders to periodically reexamine the layout, design, and décor of the building. In the fast-food industry recently, marketing managers at McDonald's, Taco Bell, and Jack in the Box had to take a hard look at retail outlets that had become outdated. It was necessary to refurbish and remodel them to look newer, more modern, and trendier. Jack in the Box undertook a 5-year-long project that started with two new prototype restaurants in San Diego. The menu was upgraded, and the facilities were completely redesigned, emphasizing a substantially higher level of customer service. These changes were made in response to a changing consumer environment and the company's desire to expand the target market to include more females and older males.[7]

The building facility houses longer-term interactions between a company and its customers. People have their favorite tables in restaurants, favorite seats in movie theaters, and preferred stores for various types of purchases. One family may feel most comfortable in a large discount store offering lower prices and fewer amenities. Another person avoids large stores and instead seeks the comfort of a carpeted floor, soft music, comfortable chairs, and other features such as a hint of fragrance or subdued lighting. In any case, it is clear that a building and its interior design do communicate to customers.

STOP AND THINK

The following is the mission statement of Coventry Health Care, which is a full-service insurance provider:

Our mission is to provide high quality care and services to our members and to be profitable in the process. Coventry Health Care is also committed to maintaining excellence, respect, and integrity in all aspects of our operations and our professional and business conduct. We strive to reflect the highest ethical standards in our relationships with members, providers, and shareholders.

1. What is the primary message that the mission statement sends?
2. What types of non-customers would have the greatest impact on Coventry Health Care?
3. What are the key customer contact points for Coventry Health Care?
4. Which of the three facility design options—quality, customization, or cost efficiency—should the organization emphasize?
5. Is it possible to emphasize profitability and remain the most ethical and high-quality health care provider?

Personal Contacts

The marketing team communicates with customers in many ways, but personal contact offers the advantage of two-way communication, which is not available through many of the other methods. The communication can be in person, over the telephone, or via e-mail. Each offers its own set of benefits and challenges with regard to customer interactions and building relationships with customers. While these interactions are primarily through sales personnel, they can also occur through call centers, service personnel, or front-line employees and sometimes even through the support staff.

Face-to-Face Communication

For almost all firms, the lifeblood of the organization is repeat business. Face-to-face communication has a great impact on whether a customer returns. Employees who provide consistent, caring attention help build loyalty, which increases the lifetime value of customers. People like doing business with friendly faces. So, in the words of Jay Miller from the Round Rock Express, a company shouldn't "entrust their business with just anybody." Face-to-face communication is a major feature in personal selling and other customer contacts. This includes occasions when the customer is satisfied, confused, dissatisfied, or, in some instances, just killing time.

Remember that according to some sources, in face-to-face communication, body language accounts for 55% of the message received, tone of voice another 36%, and the words spoken only 7%.[8] Add to this the appearance of the employee. Employees should endeavor to make a good impression, in terms of dress, nonverbal cues, and manner of speaking.

The behaviors of employees in relation to customers are critically important in determining customer satisfaction and future patronage. Figure 11.4 identifies a number of valuable

- Greet customers like guests.
- Call people by name.
- Use body language.
  - Eye contact
  - Smile
- Compliment customers.
- Listen carefully.
- Be polite.
- Reassure customers about their decisions.

Figure 11.4

Guidelines for Employee Behaviors

How does face-to-face communication affect contacts between employees and customers?

behaviors. While applications of these principles vary across different businesses and by the job responsibility of the employee, the basic concepts are useful. Treating customers as guests, calling them by name, and using body language that says "I am glad you have chosen our business" goes a long way toward solidifying relationships. Also, listening carefully, being courteous, and reassuring customers that they have made a wise decision in their selection of a particular product helps to build positive relationships with them.

Face-to-face communications are powerful. Employee dress, grooming, and personal appearance are often factors customers use to judge a person's character, honesty, trustworthiness, and ability. Marketing managers who oversee employees as they interact with customers should pay careful attention to how the contacts take place. Rewards, compliments, reprimands, advice, and role modeling are all part of the process of making sure this key component of customer interaction works in the company's favor, whether it is a clerk in a retail store or a salesperson calling on a million-dollar account.

Also, methods of face-to-face communication vary widely by culture. In some countries, standing close to someone is an indicator of trust; in others, it is a sign of aggression. The same is true for eye contact and physical contact. Any person dealing with international clients or customers is advised to first study the differences in how people interact in various countries.

Telephone Communications

The telephone is often an integral part of a business. A telephone call is often the first contact a customer makes with a business. Telephone calls are also used to make inquiries or to register complaints. Call centers, inbound and outbound telemarketers, and receptionists all interact with customers by telephone.

While the telephone offers benefits for customer communications, there are two critical disadvantages. First, many employees do not possess the telephone etiquette essential for a quality contact. Second, the telephone lacks any of the visual cues that come from the body language present in face-to-face situations. As a result, the customer may easily be misunderstood by, or misunderstand, the business employee.

Figure 11.5 provides some commonsense tips for improving telephone interactions with customers. The challenges for marketing managers are to ensure that employees in the marketing department follow the guidelines and reach every employee in the organization who interacts with customers. One bad experience with an employee can drive a customer to the competition.

Web Communications

Web communications with customers have been steadily increasing for more than a decade. Several things explain this trend. From the customer's perspective, Web communications are convenient. A Web site is accessible 24/7. Common questions or problems can often be quickly answered or resolved. Customers do not have to deal with telephone self-serve menus, delays in answering calls, transfers of calls, and difficulty in reaching the person who can answer the question or address the problem. With Web communications, this routing can be performed more efficiently.

From a company's perspective, the major advantage of Web communications is cost savings. Serving customers on the Web is considerably cheaper than serving them in person or over the telephone. High-quality customer service can be provided.

Web communications consist of two components: Web site communications and e-mail communications. Web communications involve the customer accessing a firm's Web site to gather information or to address a problem. The most common Web communication methodology is the frequently asked questions (FAQ) page, which provides a database of commonly asked questions and answers. Many Web sites provide word and phrase searches that locate answers to questions. In many instances, answers can be obtained without the need to speak with someone or even to send an e-mail.

When a customer does not find an answer using a FAQ database, the person often sends an e-mail. E-mails can be handled in two ways. The first is Web chat or live chat. The second is a delayed response. With the live chat, employees carry on instant-message conversations with customers. This type of approach can be especially helpful in dealing with problems and troubleshooting. Live chat offers the opportunity for an employee to carry on two or three conversations at the same time. The employee can respond to one customer while another customer types a response into his computer or carries out a troubleshooting step requested by the firm's technician. For individuals who are accustomed to text messaging on cell phones and instant messaging on the Internet, live chats with a company are convenient and efficient.

Although not as customer-friendly and responsive as live chats, the delayed-answer approach can also be efficient. It provides the employee time to prepare a quality response. It allows employees more time to process e-mails and normally requires fewer employees, since e-mails can be stored in a queue. Most companies have employees answer these during the night hours, when live chats are less frequent.

Figure 11.6 provides some tips on making Web communications effective. Most people are pressed for time, which means the Web site should be easy to navigate. There should be multiple means of communicating, and each should be easy to use. This reduces the potential for frustration and/or losing the customer due to Web site problems.

Web communication offers advantages that are not easily reproduced in the other methods of communication. Automated follow-up communications should be developed. E-mails can be sent to check if the problem was corrected or if the requested information was received. Follow-up e-mails can be used to thank the customer for making contact with the company and using the Web interaction method. These follow-ups are invaluable in developing stronger relationships with customers.

- Be ready to handle the call.
- Answer promptly.
- Thank customers for calling.
- View caller as a guest.
- Use courtesy titles.
- Speak with a smile.
- Speak clearly and distinctly.
- Remain calm.
- Strive to provide excellent customer service.
- Avoid dead air time.
- Take messages accurately.
- Keep customers on the topic.

Figure 11.5

Quality Telephone Etiquette

- Make the Web site easy to navigate.
- Provide multiple methods of communication.
- Make communication methods easy to use.
- Respond quickly.
- Strive for excellent customer service.
- Track correspondence to build the FAQ database.
- Follow up with automated technology.

Figure 11.6

Web Communications

Marketing Communication Tactics

As noted earlier, nearly every marketing tactic communicates in one way or another. Interactions with customers can be enhanced and improved using tactics such as advertising, consumer promotions, trade promotions, and in-store communications. When effectively combined with other company activities, relationships are built, and brand loyalty increases over time.

Advertising

Advertising has already been described in detail earlier in this book. An advertising program can easily become a "conversation" with customers in a target market. Their fears and concerns may be addressed by a single commercial. For example, if there is a persistent rumor that a store is about to close, an advertisement stating "We're not going anywhere" provides assurance to loyal customers. Some banks featured this type of commercial noting that they were financially sound and able to make loans during the recent mortgage crisis.

Ads can focus on notifying customers of great deals or be used to reinforce feelings of post-purchase satisfaction. Many advertisements simply thank customers for their continuing business. Advertising is instrumental in acquiring customers, interacting with them, and retaining them over time.

Consumer and Trade Promotions

A wide variety of consumer and trade promotions can be used. Each conveys a slightly different message. In terms of consumer promotions, coupons, premiums, contests, sweepstakes, bonus packs, price-offs, refunds, rebates, and free samples may all be directed at customers. The task of the marketing manager is to carefully consider the message that each conveys. Does it reinforce the company's mission and vision? Does it reinforce the image the company seeks to convey, or does it send a different message? For example, any company that prides itself on providing high-quality service sends a conflicting message when coupons or price-offs are frequently offered.

The same holds true for trade promotions programs. Trade allowances, trade incentives, and trade shows can all be used to maintain quality interactions with channel members. While trade promotions are necessary to remain competitive, marketing managers often consider what each communicates. Does it support the company's overall distribution strategy and way of doing business, or does it undermine the firm's long-term approach for the sake of an immediate boost in sales?

- In-store advertising (52.6%)
- Print ads (23.9%)
- Word-of-mouth communications (15.8%)
- Television ads (14.1%)
- Internet ads (10.4%)
- Direct mail (7.4%)
- Radio ads (1.8%)

Figure 11.7

Types of Advertising That Most Influenced Clothing Purchases

In-Store Communications

Approximately 70% of all final purchase decisions are made in retail stores. In a recent survey, more than half of the respondents reported that in-store signage, a display, or a point-of-purchase offer had influenced a purchase decision. This far outdistances print advertising and word-of-mouth communications.[9] A complete list of these influences is provided in Figure 11.7. As shown, in-store communication constitutes an extremely important component of marketing management. In-store marketing tactics strongly influence the customer's choice of brand to be purchased. Consequently, a number of manufacturers have increased the budget for in-store marketing materials from 3% of the total marketing budget in 2004 to almost 8% today.[10]

Before an individual walks into a business facility, she sees its exterior and its window displays. For some retailers, window displays are critically important. For others, they may not be. Some dry cleaning business owners believe that window displays, signage, and lobby appearance are not important, because customers either drive up to pick up their laundry or spend only a few minutes in the lobby. Others disagree. According to John Spomar, who owns a dry cleaning business, "A well kept, nicely dressed display window in a cleaning and dyeing establishment is as attractive and is as good an advertising feature as in any other line of business. People will give a new dry cleaning operation a chance because it looks new and smells nice."[11]

In-Store Displays

Figure 11.8 provides some tips regarding methods for creating effective store displays. A *theme* that is consistent with the retailer's image tells the person passing by what type of store it is and what type of merchandise is sold inside. It usually is best to put new items out, especially those that have been advertised or promoted through other marketing venues. Displaying *unique, colorful,* or *interesting merchandise* grabs attention. The display should be *entertaining* and *pleasing.* It must be properly lighted so that the merchandise stands out and is easily noticed. Avoid clutter in displays by limiting the number of items. *Change the display* often. For most retailers, this is every 2 to 3 weeks. Displays left too long communicate a slow, out-of-date, and boring store.[12]

In-store signage provides an excellent venue for communicating with customers. Understanding the target audience and how its members shop are keys to effective signage programs. Teens, for example, tend to be fascinated with products, other shoppers, and sales clerks in retail stores. They do not usually notice or pay attention to signage unless it is bold, large, and cutting-edge. Signs with instructions about product use tend to be ignored. Instead, teens pick up the product and experiment with it. Older shoppers, however, may be reluctant to handle a product or fiddle with it. They want signage that explains the product's benefits and how to use it.[13]

The newest and most expensive in-store marketing tactic involves carefully placing and using video screens and television monitors. Many static signs are being replaced with high-tech media. Some shopping carts now carry video screens to replace broken or unreadable signs. Spending on digital signage is estimated to double to $2.8 billion annually by 2011. Digital media within the store offers retailers the opportunity to customize messages to fit the particular retail store and the aisle where the display is located.[14]

Point-of-Purchase Displays

A point-of-purchase display, which is any form of special display that advertises merchandise, can become one of the most important components of in-store communication. Point-of-purchase displays are often located near cash registers in retail stores, at the ends of aisles, in a store's entryway, or in any other place where they will be noticed. Point-of-purchase advertising includes displays, signs, structures, and devices used to identify, advertise, or merchandise an outlet, service, or product.

Point-of-purchase displays remain highly effective tools for increasing sales, because nearly 50% of the money spent at mass merchandisers and supermarkets is unplanned. Most customers do not have a particular brand in mind when examining a product category. For food purchases, almost 90% of the decisions about brands are made in the store at the time of the purchase. In many instances, point-of-purchase materials and other in-store advertising materials influence the decision.[15]

Coca-Cola reports that only half of soft drink sales are made from the regular store shelf. The other half result from product displays in other locations in the store. Research indicates that an average increase in sales of nearly 10% occurs when a point-of-purchase display is featured. Consequently, point-of-purchase advertising remains quite attractive to manufacturers, even though more than half of the point-of-purchase displays sent to retailers are not used or are not effective.[16]

Currently, manufacturers spend more than $17 billion each year on point-of-purchase advertising materials. The largest users of point-of-purchase advertising include restaurants, food services, apparel stores, and footwear retailers. The fastest growing categories for the displays are fresh, frozen, or refrigerated foods, and professional services.[17]

- Create a theme that reflects the essence of the store.
- Make the display entertaining.
- Select merchandise carefully.
- Change the display frequently.

Figure 11.8

Tips in Creating Effective Retail Displays

- Communicate product benefits
- Communicate promotional offers
- Encourage customers to stop and look
- Communicate a clear, succinct offer
- Are integrated with brand's image
- Are integrated with other marketing messages
- Meet needs of retailers
- Fit retailers' layout, décor, and image

Figure 11.9

Effective Point-of-Purchase Displays

There has been a trend toward the use of digital point-of-purchase displays. Digital displays tend to attract more attention, and the message can be changed often and quickly. The message may be tied to special offers, to advertisements, or to particular product features.[18]

The purpose of a point-of-purchase display should be to entice a consumer to stop, look, pick up the merchandise, and then purchase it. Retailers favor displays that increase the size of the shopping basket, that is, lead customers to select more merchandise and spend more money. A manufacturer's marketing team tries to create the type of display that will increase brand sales. When a display can achieve both objectives (increased sales for both the retailer and the manufacturer), the program is successful. The guidelines featured in Figure 11.9 help to increase the probability that a point-of-purchase display will be effective.

In-store communications offer an impersonal medium for maintaining "personal" conversations with customers. Quite a few window shoppers enjoy simply walking through the store to see what has changed. Other customers who prefer shopping without the assistance of a sales clerk rely on in-store communications for information. Many retailers provide small computer terminals within the store to assist customers in attaining information about products and prices.

Public Relations

One of the key activities associated with maintaining relationships with customers is creating a quality public relations program. The public relations department oversees both internal and external communications for an organization. The three primary areas covered by public relations employees are

- monitoring messages from internal and external publics,
- responding to image-damaging news and events (damage control), and
- publicizing image-enhancing news, events, and activities.

Monitoring Messages

As noted earlier, the public relations department prepares messages and monitors contacts between the company and non-customer publics. It can become a key listening post for communications taking place with non-customer publics. Information about the types of communication that take place comes from a variety of sources, including news stories; direct contacts by mail, e-mail, and phone calls; speeches by company leaders; and reviews of meetings between the management team and other groups, such as governmental agencies, suppliers, and retail outlets. The sales force may also collect valuable information regarding the supply chain and about competitor activities. Gathering this information can provide a company's management team with valuable insights regarding public perceptions of the firm and the proactive steps to take to build or maintain a positive image.

Damage Control

Negative publicity takes many forms. There are times in which a company faces a story not based in fact or due to some unusual circumstance. Some examples of these types of problems include attempts at fraud by persons claiming to find needles in bottles of Pepsi, rumors that certain logos were Satanist or overtly sexual, and homophobic claims that various characters (Barney, Teletubbies) were created to represent homosexual interests.

Company leaders also may face problems they create themselves. Defective products, pollution, tax fraud, false or misleading advertising, practices that are perceived as discriminatory, unfair pricing, and other acts also generate negative publicity. Most of the time, the company's public relations team leads the way in framing the response.

Dealing with negative publicity is vital. When unsubstantiated charges or news about actual misdeeds reach the public, trust is lost and customers may consider choosing other companies. Lines of communication become crucial. The tactics that the public relations department can choose from include

- an apology,
- defending the company's innocence,
- providing justifications, and
- making other explanations.

An apology begins with the acknowledgement that the company did something wrong, whether by choice or by accident. It continues with a statement of regret that recognizes the behavior as inappropriate compared with what should have been done. An apology should also contain a promise to not engage in the inappropriate behavior in the future, combined with an offer to compensate the injured parties. Apologies are made both publicly and privately, depending on the offense.

Defending the company's innocence relies on evidence and proof that the company was not at fault. It can take the form of scientific evidence, statements of support by key individuals, or statements by those who were injured, removing any doubt that the company was the cause. Most of the time, the public will be skeptical. Defending a company's innocence requires powerful evidence.

Instead of placing the blame on the tire manufacturers, what type of response could have been used?

Providing justifications involves creating reasons for the inappropriate behavior that lessen the negative impact. When a restaurant serves meals that lead to food poisoning, the manager is likely to quickly place the blame on a supplier. Often this leads to counterclaims. When Ford sold a series of vehicles with defective tires, the company's CEO quickly placed the responsibility for the failure on Bridgestone/Firestone. In response, the CEO of Bridgestone charged customers with not inflating the tires to the proper pressure. In both cases, the public did not accept the justifications and blamed both Ford and Bridgestone. Both lost sales and customers.

Other explanations include those that suggest a negative event was a single-time occurrence and will not happen again, that it was an act of a disgruntled employee who has been terminated, or that it was an act of God. A few years ago, an unhappy customer phoned AOL to cancel service and taped the phone call. The recording quickly circulated to the media, as the AOL employee who took the call spent nearly 20 minutes arguing with the customer that he should not terminate the service. AOL quickly issued a press release stating that the employee had been terminated and that this type of incident would not happen again.

The public relations department may also be asked to monitor and respond to vindictive individuals and groups. Many times, false information about a company is circulated through blogs and e-mails. *Internet interventions* involve monitoring what circulates online, including discussions in chat rooms, to set the record straight and defend a company against false accusations and other complaints. Care must be used, however, to ensure that the defense comes across as honest and genuine.

The public relations function should be a key element in maintaining effective lines of communication with all the groups that interact with a company. Ignoring it can lead to declining sales, lost trust, and the eventual demise of the organization.

Publicizing Image-Enhancing Events

One key public relations function is making sure that anything that is favorable to a company receives as much attention as possible. Using press releases, press conferences, phone calls, mailers, and postings on a company's Web site, the public relations department can quickly disseminate information in two major categories: positive statements by others and company-generated events.

Endorsements come from many sources. For example, a small-town restaurant would want the entire community to know if a local newspaper chose it as "The Best Hamburger in Town." Receiving an ISO 9000 or 14,000 series quality rating would lead a company's marketing team to hold a press conference to make the announcement and to feature the award in advertisements. Positive or favorable press stories are often reproduced on a company's Web site.

Two tactics may be used to increase the impact of a positive event. The first is called **entitling**, which means making sure the company is given credit whenever favorable events take place. The second, an **enhancement**, involves increasing the value of that favorable outcome. When an Olympic athlete wins a gold medal, her sponsor may advertise that the company provided funds so that she could train for the games. Then, the enhancement comes from pointing out that winning for the United States makes everyone feel good about the country.

Many companies sponsor individual charities or perform some other altruistic activity. The responsibility of the public relations department is to make certain news of the generous act reaches the media and customers. Company-generated events may combine the efforts of the many departments in the organization, as will be described next.

Image-Building Programs

Marketing managers often take advantage of marketing programs that combine the efforts of the sales force, public relations personnel, advertising specialists, and others from the company. These programs include sponsorships, event marketing, cause-related marketing, and green marketing. By integrating the activities of the various members of a company, each of these can provide a positive customer experience that builds relationships with customers.

Sponsorships and Event Marketing

Sponsorship marketing involves the company paying money to sponsor someone, some group, or something that is part of an activity. Firms can sponsor everything from local Little League Baseball and soccer teams to national musical tours, NASCAR drivers, and professional sports stadiums. **Event marketing** is similar to sponsorship marketing, but involves the company supporting a specific event, such as an art festival, a local rodeo, or the Juneteenth Heritage Festival held every year in Grambling, Louisiana, as shown in the advertisement in this section. Event marketing is also closely related to lifestyle marketing. Both often include setting up a booth or display and having a physical presence at an event.

In North America, approximately $14.4 billion a year is spent on sponsorships and events.[19] Figure 11.10 provides a breakdown of how the money is spent. Sports represent nearly 70% of all sponsorships. Sporting events are highly popular and often attract large crowds. In addition to the audience attending the game or competition, many more watch on television.

Tostitos has maintained a sponsorship of the Fiesta Bowl in Tempe, Arizona, for over

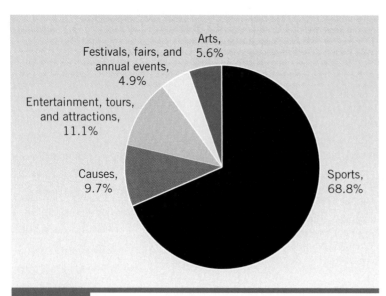

Figure 11.10   Expenditures on Sponsorships and Events

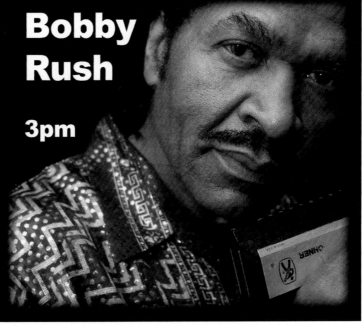

Wednesday, June 13th	Thursday, June 14th	Friday, June 15th	Saturday, June 16th	Sunday, June 17th
Opening Ceremony 5:30 p.m.	Miss Juneteenth Pageant	Community Theatre – 4:00 p.m.	Juneteenth Parade – 9:00 a.m.	Barbecue Cook-Off – 12:00 Noon
Campground Prayer Meeting	7:00 p.m. – 9:00 p.m.	All-Star Softball Game – 6:00 p.m.	Juneteenth Festival - All Day	Fishing Derby

LAW OFFICES AND TITLE COMPANY

Need more information? Call 318.247.6120 or visit www.egrambling.com
"This project partially funded by a grant from the Ruston-Lincoln Convention & Visitors Bureau."

An event marketing advertisement for a local festival in Grambling, Louisiana.

1. Determine the objective(s).

2. Match the sponsorship or event's audience profile with the firm's target market.

3. Promote the event.

4. Include the company (or brand) in all advertising and promotions by the event or sponsorship.

5. Track results.

Figure 11.11

Steps in Developing Sponsorships and Event Marketing

a decade. Patrons who attend the college football game encounter the brand in nearly every venue, from concessions and pregame parties to 30-foot-tall "bags" of chips at the main entrance to the stadium. Tostitos also advertises extensively during the television broadcast of the game.

In 2008, the horse Big Brown won two of the three legs of the triple crown. Big Brown is the nickname of UPS. The company received a great deal of free publicity as a result.

Rather than sports, Coca-Cola, Ford, and AT&T recently chose to sponsor the popular television show *American Idol*. Each company paid $35 million for the right to be part of one of the most watched TV shows, post online content, and run off-air cobranded marketing programs. Ford featured its vehicles in music videos sung by the final 12 contestants. Ford also gave away its Ford Escape Hybrid to the top two finalists. Coca-Cola made sure its branded cups were front and center on the judges' tables and that Coke graphics were visible behind the contestants while they were being interviewed. AT&T may have benefited the most from the sponsorship, as it was responsible for the text message voting each week. The company also had *Idol* downloads, ring tones, and videos of bad auditions and poor performances.[20]

Event marketing can involve sports but is often tied in with other lifestyle events. A rodeo sponsored by Lee Jeans or a music concert put on by a local radio station are marketing events. More segmented events can also be held. An Italian food festival funded by a food company is event marketing.

To maximize the return on a sponsorship or an event, a marketing manager follows the steps outlined in Figure 11.11. The first step is to determine the communication *objectives* to be accomplished before becoming involved in a particular sponsorship or event. When the objective is to reward customers, it helps to find an event major customers would be interested in attending. Objectives that are more internally oriented, especially those designed to get employees involved and boost morale, should be met by finding events internal members will enjoy. The most common goals of sponsoring include (1) helping the firm maintain its market share, (2) building a stronger brand presence in the marketplace, (3) enhancing the product or firm's image, or (4) providing a venue for interacting with customers and prospects.

The marketing manager *matches the audience profile with the company's target market.* If a firm's primary customers are men, it would be profitable for it to sponsor a participant at an event attended mainly by males. If an age range can be determined, that can also aid in the selection of an event. Marketing executives also consider the image of the individual participant or group and how it relates to the firm's image. Many bridal events have sponsors that provide gowns, tuxedos, limousine services, and DJ services.

Promoting events and sponsorships through advertisements and public relations releases allows for greater visibility. Additional effort should be given to contacting special-interest groups that would benefit from the sponsorship or event. Thus, an event such as a local Special Olympics could use commercials, press releases, and direct contact with parents and relatives of those who might participate in the event.

Marketers in firms that sponsor events often insist on *placement of the company name*, logo, and other product information in every advertisement and brochure for the occasion. Many attendees of special events keep the program as a souvenir or as something to show others. Placing the sponsor's name and message on the program generates an ad with a long life span. The sponsoring business typically works to maximize brand name exposure by connecting the firm's name with the event's marketing program. Working closely with the event management team is helpful when seeking to make sure that the sponsor's name receives prominent attention.

The marketing team *tracks the results* of the event. In addition to sales, employees can monitor how many pieces of literature were given to attendees, the number of samples distributed, and the number of visitors to the sponsor's display booth. Further, marketing research may be conducted to measure brand awareness before and after the event to see if any new brand recall or brand awareness developed.

A study by the Advertising Research Foundation (ARF) revealed that purchase intentions in buying a particular branded product dramatically changed among consumers who attended a brand-sponsored event, such as a sporting event, a walkathon, or a themed event. Further research indicated that the purchase intentions translated into sales about half the time. The ARF study involved events sponsored by companies such as Frito-Lay, State Farm, and Coca-Cola. Sports-related events tended to have the best results.[21]

Cause-Related Marketing

Cause-related marketing is a program in which a firm ties a marketing program to a charity in order to generate goodwill. American businesses contribute over $600 million each year to not-for-profits in exchange for the right to use the organization's name or logo in company advertising and marketing programs. This type of partnership agreement is based on the idea that consumers are more likely to purchase from companies that are willing to help a good cause. A survey by Cone Communications and Roper Starch Worldwide supports this belief. The findings revealed that

- 78% of consumers are more likely to purchase a brand associated with a cause they care about;
- 54% would be willing to pay more for a brand that is associated with a cause they care about;
- 66% would switch brands to support a particular cause; and
- 84% indicated that cause-related marketing creates a more positive image of a company.[22]

In the past, some companies donated to causes without necessarily thinking about the marketing benefits of such gifts. Now, most company leaders often first try to identify the advantages that may result. Although a manager may believe a charity is worthwhile, supporting that charity should, in some way, be linked to a positive outcome. Possible benefits include gaining new customers, increasing goodwill, enhancing a brand or company's image, and generating favorable publicity.

In choosing a cause, the marketing manager typically looks for issues that relate in some way to the company's business. When a good fit exists, positive reactions emerge. A company that supports an unrelated cause may find that its consumers believe that the business simply is trying to gain from the not-for-profit's reputation. This may lead some consumers to stop buying the company's products or to think that the company is trying to cover up unethical behavior. Even though most people understand that a business must benefit from the relationship, they often look dimly on businesses that they believe are exploiting a relationship with a not-for-profit organization.

Green Marketing

Green marketing is the development and promotion of products that are environmentally safe. When asked, most consumers strongly favor the concept of green marketing. One recent survey indicated that 58% of Americans try to save electricity, 46% recycle newspapers, 45% return bottles or cans, and 23% buy products made from, or packaged in, recycled materials.[23]

Although consumers favor green marketing and environmentally safe products, actual purchases of such products only occurs when all things are considered equal. Most consumers are not willing to sacrifice price, quality, convenience, availability, or performance for the sake of the environment. In fact, according to a recent study, about 40% of consumers say they do not purchase green products because they believe the products are inferior.[24]

Marketing managers normally try to align the company's green marketing strategy with the firm's target audience. In making the decision regarding the degree of emphasis to place on green marketing, managers typically examine three issues:

- The percentage of the company's customer base that prefers and will purchase green products
- Whether the brand or company can be differentiated from the competition based on its green marketing strategy and if such a differentiation offers a competitive advantage
- Whether the company's current target audience might become alienated by a green marketing approach

Many firms are environmentally friendly and provide information on company Web sites about environmental activities. The amount of effort given to publicize these activities varies

Although most consumers say they support green marketing, few actually recycle the materials they use.

widely based on the firm's target market and the products being sold.[25] For example, most people are unaware that Coca-Cola has invested heavily in various recycling programs and recyclable package designs. The activities are not publicized because some company officials fear it might reduce the product's appeal to its core audience. Another company, Starbucks, was named one of the Environmental Protection Agency's top 25 Green Power Partners because it uses renewable energy for about 20% of the power needed by its company-owned stores. The citation was posted on the Starbucks Web site, but it was buried deep in the social responsibility section.[26]

For a few companies, environmental activities can be fully integrated into the marketing approach because the primary customer base is pro-environment and supports green efforts. Honest Tea of Bethesda, Maryland, emphasizes social responsibility in every company activity, from the manufacturing process to the marketing of products. Honest Tea uses biodegradable tea bags and organic ingredients, and the company develops community partnerships. The focus of Honest Tea's marketing program is the company's concern for and support of both environmental and social issues.

In contrast, another set of firms have made the cynical decision to create a campaign of disinformation rather than making any genuine attempt at "going green." Greenwashing involves sending out information in corporate documents, via the Internet in chat rooms and on a firm's Web site, in public relations releases, and through advertisements that suggests a company seeks to become a friend of the environment while actually engaging in exactly the opposite activities. Such an approach is unethical and may, in the long term, alienate customers when they find out the truth.

In summary, these four programs require the coordinated efforts of the marketing department working in conjunction with the sales team, public relations department, and others. Image-building programs are popular because they offer a way to maintain relationships with customers, attract new customers, and pass along information regarding changes and improvements in products, services, and company operations.

STOP AND THINK

In 2008, *E. coli* was found in lettuce products in some states. Another incident resulted in tomatoes being thrown away due to fear of salmonella poisoning. Later, jalapeños were implicated as the culprit for various outbreaks.

1. Which of the responses to negative publicity should be used to counter this problem? Think in terms of responses by farmers, restaurants, and grocery stores.

2. Which of the image-building programs would work best to restore consumer confidence in these items? Again, think in terms of farmers, restaurants, and grocery stores.

3. Can you think of a method by which person-to-person communication could help repair the damage done to these products?

4. If the source of the problem was imported foods from Mexico that reached the United States, would this change your answers to Questions 1, 2, and 3?

Implications for Marketing Managers

A great deal of the external communications described in this chapter will be guided by first-level managers working with entry-level employees. The majority of personal contacts made face-to-face, by telephone, or over the Internet are handled by entry-level workers. Oftentimes, store displays and signs are either created by people on the sales floor or at least installed by them. Much of the monitoring of communications in the public relations department is conducted by first-level workers. Many of the public relations press releases are written by the same individuals. Image-building programs such as lifestyle events are likely to be handled by entry-level employees.

As a result, the job of supervising these employees becomes critical. First-level managers hold the responsibility for effectively training, supervising, rewarding, and sanctioning these workers. Those who make direct contact with the public become the "face" of the organization. To ensure the long-term stability and growth of a company, these contact points must be carefully managed.

Institutional statements, product and package design decisions, selections of building designs, and other more sweeping decisions and plans are made by managers of higher ranks. The responsibility rests with upper-level management to clearly communicate these intentions to first-line supervisors and entry-level workers. Successful external communications begin with a consistent understanding of the company's objectives and tactics at every level of the organization.

Relationship to Customer Service

When everything communicates, the importance of each of the activities and tactics described in this chapter to customer service increases. Beginning with institutional statements, a company will be well served by a mission statement emphasizing the importance of customers. Products designed to communicate functionality or aesthetic attractiveness must be backed up by a salesperson showing genuine interest and concern for the shopper. Personal contacts are critical ingredients in quality customer service programs. Carefully designed in-store communications make the shopping experience more enjoyable and easier.

Public relations programs can highlight a company's concern for its customers, society, and the environment. Image-building programs including sponsorships and event marketing, cause-related marketing, and green marketing can communicate the goal of maintaining positive relationships with a customer base over time.

In essence, customer service relies on quality communication. Without it, positive relationships with both customers and non-customers is not possible. The communication systems and tactics described in this chapter facilitate customer service.

YOURCAREER

Lisa Winter holds the title of Training and Recruitment Specialist for the Sherwin-Williams Company. She works in the Dallas, Texas, Training Center. Her primary roles are to recruit and train new employees. The new hires come to Dallas for initial training sessions, and later Lisa might visit them after they have been placed in stores. She coordinates some of the Sherwin-Williams National Sales Meetings, which are attended by about 1,300 people each year. She keeps up with individual title changes, relocations, specific training courses necessary, and more.

Sherwin-Williams is primarily a domestic company offering paints and painting supplies as well as wall and floor coverings. The corporation's annual sales exceed $7 billion in more than 3,000 retail stores. The organization's home office is in Cleveland, Ohio. The company is listed in the *Princeton Review* as one of the top U.S. companies offering entry-level jobs to college graduates.

After completing her degree, Lisa joined Sherwin-Williams as a management trainee in a retail store. She soon assumed the position of assistant manager, which lasted about 9 months, at which time she became a store manager in Albuquerque, New Mexico. She managed the store, which had $1.4 million in annual sales, for 1½ years. Lisa was then promoted to her current position and moved to the Dallas Training Center.

Lisa enjoyed her time in retail sales and management. She said, "The best part of working in our stores is that you always have someone to ask, if you don't know something.

You can ask managers, sales reps, district managers, and more. You could even ask the customers their opinions. Asking them helps in building relationships and growing sales. You get to know people this way, and they become friends." The Albuquerque store made sales to individuals wanting to buy 1 gallon of paint but also to contractors needing hundreds of gallons ready to go in less than an hour.

When asked about service failures, Lisa noted she had some experience. "Fortunately," she noted, "Sherwin-Williams gave us some training in that area. A lot of it depends on what the situation is—for example, once I accidently spilled some stain on a lady's shirt, and it was white. She was definitely upset, and so I had to do some crisis management, I had learned from my training how to keep the customer calm, separate the person from the other customers and then help them—to do whatever it takes to win the business back and win their friendship back. I discounted her some products and went the extra mile that time, and made an extra effort the next time she came back. She did come back and wasn't mad the next time."

Did college prepare her for the first few jobs after graduation? In general, Lisa believed that it did. She completed majors in both business and communications. She said that her marketing courses, as well as her communications classes in public relations, public speaking, and mass communications were helpful. "College trained me in how to interact with employees, and for some real life situations, such as financial issues. But, did it teach me how to raise my paint sales? No. But they gave me some good ideas about how I could turn things around when things were going poorly and how to work with people. I got a good overall sense of what a business would be like."

She added, "Experiencing diversity on the college campus also got me prepared for the real world. Working with an older member on a project or working with them at the store was similar. Even dealing with different levels of knowledge and experience in the classroom helped me in the real world. I knew how to face situations and what to expect, possibly. There are differences in every individual and experiencing this through college made it much more simple to experience it in the real world."

Was anything missing? "I wish I could have had more interactions with real-life employers in college instead of just professors. I wish I could have had more time and classes to pursue more business interests, such as the financial side such as reading spreadsheets and P and Ls [profit and loss statements]—that might have helped me right away in my career."

Sherwin-Williams continues to thrive. The corporation opens a new retail store on an average of 1 every 3 days. Many new graduates may soon find themselves visiting Dallas and receiving training from Lisa and others in the company's Dallas Training Center.

Chapter Summary

Communication is the lifeblood of nearly every organization. In today's marketplace, nearly everything a company does communicates in some way with external publics, some of which are customers and some of which are not. Communication with non-customers is primarily conveyed through messages and statements made by managers and by messages transmitted through the public relations department.

Communications with customers and potential customers take place at customer contact points. Some of the media used to transmit messages are personal channels, others are impersonal. Contacts are made both when the company contacts customers and when customers contact the company.

An organization's institutional statements form the framework for other messages and contacts. The mission statement, reports to stockholders, and announcements regarding a firm's strategic vision and activities all assist in creating lines of communication with various publics.

A product's appearance and package design sends an additional set of messages. Product appearance serves to create aesthetic value, symbolic value, functional value, and attention-drawing value. Private labels, which formerly were plain and uninspiring, now often feature the same clever and innovative tactics as national brands, in order to help products compete more effectively.

Business facilities can be designed to relay messages regarding quality, cost efficiency, or customization. Both product and service quality can be emphasized by the design of a facility. Facilities house long-term interactions between a company and its customers.

Personal contacts take place in face-to-face settings, by telephone, and over the Internet. Each should be carefully managed to create the best possible impression on new customers. Each should also facilitate long-term bonds between the company and its customers.

Numerous marketing programs are used to maintain communications with customers. Advertising, promotions, and in-store communications can all facilitate a new purchase or be used to keep in contact with loyal patrons. Many purchase decisions are made in the store, which makes in-store communications and point of purchase displays the vital ingredients of effective marketing programs.

The public relations department will normally be charged with monitoring messages from both internal and external publics. One key part of a public relations program is responding to negative publicity, using an apology, defending the company's innocence, providing effective justifications, or making other explanations for any negative event that comes to light. The department also publicizes image-enhancing events such as endorsements from others as well as company-generated activities.

Many image-building programs require the combined efforts of the sales force, public relations employees, advertising specialists, and others from the company. These programs include sponsorship marketing, event marketing, cause-related marketing, and green marketing. Each creates the opportunity to entice new customers and build stronger bonds with existing customers.

Chapter Terms

Aesthetic value   (p. 286)
Attention-drawing value   (p. 287)
Cause-related marketing   (p. 299)
Customer contact points   (p. 283)
Enhancement   (p. 296)
Entitling   (p. 296)
Event marketing   (p. 296)

Functional value   (p. 286)
Green marketing   (p. 299)
Greenwashing   (p. 300)
Point-of-purchase display   (p. 293)
Sponsorship marketing   (p. 296)
Symbolic value   (p. 286)

Review Questions

1. Name the non-customer publics that receive communications from companies.

2. What is a customer contact point?

3. What types of institutional statements communicate with customers and potential customers?

4. Explain the four roles of product appearance that are generated by a product and its package.

5. When designing a business facility, what three design options may be pursued? Explain each one.

6. What are the three ways in which personal contacts are made between companies and customers?

7. What role does advertising play in maintaining interactions with customers? What roles do consumer and trade promotions play in the same area?

8. What are in-store communications, and how have they changed in the past decade?

9. Describe the roles that point-of-purchase displays play in attracting customers.

11. What are the three main activities conducted by the public relations department?

12. Describe the nature of entitling and enhancement in public relations communications.

13. What four tactics may be used for damage control when there is negative publicity? Describe each one.

14. What image-building programs can be used to build strong bonds with customers? Describe each one.

15. What is greenwashing?

 CUSTOMER CORNER

Dylan and Vicky have been shopping for several hours. While enjoyable, it has been tiring. They see a pastry shop just ahead of them. A cool drink and a tasty pastry would really hit the spot right now.

The two step into the pastry shop and scan the environment. On two tables are dirty dishes and cups from previous customers. On one table is a bouquet of flowers; on the other tables are only napkin holders. One light has come loose and is dangling from the ceiling. Hearing someone talking, they turn and look toward the cash register. A young girl is sitting on a stool with her feet propped up against the pastry display case. Her hat is turned sideways, she has a straw sticking out of her mouth, and she is wearing shorts with frayed ends. Her top was probably clean when she arrived but now has several flour spots on it as well as what looks like dark berry stains.

The two look at each other and are about to turn and leave when they hear a pleasant greeting from behind the pastry display case. In unison, they turn and look. A lady in her 50s with a huge smile greets them and makes a comment that they must be tired from all the shopping. She scurries around the display case and reaches for their shopping bags instructing them to get something to eat and drink and get off of their feet and rest some.

The lady reminds Vicky of her grandma, slightly younger but very cheerful. After sitting the bags down at the table with the bouquet of flowers, she proceeds to tell them about a pastry she has just pulled out of the oven that smells so delicious. They sniff the air. They smell the items, and she is right, they smell wonderful.

Without asking if they want a piece, she hurries behind the counter to get it. As she does, she slaps the young girl's legs and tells her to get off her cell phone, they have customers.

Normally, Dylan never notices much when he walks into a business. Vicky does. She sees everything. Dylan sees nothing unless the building is caving in around him. But on this occasion, even Dylan had noticed the mixed signals this business sent to customers.

Again Dylan and Vicky look at each other. Should they leave, should they stay?

1. Discuss the physical facility of the pastry shop and the impression it made on Dylan and Vicky.

2. Compare and contrast the impression made by the young girl sitting by the display counter and the lady in her 50s.

3. In terms of communicating to customers, what aspects of this customer interaction scene convey a negative message? What aspects convey a positive message?

4. If you owned or managed this facility, what actions would you take to increase positive communications to customers?

Discussion and Critical Thinking Questions

1. Think about the last sporting event you attended. Describe all the ways in which the venue, the people, and the amenities communicated. Were the messages consistent, or were they conflicting? What suggestions would you offer to improve the message communicated by all the various factors at the sporting venue?

2. Choose one of the following companies. Access the company's Web site and print out the company's mission statement. Compare the mission statement to the layout and content of the Web site, the product package or retail store layout, and the business facility. Are the messages communicated by each consistent?
   a. Frito-Lay (www.fritolay.com)
   b. Black & Decker (www.blackanddecker.com)
   c. Kenmore (www.sears.com/kenmore)
   d. The Gap (www.gapinc.com)

3. Go to a retail store and examine the package or product appearance for each of the following items in terms of aesthetic value, symbolic value, functional value, and attention-drawing value. In your opinion, which brands had the best product appearance or package appearance? Why?
   a. Cookies
   b. Vacuum cleaners
   c. Exercise equipment
   d. Kitchen appliances

4. Figure 11.4 suggests guidelines for employee behaviors, including treating customers as guests, calling people by name, using body language, complimenting customers, listening carefully, being polite, and reassuring customers about purchase decisions. Apply the concepts to these challenging occupations:
   a. Managing a mortuary
   b. Managing a hospital emergency room
   c. Managing the financial aid department of a university

5. In-store communications have a major impact on purchasing decisions, especially in retail stores selling tangible products. Would they have the same impact in locations that sell services, such as auto insurance? Would they have the same impact on customers visiting diet centers, such as Jenny Craig? Why or why not? What kinds of in-store communications should these companies create?

6. Go to two different retail stores, one that is a large national chain, such as Target or JCPenney, and one that is small, a local retailer. Compare and contrast the in-store communication programs, including signage, layout, displays, and point-of-purchase displays. What messages are communicated?

7. Discuss how three main areas covered by the public relations department would apply to coping with an organization such as PETA, People for the Ethical Treatment of Animals, which has taken issue with the following organizations:
   a. KFC, for its methods of killing chickens
   b. Zoos, for their methods of housing animals
   c. Rodeos, for the treatment of animals used in events
   d. Movie studios, for their treatment of animals featured in films

8. Violent sports including boxing, martial arts, wrestling, and extreme fighting have increased in popularity during the past decade. Can you think of logical sponsorships for these events? Would it make sense for these sports to become involved in cause-related marketing? If so, which causes?

9. A local nightclub has decided to host a swimsuit contest, one for females and one for males. They are looking for companies to sponsor the event. For each of the following, discuss the pros and cons of the organization or company sponsoring the swimsuit contest at the nightclub:
   a. Clothing store
   b. Fitness center
   c. Auto parts store
   d. Office supply store
   e. Dine-in restaurant
   f. Independent insurance agent

Chapter 11 Case

New York Cool

What started as a simple gesture by T.L. Williams toward his sister Maybel in 1915 has become a worldwide fashion force. Williams created a method to enhance and darken eye lashes. The item caught on and was sold by mail order soon after. Today, his company has evolved into Maybelline New York and is the number one cosmetic brand globally. Maybelline products are available in over 90 countries worldwide. Maybelline officially became Maybelline New York in 2004 after being acquired by other companies earlier in the previous century.

Maybelline New York's express goal is to incorporate elements such as the size, style, color, and success that give the city its cool, captivating aura. The attitude and look combine state-of-the art technology with a keen eye for new trends. The company seeks to produce accessible, cutting-edge cosmetics. The objective continues to be to incorporate all the elements that make New York City unique into Maybelline items.

Maybelline New York products are carried in nearly every major U.S. mass market retail chain, including drugstores, discount stores, supermarkets, and cosmetics specialty stores. The company holds the reputation of being a renowned color authority that creates seasonal color collections with products in the season's hottest shades. Today, the management team also focuses on helping women feel more beautiful and recognizing their individuality and potential through education and empowerment.

Maybelline's product lines address various facets of beauty, including items for the face, eyes (and eyebrows), lips, and nails. Fashion tools such as brushes, applicators, and removers are also sold. The firm's Web site offers a "personal and product guide" page.

Women's fashion is fickle. Items that work well for teens and young women may not be the same as those best suited to other age groups. The field constantly shifts. What was highly fashionable at last year's major events (the Emmy Awards, the Academy Awards, fashion shows, the presidential inauguration) may be badly outdated in 12 months. Color preferences change with the seasons and over time. What looks good in the morning may not be suited to nighttime events. Cosmetics must coordinate with clothes and accessories to create the perfect look.

In recent years, methods of product testing have come under scrutiny. PETA has challenged using animals to test for allergic reactions to cosmetics. Products are expected to do more than simply not hurt someone's skin. Most customers look for cosmetics that are natural and will preserve beautiful skin over time.

Global influences undoubtedly will affect Maybelline's future. Staying on top of the cosmetics world will require adapting to regional, national, and worldwide fashion trends. Developing and maintaining strong brands while being in constant communication with those in the marketplace are key components of this fast-moving marketplace.[27]

1. What type of mission statement would be best suited to Maybelline New York?

2. What can the company do about customer contact points when its cosmetics are sold by retailers outside the company?

3. How does the shape and appearance of a cosmetic package communicate to consumers? What messages do you think Maybelline conveys by various product packages? Can you give some specific examples?

4. What types of image-enhancing activities are best for Maybelline New York?

5. How should the public relations department respond to special-interest groups such as PETA?

What helped Maybelline become successful?

Go to **www.sagepub.com/clow** for additional exercises and study resources. Select **Chapter 11, External Communications** for chapter-specific activities.

What has made INSIGHT, Inc. successful?

chapter 12

Distribution and Supply Chain Management

INSIGHT, Inc.: Top of Mind in Supply Chain Management

If you ask a typical consumer to name the major brands in practically any industry or product category, the question would be easy to answer. Fast foods, automobile manufacturers, insurance companies, banks, airlines, cell phone companies, brewing companies, clothing companies, and dozens of others are readily identified. If you ask the same consumer to identify the most successful supply chain management company, he is likely to be stumped. The irony is that effective supply chain management lowers costs and subsequent prices and provides a major competitive advantage to both the manufacturer and the retailer, which makes it a key part of any marketing program.

INSIGHT, Inc., a thriving supply chain management company in the United States, was founded in 1978. The firm offers products that are "designed specifically to meet the challenges companies face in the age of dynamic business, from cutting costs in supply chain networks to improving strategic and tactical decisions." The company's flagship product carries the brand SAILS. It works to help a manufacturer maintain a strong cash flow, cut costs, and deliver items efficiently.[1] The SAILS method includes a review of the location of the manufacturing facility, its capability and size, the distribution methods and policies, sourcing issues, inventory levels, peak and low seasons, and other issues before recommendations are made to create the best distribution system.

A second technology, the X-System Solver Engine, uses highly sophisticated mathematical and mixed integer linear programming techniques to create the fastest, most cost-effective delivery system possible.

INSIGHT, Inc. provides help in every aspect of the supply chain, beginning with the sources of materials to be used. The program is completed by the selection of the ideal transportation system to be used in physically moving the product to its final destination.

Company leaders view supply chain management as a key strategic ingredient.

INSIGHT, Inc.'s client list includes a variety of Fortune 500 companies, including 3 of the 5 largest beverage companies, 5 of the 10 largest electronics companies, 3 of the 5 largest petroleum companies, and 3 of the 5 largest soap and cosmetics companies. The company's client list also features major medical providers and consumer goods companies.

Customer service and customer loyalty are key factors. Over 80% of the company's customers have been served for more than 20 years. The leadership team stresses the importance of careful and sophisticated analyses to cope with complications such as globalization and fuel prices. INSIGHT offers training courses in the SAILS program and other products on a continuing basis.

As global commerce continues to expand, the challenges of delivering products in a timely manner while holding down inventory and transportation costs will undoubtedly command the attention of many company leaders. Thus, while supply chain management may seem to be a shadowy, unglamorous part of the marketing profession, its importance to the bottom line remains indisputable.

Chapter Overview

One of the unique features of marketing is that managers are directly involved in issues regarding money. On the one hand, they are authorized to spend money on a wide variety of programs, from advertising to promotions to alternative marketing tactics. On the other, they often spend money in the hope of acquiring even more money. Thus, an effective advertising campaign, practically by definition, results in increased sales. The same would be true for promotions. A discount given to a wholesaler or retailer is designed to increase the number of orders and generate additional funds.

Distribution and supply chain management programs are slightly different. It is true that money will be spent on items such as warehousing, inventory, and shipping. At the same time, often the goal is to reduce these expenditures and to be as efficient as possible. An additional complication emerges as supply chain management also involves finding ways to entice customers to purchase and then to create relationships with them over time. Successful marketing programs rely on the efficient movement of goods from the producer to the customer. When a retailer is confident that an order will be filled and shipped on time and then billed correctly, a bond quickly grows between that retailer and the manufacturer that supplies the goods.

This chapter examines the primary issues associated with supply chain management. **Supply chain management** is the process of managing the actual physical movement of products from the producer to the customer or end user. It includes selecting methods of transportation, warehousing decisions, inventory control programs, and facilitating the exchange of ownership that takes places as a product moves through the various levels of the distribution channel. The major issues in supply chain management are

- selecting a distribution system,
- establishing channels of distribution,
- managing the supply channel, and
- overseeing the physical distribution of products.

Each of these topics will be reviewed in this chapter. Implications for marketing managers and the impact on customer service quality are also discussed.

Distribution Systems

The first decision a marketing manager makes in terms of distribution is about the level of distribution desired. Three systems are possible: (1) intensive distribution, (2) selective distribution, and (3) exclusive distribution. Various factors influence this decision, including the type of product being offered, the concentration of potential buyers in an area, and management preferences.

Intensive Distribution

When the goal is full market coverage, an intensive distribution system is chosen. **Intensive distribution** means making the product available to consumers in as many different places as possible. This approach seeks to create a high volume of sales but at low gross margins. In fact, some of the locations may not be profitable, but including them preempts the competition from being the only available option in a given store or location. Consumer goods, especially convenience goods, are often intensively distributed. Staples such as soft drinks, candy, chips, milk, beer, toothpaste, chewing gum, aspirin, cough drops, and cookies are normally distributed using this approach.

Why would jewelry sellers use a selective distribution strategy?

Exclusive Distribution

The opposite of intensive distribution is **exclusive distribution**, which involves limiting the number of distributors to only one or two in each geographic area. The primary goal of the system is to develop an image of exclusivity and prestige. The approach offers the producer a high level of control over intermediaries (retailers and wholesalers) and provides the intermediaries with an exclusive geographic market. Normally, sales are lower for exclusive products, but gross margins are much higher. Specialty goods that require a unique effort to make a purchase are often distributed through exclusive retail outlets. Designer clothes, such as Prada and Armani, and automobiles, such as Lamborghini, are marketed using an exclusive distribution strategy.

Selective Distribution

A selective distribution system is in between exclusive and intensive distribution. **Selective distribution** means that a carefully chosen set of outlets carry the product. This gives the manufacturer better control over the marketing channel. The producer also hopes to achieve a reasonable level of sales and gross margins. Some clothing lines, such as Lee Jeans, Levi's, Polo, or Tommy Bahama, are offered selectively.

- Type of product
- Price
- Competition
- Brand image
- Desired product position
- Level of brand equity and brand parity
- Target market
- Image of distributors

Figure 12.1

Factors in Choosing a Distribution System

Many durable goods, including washing machines and refrigerators, are sold in a select set of retail outlets. Typically only viable, profitable outlets continue to carry such products over time.

Decision Variables

In determining the best distribution system, a marketing manager examines a number of different factors (see Figure 12.1). As noted, normally the first decision variable is the *type of product* being offered, along with the product's *price*. It would not make sense to exclusively or even selectively distribute the majority of convenience goods. High-markup luxury goods are most likely to be sold exclusively.

When a product changes categories, distribution systems may follow. For example, in the time when the Cadillac was known as the most prestigious car a person could buy in the United States, many automobile retailers desired the status as the "exclusive Cadillac dealer" in a given city. Now, Cadillac is more likely to be offered selectively.

Competition is the third decision variable. The marketing team routinely examines the distribution system used by the competition. This may result in a change. For example, in the 1960s, Titleist golf balls were sold exclusively in pro shops on golf courses. When competitors began to make inroads by offering golf balls in discount retail stores such as Kmart and Wal-Mart, Titleist was forced to follow.

A product's *brand image* also may influence the choice of a distribution system. When the emphasis is on quality, it becomes more likely that an exclusive distribution system will be the result. Exclusive distribution can help enhance an image. For instance, a high-end hair product that is sold exclusively by the most prestigious local salon may augment the image of both the hair product and the salon. Consequently, the distribution system becomes part of the overall *positioning* tactics developed by the marketing team.

Next, the marketing manager examines the *levels of brand equity and brand parity* in the industry and for the product. When brand parity exists, the most common approach is to match the competition's distribution system. This explains why snack food companies may intensively distribute items even in stores where the costs associated with delivering the items are greater than the marginal revenues received from sales. It is a mistake to believe a brand is superior and choose a system that actually harms rather than increases sales. A product being sold using an exclusive or selective distribution system when the primary competitors are using a more intensive strategy creates a competitive disadvantage.

The *target market* and the *image of the distributor,* especially the retailer, are important considerations in selecting a distribution system. There must be a match between the two. If a firm's primary target market is females between ages 30 and 50 years with incomes from $40,000 to $75,000, then the retailers chosen should target a similar market. It would not make sense to stock the product in a retail store where the primary shoppers are females between ages 15 and 30 years with incomes less than $50,000.

Successful distribution involves a partnership between the manufacturer's brand and the retail outlet. Developing partnerships can be challenging. Retailers and manufacturers often have differing goals. Retailers are concerned about increasing store sales and may be less concerned about which brands their customers purchase. Manufacturers are most concerned about the sales of the company's brands. Consequently, most manufacturers try to build strong relationships with retailers. One method is to offer the potential for higher gross margins. Also, a strong manufacturer brand name can attract customers into the store. Another enticement is dependable, reliable service.

Establishing Channels of Distribution

The second major issue in supply chain management is establishing appropriate **channels of distribution**, which are the paths goods and services take from the producer to the end user. Figure 12.2 depicts some of the more common channels of distribution.

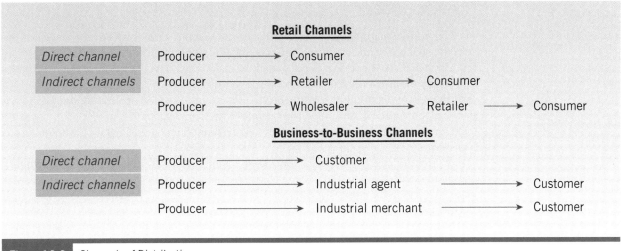

Figure 12.2 | Channels of Distribution

Direct Channels

When a producer sends products directly to the customer or end user, a **direct channel** is being used. An artist who sells his paintings directly to consumers at art fairs and over the Internet is using direct marketing. Many services, such as hair salons, restaurants, and plumbing services, use a direct channel delivery system. Also, forms of insurance and stock trade services are sold online using direct marketing distribution. Many business-to-business sales also use direct channels. Sales representatives visit client companies, complete the transaction, and arrange delivery.

Indirect Channels

The other channels of distribution are **indirect channels**, which means the goods and services go through one or more *intermediaries,* such as retailers, wholesalers, distributors, industrial agents, or industrial merchants. An artist who sells her paintings to an art store is using a retailer as an intermediary. Instead of selling her art pieces to retail art stores, she may sell them to a distributor, who then sells them to various retail outlets.

In sales to consumers as end users, large manufacturers, such as Kraft Foods, Sony, Procter & Gamble, and 3M, sell directly to retailers, such as Wal-Mart, Target, and Walgreens. The size of these manufacturers and retailers means that selling directly to them makes sense. With large-volume purchases, prices are kept lower. This approach represents the shortest channel apart from being a direct one. For large manufacturers and large retailers, bypassing the wholesaler works well. For small manufacturers and small retailers, it does not.

A *traditional marketing channel* means the manufacturer or producer moves goods through wholesalers or distributors to retailers and on to consumers. Use of the traditional channel is on the decline, as many producers seek to offer products more efficiently and at a lower cost. Internet sales have moved many traditional sales into direct transactions without the use of an intermediary. Internet companies, such as Amazon.com, have also eliminated some of the need for wholesalers.

Two kinds of intermediaries are employed in business-to-business marketing programs. An *industrial agent* is a company that represents goods without ever holding title to them. *Industrial merchants* are companies that buy merchandise and then resell it to client companies. Actually taking title means that the merchant assumes some of the risk, because goods may or may not be sold.

Dual Channels

At times, a large manufacturer, such as Sony or Panasonic, cannot effectively contact all the small retailers, convenience stores, and other outlets. Thus, in order to reach as many customers as possible, these companies sell directly to major retail outlets and employ an electronics wholesaler or distributor to market products to smaller retailers. This method is known as a **dual channel** of distribution, a *multichannel distribution system*, or a *hybrid marketing system*. Such an approach may be viewed as risky if the same company employs wholesalers for some products but not for others. Doing so can strain the relationships with wholesalers as well as retailers.

The same term, *dual channels,* applies to two other situations. The first is when a company uses both direct channels and indirect channels. Many recording companies offer direct purchasing programs for music CDs using direct-mail "clubs" and sell the same CDs in retailers such as Hastings or f.y.e.

The second is when a manufacturer or service provider sells items in both consumer markets and business-to-business markets. For example, the Hyatt hotel chain offers rooms to individual travelers but also houses conventions and conferences for companies. Most credit card companies offer credit cards to individual consumers and also to small businesses.

In today's marketplace, when a manufacturer employs multiple channels, customers enjoy an expanding array of purchase and communication options. A consumer can order an item on the Internet and pick it up at the store or have it shipped to a residence or business. These options are now expected by both consumers and business customers.[2]

Advantages of Intermediaries

There are many reasons to use intermediaries. Figure 12.3 provides some of the more common. First, using intermediaries allows a manufacturer or producer to *reach more customers*. When Sony sells electronic products to Wal-Mart, the product becomes available to the millions of consumers who shop at the over 6,000 Wal-Mart stores.

Retailers and distributors stock multiple brands of each product and then stock thousands of products. This provides customers with a much *wider assortment of merchandise*. Without the distribution channel, customers would have to contact each manufacturer directly. Thus, retailers and distributors provide consumers and businesses with *convenience* by offering wider assortments at nearby locations.

The total cost of distribution is reduced by using one or more intermediaries. If Sony shipped its electronics products to every retail store, the cost of transportation would be exceedingly high. By selling a large quantity to Wal-Mart and other large retailers and distributors, the electronic products are shipped to fewer locations. From these locations, the products are shipped to the individual stores. This reduces the total cost of moving products from Japan to each retail outlet.

Employing retailers and distributors creates a situation in which *marketing functions and costs can be shared*. The manufacturer can focus on product quality and inventory control. The retailer is often responsible for consumer credit, repairs, and service contracts. Both may share the cost of transporting and storing the products.

Disadvantages of Intermediaries

The primary disadvantages to using intermediaries include time, cost, and loss of control. The longer the channel, the greater the length of *time* it takes to move a product from the producer to the consumer. Also, each intermediary must earn some profit on the movement of the goods. Each markup increases the *cost* and price of the product. Making use of intermediaries also means that the producer loses some *control* over the product. The item may receive poor shelf space and not be pushed by retail clerks. It also becomes more difficult to control the price, as some retailers may raise the price to cover additional costs.

- Reach more customers.
- Provide a wider assortment of products to customers.
- Provide convenience for customers.
- Reduce total cost of distribution.
- Share marketing functions and costs.

Figure 12.3

Reasons for Using Intermediaries

STOP AND THINK

Organizations such as Ticketmaster, Etix.com, and Live Nation sell tickets to rock concerts, sporting events, and other gatherings by phone, through the Internet, and sometimes at walk-up counters. Using the information you have read thus far, answer the following questions:

1. What type of intermediaries are these companies?

2. How does an intermediary for services differ from intermediaries for goods, or is there a difference?

3. Besides ticketing agencies, can you think of another service-oriented intermediary?

4. Some critics complain that ticketing agencies are essentially "monopolies" over tickets, raising prices and holding the best seats for preferred customers. Is this ethical, or is it simply a business practice?

International Considerations

As more and more business is conducted on a global scale, it is important to remember that distribution systems vary widely around the world. In some countries, nearly every product is agented or represented without a transfer of title. In others, nearly all merchandise is purchased by merchant intermediaries. An individual country may be well served by a vast industrial agent or merchant company, whereas another may not have an established company in place.

Distribution, warehousing, credit terms, and shipping systems also vary depending on the region and country involved. Some countries typically do not allow or frown upon the use of credit. Retail stores in some nations do not allow for photos on packages if the product inside is sexually sensitive or is offensive due to issues of gender.

In the Pacific Rim, trading companies are common. **Trading companies** are complex marketing systems specializing in providing intermediary services, such as information flow, marketing services, and financial assistance. For example, at the wholesale level, Mitsui and Mitsubishi are large integrated trading companies that use company bottling and distribution systems to produce and dispense Coca-Cola products in Japan.

Trading companies have been very successful in Japan and South Korea. Japanese trading companies have operations all over the world in fields that include finance, distribution, technology, mining, oil and gas exploration, and information. They act as intermediaries for half of Japan's exports and two thirds of its imports. Currently, these trading companies are moving from being pure traders, or intermediaries, to becoming more financially sophisticated investment-holding companies. The largest and best trading companies are members of *keiretsus*, which are families of firms with interlocking stakes in one another. Here, the trading companies' role is to act as the eyes and ears of the whole group, spotting business trends, market gaps, and investment opportunities. The top trading companies in Japan are ITOCHU, Marubeni, Mitsui, and Mitsubishi.[3]

If a manufacturer in the United States seeks to sell products in Japan, South Korea, and other Asian countries, the manufacturer will have to deal with one of the large trading companies. Direct contact with retailers will not work. Not only would it be resisted by retailers, it would also face intense opposition from the trading companies.

Consequently, before expanding into international sales, the marketing team carefully analyzes the types of distribution channels that are available and which ones will be favored by companies and consumers in other countries. Many cultural and subcultural differences may affect the choices made in creating a distribution system.

Managing the Supply Channel

The third element of a supply chain management program is managing the supply channel. Numerous marketing functions are provided by members of the supply channel. Each manufacturer has preferences regarding which functions will be provided by other members. Some manufacturers prefer to retain control over advertising to retail customers, while others allow this function to be provided by retailers. The same holds true for shipping, storing inventory, providing credit, setting prices, and repair and servicing functions. Managing the supply channel includes four main activities:

1. Establishing channel strategies
2. Selecting a channel arrangement
3. Choosing channel partners
4. Managing channel power

Establishing Channel Strategies: Push Versus Pull

The manufacturer or producer of goods and services first establishes the channel strategies to be used. One primary choice is between a pull strategy, a push strategy, and a combination of both. A **pull strategy** means that the manufacturer focuses on stimulating consumer demand through extensive advertising and consumer promotions. The goal is to build demand.

When customers ask for a particular product, channel members stock more of that brand. Retailers and channel members carry the brands with the highest demand. When a particular product or brand generates additional customer traffic to the store, the customers who visit are likely to purchase additional products. By advertising and offering promotions to consumers, a manufacturer is building a market for its particular brand. Thus, the brand is pulled through the channel by creating demand at the end-user level.

With a push strategy, the approach is just the opposite. A **push strategy** focuses on providing intermediaries with the kinds of incentives that will lead them to cooperate in marketing the product. Various forms of trade promotions are offered to entice retailers and other channel members to purchase and stock the product and then to push it at the retail level. The idea is that when the brand is on the store shelf, consumers will see it, examine it, and purchase it.

Manufacturers often use both strategies to maximize sales and exposure for products. By building demand at the consumer level, retailers and channel members are more motivated to stock the item knowing that the manufacturer promotes its brand to end users. Offering trade promotions to channel members makes stocking the item that much more attractive, because the trade promotion often increases the retailer's or channel member's gross margin.

Establishing Channel Strategies: In-House or With Partners

Another major strategic choice is whether to use traditional intermediaries or to work to create an in-house distribution channel. The management team of a manufacturing company considers the types of partners to employ or looks at alternate strategies. The three common alternate strategies are

1. vertical integration,
2. horizontal integration, and
3. vertical marketing systems.

Vertical Integration

Vertical integration is the strategy of acquiring or merging with an intermediary in the channel, such as a supplier or a buyer. *Forward vertical integration* occurs when a manufacturer opens

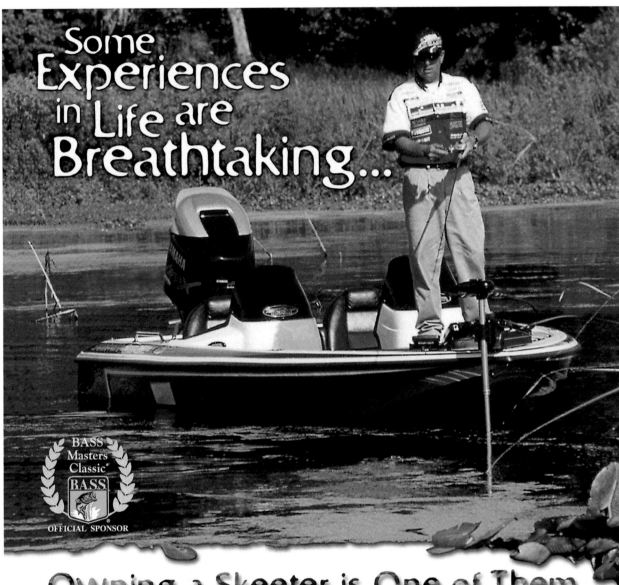

...Owning a Skeeter is One of Them.

Every angler knows the feeling of that moment when a big bass smashes your lure and takes it for a ride. You carefully battle the fish into open water and finally into your boat — and you smile, knowing that your lures, rods, reels and tackle box aren't what got you to this special place and moment in time. It was your reliable Skeeter ZX.

From the massive forward fishing platform to the mighty X-CEL transom with a powerful Yamaha bolted to it,

you know it was built tough. Designed for tournament bass fishing, it features oversized storage and rod organizing systems, optional dual console, two livewells up to 16-gallons each with a four-pump control system, built-in coolers and ergonomically perfected cockpits with backlit controls. Yep, the ZX Performance Series has it all. Hey, you can breathe now.

Eat. Sleep. Fish.

www.skeeterboats.com

YAMAHA Call 1-800-SKEETER to order a catalog, or visit your local Skeeter dealer.

Yamaha advertises the Skeeter brand of boats in many venues, including print ads.

What advantages does backward integration offer Zara?

a distribution system or its own retail stores. *Backward vertical integration* means a retailer creates a distribution system or begins manufacturing items to be sold in the store.

Zara, a popular clothing retailer, makes more than half of its clothes in-house (backward vertical integration) rather than relying on a network of suppliers.[4] Zara's clothes are created in a manufacturing center in Spain, with the sewing completed by seamstresses from 400 local cooperatives. This arrangement allows designers to closely follow which items are in demand. They talk to store managers and use scanner data to determine which clothes items are selling, and on the basis of such real-time data, they place orders and ship the inventory directly to the stores twice a week. This procedure eliminates the need for warehouses and maintaining large inventories.

In the United States, Braum's ice cream products are created on company farms and sold in company retail stores. When a company has its own suppliers, produces its own goods, and then sells them in its own stores, the company is *fully vertically integrated*.

Vertical integration strategies strengthen a company's position in the channel. Vertical integration offers the channel member control of the channel and normally increases gross margins. The potential disadvantage is that by vertically integrating, a company is entering a new business. A successful manufacturer may or may not be equally successful at retailing, and vice versa.

Horizontal Integration

Instead of vertical integration, another strategy that increases channel strength is **horizontal integration**, which is an acquisition or merger at the same level in the distribution channel. Examples of horizontal integration would be a manufacturer buying another manufacturer, a wholesaler acquiring another wholesaler at the same level in the distribution chain, or a retailer purchasing another retailer. This strategy may be problematic because it can trigger an antitrust investigation when the merger or acquisition makes the firm too large and provides any sort of monopoly power in the marketplace.

Vertical Marketing Systems

A recent development in distribution is the emergence of **vertical marketing systems**, which consist of manufacturers, wholesalers, and retailers within the same channel acting as a unified whole. Vertical marketing systems typically involve partial ownership. For example, Ukrop's Super Markets, Inc. was a founding member of Richfood Holdings, a regional mid-Atlantic distributor; SUPERVALU bought Richfood in a successful horizontal integration bid, and Ukrop's owns a proportionately smaller stake in SUPERVALU. Vertical marketing systems benefit from greater coordination achieved through common ownership.

The strategies of vertical integration, horizontal integration, and vertical marketing systems may be used either to augment or to replace current systems. When they accompany other distribution methods, channel partners are chosen carefully.

Selecting a Channel Arrangement

The second ingredient in a successful supply channel management program is the selection of a channel arrangement when the company works with partners in the distribution system. The channel arrangement guides the administration of the marketing functions that must be performed as part of the distribution program. Channel arrangements operate in one of three ways: (1) contractual, (2) administered, or (3) partnership.

A contractual channel arrangement means that a binding contract identifies all the tasks to be performed by each channel member with regard to production, delivery, sorting, pricing, and promotional support. The primary advantage of a contractual arrangement is that the various responsibilities for marketing functions are clearly delineated. This means that the manufacturer, by contract, may have a production and delivery schedule to meet. A wholesaler may be placed in charge of sorting, while the retailer provides promotional support (advertising, coupons). The contract can specify the parameters for the final price of a product.

The disadvantage is that there will be little flexibility to adjust pricing or control over other marketing functions without renegotiating the contract. In stable situations where prices remain constant and promotional programs are consistent, the contractual arrangement works well. When unexpected situations occur, it may be difficult to make changes. Also, changes in competitive tactics may be difficult to counter.

Channels adopting an administered channel arrangement approach have a dominant member in the distribution channel in terms of size, expertise, or influence. The dominant member, or channel captain, coordinates the marketing tasks provided by the channel member. The channel captain can emerge from any level of the distribution channel. A manufacturer with a strong brand pull, such as Pepsi or Kraft, could be the channel administrator. A powerful wholesaler, such as SUPERVALU, which deals with small manufacturers and retailers, can act as a channel captain. Influential retail chains, including Wal-Mart, Best Buy, and The Home Depot, can take on the role of channel captain. Hybrid structures such as Costco, a warehouse club that sells both to final consumers and to other retail outlets, may also serve as a channel captain.

A third alternative is the partnership channel arrangement. In this arrangement, the members of the channel work cooperatively together for the benefit of all firms involved. With the rise of large retailers, this arrangement has become more common. Wal-Mart has been one of the leaders in developing partnerships with vendors. By supplying each vendor with sales data and store information, Wal-Mart looks to the vendor to provide appropriate order quantities (the number of items shipped at one time to the retail store) and other marketing approaches. It is a win-win situation for both entities, because the retail information supplied by Wal-Mart provides manufacturers, such as Kraft or 3M, with important data to make production and marketing decisions.

Choosing Channel Partners

When the type of channel arrangement has been determined, the company's leadership team selects the appropriate channel partners. Most of the time, a firm's sales are greatly affected by repeat business. Typically, only 20% of sales come from new accounts. It is important, therefore, to develop solid channel partners to assist the manufacturer with customer retention at the end-user level.

Successful channel partnerships are characterized by an atmosphere of openness between the producer and the channel member, mutual trust, and a clear line of communication. The steps outlined in Figure 12.4 are the keys to developing successful channel partnerships.[5]

As with the selection of an advertising agency or any outside vendor, the first step of establishing the *objectives and criteria for selection* begins the process. The purpose is to limit factors such as one's personal preferences or friendships from influencing the choice. Establishing objectives and criteria in advance makes it more likely that the channel member that fits best will be chosen.

Next, *qualified* channel members are identified. The eligible partners are then contacted. Company leaders from both potential partners should then *share needs and wants* to see if a relationship can be developed. It must be clear that both partners will benefit from the relationship.

During the *evaluation process,* the channel member looks at the other products and brands that are being sold by the intermediary. This is especially important in terms of competing

1. Establish objectives and selection criteria.
2. Identify qualified channel members.
3. Share needs and wants.
4. Evaluate channel members.
5. Develop an integrated supply chain system.
6. Create a win-win situation for everyone.
7. Measure and analyze performance.

Figure 12.4

Steps in Developing Channel Partners

brands. In meetings with the intermediary, the channel member's representatives seek to ascertain the position its brand will hold. Only distributors or retailers that want the brand, are willing to market the brand, and will provide support for the brand are selected.

Once the channel member or members have been selected, it is time to *develop an integrated supply chain system* that ensures successful delivery of the products from the producer to the end user. This includes a data exchange system between the manufacturer and the retailer that is designed to make sure that the right mix of sizes, colors, and styles becomes available at all times.

The final component is to set up a system to *measure and analyze performance*. This includes establishing systems for problems that must be addressed. Changes in consumer or end-user wants and needs must be identified in time to correct production and marketing programs.

There are times in which a relationship with a distributor, wholesaler, or other channel member simply does not work out. Before moving on, the manufacturer's team normally analyzes the situation to see if the problem can be rectified. It is possible that moving to another intermediary will not solve the problem. Before switching, the manufacturer's manager conducts a thorough analysis of what is going on and why it is occurring. If a solid relationship with the channel member exists, a dialogue may be opened to discuss the problem and to look for ways to solve it.

Managing Channel Power

Channel members sometimes disagree on channel activities, the relative roles in the channel, and the level of rewards or profits each should receive. This includes placing the private labels next to the national brands in an attractive display, normally at a lower price. For consumers who are not brand loyal, the private brands are often selected. This may create conflict in the channel.

One of the keys to successful management of the marketing channel is to understand the nature of channel power and its proper use. Power that is exerted inappropriately leads to greater conflict and dissatisfaction among the weaker channel members. Figure 12.5 identifies five primary types of power that are present in channel relations.

Expert Power

Expert power refers to power over the other channel members based on the experience and knowledge that a channel member possesses. For example, Kraft Foods may enjoy the reputation of having a highly competent sales and marketing staff that is capable of enhancing the reputation of the Kraft brand. This reputation, based on expertise, is a source of power for Kraft when dealing with other companies in the market channel.

Referent Power

Closely related to expert power is referent power, which increases when a manufacturer, wholesaler, or retailer is well liked or respected. In interpersonal relationships, referent power is also called charisma. Referent power grows when channel members believe that an individual or the company treats others fairly. A company that has expert power may generate referent power by concentrating on what is good for everyone in the channel rather than short-term profits. A positive reputation has clout in many marketing channels.

Legitimate Power

Another form of power is legitimate power, or power based on a contractual relationship in which the duties and responsibilities of each channel member are clearly identified. Thus, through the contract, the power of one channel member over the others will be spelled out.

Reward Power

Channel conflict may also be reduced through the appropriate use of reward and coercive power. Reward power refers to power over the channel members based on anticipation of special privileges, such as financial rewards for engaging in a particular desirable behavior. Trade allowances and shipping discounts are some of the rewards that a manufacturer can provide to channel members in exchange for their cooperation. Retailers reward manufacturers with ideal

- Expert power
- Referent power
- Legitimate power
- Reward power
- Coercive power

Figure 12.5

Types of Channel Power

shelf space, with access to employees for additional training regarding a specific brand, and by their willingness to participate in cooperative advertising.

Coercive Power

Coercive power refers to power over channel members based on the ability of a channel member to remove privileges from or punish channel members for noncompliance. An example of coercive power would be threatening to change wholesalers if a manufacturer's terms for a given deal are not met. A retailer can punish a manufacturer or wholesaler by reducing shelf space, refusing to stock new items, or emphasizing another brand.

The key questions marketing managers ask about channel power include the following:

- Who has power in our marketing channel, and what are its sources?
- Which of our company's goals or objectives are linked to channel power?
- What types of channel power do we have?
- What types of channel power should we use?
- Is having channel power important to our long-term success?

Remember that "having power for power's sake" is not a viable goal. Channel power should be viewed as a tool in achieving marketing success.

STOP AND THINK

The five types of power mentioned in this section come from an article titled "The Bases of Social Power"* and were originally applied to interpersonal relationships in social organizations rather than marketing channel power differences.

1. Do you think these concepts apply equally well to both situations?
2. Can you think of other sources of channel power beyond these five? (*Hint:* in business management, control over the production process is a source of power, as is control over policy making)
3. Why is referent power the most difficult to create?
4. In what situations is reward power used ethically? In what situations is it not?
5. In what situations is coercive power used ethically? In what situations is it not?

* J. R. P. French and B. H. Raven, 1959, *The Bases of Social Power, in Studies in Social Power* (D. Cartwright, ed.), Ann Arbor, MI: Institute for Social Psychology, 150–167.

Physical Distribution

One of the best ways to deliver quality customer service is to make sure that the product arrives in the hands of the consumer on time, intact, and billed properly. Physical distribution tactics can be designed to make those things happen. From a management perspective, physical distribution begins with raw material orders and continues to the point where the finished item has left the plant and travelled through all intermediaries and made it to the final end user.

The term *logistics* applies to materials handling, inventory location, inventory control, and transportation systems. Logistics covers all the activities in the physical movement and storage of goods from the producer to the customer. The ultimate goal of a logistics program is to meet the needs of customers in a convenient and timely manner and at the best possible cost.

Logistics normally costs a firm between 10% and 35% of gross revenues. It accounts for approximately 10% of the GDP of the United States, or $1.183 billion, which makes logistics the single highest operating cost. Transportation requires the biggest portion of these costs, at $744 billion.[6]

Task	Marketing/Sales	Purchasing	Manufacturing	Other
Order status information (%)	13.1	62.3	14.8	9.8
Tracking inbound shipments (%)	6.1	61.9	19.0	12.8
Tracking outbound shipments (%)	42.9	17.6	21.0	18.5
Divergence of shipments (%)	17.2	52.6	21.5	8.7
Alerts on delayed shipments (%)	15.6	58.2	16.0	9.8

Table 12.1   Use of Logistics Information by Departments

Logistics information is critical to a firm's operation and its interactions with customers. In addition to the marketing department, logistics information is used by the purchasing and manufacturing departments, as well as other departments. Table 12.1 identifies various types of information supplied by the logistics department and specifies how much each of the other departments uses it.

The marketing and sales team tends to be most concerned with the tracking of outbound shipments. The purchasing department seeks information about order status, inbound shipments, and alerts on delayed shipments. Manufacturing wants information that relates to inbound raw materials and supplies that control production. Other departmental needs vary, but tracking of inbound and outbound shipments generates the most requested pieces of information.

Logistics programs are a classic example of a situation in which money is spent with one goal being to hold down costs and the other being to provide quality service to customers. The company described at the opening of this chapter, INSIGHT, Inc., specializes in logistics programs. Logistics plays a major part in the physical distribution tasks listed in Figure 12.6.

- Materials handling
- Inventory location
- Inventory control
- Order processing
- Methods of transportation

Figure 12.6

Tasks in Physical Distribution

Materials Handling

The first step in physical distribution is setting up a system to handle the inflow of raw materials. The management team balances the costs of orders, especially when delivery charges are present, against the cost of holding excess raw materials in storage. A company cannot afford to run out of raw materials. Reliable suppliers are a valuable resource for manufacturers. Those that constantly miss deadlines are eventually replaced.

Raw material orders are counted and prepared for use. A *bill of lading* specifies the exact amount of materials that have been sent to the manufacturer. Raw materials may take bulk form, such as coal, sheet metal, or chemicals. They can also be in the form of what are essentially finished goods that become parts of a new product. Screws, nails, prefabricated parts, and even more sophisticated items such as Intel's processors are raw materials from the manufacturer's perspective. The company's dock manager will normally be responsible for checking the actual shipment against the bill of lading to make sure that all items are present and that the items are not damaged. Then a bill for payment can be processed.

Inventory Location

Inventory location begins with identifying the most efficient and effective methods for storing finished goods before they are shipped to wholesalers, retailers, other businesses, or consumers. Normally, the rate of production does not match the demand and/or consumption. As a result, finished products are stored in warehouses until they are transported to intermediaries.

Types of Warehouses

Traditionally, the management team chooses from three alternatives: (1) a private warehouse, (2) a public warehouse, or (3) a third-party warehousing company. *Private warehouses* are owned or leased and operated by firms storing its products. *Public warehouses* are independent facilities that provide storage rental and related services for companies. Most companies use public warehouses because they are less expensive than building and maintaining private facilities. Also, the company may not need storage on a regular basis. A company conducting business in another country may also use a public warehouse. A firm expanding into a new geographic region can use a public facility until demand is sufficient for the company to build its own warehouse.

Third-party warehouses involve a firm outsourcing the warehousing function to a company that specializes in inventory and warehousing management. Many of the shipping companies now offer warehousing services. For instance, DHL ships products for companies to anywhere in the world and also warehouses products for its customers. This arrangement is especially beneficial for repair and maintenance parts that must be delivered within 24 hours. By keeping parts in the DHL warehouse, the items can be shipped quicker than if they had to be picked up and then shipped. For the marketing manager, the criteria used for selecting a type of warehouse are

- cost,
- facility size,
- access to transportation,
- closeness to the customer base, and
- closeness to the production facility.

These criteria are balanced against one another. For example, a public warehouse may offer the lowest cost yet be so far away from the transportation system that some of the cost savings are lost in the delivery process. All these items must be evaluated against the primary goal: efficiently and effectively serving customers. Marketing professionals know that there is nothing more frustrating than waiting on an order or back order for an extended period of time.

Distribution Centers

Distribution centers are not warehouses, because they are not designed to store products. Instead, they are created to facilitate the flow of goods. This reduces the costs of storage. Distribution centers often rely on an inventory control system called *just-in-time,* a method designed to move a product quickly from the production facility to the retailer or end user without stopping or staying long in a storage facility. Just-in-time inventory control will be discussed in further detail later in this chapter.

Urban Outfitters employs a distribution center. In the system, only 10% of the items that move through the center are sent to the reserve storage area. The rest are cross-docked directly from the receiving area on one side of the facility to the shipping area on the other side of the facility. They are then quickly sorted and packed for shipment.

When the merchandise arrives at the Urban Outfitters distribution facility, it is entered into Urban's enterprise resource planning system. This alerts the merchant who placed the order, signaling that the merchandise has arrived. Simultaneously, it alerts store managers throughout the system. This provides them with an opportunity to reallocate the shipment throughout the various stores if needs have changed since the order was sent.[7]

Most distribution centers are based on a design used by airlines and freight companies, such as UPS, FedEx, Norfolk Southern, and YRC. It is called the hub-and-spoke system. A warehouse is placed in a central location, the hub, and then trucks are used to move goods from the distribution center to the stores surrounding it (the spokes). For example, the Lowe's distribution center in California serves 40 stores. The hub-and-spoke system consolidates goods from different origins, breaks them into individual orders, and ships them to multiple stores, or channel members.[8]

Why would a company use a public warehouse rather than a private warehouse?

In today's marketplace, inventory location represents a major opportunity to control costs and to serve customers. The marketing team works in conjunction with other departments to make sure the system serves the company and its customers.

Order Processing

Order processing is vitally important to customer service. Order processing involves the paperwork that follows a purchase order from the manufacturer to its final destination. The standard tasks associated with order processing include

- making credit checks and giving credit approval;
- completing order forms;
- tracking the physical movement of the goods;
- providing purchase information to the salesperson, the accounting department, the shipping department, and the customer;
- verifying that the goods shipped match the purchase order and bill of lading;
- documenting any damaged or missing items; and
- submitting the final bill for payment.

Many of these functions can be facilitated by an electronic data interchange (EDI) program. At the same time, some of the responsibility continues to rest with those who physically examine the items as they are shipped and received.[9]

Inventory Control

Inventory control is the process of deciding on the level of inventory that is needed to meet demand at a reasonable cost. This includes dealing with two problems. The first occurs when too little inventory is available, which leads to lost sales, frustrated customers, complaints, and other problems. While some customers wait for a back order, most purchase a competing brand. The customer who purchases a competing brand may be satisfied with the alternative and never return to the original brand she intended to purchase.

The second problem is excess inventory, which means money is tied up in inventory. The monies spent on holding inventory are called carrying costs. Excess inventory may also lead to price reductions designed to move older merchandise. Fashions and automobiles are two examples of products whose prices are often reduced when newer products become available.

Stock Turnover

A primary factor in managing an inventory is stock turnover, which is the number of times per year the average inventory on hand is sold. A high stock turnover rate allows a company to be more efficient and reduces costs. At the same time, companies with a high stock turnover rate run the risk of insufficient inventory.

Stock turnover is calculated by dividing net sales by average inventory in retail dollars or by dividing cost of goods sold by average inventory in cost dollars. Consider the stock turnover rate calculated in Table 12.2.

Net sales ($)	3,200,000
Cost of goods sold (60%) ($)	1,920,000
Average inventory (retail $)	800,000
Average inventory (cost $)	480,000
Inventory turnover	4

Table 12.2   Calculating Stock Turnover

If net sales are $3.2 million and the cost of goods sold is 60%, then the dollar value of cost of goods sold is $1,920,000. The average inventory carried by the retailer during the year was $800,000 in retail dollars and $480,000 in cost dollars. If net sales are divided by average inventory in retail dollars, the turnover rate is 4. If the cost of goods sold is divided by average inventory in cost dollars, the turnover rate is 4. It is important for both numbers to be either in retail dollars or in cost dollars. If the gross margin or the percentage of cost of goods sold is known, then either retail or cost values can be calculated.

To understand the importance of increasing inventory turnover, consider Table 12.3. In the second column are the original numbers, showing a turnover rate of 4. If the company could increase the turnover rate to 5 through better inventory management procedures, then the average value of the inventory needed is $640,000 in retail dollars versus $800,000. If a manager is able to work with suppliers and develop an efficient inventory control system, the retailer would be able to reduce inventory levels to $500,000. This yields a turnover rate of 6.4 and provides additional funds for the firm's operations.

Company leaders search for the optimal turnover rate that allows timely delivery of products to meet customer demand without overstocking items. Finding the optimal point is difficult, and the turnover rates within industries vary widely. Some companies do an excellent job of controlling inventory, while others do not (see Table 12.4).

The average turnover rate for companies in the upper quartile in jewelry is 4.9 times per year, which means the number of days of inventory is kept approximately 74 days. In contrast, jewelry companies in the lower quartile have a turnover of only 1.6 times a year, and it takes 227 days to turn the inventory over. The difference between the upper-quartile companies and the lower-quartile companies in the wood office furniture industry and the electroplating industries is even more pronounced. The top companies in electroplating keep only 4 days of inventory on hand, turning it over 81.9 times per year. In contrast, the lower-performing companies have 39 days of inventory on hand and turn it over only 9.3 times per year.[10]

In dealing with inventory and stock turnover, retailers make decisions concerning how much merchandise to place on store shelves, how much to have in a warehouse or distribution

Net sales ($)	3,200,000	3,200,000	3,200,000
Cost of goods sold (60%) ($)	1,920,000	1,920,000	1,920,000
Average inventory (retail $)	800,000	640,000	500,000
Average inventory (cost $)	480,000	384,000	300,000
Inventory turnover	4	5	6.4

Table 12.3   Stock Turnover Rates

Industry	Turnover Rate			Days Inventory		
	Upper	Middle	Lower	Upper	Middle	Lower
Jewelry	4.9	2.7	1.6	74	137	227
Wood office furniture	23.8	9.6	5.9	15	38	62
Commercial lights	9.2	4.9	3.4	39	74	107
Electroplating, plating	81.9	25.5	9.3	4	14	39

Table 12.4   Inventory Turnover Rate and Days Inventory in Selected Industries

center, and how much to have in a back room, if such is used. Most retailers no longer have a backroom inventory. Everything is placed on the shelves as it arrives.

Inventory Management Systems

The primary goal of inventory control is to keep ordering costs and storage (carrying) costs as low as possible. Traditionally, the formula used to make this calculation was called the *economic ordering quantity,* which is designed to identify the point at which merchandise should be reordered along with the amount, or volume, to reorder. The formula assumes that the lead time, which is the amount of time it takes for an order to be processed and merchandise to be shipped, is zero. In other words, it assumes that merchandise instantly appears when it is ordered. Therefore, the manager must take into account actual lead time when making reorder decisions and using this methodology.

A second, newer approach is the just-in-time (JIT) inventory control system. JIT systems can serve two purposes. The first is to order raw materials efficiently. JIT systems allow the purchasing department to order lower quantities of raw materials with the goal of having materials arrive just when they are needed. To succeed, however, managers must be able to accurately forecast needs. When a forecast is not accurate, the supply of raw materials will be disrupted, which can halt a manufacturer's operation.

The second purpose of JIT is to reduce inventories of finished goods, thus reducing carrying and warehousing costs. Dependable delivery is an important consideration. If a company can count on timely delivery, then finished goods inventory levels can be reduced. If not, the company must carry a higher level of inventory to cover current and future anticipated needs. In addition to the reliability of the transportation system, part of the equation must correctly identify consumer demand, including peak and low sales seasons.

The retail equivalent of JIT is the quick response inventory system, which creates a supply flow that approximates consumer purchase patterns. The key to the quick response inventory system is electronic data interchange, which links the supplier's inventory system with the retailer's inventory system. By linking these two systems, the supplier knows the level of inventory available at each retail outlet. In addition, the supplier knows the sales level of each product. By monitoring the sales and inventory levels, suppliers can plan production levels to ensure a continuous supply of products to retailers.

Inventory control systems once again balance expenditures against customer needs. Too little inventory loses sales; too much inventory loses profits.

Methods of Transportation

The final task associated with physical distribution is establishing methods of transportation. Recently, the U.S. Department of Commerce reported that 60% of all Fortune 500 companies' logistics costs are spent on transporting products. One way to reduce costs and make products more affordable is to reduce shipping costs.[11] Costs also vary by the type of distribution system: exclusive, selective, and intensive. Transportation costs are highest when using an intensive distribution system.

Controlling transportation costs in terms of inbound freight to a business or distribution facility and outbound freight to a customer's business can mean the difference between a profit and a loss. Inbound transportation costs represent between 2% and 4% of the gross sales for domestic products and 6% to 12% for imported products. Outbound freight can represent 6% to 8% of the average order depending on distance and the size of the order. Many channel members receive low margins, which makes them sensitive to the shipping costs they pay. While these costs may be passed on to the final end user or consumer, they still concern the retailers and channel members receiving the merchandise.[12]

The choice of transportation method also determines how quickly goods arrive at a destination and the flexibility of loading and unloading shipments. The primary modes of transportation include trucks, rail, air, water, and pipelines (see Figure 12.7).

Trucking

Trucks transport smaller shipments over shorter distances. Trucks handle almost one third of all shipments in the United States. Trucks offer high flexibility and speed, taking products directly from the manufacturers to the retailers and other channel members. Trucking rates tend to be higher than other modes of transportation. Trucks are sometimes used in conjunction with other forms of transportation that cannot deliver a product to the customer's doorstep or to a retail outlet. Trucks carry a wide array of products, from perishables that require refrigeration units to clothing, furniture, electronics, office supplies, and even automobiles.

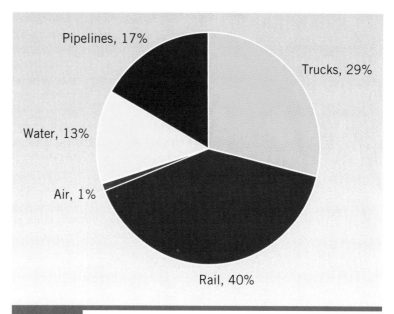

Figure 12.7 Types of Transportation and Volume of Transports

Railways

Rail accounts for 40% of all domestic shipping traffic in terms of volume. Rail is excellent for shipping over long distances high-weight, high-volume goods that have a low per-pound value, such as coal, oil, grain, and lumber, as well as more expensive items, such as large construction equipment and automobiles. Compared with other modes of transportation, rail is low cost, but it is also relatively slow. It does not offer the flexibility that trucks do because its access is limited to areas that are near or on rail lines.

What are the advantages of using trucks to transport goods?

The lower cost associated with railway freight transportation has contributed to its consistent growth as a shipping option over the past decade.[13]

Air

Air freight accounts for less than 1% of all transportation shipments in the United States. Air carriers offer high-speed shipping that is ideal for perishable products, such as cut flowers, repair and replacement parts that are rush items, and business documents. Although it is costly, air provides a means of shipping low-volume, low-weight, high-value products almost overnight. A company such as FedEx bases its entire business on air transport, banking on the capability to take products to destinations overnight. Internationally, air freight makes up a significant portion of the total freight transportation, approximately 9.5%. Domestically, however, air freight is still experiencing difficulty, as many corporations are switching from air to ground transportation in an effort to reduce costs.[14]

Water

Barges and other water freight vessels account for 13% of the total domestic traffic volume. While it is not a primary method of shipping goods in the United States, it is essential for international trade and accounts for a substantial proportion of international shipping traffic. Water, like rail, is used for transporting high-weight, high-volume products that have a low per-pound value, such as coal, oil, grain, lumber, and petroleum. Like rail, water transportation is experiencing a slow but steady increase in usage.[15]

Pipelines

Pipelines are a low-cost means of transporting liquid products from the source to the target market or processing plant in a continuous manner. Examples of pipelines are Basin, Bonito, and Capline for offshore and onshore crude oil. Perhaps the most famous pipeline is the Trans Alaska Pipeline, which runs from northern Alaska to southern Alaska across rough terrains. It transports more than 1.4 million barrels of crude oil daily. Pipelines are typically owned by the producer or by joint ventures, and they are expensive to maintain. They do provide a low-cost means of shipping liquid products, once they are in place.

Intermodal Transportation

Intermodal transportation is using two or more different transportation modes to move a particular product or shipment. Intermodal transportation has been greatly facilitated by containerization. Goods can be placed in containers at the factory, taken by truck to a train-loading facility, transported to a port, and loaded aboard a ship. After crossing the ocean, the containers can be loaded onto a truck or railway and then transported to their final destination. All these maneuvers can be accomplished using the initial containers, thus providing greater protection for the products. Labor costs are significantly reduced since all that is required is moving the container from one form of transportation to another. Unloading and loading of the goods are not necessary.

Freight Forwarders

Freight forwarders are specialized firms that collect shipments from different businesses, consolidate them into one truckload or railcar, and then deliver them to a destination. Often, the freight forwarder will pick up the goods and deliver them as well. Shipping companies

What are the advantages of intermodal transportation?

such as DHL, FedEx, and UPS are freight forwarders. They move goods for a large number of companies.

The demand for freight forwarders has escalated with the rise of e-commerce. Many Internet retailers do not even carry an inventory. Instead, they have items that are purchased drop-shipped from the manufacturer's facility directly to the customer's home or place of business. Most retailers use the services of shipping companies such as UPS and DHL.

In an effort to be competitive, a number of freight forwarders offer value-added services, such as developing distinctive competencies in terms of type of business or specific commodities. For example, Kuehne + Nagel has developed expertise in moving museum art and valuable exhibits. The company also arranges trade fairs and art exhibits. Other freight forwarders have developed strong expertise in several industry sectors, including health care, fashion, electronics, and live animals.[16]

Evaluation of Physical Distribution

To be competitive in today's global market, company leaders periodically examine the warehousing and physical distribution costs using an operational audit. The audit examines the procedures and processes used in operating the warehouse or distribution center, layout and usage of the facility, staff productivity, and freight analysis. The goals of the audit are to lower the cost per order, increase storage capacity, reduce inbound and outbound freight costs, improve service levels, and improve turnaround time.[17]

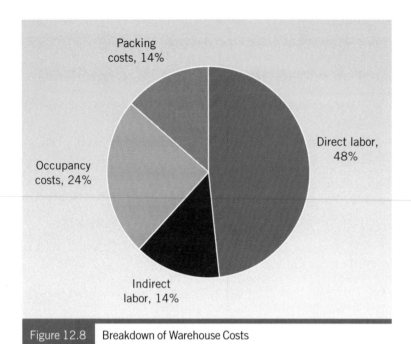

Packing costs, 14%

Direct labor, 48%

Occupancy costs, 24%

Indirect labor, 14%

| Figure 12.8 | Breakdown of Warehouse Costs |

Figure 12.8 displays a breakdown of costs associated with a distribution center or warehouse. Direct and indirect labor costs are the highest and are examined for ways to improve efficiency. Most of these labor costs are associated with picking items from bins or trucks and packing them for outbound shipping. Using automated systems for these types of activities can increase a facility's efficiency and reduce costs.

The overall costs for handling orders average between $3.00 and $5.00 per order but vary widely by industry and by company. A difference in cost of $3.00 per order versus $5.00 per order may seem small; however, it can make a major difference in annual costs. Table 12.5 provides data on six apparel companies and the costs of operating distribution centers. For Company A, the average cost per order is $5.80. The company processes 4.8 million orders a year, creating a total of $27.84 million dollars. Compare Company A with Company F, which processes more orders, 5.2 million to 4.8 million. The cost per order for Company F is only $1.40, about one third of Company A's facility costs. This translates into $7.28 million in operating costs versus the $27.84 million for Company A, a savings of over $20 million. Efficient distribution centers and logistics programs can make a difference in whether a company makes a profit or loses money.

In summary, the five tasks of physical distribution must be carefully integrated to provide the greatest level of efficiency and customer service. It is helpful to think of physical distribution as a system, as illustrated in Figure 12.9.

Company	Cost/Order ($)	Annual Orders	Total Annual Costs ($)
A	5.80	4,800,000	27,840,000
B	5.20	2,400,000	12,480,000
C	4.80	700,000	3,360,000
D	2.90	14,000,000	40,600,000
E	1.55	3,400,000	5,270,000
F	1.40	5,200,000	7,280,000

| Table 12.5 | Ordering Costs for Six Apparel Companies |

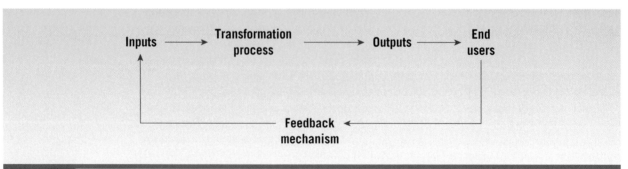

Inputs → Transformation process → Outputs → End users

Feedback mechanism

| Figure 12.9 | A Distribution System |

In this model, the inputs are the raw materials used to create goods and services. The transformation process is the actual manufacturing or value-creating method used. The outputs are the goods and services rendered, and the feedback mechanism provides relevant information about performance, in terms of both efficiencies (costs) and effectiveness (quality customer service). Using this model, the transformation process finalizes the items, which are then delivered to end users. Integrating the materials handling systems, the location of the inventory, the inventory controls, order processing, and the methods of transportation into one coherent design is the challenge for the management team, working in conjunction with marketing, production, accounting, and others in charge of physically moving goods.

Implications for Customer Service

The importance of an effective distribution system with regard to customer service has been noted in many places in this chapter. Distribution systems affect both customer acquisition and customer retention. As mentioned, when a product is not on the shelves, most customers simply move on to a competitor's brand. Consequently, stock-outs can affect customer acquisition. In terms of interactions with customers, stock-outs are likely to increase complaints, which is not the ideal form of interaction to have with customers. It may be that an appropriate analogy would be with umpires in baseball games and referees in other sports: When they do a good job, they go unnoticed. It is only when they make mistakes that they are seen. Efficient and effective product and service delivery probably does not attract a great deal of attention, but failures in this area are readily apparent.

Implications for Marketing Managers

Many of the tasks performed in the area of physical distribution are carried out by entry-level workers and first-line supervisors. Members of the sales force track orders to make sure customers are kept happy. Entry-level workers in the purchasing department handle the actual paperwork associated with orders. Dock workers load and unload shipments and examine items to make sure they are not damaged or missing. Consequently, first-line supervisors are often responsible for key elements of the physical distribution system. Therefore, they should be the first to point out the relationship between efficiently moving goods and satisfied customers.

The major decisions affecting distribution and supply chain management are made by top-level managers. The choices include selection of an exclusive, selective, or intensive distribution; the terms of channel arrangements; the type of warehouse or distribution center to be employed; methods of inventory control; and forms of transportation. Each decision should be clearly announced to all the company's department leaders. Internal communication is crucial to ensuring that these key strategic choices are carried out.

YOURCAREER

Personal Logistics

One of the most difficult problems about beginning a career can be location. Students leaving college may wish to live close to the campus or to relatives, or they may have distant new destinations in mind following graduation. Regardless, consider the following factors as part of your career plan.

Family Concerns

Families should be considered when making the initial decision about job location as well as promotions and transfers that may arise. It is important to discuss this issue with a spouse or a significant other before the choice is made. When there are children, the decision becomes more complicated. You will have to weigh career opportunities against family considerations and responsibilities. At times, you may choose to live in a location that may not be ideal because it is a good opportunity for career advancement. At other times, the family takes precedence.

Company Concerns

To advance within a company requires some tough decisions in terms of where you will be assigned. Many companies today have offices throughout the world. Some of these are not in ideal places to live. If a promotion involves living in an undesirable location, you will have to weigh the career opportunity against personal desires. It is also important to consider the ramifications of turning down the transfer or promotion. Such a decision may mean that you will be passed over the next time or that you may be viewed as not being a team player.

A difficult decision to make is concerning a move to another country. While some individuals welcome the opportunity, others are fearful. The pros and cons should be carefully considered.

One other situation may arise—a lateral transfer to another location. It is not a promotion and may not result in an increase in responsibilities or pay. At first, such a transfer to a new location may not appear to be a good idea. Before turning it down, consider what may be learned. If it is a different division of the company, you may gain considerable experience and exposure that will help prepare you for future promotions.

Personal Concerns

Because individuals differ, personal logistics will vary. The following are some personal factors that you must consider:

- Are you good at making new friends in strange locations? What about your spouse and other family members?
- Do you like the challenge of being the "new person" in a different company office?
- Are you an extrovert or an introvert, and how does this affect your feelings about moving to a new location?
- How important is your career to you? What sacrifices will you be willing to make to advance your career?

Throughout your career, you will be making a number of decisions regarding where to live and whether to accept a transfer to a new location. Carefully weigh family concerns, company concerns, and personal concerns before reaching a decision.

Chapter Summary

Supply chain management is the process of managing the actual physical movement of products from the producer to the consumer. Distribution systems can be intensive, exclusive, or selective. The decision variables that affect the choice of a system include the type of product, the price, competitive actions, the product's position, levels of brand equity and brand parity, the target market, and the image of the distributor.

Channels of distribution can be direct or indirect, to both retail customers and other businesses. Direct marketing to retail customers is on the rise, as is the strategy of bypassing wholesalers. The traditional marketing channel, which includes the producer, wholesaler, retailer, and end user, is now less common. Business-to-business channels include the use of an industrial agent, that represents goods without holding title, or an industrial merchant, that buys and resells goods.

The advantages of employing intermediaries such as wholesalers and retailers are that these systems reach more customers, provide a wider assortment of products to customers, provide convenience, reduce the total costs of distribution, and share in the marketing functions. The major disadvantages are that intermediaries add time to the movement of goods from the producer to the consumer, increase costs, and take away some of the manufacturer's control over the goods being sold.

Managing the supply channel begins with a choice between a push and a pull strategy for attracting customers. It includes choosing between in-house distribution or working with partners to move goods. In-house strategies include vertical integration, horizontal integration, and vertical marketing. Working with partners includes finalizing channel arrangements by contract, through an administered format featuring a channel captain, or through the utilization of a partnership channel arrangement.

Choosing a channel partner involves establishing objectives, identifying qualified channel members, sharing needs and wants, evaluation, developing an integrated supply chain system, creating a win-win situation with all parties, and measuring and analyzing performance.

Channel power can be managed through the application of expert power, referent power, legitimate power, reward power, or coercive power. Long-term implications suggest that reward and coercive power are less viable than the other forms.

To complete the supply chain management program, the five tasks of physical distribution must be carried out. The term *logistics* covers all the activities in the physical movement and storage of goods from the producer to the consumer, which includes the five tasks of materials handling, inventory location, inventory control, order processing, and transportation.

Chapter Terms

Administered channel arrangement   (p. 319)
Carrying costs   (p. 324)
Channel arrangement   (p. 319)
Channel captain   (p. 319)
Channels of distribution   (p. 312)
Coercive power   (p. 321)
Contractual channel arrangement   (p. 319)
Direct channel   (p. 313)
Dual channels (or multichannel distribution or hybrid marketing system)   (p. 314)
Exclusive distribution   (p. 311)
Expert power   (p. 320)
Horizontal integration   (p. 318)
Indirect channels   (p. 313)
Intensive distribution   (p. 311)
Just-in-time (JIT)   (p. 326)

Legitimate power   (p. 320)
Logistics   (p. 321)
Operational audit   (p. 329)
Partnership channel arrangement   (p. 319)
Pull strategy   (p. 316)
Push strategy   (p. 316)
Quick response   (p. 326)
Referent power   (p. 320)
Reward power   (p. 320)
Selective distribution   (p. 311)
Stock turnover   (p. 324)
Supply chain management   (p. 311)
Trading companies   (p. 315)
Vertical integration   (p. 316)
Vertical marketing system   (p. 318)

Review Questions

1. Define supply chain management.
2. What three types of distribution systems can marketing managers employ?
3. What decision variables affect the choice of a distribution system?
4. Describe all the potential direct and indirect retail distribution channels.
5. Describe all the potential direct and indirect business-to-business distribution channels.
6. What are the advantages that intermediaries offer to manufacturers? What are the disadvantages?
7. Describe the nature of a trading company and a keiretsu.
8. What is the difference between the push and pull channel strategies?
9. Describe vertical integration, horizontal integration, and a vertical marketing system.
10. Name and describe the three types of channel arrangements that channel members can create.
11. What steps are involved in choosing channel partners?
12. Name and describe the five types of channel power.
13. What are the five tasks of physical distribution?
14. Describe the term *logistics*.
16. Name the three types of warehouses that manufacturers can use.
17. What is the difference between a warehouse and a distribution center?
18. What are carrying costs? What is stock turnover?
19. Name three types of inventory control systems, and describe each one.
20. What methods of transportation can be used to physically deliver goods?
21. What is an operational audit?

CUSTOMER CORNER

Bass Pro Shops were born from a customer need. Professional tournament fishermen were often frustrated by the lack of a consistent source of specialized gear. The first Bass Pro store was a small retail outlet in Springfield, Missouri. As news of the company spread, it quickly expanded into catalog sales. A decade later, the first major Bass Pro Shop store was under construction. The Bass Pro Shop in Springfield, Missouri, also houses a museum of wildlife, a restaurant, and other amenities. It has become a local and regional tourist attraction for many outdoor enthusiasts. Now, anglers are able to shop at a Bass Pro retail store, purchase products online, or use the highly popular Bass Pro Shops catalog to purchase

nearly anything a person (a beginner or an old pro) could ever need to complete a fishing adventure.

1. What type of distribution system would best describe Bass Pro Shops'—exclusive, selective, or intensive?
2. What are the advantages of Bass Pro Shops's system of distribution, which is entirely in-house without the use of intermediaries?
3. What type of warehouse best fits the Bass Pro Shops system, or should the company use a distribution center type of approach?

How has Bass Pro Shops changed its distribution strategy to make it easier for anglers to purchase merchandise?

Discussion and Critical Thinking Questions

1. Match the following goods and services with an exclusive, selective, or intensive distribution system. Justify your answer.
   - Cough syrup
   - High-end office furniture
   - Office supplies
   - Prepaid cell phone
   - La-Z-Boy brand recliners

2. Name the channels (direct vs. indirect, type of intermediary, dual channels) that could be used in marketing the following items. Justify your answer.

   - Tickets for cruise ship vacations
   - Baseball gloves (Spalding, Rawlings)
   - Dishwasher detergent
   - Designer jeans
   - Digital photo printing

3. Which should be used, a push strategy or a pull strategy, for the following items. Justify your answer.
   - High-priced perfume
   - Candles and candle holders
   - Gardening equipment
   - Barbecue grills

4. Name the types of industries that you believe are most viable for vertical integration strategies, both backward and forward. Name the types of industries that you believe would be least viable. Explain your choices.

5. Distribution of textbooks has changed over the past two decades. In the past, all textbooks were purchased at the university's bookstore. Now most university bookstores are operated by third-party vendors. In addition, textbooks may be purchased at independent dealers located near campuses and online from sources such as Barnes and Noble and Amazon. Survey 10 students not in this class. Ask them where they purchased their books, and evaluate the prices and quality of service of each source. Write a report about the various channel outlets that are being used and what opinion the students have of each outlet. Discuss why it is important for students to have multiple places to purchase textbooks.

6. Which types of channel power would the following companies be likely to hold? Explain your answers.
   - Intel
   - AT&T

   - Ralph Lauren
   - Lowe's

7. Compare the advantages and disadvantages of warehouses and distribution centers in terms of cost, speed, and customer service.

8. How have companies such as eBay and Amazon.com changed the nature of distribution in the past decade?

9. The net sales for a company are $4,280,000, the cost of goods sold is $2,782,000, and the average inventory at retail is $800,000. What is the inventory turnover rate?

10. The net sales for a company are $12,432,000, the cost of goods sold is 58%, and the average inventory at cost is $1,073,000. What is the inventory turnover rate?

11. The net sales for a company are $7,658,000, the cost of goods sold is 70%, and the average inventory at retail is $832,000.
    - What is the inventory turnover rate?
    - If the company can reduce the inventory (at retail) by $100,000 to $732,000, what would

Chapter 12 Case

Making Movies

The glitz and glamour of the film industry fascinates many people around the world. At the same time, creating movies that make money is a tough, risky, and intricate business. As technologies continue to expand, the number of ways to package and sell films continues to grow.

The once predominant "studio system" no longer exists in Hollywood. There are still major film studios; however, in recent years, the number of independent films that have succeeded has grown dramatically. The methods to reach potential movie watchers may in part explain this phenomenon.

The standard film made by an independent filmmaker can be marketed through a series of intermediaries. A distribution company is a middleman between the theater and the producer/director/studio. Some distribution companies own the theater and do not ordinarily represent films from unknown producers or directors. Other distribution companies act as intermediaries between theater chains, independent theaters, and the studio. Many times, the major studios act as intermediaries by "picking up" the film and distributing it through theater partners.

When a distribution company is employed, the standard split of revenues may start at as much as 75% for the distributor and studio and 25% for the theater, depending on the budget of the film. A 50–50 split is common for films expected to have moderate ticket sales. Some high-profile movies that are expected to do well, such as the most recent *Batman* film, may command 90% of the revenues for the distribution company and/or studio, with only 10% going to the theater during the first week or two of the run. Over time, the split changes. By the eighth or ninth week, the theater may be keeping 90% of the ticket price, with only 10% going to the distributor and the studio.

Highly popular films also are distributed through international intermediaries. These companies handle any special regulations or intricacies of a given country. At times, the distributor may even change the name of the film. Technology is affecting international distribution systems as well. In 2008, the film *Leading to War* was offered as a complete download, using progressive streaming on the film's Web site.

Some filmmakers attempt to self-distribute movies to theaters and theater chains. It is difficult to arrange a wide distribution using this method, unless the film creates enough buzz at a film festival, such as Cannes or Sundance, or through some other form of publicity to capture theater owners' attention. A few of these films are then "picked up" by studios or distribution companies. Some of the films by Michael Moore have started independently and eventually moved into distribution companies for wider release.

New opportunities come from video/DVD rental systems. A number of films go into "direct to DVD" or "direct to video" status immediately. They are then rented by companies such as Blockbuster and Netflix.

The route traveled by other films may be even more complex. Following release to movie theaters, some are first run on pay-per-view movie channels, while others are first shown on Starz, HBO, or Cinemax. Most of these movies eventually find their way to video/DVD store shelves over time.

Movie studios also attempt to increase profits through merchandising arrangements for toys, T-shirts, hats, or action figures and tie-ins with food companies, soft drink companies, and other partners.

Among the newest challenges for moviemakers are piracy and other forms of copying. Movies that are first shown in foreign countries may be quickly pirated and may become available as videos or DVDs before the film is released in the United States. Copying technologies make it possible to take a video or DVD and copy it for friends or for resale.

As technologies for making films become more accessible to a wider number of potential filmmakers, the world of moviemaking and distribution may become even more competitive and complex. The big winners may be movie lovers, who will have more and more ways to enjoy the cinema.

How has movie making changed?

1. Name the distribution channels filmmakers and studios can use to offer movies to movie theaters and movie watchers of all types.

2. Some of the advantages of using intermediaries include reaching more customers, providing a wider assortment of products to customers, providing convenience, reducing the cost of distribution, and sharing marketing functions. Which of these apply to using intermediaries for film distribution?

3. The three disadvantages of using intermediaries are time, cost, and control. Explain how these would affect the world of film distribution.

4. In the movie distribution world, which organization might be most likely to become a channel captain, the studio, distributors, or movie theater chains? Why?

5. What role might the Internet play in movie distribution in the next decade?

Go to **www.sagepub.com/clow** for additional exercises and study resources. Select **Chapter 12, Distribution and Supply Chain Management** for chapter-specific activities.

What challenges do Vonage and other VoIP companies face?

Web Site and Internet Management

Vonage: Challenging and Changing Personal Communication

When a new firm tackles an industry's giants, business legends are born. In less than a decade, Vonage could be in the process of reaching that status. The world of person-to-person, business-to-business, and person-to-business communication, which was dominated by landlines for decades, has undergone a dramatic transformation. The primary influx of new competitors, such as cell phone providers, has carved out a large market share of the telecommunications market.

In 2002, a new method emerged. Vonage was among the first to provide broadband telephone services, also known as VoIP, or Voice over Internet Protocol. This new, award-winning technology allows a

customer to make and receive phone calls with a touch-tone telephone nearly anywhere broadband access is available. Several major retailers now offer the Vonage service, including Best Buy, Wal-Mart, and Target. The calling plans are comparable to regular phone services for both individuals and small businesses. They include unlimited local and long-distance connections, call waiting, call forwarding, automatic redial, and voice mail at one low, flat-rate monthly fee.

By 2008, Vonage hosted nearly 2.5 million customers with annual revenues reaching $225 million. In the same year, the company launched a major advertising campaign. Television ads portrayed Vonage as literally pushing traditional phone services off of the screen.

Company leaders are highly optimistic about the future of Vonage and VoIP. It was estimated that by 2008 over 250 million broadband users existed and that the number would expand to nearly 500 million by 2011. As noted in *Newsweek,* Ma Bell's kids live on the Internet, creating a lucrative new group of customers.[1]

The marketing costs of acquiring new customers have been improving. In 2007, it cost $273 to obtain a new customer. That figure dropped to $216 per customer in just 1 year. The price paid by a new customer during that time period was $24.99 per month, with the first month's service free.

This means the customer acquisitions costs were recovered in less than 1 year.

Challenges remain for Vonage's management team. First, there have been some problems with the reception in high-traffic areas and difficulties with fax transmissions. These technical glitches are likely to be resolved.

More important, Vonage now has a major competitor in the VoIP marketplace—Skype, which has the advantage of being owned by eBay. Skype offers free computer-to-computer calls for its members.

The third challenge is financial viability. In 2008, Vonage was still operating at a loss and had moved to refinance some outstanding debt. The company notes that losses were dropping quickly, from $72 million in the first quarter of 2007 to an $8 million deficit in the first quarter of 2008.

To build for the future, Vonage has begun creating new relationships, including a cobranded Internet telephone adaptor featuring a wireless router with Motorola. The company also expanded into international markets by offering free calling to Italy, France, Great Britain, and Spain, along with a launch of virtual phone numbers in other parts of Europe.

Will Vonage become the David that tackled the AT&T Goliath? Time will tell as the world of talking technology continues to evolve.

Chapter Overview

When analyzing any business operation, two helpful terms emerge: (1) necessary and (2) sufficient. Most managers now agree that a Web site is necessary. Success will be much harder to achieve without one. The key, however, may be in the word *sufficient.* Web sites that help the company to succeed do so in a value-added way. That is, Web sites must complement all other marketing and management activities and contribute something more. On the marketing side, a Web site should facilitate customer acquisition, interactions, and retention. On the management side, a Web site should also make the company more efficient and effective by providing a venue to streamline and customize operations. An insufficient Web site does not achieve these two purposes.

This chapter reviews the fundamentals of creating a Web site that surpasses being merely sufficient. Three elements are described with the goal of creating an excellent Web program. The essential ingredients that must work in concert in order to create a high-quality Web program are:

- developing the Web site functions,
- designing an e-commerce program, and
- promoting the Web site.

Creating and maintaining high-quality customer service remains the ultimate objective. Marketing managers from the top of the organization to those working each day on the site all try to find ways to turn a visit by a customer into a positive experience.

> - E-commerce
> - Customer support
> - Sales support
> - Brand support
> - Public relations support
>
> **Figure 13.1**
>
> Functions of a Web Site

Web Site Functions

Web site designs vary widely. At the core, each should be set up to serve a common set of functions, as shown in Figure 13.1. E-commerce is the most common function a Web site provides and will be discussed in detail in this section; however, the others are equally important. An effective site helps the company expand its market reach and provides customers with other valuable services. The site should assist in fully integrating a business and the channels of distribution the company uses.

Customer Support

Customer support includes any activity designed to assist customers who visit a Web site. The nature of the business or product often dictates the type of support offered. For example, DIRECTV's Web site provides a great deal of information and support for both potential customers and those who have purchased the service. Both types of customers view information about the products and services DIRECTV offers. New customers can locate providers to install the system. Ongoing customers can change service packages online. They can develop a list of favorite channels and shows and have DIRECTV send them e-mail reminders about the shows they want to watch. They may access the blog and participate in discussions with other customers about various TV shows. The site also has a trouble-shooting section for individuals experiencing technical difficulties. It has both live chat and delayed-response e-mail support for individuals requiring help or seeking technical information.

In contrast, the Tide laundry detergent Web site features "Fabric Advice" on the opening page. Customers learn how to treat common stains, including blood, coffee, ink, lipstick, oil, and pet stains. Naturally, the advice suggests Tide products as part of the solution. Special offers, online coupons, a message board, and a newsletter are also part of the site.

Sales Support

Web sites designed for sales support are normally accessed only by a company's sales staff and other employees. The goal of the site should be to provide quality information to members of the sales staff. These sites are seldom used in consumer markets unless a microsite is created that cannot be accessed or seen by consumers.

In the business-to-business sector, many Web sites are designed for sales support. These companies almost always have a different Web site or portal for e-commerce and for customers to use. Normally, the sales support staff URL will be password protected so that only the company's personnel have access. This prevents competitors from gathering proprietary information. A business-to-business Web site being used for sales support provides more than product and technical information. It also usually contains production information as well as inventory stock levels that can be used to determine approximate dates of shipping for orders.

How might DIRECTV's customer support Web site improve customer satisfaction?

Business-to-business sales support information may also be provided to the sales staff as well as internal telemarketing salespeople and customer service reps, which helps to make sure each purchase moves as smoothly as possible. A Web site may also contain internal information about customers, previous order histories, and outcomes of previous contacts.

Brand Support

A company's Web site should be devoted to supporting the company's brand or brands. This includes being attractive, easy to use, and should prominently feature the brand on each page. Any visitor can see what the brand represents and how it is different from and better than other brands. Web sites are coordinated with all other marketing activities. Advertisements and company stationery display the Web address. Also links directing customers to the site are constructed. A message can become more effective when it is portrayed across all communications in order to support the brand.

Public Relations Support

Most Web sites present some public relations information. The information may not be prominently displayed on the front page, except when an unusual event has occurred. Some releases remain on the front page only for a specified period of time. The majority of these releases are about cause-related marketing, green marketing, or an event marketing program. Where the information is posted depends on how central it is to the firm's mission and customer base. For firms such as Honest Tea that are strongly pro-environment, the type of publicity should be a major component of the Web site. For Tide, the information will be located in an area that is accessible to those interested but may not be prominently displayed.

When designing a Web site, the marketing team decides how strongly to emphasize each of these functions. The look of each Web site will be unique. The methods used to construct a site, the placement of information, and decisions regarding who will access it are carefully made before the launch of a site.

STOP AND THINK

Reread the opening vignette about Vonage, and then answer these questions:

1. What customer support might the Vonage Web site offer to retail customers and to other businesses?
2. What kind of sales support might the Vonage Web site offer to its sales and service staff?
3. Do you remember the Vonage "jingle"? If yes, does it support the brand in a positive way? If not, what can Vonage do online to build the brand?
4. Should Vonage feature a public relations event on the opening page of the Web site? Why or why not?

The Value of a Web Site

Creating and maintaining a Web program and e-commerce system takes time and can be costly. Clearly, marketing teams believe the benefits of these activities outweigh the costs. Figure 13.2 lists some of the major benefits of a Web site.

The first reason a company develops a Web site is to expand its *market reach*. A Web program should expand a business so that it does not remain limited to only nearby customers. The

Internet makes it possible to contact individuals and other businesses anywhere in the world. This expanded reach increases the company's *visibility*. With a Web site, the company becomes visible to a potentially unlimited number of individuals and businesses. By connecting a Web program to other marketing efforts, an integrated and consistent message is sent through an expanding number of venues.

A Web site provides a method to *communicate* with customers and prospective customers. It allows for both one-way communication and two-way interactions. When designed properly, a Web site becomes a powerful tool for *strengthening relationships with customers*. The key to relationship building is making use of the interaction capability of the Web.

For many businesses and consumers, a Web site is *convenient*. It can be used to gather information, to locate products, to interact with a company, and to purchase products.

For both the customer and the business operating the Web site, *cost reduction* becomes the result. Consumers and business customers save time and money when they do not have to travel to a retail outlet to finalize transactions or make telephone calls to gather information. The company hosting the Web site saves operating costs by being able to handle business over the Internet instead of through a retail outlet or channel partner. The Internet allows a retailer to reduce inventory in some locations and to customize inventory in brick-and-mortar stores to meet local needs. The Internet can offer a wide variety of products to anyone in any location. For instance, AutoZone's management team knows that certain parts should be stocked in certain retail outlets but not in others. Stocking tractor parts in major city stores does not make sense; neither does stocking Ferrari parts in rural stores. When someone from a rural area wants a Ferrari part that is not stocked locally, the situation can be handled easily through a Web site that allows the driver to order any part sold by AutoZone. The part can also be requested by an employee of a local rural store or by the person from his home. The item can then be shipped to the store or to the individual's home or business.[2]

An additional benefit exists. A Web site allows the company's management team to *integrate its channel* of distribution into a multichannel approach. Customers can order merchandise over the Web, through a catalog, or in a store. Customers can use the Web to search for information, then purchase the product through a different channel. Such seamless integration is important to ensure a high level of flexibility to customers, which may lead to greater satisfaction.

- Opportunity to expand market reach
- Visibility
- Communication
- Customer interaction
- Strengthening customer relationships
- Convenience
- Cost reduction
- Channel integration

Figure 13.2

Benefits of a Web Site

Designing an E-Commerce Program

The primary function of most Web sites is to facilitate e-commerce because these activities are now commonplace, even among brick-and-mortar stores. Marketing managers are involved from day one in developing a customer-friendly Web site. Information technology experts design a site that is easy to maintain and convenient to update. Some common activities that apply to all sites are

- building the e-commerce foundation,
- creating the e-commerce components, and
- finalizing methods of customer interaction.

- Study the competition.
- Define the target market.
- Choose a positioning strategy.
- Differentiate the site from competitors.
- Coordinate with other channel members.

Figure 13.3

Steps in Developing the E-Commerce Site

Building the E-Commerce Foundation

The first part of an e-commerce program consists of finalizing all the activities needed to effectively serve customers. This foundation requires careful planning and analysis by the marketing department working in conjunction with information technology, human resources, and public relations. Figure 13.3 identifies the steps to be followed in laying the foundation for an e-commerce site.

Study the Competition

Studying the competition constitutes the first step. The marketing team examines each competitor's Web site, making note of how it is organized, the approach it uses, and how the competition promotes products. These sites are also studied from the customer's perspective. The marketing professional studies features other sites offer that are attractive to customers and looks for features customers would like that are not being offered by competitors.

The marketing team identifies the type of cyber bait the competition uses. Cyber bait is any lure or attraction on a Web site that attracts visitors to the site and entices them to make purchases. Typically, cyber bait takes the form of free-trial offers, such as the offer from Vonage for a month's free service, or financial incentives, such as free samples, u-pons (Internet-delivered coupons), and cross-ruff or joint offers. Many hotels and airlines offer free miles or points on frequency programs when customers sign up for a special credit card. Cyber bait includes nonfinancial attractions such as free information, tips, newsletters, or games. The marketing team will try to match or exceed the competitor's cyber bait offers when the Web site goes up.

Define the Target Market

The information gained by studying the competition's Web sites makes it possible to more clearly define the target market for an e-commerce site. In term of customers, a firm has three choices:

- A new target market
- An overlap of current customers and new prospects
- Current customers

The choice of which target audience to pursue partly depends on the competitive analysis and the profile of the company's current customers. When the analysis reveals a target market not being served, it may make sense to pursue that group, even when customers in the new target market do not currently purchase the firm's products. For most companies, this represents a unique opportunity but rarely occurs..

A more common scenario is that there will be some overlap with the firm's current customers and the new target market. The degree of overlap depends on how closely the firm's current customers fit the profile of the target audience the company's marketing group seeks to pursue. Purchases made on the Internet already help marketers define the target market. Individuals over 60 years old seldom purchase products using the Internet. Individuals with lower incomes are less likely to make Internet purchases. The same holds true for individuals with lower levels of education. Thus, when launching an e-commerce site, the marketing team knows that members of the target audience tend to be better educated, earn higher incomes, and are younger. When a firm's primary market is males with college degrees who are 50 and over, there will be some overlap. Still, the majority of the firm's current customers may not be reached through the Web site. It may be, however, that the Web site can open the door for targeting younger males, and perhaps even females, depending on the product being sold.

Some e-commerce sites primarily serve the firm's current customers. While on the surface this may not make sense, it is a viable marketing approach, especially when the firm's current customers are high users of the Internet and tend to use the Internet to make purchases. Offering this direct channel provides current customers with convenience and may help to solidify their loyalty.

Most retailers now feature e-commerce sites that allow customers to order products using the Internet and arrange to have the items shipped to their homes or picked up at the nearest store. La-Z-Boy is one of the many retailers that use this tactic. When customers place orders, the local retail store becomes the point of pickup, delivery, and service. In addition to ordering furniture, customers visiting the La-Z-Boy Web site can view a virtual room planner, examine realistic fabric-to-frame applications, and use its local store locator.[3]

Choose a Positioning Strategy

After the firm's target market has been defined and the key competitors have been studied, the marketing team begins to outline the best positioning strategy. A Web site reflects the desired position. For example, an energy drink such as Red Bull will prepare a site that features fast-paced music and videos and contain links to X Games sports, motor sports, and culture pages and media mix access. The desired position reflects youth, energy, help with "all-nighters," and an active lifestyle. In contrast, Kool-Aid targets a different position in terms of image (more wholesome) and audience (kids) by prominently featuring the Kool-Aid Man cartoon character.

Differentiate From the Competition

Positioning provides some differentiation from the competition. While ideas can be gathered from visiting competing Web sites, the design of the site should be unique. The temptation to be "distinctively similar" should be avoided. Instead, the marketing team will give serious consideration to what the company can offer that will be unique, different, and appealing to customers and prospects. In the summer of 2008, the Gatorade Web site opened with a note of congratulations to Kevin Garnett for the NBA Championship. Gatorade relies heavily on celebrity endorsements. In contrast, the POWERADE Web site opened with photos of its main flavors, positioning by ingredients, and with product features.

Coordinate With Other Channel Members

Before an e-commerce site launch, the marketing team should decide how to coordinate the new site with the current channels of distribution. An e-commerce site automatically becomes a new channel of distribution (producer to end user, without intermediaries). The marketing team considers how customers might react when the company's products are currently only being sold in retail stores. The first task is to find out whether customers are willing to purchase items using the site. The manufacturer may also be concerned about the response of retailers. This is especially important if the retailer stands to lose sales and profits. In that circumstance, the retailer may not be as interested in supporting the product and in the worse case may lose interest in even stocking the item in the store.

When a manufacturer plans to sell merchandise over the Web, why is it important to coordinate the effort with other channel members?

Manufacturers typically use one of three approaches to reduce this potential source of conflict with retailers. First, products may be sold on the Internet at the same price the retailer charges. Thus, there is no financial incentive to purchase the item directly from the manufacturer. Further, the manufacturer can charge the customer shipping, which in effect means the price is higher than a purchase from a retail store. For some customers, the difference in price is acceptable because they save both time and the cost of gas by not having to make a trip to the retail store.

A second approach is to refer the customer to the closest retail store to purchase the item. The product can still be purchased online, but the e-commerce component of the site is not on the front page. The customer must locate the ordering page to make the purchase. To encourage a relationship with the retailer, the manufacturer may allow the customer to purchase the product online, but the customer must still go to a retail outlet to pick it up. Thus, the manufacturer does not offer any shipping services. This may help to maintain a better relationship with the retailer. Doing so keeps the retailer in the channel and allows the retailer to earn the same margin as it would have if the product was sold at the store.

The third alternative is to allow the customer to purchase the product through the manufacturer's Web site, but the product is shipped from the retailer's warehouse. In effect, the manufacturer's e-commerce site is just a portal to the retailer's e-commerce operation.

Other channel members and retailers will investigate the impact of e-commerce on the other distribution channels. Managers at retail operations that start accepting orders through an e-commerce site make decisions about how products will be shipped and from where. Retailers that use distribution centers and quick-response inventory systems may not initially be set up to handle online orders. Offering e-commerce may require building a warehouse to process e-commerce orders or creating a contract with a third-party logistics provider or a freight forwarder.

When Fair Indigo began operations in 2006, the company launched a Web site, its catalog, and retail outlets at the same time. The company targets socially conscious men and women ages 35 to 55. About 80% of the products are for women, since they typically purchase more clothes than men. Currently, the Web site generates about 70% of the sales; the catalog, 25%; and the retail outlets, 5%. The channels are integrated so that merchandise advertised in one venue is also promoted in the other two channels. While Fair Indigo mails catalogs to its best customers, the company also offers the catalog as a PDF file on its Web site. This allows individuals to download the catalog rather than wait for the one sent by mail. It also makes it easier to browse merchandise, because the customer does not have to scan through different pages of the Web site.[4]

One of the primary benefits e-commerce offers is reducing costs. In order to realize these savings, the firm's management team carefully plans the logistics, the warehousing, and the inventory of products to be sold online. Distribution centers (instead of more standard warehouses) are typically not prepared for e-commerce operations. E-commerce does provide an opportunity for new e-retailers that do not carry inventories. These companies can take orders and then have merchandise drop-shipped directly from the manufacturer to the person's home or business. Such an arrangement requires the marketing team to develop relationships or contracts with manufacturers to ensure there will be sufficient inventory to meet the ensuing demand.

In summary, putting up an e-commerce site is not difficult. For the program to succeed, however, the marketing team creates the best features to support the site through careful planning and coordination.

- Product database
- Internal search engine
- Shopping basket
- Payment options
- Customer tracking
- Marketing database
- Application interface
- Web site design requirements

Figure 13.4

E-Commerce Components

Creating E-Commerce Components

After the e-commerce foundation has been established, the marketing team works closely with information technology to create and finalize the various components of the e-commerce program. Figure 13.4 identifies the components involved. It is important to coordinate all the components together to make a Web site easy to visit, with the greatest degree of personal customer service possible.

The Product Database

The first task in developing an e-commerce program is to develop a product database. The product database will be similar to the company's catalog, if there is one, or the database maintained by a retail store. The product database should match items sold through the other distribution channels. A product database can consist of just a few items for a small operation or thousands of items for a large company.

Internal Search Engine

Web sites for companies selling a large number of items often feature an internal search engine. Building this type of shopping system takes time, especially when the product database contains thousands of products. An added component that is needed is a tag on each item. Each product will be tagged based on how customers search for it. Customers do not always know the proper name for a product and may type in the generic category names such as "chair" or "love seat" into the Web site's search engine. Every product should be tagged with all the names that a person might use while shopping.

Shopping Basket

A shopping basket stores the items to be purchased in a single place. The customer may review what is about to be purchased, add or delete items, and send the signal that the order is ready. The basket provides a summary of the unit price, the total units ordered, any taxes or delivery charges, and the total charge. Some also include an expected delivery date. Most Internet shoppers are familiar with the use of shopping baskets.

Payment Options

Numerous methods for making payment when using the Internet are available. It is helpful to meet the requirements listed in Figure 13.5 when building the system. First, the payment options must be *flexible*. Customers should be offered several options, such as a credit card, PayPal, Google Checkout, or other online payment system, or they should be able to use a direct bank withdrawal or bank card. Most Web sites offer two to three payment options.[5] A greater number of options increases sales. One survey by CyberSource revealed that as the number of payment options was raised, the average number of sales conversions went up. For e-commerce sites offering four or more methods of payment, sales conversion rates averaged 72%; for sites with three payment options, the conversion rate was 71%; for sites with two methods, it was 66%; and for sites with one method, it was 60%.[6]

Next, payment systems should be *acceptable,* which means the payment options are preferred by consumers and businesses. The more the payment options resemble payment options in retail stores and in placing telephone orders, the better.

Ease of use is also vital. Authorizing a payment should be as simple as clicking a box or icon stating, "Buy now," or something equally readable and understandable.

Security remains a major issue for consumers, especially as identity theft has increased. Most companies use encryption technology to ensure that information transmitted via the Internet is secure and cannot be read by others. While this provides some feeling of security, it may not be enough to entice some individuals to make a purchase. Using methods they feel comfortable with or using an alternative payment method, such as PayPal, helps.

Part of the security issue is trust. Consumers who trust a company are more likely to trust its Web operations. Trust can be generated in a number of ways. First, it can be enhanced by a strong brand name. The stronger the brand, or the greater the level of brand equity, the more likely it is that the person trusts the firm. Trust builds through product quality and service quality. It is built by efficient and positive customer interactions. A Web site can feature all the security technologies, but if a customer has a negative attitude toward the company, the person may also have a lack of trust.

- Flexible
- Acceptable
- Easy
- Secure
- Reliable
- Efficient

Figure 13.5

Requirements of a Digital Pay System

- **Basic authentication** – customers identifying themselves through a login and password
- **Cookies** – used to access personal information stored on the customer's computer and retrieve it when the customer accesses the Web site
- **Domain name** – name or e-mail used by an individual
- **IP address** – the actual numerical Internet address of the individual

Figure 13.6

Technologies to Track Web Visitors

Payment systems must be reliable and efficient. Customers are lost quickly and pass along negative word of mouth when credit cards or other payment options are not billed correctly. *Reliability* refers to the system operating properly and correctly every time it is accessed. Customers quickly become frustrated with payment systems that do not operate properly or systems that make errors in billing. Any refunds or returns are to be quickly and accurately posted to the customer's account. From the firm's perspective, the payment system should be *efficient*. It should cost considerably less to operate than taking orders by telephone or in person.

Customer Tracking

Tracking customer activity on a Web site is one of the primary advantages of having an e-commerce program. The information gathered can be used to personalize content for individuals who visit the site. Tracking can be used to evaluate consumer behavior in terms of the products individuals examine and purchase. It can be used as the basis for developing other marketing programs. The information gathered will be added to the company's database.

Figure 13.6 identifies the primary methods that can be used to track activity on a Web site. Basic authentication involves the person signing into the site using a login and password. To facilitate customer service, information can be used to personalize and customize interactions. The shopper should be able to log onto the Web site from any computer. Then, the program can track and record every visit by login number or name. Many sites for frequency programs, such as www.spg.com for the Starwood Preferred Guest program, employ basic authentication.

Another common method of tracking is through the use of cookies. Cookies access personal information stored on the customer's computer and retrieve it when the individual accesses a Web site. The major advantage of using cookies is that the customer does not have to login and does not have to remember her password. As long as the customer logs in from the same computer, the Web site recognizes the customer and pulls the individual's personal information from the customer's computer. That login information is then tied to previous tracking information stored on the company's computer. When an individual who logs in has purchased a digital camera and has examined video cameras but not made a purchase, the content can be customized to show individual video cameras or make a special promotional offer on a specific camera.

The other two means of tracking Web visitors are the domain name and the IP address. The *domain name* might be tied with a business, such as DECEnterprises.com. The *IP address* is the actual number of the person's Internet address. These two methods are used less frequently than basic authentication and cookies.

Marketing Database

The nature of a marketing database was described in Chapter 3 of this textbook. The marketing database can be used to identify various trends and types of consumers. For example, in the 1990s, humorous books (e.g., works by Dave Barry, Dilbert books, and others) were a major source of revenue for publishing companies and distributors such as Hastings, Barnes & Noble, and Amazon.com. Following the events of September 11, 2001, humor sales dropped considerably, replaced by books about family, patriotism, and other topics. The marketing database can be used to confirm such trends in order to create better offers to entice shoppers to make online purchases.

The Application Interface

Each Web site requires an application interface that connects the product database to the payment system, shopping basket, internal search engine, and other features of the site. While these are typically constructed by computer programmers, many companies purchase package solutions offered by a number of e-commerce application vendors. The application interface facilitates any search engine that allows customers to examine products. Tags are placed on items to make it easier to search for products. When a customer finds the items he wants, the item is placed into a shopping basket and can then be purchased. Amazon.com hosts an extensive application interface program.

In summary, careful coordination of all the e-commerce components leads to an easy to navigate Web site that entices consumers to inquire further and make purchases. Trips to the site are meticulously recorded, providing marketing managers access to useful information by customer, product, and target market.

Web Site Design Requirements

Another aspect of creating the e-commerce components is Web site design. Web design is critical in attracting browsers, in encouraging interaction with visitors, and in getting them to return for another visit. Figure 13.7 identifies some of the primary considerations for Web design.

The number one requirement is *quality content.* Content leads individuals and businesses to access a site. Creative graphics and fancy designs may win awards, but content is the most important feature of the design process. It helps to think about the design of the Web site from the perspective of the customer. What types of information do customers seek? What would they like to see and know? The Web site should be constructed based on the answers.

Web sites are more effective when they are *consistent.* Giving each page a similar design helps to create consistency, especially when the company's brand, logo, and advertising theme or tagline are posted on each page. One reason for maintaining consistency is that most consumers do not access a site through the home page. A study by Pindar Graphics revealed that only about 40% of visitors to Web sites first landed on the home page. The remaining 60% went first to another page within the site. Approximately 20% first accessed a category page, while 16.4% went directly to a product page, often via search engines.[7] By making the site consistent and paying attention to content on all pages, Web sites increase the probability of a pleasurable experience and a product purchase.

An *attractive* site is more likely to succeed. There is a difference, however, between being attractive and distracting. Just as an advertisement can be too "busy," a Web page may overwhelm the visitor. Too much movement or too many bright colors detracts from the content on the page.

A site should be *easy to navigate.* Links are prominently displayed on each page. Customers should be able to find products within two or three clicks. If not, they may go to a competitor's Web site. One method that is often used to speed up the shopping process is to offer an internal search engine within the site.

Personalization and *customization* are valuable assets. In addition to the company modifying the site based on customer activities within the site, customers should also have the opportunity to customize the site to fit personal preferences. This may be more difficult to do, but it can turn a casual customer into a loyal customer.

Another critical element involves creating a *living Web site* versus one that is static. Too often, content placed on the Web may be left for months or even years with the rationale that nothing has changed. Each time the customer logs onto the site, she should see something new or different. At the same time, the Web site should remain true to the principles of consistency and ease of navigation.

Finally, *maintenance* of the Web operation is crucial. The site should be accessible 24/7, and it needs to work every time. Companies such at Tealeaf Technology provide software that tracks problems with a Web site so that they can be resolved immediately. It is typically not a good idea to wait for customers to send an e-mail or make a telephone call to the company to inform them that something on the site has failed.

One recent survey revealed that 9 out of 10 people have experienced problems with online transactions. Further analysis suggests that about one third of the time, the shopper switched to a competitor's site or went offline to make the purchase. The researchers discovered that what customers defined as a problem was not always the same as those identified by Web masters and information technology experts. Customers expected "easy transactions with no failures and good feedback when issues arise." Only 3% switched to other Web sites due to slow performance. According to Rebecca Ward, CEO of Tealeaf, "a single common Web application

- Quality content
- Consistency
- Attractiveness
- Ease of navigation
- Personalization/ customization
- Living Web site
- Maintenance

Figure 13.7

Web Design Requirements

problem, such as an endless loop or business logic issue, could cost an e-business thousands if not millions of dollars, especially when hundreds, thousands, or millions of users are trying to make purchases, such as during a holiday shopping rush."[8]

Finalizing Methods of Interaction With Customers

- FAQ and Web solutions
- E-mail and live chat
- Social networks and blogs
- Customer reviews
- Customer-generated content
- Newsgroups or newsletters

Figure 13.8

Interacting With Customers

The third major component of an e-commerce program is finalizing methods of customer interaction. Beyond the foundation, displaying items for sale, creating payment systems, and the other e-commerce components, a system must be in place to allow the company to contact customers, customers to contact the company, and sometimes customers to contact each other. Figure 13.8 identifies the primary methods of interacting with customers via the Web. These concepts have already been presented in this textbook. The marketing manager makes decisions regarding the methods of interaction to be used, and the Web site is designed accordingly.

FAQs and Web Solutions

As has been noted, FAQs and Web solutions are one-way methods of communicating with customers, because customers accesses them and receive information without talking to or communicating with a specific company employee. These items are useful because they reduce service time and costs. They also provide a convenient way for customers to obtain answers and information without making a phone call or sending an e-mail. Quality FAQ and Web solution pages are produced and edited based on previous two-way interactions with customers. Problems or concerns that come up repeatedly should result in a new FAQ item, or information can be placed on a Web solution page.

E-mail and Live Chat

E-mails and live chat are easy to use and are enjoyed by many customers. The key is to ensure that the company has enough personnel to handle the volume. Live chat requires a sufficient number of employees to be available when customers access the feature. If an employee tries to handle too many customers at one time, it may slow responses and become frustrating for customers. It is also frustrating if a customer accesses live chat and receives a message that since the volume is high he must wait a considerable amount of time before an employee will be available.

Social Networks and Blogs

Social networks have become popular among Internet users. Companies can use them as a means of communicating with consumers. Two well-known social networking sites are Facebook and MySpace. Facebook has 59 million active profiles; MySpace has 110 million active profiles. Both organizations allow companies to advertise on the sites and to target ads to the interests, habits, and social friends of members based on their profiles. This means there are two methods of communicating through these sites. The first is by posting comments and responding to information placed on them. The second is by advertising on the sites.

A large percentage of the money spent on social network programs goes to advertising on MySpace and Facebook. With ad clutter now becoming a problem on these mega sites, marketing managers have begun to look for smaller social network and blog sites with a narrower focus that are a better fit with the target audience. Social networks and blogs are available for a wide variety of themes and activities. For instance, Yub.com is for shopaholics, Fuzzstar is for pet lovers, YogaMates is for individuals who like yoga, and PassportStamp.com is for avid travelers. Memberships at these specialty sites can vary from just a few hundred to millions.[9]

Heather Armstrong created a social network blog about motherhood called Dooce. It is an outlet for women to share their thoughts and frustrations about motherhood. Heather and her husband's blog quickly became highly popular, and they started selling advertising on the site. The site now contains over 850,000 avid readers, mostly mothers. The revenue generated through advertising became so large that both Heather Armstrong and her husband both left their jobs in order to run the blog on a full-time basis. JCPenney and Crate & Barrel have ads on the blog promoting furniture. Both offer decorating tips next to posts about Heather's 4-year-old daughter. Walgreens runs an ad promoting its photo-printing services next to pictures of the family dog.

The Armstrong site is just one of the thousands of social network blogs now in existence. Although men are heavy users of the Web, they tend not to visit sites explicitly for men as much as women visit sites targeted to women. Women are more likely to reach out, talk, and share on women's sites, which have attracted over 4.5 billion display ads in just 1 month to reach the 84 million visitors.[10]

National brands such as Calvin Klein, Nike, Victoria's Secret, and Ralph Lauren are increasingly featured on sites such as YouTube and MySpace. These sites allow companies to post videos, advertisements, and other marketing materials. For fashion designers, the sites provide venues for posting behind-the-scenes footage and fashion shows. People can choose which videos they wish to watch and share them with their friends. These videos are quite popular. In just 1 month, YouTube had 160 million unique visitors to its site. Many individuals went back numerous times to watch or post videos.[11]

> How can a manufacturer of jeans use social networking sites to promote its brands?

One of the fastest-growing forms of online social networking is Twitter, which is a free social networking and micro-blogging service that allows members to send and read other users' messages, more commonly known at *tweets*. Users can post tweet messages on their profile pages, which are then delivered to every user who has subscribed to them. Thus, a message is sent instantly to everyone on the user's friends circle. The user can restrict the message to just certain individuals within the circle of friends or allow the message to be sent to everyone.

Customer Reviews

Customer reviews are difficult to manage. Many sites, such as Travelocity.com, Hotels.com, and other travel sites, solicit customer reviews and comments. The same is true for Amazon.com and book reviews. Customers post both positive and negative thoughts about various books. Negative customer reviews are the ones that company leaders must think about how to handle.

The marketing department can take three approaches to handling negative information posted to a company blog or customer review page. The first is to immediately delete the posting if it is on the company's own Web site. This may be regarded by visitors as censorship. The second is for a company representative to immediately provide the company's viewpoint, on both company-run sites and other external sites. The third approach is not to provide an immediate reaction and see how other customers feel. If the negative feedback is something that a number of customers agree with, then it is probably a problem the company's leaders should address. Then, public relations releases and advertising can be used to inform customers that the problem has been resolved.

Customer-Generated Content

A company's Web site sometimes offers a place for customers to make comments about the firm's products and marketing programs. By reading customer-generated comments, the marketing team learns how customers feel about the company's products. This information may then be used to improve the product and the company's service. Dell created a Web site in which individuals submit ideas on how to improve its computer products. It actively encourages customers to share concerns, good and bad, and suggest ways to improve its products. Encouraging customer-generated content can increase brand awareness. Reebok launched a site called "Go Run Easy." The site consists of Google Maps, iTunes, Flickr, and Jumpout technologies. Runners are able to share their experiences and upload videos. They can map out favorite running trails. They can join discussion groups. The goal of the site is to engage Reebok customers with each other through a social network.

User-generated content ultimately should result in increased sales and reduced costs. As customers share experiences and comments, others may be encouraged to purchase the brand. Costs can also be reduced as customers point out problems and suggest solutions. DreamHost offers such a program on its site with a blog page. Some of these problems and solutions find their way into the company's FAQs and Web solutions. By encouraging customers to offer solutions, the company's technical staff receives additional help in solving problems. Members of the staff may join in to suggest additional solutions or to improve on a solution offered by a customer.

Rather than being intimidated by consumer-generated content, marketing managers can find ways to embrace it. They may use it to gain customer insights, boost brand loyalty, build brand awareness, increase sales, and decrease costs.[12]

How does the skin care brand Simple use its Web site to interact with customers like Priscilla?

Newsgroups and Newsletters

Two value-added methods of interaction are newsgroups and newsletters. Typically, the newsgroup is posted on a company's Web site and is often password protected to encourage individuals to log in. The newsgroup should be something that is relevant to the products being sold. For instance, a Web site that sells clothing carries fashion news. It may also have photographs of actors and actresses on the red carpet or snapshots of other famous people. For an e-commerce site selling hunting and fishing merchandise, the newsgroup may have information about these hobbies that would be interesting to participants. It might also list or provide links to various fishing tournaments or hunting sites.

A newsletter is similar but is normally sent to the person's e-mail account or is available in a PDF file for the person to download. Newsletters often contain more information about the company, its products, and its activities. Sponsorships, causes, and events supported by the company can be highlighted in the newsletter. Articles written in newspapers or magazines may be cited in the newsletter.

The skin care brand Simple has combined various value-added services to its Web site and made it interactive. The site targets 25- to 44-year-old women who are concerned about their appearance and especially about their skin. The site offers beauty tips, nutrition and fitness advice, and a "Simple Skin Health Check." For a small fee, the skin health check can provide women with an online personalized analysis of their skin. The individual fills out an in-depth online questionnaire covering all aspects of the person's lifestyle that might have an impact on her skin. The information is analyzed by a dermatologist, and the online report is compiled. To encourage women to use the site and interact with the various components, users are presented with the opportunity to earn online points through providing feedback, referring friends to the site, taking part in a survey, and participating in product trials.[13]

In summary, marketing professionals seek to facilitate customer engagement and take advantage of the power of FAQs, Web solutions, e-mail, social networks, blogs, customer reviews, customer-generated content, newsgroups, newsletters, and interactive services. Many firms believe that customers go online to search for products and want information on the Web site about products. Results from a recent study reveal that the e-commerce sites that offered a high level of customer engagement outperformed S&P 500 companies. Simple's interactive Web site is one example of a company that has developed ways to engage customers with its site. Ralph Lauren's e-commerce also does an excellent job of interacting with customers through its online *Luxury Lifestyle* magazine. The magazine encourages consumers to return to the site on a regular basis to learn about fashion, art, sports, healthy diets, and business. This type of engagement entices visitors back to the site and may lead to stronger feelings of loyalty to Ralph Lauren clothing.[14]

Promoting the Web Site

The final major ingredient in a Web site management program is promoting the site. Budgets for online advertising have steadily increased and have become a significant portion of many advertising and marketing budgets. The Internet now ranks fourth among the major media in terms of overall ad expenditures at $5.5 billion, which is 8.8% of the total ad spending (see Figure 13.9). Only television, magazines, and newspapers rank higher. The Internet is gaining in popularity because it is a highly effective means for reaching today's consumers, especially the younger, Internet-savvy market.

Companies can use a variety of ways to promote a Web site. Figure 13.10 highlights the primary methods that are available.

Banner Ads

The first way to promote a Web site is through online advertising. Banner ads have been around for some time and remain popular, accounting for 32% of online advertising. In addition to purchasing banner ads on various other sites, marketing managers consider banner ad exchanges. This is an arrangement whereby companies agree to promote each other with banner ads. Thus, a Web site for a cheerleading camp would have a banner for cheerleading clothing, and the clothing company would place a banner ad for the camp on its site.

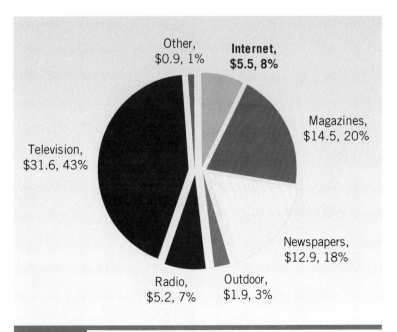

Figure 13.9   Total U.S. Advertising Expenditures (in billions)

- Banner ads
- Classified ads
- Media/video ads
- Search engine sites
- Off-line advertising
- Consumer-generated content

Figure 13.10

Methods of Promoting a Web Site

Was it helpful for Revlon to integrate both off-line and online advertising as part of the launch of the Charlie brand of perfume?

Classified Ads

A variation of banner ads is the classified ads, which now make up 17% of online ad budgets. Monster.com offers a place to advertise, as does craigslist. Many shoppers enjoy being able to look for merchandise on these sites.

Media/Video Ads

The third category of online advertising is the media/video ads. It now constitutes about 10% of online spending, but it is also the fastest-growing category. This growth will continue to escalate as mobile phones and other handheld devices are developed with increased capabilities to display videos.[15]

Search Engine Sites

When individuals look for specific information or products on the Internet, they often use a search engine. Nearly 80% of all Web traffic begins at a search engine.[16] As a result, most advertising departments incorporate search engine advertising into the budget.

The process of increasing the probability of a particular company's Web site emerging from a search is called search engine optimization. Search engine optimization can be accomplished in three different ways. The first is through a paid search insertion that comes up when certain products or information is sought.

The second approach is for the Web site to be identified through the natural, or organic, emergence of the site, which is unpaid. The idea is to develop efficient and effective organic results that will arise from the natural search process. Each search engine uses a slightly different set of algorithms to develop search lists. At the same time, these programs identify key phrases that match what the person types into the search box. To ensure that the company Web site is listed first in an organic search requires time and effort. When a Web site is first built, it is not likely that it will be listed at the top of a search. It takes time for search engines to locate the site. Some studies suggest that the impact of organic listings can be impressive. For sites that come up on the first page of a search or within the top 10, Web traffic increases ninefold. For second- and third-page listings, Web traffic increases six times. In terms of sales, the study found that being in a top 10 listing resulted in a 42% increase in sales the first month and a 100% increase the second month.[17]

The third approach is to make use of paid search ads. This form of advertising can be little text boxes that pop up when a particular word is typed in, or it can be link boxes at the top or side of a search result. Search advertising is growing in popularity, and more money is being shifted to search advertising because of its effectiveness. The typical click-through rate for online advertising is around 0.2%; for search advertising it is about 5%, which is a significant difference.[18]

Off-Line Advertising

Companies that advertise online also typically advertise off-line. Building a strong Internet brand and Web site involves integrating online and off-line advertising, which reinforce each other. This process of using traditional media to promote and attract consumers to an Internet

Web site is called brand spiraling. Television, radio, newspapers, magazines, billboards, and other media can be used to encourage consumers to visit a firm's Web site. A fully integrated advertising campaign is essential.

To push its Charlie fragrance among teenage girls, Revlon's marketing team used an integrated off-line and online advertising approach. The campaign ran across several online sites, such as GirlLand, MySpace, MTV, and the microsite created by Revlon, CharlieGirls. Ads were placed in a number of magazines encouraging teen girls to visit www.MySpace.com/charliegirls to engage with the brand through free downloads, a game, a blog, and some competitive activities. Potential customers could also go to MTV to share personal style icons and upload photos of their styles. MTV screened the submissions and posted the best ones.[19] The impact of the integrated campaign was much greater than if Revlon had used just online advertising to drive traffic to a microsite dedicated to the Charlie fragrance.

Consumer-Generated Advertising

Most ads placed on various Web sites have been generated by the company concerned. An alternative to company-produced ads that is growing in popularity is consumer-generated advertising. For instance, the 2007 Super Bowl featured a Doritos commercial that was the result of an ad-making contest for consumers. Converse, Firefox, and Diet Coke have also used video ads created by consumers. The idea behind consumer-generated ads is that the viewers of the ad tend to accept a consumer-generated advertisement as being more genuine than a company-produced commercial. Some marketing and advertising experts believe that the future of advertising is in user-generated content rather than agency-produced ads.

User-generated ads and content can offer companies several benefits when they are accepted and integrated effectively into the company's marketing outreach. What marketing managers must realize is that consumers will generate content with or without the company's participation.

STOP AND THINK

Three new venues are being used in Web site programs that involve customers creating Web content. The first is when customers review products and services. The second is when customer-generated content is posted. The third form is when customers actually create advertisements.

1. Should negative customer comments always, never, or sometimes be deleted if the company's marketing team has access to them? Why?

2. If negative customer comments remain posted, should the marketing team always, never, or sometimes respond to them on the site or in some other way? Why?

3. The four public relations approaches to damaging publicity are offering an apology, defending the company's innocence, providing justifications, and making other explanations. Do these apply to negative customer reviews? Do they apply to negative customer-generated content? Do they apply to negative customer-created advertisements?

4. Is it ethical to have a member of a company's marketing team "pose" as a customer and write positive reviews of the product? For example, authors often get their friends and family members to write positive book reviews for Amazon.com. Is this ethical? What if Sony had an employee's friend or family member write a positive review for the newest Sony camera?

International Implications

Many of today's Web site management programs incorporate both domestic and international operations. This leads to a series of challenges for the marketing team and others involved in creating and maintaining a site. The primary issues include language and slang, cultural customs, violations of protections for intellectual property, and governmental regulations.

The most basic problem to overcome is differences in language and slang. Any Web content should be translated and back-translated to make certain the messages arrive as intended. This becomes more crucial when slang becomes part of the equation. Words that are not carefully translated may end up in content in offensive ways or in ways that make the company and its brands look unprofessional or inept.

Cultural customs include the use of colors, the depiction of women and couples, the use of religious symbols, and other matters associated with everyday life. As an example, in Spain it is not unusual for the dinner hour to begin much later than in the United States. Web sites depicting dining should account for the hour when being sent to that country. Colors such as black, red, white, and violet/purple have distinct meanings in various cultures. Both black and white horses are symbols of death, depending on the culture of a given country.

Further, cultural customs dictate the payment methods used when making Internet purchases. Many times, a currency must be chosen or a currency converter employed. Also, marketers in some companies tend to rely on credit cards, while others prefer debit cards. Consequently, a cultural assimilator should carefully examine every aspect of a Web site before it goes up.

Where there are no laws protecting intellectual property, it becomes possible to copy content from a Web site onto another with a closely related name, either by cyber-squatting or by simply choosing a related name that may pop up when a search engine is used. Each company should assign an individual to protect the company's Web site materials as much as possible.

Finally, some governments regulate Web content more tightly than others. This means some sites will not be allowed. Other governments may be interested in protecting national interests. For instance, the government of France considered a ban on any Web site using only English, insisting that the page also be printed in French.

As commerce becomes more global, the use of the Internet will continue to rise. Many companies may find a greater reach of potential customers through a Web site. It is beneficial to construct sites that are appropriate for the nations involved.

YOURCAREER

It is a safe bet that the majority of today's college students are not aware of the Henkel Corporation. On the other hand, the name Duck Tape resonates with practically everyone. Duck and Loctite are two of the biggest brands managed by Vijay Shankar, as part of the adhesives division of Henkel. His wing of the company, one of the three major divisions, accounts for sales of $10 billion globally each year.

Vijay's major business customers include practically a "Who's who" of retail and home repair stores: Wal-Mart, Target, Lowe's, Home Depot, and others. The lines are also sold through office supply outlets such as OfficeMax and Staples, grocers such as the Kroger Company, and multiproduct vendors such as Walgreens and other similar chains. Adhesives are also a key ingredient in automobile manufacturing, with "somewhere close to 30 pounds of adhesives per car," Vijay reports.

The ascent to Vijay's position in Henkel took less than a decade. After graduating with an MBA degree, he joined a company called Manco, mainly because he felt an immediate affinity with the firm, its culture, and the management team.

His first position in the information technology department included working with various forms of data. The job only lasted about 6 months, as Vijay moved to the market research department, where he worked as an analyst and was then quickly promoted into a supervisory role. At that point, most of the research conducted was through secondary sources, including third-party providers such as the Nielsen Company. His three-person department also examined point-of-sale data to determine, "what was selling, where, and why." This helped the larger organization in areas such as sales, marketing, logistics, and customer service.

Vijay believed he was fortunate in this first supervisory role; his two employees were both cooperative and helpful, even though one was a former NASA member who was 10 years his senior. He suggested that the relationships worked because each had specific experience and skill sets

to contribute to the department. In 1998, Manco was sold to Henkel, and Vijay remained with the organization.

In a relatively short period of time, Vijay moved into his current position. Part of his training included immediate interpersonal contacts. "The company exposed us to customers very quickly," he reports. In fact, he was asked to make a sales pitch to the executive vice president of merchandising for Staples at the age of 25. "It was a lot of pressure, but also a great opportunity," he recalls.

Beyond the selling aspect of his job, Vijay's department spends a great deal of time working to deliver high-quality customer service. "We encounter two kinds of problems. The first is tactical, such as a shipping delay. The other is strategic, such as when a salesperson is not working well with a particular merchant." The department's response depends on the magnitude and severity of the issue. "If it is a personality issue, we make a change when it is warranted," he said, "But we are very cautious, because this affects an employee's career."

Larger problems, such as a complaint by a major customer, are handled carefully. Vijay noted that in one service crisis situation, the on-time delivery rate, which should have exceeded 99%, had dropped to 92% in one time period and even 88% in another. The department assembled a cross-functional team, including employees from sales, marketing, product sourcing, manufacturing, and distribution, to find a solution.

Vijay believes that several parts of his college training were highly helpful. He notes that courses in finance are invaluable in his current position. He also believes a variety of additional classes contributed more unique knowledge and skills, not the least of which was learning how to handle team or group members for class projects. In one situation, his team had to report to a professor that one member simply was not doing anything. "It was lousy to have to rat on someone," he noted, but at the same time he learned that similar situations would crop up in the business world.

Outside class, Vijay was involved in the campus Students in Free Enterprise (SIFE) program, as a team member and then as president. During his year as a team member, the school's SIFE team won a national championship. When he was president, the team finished third nationally. He also served as vice president of the school's MBA Association. Vijay believes that serving in the role of leader at an early age helped him considerably in his career, especially when working with diverse individuals. The SIFE team was not only composed of business students; the team recruited members from across the campus.

Vijay's division of Henkel is located in Cleveland, Ohio. In 2009, he was working hard to respond to the effects of the national and global recession. With his enthusiastic and focused approach, you can expect him to continue to succeed both personally and as leader of the Duck brand and beyond.

Chapter Summary

Web site management covers every aspect of creating and maintaining a company's Web site. The primary functions served by Web sites include customer support, sales support, brand support, public relations support, and e-commerce.

Web sites offer a number of benefits. A well-designed Web presence increases opportunities to expand market reach, creates visibility, enhances communication, strengthens customer relationships, provides convenience, and reduces costs. These benefits can also be achieved in international markets by carefully adapting the Web site to local conditions.

Developing an e-commerce program involves three common activities: (1) building the e-commerce foundation, (2) creating the e-commerce components, and (3) finalizing methods of customer interaction. Building the e-commerce foundation consists of studying the competition, defining the target market, choosing a positioning strategy, differentiating the site from competitors, and coordinating efforts with other channel members.

When the foundation is in place, the e-commerce components can be created. These include the product database, the internal search engine, the shopping basket, payment options, customer-tracking mechanisms, the marketing database, the application interface, and all Web site design requirements. The payment system should be flexible, acceptable, easy to use, secure, reliable, and efficient. Customer tracking can be facilitated using basic authentication, cookies, a domain name, or the IP address. Web design requirements include quality content, consistency, attractiveness, ease of navigation, personalization, customization, a living Web site, and a site that is easy to maintain.

Methods of interaction with customers can be one-way or two-way. They include FAQs and Web solutions, e-mail and live chat, social networks and blogs, customer reviews, customer-generated content, and newsgroups or newsletters. Each relies on quality interactions to improve relationships with ongoing customers.

A Web site can be promoted in a variety of ways. These include banner ads, classified ads, media/video ads, search engine sites, off-line advertising, and customer-generated advertising. The goal of each is to build a strong brand that connects with the Web site.

Chapter Terms

Application interface   (p. 348)
Basic authentication   (p. 348)
Brand spiraling   (p. 355)

Cookies   (p. 348)
Cyber bait   (p. 344)
Search engine optimization   (p. 354)

Review Questions

1. What are the three essential ingredients needed for a high-quality Web management program?

2. What are the main functions provided by a Web site?

3. What are the major benefits of a Web site management program?

4. What are the three basic activities found in an e-commerce program?

5. What steps are needed to develop an e-commerce site?

6. What is cyber bait?

7. What three tactics can a manufacturer use to smooth relations with retailers when an e-commerce program is being developed to market products directly to consumers?

8. What are the major components of an e-commerce program?

9. What are the basic requirements for an online pay system?

10. What is the difference between basic authentication and using cookies in tracking Web visitors?

11. What are the primary requirements for an effective Web design?

12. What venues are available for interacting with customers in an e-commerce program?

13. What methods can a company use to advertise online?

14. What is meant by the term "search engine optimization?"

15. What is brand spiraling?

16. What are the challenges in creating international Web sites?

CUSTOMER CORNER

Stella, Nicky, and Tammy had just finished an afternoon shopping trip. They decided it would be nice to enjoy some coffee and a light snack. Stella suggested Krispy Kreme. "You know," Tammy replied, "I kinda stopped going there when I started my diet. Those things are so full of calories and fat."

Stella answered, "You're right, but they are also so good!"

"I agree. They are good, but who can eat them?" Nicky added.

Their conversation seemed to follow a pattern that had affected the entire company. In the late 1990s and early 2000s, Krispy Kreme skyrocketed to fame. New store openings were often the sites of traffic jams and free publicity from local television, newspaper, and radio. In recent years, however, profits had diminished, and there was considerably less buzz. Stella wondered aloud if the company would ever "get their groove back."

1. Can Krispy Kreme use the company's Web site to generate new interest in the company?

2. Go to www.krispykreme.com, and view the site. What public relations activity does Krispy Kreme promote? In the past, the program had been highly successful. Does it still serve that function?

3. What kinds of customer support does the site offer? Should it be revised?

4. Is there any cyber bait offered by Krispy Kreme? What types could they use?

How does a company such as Krispy Kreme counter the image that its doughnuts have too many calories and too much fat?

Discussion and Critical Thinking Questions

1. What types of cyber bait would you expect to use for the following items?
   - Clothing made by Mark Ecko Enterprises
   - Golf clubs and golf balls made by Nike
   - Undergarments made by Hanes
   - Online banking services for senior citizens
   - Books sold by Barnes & Noble

2. During the 2008 Olympics, one of the most often watched sports events was women's beach volleyball. What should be the key components for a Web site promoting a women's professional volleyball league? What steps should be taken when designing the site?

3. There have been debates regarding the ethics of using cookies to track the habits of online customers. Some consider this to be an invasion of privacy. Others fear the potential for identity theft. Make an argument defending the use of cookies as a marketing tool. Make an ethical argument stating why marketers should not use cookies to track customers.

4. The following are characteristics of poor Web sites. Explain how the marketing team can address each of these issues:
   - Slow loading pages
   - Forcing Web visitors to go through numerous screens to find what they are looking for
   - Too much verbal information
   - Too many technical terms
   - Difficult and confusing navigation in the site
   - Banners and links that do not make sense
   - Fancy graphics that are distracting

5. You own a local restaurant. A local company has created a Web site that lists all area dining establishments and provides a space for customer reviews of each one. While your restaurant is consistently praised for the quality of the food, there have been numerous complaints about slow service and the lack of cleanliness. You suspect that other restaurants may be making these claims, not legitimate customers. What should you do?

6. In the mid-2000s, prior to the drastic rise in gas prices in 2008, General Motors created a space for customers to create ads for some of the company's larger vehicles. Many of the ads were positive, stressing the power and hardworking ("Like a Rock") aspects of the trucks and sport utility vehicles. A few negative ads about the environmental impact of these low-mileage vehicles also showed up on the site. General Motors's marketing team decided to leave them up. Do you agree with their decision? Why or why not?

7. You are the Web site manager for a new hot sauce for Mexican food. You have been assigned the task of creating a Web page in Spanish for customers in the United States but also to eventually expand sales to Mexico and other countries. What special challenges do you expect to encounter in creating a more international page?

Chapter 13 Case

Love Hurts

Jenny Kreidler faced a new challenge. In her new position as director of advertising for eHarmony.com, she knew that it was time to respond to the competition and to the marketplace. eHarmony employs sophisticated methods to help singles meet one another. The system begins with members answering online questionnaires, a 258-item survey. Then algorithms are used to evaluate the answers to find matches for people.

Company leaders will not publicly discuss details about how matches are made, although similarities are the key. Galen Buckwalter, eHarmony's vice president for research and development, notes, "Opposites attract, but then they attack. Differences, particularly in values, turn into perennial conflicts in long-term relationships." eHarmony boasts that 2% of marriages nationwide happen through its site, based on an online survey of more than 7,000 adults conducted by Harris Interactive and eHarmony in December.[20]

About 22 million Americans subscribe to online dating sites. JupiterResearch estimates that industry revenues totaled $500 million in 2008. At the same time, there were some dark clouds on the horizon. Jenny had been told that many have grown tired of constantly searching through ads. As evidence, industry growth was slowing dramatically. It was 77% in 2003, 19% in 2004, and only 9% in 2008.

eHarmony's primary competitor, Chemistry.com, was launched by Match.com in 2005. Chemistry.com

How should eHarmony.com react to the ads being run by competitors such as Chemistry.com?

uses neuroscience techniques to create matches for subscribers. The basis is the biology underlying romantic choices. By studying brain scans and behavioral studies, the company suggests that the type of person who is a good match will be hardwired into a person's neurons. Embedded in each brain is a "love map" that guides the choice of a mate. Chemistry.com's questionnaire is meant to decipher that map by running each profile through a proprietary computer algorithm to find that special someone who will light up those neurons.[21] While there are other online profiling services such as True.com and Perfectmatch.com, Chemistry.com has targeted eHarmony most directly in its advertisements. In a television campaign titled "Rejection," Chemistry.com ran television and magazine ads featuring young men and women explaining why their applications to join eHarmony were turned down.

eHarmony's management team responded by stating that the ads were suggesting that the company is arbitrary or discriminatory in turning people away. They demanded that the ads be changed or dropped from NBC and *People* magazine. *People* magazine's editor said that it wasn't taking sides in the feud and would continue running the ads, and NBC simply didn't respond. The Chemistry.com ad contained some fine-print qualifiers about what "1 million rejected" actually meant.

At that point, eHarmony was rejecting gays as subscribers. CEO Greg Waldorf explained that eHarmony's matching system is based on psychological research about heterosexual relationships. The company had not yet collected similar data on gay people, and the company was not confident that it can offer successful matches to same-sex couples. "I'm not saying anything precludes us from going into the same-sex market in the future," Waldorf said, "but it's not a service we offer now."[22]

In the next wave, Chemistry.com unleashed a campaign depicting eHarmony.com as out of touch with mainstream American values. The ads, which appeared in weekly newspapers and magazines, attacked eHarmony for refusing to match people of the same gender and for the evangelical Christian beliefs of its founder, Dr. Neil Clark Warren. One ad showed a sign on a beach that reads, "No gays on beach, May–September," while another featured a motel sign declaring, "No premarital sex." The copy in both ads assured readers that Chemistry.com does not judge or enforce any moral code on its members.[23]

The Chemistry.com Web site also tries to make sure that online daters pull the trigger and actually meet. Too often, company leaders suggest, two people exchange endless e-mails but never get together. Chemistry.com prods customers into making a quick date.

Jenny's first assignment was to design an advertising campaign to blunt the negative image being portrayed in Chemistry.com's advertising. She was assigned to work closely with the Webmaster to update and modify the eHarmony Web site as well.

1. What kinds of cyber bait can Jenny use on the eHarmony.com Web site to attract visitors to the site?

2. What target markets will the site serve? Can new markets be added?

3. How should eHarmony be positioned relative to other sites, and how can it be differentiated in an easy to understand way?

4. Describe how customer support, brand support, and public relations can be a part of the Web site for eHarmony.com.

 Go to **www.sagepub.com/clow** for additional exercises and study resources. Select **Chapter 13, Web Site and Internet Management** for chapter-specific activities.

part 4

Managing Customer Retention

Do you think the managers of JetBlue made the right decisions in terms of handling the crisis?

chapter 14
Customer Retention and Recovery

JetBlue: Crisis Management and Customer Recovery

In early 2007, a crisis hit JetBlue that could have been fatal to the airline's continuing operations. A massive snowstorm arrived on the East Coast of the United States, which pushed the airline into complete disarray. Some customers who had boarded the planes were forced to sit on runways for as many as 11 hours, only to have the flight eventually cancelled. A large number of flights quickly followed. Three days later, the airline's management team still had not been able to restore order. Passengers, flight attendants, and pilots were all stranded.

A wave of negative publicity emerged. Stories appeared on all the major news and broadcasting networks, which was probably made worse because the major problems took place at John F. Kennedy Airport in New York, a primary media center. The main issue seemed to be that, because of limitations on pilot flying hours and cockpit time, the airline was unable to deliver planes to relieve the backlog of passengers who were still stuck at the airport.

The incident was particularly troubling to JetBlue CEO David Neeleman. Until that week, the company had enjoyed a rich history of high consumer rankings and awards. The airline was noted for high levels of customer satisfaction for seat comfort, in-flight entertainment, and value based on low ticket prices. JetBlue scored at the top of the charts in customer loyalty in 2006.

Neeleman responded quickly and forcefully. He appeared on numerous nationally televised shows, expressing his remorse, using terms such as *mortified* and *humiliated* in the apology. He took the apology one step further: Neeleman promised sweeping reforms in JetBlue so that a similar situation would never occur again.

Even as revenues dropped due to the declining bookings that followed the negative publicity, the company moved forward. The first order of business was the posting of JetBlue's Customer Bill of Rights. The document includes three initial items,

including the statement that customers will be notified about

- delays prior to the scheduled departure,
- cancellations and their cause, and
- diversions and their cause.

To back this up, delayed departures due to what the company calls *controllable irregularity* would result in voucher payments of $25 to each passenger. An overbooking reimbursement for a passenger who does not get onto a flight is $1,000, and ground delay payments are $50 per passenger, whether an arrival is delayed or a departure problem occurs.

The sweeping reforms met with both customer approval and a great deal of positive publicity for JetBlue. One writer noted that Neeleman "couldn't have done it any better." By the summer of 2008, little more than 1 year later, JetBlue received J.D. Power's top ranking in its customer satisfaction survey for airlines. The company has received acclaim for its effort to become as environmentally friendly as possible and for its onboard entertainment package, which includes a DIRECTV package.

The lessons to be learned from the JetBlue experience include the willingness to respond to a failure quickly, to be willing to accept the blame with humility, and, most important, to work diligently to restore customer trust by fixing the problem. The template would seem to be viable for many industries beyond air travel.[1]

Chapter Overview

Marketing management, as has been noted, often involves spending money. A great deal of time, energy, and money is spent acquiring customers. The task begins with creating awareness that a brand exists. Then, the goal becomes to move prospective customers to make initial purchases. Products are refined, advertisements and promotions are created, and salespeople work diligently to entice customers to give a company's goods and services a try. All these activities require funds.

The next crucial moment occurs following the initial purchase. Will the customer come back? The ones that voluntarily return to make a second purchase have fewer marginal costs associated with the return visit. *There is nothing quite as profitable as a satisfied customer.*

The final part of this text deals with managing the customer retention process (see Figure 14.1). Chapter 14 deals specifically with customer retention and customer recovery. Chapter 15 discusses the controls that are used to manage the customer acquisition, customer interaction, and customer retention processes. Company leaders have limited marketing dollars to spend, which makes monitoring the marketing process an important component of long-term success.

The three pillars of customer retention highlighted in Figure 14.2 demand attention. Developing customer loyalty is the first. Maintaining quality relationships with loyal customers is the second. Responding to customer defections and complaints with effective recovery initiatives rounds out quality customer retention programs. These pillars are described first, followed by a discussion of the value of customer retention.

Two elements remain clear. First, providing quality customer service is the key to all three pillars. Second, entry-level workers and first-line supervisors have the most immediate contacts with customers. In simple terms, those who are entering the organization and are in the early stages of their careers often have the biggest impact on customer retention.

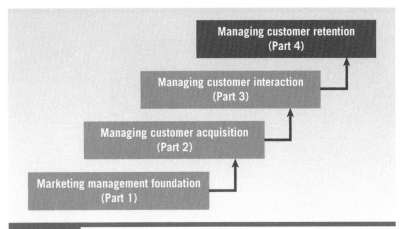

Figure 14.1   The Marketing Management Approach

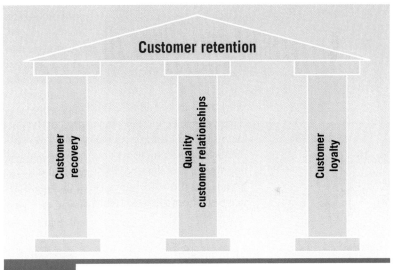

Figure 14.2   The Pillars of Customer Retention

Developing Customer Loyalty

Customer retention evolves from a series of stages. The AIDA (Awareness, Interest, Desire, Action) concept explains the initial part of this process. First, a product, service, or company captures consumer *awareness*. Next, consumers move from awareness to *interest*. When that interest grows, the customer feels *desire*. Finally, the desire spurs an eventual *action*—the first purchase of the company's product.

Once a product has been purchased, the goal becomes to motivate the customer to make additional purchases. Additional purchases can then eventually lead to brand loyalty (see Figure 14.3). At any time during this process, the customer may switch to another brand. The marketing manager's goal is to encourage the customer along the path of additional purchases rather than watching him switch to a competitor's brand.

At first, it would seem that the wisest strategy would be to encourage all the customers of a firm to move along the path of repeat purchases toward brand loyalty. Based on the material presented in Chapter 3 regarding the lifetime value of customers, however, marketing

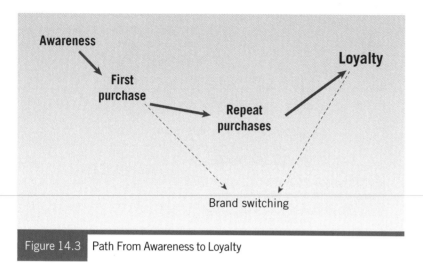

Figure 14.3   Path From Awareness to Loyalty

managers know that not all patrons are of equal value. Consequently, the goal for many marketing programs becomes to retain those who make higher levels of purchases and/or have the greatest long-term potential. In some circumstances, especially for business-to-business sales, poor customers may be let go or not strongly encouraged to make repeat purchases because they tend to cost more than the revenues they generate. Another group of customers that should be considered for retention is dissatisfied customers, if they have the potential for generating high returns. The methods used to recover these customers will be presented later in the chapter.

Types of Customer Loyalty

Customers are not all the same. Types and levels of loyalty vary. Brand loyalty consists of two components: emotional attachment and behavior or actual purchases. *Emotional attachment* means the consumer becomes connected with and attached to the brand. Emotional attachments form for any number of reasons, including pairing the product with feelings of love, happiness, nostalgia, sexiness, or the belief that buying the product helps family or friends. *Behavior* is the actual purchase of the brand. Figure 14.4 illustrates four forms of brand loyalty that result from these two dimensions.[2]

No Loyalty

Individuals who have *no emotional attachment* to a brand and who *purchase the item infrequently* have no loyalty. These consumers tend to be price-sensitive or promotion-prone consumers. They purchase the brand that is on sale or on-deal, or the one they just happen to pick up at the store. Brand names carry little or no meaning to this group. Pursuing these consumers is not practical. They do not stay with a brand, which means the costs of retaining these customers tends to be higher than the revenues generated.

Latent Loyalty

Latent loyalty involves a *high level of attachment,* but for some reason *purchase volume of the brand is low.* For example, Brandon loves Mexican food and likes to dine at El Chico. Whenever he wants Mexican food, he almost always goes to El Chico, rarely visiting any other Mexican restaurant. Brandon has a high level of emotional attachment to El Chico. Unfortunately, Brandon's wife does not like Mexican food, so they rarely go out for it. The result is that he has a latent loyalty toward El Chico. He exhibits a high level of attachment but a low level of purchases. Latent consumers may be worth pursuing because of the high level of emotional attachment. Overcoming whatever circumstances are causing the low purchase levels becomes the challenge. When the marketing team at El Chico believes that there are many customers similar to Brandon, they may consider offering a variety of American or other types of foods for family members who prefer something other than Mexican cuisine.

Inertia Loyalty

Nearly the opposite of latent loyalty is inertia loyalty, which is characterized by a *high level of purchases* but *low emotional attachment*. Many times, the purchases result from convenience or habit. For instance, Hannah almost always purchases gas at the Exxon station near her house because it is convenient. Jamie almost always uses the tanning salon near the university because that is the one she has used since she started college. Julia always buys Kraft cheese because that is what her mother bought and that is what she has always purchased. While all these consumers demonstrate repeat purchase behavior, they are not brand loyal. Their purchases are based on situational factors other than an emotional attachment to the brand. They are good customers because they tend to purchase the same brand. In Chapter 8, these were identified as *preferred-brand consumers*. They prefer a brand but have little or no emotional attachment to it.

These customers are easier candidates for competitors to try and entice into a relationship. Therefore, the marketing team looks for ways to enhance relationships with them before they drift away. They already purchase the product, which means they can be identified. The task then is to make sure that stronger emotional ties with the brand are built.

Figure 14.4 | Forms of Brand Loyalty

How does El Chico handle Brandon's latent loyalty toward the restaurant, since his wife does not like Mexican food?

Like Hannah, most customers of gas stations display latent loyalty toward a particular station. Why?

Brand Loyalty

The fourth group is *brand loyalty*. These consumers exhibit *high levels of emotional attachment* and make *high levels of purchases*. They do not substitute brands. They will travel farther or make whatever efforts are necessary to purchase the chosen brand. The company already has the consumer's attachment; therefore the key task is to reward his loyalty. Incentives to increase purchases are not necessary, are usually not effective, and may even be a waste of resources.

While moving customers to the level of brand loyalty is the ideal, it may not always be possible. For instance, in the fast food industry, extremely few customers become brand loyal to a particular chain, such as McDonald's, Wendy's, or Burger King. Therefore, the marketing manager's goal regarding these establishments is to create inertia loyalty and strive to enhance the level of emotional attachment. The objective is for the individual to purchase primarily from one particular fast food chain and develop a preference for that brand. The customer may not go to a given chain 100% of the time. Still it may be possible to attract that customer 70%, 80%, or even 90% of the time.

Factors That Generate Loyalty

Marketing managers emphasize customer retention and brand loyalty as highly desirable outcomes. They try to identify factors that lead to higher levels of loyalty. Figure 14.5 highlights activities that generate higher levels of loyalty and also create brand equity. The marketing team normally seeks to offer quality products, quality service, and comparable prices to remain competitive. Unfortunately, doing so may help create perceptions of brand parity.

Customer Relationships

To tip the scale, the marketing team looks for ways to create brand equity and to generate brand loyalty, which may be achieved, in part, by developing personal relationships with customers. When a customer feels a company cares about her personally and strives to serve her as an individual, she may start to develop an emotional attachment to the brand and move from the inertia state toward brand loyalty.

Exceeding Expectations

Building brand equity means exceeding customer expectations in some way. It may be through superior product quality, or at least perceived superior product quality. Actual product quality superiority is not necessary when consumers perceive the quality as superior. In addition to product quality, a firm may excel in service quality or offer the same quality as competitors but at a lower price. Consumers view this as a better value, and a strong emotional attachment occurs as consequence. This approach is much easier for competitors to copy, which can move the brand back to brand parity.

Expectations can be exceeded in many ways (see Figure 14.6). Expectations are set by industry standards, or by brand parity within an industry. Thus, if the average delivery time for a pizza ordered from Pizza Hut or Domino's is 30 minutes, then

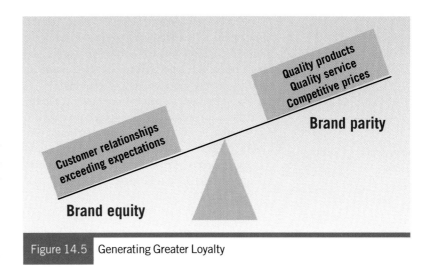

Figure 14.5 Generating Greater Loyalty

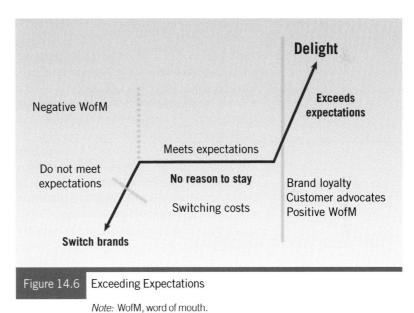

Figure 14.6 Exceeding Expectations

Note: WofM, word of mouth.

that becomes the expectation of consumers. When the average in the banking industry is free checking and free online banking for customers who maintain a minimum balance of $5,000, it becomes the expectation of consumers. In other words, consumer expectations evolve from perceptions of brand parity.

When a firm meets expectations, it only reinforces beliefs about brand parity. As a result, no compelling reason to purchase the brand again has been provided. When a customer does not have a reason to switch brands, he also has no compelling reason to stay with a brand. In terms of the four types of brand loyalty, the result becomes no loyalty. Merely meeting expectations does not produce a new level of loyalty. It also does not generate any emotional attachment to the brand. It may generate some inertia loyalty, but that loyalty comes from situational factors that are not related to exceeding expectations.

A company or brand that exceeds customer expectations will be the most likely to generate brand loyalty, create customer advocates, and foster positive word-of-mouth endorsements. For this to happen, the customer must feel delighted with the good or service because in some way the company went beyond what is average or normal. What would happen, for instance, if a car being serviced also had the interior cleaned and the exterior washed, at no extra charge, by the service department? The customer did not ask for these extras. The service department provided them as a reward for the consumer's patronage.

A check-out clerk at a grocery store exceeds expectations when he recognizes a customer from a previous visit and asks how the customer's visit with relatives went. He remembered. An emotional bond develops. At a deli, the person fixing the sandwiches recognizes a customer walking in, greets her, and asks if she is going to have the usual. By knowing what the customer usually orders, she exceeds expectations.

When superior service is provided, when superior product quality is provided, or when personal relationships are developed, customers may begin to feel an emotional attachment, and the result becomes a growing level of brand loyalty. Loyal customers turn into brand advocates, telling others about what a great place or great brand it is.

The most negative outcome occurs when a firm does not meet expectations. When this happens, a consumer becomes more likely to switch brands and engage in negative word-of-mouth communication. The decision to switch depends on the cost of switching. Switching to a new brand of jeans on the next purchase is relatively easy. To switch from cable TV to another cable TV provider or to one of the satellite providers is more difficult and involves some switching costs. As a result, the level of unmet expectations or the degree of dissatisfaction has to be greater before the individual switches.

Improving Quality

Another method of increasing emotional attachments is providing superior quality of a good or service. Most industries are in the maturity stage of the product life cycle. Finding ways to improve product quality will be difficult. Also, a product improvement may be quickly matched by competitors. The marketing team can, however, continually strive to improve service quality. This may be more difficult for competitors to duplicate because it involves changes to the firm's climate.

In improving quality, it helps to understand how it is measured and what constitutes superior quality. Examine Figure 14.7 for an illustration of quality being measured on a 10-point scale with 1 being *very dissatisfied* and 10 being *very satisfied*. Scales typically use only a 5-point or 7-point scale, but for illustrative purposes consider a 10-point scale. When asked where the midpoint of the scale would be, many individuals would reply that the midpoint is 5. Others may say the midpoint is the scale average of 5.5 (1 + 10/2). Both answers are incorrect. When satisfaction surveys are given to consumers, neither 5 nor 5.5 is the average. Instead, the average score will normally be about two thirds of the way up the scale. For a 10-point scale, the average score would be around 6.7. This is important, because if the marketing department conducts satisfaction research and finds the average level of satisfaction is 6.7, then the average has been barely met, Scores lower than 6.7 are actually less than the average. To exceed the average, the mean score on the satisfaction measure must be greater than 6.7.

One of the authors of this textbook conducts seminars on customer retention and brand loyalty for a number of businesses, such as JPMorgan Chase bank. During the seminars, he collected data from participants about their levels of satisfaction with purchases of various brands of athletic shoes, computers, pizzas, and automobile insurance. In the survey, each participant was asked to report a level of satisfaction and then to indicate the percentage of their purchases of the indicated brand. The results are shown in Figure 14.8.

Notice that when the level of satisfaction was reported as 10 out of 10, 93.2% of purchases were of that brand, which indicates a high level of customer retention. A score of 9 out of 10 leads to the percentage of purchases becoming 81.6. When the score is 8 out of 10, the percentage of purchases drops to 50.5. Satisfaction scores below 8 lead to significant drops in purchases.

When reported satisfaction scores range from 8.5 to 10, consumers are being retained. In Figure 14.8, this area is labeled as the *zone of affection*. Individuals in the zone have developed emotional attachments to the brand and reported high levels of

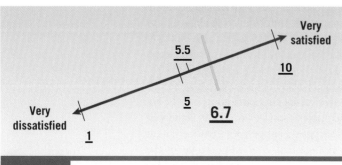

Figure 14.7   Quality Measured on a 10-Point Scale

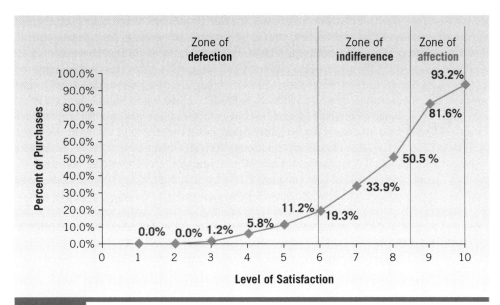

Figure 14.8 Percentage of Purchases and Level of Satisfaction

Note: Product categories measured include athletic shoes, computers, pizza, and auto insurance.

repeat purchases. Typically, this means expectations have been exceeded. The zone of affection reflects a brand or firm that has exceeded the industry standards, or the industry parity level. Customers are pleased and are more likely to express brand loyalty and become advocates.

The area of responses between 6 and 8 represent the *zone of indifference.* When the level of satisfaction reaches the 7 and 8 levels, the customer indicates some loyalty and some retention behavior; however, the consumer could still be tempted to move to a competing brand. These individuals have no strong reason to stay with a brand. Remember, a value of 6.7 is average. A score of 7 is just barely above average. That is why at 7, only about one third of these customers are willing to purchase that brand on future occasions. There may be inertia loyalty present but very little indication of brand loyalty. The reason is that expectations have not been exceeded. The company or brand's performance is no better or only slightly better than other brands, which means that consumers believe brand parity exists.

Any level of satisfaction score under 6 on a 10-point scale reflects the *zone of defection.* Not only was performance below expectations, it was also below industry norms. Therefore, on the next purchase situation, a different brand is likely to be selected.

To get a better picture of the relationship between satisfaction and financial profits, consider the table shown in Table 14.1.[3] A survey of a random sample of 4,000 customers was used to identify overall levels of satisfaction with the company. A 6-point scale from *very dissatisfied* to *very satisfied* was prepared. The company's database and financial records were added to provide the total gross profit for each level of satisfaction. As shown in Table 14.1, the "very satisfied" group made up 25% of the sample but generated 79.9% of the firm's gross profits. These customers generated an average gross profit of $800. The next group, those who indicated they were satisfied, accounted for 36% of the firm's customers and 21.6% of the firm's profit. Those who said they were somewhat satisfied generated only 2.2% of the gross profit but made up 22% of the customers.

The "dissatisfied" group of customers accounts for a total of 17% of the firm's customer base but results in a 3.6%, or $36,400, loss. The more dissatisfied the customer, the greater the loss. The financial analysis regarding this company's customers is similar to that of most companies and most brands. Individuals who are very satisfied generate the greatest percentage of gross profits because they purchase more often and purchase greater amounts. They also cost less to service.[4]

In summary, once a customer has been attracted to the point of making a purchase, the goal shifts to enticing that customer to come back. The ultimate outcome is achieved when

	Average Gross Profit ($)	Percentage of Customers	Total Gross Profit ($)	Percentage of Gross Profit
Very satisfied	800	25	800,000	79.9
Satisfied	150	36	216,000	21.6
Somewhat satisfied	25	22	22,000	2.2
Somewhat dissatisfied	−40	10	−16,000	−1.6
Dissatisfied	−70	5	−14,000	−1.4
Very dissatisfied	−80	2	−6,400	−0.6
Total (4,000 customers)			1,001,600	

Table 14.1   Financial Benefit and Level of Satisfaction

that customer becomes brand loyal. Reaching that point requires the company's marketers to begin the process of building quality relationships by exceeding customer expectations whenever possible.

STOP AND THINK

Re-read the chapter opening vignette regarding JetBlue.

1. What forms of loyalty might apply to customers prior to the snowstorm incident?
2. How would customer loyalty be affected by the delays and problems that occurred during the snowstorm?
3. What loyalty factors was JetBlue's management team seeking to rebuild after the problem occurred?
4. Is there an ethical component to JetBlue's Customer Bill of Rights? If so, what is the ethical issue? Should there be customer bills of rights in other industries?

Maintaining Customer Relationships

The second pillar of customer retention is maintaining quality relationships with customers. Many of the factors that attract customers are the same ones that retain customers. Building quality relationships with customers requires careful interpersonal attention, delivering product and service quality, responding to problems and complaints, and effectively using marketing tools such as advertising and promotional programs.

This section describes additional programs that assist in maintaining customer relationships. Some are better for customer retention than others. The marketing retention programs include cross-selling, frequency or loyalty programs, direct marketing, permission marketing, and customer relationship management programs. Each uses database information and technology to help reach ongoing customers and move them through the stages of retention to loyalty.

Cross-Selling

One method for generating additional revenue from current customers, **cross-selling**, is the attempt to sell a second or an additional product to a customer who has already purchased at least one product. When an insurance salesperson has sold an individual a life insurance policy, at some point the rep may attempt to cross-sell that customer an automobile insurance policy.

Cross-selling can enhance customer retention and help develop higher levels of brand loyalty. Figure 14.9 provides some of the reasons for using cross-selling programs. First, cross-selling may lead to *increased retention* and *increased earnings*. Consider the banking industry. Customers who have only one product with a bank, such as a checking account or home mortgage, only have about a 20% chance of being with that bank 5 years later. The retention rate improves to 80% when the customer has three or more products with the bank. It does not matter which products are used. Banks offer checking accounts, savings accounts, mutual funds, credit cards, home mortgages, automobile loans, and other financial services. The more products a customer has, the greater the attachment he has with the bank. Cross-selling additional products to current customers can help a financial institution generate sales and increase customer retention.

Cross-selling increases the *opportunities to sell additional products*. When a banking customer purchases a second product from the bank, selling the third product becomes even easier. The same holds true for the fourth product, fifth product, and so forth.

Each additional product increases the customer's *switching costs*. Once a customer has multiple products with a bank, it becomes more difficult for him to switch banks, because numerous forms must be filled out, money must be transferred, and so forth. As a result, he becomes less likely to be influenced by competing offers.

Current customers already have relationships with the company. This makes cross-selling additional products easier, especially when a current customer remains satisfied with the first product that was purchased. For customers in that zone of indifference, persuading them to add additional products may move them closer to the zone of affection. It may also move them from no loyalty to inertia loyalty and then to brand loyalty.

The final justification for cross-selling is that *it is easier and cheaper to sell a product to a current customer than it is to a new customer*. Convincing a current bank customer to take advantage of a credit card offer is easier than trying to convince someone who does not have a relationship with the bank.

While cross-selling can be used to increase customer retention, it also can cause customer defections when not handled properly. Trying to sell an additional product to someone in the zone of defection may send that customer to the competitor. This might also happen when the customer is in the zone of indifference. A customer who feels stalked or bombarded with cross-selling offers is probably going to rebel. For example, consider a customer who takes out a home equity loan. If she receives offers for additional products on an almost weekly basis, she may eventually contact a different financial institution. The marketing team should make sure that the cross-selling program does not create a situation in which current customers feel harassed. When a customer turns down an offer, it should be accurately recorded so that additional contacts are not sent out that make the same offer.

Frequency or Loyalty Programs

Frequency or customer loyalty programs help retain customers by giving rewards to those who make additional purchases. The ultimate goal is to obtain 100% of the "share of the customer" in a particular product category. This means that all the customer's purchases of a particular product or products are with one brand or company. An equally important part of frequency and loyalty programs is the gathering of spending patterns and customer profiles. These valuable data assist in developing marketing programs and communication programs and also enhance the frequency program itself.

Before developing a frequency program, marketing managers examine the full-price tag. Frequency programs offer tremendous benefits but can also become costly. The marketing team

- Increases customer retention
- Increases earnings and profits
- Increases opportunities to sell additional products
- Increases switching costs
- Customer already has a relationship with the company
- Easier and cheaper to cross-sell to a current customer than to acquire a new customer

Figure 14.9

Reasons for Cross-Selling

- Recruiting members
- Initial offers
- Administration
- Marketing programs
- Customer offers
- Database management
- Communication

Figure 14.10

Costs Related to a
Frequency Program

must be certain that the benefits and returns from the frequency program exceed the costs. Figure 14.10 summarizes the various costs involved, which range from the initial expenditures associated with launching the program to costs associated with its continued maintenance.

When a frequency program has been designed correctly and administered properly, customers shift from inertia loyalty to brand loyalty. Moving customers requires careful attention to the types of rewards or offers made and the types of communications sent to members. The rewards or offers provided through the frequency program will typically be merchandise, cash, or other items that members will value. Ensuring that this occurs requires collecting data and information from customers, which is then analyzed to determine the best offers to make. Offers vary by customer base. Typically, frequency club programs divide members into segments based on similar purchase behaviors and profiles. Targeted offers can then be made to different loyalty segments. Of course, doing this drives up costs, and as stated earlier, the benefits must outweigh the costs.

Several tactics can make a frequency program more effective. First, frequency programs are offered to all of a firm's customers. Many will not join. Those that do join may not become loyal customers. The idea is to find ways to entice the best customers and use the frequency program as a way to reward them for their loyalty.

Marketing managers for the major airlines realized that they may have made a mistake in launching frequent flyer clubs. The problem was that while almost every traveler joins, most are members of more than one program. In order to reward the best customers, most airline frequency programs now feature different levels. To reach the top level means the customer must fly a minimum number of miles per year. Those who reach this top level receive special rewards that are not available to other frequent flyer members.

To move customers to a higher level of loyalty requires engaging them in the loyalty program. They must see value and benefit in being members and in making additional purchases. This requires staggering premiums and offers. It means offering unique benefits that are not available to other members or other customers. It may be a fashion show for the Gold Members only or an early store opening for members to see new merchandise first before the public does.

Successful frequency programs feature high levels of service. When elite members of a frequency program are recognized for their loyalty and personally thanked by the company, it enhances their emotional engagement with the company and with the brand.

What is the difference
between direct
marketing and
permission marketing?

Direct Marketing and Permission Marketing Programs

Direct marketing and permission marketing programs have already been described in previous chapters of this text. Direct marketing programs can and are used to acquire new customers; however, they also represent an excellent vehicle for increasing customer retention. Direct marketing programs attempt to sell goods or services. They encourage the customer to purchase for the first time (acquisition) and to make repeat purchases (retention). They are somewhat different from frequency or loyalty programs, which are offered to members that join or sign up.

Direct marketing programs succeed when they are used in conjunction with the firm's database or with a commercial database. Instead of mass mailings of direct offers or mass e-mail offers, direct marketing programs feature a target list in which individuals or businesses that are not a good fit for the product being offered have been removed. The better the target list matches the product's target market, the more successful the direct marketing program becomes.

Permission marketing programs are a form of direct marketing. The difference is that in permission marketing, the individual or business has given permission to be contacted with offers. The advantage of permission marketing is in the consent that has been given. It means the individual has some interest in the products the company offers. Consumers and businesses should give true permission and not be tricked into signing up. Permission marketing works the best when the customer truly says, "Yes, I want to receive marketing materials and offers."

Customer Relationship Management

Customer relationship management programs generated a great deal of interest in the 1990s as an information technology tool that could be used to collect and share customer information. The ultimate goal was to increase customer retention. The basic steps of a program are to

- identify the company's customers,
- differentiate customers in terms of needs and overall value to the company,
- efficiently interact with customers, and
- customize interactions with customers.

For successful customer relationship management programs, why is it important to understand how customers interact with a company and how they purchase?

Completing these four steps effectively requires quality database technology, successful methods to interact with customers, and the ability to customize those interactions.

One of the most useful customer relationship management metrics is an RFM analysis. Through analysis of the recency, frequency, and monetary (RFM) coding, customer profiles can be built based on actual customer behavior and interactions.[5] The customization component of the customer relationship management program comes from an analysis of the various RFM segments to see what they actually purchase. This allows the marketing team to accurately understand purchase behaviors in each RFM segment. Then, marketing programs can be developed to enhance the probability that purchases will be made, thereby increasing customer retention.

The interaction component of a customer relationship management program also can be derived from an RFM analysis. Understanding when and how customers interact with the brand provides information on how the company should seek to interact with the customer. An individual who purchases primarily over the Internet and uses e-mail to interact with the company is best suited to e-mail communications. The individuals who purchase exclusively at one of the retailer's stores require personal attention from store associates and personalized offers by mail.

The Spain-based women'secret brand of lingerie used a customer relationship management program to successfully improve customer retention. The goal was to increase brand loyalty by making personalized and customized offers based on each woman's spending profile and to develop a personal relationship with her. The program was launched through a loyalty system called the "Wonderclub," or "Club WOW." The customer relationship program had the capability of warehousing data gathered from different channels, and by analyzing it, the marketing team at women'secret could better understand and manage customer transactions, behavior, and interactions. In the first 4 months of using the system, the women'secret brand tripled the number of subscribers to Club WOW.

Women'secret allows its customers to subscribe to the Club WOW loyalty program without any commitment at all, yet they enjoy all the club's benefits and advantages. Club members can earn "wow money" equivalent to 5% of their purchases, which can be used for future purchases of women'secret products. This encourages the customer to stay with the club and also to make additional purchases. Club members receive an annual "birthday surprise." They also receive discounts and special offers. Club WOW also treats its members to free exclusive concerts, festivals, and trips. The customer relationship management program allows the lingerie brand to launch timely, personalized communications based on customer-triggered events.[6] All this special treatment by women'secret was reinforced by the firm's marketing strategy to improve employee interactions with customers. This overall program was highly successful.

Problems With Customer Relationship Management Programs

Unfortunately, many companies have invested millions of dollars in software, employee training, and implementation programs only to see them fail. Many programs were not successful primarily due to the failure to develop and effectively implement strategies that related to enhancing the customer's experience. The goal of these programs seemed to be to boost sales rather than to enhance relationships.[7]

The Gartner Group, a research and advisory firm, discovered four factors that contributed to customer relationship management program failures. First, some programs were implemented before the company created a solid customer retention strategy. Market segments were not identified, which meant customization programs could not be implemented. The result was a "ready, fire, aim"–type approach rather than a customer engagement approach.

Second, rolling out the programs before changing the organization's climate to match its goals and tactics created problems. Effective programs detail how customers should be treated as well as how goods and services are to be delivered. This means that careful attention must be given to internal communications and to preparing employees to deliver the program.

Third, many programs were technology driven rather than customer driven. Technology should assist in record keeping, identification, customization, and personalization. It becomes the responsibility of employees to understand the customer and develop customized approaches that best meet the needs and personalities of each customer segment for a customer relationship management program to succeed.

Finally, the programs failed when customers felt like they were being "stalked" rather than "wooed." Bombarding customers with materials and products, even if they are personalized and customized, does not build relationships. Instead, customers are made to feel they are only wanted for one reason—to make purchases. As soon as the purchases stopped, the company was no longer interested in them. Effective customer relationship management programs work to woo customers in some fashion. While this can be done through nonpersonal channels, it is best accomplished through some type of human interaction. Relationships are best built through interactions with people, not through interactions with a program.[8]

In summary, there are many ways to maintain relationships with customers. Some methods involve the programs described in this section. The others are much less formal.

STOP AND THINK

When people think of frequency and loyalty programs, they typically think of frequent-flier miles for airlines and frequent-stay programs for hotels.

1. Are there any cross-selling opportunities in the airline and hotel industries? If so, what are they?

2. What are the connections between the direct marketing programs offered by hotel chains and airlines and frequency and loyalty programs?

3. Are the airline travel and hotel industries good candidates for permission marketing programs? Why or why not?

4. Are the hotel and airline industries good candidates for customer relationship management programs? Why or why not?

5. Name other industries that could feature frequency or loyalty programs.

Customer Recovery

The third pillar of customer retention is customer recovery. Even the companies that are most devoted to customer service encounter situations in which customers become frustrated, dissatisfied, angry, and ready to go elsewhere. Good customers are worth recovering. When the lifetime value is considered, losing a good customer can have a significant impact on a company's bottom line. The initial objective is to prevent customers from leaving; however, every firm needs a customer recovery program that seeks to win back good customers who have gone elsewhere. Consequently, customer recovery programs are designed to deal with two circumstances: (1) customer dissatisfaction and (2) customer defections.

Customer Dissatisfaction

A customer dissatisfaction incident represents an opportunity as well as a threat. The threat is that dissatisfied customers do more than move to competitors; they also often engage in negative word-of-mouth communications. Negative communication can quickly spread through social networks and blogs on the Internet. When the customer cannot be recovered, an effective customer recovery program seeks to minimize the damage.

Dealing with customer dissatisfaction involves three steps: (1) diffuse the anger, (2) seek reconciliation, and (3) restore loyalty. Angry customers cannot be reconciled and cannot be restored to any level of loyalty. Therefore, the first step in customer recovery involves *diffusing the customer's anger*. To do so requires acknowledging that the customer has a right to be upset. This does not mean the customer is right. Often the customer is wrong and does not have a valid reason for being upset. Still, the role of the customer service rep is to try to resolve the

> In dealing with dissatisfied customers, why is it important to first diffuse the customer's anger?

issue and return the customer to a level of loyalty equal to or even higher than it was before the problem occurred. Understanding why the customer is upset helps in resolving the issue. It is beneficial for customer service reps to put themselves in the shoes of the customer to understand why she is upset.

A key ingredient in diffusing anger is an *apology*. The customer wants to hear an apology. If the company has made a mistake, then admit it. If not, then apologize for the inconvenience the problem has caused. In addition to acknowledging that the person has a right to be upset and apologizing, it is important to listen carefully to what the customer says and to empathize with his situation.

Once the anger has been diffused, the customer service rep can move toward *reconciliation*. The goal is to arrive at a solution to the problem that is acceptable for the company and agreeable to the customer. The service representative can facilitate this process by asking open-ended questions, such as "What can we do to solve this problem for you?" It is important to solicit the customer's input. Often, a customer agrees to a solution that is less costly than the firm's initial offer. When a customer suggests a solution that is not acceptable to the company, then a negotiation process begins. During this step, the customer service rep should convey the feeling that she is on the customer's side, understands the problem, and wants to resolve it within the parameters of the company's policy but in a way the customer believes is fair.

When the recovery effort involves the company promising to do something, it is critical that the correction is

performed in a timely manner and within the time frame promised. It is better to not make a promise that a situation will be corrected within 24 hours than to make such a promise and then not keep it.

The recovery process should not stop when an agreeable solution has been reached and the issue has been resolved, because the customer's loyalty to the firm has not yet been restored. At that point, the service recovery process is incomplete. The company's contact person should take a further step. He should seek to restore that customer's positive feelings about the company. It is possible for an effective customer recovery effort to produce feelings of loyalty stronger than if the problem had not occurred in the first place.

Restoring loyalty begins with solving the problem as quickly as possible. The longer a problem persists, the more difficult it becomes to restore the customer's emotional loyalty. Whenever possible, provide a value-added solution. Go beyond what the customer asks. If a restaurant manager agrees to not charge a customer for a meal, he can follow up by giving the person a coupon for 50% off of her next meal. The objective is to get her to come back so the restaurant has another opportunity to provide a better level of service. If at all possible, follow up with the customer at a later date. Call her; send an e-mail; or the next time she visits the business, ask how she feels about the way the company resolved the problem.

The ultimate goal, and the opportunity, is to restore the customer's confidence in the business and to retain her by strengthening feelings of loyalty.[9] As shown in Figure 14.11, the probability of a repurchase when the customer is satisfied with how she was treated following a negative incident can be greater than if no incident had occurred.

Figure 14.12 displays the probability of repurchase in the financial services industry and customer recovery. Notice the major differences between customers who are unhappy with the recovery process and those who are satisfied with the recovery. If the problem is not handled properly, there is only about a 17% chance the person will stay with the financial institution. If it is handled well, then the percentage jumps up to almost the same point it was before the problem occurred.

Performance Research Associates conducted interviews with over 1,200 customers who had experienced problems with a service. The purpose of the research was to understand what these customers remembered about their experiences as well as to discover the actions that made them feel good about the service recovery process. In other words, what did the customer service representative do that made a positive impression and led them to feel satisfied with the process? The results are displayed in Figure 14.13.

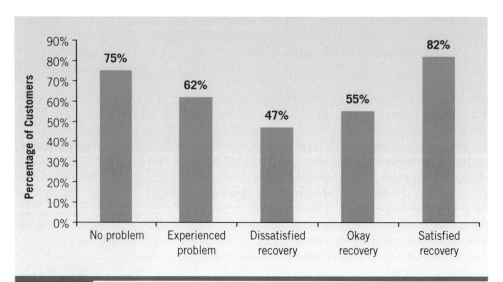

Figure 14.11 Probability of Repurchase and Customer Recovery

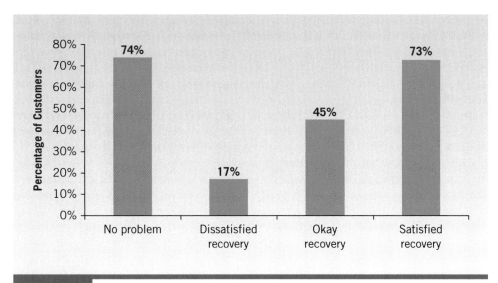

Figure 14.12   Probability of Repurchase and Customer Recovery

- Dealt with me being upset (79%)
- Apologized (69%)
- Not defensive, humble, poised (63%)
- Followed up (57%)
- Solved problem (53%)
- Admitted problem, didn't shift blame (44%)
- Acted on customer's behalf (41%)
- Listened, good communication skills (41%)
- Displayed empathy (38%)

Figure 14.13

Effective Customer Recovery

Customers who responded positively to the manner in which a company handled a problem stated that what they remembered most was how the company's service representative dealt with them. These reps were not defensive but humble and poised as they listened to the complaint. They apologized, and if the company had made a mistake, they admitted it. They did not shift the blame to the customer or to someone else. They displayed quality listening skills, effective communication skills, and showed empathy toward the customer. Note that only 53% of the time was the problem actually solved. How the customers were treated and the efforts made by the employee to resolve the problem were the most important parts of the recovery process. At the same time, note that once a company has failed a customer in a meaningful way, that customer's level of suspicion about the company will be higher. Another service failure will probably lead to a significant drop in loyalty, to the point where the customer will probably not return. The statement "Fool me once, shame on you, fool me twice, shame on me" best explains a second incident with the same customer. Thus, any airline passenger who experiences a second major problem with JetBlue will probably abandon the company.

Customer Defections

Businesses will, over time, lose customers. It is inevitable. Some customers move on, some pass away, and others drift to a competitor's brand. While the marketing department cannot influence the first two, it can influence the last one. The goal, therefore, should be to reduce customer defections, which is often called churn. A key marketing activity is reducing churn.

What happens when customers defect? For many companies, the relationship simply ends. For others, a defection launches a customer recovery effort. Figure 14.14 estimates the percentage increase in the net present cash flow in the lifetime value of customers based on a 5% reduction in churn.[10] In the banking industry, a 5% reduction in customer defections can increase customer value by as much as 85%. For auto service it is only 30%, but a 30% increase in the lifetime value of customers can make a major difference in whether a company enjoys a profit or incurs a loss.

One key to effectively reducing customer churn is brand loyalty. The greater the level of loyalty, the less likely it becomes that a customer will purchase a competing brand. The process of reducing defections begins with customer satisfaction. As Jan Carlson, president of Polaris Marketing Research Inc., notes, "Satisfying is the bare minimum that just keeps you in the game

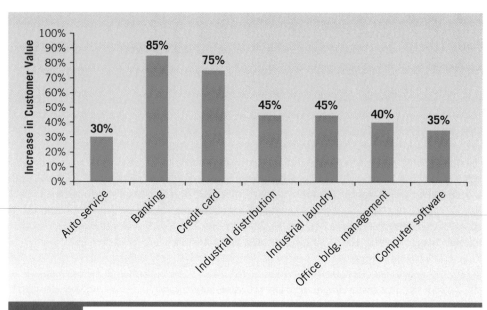

Figure 14.14   Impact of Reducing Churn by 5%

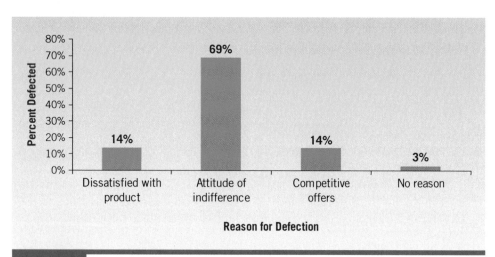

Figure 14.15   Reasons Why Customers Defect

or that allows you to play the game."[11] In other words, reducing defections must go beyond merely satisfying customers; it means exceeding their expectations and outperforming the competition. It also requires developing an emotional engagement with the brand. Otherwise, when purchases are motivated by inertia loyalty and consumers and businesses have not developed strong emotional attachments to the brand, they will leave when a competitor provides a product, price, or promotion that will better suit their needs.

Why do customers defect? The reasons may be surprising. Dissatisfaction with the product is one reason, but it only accounts for about 14% of customer churn (see Figure 14.15). The primary reason is the company's "attitude of indifference." In other words, the customer felt the company did not care about him or his business. Almost 70% of customers who defected said indifference was the reason.[12] When expectations are simply met and not exceeded, there is no compelling reason to purchase that brand in the future. There may be no reason to leave (since they may not be dissatisfied), but there is also no compelling reason to stay. This corresponds to the reason given by individuals for defecting—indifference.

Reducing churn increases profits. Therefore, marketing managers look for tactics to lessen churn. Frequency and loyalty programs, direct marketing, permission marketing, and cross-selling are all effective approaches to enhancing customer retention and reducing defections. Any program that encourages customers to make additional purchases or repeat purchases helps slow churn. The ultimate key to effective churn reduction is developing emotional engagement with customers and moving them to the brand loyalty level by exceeding expectations and developing personal relationships.

To understand the attitudinal component of churn, company leaders can use a variety of research methods. These include focus groups, customer panels, and customer surveys. The marketing team can also survey customers who make infrequent purchases and compare their attitudes toward the brand with those who make regular purchases. It is especially important to survey customers who have left—in essence to have exit interviews with these customers. When one of the authors of this textbook owned a commercial janitorial service, every time a business would call to cancel the service, the owner would make contact with that business. In that contact, the owner would seek out why the business was canceling the contract. That information was extremely valuable in improving the company's performance and in reducing defections by other customers.

Customer recovery programs represent a challenge. It is normally unpleasant to interact with someone who is angry or dissatisfied. Talking to people who have actually changed companies may be uncomfortable. At the same time, it is clear that without this third pillar of customer retention, a company's position in the marketplace becomes more tenuous.

Benefits of Customer Retention

Throughout this chapter, some of the benefits of customer retention have been noted. Figure 14.16 summarizes the primary benefits of customer retention. As shown, over time, customers increase *purchase frequencies* and the *volume of purchases*. Customer retention often results in *cross purchases*. Also as an individual continues using a business, the *cost of service* to the customer is reduced.

Many marketing experts believe that it costs five to six times more to acquire a new customer than to retain a current customer. In business-to-business relationships, transaction costs such as order processing and contract negotiations are lower. The same is true regarding transaction costs in consumer markets. Consider a consumer going to Office Depot to purchase ink for a printer. For that first purchase, the consumer examines several options and may even want to talk to a retail clerk before a purchase is made. For subsequent purchases, the consumer is not likely to need assistance.

Customers retained means fewer new customers are needed to replace the ones that are lost. Businesses that are not growing are dying. The cost of acquiring new customers is much greater than that of retaining current customers. Consequently, reducing customer turnover or defections lowers costs.

Current customers are often interested in other products a company sells. This means that the cost of cross-selling to a current customer is much lower than the cost of selling to a prospect. For a bank, it is much cheaper to cross-sell home equity loans to customers who have a mortgage loan already or even a checking account than it is to convince someone who banks at another facility to take out a home equity loan.

Current customers make additional purchases because they are satisfied with the product's performance and the company's service. This results in fewer warranty claims. It results in fewer service calls and less time spent correcting problems. The main benefit is increased sales, which, when combined with lower costs, contributes significantly to *bottom-line profits*.

Finally, highly satisfied customers become advocates and tell others about the brand or company. These *positive word-of-mouth recommendations* are the best form of advertising a firm can receive. Individuals today routinely use e-mail, blogs, and customer reviews

- Increase in purchase frequency
- Increase in purchase volume
- Increase in cross-purchases
- Positive word-of-mouth communication
- Lower service costs
- Greater profitability

Figure 14.16

Benefits of Customer Retention

to transmit positive word-of-mouth communications. A person can highlight the merits of a particular product to hundreds and even thousands of individuals almost instantly over the Internet.

Implications for Marketing Managers

Customer retention and recovery largely rests with entry-level employees and their supervisors. It is the individual salesperson, the telephone operator, the complaint department employee, the delivery person, and the service technician who meet face-to-face with customers. How the customer perceives those interactions is how the individual is likely to view the company.

Consequently, the marketing manager must use every tool at her disposal to make sure each contact point creates a positive experience. This includes numerous managerial tasks, beginning with setting up job descriptions for the purpose of recruiting that mention the personality characteristics that are most conducive to a customer-first attitude. Then, recruiting and selection processes must be geared to finding the right individuals. Training programs must be oriented to not only show employees that quality customer service is expected but also to demonstrate the methods and techniques that can be used to deliver quality service.

For those on the job, motivational programs and reward systems should honor those who exceed expectations. The climate of the entire organization should be geared to a consumer-centric focus. Communication systems should consistently deliver the same message.

Some view management as a top-down process, in which the CEO sets the tone for the entire organization. To some extent, this is true. Quality customer service is, however, more readily delivered when management also rises from the bottom up. Those who wish to be promoted must sincerely believe that providing quality customer service is the key to a positive performance evaluation that grants access to moving up.

YOURCAREER

Manager Training

One of the more common features offered by companies of any size is the manager training program. For those looking to move up on the fast track, it is important to understand how the company plans to train future managers in order to be able to take advantage of those programs. Most consist of four parts. Preparation for each part improves your odds of being successful.

Setting Goals

The majority of manager training programs include most of the following goals:

Technical skills—in sales positions, this goal focuses on the ability to make sales.

Your response: Become well acquainted with the company's performance evaluation criteria. Keep records of your success stories. Don't be shy about sharing them during performance appraisal sessions.

Managerial skills—candidates are chosen based on the potential to lead and manage.

Your response: Find situations where you can practice leading and managing. In college, these can be in the forms of clubs and sports teams. After college, joining local religious, social, and altruistic organizations and volunteering to lead offers proof that you have experience.

Conceptual skills—there are various methods by which the company may assess your ability to "see the big picture."

Your response: Review college materials related to marketing and selling. Read business journals and books related to the area in which you are employed.

Socialization—most training programs try to resocialize manager trainees to think like managers and not like their peers, who will become subordinates.

Your response: Understand that being promoted often means managing friends. Assume that this may affect these relationships.

Internationalization—many programs are designed to help train an employee for an international assignment.

Your response: Learn a foreign language that is spoken in countries where you would like to be located. Inform management of your interest to take such an assignment, if you have such an interest.

Selecting Candidates

Each company has its own criteria for selection.

Your response: Find out what the criteria are. Your track record is everything. To be chosen, there must be solid evidence that you have both technical and managerial potential.

Selecting Training Methods

Most manager training programs have two components, on-the-job and off-the-job.

On-the-job training includes *incrementally adding more duties* to an employee's job assignment, *rotating* a person to different jobs for exposure and experience, or *laterally promoting* an employee by moving the person or giving a new title or pay raise but keeping the individual at the same rank on the organization chart.

Your response: Find out which type the company uses so that you can mentally prepare for it. Volunteer for internal leadership and managerial roles, such as committee chair, head of a task force, or even leading or making a presentation at the weekly/monthly sales meeting.

Off-the-job training includes outside reading, outside education, and internal education.

Your response: Volunteer for every program the company offers.

Follow-Up

The company's HR department or your supervisor should give you progress reports.

Your response: Show enthusiasm, interest, and the willingness to work on personal weaknesses, while highlighting personal strengths.

Chapter Summary

The three pillars of customer retention are developing customer loyalty, maintaining quality relationships, and creating effective customer recovery programs. First-level employees and their supervisors have an immediate impact on customer retention.

Developing customer loyalty follows the initial purchase of a product. Four forms of loyalty exist. No loyalty means that customers are not emotionally attached to a brand and do not make frequent purchases. Latent loyalty occurs when customers have high levels of attachment but do not often make purchases. Inertial loyalty exists when customers make frequent purchases without any emotional attachment to the brand. Brand loyalty, the desired outcome, takes place when customers make frequent purchases and express attachment.

The factors that generate loyalty include developing quality relationships with customers, exceeding expectations, and continually improving quality. The opposite of brand equity, or loyalty, is brand parity, in which products and services are viewed to be essentially the same.

Loyalty is reflected in the relationships between purchase frequency and levels of satisfaction. In the zone of affection, satisfied customers can be counted on to make repeat purchases. In the zone of indifference, customers may or may not repeat purchases because they are neither satisfied nor dissatisfied. In the zone of defection, dissatisfied customers seek new purchasing alternatives.

Beyond other marketing tactics and activities, several programs may be used to retain customers. These include cross-selling, frequency or loyalty programs, direct marketing, permission marketing, and customer relationship management programs. With each, the use of data and customization helps build bonds with ongoing customers.

Customer recovery includes responding to moments of customer dissatisfaction and to customer defections. Customer dissatisfaction should be resolved by diffusing anger, seeking reconciliation, and restoring loyalty. Customer defections, or churn, require the marketing team to take steps to understand why customers have moved on, in order to respond more effectively in the future.

Customer retention offers many benefits, including increases in purchase frequency and volume and cross-purchases. Also the cost per customer of servicing accounts may be lower, which when combined with the other benefits increases profit potential. Customer retention also creates positive word-of-mouth endorsements by satisfied advocates.

Marketing managers should be involved in recruiting, selecting, and training candidates with customer-first attitudes. Reward programs and communications should emphasize the importance of positive relationships with customers. Promotions should be based, in part, on the individual's willingness to go the extra step and develop positive bonds with the firm's customers.

Chapter Terms

Churn   (p. 383)
Cross-selling   (p. 377)
Frequency or customer loyalty program   (p. 377)

Inertia loyalty   (p. 371)
Latent loyalty   (p. 370)
No loyalty   (p. 370)

Review Questions

1. What are the three pillars of customer retention?

2. Explain the characteristics associated with no loyalty, latent loyalty, inertia loyalty, and brand loyalty using the concepts of emotional attachment and purchase behaviors.

3. Which three factors contribute to greater loyalty and brand equity?

4. Which three factors contribute to perceptions of brand parity?

5. Explain the concepts of the zone of defection, zone of indifference, and zone of affection in terms of levels of customer satisfaction.

6. What is cross-selling? How does it relate to customer retention?

7. What reasons are given for using cross-selling programs?

8. What is a frequency or loyalty program? What costs are associated with developing such a program?

9. What is a customer relationship management program? What are the basic steps of such a program?

10. Why have customer relationship management programs fallen into disfavor with many marketing managers?

11. What are the two main elements of customer recovery?

12. Which three steps are involved in dealing with a dissatisfied customer?

13. Which activities are associated with effective customer recovery?

14. What is churn?

15. What are the primary reasons given for customer defections?

16. Name the primary benefits of an effective customer recovery system.

17. How can marketing managers make sure that customer recovery efforts occur in a company?

CUSTOMER CORNER

Dylan and Hailey Coffman had just returned home after a long day at work. Both were tired, and neither felt like cooking. They called a local pizzeria and ordered their favorite, one that featured ham, Canadian bacon, and pineapple. When the delivery person arrived, they paid him without first looking at the pizza. After he left, they discovered that, for the second time in a month, they did not receive what they had ordered. Dylan angrily called the pizzeria, demanding that they bring him the right pizza. The clerk who took the call replied politely, "I'm sorry, sir, but it is your responsibility to make sure you get the right one before you pay. Otherwise we might end up with customers ordering one thing and then saying they wanted something else all the time." Dylan and Hailey vowed to never order another pizza from the company.

1. Does brand parity exist in the pizza industry?

2. Which customer recovery tactics should the pizzeria have used in this situation?

3. Can you think of ways for the pizzeria to set up a system where orders are more closely tracked so errors do not occur in the first place?

4. Based on the content of this chapter, what can the local pizzeria do to create stronger brand loyalty among customers such as Dylan and Hailey?

What can the delivery person do to ensure a higher level of customer satisfaction?

Discussion and Critical Thinking Questions

1. As a marketing manager, you know that after the first purchase the goal quickly becomes to entice a second purchase in order to move the customer toward brand loyalty. Which marketing tactics do you think are best for encouraging the second, third, and fourth purchases, in the following businesses?
   - Miniature golf course
   - Restaurant
   - Furniture store
   - Insurance agency

2. Many customers are simply creatures of habit (inertia loyalty). What marketing tactics should be used to break a buyer's habit and encourage brand switching? What marketing tactics should be used to move a customer from inertia loyalty to brand loyalty?

3. Explain how the following companies can exceed customer expectations and build brand loyalty:
   - Cell phone service provider
   - Wicks and candles retail shop
   - Locally owned grocery store
   - Bowling alley

4. Ask five individuals to identify recent purchases that were made that led to a zone of defection, zone of indifference, or zone of affection. Are there any common experiences among the five that led them to the same point for each zone?

5. Customer relationship management programs involve customizing and personalizing interactions with customers, especially those with the highest profit potential. Name three industries or companies that are best suited to these programs. Name three that are not suited to the programs. Compare your answers with those of your classmates.

6. Customer satisfaction may be more difficult to detect when the bulk of purchases are made online, through companies such as Amazon.com or Travelocity. Explain how dissatisfied customers can be identified and how the three steps of dealing with dissatisfaction apply to these types of businesses.

7. Garza Uniform Services surveyed 800 customers to determine their levels of satisfaction with the company. After the survey was returned, the marketing manager matched the level of satisfaction with the total gross profit generated by the customers during the last calendar year. Table 14.2 provides this information. The first row of data has been completed. The "very satisfied" category had 178 of the 800 total customers and generated $386,000 in gross profit. This represented 55.1% of the total gross profit, an average of $482.50 per customer. Complete the table by calculating the remaining values for percentage of customers, percentage of gross profit, and average gross profit. When you have completed the analysis, write a report interpreting the results.

	Number of Customers	Percentage of Customers	Total Gross Profit ($)	Percentage of Gross Profit	Average Gross Profit ($)
Very satisfied	178	22.3	386,000	55.1	2,168.54
Satisfied	215		203,609		
Somewhat satisfied	122		85,438		
Neutral	106		46,732		
Somewhat dissatisfied	84		2,132		
Dissatisfied	53		–8,435		
Very dissatisfied	42		–15,476		

Table 14.2   Garza Uniform Services

Note: Survey of 800 customers.

Chapter 14 Case

A Taxing Situation

In the early 1940s, Henry Bloch read a pamphlet in the Harvard Library that described the challenges facing America's small businesses. He imagined a company providing comprehensive services, including collection and management, accounting, temporary workers, and tax management for small businesses. With the $5,000 that he borrowed from his aunt, Henry and his older brother Leon opened United Business Company, providing bookkeeping services from a rented storeroom office on Main Street in Kansas City, Missouri. The business struggled the first year, and Leon returned to law school. Henry kept going. He eventually landed a bookkeeping assignment for a small hamburger stand, and the business took off. Soon after, Henry's brother Richard joined him and quickly became a partner.

The business changed in 1955, when the brothers ran an ad in *The Kansas Star* advertising tax preparation services. A strong response from the public led Henry and Richard to specialize exclusively in income tax preparation. As their business expanded, the brothers began to realize that "Bloch" was difficult for customers to pronounce and spell. In 1955, the brothers incorporated and renamed their business H&R Block, Inc.

In 1956, the company opened six offices in New York and moved on to selling franchise operations in 1958. By 1963, over 1 million tax forms were prepared each year by H&R Block affiliates. The company has expanded to include other financial services and now offers consulting services along with tax services to individuals and businesses.

Marvin Harrison knew the story well. Marvin was about to open a tax preparation office. It would consist of Marvin and three other accountants. The goal was to first work with individual clients on personal income taxes as well as small business accounts. He hoped to duplicate the track record of H&R Block with his own firm.

Marvin knew that major challenges exist in the tax preparation aspect of the industry because the customer service is unique. The potential for service failures, or perceived service failures, is very high. The nature of the tax system is largely responsible for this. At the beginning of each year, companies have one month to mail tax documents, such as W-2 forms, statements of interest earned, and statements of mortgage interest paid, to individual taxpayers. The tax season runs until April 15, with a large number of people waiting until the last day to file.

Time pressure creates some of the service failures. One segment of customers wants their taxes prepared as quickly as possible in order to receive refunds. Another group waits

What challenges did Marvin face in starting his own tax preparation service?

until the last possible minute and then wants their taxes prepared on demand. Customers from either group can easily become upset if they are not served first and fast.

Tensions also result from the nature of the product (having to send money to Uncle Sam), which can easily cause resentment that transfers to the accountant doing the work.

Human errors as well as failures in the use of technology constitute the third potential cause of service failure. Numbers are easily transposed, leading to errors in calculation as well as other problems. Worries about potential audits are another source of anxiety.

In essence, someone in the tax preparation business must first understand the tax laws and codes, the deductions and exemptions, and all the technical aspects of the job, including electronic filing procedures. Then, the employee should be gifted at scheduling, expect to work long hours under time pressure, and understand she will run into more than a few unhappy people.

In Marvin's case, he also knew the fledgling business faced the challenge of the strong H&R Block brand. He had to be highly concerned with word of mouth and customer satisfaction. The company simply could not afford a series of angry clients reporting poor service. He took careful steps in the hiring process to employ only people who were friendly, upbeat, and interested in helping others.

Marvin strongly believed in what he called the four pillars of his business—promptness, courtesy, effort, and professionalism. He knew he could not offer an absolute turnaround time for returns. "We're not in the pizza business," he said. "We can't give a 30-minute guarantee." At the same time, he did think it was important to set up a tracking system to see how long each employee took to finalize a filing. Courtesy was a must. Marvin insisted that his tax preparers address customers using Mr. or Mrs. unless the client insisted otherwise. He told his team that words such as *please, thank you,* and *you're welcome* should be sprinkled liberally into conversations with customers. Effort can be measured, in part, by measuring the number of clients served combined with turnaround time. The figures should be tempered by understanding that some tax forms are much more difficult to complete than others.

Professionalism includes resistance to any attempt at tax fraud. Marvin insisted on the highest ethical standards for himself and for his staff. He gave each employee the full authority to reject a client if the staff member believed that the client was withholding information or behaved in any other suspicious manner.

1. Does brand parity exist in tax preparation services? Defend your answer.

2. How can this new business exceed customer expectations?

3. H&R Block started by offering a variety of accounting services and eventually focusing on just a few. Should Marvin attempt to create cross-selling opportunities for his company? What other services could he offer?

4. Explain how the three pillars of customer retention will be the most important factors in whether the company succeeds.

5. Discuss the concept of brand loyalty as it relates to Marvin's tax preparation service. What about inertia loyalty, latent loyalty, and no brand loyalty? How do these concepts apply to his business?

6. When Marvin finds a dissatisfied customer, what steps should he take to recover the customer, or should he? Since taxes are filed only once a year, is it worth the effort? Why or why not?

 Go to **www.sagepub.com/clow** for additional exercises and study resources. Select **Chapter 14, Customer Retention and Recovery** for chapter-specific activities.

Why is excellent customer service important for Aetna's success?

chapter 15

Marketing Control

Aetna: Making Marketing Controls Work

In 2000, Aetna, a health and medical insurance company, was losing $1 million per day. By 2005, the company had completely turned around and made profits of over $1.4 billion. How could such dramatic results be achieved? Many analysts attribute the success to the efforts and leadership of CEO Jack Rowe.

Aetna's resurgence resulted from Rowe's insistence on four pillars. First, he built the right type of leadership team. Second, the team helped develop a compelling vision for the company. Third, the leaders demanded "operational excellence" from every employee. And fourth, the company returned to its core culture, centered on employee pride.

Rowe understood the difference between managing and leading. He believed that an effective leader must be self-aware and know his or her strengths and weaknesses. To build the right type of leadership team requires enough self-confidence to select people with complementary talents and

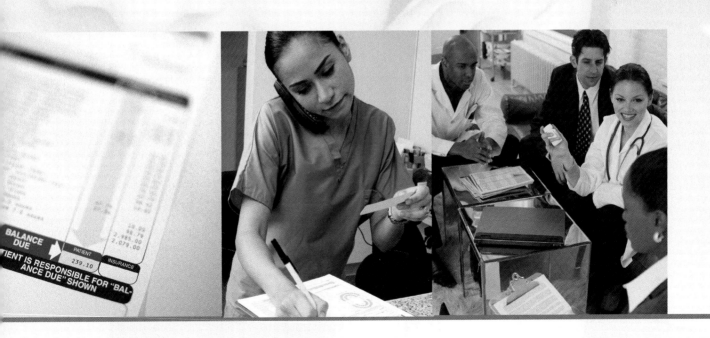

expertise. This, meant making some hard choices, such as removing nearly three fourths of the former staff.

Rowe's goal was to establish a bold vision. The idea was to rebuild Aetna into a sound, profitable company by developing excellent relationships with doctors and hospitals while providing better outcomes for patients. When he joined the company, Aetna suffered from poor relationships with every key constituency. Some doctors and health care providers were so unhappy that they had filed class-action litigation against Aetna and its competitors over billing practices. Aetna's problems with physicians also alienated patients and plan sponsors. A declining client list led to the financial misfortune that demoralized employees.

To rebuild relationships with one key group, the doctors, Rowe went against conventional wisdom and quickly settled the lawsuits over billing practices. He received a great deal of criticism for this attempt to build new bridges, but the tactic clearly worked.

Much of the operational excellence the company sought was related to marketing practices, especially understanding the customer base (markets), prices, and products, and to a renewed effort to deliver high-quality service. The key was for Aetna's

customers to once again believe they were receiving high-quality insurance products delivered with excellent service.

Rowe moved to revive the culture that had flourished earlier in the company's 150-year history. That culture had always been based on pride in Aetna's legacy of integrity and protection of the well-being of millions of Americans. "We helped people feel good about what they did—that they were an important part of the American health care system," Rowe reported.

The return to a core culture relies on constant communication. "A leader can never communicate too much," Rowe stated, "and if I'd done the managerial tasks, I wouldn't have been out communicating." To keep the lines of communication open, he set up "town hall meetings" across the country. He made great efforts to both listen and express his belief in the company's vision.

The net result of these efforts was the *Fortune* magazine "Turnaround of the Year" award in 2006. Jack Rowe has since relinquished the role of CEO, but because he provided a sound structure and sense of direction, the company remains strong with a bright future on the horizon.[1]

Chapter Overview

In management literature, two terms receive a great deal of scrutiny: efficiency and effectiveness. *Efficiency* means conducting an operation with little wasted motion or few wasted resources. In essence, management writers suggest that efficiency is "doing things right." While efficiency may be important in marketing, it cannot succeed without the other concept.

Effectiveness means conducting operations in such a way that the organization succeeds in reaching customers and keeping them. In other words, effectiveness is "doing the right things." The control process in marketing should be designed to assess both efficiency and effectiveness. Only then will the marketing team and its leaders have a quality understanding of the relative degree of success of the company, as well as what to do to make things better in the future.

In Chapter 1, the five functions of management were outlined as planning, organizing, staffing, directing, and control. Of these, planning and control have one very strong linkage: the use of *standards*. Setting standards should be a key ingredient in the planning process. In essence, the management team must specify performance targets. These targets then become the basis of control.

Control may be defined as comparing performance to standards, making corrections when needed, and rewarding success. The control process consists of four steps:

1. Restate the standard
2. Measure performance
3. Compare performance to the standard
4. Make a decision (make corrections or reward success)

Notice that the first step is to restate the standard that was set as part of the planning function. Without quality standards, both of these functions cannot operate.

Marketing control includes assessments of all marketing activities individually and collectively. The same steps apply to the marketing department's managerial controls. Both are based on the standards set in the planning process.

Control should be much more than looking at numbers. Control means carefully analyzing all the factors that have an impact on the success of the organization. Then, control includes making the right kinds of corrections that will lead to success in the future. It is also important to remember that control consists of rewarding accomplishments. Those who reach the standards should see tangible evidence that the company values their efforts.

In this chapter, planning systems as the basis of control are briefly described. Then, controls as they apply to various levels within the organization are noted, with the major focus being on marketing controls. Finally, a review of the types of corrections that are made in the marketing department, at the strategic, tactical, and individual levels is provided.

Planning Systems: The Basis of Control

Planning consists of five major activities, including scanning the external environment, forecasting future events, making decisions about which plans to undertake, carefully crafting or writing the plans, and *setting goals and standards*. Goals and standards are the performance targets that are used in the control process.

When company leaders set standards, two areas deserve particular attention. The first is making sure that quality standards are set. This is accomplished by confirming that forecasting figures are accurate. Also, difficult, attainable, measurable, and clearly stated standards are required.

Second, planning processes should not be tainted by organizational politics. Standards may be affected on the planning side by two main forms of organizational politics. The first, *hedging your bet,* involves systematically underestimating sales in order to look good or so that the standard can be easily met and then the person or department can relax. Effective standards are difficult and attainable, but not easy.

The second political problem has to do with requesting funds for the department. It is not unusual for *over-asking* to take place, which occurs when managers ask for more funding than they actually need. The term *slush fund* describes the extra monies managers hide in order to fund pet projects, spend lavishly on travel and meals, or simply have a cushion. Another method, *horse trading,* refers to trading favors for budget. Once again, the goal becomes to create excess funding for various less than ethical purposes. Company leaders seek to reduce these political activities whenever possible.

When the planning process is complete, two standards will be set for the marketing department, sales department, and public relations department. The first, *expected future sales,* sets performance standards for individual salespeople, products, brands, departments, and the overall company. The second, a *departmental budget,* sets standards regarding the maximum amount of money that can be spent on various activities. The marketing budget for advertising, promotions, events, and other functions clarifies which are the most important and to what degree.

- Company-wide performance (strategic controls)
- Strategic marketing controls
- Brands and product line controls
- Marketing function or department controls
- Individual employee controls (performance measures)

Figure 15.1

Levels of Control

Control Systems

Once a plan has been completed, the standards have been set. In current terminology, many standards are known as **metrics**, which is another term for performance measures. Remember that *metrics serve as the standards that are set during the planning process and that are to be used in the control* process. Control systems are used to monitor these metrics and other company operations in order to make corrections at the levels displayed in Figure 15.1.[2]

Strategic Controls

Strategic controls are those that apply to the CEO and any other manager involved in directing the portfolios of businesses or activities held by a single company or corporation. Typically these standards are beyond the reach of the marketing department. They include corporate profitability figures measured by return on investments, the value of a share of common stock, overall company growth in assets, and similar measures.

Various units of analysis are used to assess the strategic well-being of an organization. **Strategic business units** are clusters of activities, typically held together by a *common thread,* such as a product type or type of customer served. For many years, the 3M Corporation had one division devoted to magnetic tape (audio cassette tape, video cassette tape) and another devoted to adhesive tape (Scotch Tape, packing tape, etc.). A strategic business unit is often assessed as being a "company within the company," or as an autonomous division, responsible for its own performance.

A second, closely related approach is to evaluate the activities of various profit centers. A **profit center** is a business unit or department that is treated as a distinct entity enabling revenues and expenses to be determined so that profitability can be measured.[3] Each profit center manager is responsible for cost control, setting internal prices for items sold to other parts of the organization (known as *transfer prices*), and revenue streams.

Strategic marketing controls revolve around decisions made by the top-level management team and CEO regarding these portfolios of activities. In some companies, the assessment level includes evaluations of operations in various countries or regions of the world. Strategic responses to various conditions are described in the section regarding control corrections.[4]

Strategic Marketing Controls

The highest ranking member of the marketing department is likely to have a title such as Vice President of Marketing and Sales or Director of Marketing. This individual holds the ultimate responsibility for the strategic direction of the marketing department as well as for establishing and evaluating strategic marketing standards. The size of the company and the marketing department dictate the types of controls to be put in place. In a smaller company, sales, marketing, and public relations may all be contained in a single unit. In larger organizations, the three may each be deemed a separate department with its own manager. In any case, at the strategic level, the typical objectives and goals established for the marketing department's planning and control systems are found in the areas of

- market share,
- sales,
- profitability,
- customer satisfaction, and
- corporate and brand image.

Market Share

Market share should be assessed in a number of ways. The first criterion is **company market share**. As shown in Figure 15.2, total industry sales make up the pie and a company's market share is its slice of the pie. For a small company, such as a locally owned dry cleaning store, total sales of dry cleaning in a given area (community or even a neighborhood of a large city) are first estimated, and then an individual company's share can be derived. In this case, the total industry sales in the city where D&S Cleaners operates is $4.3 million. Since D&S Cleaners' sales totaled $655,000, the company's market share is 15.2%.

For a larger organization, determining market share involves a different kind of assessment. PepsiCo, for example, would likely estimate total sales for liquid refreshment beverages and then analyze all Pepsi products within that category to determine the market share for each brand and the company's total market share. PepsiCo also owns Gatorade, Mountain Dew, Tropicana, and Aquafina. As Figure 15.3 shows, these five brands represent 22.6% of the liquid refreshment beverage market, with Pepsi having the largest market share at 10.8%.

The marketing team at Pepsi is also likely to examine **brand market share** of all products that have the name Pepsi on them and then separately assess Mountain Dew products. Mountain Dew products are targeted at a slightly different audience than the Pepsi brand. Consequently, the marketing managers associated with Mountain Dew are likely to investigate the brand's share of the 13- to 24-year-old market for soft drinks.

Finally, Pepsi's marketing team will also assess the **product market share** for individual product categories. Figure 15.4 indicates that carbonated soft drinks account for 52.9% of the total volume of beverages consumed. Bottled water is the second largest product category, with 26.1% of total beverage sales. Sports drinks, such as Gatorade, account for 4.2% of industry sales.

The marketing team will also be interested in knowing if the overall market for soft drinks, bottled water, or sports drinks is growing, stable, or declining. In a growing market, holding market share means the company's sales will rise if they are able to maintain the same level of market share. In a stable or declining market, sales can only be increased by capturing a larger piece of the pie. This means taking share away from a competitor. Also, the entry of a new competitor or the exit of a current competitor may reshape

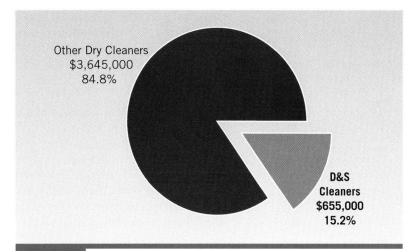

Figure 15.2 | Market Share for D&S Cleaners

Other Dry Cleaners
$3,645,000
84.8%

D&S Cleaners
$655,000
15.2%

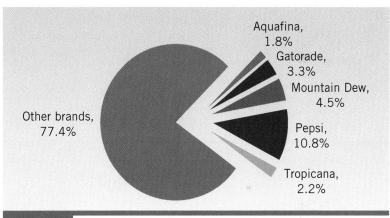

Figure 15.3 | Pepsi's Market Share of Liquid Refreshment Beverages

Aquafina, 1.8%
Gatorade, 3.3%
Mountain Dew, 4.5%
Pepsi, 10.8%
Tropicana, 2.2%
Other brands, 77.4%

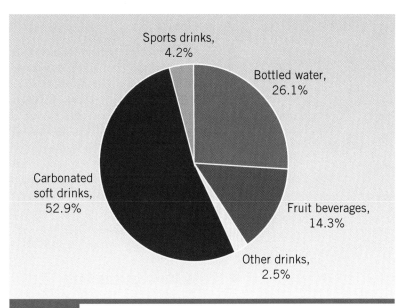

Figure 15.4 | Top Beverage Segments

Sports drinks, 4.2%
Bottled water, 26.1%
Fruit beverages, 14.3%
Other drinks, 2.5%
Carbonated soft drinks, 52.9%

the overall market by either adjusting total industry sales or affecting the market shares of individual brands. Top-level marketing officials investigate all the relevant factors associated with companywide, brand, and individual product market share.

Sales

Sales figures are evaluated using roughly the same levels of analysis as market share. First, *overall sales* constitute a general measure of the well-being of the sales department and the total organization. Overall sales may be examined using dollar figures or product units. For example, an automobile manufacturer such as Hyundai will report total sales in either U.S. or Korean currency, as well as sales in terms of the total number of vehicles sold.

Sales are also tallied by *brand* or *product line*. Thus, a marketing manager for a company such as Levi Strauss examines sales of Dockers as well as Levi's and Signature by Levi Strauss & Co. Hallmark's marketing team studies sales of the Hallmark line as well as the Shoebox line. Kraft sales figures are reported for its lines of cheese as well as for other product lines, including Maxwell House and Planters.

The third level of sales analysis consists of figures for *individual products*. Pepperidge Farm will report figures for Goldfish Crackers and each variety in its Distinctive Cookies line.

Sales figures should be examined in various contexts. First, current sales will be compared with *past sales*. This includes annual sales (2011 vs. 2010) as well as monthly or seasonal sales (March 2011 vs. March 2010; Christmas season 2011 vs. Christmas season 2010) and trends, such as a trend line representing sales over the past 5 years. Sales are also studied in relationship to *competitor sales*. This includes company versus company sales, brand versus brand, and product versus product.

Profitability

Profitability is a criterion that can be applied to the overall organization (strategic control) as well as to particular areas. In marketing, the standard assessments of profitability are made in the following areas:

- Product
- Territory
- Customer
- Segment
- Trade channel
- Order size

Assessments of profitability include figures that reflect the return on investment on various company activities. Two methods that have been described and used in this textbook are (1) the cost of customer acquisition and (2) a break-even analysis or the contribution margin approach.

The *cost of customer acquisition* figures reflect how much was spent on advertising or a specific promotion in order to attract a new customer. The lower the number, the more efficient the marketing program has been. A *break-even analysis* indicates the number of sales that must be made to cover the cost of a marketing program. Each dollar of sales contributes to covering the costs of the program up to the break-even point. Additional sales are then profits.

The marketing manager bears in mind that profits are never the solitary goal for any of these programs. A product early in its life cycle may lose money. The same holds true for a product being introduced into a new territory or being offered to a new market segment. Careful judgments are made regarding profits in light of these and other factors, such as costs, especially during times when costs of raw materials or shipping rise.

Customer Satisfaction

Many marketing departments conduct continual assessments of customer satisfaction. A wide variety of techniques may be used to evaluate this variable. Figure 15.5 lists some of the methods used to study customer satisfaction. Data-capturing techniques make it possible to assess satisfaction levels of high-, medium-, and low-purchase-volume customers.

Marketing managers realize that customer satisfaction should be continually monitored to yield the best information. By tracking customer satisfaction over time, the marketing manager can identify trends and problem areas. The goal of control is to correct, as quickly as possible, any variances that are negative. Declining customer satisfaction demands immediate attention before sales are adversely affected.

Formal methods of studying satisfaction, such as surveys, are extremely valuable, but so are informal, or qualitative, methods such as monitoring blogs, customer-generated reviews, and customer-generated commentaries online. While at times these may be uncomfortable to read, they can be extremely helpful because the comments reflect what customers are saying to other consumers about the company, its products, and its people.

Another facet of customer satisfaction that should be considered is comparative information. Data collected on customer satisfaction can tell a marketing manager what customers think about a company or brand. Comparative data assist the marketing team in understanding how customers view the company in relation to the competition. Consider the following average customer satisfaction scores for Sharp Auto Repair Services:

Customer reactions to the company or purchase experience
- Evaluation cards given during or after a purchase
- Postpurchase follow-up
- Surveys (telephone, online, in-store, mail, mall)
- Blogs and customer-generated reviews

Negative customer responses
- Product returns
- Warranty work on products
- Complaints (in person, mail, online, blogs, reviews)

Positive customer responses
- Repeat purchases
- Complimentary remarks (in person, mail, online, blogs, reviews)

Figure 15.5 | Assessing Customer Satisfaction

Quality of repair: 6.8

Treatment by service personnel: 7.1

Reliability of service: 6.4

Price of service: 7.2

Time for repair: 6.3

A 10-point scale was used in this survey. The marketing manager at Sharp Auto Repair Services may assume that, based on these results, the company is doing well. All scores are above the midpoint. Remember that in most surveys of customer satisfaction, the actual midpoint is about 6.6, as was described in Chapter 14. That means "time for repair" and "reliability of service" are below the average in these responses.

Additional information can help the marketing manager assess the shop's operations, including competitor scores. Table 15.1 compares Sharp with three of its competitors. Of the four companies, Sharp ranks the lowest in quality of repair, reliability of service, price of service,

Satisfaction Criteria	Sharp	Competitors		
		A	B	C
Quality of repair	6.8	7.4	7.2	7.5
Treatment by service personnel	7.1	6.2	6.9	8.1
Reliability of service	6.4	6.8	6.5	8.3
Price of service	7.2	7.5	7.3	7.2
Time of repair	6.3	8.3	7.3	6.4

Table 15.1 | Comparative Customer Satisfaction for Sharp Auto Repair Services

and time of repair. While Sharp ranks second in treatment by service personnel, the company is a full point behind Competitor C. The competitor analysis reveals that when a customer makes a decision regarding where to take her vehicle for a repair, Sharp is considered inferior to three of its competitors.

Corporate and Brand Image

The marketing manager's assessment of the corporate and brand image influences a variety of future decisions. Evaluations of *share of mind* and *share of heart,* as noted in Chapter 2, give the marketing team a sense of a product or the company's position. Understanding a corporation's image requires additional inquiry. To investigate, various forms of consumer research may be employed. These include both primary and secondary sources.

Primary sources include surveys, interviews, and focus groups. The researcher may visit with or survey both customers and non-customers. Also, members of the local community may be contacted by smaller companies. Further primary information may be captured through communications with members of the marketing channel. Manufacturers contact distributors, wholesalers, and retailers. Retailers can also gain information from wholesalers or the manufacturer.

Secondary information is collected from various media. Magazine and newspaper articles, television stories, and comments on Web sites and in Internet chat rooms may yield helpful information about how outsiders perceive the company and its brands. As part of the control process, these questions about image are asked

1. Does this company portray the desired image?
   a. If yes, then what can be done to strengthen and build the image?
   b. If not, what should be done to improve or correct the image?

In summary, the strategic level of control in the marketing department includes the evaluation of the most general features of a marketing program, including market share, sales, profitability, customer satisfaction, and corporate/brand image. The control process must also address other activities and individuals. The next level, in many companies, is analysis of the successes (or failures) of brands and product lines.

Brands and Product Lines

As has been noted, three primary objectives with regard to brands are to build awareness, brand loyalty, and brand equity. When a company only carries a single brand, the goal for the brand is also a companywide goal. Most large firms manage a portfolio of brands, each to be assessed individually. Then, product lines and individual products can be studied.

Brand Awareness

Measuring brand awareness means finding out how many consumers or businesses are aware of a company's products. Creating awareness takes place during the first stage of the purchase decision process. Brand awareness can be built through an advertising program, through both traditional and new promotional efforts, and by activities carried out by the public relations department.

Companies can measure how many individuals are exposed to a marketing message. With regard to advertising, *ratings* of various programs offer a rough idea as to how many viewers potentially saw or heard a commercial. *Circulation figures* provide similar information for newspapers and magazines. *Traffic counts* assess exposures to billboards and other outdoor advertising programs. All these methods measure gross impressions or exposures; but this does not, however, guarantee that the consumer has become aware of the brand.

More reliable measures of exposure may be Internet *Web site hits* that give some indication about how many people visited a site. The *number of visitors to a booth* is an indicator of the success of a lifestyle marketing program, a company-sponsored event, or some other promotional program. Similar measures of awareness can be used for newer approaches, such as buzz marketing programs and guerrilla marketing tactics. Again, these techniques measure exposure, which is necessary for brand awareness to occur.

Brand awareness can be measured directly in a number of ways, including *telephone surveys, mall intercepts,* and *Internet questionnaires.* The marketing team will probably be interested in brand awareness statistics, because awareness creates the foundation for future marketing efforts. Without awareness, moving customers to liking a brand, making purchases, and building loyalty is not possible. In simple terms, a customer will not buy a product if he does not know that the product exists.

Awareness measures also provide evidence regarding the success of an advertising or marketing campaign. For instance, if a series of ads are placed in a magazine with a circulation of 3 million and survey research indicates that only 17% of the magazine's readers are aware of the brand after 3 months of running the ads, then for some reason the ad is not being noticed or is not being processed effectively. A similar analysis can be performed for any type of marketing campaign.

Brand Loyalty

Brand loyalty occurs when the customer has moved beyond awareness to liking and preferring a brand. Loyalty involves an emotional attachment to the brand. It indicates a higher level of success. A loyal customer is one who will, under almost all circumstances, choose a particular brand or company. The primary indicator of brand loyalty is *repeat business* along with positive word-of-mouth recommendations

What are the benefits of customer loyalty?

Two additional measures of loyalty were first described in Chapter 3, lifetime value and RFM (recency, frequency, and monetary value). *Lifetime value* captures the benefits of a customer's repeat business in terms of purchases and provides a monetary indication of the customer's loyalty. RFM indicates how recently the customer last made a purchase, the frequency of purchases, and the monetary value of those purchases. While both of these instruments measure purchase activity, they cannot measure the emotional attachment. As was presented in Chapter 14, in the case of latent loyalty, for example, a customer shows low purchase activity but has a strong emotional attachment to a brand.

Brand loyalty offers additional benefits. The primary advantage is word-of-mouth endorsements to family members, friends, and even individuals the loyal customers do not know. This can be in the form of personal recommendations, but can also occur through blogs, customer reviews, and customer-generated ads and commentaries on the Internet. Discovering that a product or brand has a loyal set of followers means knowing that the potential for attracting new customers is higher. Conversely, when brand loyalty is low, the marketing team realizes that most customers are being influenced by price, promotions, or other factors more than by the brand name.

Brand Equity

The perception that a product or brand is different and better means brand equity exists. The marketing team can collect information about brand equity through various *market research* tools, including *surveys, questionnaires,* and *focus groups.* Both brand loyalty and brand equity figures should be tracked over time, which gives the marketing manager a better sense of how a brand has fared and the direction it

is heading. Several companies provide assessments of brand equity, including Bioinformatics, Landor, and Power Decisions Group. These firms can be located online.

Brand equity takes time to build. It can be reversed by bad publicity, product failures, or other unfortunate events. Consequently, the marketing team works hard to defend and build on the perception that not all products in a class are equal.

In summary, these three brand objectives are primary goals and standards. More favorable numbers for each one represent successful marketing of the brand. When a series of brands is offered by a single company, the analysis requires careful consideration of how the brands interact and support (or hurt) one another.

Evaluating New Products and Brand Extensions

New products and brand extensions have not had time to develop any level of loyalty or brand equity. For brand extensions, there will be carryover effects from other products because of the brand name. When Nabisco offers a new flavor or brand of crackers, there will be a level of brand equity and latent brand loyalty because of the Nabisco name. For new products, in addition to measuring awareness, other beneficial metrics include

- rate of trial,
- repeat purchase rates, and
- cannibalization rate.

The *rate of trial* indicates the success of the marketing launch of the product. The more critical measure is the *repeat purchase rate*. A consumer may be willing to try a product because it is being offered at a 35% discount. The acid test of success is the percentage of consumers who try the product and then purchase it again, at full price. If only 10% repurchase the product, then the marketing manager may become concerned. If the repurchase rate is high, then the product is a success.

For companies with multiple products that produce a line extension, the *cannibalization rate* is an important measure. The cannibalization rate reflects the degree to which this new product affects sales of other products. When Nabisco introduces a new flavor of crackers, Nabisco's marketing team will measure the sales of the new flavor combined with sales of related flavors. If 75% of the sales of the new flavor come from consumers who switch from other Nabisco crackers, then there is a high rate of cannibalization. This does not necessarily mean the new flavor is a failure, but it is a concern.

STOP AND THINK

Campbell's Soups dominate the marketplace of condensed canned soups.

1. Does this mean Campbell's has brand equity or simply a large market share?

2. Campbell's has created brand extensions by adding the Chunky soups, Microwavable soups, Select Harvest soups, and Healthy Request soups. Discuss the addition of all these product forms in terms of potential dilution of brand equity.

3. Could these additional product lines generate a larger soup market, take away sales from competitors, or simply cause cannibalization? What metrics can be used to evaluate these concepts?

4. Compare the previous Campbell's tagline, "Soup is Good Food," to the current motto, "Nourishing people's lives everywhere, every day." What does this say about the company's scope of operations?

Marketing Function or Departmental Controls ───

The five primary functions carried out under the leadership of a director or vice president of marketing are marketing activities, sales activities, advertising and promotional activities, distribution activities, and the public relations function. In larger companies, these may be divided into separate units, and even in midsize companies, the public relations work may be performed by a separate department.

Sales Activities

Control programs account for the effectiveness of the sales force. Some of the figures collected indicate how effectively members of the sales team are doing in terms of actual sales. As noted in Chapter 9, these include assessments of

- input measures,
- output measures, and
- financial measures.

Input measures begin with an analysis of *presales activities,* including amount of time spent in preparation, the number of contacts made, the number of prospects identified, and the number of prospects evaluated. An analysis of *selling activities* assesses the number of sales calls made, the number of sales presentations made, time spent on presentations, prospects contacted, and prospects converted. *Postselling activities* include the number of follow-up contacts made and notes of thanks that are sent to buyers. *Nonselling activities* are assessed in terms of the number of samples distributed, the number of sales meetings attended, and the number of team sales contacts. These metrics are assigned to individual salespeople and may be aggregated to assess the effectiveness of the overall sales force.

Output measures are broken into two categories, accounts and orders. *Accounts* are measured by the number of new accounts, the number of accounts placing orders, the number of active accounts, and the number of lost accounts. *Orders* are evaluated based on the number of orders, the average size of orders, the number of new orders, and the quality of each product sold. Again, these figures reflect success at the individual and departmental level.

Financial measures assess the volume of sales, the gross margin of the sales volume, and the contribution margin of each salesperson.

The manager of the sales force can be evaluated based on the *turnover rate* of the sales staff. Too many individuals quitting or a large number of terminations indicate that the right people are not getting the job or that the sales force is not properly motivated, prepared, or compensated. Also, *sales force expenditures* indicate whether the sales manager is properly overseeing the use of company resources.

Advertising and Promotional Activities

Advertising and promotions represent areas in which funds are spent, and at times, it is difficult to determine whether the monies have been spent wisely. Company leaders still want to have some

How can company managers evaluate salespeople?

Advertising to Sales Ratios		Revenue Per Ad Dollar	
Amusement parks (%)	8.4	Yum! Brands ($)	20.30
Beverages (%)	7.8	Burger King ($)	17.00
Fast foods (%)	6.9	Wendy's ($)	16.60
Perfume and cosmetics (%)	8.9	McDonald's ($)	15.40
Women's clothing (%)	3.4		

Table 15.2 Advertising and Promotional Expenditures

idea about the effectiveness of advertising and promotional activities. Some of the metrics used to evaluate these efforts include

- advertising and/or promotional cost measures,
- psychological responses, and
- behavioral responses.

Advertising and promotional costs may be evaluated in a number of ways. The two most common are percentage of sales and revenue per ad dollar. To calculate the *percentage of sales,* consider a fast-food chain that spends $1.8 million on advertising and promotional activities and generates $28 million in revenues. The advertising and promotions expenditures represent 6.4% of the company's revenues. This number is useful because it can be compared with the industry average and against specific competitors. Table 15.2 shows that the average advertising-to-sales ratio for fast-food establishments is 6.9%. This particular fast-food chain is spending slightly less than the industry average.

To calculate the *revenue-per-ad-dollar* ratio, the process is reversed. Sales totals are divided by the advertising dollars. The results indicate the amount of revenue that was generated by each $1.00 spent for advertising and promotions. When this calculation is made, the outcome suggests that the fast-food chain is generating $15.56 for each dollar. This number is valuable because it is a measure of advertising's effectiveness. The right side of Table 15.2 displays four fast-food restaurants in terms of revenue per ad dollar. Yum! Brands, which operates KFC, Pizza Hut, Taco Bell, A&W, and Long John Silver's, is the industry leader, generating $20.30 in revenue for every $1 spent in advertising. A revenue-per-dollar value of $15.56 would place a chain behind Wendy's and ahead of McDonald's in advertising effectiveness.

Psychological responses to advertising programs are evaluated using tools and research methods specific to the field. They include evaluations of consumer *recognition* and *recall* of advertisements, degrees of *persuasion, emotional responses,* and *liking.* These reactions are evaluated by individual campaigns as well as over time.

Behavioral responses to advertisements and promotional efforts are more tangible. They include increases in *sales,* the number of new *inquiries,* increases in *store traffic,* the number of *coupons redeemed, entries* into contests or sweepstakes, *premiums redeemed,* increases in *order size,* the number of *bonus offers accepted,* and *visits* to a booth or display.

Behavioral responses consist of observable reactions to promotions and advertisements; psychological responses are more difficult to measure because they are not tangible. Psychological responses may take longer to develop in customers. Still, both types of response should be considered as part of the evaluation, along with any other calculations of effectiveness.

Distribution Activities

Distribution channels may be evaluated at the strategic level as well as at the department level. The terms efficiency and effectiveness both apply to the assessment of distribution activities. At the functional level, the standard measures of distribution effectiveness include

How does a retailer evaluate the distribution channel that delivers products to be stocked on store shelves?

- average delivery time,
- percentage of stores carrying a product (vs. target),
- month of inventory in dealer's possession, and
- distribution cost per unit.

It isn't just pizza companies that seek a quick *delivery time,* although they may be the most famous for keeping such standards. A quick and courteous delivery can go a long way toward developing positive relationships with a customer. Many Sears retail stores have systems in which sales are made in the store and then the customer is directed to a pickup window at another location. The windows feature displays indicating the percentage of times items were delivered to the customer's car within 5 minutes. Also, the employee who will bring the item out of the warehouse and to the customer is named on the posting, along with a running clock that states how much time has passed since the customer requested delivery.

The *percentage of stores carrying a product* reflects on both the sales force and the distribution team. One sure way a manufacturer can lose a retail store is to feature slow, inaccurate deliveries. It does not take long for the retailer to find a replacement item for the available shelf space.

The *months of inventory carried by the retailer* notes the volume of purchases. It also suggests a reduction of risk for the manufacturer. Any merchandise held by the retailer has been paid for and is inventory the manufacturer does not have to store, which reduces carrying costs.

Distribution costs per unit represent the costs of paperwork and storage, as well as carrying charges and transportation costs. It is calculated by dividing the total annual distribution expenses by the total number of units sold, which yields a cost-per-unit figure. Distribution costs represent an efficiency issue. When the cost per unit is combined with average delivery time, both time and money have been evaluated for the distribution function.

Public Relations Activities

The public relations department is assigned the tasks of promoting positive, image-building events and of limiting the effects of negative, image-damaging situations. The standard tools used to evaluate public relations begin with noting the number of hits a company receives in the media. A *hit* is the mention of a company or its employees in a news story or public service announcement. Additional tools of analysis include

- counting clippings,
- calculating impressions, and
- calculating advertising equivalence.

Counting clippings means counting the number of hits in a given time period, typically in terms of a month, a season, or an annual total. Presumably, the larger the number, the better. *Calculating impressions* requires the manager to estimate the total audience that saw a hit. If a newspaper has a circulation of 40,000 copies with an average of two readers per copy, a hit would create 80,000 impressions. A radio station that runs a public service announcement featuring the company's name with an average listenership of 20,000 adds that many more impressions.

Advertising equivalence estimates the cost of buying a hit on any given medium. A newspaper hit that covers 4 column inches in the paper would generate the equivalent of a 4-column-inch advertisement. A 10-second hit on a television newscast would be evaluated at the rate of a 10-second television commercial.

The public relations team should also be evaluated in light of the number of favorable and unfavorable mentions. Bad publicity may not hurt a high-profile entertainer or personality, but it can be devastating to a business organization.

Individual Controls (Performance Appraisal) ———————

Performance appraisals are used to evaluate individual employees with many goals in mind. The first, naturally, is to gather information on how well each person is doing on a given job. Second, the system often will be used to make decisions regarding which individuals are qualified to receive promotions. Third, performance appraisals are often linked to the pay system and affect decisions about pay raises. Consequently, the most important features of a performance appraisal program are

- perceptions of relevance,
- perceptions of fairness, and
- perception that rewards are tied to performance.

Perceptions of relevance fall into two categories. The first, believing that the top management team "buys in" and considers performance appraisal to be an important process and not just a procedural matter, can only be communicated by those of higher rank. The second is the belief that high marks on a performance appraisal will lead to a promotion, pay increases, and other organizational benefits.

Perceptions of fairness emerge from confidence that the system does not play favorites based on seniority, nepotism, or internal politics. Each employee should believe that the company seeks to reduce manipulation of results and minimizes undue influence from those who simply want to have their friends receive the best evaluations.

The *perception that rewards are tied to performance* may be the most critical element. When employees believe that high marks on an evaluation lead to pay raises, bonuses, and other perks, they also will believe that the company values their efforts. When they do not, the system probably does little to influence organizational outcomes.

One of the more popular methods for setting standards and assessing performance at the individual level is **management by objectives**, which is a participative goal-setting program. The program requires each individual to prepare a personal list of goals each year, in conjunction with a supervisor. Then, the employee will be evaluated based on the attainment of those goals. Management by objectives programs require several characteristics in order to be successfully operated. The same characteristics apply to many other aspects of planning and control. They include the concepts displayed in Figure 15.6.

As was just noted, *top management emphasis* makes the system seem more important in the eyes of individual workers. Employees are "signal readers." When top management stresses that an activity is important, the activity receives attention. When top management ignores a process, workers are likely to follow suit.

All planning and control systems should be *systematic*. They should be built into the calendar. Every employee, from the CEO to the janitor, should know when plans are made and standards are set. They should also know when their performance will be evaluated.

Quality standards must be set at every level. Management experts emphasize the following characteristics of quality standards:

- Difficult
- Attainable
- Clearly stated
- Measurable
- Flexible

These concepts apply equally well to standards set by top managers, functional leaders, and department heads.

Management by objectives programs gain value when employees can somehow *link individual goals with company goals*. For example, learning a foreign language makes an employee more valuable to the organization. When a person succeeds in reaching such an individual goal, the outcome should also affect organizational outcomes, such as being considered for a promotion or an international assignment.

Performance appraisal systems are more than just control systems. They are lines of communication that can be devoted to helping employees succeed and enhance their individual careers. They also determine employee behaviors and influence how employees view and treat customers.

- Top management emphasis
- Systematic approach
- Ability to reward performance
- Quality standards
- Personal objectives linked to company objectives

Figure 15.6

Characteristics of Effective Control Systems and Management by Objectives Programs

Types of Corrections

When the first three steps of the control process are complete, the standards have been set, performance has been measured, and a comparison has been made between the established standard and actual performance, the final step of control is to either reward success or make corrections. Corrections take place at strategic, tactical, and individual levels.

Strategic Corrections

Strategic management at the top level of the company will focus on either a resource-based approach to strategic direction or a competitive approach. The resource-based approach focuses on the organization's **core competence**, which is the most proficiently performed internal activity that is central to the firm's strategy and competitiveness. Core competencies are based on knowledge and people, not on capital and assets. In this approach to strategic management, the goal becomes to develop a **distinctive competence**, which is something a company performs at

How can this retail store in the French Quarter in New Orleans be differentiated from others?

a level that is better than all rivals. In marketing terms, this equates to *brand equity* because it creates competitive superiority.[5]

The second perspective regarding strategic management is the choice of one of the four generic competitive strategies found in the marketplace. These are overall guidelines for the entire organization.

Low-cost provider strategy—seeking to achieve the lowest overall costs as compared with competitors and therefore being able to compete with price

Broad differentiation strategy—seeking to make the organization's products unique when compared with competitors' products, therefore being able to compete based on those differences

Best-cost provider strategy—giving customers the most value for their money, combining some uniqueness with lower costs and lower prices

Focused (market niche) strategy—concentrating on a market segment and outcompeting rivals based on price or some form of differentiation

In marketing terms, differentiation is the attempt to make goods and services that are different and better, which matches the concept of building *brand equity*. Low-cost provider strategies are designed to compete with price, which assumes *brand parity* exists. The hybrid of these methods would be the best-cost provider strategy, which is employed by numerous companies seeking to be both distinctive and price competitive.[6]

In terms of control systems, the CEO and top management team's responsibilities to the organization are to create the correct strategic responses to various company and environment circumstances. The core decision will be whether to pursue a rapid-growth strategy, a slow-growth strategy, a strategy of remaining stable, or a decline strategy.

Rapid-Growth Strategies

Rapid-growth strategies are pursued when the top management team identifies an opportunity. Rapid-growth strategies include *mergers, acquisitions,* and *takeovers* of other companies. A second strategy, *vertical integration,* means taking over a new aspect of the marketing channel, such as when a manufacturer either sets up its own distribution systems or opens its own retail outlets. Another approach, *horizontal integration,* widens relationships with distributors with the goal of increasing market share and/or controlling the channel of distribution. Another form of rapid growth takes place through cooperative agreements between firms to mutually market products or to create *joint venture* arrangements. *Globalization* is another alternative for rapid growth.

Slow-Growth Strategies

When a company's environment and internal circumstances indicate that rapid growth is not advisable, the top management team often chooses a slow-growth approach. Two of the most common approaches are incremental growth and efficiency or profitability strategies. *Incremental growth* involves the firm seeking either to add more customers in existing markets or to gradually expand into new markets. *Efficiency strategies* seek to build profits by eliminating waste or finding new ways to do things that take less time or use fewer resources.

Stability Strategies

When companies operate in mature, highly competitive markets, top management may select a stability approach that is designed to maintain the status quo. This approach may involve *long-term contracts* with suppliers and/or retail outlets to ensure the continuing relationships between various companies. It may seek to develop strong *relationships with customers,* and even use contracts to ensure stability. Stability strategies also include *refinancing company debt* to take advantage of favorable interest rates, *repurchasing stock* to ensure ownership without the possibility of hostile takeovers, and *retiring debt* to open credit lines for the future.

Decline Strategies

When the control system indicates major threats to a firm's well-being, the strategic response will be to find ways to keep the organization functioning. Strategies for decline include divestments, liquidation, and a series of efforts known as retrenchment programs. In general, these responses are designed to raise cash or capital for the company and to cut costs or programs that operate at a loss.

A *divestment* means that an organization sells off part of the company. A divestment yields cash for the selling company. The part that is sold is viewed by the purchasing company as an opportunity to expand or to take a failing enterprise and turn it around.

When *liquidation* takes place, the company stops an operation and sells off the component parts. Many times, liquidation is used when the company's management team is unable to complete a divestment deal. For example, BFGoodrich had decided to divest a tire-manufacturing operation in Miami, Oklahoma. Several deals were nearly completed, but at the eleventh hour each one fell through. Finally, company leaders decided it was best to close the plant; sell the building, equipment, delivery trucks, and other assets; and simply move on.

Retrenchment or turnaround programs have one common denominator: the objective of becoming smaller but stronger. This can be accomplished by

- reducing outlets,
- reducing the number of products and services,
- eliminating entire markets, and
- eliminating employees.

Many firms have survived and eventually thrived by first cutting back locations and/or markets. The hamburger chain White Castle is one example; the retailer Kmart is another. In 2008, Starbucks adopted the same strategy. By concentrating efforts on the most profitable units and cutting those that are not doing well, the firm gears up for future growth.

Possibly one of the more famous examples of retrenchment by reducing products occurred when Chrysler cut nearly 500 products from its lines as part of a major reorganization in the 1980s. The goal was to only sell items the company had expertise with and some type of technological or market advantage. Poor-performing products or services often distract managers and employees with little return. Eliminating them solves this problem and helps workers concentrate on the items that give the organization the best chance for success.

Eliminating employees is known as *downsizing*. The impact on morale will be negative. At the same time, it may be the only recourse available to a company.

In summary, strategic plans are made as the result of a careful analysis of the environment combined with an examination of the company's current situation. Strategic controls are designed to provide the types of information that will guide these decisions as the organization moves forward.

Tactical Corrections

Strategic responses are the most dramatic and sweeping types of corrections made in control systems. They are normally accompanied by various tactical responses. Tactical corrections may be developed by brand, by product, and by function.

Product Line Tactics

One of the marketing team's constant concerns is making sure that the firm's products have an optimal impact on the market. Tastes change over time and product lines are adjusted to meet the newest needs. In men's fashion, henley shirts were quite popular for a series of years. More recently, however, this fashion trend has waned and casual shirts are more likely to be polo or golf shirts. In washing machines, front-loading machines have captured a significant market share because they are more energy efficient. Musical recordings were made on vinyl albums for many years but moved first to cassette tapes and then to CD and MP3 formats. Some artists have begun to move back to vinyl, expressing the belief that the sound is "warmer" or "richer." Product line adjustments are made in two ways:

1. Cutting or adding depth to a product line

2. Cutting or adding breadth to product lines (brand extensions or deletions)

Adding *depth* to a product line means creating supplementary products within the line. A simple example would be adding a new flavor to the Kool-Aid line of products, either in the unsweetened or sweetened package lines. Cutting depth would be reducing the number of products in a line.

Adding *breadth* to product lines is the process of creating a new line or set of lines. When Nabisco added a line of low-sodium crackers, greater breadth was created. Cutting breadth would be the elimination of a line, as when General Motors stopped producing cars with the Oldsmobile, Pontiac, and HUMMER brands.

A third brand tactic is brand repositioning. This tactic may take more time. It involves creating a new perception of the brand in the mind of the typical consumer. Brand repositioning often requires product improvements, improvements in customer service, additional advertising and promotion, and employee retraining.

Product-Based Tactics

There are times when tactical responses are aimed at a single product rather than a line of products. Many product-based tactics result from changes in the marketplace. In the insurance industry, standard whole life insurance policies dominated sales for many years. Then, many firms began to focus on term life insurance. Currently, insurance policies are often hybrids designed to achieve more than one personal goal. Instead of simple protection against financial hardship due to death, life insurance packages now may be used to build wealth by saving for the future, to protect the family in case of death, and in some instances to provide relief from income tax.

Many product-based tactics occur when an item seems to be near the end of its life cycle. Several approaches have been identified as tactics to extend a product's life cycle. These same tactics may, however, be used to strengthen sales of a product in any stage of the cycle. They include

What type of product line tactics can be used by Sony and other manufacturers of MP3 players and radios?

- finding new users,
- finding new uses for the product, and
- encouraging more frequent uses.

Finding new users means identifying new target markets for the product. When the classic Pong game began to lose popularity, the video game market was expanded by the development of new games for adults to play. Market research and focus groups may help to identify potential new users. In recent years, many products that were only targeted to women, in the areas of hair care, skin care, and even nails, are now also marketed to men.

Finding new uses for the product may be difficult, but this does happen. Over the years, the product ARM & HAMMER Baking Soda has been promoted as an odor killer to be used in the refrigerator, in pet boxes, in carpet cleaning products, and also in toothpaste. Hydrogen peroxide not only kills germs, it also lightens hair and now is considered to be a whitening agent in toothpaste. Avon's Skin So Soft has been extended into a line of insect repellants.

Encouraging more frequent uses comes from finding new times and places for a product to be consumed. Orange juice marketers attempted this approach with the classic "It's not just for breakfast anymore" tagline. Southwest Airlines' "Wanna get away?" promotions encourage flying more often.

Perhaps the most common product-based tactic is to offer some new feature. The *new and improved* approach can be marketed through advertising, changes in the package, or promotional tactics such as coupons for the new version, free samples, and so forth. The laundry detergent market has shifted to more concentrated forms featuring smaller packages. Many restaurants now offer heart-smart variations of foods to be served. Product improvements create the opportunity for the marketing team to creatively reintroduce the item to the public.

Functional Tactics

Additional tactics are created in the marketing functions, such as advertising, promotions, and selling. *Advertising tactics* revolve around creating a new theme, tagline, or some other new approach, such as shifting advertising dollars to new media. In the past decade, many firms have begun to allocate more dollars to Internet advertising and alternative media and fewer funds to the more traditional outlets.

Promotional tactics include adjustments to the types of promotions offered to consumers, businesses, and channel members. In hard economic times, coupons, bonus packs, and price-offs may be emphasized for customers seeking to cut back but remain brand loyal. When shipping costs rise due to increasing fuel costs, business-to-business customers may be enticed by free or discounted shipping offers. Trade promotions may have to be increased to provide channel members with greater incentives to stock and push a product.

Personal selling tactics will require changes when a company's strategic direction changes, or when control systems indicate that the current sales approach is not working. Instead of emphasizing price, the sales force may move to a greater emphasis on quality, delivery, or some other aspect of the purchase decision. As illustrated in Chapter 9, a change in the ways salespeople are compensated may also alter the sales approach used.

Distribution tactics accompany other marketing efforts. The goal is to make sure that products are being delivered efficiently to the end user. As various markets change, the delivery system tactics can be altered to fit them. Two of the most common delivery system tactical responses are (1) to change channel arrangements and (2) to change the actual channel used.

Channel arrangements can be altered by creating new distribution systems or finding new distributors. New distributors may be identified when the marketing team is dissatisfied with current distributors. *Changing the channel* most often involves creating a direct marketing program, normally through a Web site. Direct marketing may be used to accompany other methods of distribution. Channels are also changed when firms undertake vertical integration strategies.

Individual Rewards and Corrections

When considering individual corrections, the first thing to remember is that individuals are evaluated at every level of the organization. Performance appraisals apply to entry-level workers, first-line supervisors, middle managers, top management, and the CEO. As was noted, the fourth step of control is to make a decision. The decision involves either (1) rewarding or (2) correcting. Corrections are made at every level and include all the potential courses of action noted in this chapter. Rewards are granted to individuals. Before describing corrections, rewards should be considered.

Rewards for Performance

When an individual has met or exceeded performance expectations, rewards should follow. The forms rewards take vary by level. The common denominator is that rewards serve as motivation for the future. At the *top management and CEO level,* rewards often include

- stock options or percentage of ownership plans,
- bonuses,
- major company perks such as homes or cars or vacation resort stays, and
- a longer-term contract or contract extension.

Middle managers and *first-line supervisors* receive more modest rewards. Some of the more common include

- stock purchase plans,
- use of a company car,
- pay raises,
- bonuses,
- permanent personal parking space, and
- consideration for further promotion.

Individual employees also should be rewarded. Among the rewards granted to these employees are

- pay raises,
- bonuses,
- increased vacation time,

What makes individual rewards important for employees such as Abby?

- preference in choosing a vacation time period (e.g., over Christmas or spring break),
- more desirable hours (not having to work on weekends; day shift instead of the second or third shift),
- consideration for promotion,
- a personal parking space for a period of time (often 1 month), and
- a plaque for employee of the month.

Information regarding the performance appraisal results will be filed with the individual's records in the human resources department. Over time, this creates a track record of the employee's career. This information can then be used in the future.

Individual Corrections

Individual corrections are made at the level in which performance is being evaluated. For *top managers and the CEO,* corrections may include retraining, reassignment, or, in an extreme case, termination or demotion. The same would be true for *middle managers.*

At the *first level of supervision* and for *individual employees,* corrections include additional training, mentoring, coaching, or counseling, exposure to role models, providing new incentives, setting more concise goals, and at times using the discipline system when rules have been violated. Termination is the final resort for an unsuccessful employee.

As has been noted throughout this textbook, part of the reward system should be geared to how well the individual, no matter what the rank, provides quality customer service. When the employee makes a concerted effort in this area, rewards should follow. When the employee is deficient, corrections are in order.

Implications for Marketing Managers

At the first level of supervision, two problems often accompany the control system. The first is *overemphasizing the short term*. Quotas and deadlines take on exaggerated meaning, and the temptation is to overwork and press employees to hit short-term targets at the expense of long-term results. For example, a sales manager who knows that the department will not reach its annual sales standard may encourage salespeople to push too hard with clients, getting sales but losing trust and damaging the company's image and long-term relationships with customers.

The second potential problem is *overemphasis on a single number* rather than all the results of an evaluation. For example, in advertising, overemphasizing the increase of sales following an advertising campaign may neglect the fact that the brand loyalty was built or that other factors, such as the season of the year, may have had an impact. The same holds true for supervising salespeople and only noting sales quotas while ignoring paperwork, returning calls, handling returns and complaints, and other crucial activities. The supervisor's responsibility is to see the forest, not just a tree.

At a more general level, but also including first-line supervisors, several characteristics help to ensure that a control system is successful. These include

- seeing the big picture,
- encouraging participation,
- using the system for diagnosis,
- remaining flexible for changing circumstances, and
- staying future oriented.

As just noted, managers of all levels should think of control as a means to guide the entire organization and to make sure that all the component parts are working together efficiently and effectively. This means *seeing the big picture* rather than getting lost in the details.

Participation should be encouraged in both planning and control operations. When employees help set standards, they are more committed to reaching them. When employees help to measure performance, they see the system as being fairer. Participation creates a "buy-in." Better relationships between supervisors and employees become possible.

An effective control system is one that is used to *diagnose problems* rather than lead to punishments. When employees trust that the system will help them improve their efforts, they do not fear it. Instead, they will view control as a tool to help them succeed.

Remaining *flexible* allows the manager to say that standards are not carved in stone. If circumstances change, the best course of action is to first set new, realistic standards based on a changing environment. This becomes the best rationale for developing both plans and contingent plans. Preparedness should be part of any planning and control system.

The final challenge is to always stay *focused on the future*. Looking back, placing blame, and offering excuses are easy and inviting traps. They do not help the individual or the company. Successful marketing requires being future oriented at all times. The past can be a teacher, but planning for the future is the key.

YOURCAREER

Marketing Yourself

In any type of job search, one of the keys to success is taking advantage of the one item you can control the most—yourself. Some of the ways to effectively market yourself include the following.

Goal Setting

Many students, especially college seniors, tend to use a "buckshot" type of approach to finding the first job. Sending out large batches of resumes to anyone and everyone dilutes your time. First, write down the most important features that first job would have. Brainstorm, and then carefully consider the list. Then, devote the greatest amount of effort to the companies that offer the types of positions that are the best personal fit.

Preparation, Part A: The Résumé

Take the time to consult with an expert on the preparation of a résumé and cover letter. Don't assume you know what is best. The more trained eyes that see the résumé before it is sent out, the better the odds you will find any flaws or mistakes.

Preparation, Part B: Personal Appearance

Dress professionally. If you are not used to wearing a suit or dress clothing, practice. Looking awkward in professional attire does not present a good impression. Consider how important it is to make a fashion statement with the other aspects of your appearance. If that earring or piercing matters, make sure you are applying to the types of companies that would not object.

Preparation, Part C: Research

Before making personal contact with an employer, take the time to learn as much as you can about the firm. You should be able to present two items at a minimum: (1) that you have some knowledge of the nature of the company and (2) that you can demonstrate how your skills and talents fit with and meet the needs of that specific company.

Practice

Sometimes, the first interview offer you will receive is not with a company that is an ideal fit. Go to the interview anyway. Any time or place in which you can practice interviewing skills is helpful. It may be worthwhile to conduct a practice interview with someone taping or making a digital image. This may help with fidgeting, clearing your throat, saying "ah" or "um," and other distracting habits. Bear in mind that a job interview is quite similar to a sales call. The only difference is that the product/service you have to offer is your training, skills, and the interpersonal skills you display during presentations.

Perseverance

As this textbook is being written, the nation's economy is sagging. This means it may take more time than ever to obtain a position. Do everything you can to burnish your confidence. Keeping your head up and believing in yourself may give you just the edge needed to make the best impression.

Chapter Summary

A control system should be designed to assess levels of both efficiency and effectiveness of a company's operations. Control consists of comparing performance to standards, making corrections as needed, and rewarding success. Standards are the key ingredients in both planning and control systems.

Setting quality standards means eliminating or reducing organizational politics. When a manager hedges his bet, the standard is being set artificially low to make it easier to achieve the desired results. Over-asking and horse trading are designed to generate slush funds for a given manager's department.

Control systems use metrics across various activities. The levels of control include strategic control, strategic marketing controls, brand and product line controls, marketing function or department controls, and individual employee controls through performance appraisal. Strategic controls are those that apply to the CEO and the top management team.

Strategic marketing controls set standards or metrics and then assess performance in the areas of market share, sales, profitability, customer satisfaction, and corporate and brand image. Brands are evaluated using the concepts of brand awareness, brand loyalty, and brand equity. New products are assessed by examining rates of trial, repeat purchase rates, and cannibalization rates.

The marketing functions that are part of the control systems feature marketing activities, sales activities, advertising and promotional activities, and distribution activities. Individual controls must reach the standards of perceptions of relevance, perceptions of fairness, and perceptions that rewards are tied to performance.

The types of corrections made in control include strategic corrections, tactical corrections, and corrections at the individual level. Strategic corrections include strategies based on resources or on core competencies. Also, strategic plans that result from control systems analyses are designed to create rapid growth, slow growth, or stability or to deal with decline through divestment, liquidation, or retrenchment. Tactical corrections are developed by brand, by product, and by function or activity. Individual corrections are made by developing activities for top management, middle managers, first-line supervisors, and individual employees. When any of these individuals succeed, rewards should follow.

Chapter Terms

Best-cost provider strategy   (p. 410)
Brand market share   (p. 399)
Brand repositioning   (p. 412)
Broad differentiation strategy   (p. 410)
Company market share   (p. 399)
Competitive superiority   (p. 410)
Core competence   (p. 409)
Distinctive competence   (p. 409)
Focused (market niche) strategy   (p. 410)

Low-cost provider strategy   (p. 410)
Management by objectives   (p. 409)
Marketing control   (p. 397)
Metrics   (p. 398)
Product market share   (p. 399)
Profit center   (p. 398)
Strategic business units   (p. 398)
Strategic controls   (p. 398)

Review Questions

1. Define control and list the four steps of control.

2. Define the terms "hedging your bet," "over-asking," and "horse trading."

3. What are the five main levels of control?

4. What five main areas are assessed as part of the strategic marketing control process?

5. Name the four metrics used to assess products and product lines.

6. When measuring sales activities, what types of measures may be used?

7. When measuring advertising and promotional activities, what types of measures may be used?

8. Describe the metrics used to assess distribution activities.

9. Describe the three metrics used to assess public relations activities.

10. What three perceptions are important when designing individual controls or a performance appraisal system?

11. Describe the characteristics that apply to management by objectives programs and to planning and control systems in general that can make them successful programs.

12. Describe the terms "core competence," "distinctive competence," and "competitive superiority."

13. What are the four generic competitive strategies?

14. What strategic corrections can be made?

15. In what three areas are tactical corrections made?

16. What types of rewards can be given for successful performance for top managers, middle managers, first-line supervisors, and entry-level employees?

CUSTOMER
CORNER

Carlos Lopez loved doughnuts. Unfortunately, he lived on a very tight budget. Carlos knew that his local grocery store, Dilbert's, would box up any doughnuts that had not been sold during the day and put them out at 11:00 p.m., as "day old," for the next day's business. These were dramatically discounted, and customers could buy them at the reduced price between 11:00 p.m. and midnight, when the store closed.

One night, following his son's high school football game, Carlos decided to make a quick stop at Dilbert's to pick up milk. He left his family waiting in the car and entered the store. It was 10:52 p.m. He noticed that the bakery had already boxed up the next day's supply of doughnuts, but they were stored behind the bakery counter. Carlos was more than willing to wait a few more minutes to buy them, even if it seemed a little silly to do so. He wanted to know what his choices would be, so he leaned over the counter and began checking the boxes. A bakery employee quickly rushed up.

"You can't have those yet," the employee said sharply.

"I know," Carlos replied, smiling, "I was just getting a sneak peak."

"It's not 11:00," the baker growled. "You have to wait."

Now Carlos was annoyed. "Tell you what, why don't you keep your *@%#* doughnuts, and go to hell while you're at it!" He stomped out of the store and vowed not to go back. Little did the bakery employee know, but the Dilbert's store manager saw the entire incident.

1. What level of control is involved in this incident?

2. What type of correction should be made?

3. Is there anything the store manager could do to make sure similar incidents do not happen in the future?

4. If Carlos was clearly Hispanic, do you think other forces may have been involved?

What type of controls can Dilbert's manager establish to prevent another incident such as the one with Carlos?

Discussion and Critical Thinking Questions

1. In more mature markets, perceptions of brand parity are more likely, and sales in the overall market are more likely to grow only slowly or incrementally. What marketing tactics are more likely to be used when these conditions exist? How would this affect planning and control system metrics?

2. When a customer has a negative shopping experience, that customer is likely to tell, on average, 11 other people about it. When a customer has a positive shopping experience, the customer is only inclined to tell, on average, 4 other people about it. How should this affect a manager's analysis of customer satisfaction?

3. As director of marketing, it is your job to integrate information. Explain how metrics regarding sales activities interact with metrics regarding advertising and promotion activities as well as with metrics for distribution system activities.

4. The four components of a marketing system are inputs, transformation processes, outputs, and feedback mechanisms. Apply these components to concepts regarding core competencies and distinctive competencies. Apply these components to concepts regarding the five generic competitive strategies.

5. One of the more common failures of first-line supervisors is the tendency to "promise and not deliver." Explain how this affects both planning and control system activities.

Chapter 15 Case

Victoria's Secret: Pushing Up Sales During Tough Times

What happens to a cultural icon when a recession hits? Many managers in well-known national corporations faced this question as a strong recession affected both the United States and nations around the world in late 2008 and early 2009. The Christmas 2008 shopping season was dismal. Many retailers faced difficult times, dropping prices to the bare minimum in the hopes of generating sufficient cash flow to stay in business. Some were able to survive the storm; others, such as The Sharper Image, Goody's, Steve & Barry's, and Circuit City, did not.

Against this backdrop, the management team at Victoria's Secret would naturally be forced to assess the company's prospects. The retail chain is part of a larger set of brands held by Limited Brands that also includes Bath & Body Works, C.O. Bigelow, The White Barn Candle Co., Henri Bendel, and La Senza. All these retailers target women in their marketing efforts as well as the men seeking to please them.

Victoria's Secret was formed by Roy Raymond, a business student with a degree from Stanford, who was frustrated by the process of trying to buy lingerie for his wife without feeling uncomfortable or embarrassed. Victoria's Secret stores are designed to achieve a quality shopping experience that would be similar to visiting a "Victorian boudoir."[7] The goal was to make males feel as equally at ease as their female partners when shopping for Christmas presents, Valentine's Day gifts, and purchases for other romantic occasions such as a birthday or wedding anniversary.

Over the years, the company gained a great deal of notoriety through a variety of tactics. The models were among the first to be featured in commercials for bras, following the loosening of advertising regulations in the early 2000s. More recently, the Victoria's Secret fashion show online, as well as company advertisements during the Super Bowl, received a massive amount of attention, which led to free publicity and a great deal of buzz. The company clearly enjoys powerful brand recognition and recall as a result of these efforts.

Victoria's Secret has chosen to employ beautiful, but not celebrity, models. At the same time, being selected to wear the company's products has become an entryway to greater recognition for someone entering the world of modeling.

Currently, the store features bras, panties, sleep and lounge clothing, other fashion clothes, shoes, swimwear, beauty products, and the PINK line. The company has achieved a dominant position in the marketplace through a strong emphasis on customer service that stresses frequent staff attention and upselling during the shopping visit. The company's in-store credit card provides access to customers for marketing offers and other messages.

The question for Victoria's Secret's marketing team is, "What happens when times are tough?" Clearly customer shopping and buying habits shifted in early 2009. Of note, sales of men's underwear dropped significantly during the first quarter of the year. Would Victoria's Secret suffer a similar fate? Is women's fashion underwear a necessity or one of those "small" luxuries that people may buy instead of larger purchases, such as expensive dinners, vacations, and other indulgences?

1. What is the strategic approach employed by Victoria's Secret since its inception? Does such an approach create an advantage or a disadvantage during a recession?

2. What product line tactics might the company use in response to the recession?

3. What brand tactics might the company use in response to the recession?

4. Should Victoria's Secret adjust the company's advertising approach during this time? Should the company offer a greater number of promotions, such as price-offs, coupons, or bonus packs? Why or why not?

5. Should incentives for salespeople be changed during this time period? If so, how?

What might keep Victoria's Secret successful during a recession?

Go to **www.sagepub.com/clow** for additional exercises and study resources. Select **Chapter 15, Marketing Control** for chapter-specific activities.

Appendix A

Analyzing a Case

While there is no one magic way of analyzing a case, Figure A.1 provides a general outline of the components that should be present. The goal of a case analysis is to determine the problem or situation the organization faces, to generate some feasible alternative solutions, and to select the best strategy. A quality solution requires a careful analysis and understanding of the case.

- Executive Summary
- History or Introduction
- SWOT Analysis
- Case Analysis
- Marketing Problem
- Alternative Solutions
- Recommendation
- Implementation
- Appendix

Figure A.1 Components of a Case Analysis

Executive Summary

The executive summary appears first on this list of components; however, it is actually written last. It is a summary of the report for executives to read. The report should be 1 to 2 pages in length. After an executive reads this section, she would have a basic grasp of the entire report. This is not a teaser designed to get someone to read the report. Instead, the goal is to highlight what the report is about, the problem being faced, and the recommended solution. If the executive desires more detail, she can then examine additional sections.

History or Introduction

This section contains a history or a brief introduction to the case. It should provide sufficient information to allow the reader to get a solid grasp of the case and the situation being encountered by the company or organization. It should be written assuming that the reader did not read the case and knew nothing about the company. The wording should provide background information for the case analysis.

SWOT Analysis

The SWOT analysis is important because it provides a clear understanding of the company or organization in the case. The key to preparing a quality SWOT analysis is to understand each component. Note that the "Strengths and Weaknesses" are internal to the organization and the "Opportunities and Threats" are external factors.

A strength is something the company does well that makes it unique and stronger than its competitors. It can be a superior marketing team or a superior product. It might also be its position in the marketplace or the market share the brand or company holds.

Weaknesses are characteristics of the company that make it vulnerable. These are things that can do potential harm to the firm. These might include excessive debt, poor market position, or inferior product quality. Understanding weaknesses is important because, if left uncorrected, they can lead to new problems in the future.

Opportunities are external to the firm. These exist for all firms in the industry. Examples might be an interest in health care products by individuals of age 50 and over or an increasing interest in green products. When opportunities are identified, ask the question whether the opportunity is available to every firm in the industry. If so, then it is an opportunity. If not, then it is likely a strength or perhaps a strategy. Some students and marketing professionals confuse opportunities with strategies. "The opportunity to expand a company's product offerings through a flanker brand" is a strategy, not an opportunity. The opportunity may be that a specific market is receptive to a cheaper version of a product.

Threats are similar to opportunities in that they are external and faced by all companies in the industry. If raw material costs are increasing and all firms in the industry face that problem, it is a threat. When evaluating threats, consider everything that would affect the industry as a whole.

Case Analysis

Once the SWOT analysis is complete, it is time to analyze the rest of the information provided in the case. Each case will be different. Some mention financial or accounting information. Others present marketing information to be studied. Other cases contain internal personnel or operations information. Examine each piece of information provided in light of the SWOT analysis and what it tells you about the firm. This is not a summary of information. That should have been presented earlier. It is an analysis, which implies that the information is being interpreted. It should provide additional information that will help in identifying the problem and proposing potential solutions.

Marketing Problem

By the time the reader reaches this point, she should have a grasp of the case and be able to identify the problem faced by the company. It should have become evident during the analysis. To ensure it is clear, state the marketing problem clearly. Be sure it is the problem the company is facing, not a symptom. Declining sales, declining market share, and eroding brand image are all symptoms. The problem is what is causing these conditions.

Think in terms of going to a medical doctor with a fever, runny nose, and cough. These are symptoms. The doctor then runs medical tests and perhaps performs a physical exam. Using your symptoms and the information gathered from the tests and exam, the physician will be able to diagnose the problem. It might be a cold, it might be pneumonia, or it might be a more serious problem, such as cancer. Once the correct diagnosis is determined, the physician can then prescribe the proper treatment.

A case analysis follows a similar format. Based on information presented in the SWOT and case analysis, the marketing problem should be identified. It might be the emergence of a new product that is superior or it could be a shifting of consumer interests and desires. Identifying the problem is extremely important. Treating symptoms only provides a temporary Band-Aid-type fix. Treating the problem provides the organization with a long-term strategy and solution.

Alternative Solutions

With the problem clearly identified, assess the possible courses of action the firm can take. It is important to generate several potential solutions. Make sure that they are feasible and that they would sufficiently solve the problem the company is facing.

Once feasible alternatives have been identified, examine each one. List the pros and cons of each. Discuss the benefits of following each strategy as well as the risks involved. In this analysis, it is a good idea to go back to the SWOT analysis. How will each alternative build on a strength or take advantage of an opportunity? Alternatively, a solution may minimize a weakness or overcome a possible threat.

It is not sufficient merely to state the alternatives. A clear and concise analysis of each alternative must be presented. Keep in mind that for most cases, one alternative is the "status quo," which is to continue doing what the company is doing. At times that may be acceptable, but this is not likely. A change of direction is needed to get the company back on a solid foundation or to minimize a threat.

If alternative solutions are suggested, they should be mutually exclusive. This means that only one alternative will be chosen. It should not be a potpourri of ideas. In making each alternative mutually exclusive, it may be necessary to have similar subcomponents or implementation strategies.

Recommendation

As was the case in the section that presents the marketing problem, by the time the reader arrives at this section she should know what the recommendation will be. The analysis of each alternative should provide the reader with evidence on which one is the best. The recommendation should be clearly stated, followed by a justification for using the alternative and a statement about why is it better than the others.

Implementation

This section provides the tactical and operational details regarding how the solution will be carried out. In most case analyses, the recommendation is a strategy. It is long term. The implementation is the tactics and operations that the company will use to ensure that the strategy is successful. It is also a good idea to describe control measures that will be used to determine if the strategy is successful or not.

Appendix

This section provides the support materials that you used in the case but did not want to place in the written part of the case.

Appendix B

CASE 1

Sara Lee Corporation

Umit Akinc, Calloway School of Business and Accountancy, Wake Forest University
Jack Meredith, Babcock Graduate School of Management, Wake Forest University
Kirk Nelson, Sara Lee Corporation

In mid-2004, Kirk Nelson, Supply Chain Analyst in the Wal-Mart Account Division of Sara Lee Corporation's Customer Management Group in Winston-Salem, North Carolina, pored over the new sales data he had just received on their Girls' Panty (GP) line. He wanted to be well prepared with the latest information before his meeting with his boss, Dudley Gentry, Director of the Female Underwear and Sleepwear category for the division. Wal-Mart stores allocated Sara Lee's GP line, like many other product lines, a certain shelf space at each store where the line was offered. If a particular style did not perform well, not only would Sara Lee not achieve its revenue objectives, but Wal-Mart would not achieve its total margin dollar goals. This carried the risk of losing precious shelf space at Wal-Mart stores, and worse, possible reallocation of the space to a competitor's product.

It was Kirk's responsibility to monitor and analyze the sales data to ensure that Sara Lee was using shelf space allocated to the GP line effectively. The task was complicated, however, due to the constant changes not only in demand, but also in competitors' offerings as well as Sara Lee's own product changes. As Kirk explained, "our product assortment is constantly changing, based on consumers' interests and sales. From time to time, we may have to discontinue a style because it is no longer economical to produce, or because consumers' desire for that product has declined. This allows us to offer new styles with broader appeal."

Specific styles in the GP line had a life cycle of two to three years with more frequent (about every six months) print and color changes. It was therefore extremely important to time the new major style introductions and color print changes correctly to keep the product line fresh and performing to the satisfaction of both Sara Lee and Wal-Mart. One constant danger was the possibility of introducing styles, colors, or print and packaging combinations that competed with and cannibalized existing products or each other.

That was the dilemma facing Kirk now. The company had recently introduced two new GP styles; however, they might be cannibalizing an older style that had been selling well. In addition, another new style was now ready for introduction, but Kirk was unsure which style it should replace. He hoped that an analysis of the sales data would help him with this decision.

Sara Lee's roots trace to 1939 when Nathan Cummings, a small wholesaler, acquired C.D. Kenny Company, a small wholesale distributor of sugar, coffee, and tea in Baltimore with net sales of $24 million. Upon later acquiring Sprague, Warner & Company in 1942, the company moved its headquarters to Chicago and changed its name to Sprague Warner-Kenny Corporation. The company began trading its common shares on the New York Stock Exchange, and the stock split three-for-one in 1946. The stockholders voted to change the corporation's name to Consolidated Foods Corporation in 1954 to emphasize its diversified role in food processing, packaging, and distribution and to better identify with multiple segments of the food industry. In 1956, Consolidated Foods acquired Kitchens of Sara Lee and 34 Piggly Wiggly supermarkets. This event marked the entry of Sara Lee into the retail food business for the first time. The

Copyright © 2007 by *Case Research Journal* and Umit Akinc, Jack Meredith, and Kirk Nelson. Preparation of this case was partially supported by the Babcock School of Management Research Program and the Calloway School of Business and Accountancy Summer Research Grant Program.

decade of the 1960s continued the growth of the corporation with various acquisitions that firmly established the company in the food industry and catapulted it into a diverse set of businesses. Among these acquisitions, those of both Gant and Country-Canadell were significant because they marked the entry into the general apparel and women's intimate apparel businesses, respectively.

Growing by acquisitions continued in the decade of the 1970s. One of the company's most important acquisitions occurred in 1979 when it bought Hanes, a well-known manufacturer/marketer of women's hosiery, foundation garments, swimwear, men's and boys' underwear, and cosmetics (brands include L'eggs, Bali, Hanes, L'erin). In the mid 1980s, Hanes (now as a division of Consolidated Foods) introduced the Hanes Her Way brand of women's apparel, starting with women's panties and expanding to other categories. Hanes Her Way quickly became a $100 million brand by itself. In 1985, Consolidated Foods changed its name to Sara Lee Corporation to reflect the growing consumer marketing orientation of the company and to emphasize around the world its high-quality, well-known branded products. Sara Lee Corporation celebrated its 50th anniversary in 1989 with sales topping $10 billion and record earnings. Meanwhile, Hanes signed an up-and-coming, young basketball player from the University of North Carolina who had recently moved to Chicago—Michael Jordan—to serve as a spokesperson. Hanes introduced the new logo and advertising campaign in 1992, letting consumers know that "Just wait'll we get our Hanes on you." By 1997, Hanes' worldwide brand sales surpassed $2 billion with high quality, affordable, casual clothing for today's everyday lifestyle. The pace of new acquisitions in food, apparel, and personal care products continued in the decades of the 1990s, with net sales reaching $20 billion in 1998, and continuing into the new century.

Company Business and Strategy

Sara Lee's modest origins had been in domestic food processing and distribution. By mid-2004, it had become a global corporation with 150,400 worldwide employees, operating in 58 countries and selling in over 200. By this time, it derived 39 percent of its sales revenue and 47 percent of its profits from outside the United States. The growth and diversification of the corporation into a global conglomerate is a result of many acquisitions in the last century as well as changing economic conditions.

Recent global competitive forces had become an important influence on the company's basic character and its competitive focus. Strong brand development and marketing has always been the major focus for Sara Lee. However, overseas competition from such emerging regions as Eastern Europe, South East Asia, and the Middle East, powered by newer technology and cheap labor, had made it increasingly difficult for U.S. manufacturers to compete. Sara Lee's operations, particularly in the apparel business, were no exception. Thus, the company started moving some of its apparel manufacturing to these regions, expanding its operational base into 55 countries. In doing so, however, the company found itself manufacturing a smaller and smaller percentage of the volume it markets globally. As a result, Sara Lee decided to relinquish its focus on manufacturing apparel products and instead concentrate on developing and marketing its high quality, market-leading, repeat-purchase, brand-name products.

At the turn of the millennium, Sara Lee also realized that the company had overexpanded into too many product areas. Thus, in 2000, a new initiative to "reshape" Sara Lee emerged, with the goal of narrowing the company's focus to a smaller number of consumer packaged-goods segments. To implement this strategy, Sara Lee divested some of its manufacturing operations while adding some others to build leadership brands in the core categories of packaged meats, bakery, coffee, tea, underwear, intimate apparel, hair and body care, shoe care, and air fresheners.

This strategic realignment culminated in three broad strategic business areas:

- Food and Beverage
- Branded Apparel
- Household Products

In the apparel business, Sara Lee marketed a global portfolio of basic, nonfashion apparel brands, which it distributed largely through mass marketers such as Wal-Mart, Target, and Kmart. This product line occupies the marketing space below the high fashion segment (e.g., Victoria's Secret, Yves St. Laurent) but above the no-name apparel. Sara Lee's major brands in the intimates/underwear segment, for example, included Bali, Barely There, Gossard, Lovable, Playtex, Unno and Wonderbra; in the legwear category it had L'eggs, Hanes and Just My Size brands; and the sportswear category included such well-known brands as Champion and Outer Banks.

Hanes had been making comfortable, quality products in underwear, socks, and casual wear for the whole family for over 100 years. Hanes Knit brand was the corporation's largest brand and also the world's largest apparel brand, with total annual sales of $2.2 billion in fiscal 2002. *Hanes Her Way,* one of Hanes Knit brands, alone had sales revenue of $750 million in the same year.

The GP Line

Underwear for everyone in the family had been a significant portion of Sara Lee's apparel business, and consumers had known its brands for several decades. Under the general Hanes brand, Sara Lee marketed a broad line of underwear for girls aged between four and 12. The GP line included three types of cuts referred to as *silhouettes*—Brief, Bikini, and Hipster. Each silhouette came in up to three price levels, called *programs,* which could be Basic, Fashion, or Character, which covered, respectively, the "good," "better," and "best" spectrum of the market. The three cuts not only differed in the use of quality of materials and other frills such as fancy elastic, lace, etc., but also in the company's brand equity in them. Pricing, therefore, reflected these differences.

For instance, Basic was the economy line, which came either in plain or simple prints such as butterflies or flowers. The next step up was the Fashion program, which came in more elaborate prints based on various themes such as beach, sandals, travel, days of the week, etc. The highest program level was Character, based on popular cartoon characters such as Strawberry Shortcake, Winnie the Pooh, and Barbie. This last category targeted the younger slice of the 4–12 age group. Because a licensing fee to the cartoon characters was involved, Sara Lee had higher brand equity in this line, commanding higher prices.

Of the three silhouettes, only the Briefs were offered in all three programs: Basic, Fashion, and Character. The Bikini and Hipster silhouettes were only available in the Basic and Fashion programs. Each combination of silhouette and program also came in various packaging configurations and prints. For instance, Basic targeted the economy buyer and came mostly in packages (called "units") of six or nine with simple printing. The higher-priced Fashions were available in a 6-pack configuration whereas the high-end, highest-priced Characters were only sold in packages of three.

Sara Lee marketed these products largely through mass marketers such as Wal-Mart and Target, but also (though on a much smaller scale) through smaller department stores and independent stores at shopping malls. Fruit of the Loom was Sara Lee's primary competitor in the underwear category. It offered similar products to Sara Lee's at both mass merchandisers and smaller stores.

The Wal-Mart Account

As of mid-2004, Sara Lee and Wal-Mart had enjoyed a close and growing supplier-customer relationship for many years. Wal-Mart was not only a significant distributor for Sara Lee's apparel line, but also for the Sara Lee brands in food and beverages as well as household items. Sara Lee brands in all three categories (apparel, food and beverages, and household products) accounted for a sizable portion of Wal-Mart's total sales. Total apparel sales to Wal-Mart alone exceeded $1.3 billion in the 12 months prior to mid-2004. In this relationship, Sara Lee had in Wal-Mart a strong distribution

channel partner with deep market penetration, while Wal-Mart relied on Sara Lee's wide portfolio of well-known and established brand names. The ability of Sara Lee to reliably supply Wal-Mart with wide product lines at competitive prices was crucial to Wal-Mart since these capabilities translated into "everyday low prices" and high availability of products—two of Wal-Mart's success factors.

Sara Lee managed this important relationship with one of its biggest customers by an elaborate sales organization consisting of, for example, more than 40 professionals just in the apparel segment. Sara Lee's Wal-Mart Account apparel team was organized around the categories of products sold (see Exhibit 1) and was headed by its own President. One of the most important duties of the Analysts was to monitor the sales data closely to ensure that the precious allocated retail space in Wal-Mart's stores was being utilized as effectively as possible. Since in the short-term, the space allocated to GP styles was fixed, it was important to stock that space with an "optimal" assortment of styles. Generally, introducing a new style required terminating an existing style. Furthermore, it was a distinct possibility that Wal-Mart would take back part of the display space if the product was not performing in terms of total margin. This meant that the Analyst was responsible for making recommendations regarding both which styles to discontinue and which new styles to add.

The Analysts were also responsible for monitoring the sales of the product lines that were assigned to them and initiate inventory replenishment actions to ensure that products achieved a high "fill rate," i.e., the proportion of customer requirements filled immediately. Wal-Mart shared its demand forecasts for various products with its appropriate suppliers but expected a maximum two-week delivery lead time on most items. Because most of the GP line came from as far away as China, the two-week lead time created a supply chain challenge. Managing this long supply chain while still meeting Wal-Mart's delivery standard was complicated by at least two factors. First, Sara Lee dealt with a multitude of suppliers in various countries on different continents (China, India, Pakistan, Turkey, Egypt) who were subject to all sorts of disruptions due to such things as strikes, unrest, cultural traditions, religious holidays, etc., as well as the common manufacturing difficulties of maintaining quality, material flows, equipment, and labor. Second, the supply lines were very long, crossing international borders and oceans resulting in delivery times to Sara Lee as long as six months for some items. These factors made the supply time relatively long and highly unpredictable.

To meet this supply chain challenge—supplying Wal-Mart within two weeks with products whose supply chains were long and unpredictable—Sara Lee operated a number of distribution centers and tried to maintain appropriate inventories. In order to achieve the delivery performance that Wal-Mart expected and still control the inventory investment, Sara Lee relied on good forecasts going out to six months or longer.

Exhibit 1   Sara Lee's Sales Force Organization for the Wal-Mart Account

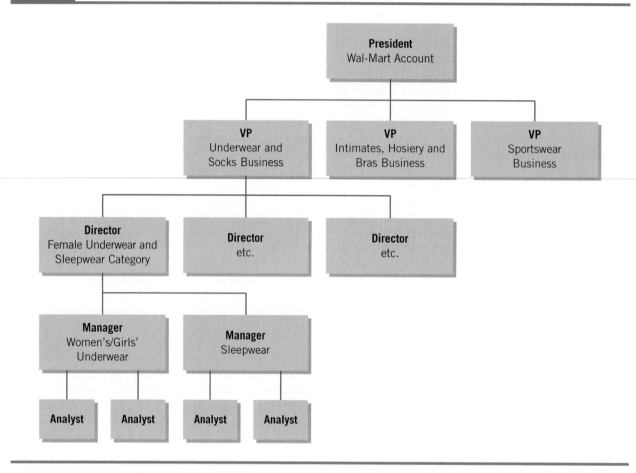

Source: Sara Lee records.

In the Wal-Mart Account division, Kirk Nelson reported to the manager of Women's and Girls' Underwear, who in turn reported to Dudley Gentry, Director of the Female Underwear and Sleepwear Category. As of mid-2004, Wal-Mart offered the GP line at more than 2,300 stores. At each store, the packages were presented to consumers in "modules" resembling columns and rows of pigeonholes, where each column was assigned to a particular style (silhouette, program, and packaging combination) that ranged up to a dozen or so. Different sizes, depending on the style, occupied specific shelves in each of the columns. Each style of silhouette, program, packaging combination, and size was assigned a unique SKU for accounting and inventory management purposes. In this display arrangement, the "columns" allocated to the Hanes brand GP line from Sara Lee stood side by side with those allocated to the Fruit of the Loom line. Although Wal-Mart also carried an assortment of lower priced, private brands of underwear, these were not regarded as directly competing products.

Each week, Kirk got a weekly retail sales report from Wal-Mart. The format of this report modeled the module display used at the stores. Each column detailed the average unit (i.e., package) sales per store for each group (silhouette, program, and packaging) for each size.

Cannibalization and Replacements

One of the GP line's longest-running styles had been FashionBikinis sold in 6-pack units at a retail price of about $6.90 per unit. Sara Lee's net profit margins in the GP line were about the same for all styles and can be assumed to duplicate the average in the children's apparel industry, about 2–3 percent. Among similar products (both Sara Lee and other brands), this product had been performing well in

Wal-Mart stores since the start of calendar year 2001, though clearly nearing the end of its life cycle. Kirk was considering this product as a benchmark to evaluate the performance of other styles. On average, 6,000 units sold each week across 2,300 stores translated into about $18 of revenue per store each week for this product, just one of half a dozen styles sold in this product line.

In November 2002, Sara Lee had introduced a similar product—a FashionBrief version of the 6-pack FashionBikinis—and started selling it in the same Wal-Mart stores. The Fashion style had been so popular in the Bikini line that it seemed logical to introduce it in the Briefs line as well. Because this product was somewhat similar to the successful FashionBikinis, differing only in the silhouette, there was some concern whether the FashionBrief version would "cannibalize" sales of the FashionBikini product. On the other hand, since the Brief silhouette primarily sold to younger girls whereas the Bikini silhouette sold to older girls, the two styles might actually complement one another rather than competing with one another. Weekly unit sales (all sizes combined) for these two products from their introduction to mid-2004 are given in Exhibit 2.

Back in August 2003, Kirk had noticed that one of the BasicHipster styles—a 6-pack economy package that had been in the stores for a number of years—was not doing well. Looking at the sales figures, Kirk felt that they had to replace this style quickly or they would run the risk of losing the space in the Wal-Mart stores to a competitor. Unfortunately, Sara Lee did not yet have an updated BasicHipster to replace this style. Reluctantly, Sara Lee decided to replace it with the new FashionBikini style they had been preparing in anticipation of the end of the existing FashionBikini's life cycle. The "New FashionBikinis" differed from the existing FashionBikinis primarily by having more current print themes and more exciting colors. Given the still limited supply of these New FashionBikinis, they decided to substitute it at only 1,700 Wal-Mart stores where the BasicHipster's performance was the poorest. They knew that this product did not replace the discontinued Hipsters well and that it could, in fact, cannibalize the very successful FashionBikinis. However, as Kirk put it, they had no choice—they had to keep the spot until a proper replacement for the BasicHipster was available and his task, after all, was to maximize total sales in the GP line. Weekly unit sales for these New FashionBikinis are also given in Exhibit 2.

Now that these potentially competing products had been on the shelves for a reasonable period, Kirk felt that it was time to do a more extensive analysis of the sales patterns of the three products to determine if any cannibalization of the original FashionBikinis had been occurring. If this was indeed the case, it was important to keep the newer products on the shelves only if they were creating additional incremental revenue and meeting Wal-Mart's margin dollar expectations.

Checking the values in Exhibit 2, Kirk could see that there was much variability in the weekly sales of all these products, which did not surprise him. Kirk's experience with sales of similar products indicated that the products tended to exhibit various persistent seasonal ups and downs with two pronounced peaks corresponding to the "back-to-school" and "Christmas" seasons. To see these patterns more clearly, Kirk used a spreadsheet software package to plot, in Exhibit 3, the weekly sales data in Exhibit 2 for the three products for each year. As he expected, every product in every year exhibited the same seasonality.

Kirk decided it was now time to begin the data analysis. To see the effect of the FashionBriefs introduced in 2002 on the sales of FashionBikinis, Kirk graphed the weekly sales data for the FashionBikinis before and after the introduction of the FashionBriefs, as shown in Exhibit 4a. Kirk did not believe that this would necessarily be an accurate assessment of the impact of FashionBriefs on the FashionBikini sales, but it was always useful to look at a plot of the data before trying to analyze it. To begin, he thought he would simply calculate the average weekly sales of FashionBikinis for the year *before* the FashionBriefs were introduced and compare it to the entire year *after*. He reasoned that by looking at two entire years' sales, he would be comparing *annual* average sales not influenced by any seasonal fluctuations. He found that the average weekly demand for the entire year preceding the introduction of the FashionBriefs had been 4,853 packages and for the year immediately following the introduction, the average weekly sales had jumped to 5,955 packages, a 23 percent increase. Rather than hurting the sales of the FashionBikinis, it appeared that the new FashionBriefs were actually *helping* sales.

When he mentioned this 23 percent increase to Dudley Gentry at lunch the next day, Mr. Gentry seemed pleased that the FashionBikini sales had risen, but wondered if the increase was solely attributable to the introduction of the FashionBriefs. For example, if the sales for FashionBikinis were trending upwards anyway, then the difference observed may have been due to this trend and not the result of the new style introduction. He said that, although it did not appear to be so, it was still possible that the FashionBriefs were cutting into the sales of the FashionBikinis and the upward trending FashionBikini sales were hiding the cannibalization.

To see if there was any significant trend in the sales, as Dudley suspected, Kirk used the software package's "linear trend" feature to add a rough trend line to the graph, as shown in Exhibit 4a. There did indeed seem to be an upward trend in the data, but it seemed to continue even after the new product introduction. Still, perhaps the trend was even higher *before* the introduction of the FashionBriefs and the introduction of the new product had reduced the growth rate. Unfortunately, the seasonality in the data made it difficult to see what was happening. Hence, Kirk decided to look at the cumulative sales (Exhibit 4b) and plot a trend line through the cumulative sales up to the introduction of the FashionBriefs, and then extend it on to see if sales increased faster than this line.

Exhibit 2	Weekly Unit Sales of the Three Products

	FashionBikinis				FashionBriefs				New FashionBikinis			
Week	2001	2002	2003	2004	2001	2002	2003	2004	2001	2002	2003	2004
1	3091	3723	3549	4319			3776	4566				1734
2	3449	4207	4019	4780			4471	5125				1971
3	3370	4110	3900	4545			4494	4947				1931
4	3479	4199	4001	4542			4746	4999				1983
5	3569	4211	4118	4544			5000	5053				2023
6	3557	4121	4095	4399			5079	4943				1983
7	3484	3951	4010	4199			5058	4781				1928
8	3580	4010	4129	4203			5243	4831				1956
9	3681	4163	4352	4293			5493	4963				2021
10	3765	4205	4558	4409			5635	5118				2110
11	4074	4416	5010	4667			6116	5400				2228
12	3359	3690	4211	3811			5086	4472				1852
13	3171	3481	4028	3557			4845	4253				1766
14	3378	3703	4330	3764			5197	4552				1899
15	3037	3389	3977	3377			4791	4163				1745
16	2994	3370	4060	3371			4909	4239				1775
17	3469	3865	4790	3946			5787	4969				2082
18	3934	4318	5516	4587			6645	5700				2407
19	4422	4824	6255	5279			7454	6406				2717
20	4582	4931	6460	5579			7626	6605				2812
21	4914	5263	7022	6115			8118	7040				3010
22	5334	5698	7891	6916			8850	7676				3286
23	5546	5967	8462				9224					
24	5582	6009	8842				9289					
25	5816	6237	9343				9551					
26	6324	6757	10343				10451					
27	8132	8672	13250				13270					
28	8998	9795	14230				14193					
29	8302	9054	12739				12616					
30	7462	8185	11117				11074					
31	5814	6417	8569				8487					
32	4232	4843	6036				5938					
33	2627	3072	3808				3722					
34	2755	3204	3905				3822					805
35	3017	3416	4152				4089					922
36	3184	3541	4266				4195					1007
37	3182	3488	4165				4113					1039
38	3336	3622	4294				4252					1126
39	3378	3635	4373				4290					1192
40	3684	3867	4795				4660					1359
41	4003	4150	5228				5045					1541
42	4163	4264	5443				5232					1667
43	4857	4864	6407				6141					2025
44	5066	5108	6742				6460					2188
45	6201	6226	8280				7947					2744
46	7905	7898	10502				10213					3586
47	9521	9394	12322			1415	12330					4393
48	6169	6117	7353			4965	7517					2690
49	2982	2933	3464			2387	3599					1321
50	2763	2713	3171			2274	3310					1236
51	2927	2869	3472			2590	3602					1355
52	4583	4215	5258			3998	5378					2031
53	4129	3784				3804						

| Exhibit 3 | Seasonal Pattern of Sales |

Weekly Unit Sales

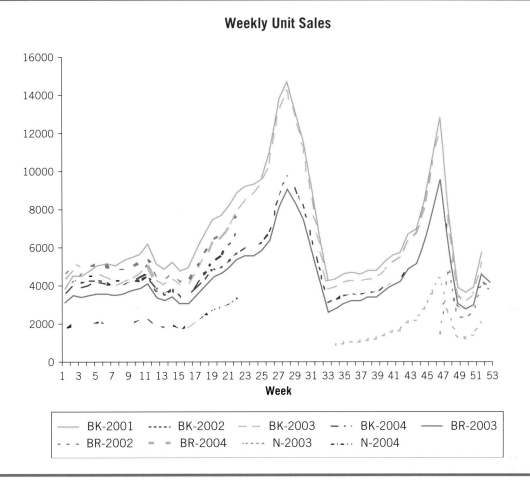

BR: FashionBriefs; BK: FashionBikinis; N: New FashionBikinis.

The Styles-to-Offer Decision

Back in his office, Kirk wondered how he might account for the possible increase in FashionBikini sales. Solid decisions on which styles to continue and which, if any, to drop, would require a more detailed and sophisticated analysis. He had to find a way to account for any sustained trend as well as the seasonal fluctuations in the data before he could make a convincing argument about the possible negative or positive effect of one style or another.

In addition, an e-mail message Kirk received informed him that a proper replacement for the BasicHipster was now available. He could recommend using it to replace either the old or the New FashionBikinis, as originally planned. However, considering the higher margins of the

FashionBikinis compared to the BasicHipsters, Kirk was wondering whether this was the rational thing to do. Of course, the decision depended on the degree to which the two FashionBikinis (old and new) were working well together; i.e., without substantial cannibalization. If there was some cannibalization, he could recommend replacing one of the FashionBikinis with the new BasicHipster. However, which one should it be? Alternatively, if the New FashionBikinis were not cannibalizing the old FashionBikinis in a way that undermined the total revenues, perhaps both FashionBikinis might be carried side by side in all Wal-Mart's stores.

Finally, Kirk wondered if he could also use the analysis to forecast overall revenue expectations for these lines, and perhaps even unit sales of each style combination so their warehouses could maintain adequate supplies to keep Wal-Mart's stores replenished.

Exhibit 4a   Fashion-Bikini Sales for 2001–2004

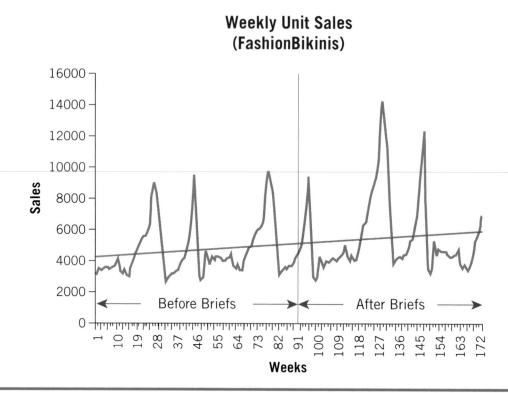

Weekly Unit Sales (FashionBikinis)

Exhibit 4b   Cumulative Fashion-Bikini Sales for 2001–2004

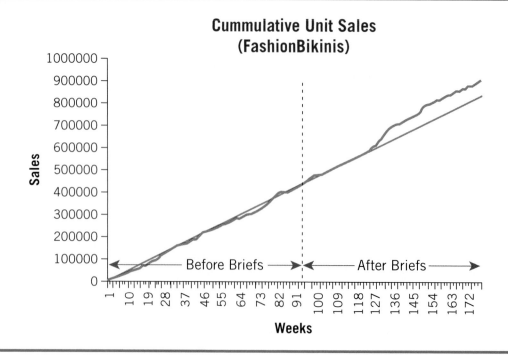

Cummulative Unit Sales (FashionBikinis)

CASE 2

Cowgirl Chocolates

John J. Lawrence, University of Idaho
Linda J. Morris, University of Idaho
Joseph J. Geiger, University of Idaho

Marilyn looked at the advertisement—a beautiful woman wearing a cowboy hat in a watering trough full of hot and spicy Cowgirl Chocolates truffles. The ad would appear next month in the March/April edition of *Chile Pepper* magazine, the leading magazine for people who liked fiery foods. The ad, the first ever for the business, cost $3,000 to run, and Marilyn wondered if it would be her big mistake for 2001. Marilyn allowed herself one $3,000-$6,000 mistake a year in trying to get her now 4-year old business to profitability. Two years ago, it was the pursuit of an opportunity to get her product into Great Britain on the recommendation of the owner of a British biscuit company who loved her chocolates. Despite significant effort and expense, she could not convince anyone in Great Britain to carry her chocolates. Last year, it was her attempt to use a distributor for the first time. It was a small, regional distributor, and she had provided them with $5,000 worth of product and had never gotten paid. She eventually got half her product back, but by the time she did, it had limited remaining shelf life and she already had enough new stock on hand to cover demand. She ended up giving away most of what she got back.

Marilyn knew it took time to make money at something. She was now an internationally celebrated ceramicist, but it had taken 20 years for her ceramic art to turn a profit. She also knew, however, that she could not wait 20 years for her foray into chocolates to make money, especially not at the rate that she was currently losing money. Last year, despite not paying herself a salary and occasionally bartering her art for services, the small business's revenues of $30,000 did not come close to covering her $50,000+ in expenses. Although her art did not make money for a long time, it did not lose that kind of money either. Her savings account was slowly being depleted as she loaned the company money. She knew that the product was excellent—it had won numerous awards from the two main fiery food competitions in the United States—and her packaging was also excellent and had won awards itself. She just was not sure how to turn her award-winning products into a profitable business.

Company History

Cowgirl Chocolates was started in Moscow, Idaho, in 1997 by Marilyn Lysohir and her husband, Ross Coates. Marilyn and Ross were both artists. Marilyn was a nationally known ceramicist and lecturer; Ross was also a sculptor and a professor of fine arts at a nearby university. They had started publishing a once-a-year arts magazine in 1995 called *High Ground*. *High Ground* was really a multimedia product— each edition contained more than simply printed words and pictures. For example, past editions had included such things as vials of Mount St. Helens ash, cassette tapes, seeds, fabric art, and chocolate bunnies in addition to articles and stories. One edition was even packaged in a motion picture canister. With a total production of about 600 copies, however, *High Ground* simply would not pay for itself. But the magazine was a labor of love for Marilyn and Ross, and so they sought creative ways to fund the endeavor. One of the ways they tried was selling hot and spicy chocolate truffles.

The fact that Marilyn and Ross turned to chocolate was no random event. Marilyn's first job, at age 16, was at Daffin's Candies in Sharon, Pennsylvania. The business's owner, Pete Daffin, had been an early mentor of Marilyn's and had encouraged her creativity. He even let her carve a set of animals, including an 8-foot-tall chocolate bunny, for display. Her sculptures proved irresistible to visiting youngsters, who would take small bites out of the sculptures. It was at this point that Marilyn realized the power of chocolate.

In addition to loving chocolate, Marilyn loved things hot and spicy. She also was aware that cayenne and other chilies had wonderful health properties for the heart. But it was her brother who originally gave her the idea of combining hot and spicy with chocolate. Marilyn considered her brother's idea for a while and could see it had possibilities, so she started experimenting in her kitchen. She recruited neighbors, friends, and acquaintances to try out her creations. Although a few people who tried those early chocolates were not so sure that combining hot and spicy with chocolate made sense, many thought the chocolates were great. Encouraged, and still searching for funding for *High Ground,* Marilyn found a local candy company to produce the chocolates in quantity, and she and her husband established Cowgirl Chocolates.

The name itself came from one friend's reaction the first time she tasted the chocolates. The friend exclaimed, "These are cowboy chocolates!" Marilyn agreed that there was a certain ruggedness to the concept of hot and spicy chocolates that matched the cowboy image, but thought that *Cowgirl* Chocolates was a more appropriate name for her company. Marilyn found the picture of May Lillie that would become the Cowgirl Chocolates logo in a book about cowgirls. May Lillie was a turn of the century, pistol-packing cowgirl, and Marilyn loved the picture of May looking down the barrel of a pistol because May looked so tough. It certainly was not hard to envision May adopting the Cowgirl Chocolates motto—"Sissies Stay Away." That motto had come to Marilyn when a group of friends told her that they really did not like her hot and spicy chocolates. Marilyn was a little disappointed and hurt, and thought to herself, "Well, sissies, stay away. If you don't like them, don't eat them."

The Product

Cowgirl Chocolates sold its hot and spicy creations in three basic forms: individually wrapped truffles, chocolate bars, and a hot caramel dessert sauce. The individually wrapped truffles were available in a variety of packaging options, with most of the packaging designed to set Cowgirl Chocolates apart. The truffles could be purchased in gift boxes, in drawstring muslin bags, and in a collectable tin. According to Marilyn, this packaging made them "more than a candy—they become an idea, an experience, a gift." The truffles were also available in a plain plastic bag from Cowgirl Chocolates' Web site for customers who just wanted the chocolate and did not care about the fancy packaging. The chocolate bars and truffles were offered in several flavors. The chocolate bars were available in either orange espresso or lime tequila crunch. The truffles were available in plain chocolate, mint, orange, lime tequila, and espresso. The plain chocolate, mint, and orange truffles were packaged in gold wrappers; the lime tequila truffles were packaged in green wrappers. The espresso truffles were the hottest, about twice as hot as the other varieties, and were wrapped in a special red foil to give customers some clue that these were extra hot. Cowgirl Chocolates' full line of product offerings is described in Exhibit 1.

Marilyn was also in the process of introducing "mild-mannered" truffles. Mild-mannered truffles were simply the same fine German chocolate that Marilyn started with to produce all of her chocolates, but without the spice. Marilyn had chosen silver as the wrapper color for the mild-mannered truffles. Although friends teased her about how this did not fit with the company's motto—Sissies Stay Away—which was integrated into the company's logo and printed on the back of company t-shirts and hats, she had decided that even the sissies deserved excellent chocolate. Further, she thought that having the mild-mannered chocolate might allow her to get her product placed in retail locations that had previously rejected her chocolates as being too spicy. Marilyn was the

first to admit that her chocolates packed a pretty good kick that not everybody found to their liking. She had developed the hot and spicy chocolates based primarily on her own tastes and the input of friends and acquaintances. She had observed many peoples' reactions upon trying her hot and spicy chocolates at trade shows and at new retail locations. Although many people liked her chocolates, the majority found at least some of the varieties to be too hot. In general, men tended to like the hotter truffles much more than women did. Marilyn knew her observations were consistent with what information was available on the fiery foods industry. Approximately 15 percent of American consumers were currently eating hot and spicy foods, and men were much more inclined to eat hot and spicy foods than were women. In addition to introducing mild-mannered chocolates, Marilyn was also thinking about introducing a chocolate with a calcium supplement aimed at women concerned about their calcium intake.

All of Cowgirl Chocolates' chocolate products were sourced from Seattle Chocolates, a Seattle-based company that specialized in producing European-style chocolate confections wrapped in an elegant package fit for gift giving. Seattle Chocolates obtained all of its raw chocolate from world-renowned chocolate producer Schokinag of Germany. Seattle Chocolates sold its own retail brand and provided private label chocolate products for a variety of companies including upscale retailers like Neiman Marcus and Nordstrom. Seattle Chocolates was, at least relative to Cowgirl Chocolates, a large company with annual sales in excess of $5 million. Seattle Chocolates took Cowgirl Chocolates on as a private label customer because they liked and were intrigued by the company's product and owners, and they had made some efforts to help Cowgirl Chocolates along the way. Seattle Chocolates provided Cowgirl Chocolates with a small amount of its table space at several important trade shows and produced in half batches for them. A half batch still consisted of 150 pounds of a given variety of chocolate, which was enough to last Cowgirl Chocolates for 6 months at 2000 sales rates. Marilyn hoped that she could one day convince Seattle Chocolates to manage the wholesale side of Cowgirl Chocolates, but Seattle Chocolates simply was not interested in taking this on at the current time, at least in part because they were not really sure where the market was for the product. Marilyn also knew she would need to grow sales significantly before Seattle Chocolates would seriously consider such an arrangement, although she was not sure exactly how much she would have to grow sales before such an arrangement would become attractive to Seattle Chocolates.

The chocolate bars themselves cost Cowgirl Chocolates $1.04 per bar, while the individual chocolate truffles cost $0.13 per piece. Seattle Chocolates also performed the wrapping and packing of the product. The chocolate bar wrappers cost $0.06 per bar. The wrapper design of the bars had recently been changed to incorporate dietary and nutritional

| Exhibit 1 | Cowgirl Chocolates Product Offerings with Price and Cost Figures |

Item	Approximate Percentage of Total Revenues	Suggested Retail Price[1]	Wholesale Price[1]	Total Item Cost (a + b)	Cost of Chocolate or Sauce (a)	Cost of Product Packaging[2] (b)
Spicy Chocolate Truffle Bars (available in 2 flavors: orange espresso or lime tequila crunch)	50%	$2.99	$1.50	$1.16	$1.04	$0.12
¼-Pound Muslin Bag (13 truffles in a drawstring muslin bag-available in 3 flavors: assorted hot, lime tequila, and mild-mannered)	16%	$6.95	$3.50	$2.35	$1.69	$0.66
½-Pound Tin (assorted hot and spicy truffles in a collectable tin)	12%	$14.95	$7.50	$4.78	$3.25	$1.53
Hot Caramel Dessert Sauce (9.5-oz. jar)	10%	$5.95	$3.50	$2.50	$2.00	$0.50
Sampler Bag (4 assorted hot truffles in a small drawstring muslin bag)	7%	$2.95	$1.50	$0.97	$0.52	$0.45
¼-Pound Gift Box (assorted hot truffles or mild-mannered truffles in a fancy gift box with gift card)	~1%	$8.95	$4.50	$2.95	$1.69	$1.26
1-Pound Gift Box (assorted hot truffles or mild-mannered truffles in a fancy gift box with gift card)	~1%	$24.95	$12.95	$9.05	$6.37	$2.68
Gift Bucket (tin bucket containing ¼-pound gift box, 2 truffle bars, and 1 jar of caramel sauce)	~1%	$39.95	$20.95	$11.02	$5.77	$5.25
Gift Basket (made of wire and branches) and containing ½-pound tin, 2 trufflebars, 1 jar of caramel sauce, and a T-shirt	~1%	$59.95	$30.95	$23.06	$15.29[3]	$7.77
Nothing Fancy (1-pound assorted hot truffles or mild-mannered truffles in a plastic bag)	~1%	$19.50	N.A.	$7.42	$6.37	$1.05

Notes:

1. Approximately 1/3 of sales were retail over the Cowgirl Chocolates Web site; the remaining 2/3 of sales were to wholesale accounts (i.e., to other retailers).

2. Packaging cost includes costs of container (bags, tins, or boxes), labels, and individual truffle wrapping. Packaging cost assumes Marilyn packs the items and does not include the packing and labeling fee charged by Seattle Chocolates if they do the packing ($1.00 per ½-pound tin or 1-pound box; $0.75 per ¼-pound box; $0.25 per ¼-pound bag; $0.20 per sampler bag).

3. This cost includes the cost of the T-shirts.

information. Although such information was not required, Marilyn felt it helped convey a better image of her chocolates. The change had cost $35 to prepare the new printing plates. Including the materials, wrapping the individual truffles cost $0.02 per piece.

The distinctive muslin bags, collector tins, and gift boxes also added to the final product cost. The muslin bags cost $0.35 each for the quarter-pound size and $0.32 each for the sampler size. The tamper-proof seals for the bags cost an additional $0.05 per bag. The minimum-size bag order was 500 bags. As with the chocolate bar wrappers, Cowgirl Chocolates had to buy the printing plates to print the bags. The plates to print the bags, however, cost $250 per plate. Each color of each design required a separate plate. Each of her three quarter-pound bag styles (assorted, lime tequila, and mild-mannered) had a 3-color design. One plate that was used to produce the background design was common to all three styles of bags, but each bag required two additional unique plates. There was also a separate plate for printing the sampler bags. Marilyn was planning to discontinue the separate lime tequila bag and just include lime tequila truffles in the assorted bag as a way to cut packaging costs. The lime tequila bags had been introduced a year ago. Although they sold reasonably well, they also appeared to mostly cannibalize sales of the assorted bags.

The collectible tins cost $0.80 each, and the labels for these tins cost $0.19 per tin. The tape used to seal the tins cost $0.04 per tin. The minimum order for the tins was for 800 units. The company that produced the tins had recently modified the tin design slightly to reduce the chance that someone might cut themselves on the edge of the can. Unfortunately, this change had resulted in a very small change to the height of the can, which left Cowgirl Chocolates with labels too big for the can. Each label currently had to be trimmed slightly to fit on the can. The alternative to this was to switch to a smaller label. This would require purchasing a new printing plate at a cost of about $35 and might require the purchase of a new printing die (the die holds the label while it is printed), which would cost $360. Marilyn also had hopes of one day being able to get her designs printed directly on the tins. It would make for even nicer tins and save the step of having to adhere the labels to the tins. The minimum order for such tins, however, was 15,000 units.

The gift boxes, including all of the associated wrapping, ribbon, and labels, cost about $1.70 per box. The gift boxes did not sell nearly as well as the tins or bags and were available primarily through the Cowgirl Chocolates Web site. Marilyn was still using and had a reasonable inventory of boxes from a box order she had placed 3 years ago.

Marilyn currently had more packaging in inventory than she normally would because she had ordered $5,000 worth in anticipation of the possibility of having her product placed in military PX stores at the end of 2000. Seattle Chocolates had been negotiating to get their product into these stores, and there had been some interest on the part of the PX stores in also having Cowgirl Chocolates products. Given the 6- to 8-week lead time on packaging, Marilyn had wanted to be positioned to quickly take advantage of this opportunity if it materialized. Although Marilyn was still hopeful this deal might come about, she was less optimistic than she had been at the time she placed the packaging order.

Marilyn was concerned that the actual packing step was not always performed with the care it should be. In particular, she was concerned that not enough or too many truffles ended up in the bags and tins, and that the seals on these containers, which made the packages more tamper resistant, were not always applied correctly. Each quarter-pound bag and gift box was supposed to contain 13 individual truffles; each half-pound tin was supposed to contain 25 individual truffles; and each 1-pound gift box was supposed to contain 49 individual truffles. The tins, in particular, had to be packed pretty tightly to get 25 truffles into them. Marilyn had done some of the packing herself at times and wondered if she would not be better off hiring local college or high school students to do the packing for her to ensure that the job was done to her satisfaction. It could also save her some money, as Seattle Chocolates charged her extra for packing the tins and bags. The tins, in particular, were expensive because of the time it took to apply the labels to the top and side of the tin and because of the extra care it took to get all 25 truffles into the tin. Seattle Chocolates charged $1 per tin for this step.

Marilyn made the caramel sauce herself with the help of the staff in a commercial kitchen in Sandpoint, Idaho, about a 1/2-hour drive north of Moscow. She could make 21 cases of 12 jars each in 1 day, but including the drive it took all day to do. As with the chocolate, she used only the best ingredients, including fresh cream from a local Moscow dairy. Marilyn figured her costs for the caramel sauce at about $2.50 per jar, which included the cost of the ingredients, the jars, the labeling, and the cost of using the Sandpoint kitchen. That figure did not include any allowance for the time it took her to make the sauce or put the labels on the jars. She was considering dropping the caramel sauce from her product line because it was a lot of work to produce, and she was not sure she really made any money on it after her own time was factored in. She had sold 70 cases of the sauce in 2000, however, so she knew there was some demand for the product. She was considering the possibility of offering it only at Christmas-time as a special seasonal product. She was also looking into the possibility of having a sauce company in Montana make it for her. The company produced caramel, chocolate, and chocolate-caramel sauces that had won awards from the fancy food industry trade association. Marilyn thought the sauces were quite good, although she did not like their caramel sauce as much as her own. The company would sell her 11-ounce jars of any of the sauces, spiced up to Marilyn's standards, for $2.75 per jar. Marilyn would have to provide the labels, for which she would need to have new label designs made to match the jar style the company was set up for, and she would also have to pay a shipping cost of $70 to $90 per delivery. The company requested a minimum order size of 72 cases, although the company's owner had hinted that they might be willing to produce in half batches initially.

All of Cowgirl Chocolates' products had won awards, either in the annual Fiery Food Challenges sponsored by *Chile Pepper* magazine or the Scovie Award Competitions sponsored by *Fiery Foods* magazine (the Scovie awards are named after the Scovie measure of heat). All in all, Cowgirl Chocolates had won 11 awards in these two annual competitions. Further, the truffles had won first place in the latest Fiery Food Challenge and the caramel sauce won first place in the latest Scovie competition. The packaging, as distinctive as the chocolate itself, had also won several awards, including the 2000 Award for Excellence for Package Design from American Corporate Identity.

Distribution and Pricing

Marilyn's attempts to get her chocolates into the retail market had met with varying degrees of success. She clearly had been very successful in placing her product in her hometown of Moscow, Idaho. The Moscow Food Co-op was her single best wholesale customer, accounting for 10 percent to 15 percent of her annual sales. The co-op sold a wide variety of natural and/or organic products and produce. Many of its products, like Cowgirl Chocolates, were made or grown locally. The co-op did a nice job of placing her product in a visible shelf location and generally priced her product less than any other retail outlet. The co-op sold primarily the chocolate bars, which it priced at $2.35, and the quarter-pound muslin bags of truffles, which it priced at $5.50. This compared to the suggested retail prices of $2.99 for the bars and $6.99 for the bags. The product was also available at three other locations in downtown Moscow: Wild Women Traders, a store that described itself as a "lifestyle outfitter" and sold high-end women's clothing and antiques; Northwest Showcase, a store that sold locally produced arts and crafts; and Bookpeople, an independent bookstore that catered to customers who liked to spend time browsing an eclectic offering of books and drinking espresso before making a book purchase.

Marilyn was unsure how many of these local sales were to repeat purchasers who really liked the product and how many were to individuals who wanted to buy a locally made product to give as a gift. She was also unsure how much the co-op's lower prices boosted the sales of her product at that location. At the co-op, her product was displayed with other premium chocolates from several competitors, including Seattle Chocolates' own branded chocolate bars, which

were priced at $2.99. Marilyn knew Seattle Chocolates' bars were clearly comparable in chocolate quality (although without the spice and cowgirl image). Some of the other competitors' comparably sized bars were priced lower, at $1.99, and some smaller bars were priced at $1.49. Although these products were clearly higher in quality than the inexpensive chocolate bars sold in vending machines and at the average supermarket checkout aisle, they were made with a less expensive chocolate than she used and were simply not as good as her chocolates. Marilyn wondered how the price and size of the chocolate bar affected the consumer's purchase decision, and how consumers evaluated the quality of each of the competing chocolate bars when making their purchase.

Outside of Moscow, Marilyn had a harder time getting her product placed onto store shelves and getting her product to move through these locations. One other co-op, the Boise Food Co-op, carried her products, and they sold pretty well there. Boise was the capital of Idaho and the state's largest city. The Boise Museum of Fine Arts gift shop also carried her product in Boise, although the product did not turn over at this location nearly as well as it did at the Boise Co-op. Other fine art museum gift shops in places like Missoula, Montana; Portland, Oregon; and Columbus, Ohio carried Cowgirl Chocolates, and Marilyn liked having her product in these outlets. She felt that her reputation as an artist helped her get her product placed in such locations, and the product generally sold well in these locations. She thought her biggest distribution coup was getting her product sold in the world-renowned Whitney Museum in New York City. She felt that the fact that it was sold there added to the product's panache. Unfortunately, the product did not sell there particularly well, and it was dropped by the museum. The museum buyer had told Marilyn that she simply thought it was too hot for their customers. Another location in New York City, the Kitchen Market, did much better. The Kitchen Market was an upscale restaurant and gourmet food takeout business. The Kitchen Market was probably her steadiest wholesale customer other than the Moscow Co-op. The product also sold pretty well at the few similar gourmet markets where she had gotten her product placed, like Rainbow Groceries in Seattle and the Culinary Institute of America in San Francisco.

Marilyn had also gotten her product placed in a handful of specialty food stores that focused on hot and spicy foods. Surprisingly, she found, the product had never sold well in these locations. Despite the fact that the product had won the major fiery food awards, customers in these shops did not seem to be willing to pay the premium price for her product. She had concluded that if her product was located with similarly priced goods, like at the Kitchen Market in New York City, it would sell, but that if it stood out in price then it did not sell as well. Marilyn was not sure, however, just how similarly her product needed to be priced compared to other products the store sold. It seemed clear to her that her $14.95 half-pound tins were standing out in price too much in the hot and spicy specialty stores that thrived on selling jars of hot sauce that typically retailed for $2.99 to $5.99. Marilyn wondered how her product might do at department stores that often sold half-pound boxes of "premium" chocolates for as little as $9.95. She knew her half-pound tins contained better chocolate, offered more unique packaging and logo design, and did not give that "empty-feeling" that the competitor's oversized boxes did, but she wondered if her product would stand out too much in price in such retail locations.

Several online retailers also carried Cowgirl Chocolates, including companies like Salmon River Specialty Foods and Sam McGee's Hot Sauces, although sales from such sites were not very significant. Marilyn had also had her product available through Amazon.com for a short time, but few customers purchased her product from this site during the time it was listed. Marilyn concluded that customers searching the site for music or books simply were not finding her product, and those who did simply were not shopping for chocolates.

Marilyn also sold her products retail through her own Web site. The Web site accounted for about one-third of her sales. She liked Web-based sales, despite the extra work of having to process all the small orders, because she was able to capture both the wholesale and retail profits associated with the sale. She also liked the direct contact with the retail customers, and frequently tossed a few extra truffles into a customer's order and enclosed a note that said "A little extra bonus from the head cowgirl." Marilyn allowed customers to return the chocolate for a full refund if they found it not to their liking. Most of her sales growth from 1999 to 2000 had come from her Web site.

The Web site itself was created and maintained for her by a small local Internet service provider. It was a fairly simple site. It had pages that described the company and its products and allowed customers to place orders. It did not have any of the sophisticated features that would allow her to use it to capture information to track customers. Although she did not know for sure, she suspected that many of her Internet sales were from repeat customers who were familiar with her product. She included her Web site address on all of her packaging and had listed her site on several other sites, like saucemall.com and worldmall.com, that would link shoppers at these sites to her site. Listing on some of these sites, like saucemall.com, was free. Listing on some other sites cost a small monthly fee. For the worldmall.com listing, for example, she paid $25 per month. Some sites simply provided links to her site on their own. For example, one customer had told her she had found the Cowgirl Chocolates site off of an upscale shopping site called Style365.com. She was not sure how much traffic these various sites were generating on her site, and she was unsure how best to attract new customers to her Web site aside from these efforts.

Marilyn had attempted to get her product into a number of bigger name, upscale retailers, like Dean & DeLuca and Coldwater Creek. Dean & DeLuca was known for its high-end specialty foods, and the buyers for the company had seemed interested in carrying Cowgirl Chocolates. The owner, however, had nixed the idea because he found the chocolates too spicy. One of the buyers had also told Marilyn that the owner was more of a chocolate purist or traditionalist who did not really like the idea of adding cayenne pepper to chocolate. Marilyn had also tried hard to get her product sold through Coldwater Creek, one of the largest catalog and online retailers in the country that sold high-end women's apparel and gifts for the home. Coldwater Creek was headquartered just a couple of hours north of Moscow in Sandpoint, Idaho. Like Dean & DeLuca, Coldwater Creek had decided that the chocolate was too spicy. Coldwater Creek had also expressed some reservations about carrying food products other than at its retail outlet in Sandpoint. Marilyn hoped that the introduction of mild-mannered Cowgirl Chocolates would help get her product into sites like these two.

Promotion

Marilyn was unsure how best to promote her product to potential customers given her limited resources. The ad that would appear in *Chile Pepper* magazine was her first attempt at really advertising her product. The ad itself was designed to grab readers' attention and peak their curiosity about Cowgirl Chocolates. Most of the ads in the magazine were fairly standard in format. They provided a lot of information and images of the product packed into a fairly small space. Her ad was different: It had very little product information and utilized the single image of the woman in the watering trough. It was to appear in a special section of the magazine that focused on celebrity musicians like Willie Nelson and The Dixie Chicks.

Other than the upcoming ad, Marilyn's promotional efforts were focused on trade shows and creating publicity opportunities. She attended a handful of trade shows each year. Some of these were focused on the hot and spicy food market, and it was at these events that she had won all of her awards. Other trade shows were more in the gourmet food market, and she typically shared table space at these events with Seattle Chocolates. She always gave away a lot of product samples at these trade shows and had clearly won over some fans to her chocolate. But although these shows occasionally had led to placement of her product in retail locations, at least on a trial basis, they had as yet failed to land her what she would consider to be a really high-volume wholesale account.

Marilyn also sought ways to generate publicity for her company and products. Several local newspapers had carried stories on her company in the last couple of years. Each time something like that would happen, she would see a brief jump in sales on her Web site. *The New York Times* had also carried a short article about her and her company. The day after that article ran, she generated sales of $1,000 through her Web site. More publicity like the *New York Times* article would clearly help. The recently released movie *Chocolat* about a woman who brings spicy chocolate with somewhat magical powers to a small French town was also generating some interest in her product. A number of customers had inquired if she used the same pepper in her chocolates as was used in the movie. Marilyn wondered how she might best capitalize on the interest the movie was creating in spicy chocolates. She thought that perhaps she could convince specialty magazines like *Art & Antiques* or regional magazines like *Sunset Magazine* or even national magazines like *Good Housekeeping* to run stories on her, her art and her chocolates. But she only had so much time to divide between her various efforts. She had looked into hiring a public relations firm but had discovered that this would cost something on the order of $2,000 per month. She did not expect that any publicity a public relations firm could create would generate sufficient sales to offset this cost, particularly given the limited number of locations where people could buy her chocolates. Marilyn was considering trying to write a cookbook as a way to generate greater publicity for Cowgirl Chocolates. She always talked a little about Cowgirl Chocolates when she gave seminars and presentations about her art, and she thought that promoting a cookbook would create similar opportunities. The cookbook would also feature several recipes using Cowgirl Chocolates products.

In addition to being unsure how best to promote her product to potential customers, Marilyn also wondered what she should do to better tap into the seasonal opportunities that presented themselves to sellers of chocolate. Demand for her product was somewhat seasonal, with peak retail demand being at Christmas and Valentine's Day, but she was clearly not seeing the Christmas and Valentine sales of other chocolate companies. Seattle Chocolates, for example, had around three-quarters of its annual sales in the fourth quarter, whereas Cowgirl Chocolates sales in the second half of 2000 were actually less than in the first half. Likewise, although Cowgirl Chocolates experienced a small increase in demand around Valentine's Day, it was nowhere near the increase in demand that other chocolate companies experienced. Marilyn did sell some gift buckets and baskets through her Web site, and these were more popular at Christmas and Valentine's Day. The Moscow Co-op had also sold some of these gift baskets and buckets during the 2000 Christmas season. Marilyn knew that the gift basket industry in the United States was pretty large, and that the industry even had its own trade publication called the *Gift Basket Review*. But she was not sure if gift baskets were the best way to generate sales at these two big holidays; she thought that she could probably be doing more. One other approach to spur these seasonal sales that she was planning to try was to buy lists of e-mail addresses that would allow her to send out several e-mails promoting her products right before Valentine's Day and Christmas. She had talked to the owners of a jewelry store about sharing the expense of this endeavor and they had tentative plans to purchase 10,000 e-mail addresses for $300.

What Next?

Marilyn looked again at the advertisement that would be appearing soon in *Chile Pepper* magazine. The same friend who had helped her with her award-winning package design had helped produce the ad. It would clearly grab people's attention, but would it bring customers to her products in the numbers she needed?

Next to the ad sat the folder with what financial information she had. Despite having little training in small business accounting and financial management, Marilyn knew it was important to keep good records. She had kept track of revenues and expenses for the year, and she had summarized these in a table (Exhibit 2). Marilyn had shared this revenue and cost information with a friend with some experience in small business financial management, and the result was an estimated income statement for the year 2000 based upon the unaudited information in Exhibit 2. The estimated income statement, shown in Exhibit 3, revealed that Cowgirl Chocolates had lost approximately $6,175 on operations before taxes. Combining the information in both Exhibit 2 and 3, it appeared that the inventory had built up to approximately $16,848 by December 31, 2000. Marilyn had initially guessed that she had $10,000 worth of product and packaging inventory, about twice her normal level of inventory, between what was stored in her garage turned art studio turned chocolate warehouse and what was stored for her at Seattle Chocolates. However, the financial analysis indicated that she either had more inventory than she thought or that she had given away more product than she originally thought. Either way, this represented a significant additional drain on her resources. In effect, cash expended to cover both the operational loss and the inventory buildup was approximately $23,000 in total. When Marilyn looked at the exhibits, she could better understand why she had to loan the firm money. The bottom line was that the numbers did not look good, and she wondered if the ad would help turn things around for 2001.

If the ad did not have its desired effect, she wondered what she should do next. She clearly had limited resources. She had already pretty much decided that if this ad did not work, she would not run another one in the near future. She was also wary of working with distributors. In addition to her own bad experience, she knew of others in the industry who had had bad experiences with distributors, and she

| Exhibit 2 | Summary of 2000 Financial Information (unaudited) |

Revenues

Product Sales	$26,000
Revenue from Shipping	4,046[1]
Total Revenues	$30,046

Expenses (related to cost of sales)

Chocolate (raw material)	$16,508
Caramel (raw material)	2,647
Packaging (bags, boxes, tins)	9,120
Printing (labels, cards, etc.)	3,148
Subtotal	$31,423[2]

Other Expenses

Shipping and Postage	$ 4,046
Brokers	540
Travel (airfare, lodging, meals, gas)	5,786
Trade shows (promotions, etc.)	6,423
Web Site	1,390
Phone	981
Office Supplies	759
Photography	356
Insurance, Lawyers, Memberships	437
Charitable Contributions	200
Miscellaneous Other Expenses	1,071
State Taxes	35
Subtotal	$ 22,024
Total Expenses	$ 53,447
Cash Needed to Sustain Operations	$ 23,023[3]

Estimated Year-End Inventory (12/31/00)

Product Inventory	$ 9,848
Extra Packaging and Labels	7,000
Total Inventory	$16,848

Notes:

1. The $4,046 revenue from shipping represents income received from customers who are charged shipping and postage up front as part of the order. Cowgirl Chocolates then pays the shipping and postage when the order is delivered. The offsetting operating expense is noted in "Other Expenses."

2. Of this amount, $14,575 is attributed to product actually sold and shipped. The remaining $16,848 represents leftover inventory and related supplies (i.e., $16848 + $14575 = $31,423).

3. Marilyn made a personal loan to the firm in the year 2000 for approximately $23,000 to sustain the business's operations.

| Exhibit 3 | Cowgirl Chocolates Income Statement (accountant's unaudited estimate for year 2000) |

			% of Sales
Revenues			
Product Sales	$26,000		
Miscellaneous Income	$ 4,046		
Total Net Sales		$30,046	100%
Cost of Sales (shipped portion of chocolate, caramel, packaging, and printing)		$14,197	47%
Cross Margin		$15,849	53%
Operating Expenses			
Advertising and Promotions			
Trade Shows	6,423		
Web Site	1,390		
Charitable Contributions	200		
Subtotal		8,013	27%
Travel		5,786	19%
Miscellaneous		1,071	4%
Payroll Expense/Benefits @ 20%	(no personnel charges)	—	0%
Depreciation on Plant and Equipment	(no current ownership of PPE)	—	0%
Continuing Inventory (finished and unfinished)	(not included in income statement)	—	0%
Shipping and Postage		4,046	13%
Insurance, Lawyers, Professional Memberships		437	1.5%
Brokers		540	1.8%
Office Expenses (phone, supplies, photography, taxes)		2,131	7%
Total Operating Expenses		22,024	
Grand Total: All Expenses		$36,221	
Profit Before Interest and Taxes		($6,175) [see note]	
Interest Expense (short term)		—	
Interest Expense (long term)		—	
Taxes Incurred (Credit @ 18%, approximate tax rate)		($1,124)	
Net Profit After Taxes		($5,051.15)	
Net Profit After Taxes/Sales			–17%

Note: The ($6,175) loss plus the $16,848 in inventory buildup approximates the cash needed ($23,023) to cover the total expenses for year 2000.

did not think she could afford to take another gamble on a distributor. She wondered if she should focus more attention on her online retail sales or on expanding her wholesale business to include more retailers. If she focused more on her own online sales, what exactly should she do? If she focused on expanding her wholesale business, where should she put her emphasis? Should she continue to pursue retailers that specialized in hot and spicy foods; try to get her product placed in more co-ops; expand her efforts to get the product positioned as a gift in museum gift shops and similar outlets; or focus her efforts on large, high-end retailers like Coldwater Creek and Dean & DeLuca now that she had a nonspicy chocolate in her product mix? Or should she try to do something entirely new? What more should she do to create publicity for her product? Was the cookbook idea worth pursuing? As she thought about it, she began to wonder if things were beginning to spin out of control. Here she was, contemplating writing a cookbook to generate publicity for her chocolate company that she had started to raise money to publish her arts magazine. Where would this end?

CASE 3

GoodLife Fitness Clubs

Gordon H. G. McDougall, Wilfrid Laurier University

"These retention rates are poor. I need to do a better job of keeping members," thought Krista Swain, manager of the GoodLife Kitchener Fitness Club in Kitchener, Ontario, as she reviewed her retention rates for the 1999-2000 fiscal year.

As she was analyzing the report, Jane Riddell, chief operating officer, entered her office. Krista looked up and said, "Hi Jane. I've just been looking over the retention rates for the clubs. I'm not happy with my numbers."

"Neither is the head office," Jane replied, "and that's why I'm here today. You run one of our best clubs, and yet your retention rates are around 60 percent, the average for the 40 GoodLife Clubs. We lose 40 percent of our members each year. By improving your club's retention rates from 60 percent to 65 percent, based on last year's figures, gross revenues would increase by over $35,000. You are one of our top performers, and you should be leading the way."

"I agree," said Krista. "We have to figure out how to keep the members enthused and show that the club offers them value."

"That's what I wanted to hear," replied Jane. "As a first step, let's both think about this and meet again next week with some ideas. Then I'd like you to prepare a retention plan that will be the model for all the clubs."

The Fitness Market

In a national study, the Canadian Fitness and Research Institute found that most Canadians believed that physical activity was beneficial in preventing heart disease or other chronic conditions, in reducing stress, and in maintaining the ability to perform everyday tasks with aging. However, physical inactivity remained pervasive in Canada, with 63 percent of adults age 18 and older still considered insufficiently active for optimal health benefits in 1998.[1]

The study also revealed that for a variety of reasons most Canadians tended to "talk" positively about the importance of physical activity but didn't "walk the talk." The most popular physical recreation activities were walking (86 percent of Canadians had participated at least once in this activity within the past 12 months), gardening (75 percent), swimming (57 percent), bicycling (55 percent) and home exercise (50 percent). Exercise class/aerobics was ranked thirteenth

(21 percent) with significantly more women (33 percent) than men (9 percent) participating.

Although the overall physical activity of Canadians was relatively low, the fitness market was growing at approximately 6 percent a year. The growth was due to demographic changes (baby boomers were increasingly interested in maintaining a good level of physical fitness), marketing (increasing numbers of health/fitness clubs extolling the benefits of fitness through their programs), and individuals selecting fitness clubs over other physical activities as their choice for exercise.

Industry estimates were that about 10 percent of the Canadian population belonged to a health club. However, there was considerable "churning" (the percentage of members lost in a month or year); many Canadians had good intentions and joined a club, only to leave at the end of their membership for a variety of reasons. Industry research revealed the following major reasons for leaving: decline in interest, took too much time, too hard and didn't like the club. It was estimated that on an annual basis the average health/fitness club in Canada lost between 36 percent to 45 percent of its members.

Another reason for the high average churn rates was that many clubs, referred to as "factories," did not take a professional approach in managing their operations. Typically, a sports personality (e.g., a retired hockey player) would own these "factories" and offer low initial memberships to get people into the club. These clubs had few trained instructors, frequent equipment breakdowns, and poor facilities maintenance. These clubs often failed within a year or two, leaving customers with a valid membership and no facility.

GoodLife

The Philosophy and Goals

In March 1979, David Patchell-Evans established GoodLife as a sole proprietorship. "Patch," as he was called, saw an opportunity. Canadian fitness clubs were largely cash and sales oriented with little emphasis on scientific fitness or member retention. By May 2000, Patch had built this privately owned fitness company to over 40 clubs (10 were franchises, the rest were company owned) in Ontario and Quebec. GoodLife had the largest group of fitness clubs in Canada with over 70,000 members. (Appendix 1 provides more details on the philosophy and growth of the GoodLife Clubs.)

From the beginning, the company's goal was to provide the best in equipment, facilities, and service with a well-trained staff. The goal was based on high-quality service with education and training, superior cleanliness, and programs that made the individual a member for life based on their "needs and goals." The GoodLife motto, "Measurable Constant Improvement," underlaid its plan to grow to 100 clubs by 2004.

Head Office

The head office was located at the Galleria Mall Fitness Club in London, Ontario. Head office personnel numbered approximately 40, led by "Patch," Jane Riddell, chief operating officer, and Maureen Hagen, national director of fitness. Head office's main role was to provide leadership and support for the franchisees and company-owned clubs. Among the group's major activities were determining the advertising strategy, designing new fitness programs, ensuring that all clubs maintained quality standards, providing training programs for staff, and keeping all club managers abreast of the latest trends and issues in the fitness industry.

One of Jane Riddell's responsibilities was the design and management of GoodLife University, where each month 50 to 60 new associates went through a 1-week program. The training included an orientation to GoodLife (basic knowledge of GoodLife and its philosophy), personal training (skills required to assist members as a personal trainer), and computer program training. When club managers hired the associates, they typically spent their first few weeks "learning the ropes" at the club and then attended the university program. Jane led some of the training sessions and evaluated the participants, some of whom failed and left GoodLife.

Jane was generally pleased with the caliber of the participants. She rated about 70 percent of them as good to great and 30 percent as poor. In the past, the GoodLife clubs had focused on hiring physical education and kinesiology graduates. However, as the economy improved in the late 1990s, these graduates chose other job opportunities, requiring GoodLife to broaden its hiring criteria. Now GoodLife hired individuals with the "right" attitude (i.e., customer focused). However, the attitude of some new employees was that this was not a "real" job or a career. Rather it was a fun place to be for a while, a "cool," easy job until they got a "real" job. Jane felt that this was part of the issue of employee retention at GoodLife. In the past 2 years, employee turnover had increased, and last year 600 employees (out of a total of 1,400) had left GoodLife. Jane estimated that most of the employee retention problem was GoodLife's "fault"—they either hired the wrong people, or didn't do enough to keep them.

Advertising spending, at 6 percent of revenues, used a "call to action" versus a "branding" approach. The call to action used variations on "$99 for 99 days," "one month free," "no initiation fee," or "save now."

The company allocated advertising expenditures by season (winter, 40 percent; summer, 25 percent; and October to December, 35 percent), which reflected the general interest level of people in joining a fitness club. Each month headquarters evaluated each club on sales targets—the new members obtained through internal marketing (e.g., referrals or *Yellow Pages*), external marketing (e.g., newspaper, flyers, radio, or television), and walk-ins (e.g., potential member walks into the club and asks about memberships). This information, along with conference calls with the regions, set the regional advertising allocation.

GoodLife's commitment to club members, staff, and community resulted in numerous awards and achievements. GoodLife was the first to bring many innovations to the fitness industry, including the Fit Fix training concept and the PUNCH program. GoodLife raised over $500,000 annually for various charities and supported a wide range of community activities.

The GoodLife Staff

GoodLife's size (over 1,400 associates) and rapid growth provided many opportunities for advancement. The career path at GoodLife could take an associate to any number of areas: group exercise classes, personal training, sales, administration, management, accounting, and even to owning one of the clubs.

Compensation consisted of a base salary plus club sales commissions and bonuses. The club sales commissions were based on the number of memberships sold per week against a target. Depending on the type of membership sold and/or specialty programs sold, the associate could receive a commission on sales ranging from 5 percent to 15 percent. Bonuses were based on weekly targets set for the individual club. Depending on the hours and shifts worked by the staff, if the goals were met, the staff member could earn a bonus of $15 or $25 per week. As well, there was an employee referral bonus: Any current staff member who referred an individual for employment with GoodLife could receive a bonus of $100, or $200 for individuals hired on a part-time or full-time basis. Finally, there were incentive programs for good ideas. The rewards, called "Patch Bucks," could be redeemed for fitness conferences.

GoodLife offered company awards on a monthly and yearly basis. On a monthly basis, awards were given to (1) group exercise coordinator (gift and plaque), (2) manager of the month ($200 and plaque), (3) associate ($100 and plaque), (4) sales manager ($200 and plaque), (5) sales associate ($100 and plaque), (6) personal training associate ($100 and plaque), and (7) customer service representative ($100 plus plaque). On a yearly basis, awards were given to (1) manager (free fitness conference, valued at $2,500), (2) group exercise instructor, and (3) group exercise coordinator.

GoodLife Kitchener

The New Location

In September 1998, the GoodLife Kitchener Club reopened on the second floor of an indoor mall in downtown Kitchener,

Exhibit 1	GoodLife Kitchener Club—Membership by Month

Month	Members Lost During Month	Members Gained During Month	Net Members Gained During Month	Members (at end of month)	Retention Rate per Year (%)	Loss Rate per Month (%)
March '99	–	–	–	1900	–	–
April '99	58[a]	163	105	2005	63.5[b]	3.0
May '99	61	158	97	2102	64.0	3.0
June '99	73	156	83	2185	59.4	3.4
July '99	75	155	80	2263	60.9	3.3
August '99	68	150	82	2341	65.2	2.9
September '99	70	168	98	2423	64.8	2.9
October '99	108	196	88	2521	48.5	4.3
November '99	91	220	129	2609	57.9	3.5
December '99	90	223	133	2738	60.1	3.3
January '00	103	244	141	2871	56.4	3.6
February '00	99	238	139	3012	60.1	3.3
March '00	113	234	121	3151	56.4	3.6
Annual Average					59.8[c]	3.4

Source: GoodLife Fitness Clubs.

a. At the beginning of April, the club had 1,900 members. The monthly loss rate for April is 3.0% (based on a yearly retention rate for April of 63.5%, which is a yearly loss rate of 36.5%). The club lost $1,900 \times .03 = 58$ members in April.

b. 63.5% of the members as of April '98 were still members as of April '99; 36.5% were no longer members.

c. The average retention rate for the year shown is 59.8%; average loss rate per month is 3.4% $(1 - .598 = .402/12)$.

Ontario. Prior to that, it was located two blocks away in a relatively small (12,000 square feet) and poorly designed facility. The new facility was larger (30,000 square feet), had an open concept design, and an extensive range of equipment and programs. Over the next 18 months, membership increased dramatically under Krista Swain's guidance. As of May 2000, the club had 3,500 members, an increase of 2,300 over the original 1,200 members who moved from the old club.

Krista, a 1995 graduate in kinesiology and physical education from Wilfrid Laurier University in Waterloo, Ontario, worked for GoodLife as a fitness instructor while she was attending the university. After graduation, she joined the GoodLife Waterloo Club as a service trainer. In addition, she handled corporate sales for the GoodLife Women Only Club in Kitchener. Within 10 months, she was appointed manager of the GoodLife Kitchener Club and was actively involved in the transition from the old to the new location. When asked how she had rapidly advanced to club manager, she said:

I have a passion for fitness and I'm committed to the company. I'm convinced that the GoodLife values, mission, and philosophy are right; I truly feel that we are helping people at GoodLife. I like working with people. My role is to be a coach and mentor, and I lead by example. I think the staff understand my goals and respect me because I respect them. Sometimes I

can't believe what the staff are willing to do to help the club and the members. But I'll also say, if you are not a top performer, you won't fit in at GoodLife.

In early 2000, the Kitchener club was signing up over 230 new members per month (Exhibit 1). At the same time, the club was losing about 100 members per month for a net gain of about 130 members. On an annual basis, the club was losing 40 percent of its members. Overall, the rapid growth in membership had a very positive impact on revenues, which increased by over 60 percent between June 1999 and March 2000 (Exhibit 2).

The Associates

The Kitchener club's 40 associates (10 full-time, 30 part-time) worked in four groups: sales, customer service, personal training, and service.

- The four sales associates (all full-time) were responsible for getting new members.
- Customer service employees, who were primarily part-time, worked the front desk.
- Personal trainers worked with individual club members on fitness programs.

| Exhibit 2 | GoodLife Kitchener Club—Selected Revenues and Expenses |

	June 30 '99 Month	June 30 '99 YTD (12 months)	March 31 '00 Month	March 31 '00 YTD (9 months)
Revenues	(%)	(%)	(%)	(%)
Membership	88.9	88.2	86.9	83.3
Services[a]	9.3	10.2	11.9	15.5
Other	1.8	1.6	1.2	1.2
Total Revenues	100.0	100.0	100.0	100.0
Expenses				
Sales Wages and Commissions[b]	10.5	12.1	8.3	8.9
Service Wages and Commissions[c]	9.0	7.1	5.3	12.3
Service and Other[d]	19.4	28.6	20.4	17.1
Total Direct Expenses	38.9	47.8	34.0	38.3
Manager Controlled[e]	9.2	15.6	4.8	10.4
Administrative[f]	31.8	31.1	26.3	32.6
Total Expenses[g]	79.9	94.5	65.1	81.3
Members	2,200		3,200	
Total Revenue ($)	120,000	1,004,000	195,000	1,177,000

Source: GoodLife Fitness Clubs.

a. Includes personal training, specialty programs, tanning, and pro shop
b. Related to new membership sales
c. Includes personal training and member services
d. Includes service staff wages and expenses
e. Includes utilities, supplies and services
f. Includes advertising, administrative management, rent, realty taxes, equipment leasing
g. Not included are depreciation, amortization, interest, and taxes

- Service employees introduced new members to the club and its philosophy through a series of programs on fitness and equipment use.

All employees were involved in selling. Although the sales associates were dedicated to selling new memberships, the personal trainers spent time encouraging members to sign up for personal training. The customer service employees would sell tanning programs and other services to members. Typically, each group or individual had sales targets and earned bonuses and commissions based on meeting those targets.

Most of the employees earned a base salary of $8 per hour plus bonuses if they achieved the weekly targets. As an example, a sales associate might have a target of eight new members per week. If the target were achieved or exceeded, the associate could earn $1,250 or more every 2 weeks. Customer service staff could earn up to $25 per week if they met targets that included phoning members to remind them of upcoming events, encouraging them to use the club, and selling various club products and services such as tanning. Personal trainers could make up to $27 per hour

for personal training in addition to their base pay of $8 per hour. The more members the trainer signed up, the more hours he/she spent in personal training.

Through these incentive programs GoodLife encouraged its staff, particularly the sales associates, to be entrepreneurial. As Krista often said, "The staff have to make things happen; they can't wait for them to happen. Both GoodLife and the staff do better when they make things happen."

As noted, GoodLife had formal training programs for new employees. In addition, Krista spent time with the new employees teaching them the technical side of the job and establishing the norms and culture of the club. By emphasizing what was important to her, Krista hoped they would understand the importance of excellent customer service. "If I can show the new employees what's important to me, and get them to trust me, they come on board and are part of the team. For example, we hold weekly staff meetings where we discuss a number of issues, including how to improve the club. People don't miss the meetings. Every once in a while, a new associate decides not to come to the meetings. The team lets him or her know that's not acceptable. Those people either become part of the team or decide to leave GoodLife."

Employee turnover at the Kitchener GoodLife Club was slightly better than the average across all the GoodLife clubs. In the past year, Krista had a turnover of about 35 percent, with the rate for full-time slightly lower than for part-time. Part-time turnover was higher, in part, because many of the part-time employees were students who left to go to university or left after completing their degree programs.

Like Jane Riddell, Krista was concerned about employee turnover, but she wasn't sure what actions could improve the situation. She had noticed that some new employees were surprised at the amount of selling involved in their positions. She also felt that some employees were not satisfied with the base salary of $8 per hour.

Typically, when an employee left, Krista needed to hire a new associate relatively quickly. She would place an ad in the local paper, *The Record;* get some applications; conduct interviews; and hire the individual she felt was most suited for the position. With full-time employees, Krista was not always happy with the pool of applicants she interviewed, but there was always the pressure of filling the job, which had to be balanced against the quality of the applicants. With the economy improving and a low local unemployment rate, it was sometimes difficult to attract high-quality applicants.

The Members

Most new members joined the club through referrals. When an individual asked about joining the club, a sales associate would show them the club and discuss the benefits of membership and the GoodLife philosophy. Assuming the individual decided to join, the sales associate would ask if he or she had any friends who might be interested in joining the club and, if so, they would receive a free membership for 1 week. Typically, the associate tried to get five referrals. The associate would then contact these people, offer the free 1-week membership, and set up a meeting with them if they accepted. The cycle was repeated with each new member. On average, the sales associates converted between one or two of the five contacts to new members. Referrals generated between 60 percent and 80 percent of all new members.

The price for a new membership varied depending on the promotion option. The two main options were (1) a $199 initiation fee, the first 6 months free, and $40 per 4 weeks after that or (2) the initiation fee was waived and the member paid $40 per 4 weeks. Payments were on a biweekly basis through an automatic payment plan that the member signed. The new member also paid a total of $54 for the membership card ($15) and a processing fee ($39). A new member could also decide to join for a 3-month period for $180. Members could also decide to pay once a year and not use the automatic payment plan.

When an individual joined the club, an associate from the service group would take the new member through three programs as an introduction to the club and the GoodLife approach to a healthy lifestyle. The three programs were (1) Fit Fix 1—an introduction to strength training, (2) Cardio—basic information about cardiovascular training principles, and (3) Fit Fix 2—adding exercises to the member's program. Any new member could also have a fitness assessment (including resting heart rate and body fat measurements). After 6 weeks, the new member could also have a second fitness assessment to track his/her progress.

The club offered a wide range of cardio equipment, weights, and personal training programs. Members could participate in over 20 aerobics programs each week, from Steps 'n Abs to Circuit Training to Newbody to PUNCH. On average, 12 members were participating in each program. Typically, members had been going to these programs for years, and few new members joined any program. The club attempted to address this issue with new members by having a "new members only" aerobics class. On average, the club would get 50 new members to sign up for the program, 15 would show up for the first class, and it would be down to six people when the class ended in 12 weeks.

This issue reflected a broader problem common to most of the GoodLife Clubs, often referred to as the "20–20–60 phenomenon." Twenty percent of the club members were hard-core fitness and health people. These members came three or more times a week, were serious about their training, and would tolerate a lot (such as uneven service) as long as it didn't interfere with their training. The second 20 percent were the new members. They were enthusiastic, wanted to get fit, and over time they either became committed or not. The largest group, the remaining 60 percent, were those members who came on an irregular basis. The club staff didn't know their names; these members often were not sure how the equipment worked or what they should be doing; and they often wouldn't ask for help. Even when they stopped coming, this group kept their membership for a period until they decided to cancel. When one came to cancel, an associate tried to get her or him to stay, usually with little success.

Krista and other associates at GoodLife believed that getting members to feel that they were part of the GoodLife Club was important in retaining them. Krista believed that many of the 60 percent probably never felt they were part of the club because they didn't know many or any of the other members or the staff. Krista remembered that although many of the 1,200 members from the old club liked the new facility, they felt that the club was more impersonal. In particular, as the membership grew, the "original" members felt less at home. Krista estimated that, within a year, about 50 percent of these members had left the club.

The advertising for GoodLife consisted of an ad in the *Yellow Pages* and ads in a local free weekly newspaper, *The Pennysaver.* Local businesses were targeted with brochures offering specials. Krista felt that most of the new members came from the referral program and *Pennysaver* ads. As she said, "*The Pennysaver* ads get the phones ringing."

Although Krista believed that overall the members were satisfied with the club, she felt there was always room for improvement. For example, members sent her about 14 written complaints or concerns every week through the suggestion box. Each week, the front office staff received about a dozen verbal complaints. Most complaints or concerns dealt with equipment problems (e.g., equipment not working properly) and a few dealt with staff (e.g., a particular staff member was not friendly). Krista dealt with the complaints as they arose.

Competition

In the Kitchener/Waterloo (K/W) area (Kitchener and Waterloo are twin cities), there were about 15 fitness/exercise clubs serving a population base of 450,000 people. The Kitchener GoodLife Club had four major competitors:

- The two YMCAs in K/W offered aerobic programs and had workout areas. The "Ys" had a good reputation as being friendly, family-oriented clubs. The annual membership fee ranged from $400 to $650 depending on the type of membership and the services requested.
- The International Family Fitness Centre was also located in downtown Kitchener within three blocks of the GoodLife Club. It offered equivalent facilities to the GoodLife Club, was of a similar size, and had over 40 programs a week. Its membership rates were very similar to those of GoodLife.
- Popeye's Gym previously had a reputation as a male-oriented facility where bodybuilders worked out. However, the image was slowly changing to a men's and women's fitness club that offered aerobic programs and a variety of weight and training machines. It was located approximately 3 kilometers from downtown Kitchener and was open 24 hours a day. The membership fees were approximately $350 per year.

Customer Retention

As Krista prepared for the meeting with Jane, she knew that improved customer retention rates were possible but was uncertain as to what actions would be most effective. She identified three major areas that she could address: employee turnover, a new bonus system, and swipe card technology.

Employee turnover, at over 40 percent, created a lack of stability at the club. Every time a new employee started, he or she did not know any members. Over time, the new employee would learn the members' names (often those who visited frequently). If the employee left, so did the knowledge. Krista had always felt that members would have a greater sense of "belonging" to the club if the front desk staff could greet them by name. Although many of the front desk staff knew some of the members by name (most of these members were the hard-core regulars who came frequently), most of the front desk staff were part-time associates or had recently joined GoodLife; therefore, they knew relatively few members by name. Further, because most of the "60 percent" group came infrequently, few staff knew their names.

Krista had two ideas for reducing employee turnover, both based on increasing wages. Increasing the hourly base rate from $8 to $9 for most employees (excluding managers and sales associates) would add about $4,000 per month to wage costs. The problem was that, although she knew that employee turnover would decline, she did not know by how much, nor did she know the effect on retention rates. A second option was to focus only on the front desk employees who greeted members. Increasing their rate to $9 would increase monthly wage costs by about $1,000. She preferred this option because the front desk associates greeted all the members as they entered and swiped their card. With the increase in their wages, Krista would ensure that the front desk staff knew that an important part of their job was to greet members by name.

Next, Krista considered introducing a bonus plan for increasing customer retention. Virtually all the targets and bonuses at GoodLife focused on increasing sales, reflecting, in part, Patch's aggressive growth targets. Although she did not have a specific plan in mind, Krista felt that an allocation of at least $1,000 to bonuses for increased retention was feasible. Her initial idea was that for every percent increase in retention rates per month (e.g., from 60 percent to 61 percent), staff would receive $200 in bonuses. Krista was uncertain how the target should be set—on an individual or group basis. The front desk staff had the most contact with members, but potentially all the employees could be involved. What was important to Krista was that the associates have a goal and a bonus attached to customer retention. She knew that this plan would get the associates to focus more of their efforts on customer retention.

Krista felt that better use of the swipe card information could improve retention. Members swiped their membership card when they visited the club. A valid card allowed a member to go through a turnstile; a nonvalid card (because it had expired) did not release the turnstile. Krista knew that other information (e.g., number of member visits) was available, but no one at the club or head office had developed a software program to track member visits. Krista contacted two software companies, one of which offered a membership management program that would provide interface with swipe scanners and provide reports on members' frequency of visits, along with a host of other member information. The cost ranged from $3,500 for a license for five sites up to $8,500 for unlimited site use.

One of the targets for the front desk associates was to make "motivation" calls to members each week. Associates would call a specified number of members to reach their target. The associates would begin anywhere on the member list (a binder at the front desk) and begin calling members to encourage them to use the facilities or inform them of special events. After the call, the associate would record the date called and his or her name next to the member's name. Ideally, all members were called once every 6 weeks, but this didn't always happen.

With the new software system, reports could identify members who had not visited the club for a particular period. Staff could then contact members who had not visited for a specific time period, such as 3 weeks or 4 weeks. Krista felt that this would substantially improve the existing approach and would improve member retention rates.

Krista knew that there were other available approaches or tactics to improve retention rates. In particular, any activities that built a greater sense of "community" would increase interaction between members and a sense of "belonging." But it was difficult to find the time to figure it out. Managing a club with 3,500 members kept her very busy making sure everything was running smoothly, and she spent most of her time "doing" not "planning."

A week later, Jane met Krista in her office. Jane started the conversation. "Let me review the situation. As I mentioned last week, if we could improve your club's retention rates from 60 percent to 65 percent, based on last year's numbers, gross revenues would increase by more than $35,000. In this business, most of the costs tend to be fixed, probably about 60 percent of revenues, so most of the revenue would be profits. If we could do that for all the clubs, it would be great for business, and I think we would have more satisfied members. Just to put this in perspective, on average, we have about 2,000 members per club."

Jane continued, "In the past year, the story has been about the same for most of our clubs. For every 100 new members signed up each month, we have about 40 people who don't renew or cancel their membership. We spend a lot on marketing to get them in the door. Then we spend time with them setting up an exercise or training program. They are enthusiastic to begin with; then they stop coming to classes or exercise. They cancel or don't renew when their membership comes up. When they cancel, we ask them why they are leaving. The most common reasons are that they don't have enough time or they can't fit it into their schedule. I think that about 30 percent of the time, they have a good reason for leaving, such as they are moving out of town. I think that 70 percent of the time, we could have done something to keep them with the club.

"From a head office point of view, we have had a number of debates about the amount of advertising we do, which is about 6 percent of revenues. That's a lot of money and sometimes we think that we should be spending more of that in staff training. Another question is—what type of training would be most effective?

"Let me mention one other issue we are concerned about," Jane continued. "We don't use the swipe card to collect data. We need to do more with that."

"That was one of my thoughts," Krista replied. She then told Jane about the software program's capabilities and costs.

"Very interesting," replied Jane. "That's certainly something to consider." Krista then presented her other ideas to Jane. As she finished, Krista said, "I think my cost estimates wouldn't be too far out of line for our average club."

Then Krista added, "Sometimes I think that maybe we should focus more on service than sales. As an example, my front desk staff have sales targets and other assignments as well as greeting members. Also, there are few opportunities for the staff to walk around and just talk to our members and see how they are doing. That's why I suggested a bonus plan based on increasing retention rates. We have very aggressive growth targets for each club and plan to add a lot more clubs. As an organization, we are really getting stretched. Most of our time is spent on growth, not service."

"Yes, but the strategy has worked well so far," Jane replied. "I'm not sure if we could justify adding more staff to focus on service; we would need to see a payback. But it's another interesting idea."

Krista and Jane continued the discussion and then decided that Krista would prepare a customer retention plan for the Kitchener GoodLife Club with the goal of increasing retention rates by 5 percentage points or more within 6 months. "I want to at least get the average retention up to 65 percent," Jane said. "As I mentioned last week, we'll use this plan as the model for all the clubs."

As Jane left, she said, "Krista, I have every confidence in you. I'm going to send an assistant manager from the other Kitchener club down here to help you run the club while you work on the plan. I look forward to positive results."

After Jane left, Krista sat down and began thinking about the approaches she could take to increase retention rates. She had always liked a challenge, and she knew that she would do her best to meet this one.

Appendix: Muscle Mania

David Patchell-Evans may not be a natural athlete, but he's a confirmed fitness fanatic. He works and dreams physical fitness. Even his vacations are spent pursuing extreme sports such as mountain climbing or skiing. But that wasn't always the case. In his first year at university, a motorcycle accident paralyzed the right side of his body. Following extensive rehabilitation, Patchell-Evans was determined to return to full physical fitness. He took up rowing and eventually became a five-time Canadian rowing champion and a member of the 1980 Canadian Olympic team.

Those experiences taught Patchell-Evans the role health and fitness play in creating a satisfying life and fostered a life-long commitment to sell the idea to others. In

1979 he bought a workout club in London, Ontario, and began implementing his vision: to provide customers with an affordable club offering state-of-the-art equipment and, more importantly, knowledgeable staff eager to teach them how to get the most from it. "The opportunity in the marketplace," he says, "was to provide service."

In an industry notorious for dubious claims and fly-by-night operators, GoodLife Fitness Clubs has built its business on highly trained staff, innovative programming, and reinvesting in its facilities. In 20 years, it has become Canada's largest health club chain, with 42 clubs, 100,000 members, and 1998 sales of $40 million. In an industry that's adding new clubs and members at 9% a year, GoodLife is growing at almost three times that rate. By 2004 Patchell-Evans goal is to have 100 facilities.

To reach the goal Patchell-Evans will rely on the same philosophies on which the chain was founded: providing health, fitness, and self-esteem so that people feel better about themselves. It is part of the strategy to raise the bar of service excellence and bring a new professionalism to an industry where clubs were traditionally run by sports jocks with little business training. The GoodLife philosophy of ensuring consistently high standards in every club goes a long way to building brand loyalty among the members. "When people work out, they want to know that the shower will be clean, the equipment is going to work, and the staff know what they are talking about."

That philosophy has served GoodLife well as the chain expanded, opening new clubs and buying others that were doing poorly in strong locations. "One of the ways we grew in the early days was to take over clubs that really nobody else wanted to touch," Says Jane Riddell, GoodLife's vice president and director of franchising. "A classic example is our club at the corner of Queen and Yonge Street in downtown Toronto. When we took over the club, the membership was languishing around 100, and the facility was losing $60,000 a month. The club needed refurbishment and new equipment, but it had huge potential, with its high-profile location in a dense work population." GoodLife invested $400,000 and the facility is one of the firm's most financially successful clubs with a membership of 3,000.

One fitness expert says, "GoodLife developed a niche underneath the well-established clubs. Patchell-Evans runs a professional organization and he has a well-honed management style that includes business and financial acumen. The old-style clubs were run by squash players or golfers." One example was the innovative client billing system. While most fitness clubs demanded an upfront annual fee, Patchell-Evans debited monthly membership fees ranging from $30 to $50. Members like the system because it eliminates the needs for large upfront payments, and it stabilizes cash flow for GoodLife, which is attractive to lenders and investors.

The key to any fitness club's success is attracting and keeping members. At GoodLife it starts with the staff. Some 75% of its 1,200 employees hold kinesiology or physical education degrees. In addition to competitive salaries, staff benefit from ongoing training—GoodLife's annual education and training budget exceeds $2.4 million—and recognition for individual achievement, such as a weekly top performer's list. "Good staff retention leads to good membership retention," says Jane Riddell. "Members don't have a relationship with a treadmill or a whirlpool. They have a relationship with the staff." That commitment to human resources gives GoodLife an edge, says the industry expert. "GoodLife has good equipment, but they also have a very proactive staff with an attitude that says they want to help you out. The club's employee training program is probably more extensive than any other in the industry. It's difficult for an independent operator to compete with this."

In 1998 GoodLife was recognized for its mandate to provide leading edge programs. The U.S.-based International Dance Exercise Association named the club's fitness director, Maureen Hagan, program director of the year for her creative programming and leadership abilities. Hagan's innovations include Newbody, a low-impact, cardiovascular conditioning class designed for both fit and "underactive" participants.

Programming and services are also tailored to fit the demographics of each club. Some 70% of members are women, reflecting the club's focus on aerobics programs, to which women tend to gravitate. To ensure that women enjoy a high comfort level, GoodLife designated more than a dozen clubs for women only, where they are provided with such services as daycare, tanning facilities, and individual change rooms. GoodLife was one of the first clubs to develop the trend to women-only sections and clubs. As an example, GoodLife recently spent $500,000 upgrading the facility and equipment of a women's club in Cambridge, Ontario.

This formula to exceed customers' expectations is the foundation for GoodLife's aggressive growth plans for the future. Two trends will help the growth: industry consolidation, where GoodLife has achieved a critical mass, and an expanding market, where the number of people who will work out in clubs will increase substantially because the baby boomers want to stay in shape.

A challenge for Patchell-Evans is finding staff to keep pace with growth. "There was a time," he says, "when we had a bigger pool of people waiting for the next manager's job." To that end he says GoodLife will focus on giving staff the skills and knowledge they need to get to a higher level within the firm. "Staying on the cutting edge of the industry is a challenge, but it's also a passion for me," says Patchell-Evans. "Running a business is like a sport. You're driven to go fast, go hard, and find the ways you can do it better."

Source: Excerpts from Louise Dearden, "Muscle Mania," *Profit*, May, 1999, 46–49.

Endnote

1. Canadian Fitness and Research Institute, Canadian Physical Activity Monitor, 1998.

CASE 4

Suburban Hotel Development

Choosing a Franchise Brand

John W. O'Neill, The Pennsylvania State University

Qu Xiao, The Hong Kong Polytechnic University

Anna S. Mattila, The Pennsylvania State University

On a sunny Saturday morning in July 2005, Clarke Blynn, President of Gulph Creek Hotels, a Wayne, Pennsylvania-based hotel development and management company, was analyzing the feasibility of purchasing 6.22 acres in the Providence Corporate Center business park in Collegeville, PA, to develop a hotel. Business parks in the greater Philadelphia area had been growing, and Clarke's five existing hotels, all located close to commercial centers in suburban Philadelphia, were performing well. As the hotel industry recovered from the downturn caused by September 11, 2001, hotel projects had once again become darlings of many commercial banks, and financing was becoming available to outfits like Clarke's. Clarke believed that Gulph Creek might want to take advantage of the optimistic environment.

After meeting with Andy Detterline of the Providence Corporate Center, Clarke believed that the location might have potential as a feasible hotel site, even though it was relatively remote compared to urban Philadelphia. Based on his discussions with Andy, Clarke figured that the land would cost him about $2 million. Clarke also met with Fred Bonsall of Bonsall-Shaferman Architects and Lee Milligan, the local township's planning and zoning administrator. Fred drew up a site plan and determined that, based on the zoning regulations in Collegeville, the proposed site could accommodate a 130-room hotel. Clarke then met with James Gentile of North Star Construction Management who drew up the proposed hotel's preliminary development budget. Based on the construction market in the greater Philadelphia area and Clarke's history and preferences regarding hotel facilities, James estimated a construction cost of around $84,000 per room.

With the above information, Clarke knew that the next task would be determining the franchise brand for the hotel. As a veteran of the hotel industry, in which over 65 percent of properties were franchises,[1] Clarke knew that an appropriate brand name was essential for obtaining bank financing. Without knowing which brand he would flag, he would be unable to explore the financing options that banks could offer. Moreover, Clarke was fully aware that significant differences existed among brands, and he believed that a good name would be important to the hotel's success. The question was, Which brand should he choose? The site specifications and the hotel's capacity left Clarke with what he believed were three viable candidates: Hampton Inn, Courtyard by Marriott, and Best Western. Clarke met with his partner, Doug McBrearty, regarding his ideas for the proposed hotel project, and Doug's first question was, "If we develop that site, what brand do you think we should go with?"

Background of Gulph Creek Hotels

Gulph Creek Hotels specialized in the development, acquisition, and management of hotels in the Greater Philadelphia area. Cofounded by Clarke Blynn and Doug McBrearty in 1995, by 2005 Gulph Creek had about 200 employees and owned and operated five Hilton franchised hotels in suburban Philadelphia, including three Hampton Inns, one Hampton Inn & Suites, and one Homewood Suites.

Clarke and Doug had had experience in the hospitality industry before teaming up. Clarke received a bachelor's degree from the School of Hotel Administration at Cornell University in the late 1970s. He had worked for GF Management, which owned and operated full-service and limited-service hotels across the country. He was also a consultant at the Philadelphia office of PKF Consulting, a leading hospitality consulting firm. Having completed a number of market and feasibility studies in the region, Clarke had knowledge of the hotel markets throughout the Philadelphia area. Doug, as a graduate of the hotel and restaurant management program at The Pennsylvania State University in the mid 1970s, worked for Sheraton Hotels and GF Management. Before joining forces, Clarke and Doug crossed paths under two different circumstances: Clarke conducted a market study for the Sheraton Society Hill when Doug was its general manager, and the pair met again at GF Management.

Local operation of their hotels was a core strategy that contributed to their success. The company had decided it would concentrate only on the greater Philadelphia market. Clarke believed that by staying local, Gulph Creek maintained the highest level of management effectiveness, and consequently enjoyed an advantage over national hotel operators. According to Doug, Gulph Creek's focus reflected a historical lesson learned in the early 1990s, when the hotel industry was suffering: "The people we saw get in trouble in the early 1990s were the ones who were spread too far apart." "We're at all of our properties at least once a week," Clarke was very proud of being able to say about Gulph Creek's upper management. In 2005, encouraged by the promising outlook for the hotel industry nationwide, Clarke was particularly optimistic about Gulph Creek's potential for expansion in the greater Philadelphia area.

Proposed Hotel Overview

Site Evaluation

The potential site was along Campus Drive, near the east side of US Route 422, a regional highway linking King of Prussia (a large Philadelphia suburb) and Philadelphia, to the southeast, with Collegeville and Pottstown, PA, to the northwest. The site was within the 121-acre Providence Corporate Center, adjacent to the 230-acre world headquarters for Wyeth (pharmaceuticals). Wyeth had purchased its site and constructed facilities since 2000. As of 2005, Wyeth employed a workforce of approximately 3,200 people within the subject site's township and occupied 1.2 million square feet of space. US Route 422 was a developing commercial and residential corridor, anchored by four major company facilities: Wyeth, GlaxoSmithKline, SEI Investments, and Quest Diagnostics. A fifth major development was planned for two parcels totaling 147 acres at the northeastern quadrant of the intersection of US Route 422 and Route 29, just north of the subject site. The subject site was located approximately 10 miles northwest of King of Prussia, 32 miles west of Philadelphia, and 31 miles northwest of the Philadelphia International Airport. Clarke expected that Wyeth would be the primary commercial transient and group demand generator for the proposed hotel. The closest potentially competitive hotel was a Hampton Inn & Suites located approximately three miles southeast of the subject site along Route 422.

Clarke considered the site to be advantageous for hotel operations for the following reasons:

- Its location provided guests with good access to area companies, including GlaxoSmithKline, SEI Investments, and Quest Diagnostics, King of Prussia/Valley Forge amenities, and a growing population base.
- Wyeth operated a 16,000 square-foot day conference center (meeting rooms) at its world headquarters and a 52,000 square-foot Learning Center (training facility) 0.2 miles from its world headquarters and virtually adjacent to the subject site.
- The site was in the Providence Corporate Center.
- The site had an accessible location with respect to the proposed commercial development along US Route 422.
- The site was proximate to Ursinus College, area catering facilities, bedroom communities, and the area's tourist destinations, all modest but potential sources of weekend and seasonal leisure demand.

On the other hand, Clarke was aware of that the site had the following disadvantages:

- The potential for future hotel development along US Route 422 including developable sites near both the subject site and the existing Hampton Inn & Suites. Clarke knew that additional hotel supply would further dilute lodging demand in the US Route 422 corridor and could cause an erosion of room rates.
- The site was not exactly located in Valley Forge/King of Prussia, the location of the area's major concentration of lodging demand generators and a potential source of overflow demand for the proposed hotel. The site was approximately ten miles from Valley Forge/King of Prussia.
- The hotel probably would be heavily dependent on Wyeth as a primary source of demand.

Area Analysis

Clarke collected economic and demographic statistics for the greater Collegeville area. His analysis indicated a cautiously optimistic economic prognosis for the market, with slow-to-moderate growth anticipated.

Relevant Demographic and Social Statistics

The populations of the Collegeville Borough, Montgomery County, and state of Pennsylvania, according to the 2000

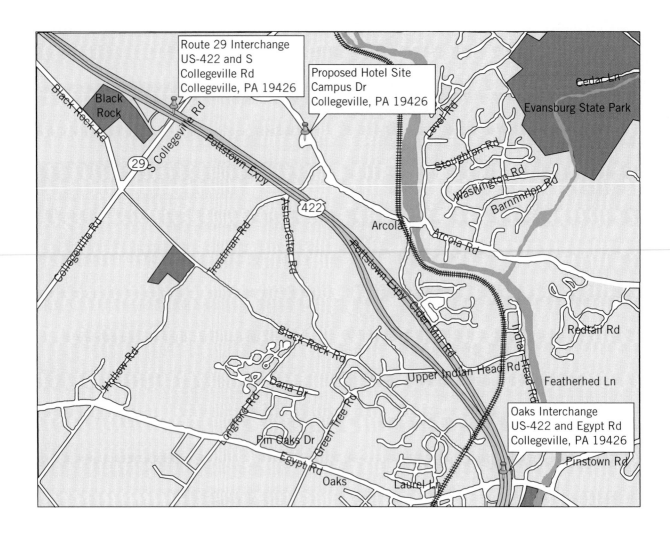

Census, were 4,682, 4.7 million, and 12.3 million persons, respectively. The population of the Borough and County increased marginally at a compound annual growth rate of 1.0 percent, compared with 0.3 percent at the state level from 1990 to 2000.

The population, age, and household income data for the subject market area are presented in Figure 1. The demographic profile area was indicative of a low-density population base with mid to upper-scale incomes. By 2010, the population of the Collegeville Borough was projected to increase to 4,900 residents while the population of Upper Providence Township was projected to increase to 18,400 (from 15,400 in 2005).

Tourism

Though not exactly a tourism Mecca, Montgomery County offered a variety of attractions, from its scenic beauty and outdoor recreational opportunities to its history and museums, fairs and festivals, and shopping venues. Among the area's tourist attractions that drew leisure travelers were Valley Forge National Historical Park, Ursinus College,

King of Prussia Mall, and Plymouth Meeting Mall. In addition, Philadelphia area attractions (including the Historic and Waterfront Districts, Independence Hall, the National Constitution Center, the Liberty Bell Center, Old City, Chinatown, the Parkway/Museum District, the University City District and South Philadelphia Sports Complex) provided a variety of activities for leisure travelers.

Hotel Market

There were a large number of hotels, motels, and lodging establishments in the Valley Forge, King of Prussia, Great Valley, and Pottstown (northwest of Collegeville) areas of Pennsylvania, though none was actually located in Collegeville. However, based on their locations, quality of facilities, brand affiliations, rate structures, and market segmentation, Clarke believed that seven hotels in the area would compete with his proposed hotel. These seven comprised 1,156 rooms, and included the Hampton Inn &

Radius from Routes 422/29	Population	Median Age	Median Household Income
One Mile Radius	1,354	35.2	$74,375
Three Mile Radius	28,135	36.0	$66,238
Five Mile Radius	79,245	36.3	$63,791

Figure 1 Demographic Trends

Source: CACI, 2005.

Hotel	Guest Rooms
Hampton Inn & Suites—Oaks	107
Courtyard by Marriott—Valley Forge/Wayne	150
Homewood Suites—Valley Forge	123
Desmond Hotel—Great Valley	194
Wyndham Hotel—Valley Forge	229
Sheraton Hotel—Park Ridge	265
Residence Inn—Valley Forge/Berwyn	88
Total	**1,156**

Figure 2 Competitive Hotel Supply

Source: Hospitality Advisory Services, LLC, 2005.

Suites—Oaks, Courtyard by Marriott—Valley Forge/Wayne, Residence Inn—Valley Forge/Berwyn, and Homewood Suites—Valley Forge. The Desmond Hotel—Great Valley, Sheraton Hotel—Park Ridge and Wyndham Hotel—Valley Forge, were also in the competitive supply due to their proximate locations with respect to Collegeville and comparable market position. The Sheraton and the Desmond Hotels captured a significant percentage of Wyeth's demand. Each hotel in the competitive set also captured demand from other employers such as GlaxoSmithKline and SEI Investments. A listing of the competitive hotels in the subject market area, in order of their likely competitiveness with the subject property, is presented in Figure 2.

Among the seven competitors, Clarke believed that the proposed hotel's primary competitor would be the Hampton Inn & Suites—Oaks, located approximately three miles south of the subject site. Hampton Inn & Suites—Oaks achieved strong midweek occupancies and Average Daily Rates (ADRs) as the only hotel in the US Route 422 corridor between Pottstown and Valley Forge. In fact, Clarke believed that if it were not for the fact that Gulph Creek already owned a number of Philadelphia area Hampton Inns, thereby having a tight relationship with the parent organization, a Hampton Inn franchise probably would not be available to him at the subject site. This 107-room Hampton Inn & Suites was located at the Oaks Interchange of US Route 422. The hotel was a five-story, interior-corridor facility that opened in 1999 and offered 31 suites with kitchens. Willow Valley Associates, a small regional hospitality company based in Lancaster, PA, managed the property. The hotel's published rates ranged from $115 on weekends to $139 during midweek. However, with an ADR in the low $100s (lower than the published rates because of negotiated, high-volume corporate rates), this hotel had the lowest ADR in the competitive market. Hampton Inn & Suites—Oaks' market mix was 70 percent business/commercial demand, 15 percent leisure/transient demand and 15 percent group. The hotel captured limited extended-stay demand despite its 31 suites with kitchens.

Prior to 2005, the seasonality of demand and capacity constraints of the competitive supply restrained the annual market occupancy at approximately 67 to 68 percent. Clarke noted that the majority of the hotels within the competitive

set were built in the 1980s. In spite of recent renovations, the competitive properties typically catered to some demanding clientele and were showing signs of aging. The limited demand growth in the Valley Forge/King of Prussia area had limited the ADRs that the competitive hotels could charge.

Trends in Hotel Room Night Supply and Demand

Except for the addition of the Homewood Suites—Valley Forge in February 2005, the total supply of guest rooms had been stable over the past several years. The hotels served three primary demand segments: leisure travelers, commercial travelers, and groups/meetings.

Figure 3 summarizes the occupancy percentage, ADR, and RevPAR (calculated as ADR multiplied by occupancy percentage) statistics for the competitive set based on Clarke's discussions with management and others related to the properties, as well as information purchased from Smith Travel Research.

2005 Market Performance

The Oaks/Valley Forge hotel market seemed to be recovering slowly, as market demand increased 5.6 percent from 127,652 occupied room nights during the first half of 2004 to 134,746 occupied room nights during the first half of 2005. Market occupancy percentage declined 3.9 percent during the first half of 2005 due to the increase in available guest rooms with the opening of the Homewood Suites—Valley Forge in February 2005. The recent market revenue trend had been positive as well, with the market experiencing a 9.4 percent increase in room revenues during the first half of 2005. The market experienced a RevPAR decrease of 0.5 percent during the first half of 2005 due to the previously discussed occupancy percentage decrease. In short, the additional rooms at the new Homewood Suites—Valley Forge appeared to be slowly getting absorbed in the market.

Collegeville, PA Area					
Year	Demand	Supply	Occupancy	ADR	RevPAR
2001	255,037	377,045	67.6%	$121.11	$81.87
2002	252,525	377,045	67.0%	$115.24	$77.21
2003	253,848	377,045	67.3%	$113.07	$76.09
2004	256,820	377,045	68.1%	$117.70	$80.15
CAGR*	0.2%	0.0%	0.2%	(0.9%)	(0.7%)

Figure 3	Demand and ADR Estimates, 2001 Through 2004

Source: Smith Travel Research, 2005.

*Compound Annual Growth Rate

Segment	Room Nights	Percent of Total Demand
Commercial	149,900	58
Group/Meeting	74,000	29
Leisure	32,800	13
Total	256,800	100%

Figure 4	Estimated Relationship of Market Supply and Demand

Source: Hospitality Advisory Services, LLC, 2005.

Notes: Room nights are rounded to the nearest hundred.

Totals may not add due to rounding.

Demand Analysis

Based on market research and calculations conducted by Clarke, the total demand and the estimated mix of demand into market segments for 2004 are presented in Figure 4.

Clarke had also conducted an analysis of the trends of each of the identified demand segments—commercial, group/meeting and leisure.

Commercial Demand

Commercial demand, including business-related and government-related demand, represented the largest of the three demand sources in the area. Transient commercial demand in the competitive market was largely comprised of traveling salespeople, manufacturing representatives, and area companies' employees.

Group/Meeting Demand

Group demand consisted of small corporate groups, training groups, social groups, and sports teams. Wyeth generated significant group demand for training and meeting functions. Social events, amateur sporting events, and reunions generated additional group demand. All of the competitive hotels offered discounted weekend rates to appeal to groups due to the market's limited number of leisure attractions. According to Clarke's discussions with special event venues in the area, growth in this market segment had been slightly negative over the past few years, but as corporate group demand rebounded, it was expected that this segment was poised for growth.

Leisure Demand

Leisure/transient demand was a small segment due to the limited tourist/visitor sites in the area. Valley Forge Park, Ursinus College and through travelers generated demand.

Valley Forge hotels captured overflow demand from visitors to historic and cultural sites in the Philadelphia area and shopping/restaurants at the King of Prussia Mall. Growth in this market segment had been slightly positive over the past few years, and positive growth was expected to continue.

Future Hotel Supply

There were a number of proposed hotels (in addition to the subject hotel) in the planning stages. A summary of these projects follows:

- A 123-unit Homewood Suites opened in February 2005 near the intersection of Trooper and Egypt Roads in the subject market area, as part of a mixed-use development that included a number of restaurants.
- Developers had proposed a 120- to 124-room Hilton Garden Inn for the Oaks interchange across from the existing Hampton Inn & Suites. However, due to site and zoning constraints, they had put the project on hold.
- Willow Valley Associates, the owner/operator of the existing Hampton Inn & Suites was also considering the development of a Hilton Garden Inn for sites at the Oaks and/or Royersford interchanges. However, the developer had put the project(s) on hold.
- A hotel project had been rumored as a component of a 121-acre site at the northeastern quadrant of the intersection of US Route 422 and State Route 29.

Despite strong interest from developers, the likelihood of hotel development in the area was reduced by the lengthy and costly development approval process, and financing hurdles. Clarke believed that many of the projects in the preliminary stages of development would encounter delays and/or never come to fruition.

Hotel Franchising: The Three Brands

Since Holiday Inn initiated hotel franchising in the 1960s, the hotel industry had become one of the country's ten most successful industries in franchising.[2] As a highly experienced hotel franchisee (developer and owner), Clarke was well aware of all the benefits of a hotel franchise, such as recognized brand name, standards and quality control, marketing programs, central reservation systems, technical assistance, operational and managerial assistance, and access to financing. Consequently, joining a franchise could significantly increase a hotel's market share. On the other hand, Clarke knew that all those benefits came with costs, including franchise fees, limited flexibility in operations, and possible liquidated damages. Based on his experience, available information regarding the site, and capacity specifications of the proposed hotel, Clarke believed that the following three brands would be his best franchise candidates:

Hampton Inn

Holiday Inn launched the Hampton Inn brand in 1984. This brand was the first "limited-service" hotel in what became the hottest and most profitable industry segment as business and leisure travelers alike looked to reduce their travel costs.[3] Recognized as one of the most successful brands in the limited-service segment, Hampton Inn aimed to satisfy guests who placed importance on a clean, well-maintained room, consistent service quality, and value, but were not concerned with the availability of extra amenities such as restaurants and lounges. Therefore, Hampton Inn specializes in lodging that combined clean, safe, and comfortable rooms with a relatively affordable room rate, about 30 to 40 percent less than a typical Holiday Inn hotel room. Aside from a free continental breakfast, Hampton Inn hotels had no food and beverage (F&B) operations and usually co-located with a known brand-name restaurant or were developed in areas served by restaurants. The absence of F&B facilities and staff resulted in sharply lower operating costs and lower capital costs than those of full-service hotels. In the early 1990s, the average construction cost per room for Hampton Inn was around $31,000, less than half of the cost of a standard guest room in full-service hotels.[4]

The initial Hampton Inn prototype featured 100–130 guest rooms and targeted secondary and suburban markets with a population of over 50,000 people. The brand became so successful in the hotel franchising market that it flagged over 150 properties, 90 percent of which were franchises, within four years of its birth. In 1989, Hampton became the first hotel chain in the industry to offer its guests an unconditional, 100-percent-satisfaction guarantee permitting any employee to give guests their money back if not satisfied. Hampton Inn reported that the guarantee itself cost very little (0.3 percent of sales), and for every dollar returned

to customers, the organization got back eight dollars from repeat sales.[5]

In 1999, Hilton acquired Hampton Inn as one of its seven brands. The brand's guests consisted of 51 percent leisure travelers and 49 percent business travelers. In 2004, Hampton Inn had 1,255 properties and 127,543 rooms, and was ranked the world's 5th largest hotel brand. Hilton franchised all but 34 of the 1,229 Hampton Inn hotels in the U.S. In 2004, Hampton Inn's U.S. systemwide average daily rate (ADR) was $81.64; occupancy percentage rate, 68.3 percent; and rooms revenue per available room (RevPAR), $55.73. While Hampton Inn did not charge a reservation fee, the monthly royalty and marketing fees cost franchisees about nine percent of total room revenue, which was one of the most expensive hotel franchises.

In 2004, as Hampton Inn approached its 20th year, the brand initiated a $100 million project, called "Make It Hampton" (MIH), which transformed nearly every aspect of the chain's facilities, amenities and services. Based on a two-year study involving franchises, guests and employees of approximately 100 properties, MIH called for up to 127 individual changes in each of over 1,200 properties to ensure competitiveness. Among the changes were new graphics and décor, new guestroom and bathroom amenities, and an enhanced breakfast menu with eight new hot items (previously only cold items had been available).[6]

Courtyard by Marriott

Courtyard by Marriott was Marriott's first moderately-priced lodging brand and was well regarded as an example of a research-based lodging product. In the early 1980s, when Marriott development executives realized that the growing saturation of its traditional upscale hotels in major geographical markets necessitated the development of a new hotel product for midmarket and suburban sites, the company had little experience with price-sensitive guests. After spending one year and over $300,000 in focus-group interviews, Marriott executives found that the midmarket guests wanted a hotel to be as much like home as possible, and wanted functional guest rooms that would facilitate both business and socializing.[7]

With this information in hand, Marriott conducted a tradeoff study, developed the product mix, built a prototype guest room at its corporate headquarters and showed it to hundreds of people. Marriott positioned Courtyard by Marriott to serve business travelers who wanted moderately-priced hotels of consistent high quality, and pleasure travelers who wanted an affordable room that was a safe base of operations. The first Courtyard hotel opened in 1983. Courtyard hotels typically ranged in size from 80 to 200 rooms and featured a limited-menu restaurant, lounge, small meeting spaces, an exercise room, and a swimming pool, all of which aimed to satisfy the guests' needs for a residential feel and a functional hotel. Guests involved in the initial research process selected many of the facilities and amenities, from patios and balconies to couches and closet doors, which most moderately-priced hotels did not have.[8]

Although Courtyard was effectively competing with both full-service and limited-service brands such as Hilton Garden Inn, Holiday Inn, and Hampton Inn, market analysts could not agree under which segment to classify the Courtyard brand. In 1994 and 1995, Courtyard by Marriott was continuously ranked by *Hotel & Motel Management* among the top ten in the "Top 40 U.S. Economy/Limited-Service Chains" together with Comfort Inn, Hampton Inn, and Holiday Inn Express. However, most of the research after 2000 tended to classify it in the full-service category. J.D. Power and Associates had classified Courtyard by Marriott as one of the "Mid-Priced Hotel Chains with Full-Services," competing with Holiday Inn, Best Western, and Ramada. Due to Courtyard's relatively high market position in terms of ADR, Smith Travel Research listed Courtyard in the "Upscale" category, which also consisted of full-service hotel brands such as Crowne Plaza, Radisson, and Wyndham.[9] Many analysts considered Courtyard as a newer full-service concept, which provided full-size guest rooms but limited the size of the lobby, F&B facilities, and meeting spaces. Through reducing investment and operating costs, Courtyard hotels were competitors with older, midmarket, full-service hotels, and with limited-service hotels as well.

Courtyard was the world's 12th largest brand with 608 properties and 87,041 rooms worldwide in 2004, including 550 hotels in the United States. With a 2004 systemwide ADR at $97.18, RevPAR at $69.35, and occupancy rate at 71.4 percent, approximately half of the U.S. properties were company-owned and the other half were franchises. Typically, the franchise cost of Courtyard by Marriott included royalty, marketing, and reservation fees, which would cost franchisees approximately eight to nine percent of total annual room revenues and as such was one of the expensive hotel franchises.[10]

After 17 years operating in the midscale market, Courtyard by Marriott announced the "reinvention of the brand" in 2000 in response to travelers' changing needs. Once again, the opinions and preferences of business travelers as well as franchisees played a significant role in this "reinvention" process. The new hotel elements included a more functional lobby with flexible furniture and amenities, a walk-around front desk for more guest interaction and personalized service, a fully equipped "business library," and 24-hour "grab-and-go" pantry-style food service. All Courtyard hotels (both Marriott-managed and franchised properties) would complete the revamped design by the end of 2005.[11]

Best Western International

Compared to most hotel brands, including Hampton Inn and Courtyard by Marriott, Best Western International was a unique concept because technically it was a membership association rather than a franchise system. Best Western was founded in 1946 by M. K. Guertin, a California motel owner with a simple concept: independent hotel owners united to promote their properties and to increase profitability. The organization began as an informal link between properties with each hotel recommending other lodging establishments to travelers.

The original "referral system" consisted of phone calls from one front desk operator to another. During the 1950s, the loosely-knit organization grew from 50 to nearly 500 properties, and then increased to over 700 properties in the 1960s when the brand started recruiting members in Europe and launched its central reservation system with toll-free numbers dedicated to travel agents and business and leisure travelers. In the 1970s, Best Western decided to drop its referral organization image and began competing directly with other major hotel chains.

Gradually, the corporate identification of "World's Largest Hotel Chain" was established and the name "Best Western" began to be recognized as a brand. By the end of 2004, Best Western had over 4,200 member hotels with 315,000 guest rooms in 79 countries. In 2004, the 2,200 Best Western properties in the United States had a systemwide ADR at $75.21, occupancy rate at 60.9 percent, and RevPAR at $45.78. The average property size was 79 rooms in the United States, 68 rooms in Europe, and 39 rooms in Australia. Only 25 percent of Best Western properties were considered full-service hotels in 2004.[12]

Best Western remained a nonprofit membership association operating on a cost-recovery basis. Each member of Best Western paid an annual fee and members had to approve major policy changes. Best Western had differentiated itself from other brands as an owner-oriented organization with several important advantages and disadvantages. The two most recognized differences were its competitive fee structure and annual renewable contract. Most other major brands required a total franchisee cost (including royalty, marketing, and reservation fees) of seven or more percent of total room revenue, while the total annual membership cost of Best Western was less than three percent. In addition, unlike other hotel franchise agreements that required commitments of five or more years, Best Western memberships were renewable annually without any liquated damages.[13]

Compared to other brands, Best Western had the least strict standards regarding physical plants, facilities, and operations. It invested a large portion of its membership fees revenue in its reservation system because, except for building the brand name, the tradition of Best Western focused on generating more reservations. Best Western had one of the most productive hotel Web sites in the industry. Therefore, by combining relatively low fees, short contracts, a globally recognized brand name, and a worldwide reservation system, Best Western offered its members benefits similar to those of other brands but still enabled them to retain a fair amount of flexibility and entrepreneurial independence.[14]

Best Western's portfolio ranged from four-star, upscale, full-service hotels to one-star, limited-service hotels, and the nightly room rates varied significantly from over $200 to less than $50. Therefore, quality consistency and brand level guest satisfaction were particularly keen challenges for Best Western. Best Western's research showed that hotel guests liked the organization and its tradition, but did not like the inconsistency among properties. To improve quality and consistency, Best Western conducted research, in which over 1,400 travel agents and guests selected the most important amenities and services in a hotel. Then, in 2001, Best Western launched the hotel industry's largest ever quality and brand enhancement initiatives, known as "Best Requests Global Standards." A set of "Best Requests" amenities and services (16 for North America hotels and 14 for international properties), including breakfast and in-room hair dryer, etc., were fully implemented in all Best Western hotels by 2003.[15]

Brand Differences

Realizing that significant differences existed among brands, Clarke collected additional information from several other reliable third-party sources. He believed he should assess a brand's overall competitiveness based on a number of key aspects, including franchise fees, loyalty programs, guest satisfaction, and word-of-mouth (WOM) influences.

Franchise Fees

Franchise fees typically included a onetime initial fee, a monthly royalty fee, a marketing fee based on a certain percentage of the room revenue, and a monthly reservation fee based on the reservations received from the franchisor's reservation system. A comparison of the franchise costs of Hampton Inn, Courtyard by Marriott, and Best Western is presented in Figure 5.

Loyalty Program

Clarke knew a brand's loyalty program was essential to develop and retain guests' commitment to the brand. Therefore, he collected a summary of the loyalty reward programs for the three brands as shown in Exhibit 1.

Guest Satisfaction and Market Metrix Hospitality Index

Guest satisfaction had been a key factor contributing to the success of Gulph Creek Hotels. Indeed, Clarke and his executive team had been very proud of the fact that their hotels were well known for their high guest satisfaction scores. To gain an in-depth understanding of guest satisfaction associated with the Hampton Inn, Courtyard by Marriott, and Best Western brands, Clarke purchased a recent issue of the Market Metrix Hospitality Index (MMHI), the largest and most in-depth measure of guest satisfaction for many segments of the hospitality industry, including hotel, car rental and airline. The details are shown in Exhibit 2.

Online Word-of-Mouth Influences

During his 30+ years working in the hotel industry, Clarke had seen the power of word-of-mouth (WOM) on both good and bad brands. As the Internet made communications among strangers easy, many Web sites became particularly influential regarding hotel guests' brand decisions. Having talked to numerous guests in his Hampton Inn properties, he realized that guests were becoming increasingly sophisticated in determining their hotel choices. A few negative comments posted on third-party Web sites was unlikely to be detrimental to brand image, yet a relatively large number of complaints regarding different properties of a specific

	Parent Company	Segment	Initial Fee	Royalty Fee	Marketing Fee	Reservation Fee
Hampton Inn	Hilton	Midscale w/o F&B	$50,000 minimum	5.0%	4.0%	None
Courtyard by Marriott	Marriott	Upscale	$50,000 minimum	5.5%	2.0%	1.0%
Best Western	Best Western	Midscale with F&B	$42,250 for 100 rooms	$3,761 for 100 rooms	$28,653 for 100 rooms	$14,600 for 100 rooms

Figure 5   Comparison of Brands

Source: Hotel & Motel Management, 2005.

Note: Royalty, marketing, and reservation fees are expressed as a percentage of room revenues (daily room revenue = ADR x occupancy rate x number of rooms available)

Exhibit 1   Comparison of Loyalty Reward Programs

HILTON HHONORS

Benefits/Structure

Earn 10 points per dollar spent at Hilton Hotels, Conrad Hotels, Doubletree, Embassy Suites, Hampton Inns & Suites, Homewood Suites.

Free nights: 7,500 points to 45,000 points (more points required for luxury brands and packages)

Earn points and miles for each stay

- 10 HHonors points per dollar
- 500 airline miles per stay at high-end properties and 100 miles at midscale properties

Three tiers:

- Silver: (10 nights/4 stays)—15 percent point bonus
- Gold: (36 nights/16 stays)—25 percent point bonus
- Diamond: (60 nights/28 stays or earn 100,000 points/year)—50 percent point bonus

Points can be redeemed for:

- Miles with more than 60 airline partners
- Vacation packages
- Amtrak
- Car rentals
- Cruises
- Mypoints
- Disney and Universal Rewards
- Merchandise and retail certificates

Soft benefits based on tier level:

- Silver: Complimentary health club privileges, check-cashing privileges, VIP-only rewards
- Gold: Add room upgrades
- Diamond: Add guaranteed availability, no blackout dates, reward-planner (concierge) service

Earn Partners: Points can be earned through co-branded American Express and Citibank Visa products, Membership Rewards, Diners Club, Mypoints, Amtrak, three major U.S. airlines, Critic's Choice video, Avis, National, *USA Today* and others.
Membership Rewards points and Diners Club points can also be converted for HHonors points.

Blackout dates and capacity controls apply.

Points can be purchased.

Points are forfeited after 12 months of inactivity.

Notes/Results

- Hilton Brand: 499 hotels, 148,000 rooms
- Doubletree Brand: 160 hotels, 43,000 rooms

MARRIOTT REWARDS

Benefits/Structure

Earn 10 points per dollar spent at Marriott, Renaissance, Courtyard, SpringHill Suites and Fairfield Inn. Earn 5 points per dollar spent at Residence Inn and Towne Place.

Can choose to earn points or miles directly. Three miles per dollar spent at most brands, or 1.0 SWA credit/stay.

Free nights: 7,500 points to 35,000 points (more points required during blackout or low availability dates)

Other rewards:

- Car rentals (from 30,000 points for three-day weekend)
- Cruise, travel, golf, ski, spa, theme parks, theater (mostly UK)
- Merchandise (Best Buy, Sony and others)
- Retail certificates (mostly UK focused)

Three tiers:

- Silver: (15 nights)—20 percent bonus
- Gold: (50 nights)—25 percent bonus
- Platinum: (75 nights)—30 percent bonus

Earn Partners:

- Marriott Signature Visa
- Hertz
- Amex Membership Rewards
- AT&T
- Diners Club
- Skymall

Soft benefits:

- All members: Priority check-in, room guarantee, newsletter with special offers, member exclusive specials
- Silver tier: Reservation guarantee, special 1–800 number, priority room selection, late check-out, 10 percent weekend discount, check cashing, 10 percent gift shop discount
- Gold tier: free local phone and fax, access to concierge lounge, free continental breakfast, exclusive offers, room upgrade
- Platinum tier: Guaranteed availability, free gift

(Continued)

| Exhibit 1 | (Continued) |

- Embassy Suites: 170 hotels, 42,000 rooms
- Hilton Garden Inn: 155 locations
- Homewood: 195 locations
- Hampton Suites: 1,000+ locations
- Conrad Hotels: 15 Hotels

Points may be purchased.

Points do not expire.

Notes/Results

- 2,300 eligible Marriott properties in 63 countries

BEST WESTERN GOLD CROWN CLUB

Benefits/Structure

Earn one point per dollar spent.

Global Free Night Award starting at 800 points.

North American Awards include: 60 retail, dining, and travel award partners such as Home Depot, Target, Roots; seven airline partners; and U.S. Savings Bonds. Global Cheques are available for $50 (1,200 points), $25 (650 points), and $15 (500 points). Gas cards available. Merchandise available.

Primary reward is the Global Free Nights voucher:

- No blackout dates
- More award inventory than almost all other hotel reward programs
- Redeemable at over 4,000 hotels in 80 countries
- Takes about 10 nights to earn (based on $80 average rate)
- Hundreds of hotels worldwide at 800-point award level

Members can choose between earning points or airline miles for each stay. Points can also be converted to miles in 1,000-point increments.

Partnerships: Convert Air Canada Aeroplan miles to free nights. Convert Amex or Diners Club points to Gold Crown Club points.

250 airline miles per stay in North, Central, and South America, and Asia. American AAdvantage miles may be earned in Sweden and UK.

Elite Tiers:

- Diamond: (30 qualified nights)—earns 15 percent bonus points
- Platinum: (15 qualified nights)—earns 10 percent bonus points

Elite Benefits:

- Quarterly recognition gifts
- Exclusive offers
- Dedicated level-exclusive priority service

Complimentary room upgrades, early check-in and late check-out privileges (upon availability), point-pooling for individuals with the same address.

No blackout dates.

Points expire after 12 months of no activity.

Notes/Results

- In 2002, Gold Crown Club re-launched and extended to include overseas properties.
- Now over two million members.
- Elite Status members have doubled since re-launch.
- Over 4,000 locations in 80 countries.

Exhibit 2 MMHI Overview (January 2004–December 2004)*

	Customer Satisfaction	Emotions	Very Likely To Return	Loyalty Program Strength	Reported Price
Luxury					
Average	87.0	84	60%	4%	$177
W Hotels	88.8	90	66%	7%	$174
Loews	87.8	81	48%	3%	$180
Four Seasons	87.6	82	71%	3%	$203
Ritz-Carlton	87.3	85	77%	0%	$222
Fairmont	86.7	83	58%	1%	$163
Intercontinental	86.3	82	51%	0%	$150
Grand Hyatt	84.5	83	47%	11%	$150
Upper Upscale					
Average	84.5	80	57%	8%	$123
Walt Disney World Resorts	90.5	87	80%	5%	$136
Renaissance	88.6	83	56%	6%	$121
Westin	86.0	81	54%	12%	$140
Omni	85.1	80	44%	5%	$124
Embassy Suites	84.3	79	66%	7%	$118
Marriott Hotels	83.9	78	65%	16%	$120
Hyatt	82.9	77	49%	7%	$124
Hyatt Regency	82.3	77	54%	6%	$131
Sheraton	82.3	77	49%	8%	$114
Doubletree	81.8	78	54%	7%	$104
Hilton	81.7	77	53%	11%	$119
Upscale					
Average	83.4	78	55%	6%	$104
SpringHill Suites	88.8	83	64%	14%	$91
Outrigger Hotels	86.8	82	73%	0%	$116
Hilton Garden Inn	84.4	78	63%	13%	$101
Crowne Plaza	84.3	79	56%	5%	$119
Wyndham	83.3	78	50%	10%	$112
AmeriSuites	83.0	76	50%	2%	$82
Courtyard By Marriott	82.5	77	63%	10%	$95
Radisson	80.7	76	46%	2%	$104
Adam's Mark	76.7	72	31%	2%	$112
Midscale w/F&B					
Average	79.7	73	44%	4%	$80
Four Points	83.8	78	51%	4%	$87
Red Lion	82.0	76	42%	3%	$82
Holiday Inn Select	81.2	75	47%	6%	$93
Quality	79.8	74	49%	8%	$72
Best Western	79.7	74	51%	3%	$76

(Continued)

Exhibit 2   (Continued)

	Customer Satisfaction	Emotions	Very Likely To Return	Loyalty Program Strength	Reported Price
Holiday Inn	79.5	74	54%	8%	$86
Clarion	78.4	72	40%	2%	$82
Ramada	78.3	70	37%	2%	$73
Executive Inn Hotels	78.3	72	32%	0%	$76
Howard Johnson	76.4	67	39%	1%	$75
Average	84.0	77	60%	7%	$77
Wingate Inn	91.2	83	73%	3%	$78
Drury Inns	90.4	82	68%	6%	$80
Hampton Suites	87.7	81	65%	10%	$92
Country Inns & Suites by Carlson	87.6	81	67%	5%	$81
Sleep Inn	84.5	78	68%	10%	$66
Hampton Inn	84.1	77	73%	12%	$81
Baymont Inns and Suites	83.9	77	59%	3%	$67
Amerihost Inn	82.9	76	50%	3%	$79
La Quinta Inns	82.9	76	61%	7%	$69
Comfort Suites	82.8	76	59%	9%	$80
Fairfield Inn by Marriott	82.5	75	64%	11%	$76
Holiday Inn Express	82.3	76	62%	11%	$78
Wellesley Inn and Suites	81.4	76	44%	6%	$68
Shilo Inns	81.3	75	48%	0%	$87
Comfort Inn	79.6	74	56%	8%	$70
Comfort Hotel	78.3	71	45%	5%	$74

(Midscale w/o F&B)

Source: Market Metrix, LLC, 2005.

* The MMHI Overview, a product from Market Metrix Hospitality Index (MMHI), presents the major hotel brands' satisfaction performance during 2004. Based on 35,000 customer interviews conducted each quarter, the index has unprecedented breadth and depth. Industry results are compiled into quarterly reports, which are available for purchase. With MMHI, hoteliers like Clarke can measure a brand's stand-alone performance and dynamically benchmark its rating against those of competitors and highly ranked companies within and across other hospitality industries. The MMHI consists of the following four types of information, plus the average price reported by the customers.

Customer Satisfaction: This score is the average score of 13 product and service questions and is highly correlated with repeat behavior and word-of-mouth recommendations. The customer satisfaction component of the Market Metrix Hospitality Index provides accurate scores and comparable results for all major hotel brands.

Emotions: The numbers in this category indicate the average score for 16 key emotions. This section is designed to identify which segments and brands deliver the emotions that drive guest loyalty.

Very Likely to Return: This is the percentage of guests that say they are very likely to return. Along with "Very Likely to Recommend," it is a key component of a "Secure Customer."

Loyalty Program Strength: This score indicates the relative success of a brand's loyalty program compared to other programs in the hotel industry. This measure combines the percentage of guests who are members of a brand's loyalty program and the importance of that program (to the guest) in selecting that hotel brand.

brand was easily interpreted as "stay away from this brand." Therefore, Clarke hired an external consultant to research what guests were saying about the three brands of interest. After researching a number of the most popular hotel evaluation Web sites, the consultant indicated that the TripAdvisor site (www.tripadvisor.com) was the most influential with more than 250 hotel reviews for each of the three brands. The consultant provided Clarke with a summary of the average rating of each brand on www.tripadvisor.com as shown in Figure 6.

Average Score*		Score Range*	Rank
Hampton Inn	3.59	3.0–4.0	2
Courtyard by Marriott	3.92	3.5–4.5	1
Best Western	3.08	2.5–3.5	3

Figure 6   Comparison of Online Reviews

Source: www.tripadvisor.com, 2005.

*The highest possible score was 5.

Clarke's Task

Clarke planned an executive meeting on the upcoming Monday to discuss the branding issue with Doug. Clarke needed to develop a brand recommendation before going to the meeting. However, he knew that he had more work to do to decide which hotel brand would be the best fit. Initially, he decided that he needed to analyze the market and compare the three brands from a brand equity perspective. Although Clarke was company president, he expected that Doug would ask many detailed questions before agreeing or disagreeing with his choice. Clarke walked into his office, pulled out all the reports and analyses he had collected, and began his decision-making process.

Notes

1. Rushmore, S. (Summer, 1997). "Hotel franchising: How to be a successful franchisee," *Real Estate Journal*, p. 56.

2. Brown, J. R., and Dev, C. S. (1997). "The franchisor-franchisee relationship," *Cornell Hotel and Restaurant Administration Quarterly,* 38 (6), pp. 30–38.

3. Connolly, D. J. (1998). "Limited-service/economy lodging sector faces challenges ahead," *FIU Hospitality Review,* 16 (1), pp. 67–79.

4. Taninecz, G. (February 4, 1991). "Hampton Inns calling its shots," *Hotel & Motel Management,* pp. 3, 48–49.

5. Powers, T. (1995). *Introduction to Management in the Hospitality Industry.* New York: John Wiley & Sons, Inc.

6. *Lodging Hospitality.* (March 1, 2004). "Hampton Inns ups the ante," p. 8.

7. Koepper, K. (October, 1988). "Creating hotel services for the mid-market psychology," *Lodging,* 14, pp. 54–57.

8. Hart, C. (1986). "Product development: How Marriott created Courtyard," *Cornell Hotel and Restaurant Administration Quarterly,* 27 (3), pp. 68–69.

9. Hasek, G. (July 24, 1995). "Limited's success," *Hotel & Motel Management,* pp. 36–37; Troy, T. N. (July 25, 1994). "Standing strong," *Hotel & Motel Management,* pp. 14–15; J. D. Power and Associates. (August 28, 2000). "Omni Hotels, Embassy Suites, Courtyard by Marriott, Hampton Inn and Fairfield Inn are Tops in Respective Segments When Ranked for Customer Satisfaction," retrieved from http://www.hotelonline.com/News/PressReleases2000_3rd/Aug00 _SegmentLoyalty.html; Lomanno, M. V. (March 13, 2005). "U.S. lodging industry overview," Presentation at 2005 Hotel Investment Conference, Atlanta, GA.

10. *Hotel & Motel Management.* (May 16, 2005). "Special report: Franchising survey," pp. 26–28; Rushmore and Baum, op. cit.

11. Walsh, J. P. (August 14, 2000). "A fresh, new face," *Hotel & Motel Management,* pp. 3, 33.

12. Higley, J. (May 1, 2006). "Best Western concentrates on consistency," *Hotel & Motel Management.* pp. 1, 38–39.

13. Best Western International. (2005). http://www.bestwestern.com/aboutus/memdev/index.asp; Lomanno, op. cit.

14. Higley, op. cit.

15. Hotel Online. (January 16, 2001). "Best Western unveils new global standards; Sixteen amenities and services now policy worldwide," retrieved from http://www.hotelonline.com/News/PR2001_1st/Jan01_BestWestern55.html.

CASE 5

EMR Innovations

Kay M. Palan, Iowa State University

Eric Reynolds stood inside the door to his RV repair shop and surveyed the activities. He and his wife Mary were avid RVers and had combined their love of RVing with business by starting an RV repair business out of their home in 1995. In 1999, the business was large enough to allow them to open their own shop in Amana, Iowa. By 2002, the business had steadily grown, but he and Mary wanted more—they wanted to be "the" supplier of innovative RV products. To that end, they had developed their first product, the Lock-Awn antibillow device for RV patio awnings. In fact, Eric mused, he and Mary had invested about $10,000 of their own money to develop a prototype product. They had even sought assistance from an industry research center located at a nearby university with respect to developing the prototype. Now, in late fall 2003, Eric and Mary had a working prototype, and preliminary feedback from some of their RV repair customers who had seen the product was very positive.

However, even though potential customers seemed to like it, Eric and Mary were unsure about whether or not the Lock-Awn product would be successful. In the last several months, they had become aware of a potential competitor selling a similar product. While Eric and Mary believed the Lock-Awn was superior to the competitor's product, they were uncertain if potential customers would feel the same way. Money was too tight for the Reynolds to risk market entry without a better grasp of the Lock-Awn's market viability.

Mary, who did the bookkeeping for the RV repair shop in between caring for their three children, looked up from her desk and saw Eric. She walked over to him and placed her hand on his shoulder. "What are you thinking about?" she asked.

Eric turned and said, "I just wish I knew for certain if investing more money in the Lock-Awn is the right thing to do. I think we need to know more about how we would actually market it before we can seek additional funding. That manufacturing consultant we've talked with said the next step was to decide on a marketing strategy."

Mary nodded her agreement, stating, "I've been thinking the same thing. I know you've got your hands full with the shop right now, so I'll start reviewing the information we have about customers and competitors and start thinking about how we would market the Lock-Awn. Hopefully, in a few weeks we can make sense of it all and decide on a marketing strategy."

The RV Industry

Recreational vehicles (RVs) were vehicles that combined transportation and temporary living quarters for recreation, camping, and travel. According to Web sites that Mary found (RV Central and RV Hotline Canada), interest in RVs dated back to the early 1900s when nature enthusiasts customized their own vehicles with such accessories as bunks, storage lockers, and cooking capabilities, in order to see the country. When roads began to improve in the 1920s, RV enthusiasm grew and did not diminish during the Depression. After World War II, the RV industry flourished. Enthusiasts could build their own RVs with home kits or could purchase readymade motor homes. However, it wasn't until the 1960s that the term "RV" was coined as a marketing tool.

By 2000, the RV industry consisted of 135 RV manufacturers and more than 200 suppliers of component parts and services. There were two main RV categories—motorhomes (motorized) and towables (towed behind the family car, van, or pickup). Purchased new, towables were the least expensive. Towables included folding camping trailers, ranging from $5,000 to $10,000, and truck campers, affixed to the bed or chassis of a truck, at an average sticker price of $10,500. Conventional travel trailers, which were also towed, cost about $13,000, while fifth-wheel trailers (towed by a vehicle equipped with a device known as a fifth-wheel hitch) ranged from $25,000 to over $80,000. Motorhomes were considerably more expensive than towables, ranging from $35,000 for Class C motorhomes (built on a van cutaway chassis) to over $500,000 for the most luxurious Class A motorhomes (built on a specially designed motor vehicle chassis).

According to the Recreational Vehicle Industry Association (RVIA), nearly 7.5 million households in the U.S. owned an RV in 2002, and RV sales were expected to hit a 25-year high in 2003. RV shipments, shown in Exhibit 1, had steadily grown, although there were occasional decreases in shipped units, which tended to coincide with increases in gasoline prices. Although it was difficult to find hard-and-fast numbers detailing exactly how many of which types of RVs were owned by U.S. households, data from a 2001 survey suggested the breakdown of RV ownership in Figure 1.

Nonetheless, the economic forecast for the RV industry was positive. There was renewed interest in domestic

Exhibit 1	Total RV Shipments: 1986–2002 (Units in Thousands)

Year	Shipped Units
1986	189.8
1987	211.7
1988	215.8
1989	187.9
1990	173.1
1991	163.3
1992	203.4
1993	227.8
1994	259.2
1995	247.0
1996	247.5
1997	254.5
1998	292.7
1999	321.2
2000	300.1
2001	256.8
2002	311.0

Source: Recreation Vehicle Industry Association (RVIA), RVIA Facts, RV Shipments Data, http://www.rvia.org/media/ShipmentsData.htm.

ground travel in the U.S., resulting in more people taking driving vacations than ever before. The aging baby boom generation, which had greater buying power relative to previous generations, was buying more RVs as it neared retirement. Moreover, low interest rates since 2001 encouraged Americans to purchase big-ticket, leisure items.

The RV Culture

According to a 2001 University of Michigan study commissioned by the RVIA, RV enthusiasts were growing in numbers. In 2001, nearly 7 million U.S. households owned an RV, which translated to almost one RV in every 12 households, although the RVIA estimated that there were as many as 30 million RV enthusiasts in the U.S., which included RV renters. Although people of all ages owned RVs, the largest segment was the 55 and older crowd, with about 10 percent of the RVs, closely followed by the 35- to 54-year-olds who owned 8.9 percent of the nation's RVs. The fastest growing segment of the RV market was the baby boomers. By 2010, the RVIA projected that there would be 8.5 million RV-owning households.

The same University of Michigan study identified the typical RV owner as 49 years old, married, owning his/her own home, and having an annual household income of

Type of RV	Estimated ownership[1] (percent)	Estimated number in U.S.[2]
Folding camper trailers	24	1,800,000
Truck campers	5	375,000
Travel trailer (includes fifth-wheel trailers)	47	3,525,000
Class C motorhomes	8	600,000
Class A motorhomes	16	1,200,000

Figure 1	Estimated Breakdown of RV Ownership

1. Estimated from data taken from 2001 RVIA industry survey.

2. Based on 7.5 million estimated households owning RVs in 2002

$56,000. RV owners spent their disposable income on traveling an average of 4,500 miles and 28–35 days annually. The RVIA further noted several reasons why people chose RVs as a way to travel:

- Convenience, flexibility, and freedom to go where they wanted, when they wanted, without having to plan in advance.
- Comfort and amenities of home while on the road or at a campground.
- Enjoyment of traveling together as a family.
- Affordability—even factoring in RV ownership, a family of four spent up to 70% less when traveling by RV (according to a cost-comparison study conducted in 2000 by PKF Consulting).
- Accessibility to enjoying outdoor getaways—the beach, mountains, parks, tourist attractions.
- Versatility of vehicle—in addition to traveling, the RV was used for shopping, tailgating, and pursuing special hobbies.

Two thirds of RV owners purchased a previously owned vehicle. RV owners tended to keep their RVs a long time—nearly 25 percent owned their RVs for 10 or more years. The average age of used RVs when purchased was 11.6 years.

RVers were an adventuresome group. From their own experience in the RV business, Mary knew that some RVers lived full-time on the road, traveling from place to place, absorbing the sights and sounds wherever they happened to be. Many of these people were retired couples who wanted to see the country. Others traveled for part of the year; for example, it was common for retirees in the Midwest to spend spring/summer in the Midwest, and fall/winter in warmer climates. They would use their RV as their residence during the fall and winter months. Still others took a week or two here or there for short vacations. In 2003, *Workamper News,* an RV publication, estimated that approximately 750,000 Americans lived and worked out of travel trailers, truck campers, or motor homes full-time—it called these people "work-ampers," individuals motivated to earn a living but without being tied down to either one address or to an employer.

RVers were well connected through a variety of networking groups and forums. In her research, Mary found countless Web sites devoted to members of RV clubs. Members formed clubs based on type of RV ownership (e.g., Gulf Streamers International RV Club), travel and leisure interests (e.g., Happy Camper Club), geographic location (e.g., Carolina Cruisers), or other demographics (e.g., The Handicapped Travel Club). There were numerous Web sites devoted to answering RV questions that also featured chat rooms, which encouraged informal networking among RVers.

Regardless of how many months of the year RVers lived on the road or what their specific purpose was, all of them wanted their accommodations to be as comfortable as possible and, Mary knew, were willing to spend money on products that improved their RVs. There were literally dozens of companies that manufactured and sold RV gadgets and accessories like auxiliary fuel tanks, power booster equipment, and anti-sway trailer hitches (RVInfo). Some RVers invented their own gadgets to improve RVs, and then peddled these inventions to other RVers they met on the road. In some instances, this led to substantive businesses. One such RVer, Richard Dahl of Roseburg, Oregon, invented a water filter for RV plumbing systems and subsequently sold the $30 filter, which he manufactured himself, at trailer parks, campgrounds, and motor-home shows. Eventually he expanded his product line to 300 items, created The RV Water Filter Store, and made more than enough to pay for his and his wife's travels, plus $30,000 or so left over each year for fun (Henricks 2003). What Dahl discovered was that RVers were more than willing to purchase accessories like his water filter when they appreciated the benefits.

EMR Innovations

Eric and Mary Reynolds hoped to be as successful as Richard Dahl had been. Being acquainted with RVs through both personal experience and through their repair business, Eric and Mary discovered that most RVs suffered from design flaws. Some were minor inconveniences, but others were dangerous.

One such problem was with patio awnings, which were standard equipment on virtually all RVs, including motor homes, fifth-wheel trailers, and travel trailers. A very small percentage of RVs had motorized awnings, but most RVs had manually operated awnings, which had a propensity to become unwound while the RV was in motion or parked. The awnings, which were 8 feet wide and up to 22 feet long, could billow in the wind, either startling the driver or causing the driver to lose control and cause accidents (Siuru, RV Awning Care). In fact, although Eric could not find specific numbers

on exactly how many accidents the billowing problem had caused, he had found several RV Internet forums and chat rooms where the string of discussion focused on the awning billowing problem. Many RVers reported trying to fix the problem with things like duct tape and Velcro. Eric saw an opportunity to create a permanent and practical fix for the many RV owners who still had to deal with the awning problem.

Thus began the idea for EMR Innovations. Eric believed that he could design a product that would lock awnings in place and be affordable. Moreover, he readily identified several other RV design flaws that EMR Innovations could address: sewer hookups, a battery fluid indicator cap, an all-in-one tow tester, an RV essentials toolkit, and a streamlined brake control device. Some of these devices Eric had already designed for use on his own RV while others were just ideas. However, he was certain there was a market for all these products.

Both Eric and Mary thought that the best product to introduce first to the market was the Lock-Awn device. Given RVers' concerns about this problem, it made sense that the product would sell. They had invested $10,000 so far to design and perfect a prototype. In addition, they had invested a lot of their time. However, if they proceeded to introduce the product, they needed an infusion of cash, either from an investor or through a bank loan. Although they did not have a well-formulated business or marketing plan, they roughly estimated that they needed about $200,000 to begin production, distribution and promotion. The local bank estimated that the Reynolds' RV repair business was worth $800,000 to $900,000, so Eric and Mary planned to use that as collateral for a loan if necessary. Their credit history with the bank was excellent, and they had no outstanding debt other than their house mortgage. If they borrowed $200,000 from the bank, Eric and Mary wanted to repay the loan within two years, even though the bank would be willing to give them anywhere from three to seven years, because they just didn't want any debt hanging over their heads any longer than necessary.

Eric and Mary had talked with a nearby manufacturer about producing the Lock-Awn, although they had not formalized any agreement. To begin, they planned to manage EMR Innovations themselves with part-time workers to help with production—Mary would manage inventory and shipping, and Eric would manage sales. However, they thought that eventually, as the business grew, they would hire a full-time office manager and additional help for shipping. This would permit them to focus on marketing and sales, and would free up some of Eric's time to develop new products. However, they knew this would not happen right away. For the first year or two at least, they did not think they would need to hire additional help. The profits from the RV repair business, while not large, were sufficient to maintain their current modest lifestyle and support their involvement in EMR Innovations.

EMR Innovations was just an idea—it was not formalized into any type of organization (e.g., sole proprietorship or Subchapter S corporation).

Now in their mid-30s, neither Eric nor Mary had attended college or taken business courses. High school sweethearts, they had married and started their family when they were young. Eric trained and worked as a mechanic and, given his love for RVs, had found it natural to begin an RV repair business. Mary had always been a stay-at-home mom, but had helped Eric by taking on the bookkeeping responsibilities. Now that their youngest child had started kindergarten, Mary found herself with more time to devote to beginning EMR Innovations. What Eric and Mary knew about business was what they had learned by owning the RV repair business, so they felt challenged by all of the details necessary to develop, manufacture, and sell a new product. Mary appreciated that they didn't know everything there was to know about operating a business, but she knew that both she and Eric had common sense, a strong work ethic, and the desire to succeed.

The Lock-Awn Antibillow Device

Manually operated patio awnings on RVs consisted of a long aluminum roller tube with two spring-loaded end-cap assemblies, the awning fabric, a locking cam or ratchet on the front spring, two vertical awning arms, and an awning rod. The awning rod or wand, separately stored, disengaged the awning's locking mechanism. The user pulled a strap attached to the awning fabric to extend the awning for use. In windy conditions, when the awning was stored or retracted, the force of the wind could cause the locking cam mechanism to fail by overcoming the spring tension. This, in turn, could cause the aluminum cam to break. The aluminum teeth could also become so worn that they no longer held. Or, the lock could break. Any of these scenarios caused the fabric roller tube to come loose, allowing the awning fabric to release and billow in the wind.

The Lock-Awn antibillow device consisted of three main components—a catch that attached to the awning arm, a lock rod with a spring-loaded handle, and a two-piece roller tube collar. Eric had designed the spring-loaded handle to keep constant tension on the awning roller tube to minimize friction wear from the wind and road rattle; thus, the Lock-Awn would protect the internal awning mechanisms from wear and tear *and* would prevent billowing. Mary was especially excited because the Lock-Awn replaced the awning rod, which she (and all the RVers she knew) found to be very inconvenient to use and store. The Lock-Awn would operate the awning lock and pull the awning strap when extending the awning for use.

Eric had put great thought and care into designing and developing the Lock-Awn. The device had the following features:

- Heavy-duty injection molded U.V. and weather resistant collar and handle

- Nickel-plated steel lock rod
- Ergonomically designed handle
- Heavy-duty spring and rivet components
- A 30-day, 100% satisfaction guarantee and a 90-day limited warranty against defects in parts or workmanship
- Embossed company and product logo on the formed handle with contact information

Moreover, the Lock-Awn took only a few minutes to install, would work on either the right or left spring assembly of RV awnings, and did not detract from the RV's appearance.

Production costs for the Lock-Awn included a one-time investment of $40,000 for the mold and tooling. In addition, material cost for each unit was $5.95, packaging cost per unit, $0.75, and labor cost per unit, $5.90. Labor cost was calculated by dividing monthly projected part-time payroll costs, including wages and taxes, for part-time production workers by estimated Lock-Awn units produced per month. Eric and Mary thought of this as a variable cost because the workers' hours would fluctuate with demand. There would also be costs for packaging and assembly equipment ($3,500), office equipment ($1,000), product liability insurance ($5,000/year), building lease ($1,500/month), utilities (estimated to be $400/month), and standard commercial insurance ($1,000/year). Eric and Mary's time was also worth something, though that was more difficult for them to quantify. Mary figured she would eventually devote about half of her workweek (20 hours) to EMR, and to replace her would cost roughly $300/week. Mary further assumed that Eric would also put in about 20 hours a week into marketing the Lock-Awn, and to replace his time in the RV repair business would be about $600/week.

Eric had considered and rejected patenting the Lock-Awn because he didn't think patent protection was worth the $10,000 investment. He believed they could better protect their competitive advantage by penetrating the market.

Competitors

There were many do-it-yourself homemade versions of awning locks—Eric and Mary found many described on RV Internet chat sites, and they had seen some themselves on their RV travels. As one might expect, the homemade versions varied in sophistication, level of function, attractiveness, and ease of use. The most common homemade "fix" was to use rope to tie up the awning, which people did when their awnings had already been damaged by billowing. More sophisticated versions utilized dog-collar, metal-strap devices to secure the awning. Although some of these homemade devices provided protection, in Eric and Mary's opinion all of the do-it-yourself devices were lacking in some way, either in appearance, ease of installation, or ease of operation.

Eric found one commercial product designed to prevent billowing, the "AwningSaver," which a small company in Texas sold by mail order. The company had first offered the AwningSaver in 2001, but did not distribute it widely. However, some of the RV Internet chatters mentioned they had purchased the product. According to the company's materials, the AwningSaver worked by locking the awning roller tube to the awning arm. The device was permanently clamped to the awning arm, and a brake clamp gripped the roller tube end securely, preventing rotation of the tube. The user opened the brake clamp with the standard awning wand.

Neither Eric nor Mary believed the AwningSaver was a credible threat to the Lock-Awn. After examining one of the AwningSaver devices themselves, they believed that the product would prevent billowing. But, they found it difficult to operate, contrary to the company's claims, and they thought the AwningSaver had a "homemade" look to it when installed, which Eric and Mary found unappealing. As Mary said, "why would you want to put something that looks cheap on a motor home that cost $100,000?" In addition, Eric and Mary thought the AwningSaver was overpriced—it retailed at $59.95 plus $7.50 for shipping, for an assortment of bolts, nuts, washers, and clamps that could be purchased for under $5 from any hardware store.

Marketing and Distribution of the Lock-Awn

When Mary finished collecting information about RVers and competitors, she began to research information she could use to develop a marketing mix. Mary thought there were three viable distribution channels. First, they could sell the Lock-Awn as a mail-order product, much as the AwningSaver, passing the shipping costs on to the buyer. This would require a good Web site and knowledge about how to get the Web site highly ranked on search engines. Neither Eric nor Mary had that knowledge, but Mary thought that perhaps they could use the plethora of RV-related Web sites to direct Internet traffic to a Lock-Awn Web site. Mary contacted a regional company well-known for its Web site design and management and discovered that a basic five-page Web site design and hosting would cost $600, while search engine optimization would cost a minimum of $1,795 per year. If they wanted customized features on their Web site, the cost could go as high as $2,000–$3,000.

A second possibility was to attract individual dealers from the Workampers group. This group, at 70,000 members, lived full-time in their RVs and looked for business opportunities they could conduct from their RVs. "Who better to sell the Lock-Awn to RVers than people who live in their RVs all the time?" thought Mary. They could recruit Workampers through the Workamper publication and Web site (a one-time ad cost $100). They would advance qualified applicants ten Lock-Awn units on 30-day net terms. EMR would also provide promotional materials and one free display unit for the dealers to install on their own awnings. Workampers would earn a 25 percent margin (a 25 percent discount off the retail price) on each Lock-Awn unit they sold. Mary thought that Workamper dealers could not only make money by selling the Lock-Awn devices, but they could also charge to install the Lock-Awn to earn some additional income. Dealers also had the option to sell the product to retail distributors, such as RV repair shops or campground stores.

A third distribution method was to use an established distributor that already sold RV accessories, such as Camping World. Camping World was the largest RV aftermarket retailer in the U.S. Mary thought that without a strong sales record, it would be difficult to get Camping World to sell the Lock-Awn. Still, she recognized it as a possibility, if not right away, then at least in the future. Mary was not sure what kind of margin Camping World required, but she assumed that they would dictate the terms, not the Reynolds.

As she considered the distribution options, Mary figured that she and Eric would probably use some combination of direct selling and the Workampers (indirect selling). She also assumed that for the first few months EMR Innovations was officially open, there would be no sales, as they implemented their distribution systems. Mary quickly projected what the sales of the Lock-Awn might be for the first couple of years (Exhibit 2), given that it would take a few months to establish the sales channels and that EMR Innovations was a small company. These projections were very modest, amounting to only 0.02 percent of the entire U.S. RV market (7.5 million households) by the end of the second year. Mary had no idea how many Lock-Awns would be returned under the 30-day satisfaction guarantee or 90-day warranty, but to be safe, she thought maybe a 0.5 percent return rate was a reasonable expectation.

To support selling efforts, Mary knew it was important to increase awareness for the Lock-Awn. She researched several different ways to do this:

- Advertise in popular RV magazines, such as *Motor Home* and *Trailer Life*. The combined circulation of these two publications was 1.5 million. A 1/3 page, black-and-white ad inserted four times would cost $25,000.
- Advertise on RV-related Web sites. Some would include links to other Web sites. Some would include ads on their sites for minimal or no cost.
- Develop promotional brochures detailing the awning billowing problem and the benefits of the Lock-Awn in addressing this problem. They would make the brochures available to dealers and RV parts

| Exhibit 2 | EMR Sales Projections in Units—Years 1 and 2 |

Year 1 Month	1	2	3	4	5	6	7	8	9	10	11	12	Total Unit Sales
Direct Sales	0	0	0	100	300	400	500	500	600	600	600	600	4,200
Indirect Sales	0	0	0	20	40	100	300	350	500	500	500	500	2,810
Total Sales	0	0	0	120	340	500	800	850	1,100	1,100	1,100	1,100	7,010

Year 2 Month	1	2	3	4	5	6	7	8	9	10	11	12	Total Unit Sales
Direct Sales	650	650	650	650	650	675	675	675	675	675	675	675	7,975
Indirect Sales	550	550	550	550	550	575	575	575	575	575	575	575	6,775
Total Sales	1,200	1,200	1,200	1,200	1,200	1,250	1,250	1,250	1,250	1,250	1,250	1,250	14,750

Source: Eric and Mary Reynolds.

distributors throughout the country. For high-quality 4-color brochures, design and printing costs would be about $1,500 for 10,000 brochures, according to some printing Web sites Mary consulted.

- Promote and demonstrate the Lock-Awn at RV shows and rallies. These types of shows attracted RV enthusiasts either for the purpose of learning more about RVs or for social gathering (traveling) with other RVers. Virtually every state had an RV show every year, and numerous rallies were sponsored throughout the company by RV clubs and organizations. Mary estimated that registration and travel costs for each show would be approximately $1,800, and that they could go to four regional shows annually.
- Ask RV trade publications to evaluate and feature the Lock-Awn in new product spotlight columns.
- Generate discussion about the Lock-Awn in RV chat rooms.
- Use the networking systems of RV clubs to spread information about the Lock-Awn device.

Conclusion

Eric and Mary carved some time out of their busy schedules a few weeks later to look at the marketing information Mary had put together. As she summarized her findings, she explained, "We need to decide which RVers are most likely to buy the Lock-Awn. And we have to decide how much we want to charge and how to distribute it. Once we've done that, we should be able to have a better idea about whether or not we can make money selling the Lock-Awn."

Eric was quiet for a moment, sighed, and then replied, "I know the Lock-Awn is a good product, and I think all RV owners should install it on their RVs, but I guess we can't

build a business on what I think. So, let's really look at this information and consider our options with respect to how we would market the Lock-Awn."

"Yes," Mary said, "we have to. Otherwise we can't really know if we should do this or not."

Focused on their decision-making task, Mary and Eric began to review the market data piece by piece. Both knew the future of EMR Innovations depended on what the data told them.

References

AwningSaver, retrieved from http://www.awningsaver.com, January 4, 2006.

Henricks, Mark (2003), "RV-Based Businesses Can Be 'Going Concerns,'" *WSJ.com Startup Journal,* October 31, retrieved from http://www.startupjournal.com/startuplifestyle/200309101ifestyle.html.

Recreation Vehicle Industry Association (2001), *2001 National Survey of Recreation Vehicle Owners,* conducted by Dr. Richard Curtin, University of Michigan.

Recreation Vehicle Industry Association (RVIA) RVIA Facts, http://www.rvia.org/ media/fastfacts.htm.

Recreation Vehicle Industry Association (RVIA) RVIA Facts, http://www.rvia.org/ media/shipmentsdata.htm.

RV Central, RV History, retrieved from http://www.rvcentral.com/rv_history.htm, June 2, 2005.

RVHotlineCanada.com—From Past to Present, retrieved from http://www.rvhotlinecanada.com/rvhistory.asp, June 2, 2005.

RVInfo: Your RV News and Information Portal, RV gadgets and accessories, retrieved from http://www.rvinfo.net/rvgadgets.html, February 26, 2006.

Siuru, William D., Jr., "RV Awning Care: Protect this Expensive Investment," *Woman Motorist,* retrieved from http://www.womanmotorist.com/index.php/news/man/3062/event=view, January 4, 2006.

CASE 6

Total Quality Logistics

Sales Force Management

David W. Rosenthal, Miami University

In June 2005, Ken Oaks, President, Debbie Strawser, Human Resources Director, and Kerry Byrne, Executive Vice President, sat in Total Quality Logistics' (TQL) conference room to discuss the company's sales management practices and organization. They expected the sales force to roughly double in size in the coming year and wanted to be prepared for that growth.

TQL offered freight brokerage services to companies that needed to send or receive shipments by truck. Its brokers were responsible for finding truck shipments or "loads," matching them with trucks, referred to as "carriers," and coordinating the entire process to make certain that the carriers picked up the loads and delivered them in good condition and on time.

Since Ryan Legg, CEO, and Ken Oaks had founded the company in Milford, Ohio, in 1997, it had grown to employ roughly 130 salespeople. The three executives were concerned that the sheer size of the firm could begin to erode the quality of service they provided. Kerry Byrne described the management team's thinking regarding the sales organization:

> What we really need is to break the sales organization down. It was 20 salespeople, then it was 40, then 60. It is really hard to push the accountability down; there is no one to push it to. It is too much for the high-level sales managers to cover, just too many people.

For much of the company's history Oaks or Legg had maintained direct oversight of every broker. Although the company was still small, such direct management had become impossible. It was important to ensure that the salespeople continued to perform according to the company's best practices because the company relied on its reputation for integrity and outstanding service as differentiating features in the highly competitive freight brokerage field. (Exhibit 1 presents the company's sales organization.)

TQL's managers considered the availability of qualified employees, their training, support, and management to be the major constraints to the company's continued growth. Management expected company revenues to exceed $150 million in 2005. The number of employees was approaching 200, and they believed it was important groundwork for even more growth.

Recently, the company had organized the brokers into nine teams, designating each with a color and assigning an experienced broker to oversee the team. However, the team leaders had not yet been assigned formal duties or responsibilities or given any formal authority. Today's meeting was to decide what, if any, formal structure the company would implement. One option was to establish a new layer of sales management, making the nine team leaders salaried managers. At the other end of the spectrum, they could decide that no changes were necessary at this time. Other options fell between the two extremes; for example, adding a smaller number of managers or creating specialized positions for training.

The Freight Brokerage Industry

Simply stated, freight brokers provided a service. They matched loads with carriers. For example, JTM Meats, a food processor in Cincinnati, might need to ship a truckload of frozen meats to the Jewel T supermarket distribution center in Chicago, Illinois. JTM would call and inform its TQL Account Executive (AE) that it had a shipment that would be ready at a certain time and needed to be delivered by a certain time. The AE would set a price for handling the shipment and then find a carrier who was willing and able to transport the load to Chicago in the allotted time. The AE would negotiate a fee for this service with the carrier. TQL earned its money by charging JTM Meats more than it cost TQL to contract with a carrier to make the delivery.

Once the carrier had delivered the shipment, the AE would likely be involved in arranging another load for the carrier to bring back to Cincinnati or some other destination. Shippers did not always have the time, expertise, or communications network to find the best carriers or to negotiate the best terms for a given load. Similarly, having delivered a load, a carrier could find itself with an empty truck, many miles from home, with no prospects for a new shipment.

Exhibit 1   Total Quality Logistics, Inc. Sales Organization

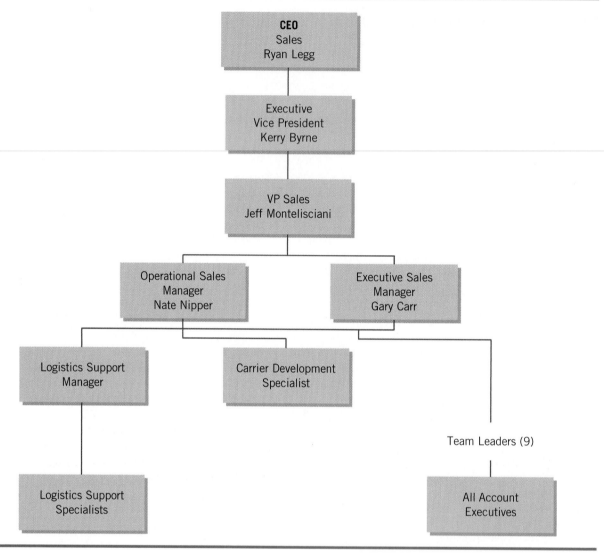

Source: Company records.

Brokers created value for shippers and carriers by developing a network of contacts, making the appropriate connections, and negotiating rates that included a fee for their services.

The freight brokerage market was large and growing. Industry estimates were that third-party brokerage companies controlled approximately 20 percent ($50 billion) of the $255 billion truckload and less-than-truckload (LTL) freight market. The freight brokerage industry was highly fragmented; a broker was often simply an individual with a telephone, a computer, and the necessary personal relationships to connect a carrier and a load. Large companies such as C. H. Robinson had the advantage of offering international, intermodal, warehousing, consulting, and other third-party logistics (3PL) services. Other firms often specialized by geographic region, type of freight (e.g., produce versus dry goods) or carrier (refrigerated or "reefer" versus liquid or bulk).

The trucking industry was similarly fragmented. Industry estimates indicated that there were more than 320,000 trucking companies in the U.S., of which 82 percent operated fewer than 20 trucks.

Ken Oaks and Ryan Legg met in 1990. Ken was a buyer and selling agent for the Castellini Company, a Cincinnati-based produce wholesaler, and Ryan was a freight broker with RWI, a Castellini subsidiary.

Exhibit 2 | TQL Employee Growth*

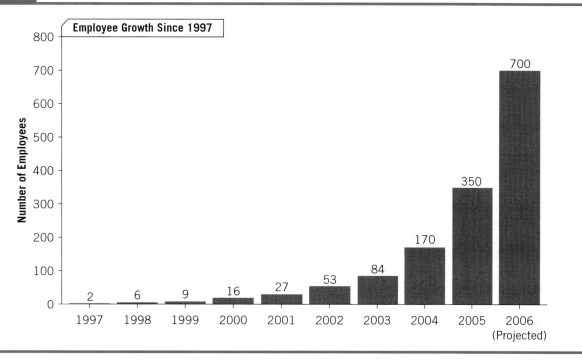

Source: Company records.

*2005 entry is anticipated number at year-end.

Oaks described his start and the motivation for founding TQL:

> Ryan and I talked all the time about starting our own thing, whatever it would be, mainly because we were both selling and we weren't making commission. We were both doing great at selling and every year our numbers were way up, but we didn't feel that we were being compensated properly. We loved our jobs and the business, and we finally decided that there was definitely room for more people in this industry.

Legg elaborated:

> I used to give a lot of freight to freight brokers and I had a terrible time with them. I'd visit them and see that their business was successful but I often found that they gave horrible service and they just weren't very ethical. You couldn't get hold of them on weekends and they didn't really follow up to make sure the truck and shipment actually arrived on time, but they were still doing business. Ken agreed, and that's when he said, "Well, I know we can do that." We decided that being on the customer side, we knew what they expected, and we weren't getting that service.

The company had revenue of $1 million in 1997, which was a little more than Legg and Oaks had expected in their

first year. Revenue jumped 48 percent from 2001 to 2002, to $32 million, which was sufficient for TQL to be named the fastest growing TriState (Ohio, Kentucky, Indiana) private company, according to *Cincinnati Business Courier* research. The company expected to double the number of employees from 170 (2004) to 350 (2005). Revenue reached nearly $50 million in 2003 and over $100 million for 2004. (See Exhibit 2 and Exhibit 3.)

The company had over 1,000 customers including Fortune 500 companies such as Wal-Mart, SUPERVALU, Kroger, Fleming, ConAgra, Sara Lee, Publix Super Markets, Spartan stores and Chiquita. Customers also included small and medium-sized businesses such as JTM Food Group, Gilardi Foods, Hillshire Farms and Kahns. The company contracted for a wide variety of loads ranging from frozen dinners, produce, and general commodities to heavy equipment and lumber. TQL brokered shipments to and from the 48 contiguous states plus Canada and Mexico.

The TQL Advantage

TQL's founders believed its competitive advantage stemmed from three factors.

Exhibit 3   TQL Revenue Growth*

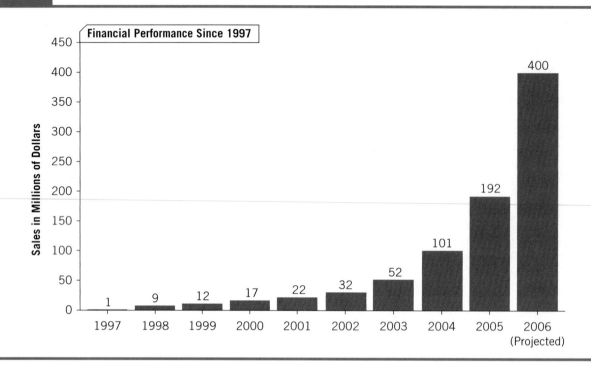

Financial Performance Since 1997

Source: Company records.

*2005 entry is anticipated number at year-end.

Honesty

The owners attributed the company's growth to hard work and an emphasis on honesty. "Reputation is everything in this line of work, so we do absolutely everything possible to keep ours," said Oaks. "There are lots of unethical people in this industry. They'll over promise, saying that a truck will be there in a couple hours when they have no idea where it is."

The company had formalized its commitment to maintaining an excellent reputation by establishing its "Five Winning Principles":

1. Pledge integrity.

Commit to the highest ethical standards, and don't compromise them. Ethical and professional behavior is the bedrock of our company.

2. Exceed expectations.

Seek to achieve not only what is asked, but also use creativity to provide solutions above and beyond what is expected. There is little traffic on the extra mile.

3. Recognize the value of teamwork.

Fidelity to a team ethic results in personal achievements beyond one's individual capabilities and respects differences among individuals. The only way we can be the one-stop source providing the best overall service for our clients is to pool the talents of our people.

4. Be forthright about conflict.

Inform clients of real or perceived conflicts. Always choose the harder right over the easier wrong.

5. Maintain balance in life and business.

To be our most productive, we must maintain a healthy balance among our priorities for clients, family, faith, community, and self.

Evidence of the company's commitment to its reputation was also clear in a number of industry ratings and certifications that noted TQL as being in the top one percent of all companies registered in integrity, pay practices, and credit worthiness, and as having the best practices among logistics industry members.

Access and Communication

Prior to founding TQL, Legg and Oaks found it difficult to get a straight answer from brokers, and that brokers were often unavailable when needed most. At TQL, dispatchers took calls through nights, weekends and holidays, and the company expected brokers to be on call for a customer at all times. The company's ability to deal with problems quickly had helped it land one of its major customers, JTM Food Group. In 2000, JTM Director of Distribution Paul Burton received a cold call from Oaks on a day when Burton needed help. "I had had problems moving some loads, and he made that the most important part of his day," Burton said. "I started him out with a problem, and he solved it." Burton was so impressed that he used the company as JTM's major freight broker, to the tune of about $1 million of business annually.

A conversation with one of TQL's freight brokers in a rare off-the-phone moment amplified the founders' perspective:

> At TQL, a customer gets a one-on-one relationship with their broker. They know they are going to talk to the same guy, every time. If they have a question, they are going to call my cell phone and they know that I am going to be available 24–7–365. I am personally responsible for any problems with a customer's load. Every load has a specific broker, a person, attached to it. Loads are not let out to a group of dispatchers like you might find at a large trucking company, where if you have a problem you would first have a hassle just to find the person responsible for that piece of business. With TQL, you know who you are dealing with, every time. That allows us to get to know the customer, and their specific needs and the little details of providing the best service to them. For example, I might know that the load is supposed to be there by 9:00 A.M., but if I get it there just a few minutes early, I can get offloaded immediately rather than having to wait. That is good for everybody.

> We communicate with everyone in the channel. We offer 24/7 dispatch to make sure your truck is on the road. We make "check calls" every morning between 8:00 and 9:00 A.M. so that we know where every shipment is. We have cell phone numbers for every driver. We are going to make sure that load gets there on time and in good shape if it is humanly possible. And if it isn't, you are going to know about it ahead of time.

Carrier Business Practices

As a brokerage company, TQL dealt with customers and with carriers as well. TQL management considered the relationships with the carriers from dispatchers all the way to the individual truck drivers to be as important as their relationships with their customers. Oaks commented:

> From experience on the truck side, we know how to treat truckers and drivers. A lot of brokers talk very badly to drivers, and that's another part of the business that you've got to take care of.

> On the Load Program it will show the history we have with them, how many loads we've done, and what their on-time percentage is. (The Load Program

was the company's custom database that included data on all carriers and customers served by TQL. The Load Program was a sophisticated customer relationship management system that kept track of all contact information, history of transactions, pricing, payments, call data, performance measures, credit ratings, locations, broker assignments, and other pertinent comments and conditions.)

The Load Program software required certain fields for each transaction, and therefore controlled the information generated and the activities of the sales force. The records generated by the Load Program were used to document contracts, to account for payments and commissions, for reference in case of claims, and for research and analysis. Every transaction was recorded in the Load Program. Further, no carrier not certified by management could be used by a broker, and all of the certified carriers were listed in the Load Program, along with the necessary contact information.

Legg added:

> The carriers' dispatchers decide whether to take a load or not. It is based on the money, what we're paying on the load, where it's going, and probably the commodity. They also look at our history with them, and how quick we've paid the company.

> Here's an example of something unethical brokers will do. They'll have a load picked up on Friday to be delivered Tuesday. The run is only two days long, but the receiver can't unload it until Tuesday—and the broker knows that. Well, they don't tell the carrier this, so the trucker is expecting to drop it on Sunday or first thing Monday. So, Saturday or Sunday the broker will call the carrier and say, "Gosh, they don't have enough room until Tuesday!" But it's already on a truck and, the truck is already almost there. The trucker says, "You need to pay me $250 for the extra time and labor!" But the broker says, "Well, I can't do that, but I'll give you $50." The driver maybe had plans to go home, or had to reload for one of their best customers, and they would never, ever have taken that load to deliver on Tuesday. We don't do that.

> Ken and I realized from the very beginning how important carriers are, and a lot of brokers don't. They think they'll just find another truck. Well, in this day and age, there are credit agencies and if you treat carriers wrong it'll catch up to you. Money is a big thing with the carriers, particularly the smaller firms. They don't have a lot of cash or credit, 20–30 days, but on average it would probably be 45 days before the carrier would get paid. But we pay all of our trucks right away up until 21 days. Plus, after they pick up a load we'll advance them 40 percent of the fee for fuel or

costs. Some brokers will not do that. If they break down on the side of the road and need money for a tire, we'll give them an advance on the load.

And, it is not just the credit. If you have a carrier that has 40 trucks running our lanes (routes), and we treat them right and talk to their drivers and are personal with the drivers, they're going to want to haul for us. Truck drivers talk to people all day on the road, and if they like someone they're going to tell the dispatcher they want to haul for them. The dispatchers want their drivers to be happy, so if a dispatcher gets a load from a broker who treated a driver badly, they're not going to haul for them. And we want drivers to haul for us. You want a great relationship with CEOs of our customers, but we treat truck drivers the same way.

The Selling Task

Four elements made up the selling task: customer acquisition, finding a carrier, rate negotiation, and project management.

Customer Acquisition

The broker position at TQL was almost entirely comprised of telephone sales. Brokers identified potential customers, researched them—often online or through industry references—and made cold calls to introduce TQL and solicit loads. Once a broker had identified and contacted a potential customer, the account was "protected" for a 90-day period, after which it became open for other brokers to call, unless the original broker had been successful in generating a load. If a load had been forthcoming, the broker kept that account permanently.

The prospecting phase of the selling process often took multiple calls just to break through and have a conversation with the person responsible for truck shipments. Decision makers at shippers could receive as many as 40–50 calls per day from competing sales people asking for their freight business. The initial contact call involved qualifying the customer for truckload shipments, type of freight, etc., and then sending the TQL Customer Packet, which included information on TQL certifications, insurance, practices, and accomplishments. A few days later, the broker would contact the customer again, and begin asking for loads. It often took as many as 20 calls before a first-time customer would agree to ship with TQL. Most often, however, the first shipment would occur as the result of a customer emergency.

Legg described the customer acquisition process:

They'll look at our rates, and usually when they give us a shot it'll be when they're in a bind. They're not going to say, "Okay, here's some business." It takes some time to build rapport; probably five or ten phone calls. You do the typical sales routine to let them know you are available and interested in them, and usually it's an afternoon when a truck falls out on them (can't make a pick up), and they'll call us. That's how you get your foot in the door. Beautiful thing about this business, there are always problems.

Once we get in the door, they won't take away all of the business from the competitor and give it to us, but they'll keep us in the loop. If that guy got ten loads a week, now they are getting nine and we're getting one. Then it's up to the broker to keep calling, and to provide better communication, better service, and more attention to gain a greater share.

Finding Carriers

The broker's second focus involved finding trucks to handle the freight on specific lanes. Legg described the firm's treatment of truckers:

We actually deal with (carriers) from JB Hunt, huge, to a guy who has two trucks. But what we do with those guys as far as services, we treat them the way we would want to be treated. We don't lie to them, we don't mislead them. We tell them this is the deal, either I know or I don't know, no maybes or gray areas, all black and white.

We have our primary carriers, the guys we use day in and day out, with whom we have built rapport. We've done business with them, we know the drivers, we know how they perform. We're probably talking to them just as much as a customer. We go to them first. We know they'll be on top of it. If they can't handle it then we'll go to our secondary carriers. We still know everything is fine, we just don't talk to them every day.

A variety of industry conditions had combined over the previous three years to limit the availability of trucks. New regulations limited the number of hours drivers could spend on the road. Weakness in the economy and fuel price increases had driven less profitable trucking firms out of business. TQL brokers generally believed that the major constraint to growth on a day-to-day basis was finding more trucks. Company policy required that top managers evaluate all carriers before brokers could use them. Once managers certified carriers, the Load Program listed them as available for use.

Rate Negotiation

There were considerable variances in the prices charged to customers and in the payments made to carriers. Lanes that easily supported consistent fronthaul and backhaul opportunities permitted lower payments to truckers. Length of haul played a role as well. Commodity type also affected pricing. Because of its perishability, produce generated high shipping costs and high carrier payments. Contracts, ongoing relationships, timing, availability of trucks, and a myriad of other factors all played into the negotiations and price setting. On average, however, a load resulted in about $2,000 cost to the shipper. Industry estimates were that brokers earned about a 7–10 percent gross margin, although TQL generally tried to maintain somewhat higher margins because of its service levels.

TQL brokers were effectively in charge of their own pricing. Stories abounded about taking a load for a shipper below the trucking cost in order to gain a new customer, or to remind an established customer of the value of dealing with TQL. Similarly, if there had been a problem with an earlier shipment, a broker might quote a low price as a "make good." Similarly, a broker might pay a carrier a greater than normal fee to entice them to take an unattractive load, or to make up for a previous problem. In the long run, however, the brokers tried to strike a balance based on fairness, quality service, and mutually beneficial relationships.

Project Management

The fourth part of the selling task involved monitoring the load. Brokers were in contact with drivers at least twice a day, and often more, keeping track of the pickup, progress along the route, conditions of the truck and load. They also provided directions, and relayed information to customers and receivers as needed. Effectively, each load was a "project" and the broker played the role of "project manager" to assure a satisfactory conclusion. Oaks described the company's dedication to service:

> While our prices are often higher than our competitors', we can save customers money—not on the transaction but on the efficiency. We save the time of the guys at the warehouse in loading and unloading. If we say our truck is going to be there at three, it is going to be there at three o'clock, or else you get a call way before three letting you know it's going to be there at four. So, we keep in contact with the drivers and dispatchers the whole time, and make sure we know exactly what is going on so we can get the information to the customer. That way, they won't be throwing their money out the window for labor or whatever.

The Broker (Account Executive) Position

The Account Executive (AE), or broker, was the key player in TQL's business. Account Executive Trainees (AETs) received training on company policy, use of the Load System, and some general selling guidelines and principles, including the number of daily calls TQL expected them to make (120). After the initial training phase, which consisted of about two weeks, each AET began working with a specific AE. AETs assisted in managing that AE's customer base, prospecting, communicating with customers, tracking truck locations, and coordinating pickups and deliveries.

The "apprenticeship" the AETs served under their respective AEs was an important training stage. AETs worked closely with their AEs and learned by doing. The AEs provided close supervision because their actual accounts and carrier relationships were on the line. The relationships were usually close and supportive, and by the time the AET was ready to strike out on his/her own, he/she had developed a good working knowledge of the business, critical relationship-building skills with carriers and customers, problem-solving abilities, and a network of colleagues upon whom they could call for advice or assistance.

Once AEs reached a certain sales level, the company assigned an assistant. As AEs attained higher levels of sales, additional assistants joined their teams. The team grew as sales warranted. Some salespeople had teams of seven or more and earned over $600,000 a year themselves. Generally, assistants and trainees handled the carrier procurement and some project management sides of the brokerage task, leaving the cold calling, solicitation of loads, and customer relationship building to the AEs. Experienced AEs generally spent about 40 percent of their time on solicitation of loads and relationship building with existing accounts, another 40 percent on project management and problem resolution, and ten percent each on prospecting new accounts and carrier procurement. New AEs often spent 90 percent of their time cold calling new accounts for loads.

Over the years, some AETs had found that they were more skilled at finding trucks and managing the relationships with carriers than at developing loads. Other skilled candidates had been uncomfortable with the uncertainty of entirely commission-based position. An LC supported an AE by selling loads to carriers, negotiating, tracking, updating information, managing calls, and solving problems on the carrier side of the business. LCs worked with specific AEs and were included as an integral part of their team. The company generally paid LCs straight salary, but they could also earn bonuses based on team performance.

Recruitment and Selection

The characteristics the company sought in a candidate included: PC skills, typing, exceptional phone skills, teamwork skills, written and verbal communication skills, organization, customer service orientation, sense of urgency, attention to detail, a strong work ethic (giving 110 percent at all times), dependability, focus, ability to multitask, strong determination, and an entrepreneurial spirit.

Oaks expressed the desired attitude through an e-mail provided to trainees:

If you asked me how Ryan and I became so successful so fast, I would reply as follows: In the beginning, we were in early, we worked late every night, we worked all day Saturday and part of Sunday (and that was just selling, we did the billing after that). We were there when no other brokers were. We called prospects multiple times all through the day until 7:00 P.M. We were in calling our prospects every Saturday and Sunday to see if anyone else fell out on them and, if so, we stayed until we got them covered. We were willing to do whatever it took to get business established. We never missed work because we were a little sick, and would have missed only if we were extremely sick. The customers and prospects were amazed at our dedication to them, and we built relationships. We built our base and then expanded it from there.

Now it is up to you.

If you think getting established is easy, you are mistaken. It takes incredibly hard and long work. Ask Jeff M., Nathan, Mike N., Royce, Tony, David, Fuhrman and others—they have mirrored our ways. This is also how they became successful so quickly. They were in your shoes once. They are no smarter than you. Pay your dues, especially in the beginning, if you want to excel.

Over the years, we have had to let a few salespeople go, and they all shared one common belief—they just weren't having any luck getting accounts. They failed to realize that luck has nothing to do with success. These individuals did not go the extra mile to build a customer base. Nobody ever saw them on a Saturday when they were not scheduled to work, and rarely were they here after 5:00 P.M. or before 8:00 A.M. during the week. Success doesn't "happen," it is a result of hard work, perseverance, and dedication. Make your own bed.

One more thing: The successful people did not ever, ever make excuses such as, "I'm getting offered loads and can't get trucks cheap enough," or, "I'm so depressed because I can't get sales." They never had time to feel sorry for themselves because they were constantly on the phone hustling, doing it!

In its recruiting literature, the company claimed "TQL Only Hires the Best of the Best" and indicated that a "target potential candidate for TQL possesses one or more of the following:"

Background in sports (college preferable)	Sales experience
Military "special forces" background	Leadership experience
Transportation/ Logistics background	College experience (degree)
Former traffic manager	Strong work ethic
Former dispatcher	Hunger for success

The company recruited primarily from local and regional colleges through an established network of contacts among faculty members and career placement offices. It also solicited candidates from employees and advertised open positions in local and regional media.

The recruitment and selection process consisted of five phases. Candidates submitted a résumé and an HR manager interviewed them via telephone. In this call, the interviewer asked the candidate to sell something. Interviewers were reportedly almost combative in this process. TQL required multiple letters of recommendation. Candidates had to pass a geography test (naming all 50 states on a map) with 100 percent accuracy. Candidates had a short time to develop a list of potential customers and to provide statistics on the trucking industry. Lastly, they visited the facility to interview in person. A committee comprised of Legg, Oaks, and Vasseur conducted nearly all interviews and had to come to a consensus to make an offer.

The management team believed that the five-phase process did a good job of weeding out weak candidates, and preparing those chosen for the tasks inherent in the AE position. The telephone interview tested selling and communication skills, telephone demeanor, and assertiveness. The letters of recommendation required diligence and timeliness. The geography test focused on learning shipping lanes. The research assignment also required a timely return and tested the candidate's ability to identify potential new business and to use appropriate research resources. Management believed the company's four percent turnover rate, high levels of compensation, and growth were indicators that the hiring process was successful.

Compensation

AEs earned commission on the difference between the rates they negotiated with customers and carriers. For example, a customer might need a load delivered from St. Louis, Missouri, to Atlanta, Georgia. The AE for that account would negotiate a price and terms of the pickup and delivery, etc. If the shipping cost were $2,000, the AE might then negotiate a payment of $1,800 with a carrier. The AE would then receive a 30 percent commission on the $200 difference, for a total commission of $60.

AETs received a straight salary but had the goal of moving to commission-only compensation within a year, along with promotion to the AE position. TQL paid AE commissions equal to 30 percent of gross profit on loads, payable when the customer paid. The company could also charge an AE's commission account for 30 percent of any costs paid by TQL in the event of a customer bad debt or cargo claim not collected from the carrier. Recently, the company had cut the commission rate to 25 percent, but it continued to pay the old rate in some instances.

In 2003, ten out of 41 salespeople made over $100,000, and 22 of the 41 were new salespeople in 2003. The average sales executive commission among first-year brokers was $70,000, second year—$100,000, and third year—$115,000.

The benefits package was relatively standard and included a company cell phone, vacation, health insurance, dental coverage, life insurance, disability coverage, and retirement.

Physical Facilities

The company was growing rapidly, roughly doubling in size each year, and a year before, had moved into a new, 30,000-square-foot facility in Milford, Ohio. In the intervening year, it had been necessary to double the size of the building, and the new extension had just opened a few weeks ago.

The new facilities were very different from the cramped conditions of the previous location. There, desks had been jammed into whatever space was available, and the place was dark, cramped, piled with files, records, and the accumulated junk of years.

The new building largely consisted of a vast, open expanse of waist-high dividers that did nothing to obstruct the view. Teams of brokers and assistants worked in "bays" around multiple phones and computer screens. The buzz of phone conversations, computer keyboards, and shared discussions across the maze was evidence of the rapid pace and high energy level.

The general atmosphere was light and open. Two sides of the rectangular space were glass, providing views of the surrounding countryside. The other two sides of the perimeter were comprised of offices for accounting, IT services, training rooms, meeting rooms, executive offices, a large lunchroom and even an exercise facility. Management specifically wanted to provide employees with amenities to make it easy for them to stay on site.

Sales Organization

As the company grew, Ryan Legg and Ken Oaks looked to senior AEs to take on additional responsibilities. On January 1, 2004, the company promoted Jeff Montelisciani to Vice President of Sales. He was the company's top salesperson at the time. His duties included the continued coverage of his major accounts, but also extensive travel in support of new customer development and ongoing customer support. Montelisciani traveled over half the time, and his customer visits were an important part of the process of gaining new, large accounts. Other brokers had the opportunity to get into the field and actually meet their customers only rarely. However, in a number of instances, the personal face-to-face interaction with Montelisciani or Legg had proved to be the difference in obtaining trial business from a customer. Montelisciani also was responsible for advising other AEs and for decisions when questions of policy or problem resolution occurred.

Nate Nipper was the company's top salesperson on September 13, 2004, when he was promoted to the position of Operational Sales Manager. Nipper was responsible for handling claims and insurance issues. The company handled all insurance claims as part of its "one-stop shopping" service. Essentially, TQL guaranteed that a customer's load would arrive on time and in good condition. If the carrier damaged or lost a load, TQL would pay the customer the load's value or the appropriate adjustment and would then seek redress from the carrier, insurance company, or other responsible party. This practice significantly reduced customer risk, and was another reason customers regarded TQL's service highly. However, it also added a great deal of potential risk exposure when TQL contracted to handle a load. As a result, the company was very careful about the carriers it used, the insurance the carriers had, and the value and types of loads it would accept. For example, the company would not accept a load of cigarettes because of the high value and the potential for loss. On matters related to the area of insurance, all AEs reported to Nipper.

Gary Carr was also one of the company's top ten AEs and had been with the company for a number of years when Legg and Oaks promoted him to the position of Executive Sales Manager on January 1, 2005. His combination of performance and longstanding relationships made him an obvious choice to become a manager. Legg and Oaks had asked him to take on some of the sales management duties including providing input on hiring decisions, handling customer problems and issues beyond the abilities of less experienced AEs, providing training, instruction, and mentoring. On matters related to general sales or sales management, all AEs reported to Carr.

Montelisciani, Nipper, and Carr all received a compensation mix of salary and bonuses. Their salaries were proportional with their prior level of sales commissions, and they could earn bonuses based on corporate attainment of income targets. Their new compensation plan allowed them to earn total pay that was consistent with their compensation levels as AEs.

Kerry Byrne had joined the company in March, 2005. He had been in client management with 5/3 Bank in Cincinnati for 15 years and had a background in both personal and corporate finance. He and Oaks had known each other since grade school. He had been instrumental in the construction of TQL's initial business and financial plans, and was a natural choice to join the company to contribute both financial and client service perspectives.

J. J. Blum had also been a top AE and rose to the position of Training Manager in summer 2004. He was responsible for the formal portion of the training program and for managing the Logistics Coordinators.

Discussion of an Additional Management Level

In late 2004, the management team had begun discussing the idea of creating a more formal sales management organization. The managers were concerned that the company was growing too large for the direct AE management contact that had been the practice. While there were, as yet, no serious signs of weakening performance, the general consensus was that it was only a matter of time before sheer numbers made the current structure untenable.

By late January 2005, the management team had decided to experiment with the sales force structure by breaking the sales force into a number of teams. A "team captain" would head each team, and there would be a backup. Management had selected individuals who had shown leadership, who were successful, and who had "credibility on the floor" to fill the positions.

Management selected teams based on several factors including commodity focus and existing relationships. Several teams dealt exclusively with produce, others with mostly dry goods, and others mostly with frozen goods. One of the goals was to generate more interaction within teams. Organizing by commodity made sense because each commodity tended to use different types of trucks, and different lanes. TQL had also taken care to support natural groupings that already existed. For example, an AE who had a couple of assistants and a logistics coordinator would all be on the same team.

Members met to discuss the new structure and how the teams would work together. In addition, some captains suggested social gatherings, while others focused on team members coming to them with questions or problems.

By May, the experiment had been underway for over two months and Byrne, Strawser and Oaks met to discuss future steps the company would take in managing the sales force. Kerry Byrne summed up the purpose of the meeting:

Up to now, the team concept has been a purely volunteer thing. Captains don't have formal responsibilities, and they don't receive any additional compensation. What we are trying to do is solidify this and create some structure that makes sense for us in going forward. The discussion is about what the actual job will look like. What do we think that we want them to do? How will we compensate them? Part of the problem is that the team captains still have their own individual books of business, and most of them are pretty successful. That makes it hard to continue paying them at their current levels if they stop selling in order to manage.

The existing managerial roles had evolved more or less on an "as needed" basis, and reflected specialized duties rather than day-to-day supervision. Oaks observed:

The managers we have now are all specialized. Nate is great at taking claims, Gary is great at handling the scheduling and customer complaints and general supervision, Jeff is great at working on acquiring large, new customers. If we want to, we can bring someone up, possibly to take care of all the first-year guys, mentor those guys, and be the coach. We can't expect one guy to be able to be good at all of that. Why don't we just go ahead and do what we are doing; bring up guys, have them in charge of particular things, and still have the teams?

Debbie Strawser, Human Resources Director, was concerned, however, about the impact of growth and the increasing span of control. First, she was worried over training, both initial and ongoing.

We have a lot of classwork that first six months. The second six months we do one 4-hour class on prospecting and that is the only classroom piece they get. Sales is an area where I think you need some one-on-one, me sitting with you and saying, 'You know what, here's how you might have done that better.' We are doing some of that, but nobody has enough time to do as much as needs to be done. From six to twelve months, they are not getting enough direction. They are not getting enough mentoring.

Byrne agreed, and added his concern over the continuing development of experienced brokers:

It is a basic sales management issue. How do we enhance productivity? And it is a big problem. With as many people as we have now, we are kind of throwing them out of the nest. They are off the training program and on their own, but they are not getting a lot of direction. It is just sink or swim. Can we provide some more coaching during that 6–12 month period? Also, there is the experienced $4,000 per week guy—how do we get him to $6,000 or $7,000? We *completely* ignore those folks because they are doing okay. At $4,000 and they have been here for a year and a half? They could probably do a whole lot better than that. We just haven't had the resources and the structure in place to have somebody spend time pushing them and coaching.

Oaks agreed that training should be a company focus, but was more concerned about ongoing mentorship and "developing the top folks." He had had a recent conversation with a friend on the subject. This friend pointed out the obvious math, "If you increase a guy who is doing $10,000 by 20 percent, what do you get? If you increase someone who is doing $4,000 by 20 percent what do you get?" Ken believed that the company practice of creating "manager specialists" should continue. However, he was concerned about who might fill a high-end training position, and the reception that person might receive. He concluded, "In fact, nobody here would be right for that spot."

Byrne supported that view:

That's right, because this is a tough crowd. Their attitude would be, "this has to be the right person for me, somebody who has an understanding of the transportation industry." It has to be somebody with credibility.

Strawser's second concern was that the span of control was growing so large that managers could no longer handle their managerial functions effectively. The sheer volume of work created by the increasing numbers of account executives, trainees and logistics coordinators was becoming overwhelming. She had drafted a "job description" to point out the duties and responsibilities of a potential sales manager (Exhibit 4). In general, these tasks included involvement in recruiting and selection, evaluation and promotion of

Exhibit 4

(DRAFT)

Responsibilities include (but not limited to):

- Weekend and after-hour shifts
- DAT/Transcore
- Cincinnati Reds tickets
- Phase five interviewer
- Sales interns and coops
- Sales meetings with brokers
- Role playing with assistants two weeks before they are approved to start cold calling
- Periodic fill in on sales trips with brokers
- Daily sales operations
- Monitor phone times of brokers
- Convention/associations coordinator involving customers
- Inactive customers: contact why no business
- Customer list/inactive prospects
- First delivered load/contact customer
- Customer contracts review
- Daily attendance
- Working on advertising options
- Customer rate confirmations (being turned in)

The following should be directed to the Executive Sales Manager, Gary Carr. (In case of absence contact Nate Nipper.)

- Carriers/customers asking for a manager
- Questions on lanes/rates/quotes
- Questions on after-hour shifts
- All attendance issues: late, sick, weather, etc.
- Questions on inactive customers/prospects
- Any new customer/prospect calling in on customer service
- Problem carrier approval
- Waiving comcheck fees
- Cincinnati Reds ticket requests

Source: Company records.

trainees, assignments of personnel and accounts, scheduling, monitoring adherence to policies, and some customer contact and support. She noted:

> I'm still worried about span of control. We are okay today, but I am worried that shortly we are going to get beyond a good span of control. As we get bigger, somehow we are going to have to divide it up a little. When we have 100 brokers out there, one person is not going to be able to handle it.

Another issue was that of compensation. If the company created a new layer of management, the additional overhead would be a significant cost to the firm. Top performers who would be candidates for a management position simply earned so much in commission that the company could not afford to pay them at the same level for management duties. The time required to be a successful broker limited the ability to take on additional managerial roles at a significant level. Views on captains' compensation ranged from zero, to recognition, to travel incentives, to a $10,000 salary increment. One thought was to make this role a qualifying "stepping stone" to be promoted to the next "official" sales management position. There had been some discussion among the management about the need to create a "career path" for senior brokers, reflecting concern that over time brokers would "burn out" from their normal duties.

Conclusion

As the meeting ended, the three executives returned to their offices, to other meetings and responsibilities. Each considered the meeting to have been a good exchange of ideas, but they had finalized nothing. The questions were still on the table. Should they formalize the management function over the sales force, creating nine new management positions? If so, how should they pay the managers, and what would happen to their accounts? Should they maintain the informal "team captains" positions, and wait for the sales force to grow further before selecting a captain to move into a new position? Might they take a middle route and add a smaller number of managers, perhaps to deal with specific functions? Were there other things that they should change in their sales management system? For that matter, things were going so well, did they really need to do anything at all? They were all agreed on one thing, the company would continue to grow rapidly and they didn't want to be unprepared. Another meeting would be scheduled in a few weeks to continue the discussion and come to a consensus on a direction.

CASE 7

Clearwater Technologies

Susan F. Sieloff, Northeastern University
Raymond M. Kinnunen, Northeastern University

At 9:00 A.M. on Monday, May 2004, Rob Erickson, QTX Product Manager; Hillary Hanson, Financial Analyst; and Brian James, District Sales Manager; were preparing for a meeting with Mark Jefferies, Vice President of Marketing, at Clearwater Technologies. The meeting's objective was to establish the end-user pricing for a capacity upgrade to the QTX servers Clearwater offered.

No one was looking forward to the meeting because company pricing debates were traditionally long and drawn out. Because there had already been several meetings, everyone knew that there was no consensus on how to determine the appropriate price, but company policy insisted on agreement. Only one price proposal went forward, and it had to represent something everyone could accept.

When Jefferies called the meeting, he commented:

We've struggled with this pricing issue for several months. We can't seem to all agree on the right price. Finance wants the price as high as possible to generate revenue. Sales wants it low to sell volume. Product management wants the price to be consistent with the current product margin model. We've debated this for quite a while, but we need to finalize the third quarter price book update before June in order to get it into print and out to the sales force. We need to get this done.

Clearwater Technologies, Inc. History

Clearwater Technologies, Inc. was a small, publicly traded technology firm outside Boston. It was the market share leader in customer relationship management (CRM) servers for sales staffs of small to medium-sized companies. Four MIT graduates had founded the company when they saw an opportunity to meet a market need that larger firms ignored. Unlike the CRM systems from Oracle or SAP, Clearwater customized the QTX for companies with sales forces of 10 to 30 people. Clearwater had been first to market in this particular segment, and QTX sales represented $45 million of its $80 million sales in 2004.

The QTX product line represented Clearwater's core franchise. Clearwater's premium-priced products were renowned for high reliability in performance supported by free lifetime technical support. The QTX line held 70 percent of its mature market. To date, competition in this market had been minimal, because no competitor had been able to match Clearwater's general functionality, and Clearwater held a U.S. patent on a popular feature that directed faxed documents to a specific salesperson's email rather than a central fax machine.

Since 1999, Clearwater had used the cash generated by the QTX line to support engineering-intensive internal product development and to buy four other companies. None of these other businesses had achieved a dominant market position or profitability, so maximizing the QTX cash flow remained a priority.

The QTX Product

QTX was a sales support server that allowed multiple users to simultaneously maintain their sales account databases. These databases covered contact information, quote histories, copies of all communications, and links to the customers' corporate database for shipping records. The basic QTX package consisted of a processor, chassis, hard drive, and network interface, with a manufacturing cost of $500. The package provided simultaneous access for 10 users to the system, referred to as 10 "seats." Each seat represented one accessing employee. The product line consisted of 10-, 20-, and 30-seat capacity QTX servers. Each incremental 10 seats required $200 of additional manufacturing cost. Yearly sales were at the rate of 4,000 units across all sizes. In initial sales, approximately 30 percent of customers bought the 30-seat unit, 40 percent bought the 20-seat unit, and 30 percent bought the 10-seat unit. Customers who needed more than 30 seats typically went to competitors servicing the medium-to-large company market segment.

Clearwater set a per seat Manufacturer's Suggested Retail Price (MSRP) that decreased with higher quantity seat

Number of Seats	MSRP to End User	VAR Price	Unit Cost*	Unit Margin**
10	$8,000	$4,000	$500	87.5%
20	$14,000	$7,000	$700	90.0%
30	$17,250	$8,625	$900	89.6%

Table 1   *Unit cost reflects additional $200 for memory capability for each additional 10 seats.

**Margin = VAR Price—Unit Cost VAR Price

Number of Seats	Original Unit Cost	Original Unit Margin	Actual Unit Cost	Actual Unit Margin
10	$500	87.5%	$900	77.5%
20	$700	90.0%	$900	87.1%
30	$900	89.6%	$900	89.6%

Table 2

purchases, reflecting the customer perception of declining manufacturing cost per seat. Clearwater also saw this as advantageous because it encouraged customers to maximize their initial seat purchase.

Clearwater typically sold its products through Value Added Resellers (VARs). A VAR was typically a small local firm that provided sales and support to end users. The value added by these resellers was that they provided a complete solution to the end user/customer from a single point of purchase and had multiple information technology products available from various vendors. Using VARs reduced Clearwater's sales and service expense significantly and increased its market coverage.

These intermediaries operated in several steps. First, the VAR combined the QTX from Clearwater with database software from other suppliers to form a turnkey customer solution. Second, the VAR loaded the software with customer-specific information and linked it to the customer's existing sales history databases. Finally, the VAR installed the product at the customer's site and trained the customer on its use. Clearwater sold the QTX to resellers at a 50 percent discount from the MSRP, allowing the VARs to sell to the end user at or below the MSRP. The discount allowed the VARs room to negotiate with the customer and still achieve a profit (Table 1).

The Upgrade

Initially, the expectation had been that the 30-seat unit would be the largest volume seller. In order to gain economies of scale in manufacturing, reduce inventory configurations, and reduce engineering design and testing expense to a single assembly, Clearwater decided to manufacture only the 30-seat server with the appropriate number of seats 'enabled' for the buyer. Clearwater was effectively 'giving away' extra memory and absorbing the higher cost rather than manufacturing the various sizes. If a customer wanted a 10-seat server, the company shipped a 30-seat capable unit, with only the requested 10 seats enabled through software

configuration. The proposed upgrade was, in reality, allowing customers to access capability already built into the product (Table 2).

Clearwater knew that many original customers were ready to use the additional capacity in the QTX. Some customers had added seats by buying a second box, but because the original product contained the capability to expand by accessing the disabled seats, Clearwater saw an opportunity to expand the product line and increase sales to a captive customer base. Customers could double or triple their seat capacity by purchasing either a 10- or a 20-seat upgrade, and getting an access code to enable the additional number of seats. No other competitor offered the possibility of an upgrade. To gain additional seats from the competitor, the customer purchased and installed an additional box. Because customers performed a significant amount of acceptance testing, which they would have to repeat before switching brands, the likelihood of changing brands to add capacity was low.

The objective of this morning's meeting was to set the price for the two upgrades.

As QTX product manager Rob Erickson stopped to collect his most recent notes from his desk, he reflected:

What a way to start the week. Every time we have one of these meetings, senior management only looks at margins. I spent the whole weekend cranking numbers and I'm going in there using the highest margin we've got today. How can anybody say that's too low?

He grabbed his notes, calculator, and coffee and headed down the hall.

From the other wing of the building, financial analyst Hillary Hanson was crossing the lobby towards the conference room. She was thinking about the conversation she had late Friday afternoon with her boss, Alicia Fisher, Clearwater's CFO. They had been discussing this upcoming meeting and Alicia had given Hillary very clear instructions.

I want you to go in and argue for the highest price possible. We should absolutely maximize the profitability on the upgrade. The customers are already committed to us and they have no alternative for an upgrade but with us. The switching costs to change at this point are too high since they've already been trained in our system and software. Let's go for it. Besides, we really need to show some serious revenue generation for the year-end report to the stockholders.

Hillary had not actually finalized a number. She figured she could see what the others proposed and then argue for a significant premium over that. She had the CFO's backing so she could keep pushing for more.

From the parking lot, Brian James, the district sales manager, headed for the rear entrance. He, too, was thinking about the upcoming meeting and anticipating a long morning.

I wish marketing would realize that when they come up with some grandiose number for a new product, sales takes the hit in the field. It's a killer to have to explain to customers that they have to pay big bucks for something that's essentially built in. It's gonna be even tougher to justify on this upgrade. At least with the QTX, we have something the buyer can see. It's hardware. With the upgrade, there isn't even a physical product. We're just giving customers a code to access the capability that's already built into the machine. Telling customers that they have to pay several thousand dollars never makes you popular. If you think about it, that's a lot of money for an access code, but you won't hear me say that out loud. Maybe I can get them to agree to something reasonable this time. I spent the weekend working this one out, and I think my logic is pretty solid.

Price Proposals

Once everyone was settled in the conference room, Rob spoke first:

I know we have to come up with prices for both the 10-seat and 20-seat upgrades, but to keep things manageable, let's discuss the 20-seat price first. Once that number is set, the 10-seat price should be simple. Because the margin on the 30-seat unit is the highest in the line, I think we should use that as the basis to the price for the upgrade.

He went to a white board to show an example:

If a customer is upgrading from a 10-seat unit to a 30-seat unit, they are adding two steps of capacity

costing $200 each to us, or $400. $400/10.90 = $4,000 to the reseller, and $8,000 to the end user. We keep the margin structure in place at the highest point in the line. The customer gets additional capacity, and we keep our margins consistent.

He sat down feeling pleased. He had fired the first shot, had been consistent with the existing margin structure, and had rounded up the highest margin point in the line.

Brian looked at Rob's calculations and commented:

I think that's going to be hard for the customer to see without us giving away information about our margins, and we don't want to do that, since they are pretty aggressive to begin with. However, I think I have solved this one for us. I've finally come up with a simple, fair solution to pricing the upgrade that works for us and the customers.

He walked over to a white board and grabbed a marker:

If we assume an existing 10-seat customer has decided to upgrade to 30-seat capability, we should charge that customer the difference between what the buyer has already paid and the price of the new capacity. So . . ."

New 30-seat unit	$17,250
Original 10-seat unit	*$8,000*
Price for 20-seat upgrade	$9,250

It's consistent with our current pricing for the QTX. It's fair to the customer. It's easy for the customer to understand and it still makes wads of money for us. It also is easy for the customer to see that we're being good to them. If they bought a 20-seat box in addition to the 10-seat box they already have, it would be costing them more."

He wrote:

New 20-seat unit $14,000

A new unit provides customers with redundancy by having two boxes, which they might want in the event of product failure, but the cost is pretty stiff. Upgrading becomes the logical and affordable option.

Hillary looked at the numbers and knew just what she was going to do.

That all looks very logical, but I don't see that either of you has the company's best interests at heart.

Brian, you just want a simple sale that your sales people and the customers will buy into, and Rob, you are charging even less than Brian. We need to consider the revenue issue as well. These people have already bought from us; are trained on our hardware and software and don't want to have to repeat the process with someone else. It would take too long. They've got no desire to make a change and that means we've got them. The sky is really the limit on how much we can charge them because they have no real alternative. We should take this opportunity to really go for the gold, say $15,000 or even $20,000. We can and should be as aggressive as possible.

All three continued to argue the relative merits of their pricing positions, without notable success. Jefferies listened to each of them and after they finished, he turned to a clean white board and took the marker.

I've done some more thinking on this. In order to meet the needs of all three departments, there are three very important points that the price structure for these upgrades must accomplish:

1. The pricing for the upgrades shouldn't undercut the existing pricing for the 30-seat QTX.

2. We want to motivate our buyers to purchase the maximum number of seats at the initial purchase. A dollar now is better than a potential dollar later. We never know for sure that

they will make that second purchase. If we don't do this right, we're going to encourage customers to reduce their initial purchase. They'll figure they can add capacity whenever, so why buy it if they don't need it. That would kill upfront sales of the QTX.

3. We don't want to leave any revenue on the table when buyers decide to buy more capacity. They are already committed to us and our technology and we should capitalize on that, without totally ripping them off. Therefore, while Hillary says 'the sky's the limit,' I think there is a limit and we need to determine what it is and how close we can come to it.

If we assume that those are the objectives, none of the prices you've put together thus far answers all three of those criteria. Some come close, but each one fails. See if you can put your heads together and come to a consensus price that satisfies all three objectives. OK?

Heads nodded and with that, Jefferies left the conference room. The three remaining occupants looked at one another. Brian got up to wipe the previous numbers off the white boards and said:

OK, one more time. If our numbers don't work, why not and what is the right price for the 20-seat upgrade?

CASE 8

Buzz Marketing: Kayem Foods, Inc., Al Fresco Chicken Sausage

Robert F. Young, Northeastern University

Raymond Kinnunen, Northeastern University

In November 2004, Matt Monkiewicz, Director of Marketing for Kayem Foods, Inc., had to decide whether to implement another "buzz" marketing campaign in 2005 for a small but fast-growing product, Al Fresco chicken sausage. In a very short time, Al Fresco had become the number-one brand in its niche market. However, it was not clear whether this was due to the buzz campaign or to other marketing activities implemented by the firm. Although the sales increases had been impressive, it was not clear how much more growth Kayem could expect from this rather unusual marketing tactic.

Monkiewicz explained:

> We seem to have a real winner with this Al Fresco product, albeit in a very small product market segment with limited penetration. The challenge is how to sustain the growth and increase market share and to do so with a very limited marketing budget.

Monkiewicz had observed that the retail trade, whose support was so important for all of the company's brands, had been unimpressed with the buzz campaign. The sales force reported that supermarket executives and food distributors had been unwilling to increase buying and support for the brand based only on the campaign.

For 2005, the alternative was to use the limited marketing budget for more traditional marketing support activities, such as limited magazine advertising, consumer coupons, or more point-of-purchase material. In addition, Monkiewicz was considering an advertising campaign in supermarket trade magazines aimed at retail food buyers and merchandising executives. He thought that many of these decision makers were unaware of the sales and profit potential Al Fresco offered.

Monkiewicz commented:

> I have two weeks to make a decision on where to spend the marketing dollars. I realize that this is a small niche market and that others have differing opinions on the sales results. I really think, however, that buzz marketing could have a lasting effect on sales—especially if we do it again.

Kayem Foods

Kayem Foods, Inc., was a medium-sized, privately held, and family-controlled meat processing company located in Chelsea, Massachusetts. For almost 100 years, the firm had experienced success as a processor and distributor of fresh delicatessen meats, hot dogs, and sausage. Historically, the firm's trading area had been primarily New England and parts of the Mid-Atlantic area. In its fiscal year ending February 28, 2004, annual sales had been approximately $140 million. Of that amount, approximately 60 percent was from meat products sold under several brand names, and the remainder was from private label supermarket products made for other manufacturers and merchandise that Kayem sold acting as a distributor.

While Kayem's top-selling product was hot dogs, it also sold a variety of other meat products that included bologna, salami, sausage, kielbasa, and hams. Its products were sold under several different brand names, with Kayem being the most well-known. Table A shows the company's principal brands and their relative percentage of the firm's volume.

Some of the company's brands competed on price, such as MeisterChef. Other brands were holdovers from firms that Kayem had acquired and retained due to regional loyalty. For instance, McKenzie products had a strong following in Vermont and upstate New York.

Distribution

The company sold its products primarily through supermarkets and other retail food stores, mostly in the Northeast. In the last two years, it had made a concerted effort to obtain distribution in the Midwest and Southeast. It had also obtained some supermarket distribution in California and Florida.

Kayem sold most of its volume directly to the major food chains and food wholesalers. Its trucks made weekly and sometimes more frequent deliveries to its major New England customers. In addition to food retail outlets, Kayem sold approximately $15 million annually to the food service industry (e.g., universities, hospitals, corporate dining services, and restaurants).

Brand	Percent of Total Sales	Products
Kayem	15.7	Hot dogs, bologna, bratwurst, salami, ham, turkey, roast beef
Genoa	6.9	Fresh pork sausage, salami
McKenzie	2.9	Bacon, ham, roast beef
MeisterChef	6.8	Hot dogs
Schonland	2.2	Hot dogs, link sausage
Triple M	6.0	Whole hams, roast beef
Al Fresco	1.3	Gourmet chicken sausage
Copack	19.3	Products made for other branded processors
Private Label	26.6	Products made for supermarket private label
Resale	12.3	Products of other manufacturers, distributed by Kayem

Table A   Kayem Sales, by Brand, Fiscal Year Ending February 28, 2004

Source: Company Documents.

Since the company's founding, the marketing strategy had been to focus its product offerings on high-quality hot dogs and fresh delicatessen meats. Therefore, over 80 percent of the firm's volume through supermarkets was at the delicatessen counter.

In recent years, Kayem had achieved some success with hot dogs and sausage packaged and sold in supermarket refrigerator sections. For instance, although deli counters sold most of the volume in Kayem hot dogs (the company's highest volume product), in many supermarkets the customer could find an 8-pack or 24-pack of Kayem hot dogs in the refrigerator section along with other branded hot dog packages.

The firm's emphasis on the deli counter was consistent with its competitive positioning of freshness and high quality. Thus, many supermarkets had found its products, especially the Kayem brand, to be a staple of their delicatessens' offerings.

The Sausage Market

Consumers had used sausage as a staple at all three meals for many years, often serving it as the main entrée or as a complement to other centerplate dishes.

The sausage category had recently experienced only modest growth. In 2003, the sale of sausage served at breakfast had grown approximately 2 percent, and sausage for dinner grew approximately 4 percent. In 2003, retail sales of all sausage totaled $2.4 billion. Approximately 60 percent of this volume was dinner sausage, 33 percent was breakfast sausage, and the remainder was frozen sausage, for use with either meal.

The fastest growing product segment had been specialty sausage. This subcategory represented about 20 percent of the dollar volume. It included chicken sausage, turkey sausage, pork sausage with various flavorings such as jalapeño or apple, cheese sausage, and kielbasa. Consumers seemed to like these differentiated products because of their desire for variety in the menu, and in some cases to serve sausage products that were lower in fat content. These specialty products had experienced 10 percent growth in 2004. Another fast-growing product area was lowfat/lean sausage, which comprised approximately 19 percent (in dollars) of all sausage sold.

On a national level, three large brands dominated the sausage market: Hillshire Farms (dollar share of national market—18.3 percent), Johnsonville (13 percent), and Ball Park (13.2 percent). However, in New England, Hillshire (46 percent share of market), and Perri (20 percent share of market), were the dominant players. In this market, Kayem (with its several brands) was number three in share with 7 percent. Al Fresco alone had a 5.3 percent share in New England.

Families at all income levels consumed sausage. In 2004, 59 percent of all households bought sausage at least once. Of those who purchased sausage, the average expenditure was $16.95 annually per family. Per capita consumption was considerably lower among senior citizens. Residents in the South ate the most sausage, followed by those living in the Northeast. Sausage sales varied seasonally with approximately one third of all dinner sausage sold during the three summer months. Breakfast sausage sales peaked during the holiday season, November–January.

Traditional retail food outlets accounted for most sausage sales. The major firms had professional salespeople who called on supermarkets and food wholesalers in order to sell the sausage as well as their other meat products.

Consumer advertising for sausage was limited. Hillshire Farms spent approximately $29 million per year on advertising for all of its products, which included sausage, bacon and luncheon meats. Most of this spending was on television advertising. Johnsonville spent about $13 million on advertising for all of its broad product line. Of this, $8 million was for television and $3.5 million for radio. Emeril, a small producer of specialty sausages, including chicken sausage, spent about $1 million per year, mostly in magazines. In the previous year, Aidell, a West Coast producer of chicken sausage, had run a magazine campaign, spending approximately $200,000.

Kayem's primary sausage brand was Genoa. Limited sample taste tests indicated that consumers considered the product to be the equivalent in both taste and quality to the market leaders, although it did not have any distinguishing characteristic. It had become a commodity product. Retailers used it as a control brand, pricing it aggressively below their own brands. As a result, they often sold the brand at a substantial discount or with substantial promotional allowances. Genoa had low brand awareness and was operating at breakeven financially.

Because the chicken sausage category was small, it was difficult to obtain many specifics about competition. Aidell, made by a small West Coast meat processor, was one of the leading national brands, with about 30 percent share. It had particularly strong distribution in food specialty stores such as Whole Foods. Sara Lee sold its Emeril brand as part of its overall sausage marketing program. Gerhard was a small specialty company in California. Analysts estimated that about one half of the chicken sausage dollar volume was private label.

Profit Concerns

In recent years, Kayem's profit margins had been eroding. Gross margin for the company had been declining for several years due to supermarkets gaining "power" through consolidation and demands for greater discounts and promotional allowances from suppliers. Declining gross margin was particularly acute for small and medium-sized purveyors due to their relatively weak bargaining positions.

Manufacturers with particularly strong consumer brand franchises were in a position to resist the pressure for price concessions. However, while Kayem Foods had a local following for some of its brands, such as Kayem hot dogs, its mix of business between high-margin and low-margin brands was not strong enough to produce the profits that the firm wanted. Price competition from other manufacturers along with the pressure from supermarkets kept profits below expectations.

In addition, in recent years Kayem had developed a significant volume in both private label and copack business (see Table A). These activities were not producing the profits that the firm wanted. The private label activity had been at a financial breakeven for the last two years. Copack was below breakeven and only slightly above variable costs.

Al Fresco

One response to this profit dilemma was to develop distinctive branded products. If the firm could have a well-recognized "demand brand," it could potentially obtain higher prices and better margins and open doors in new markets. Therefore, the company had decided to develop a gourmet product line that, if successful, would be able to command higher margins.

To make a significant entry into the gourmet food category, Kayem introduced the Al Fresco brand in 1999. The product line consisted of fresh pizza (since discontinued) and gourmet chicken sausage. The strategy was to produce differentiated, high-quality goods for the refrigerator section of supermarkets. Kayem positioned the Al Fresco fully-cooked chicken sausage as a convenient, all-natural, low-carbohydrate, lowfat main meal entrée. Promotion emphasized product freshness and natural ingredients. A main selling point was that Al Fresco chicken sausage had 75 percent less fat than traditional pork sausage. The product was available in seven flavors: roasted garlic, teriyaki ginger, sun dried tomato and basil, spicy jalapeno, garden primavera, sweet apple, and sweet Italian.

With its high quality, healthy attributes, freshness, and distinctive flavors, Kayem management thought that the product could command a premium price. It priced the products at $3.58 per pound (at factory) with a $1.60 per pound contribution margin. The typical package size was 0.75 pounds, with four sausages. This resulted in a higher retail price than similar products. Table B shows typical prices at retail.

The chicken sausage segment was small by most measures. Total category sales were about $75 million per year; however, it was growing at about 12 percent a year. The target market for Al Fresco chicken sausage was the 25- to 54-year-old woman who was health conscious. This attitude translated into a preference for all natural foods and a concerted effort to reduce fat consumption. In addition, she liked gourmet foods and tended to be very interested in foods and food preparation.

For the past several years, the marketing campaign for Al Fresco had consisted of small ad placements in trade magazines and publicity efforts that included cable TV food shows. The marketing communications budget for 2004 was

	Cost	Package Size
Al Fresco, chicken sausage	$4.49	12 ounces
Johnsonville, pork sausage	3.89	one pound
Perri, hot Italian pork sausage	3.99	one pound
Shaw's, turkey sausage	4.49	one pound
Shaw's, pork sausage	2.49	one pound
Aidell, chicken and turkey sausage	5.99	12 ounces

Table B   Typical Retail Prices

Source: One-time survey in Boston area supermarket by case writer, February 2004.

$90,000. The sales force had enthusiastically presented Al Fresco to supermarket buyers and wholesalers by offering a onetime, buy-in allowance of 10 percent off the regular price for the period November 1, 2003, to January 31, 2004. These efforts had met with only limited success. A similar promotion was offered from June 1, 2004, to August 31, 2004, to offer Al Fresco at 10 percent off to the supermarket if the managers agreed to carry at least three of the flavors. This latter period coincided with the buzz campaign discussed below.

Buzz Marketing

Soon after the company launched Al Fresco, it became apparent to Monkiewicz that the marketing budget was inadequate to make a substantial impact using traditional media. Accordingly, he sought a means to promote the brand on a small budget but still have an impact on his target market. As he explored various alternatives, he learned about a relatively new marketing firm called BzzAgent. This firm had developed a technique to create word-of-mouth advertising ("buzz") for unique products or brands.

BzzAgent had 60,000 BzzAgents. These agents volunteered to try a new product and then talk with friends and acquaintances about the product and their experience with it. The conversations relied on the agent's own creativity and his/her enthusiasm for the product. They were not paid, but rather earned points towards a variety of premiums, although only a small fraction (fewer than 10 percent of agents ever claimed their premiums). The motivation for the BzzAgents' activities seemed to be that these people enjoyed being innovators and liked to talk about new and interesting products. BzzAgent found that many of its agents made their "buzzing" part of their social networking.

BzzAgent would only work with companies or products that were compelling, interesting or different. The company had learned that its system worked only when its BzzAgents had strong beliefs about the product or brand. The firm turned down 80 percent of the requests from companies to have their products or brands "buzzed." BzzAgent had implemented successful campaigns for many firms including Anheuser-Busch, Lee Jeans, Penguin Publishing, and Ralph Lauren.

There were two underlying premises to buzz marketing. Marketing managers generally agreed that promotional messages or product endorsements were much more credible when delivered in person by a friend or acquaintance with no business interest in the product. This was consistent with the reported decline in the credibility of mass media advertising.

Second, people liked to talk about new products or services they had "discovered." Marketing studies showed that if people were pleased with a product, they enjoyed relaying that information to friends and relatives and would often do so with enthusiasm.

Monkiewicz decided to use a buzz campaign as part of Al Fresco's 2004 marketing efforts. The campaign cost $47,000 in addition to the cost of the coupons. The entire marketing communications budget for Al Fresco was $90,000. He worked with BzzAgent to create a 12-week campaign the company would implement from June 23 to September 15, 2004. The firm would employ 2,000 of its agents in New England, New York, New Jersey, and selected cities in Ohio, Pennsylvania, and North Carolina. Each agent would have three coupons for a free package of Al Fresco Chicken Sausage for themselves, as well as ten coupons worth $1 off on the purchase of two packages that they would give to buzz targets. In addition, BzzAgents had a brochure with a list of suggested activities, including serving Al Fresco to guests, taking it to a party/cookout, using it as an added ingredient in their favorite entrée recipe, and taking it to work.

The BzzAgents were to try the product themselves and then relate their experience to friends and acquaintances. The goal was to have every agent talk with 10 people. After the campaign was over, BzzAgent provided Monkiewicz with a detailed summary of activities and results. Although he was quite pleased with the overall outcome, he was unsure how to evaluate the results.

Summary of Results of the Buzz Campaign

BzzAgent recruited 2,000 agents in the selected areas. Of these, 77 percent were female, and the average age was 35. While 32 percent of the agents ate sausage at least once a week, 57 percent had never eaten chicken sausage prior to the campaign, and 91 percent had never heard of Al Fresco chicken sausage. However, 43 percent had heard of Emeril's chicken sausage

Of the agents recruited, 758 sent reports regarding their activities. There were 1,647 BzzReports completed and there was a total of 8,470 buzz hits. In other words, each report averaged 5.1 reported hits. A buzz hit was a conversation or activity about Al Fresco sausage. A follow-up survey revealed that reporting BzzAgents had an additional 3.5 buzz hits that they did not record. The fact that BzzAgents were not compensated on a per-hit basis may explain the lack of reporting. Most of the conversations took place in the home (Table C).

Agents held conversations with a wide variety of people. Forty-nine percent of people buzzed were friends or social acquaintances (Table D).

Of all the buzz activities reported, 16 percent were reported at a party or other social occasion. However, such occasions accounted for 32 percent of all buzz hits. Eighty seven percent of agents reported giving away at least one coupon. Of those reporting, the agents gave away an average of 6.8 coupons.

Place	Percent
Home	41
Social Location	16
Work	15
Grocery Store	10
Other	18

Table C Conversation Locations

Source: Company Documents.

Who	Percent
Friend	40
Relative	24
Stranger	11
Acquaintance	9
Other	16

Table D Subjects Reached

Source: Company Documents.

	Percent of Shares	
	4/27/04	9/1/04
Al Fresco	41	42
Aidell	42	31
Emeril	10	19
Gerhard	7	8

Table E Market Shares for Branded Chicken Sausage

Source: Company Documents.

Note: that these measures are only four months apart.

Seventy-two percent of the BzzAgents reported that they had had difficulty finding the product in the supermarket. This meant that they had to either ask the store manager for the product or go to a different store. Twenty-three percent were never able to find the product.

BzzAgents filed reports of their conversations. These seemed to be very enthusiastic in most cases, although there were complaints of difficulty finding the product in their favorite supermarket. Appendix A shows a sampling of the reports.

In summary, the BzzAgents reported that they personally liked the product. They enjoyed the variety of flavors as well as the ease of preparation. They also reported that they viewed Al Fresco as part of a healthy lifestyle. Of those reporting, 65 percent said they were likely to purchase Al Fresco again.

Sales Results

During the buzz campaign, Kayem sales people were engaged in efforts to obtain new distribution for the product. They were able to offer trade discounts to supermarkets taking on the product for the first time. In addition, Kayem ran a few advertisements for Al Fresco in trade publications. These emphasized Al Fresco's leadership position and pointed out the profit potential.

Nationally, for the period November 1, 2002, to October 30, 2003, sales for Al Fresco were 0.80 million pounds. From November 1, 2003, to October 30, 2004, sales were 1.26 million pounds. It was not possible to isolate sales by the particular markets where BzzAgent had implemented its program. According to ACNielsen, Al Fresco had become the number one selling branded chicken sausage in the United States by late July 2004. Estimates of shares derived from store audits are shown in Table E.

Dollar sales for Al Fresco are shown in Table F.

Date	Sales in $ (000)
September, 2003	$197
October, 2003	205
November, 2003	196
December, 2003	187
January, 2004	297
February, 2004	257
March, 2004	262
April, 2004	366
May, 2004	323
June, 2004	368
July, 2004	500
August, 2004	399
September, 2004	453
October, 2004	575

Table F Sales by Month of Al Fresco Chicken Sausage (factory shipments)

Source: Company Documents.

Note: that Kayem's fiscal year ends February 28.

Additional Issues

Monkiewicz was quite pleased with the overall results of the buzz campaign. However, he was not certain how much of the sales increase in the brand had been due to this effort. Prior to the campaign, the brand had developed substantial momentum with a minimum of advertising support. In addition, the sales force had been making a special effort during the campaign period. They had offered special discounts and allowances to obtain new distribution. Thus, it was not possible to isolate the specific effect of the buzz campaign.

Decision

Because sales of Al Fresco had been increasing significantly, Monkiewicz had convinced Kayem's president that a substantial increase in the advertising budget was justified. Thus, the FY 2006 (March 1, 2005—February 28, 2006) budget would be $185,000. Monkiewicz was considering running another buzz campaign in geographic areas not covered in the recent campaign. This would entail a fee of approximately $60,000, plus another $12,000 to $15,000 to reimburse retailers for coupons that consumers redeemed.

Alternatively, he thought that a series of trade advertisements might be productive. These would target supermarket executives and buyers. Monkiewicz thought that there was now an Al Fresco story to tell. He thought he could make an impact on food retailing decision makers by telling them about the brand's sales and profit potential. It was now the number one chicken sausage brand, and he needed to tell that story. He believed it would cost approximately $80,000 for this effort to have any impact.

As Al Fresco's sales had grown, the sales force began asking for more price-oriented promotions. Accordingly, Monkiewicz was thinking about distributing consumer price-off coupons. Kayem would probably have to spend about $90,000 for this effort to be effective.

Several supermarket executives had said that advertising in specialty food magazines might help generate sustained demand for the brand and it was customary in the food business to advertise new products in such media. These ads announced the product to the consumer and built specific demand for the brand, often persuading supermarket executives that consumers would be looking for and expecting the brand to be on the shelf.

A full-page color advertisement in high-circulation food magazines such as *Better Homes and Gardens* (circulation approximately seven million) would cost about $359,000 and was thus out of the question. A quarter-page ad in the same magazine would be approximately 30 percent of that figure. Although such advertising would achieve wide exposure for

Exhibit 1   Media Cost and Circulation for Magazines

	Circulation	Cost of a Single Insertion Full Page, Four-Color Ad
Better Homes and Gardens	7.6 million	$359,000*
Food and Wine	0.9 million	$66,275*
Cooking Light	1.7 million	$96,400*

Source: Publishers' Web sites.

*The cost of a four-color, one-half page advertisement was approximately 60 percent of the full page and the cost of a four-color, one-quarter page advertisement was approximately 30 percent of the full page.

Al Fresco, the cost still seemed to be beyond what the brand could support. In order for the ads to be effective, Monkiewicz thought that the potential customer would have to be exposed to the Al Fresco message at least two or three times.

For a more focused campaign, Monkiewicz thought that perhaps food specialty magazines might be effective in reaching Al Fresco's potential customer. The readers of these magazines had the approximate demographic profile of the Al Fresco customer. The costs for two such magazines representative of that category are shown in Exhibit 1. In addition to creating multiple exposures, Monkiewicz thought that Al Fresco would have to be in two or three of these smaller circulation magazines in order to achieve effective reach.

In considering a follow-on buzz campaign, Kayem's sales executives raised some concerns about the reaction of supermarket buyers. The sales force reported that retail executives were unimpressed with the buzz campaign. They were skeptical about its ability to build sustainable brand demand. The Kayem sales executives said that they had not been able to use the buzz campaign alone to get additional placements or to expand shelf space with established customers. Supermarket merchandising managers believed that either national advertising or price-oriented consumer coupons would be more effective. They thought that Al Fresco needed more of the traditional mass media and sales promotion activities to create more demand at the consumer level. They cited the success that Johnsonville and Hillshire Farms had experienced with their several offerings in the pork sausage category. These supermarket executives commented that those brands' sales success was tied closely to their big customer advertising budgets, along with extensive coupon and other price promotion programs.

In the sausage category, it was common practice to advertise branded products in various women's service and food-oriented magazines. In addition, during peak holiday selling seasons, most of the leading sausage brands would offer a variety of sales promotions, such as coupons, free offers, and bonus packs. The attractiveness of such programs was often influential in the supermarket buyers' decisions regarding shelf space and retail advertising locations.

Monkiewicz was very familiar with "traditional" marketing methods for food products and how much such activities cost. He thought that Al Fresco was approaching the point where it could utilize such programs; however, at this time, he was concerned that the budget was not going to be large enough to create sufficient impact. It seemed that buzz marketing had helped stimulate the dramatic growth in the brand but his own sales force, several of his major customers, and a few friends around the office continued to be skeptical.

Monkiewicz was also aware of some recent criticism in the public press about the ethics of BzzAgent-type marketing. In essence, companies employing buzz marketing were using peoples' friendship and acquaintance networks to promote their own interests. In most instances people being approached about Al Fresco were not aware that they were about to be "buzzed," and some people wondered if this activity was taking unfair advantage of personal relationships.

Monkiewicz concluded:

It is very clear to me that I have to make a difficult tradeoff. If I use the BzzAgents again, I will have to forgo some other seemingly useful marketing activity. If there had not been so much skepticism I would go with the buzz campaign again. However, there are good reasons to consider the other alternatives.

Appendix A: Excerpts From Verbatim Reports of BzzAgents

Flavor Comments

"Had some friends over for dinner this evening and the whole evening was a hit thanks to the Al Fresco jalapeño pizzas I served. I used my basic pizza recipe and replaced the veggie toppings with Al Fresco jalapeño sausage. I got many comments about this is the best pizza I ever had."

"Dinner last night was fabulous mostly because of the wonderful Al Fresco chicken sausage."

"I saw my friend Lena and her cousin yesterday. I had recently had apple flavored sausages that Al Fresco makes and I was raving to her about them. Lena is on a diet, so she said she could not eat it. I explained that it was low fat. I think that Lena will try some."

"I had my boyfriend over for a romantic dinner. I decided to cook up the rest of the sausage. My boyfriend was so excited about the sausage that he thought it was gourmet or homemade. I told him it was Al Fresco. I told him it was made out of chicken. He didn't believe me. I had to pull out the package and show him."

"I made dinner for my mom, aunt, and her family and they thought it was WOW. The children, ages four and seven, wanted more and more."

"Last night I tried the sausages for the first time. I bought the teriyaki/ginger ones. The sausages were a little bit spicier than I had expected but I enjoyed them quite a bit. They were not greasy at all. I made this dinner for myself and my husband. He also enjoyed it."

"I made a dish that consisted of the Al Fresco chicken sausage. I cooked the sausage and then added fried onions, mushrooms, and broccoli and served it over some rice. It made a great dinner for me and my family."

Ask the Manager

"I guess by now people know I really like Al Fresco Chicken Sausages. I talk about them a lot. I stopped by Sam's Club after work yesterday. Our Sam's Club always has free food samples all over the store. I went to customer service and asked for the manager. When the manager came to the service desk and I asked the manager why I never ever find Al Fresco Chicken Sausages being cooked and served at the demonstration tables. He had never heard of Al Fresco so I told him all about how excited I was about the product and about all of the flavors. The manager promised that he would look into Sam's Club bringing in Al Fresco."

"I saw on the BzzAgent Web site that Al Fresco was available at ACME markets. I was disappointed to learn that my local ACME did not carry the products. I approached the night manager (an older woman) and showed her the coupon with the recipe attached. I told her that I was looking for a new sausage that a friend had recommended. In typical night shift fashion she asked if I had looked back in the meats section—yes, I had. Well, if it is not back there, we probably don't carry it. I asked her to please go back with me to make sure I wasn't missing it. She walked back with me and I explained that I had seen a few types of sausage but that none were like Al fresco. She did pull out the Emeril sausage, but I told her I wanted Al Fresco. She expressed her apologies. I told her that I would most likely try the neighboring ShopRite. I had just wanted to try my hometown store first. She asked if she could take the part of the coupon with the picture. I thanked her and she said she would consider stocking it."

"I frequent Pathmark Supermarket about twice a month. During the whole campaign I constantly checked their meats to see if they would start carrying this product. I never thought to ask until you e-mailed me with the form. That was a light bulb for me. I did make use of it. The manager said he'd never heard of it before and was definitely going to look into it. I should see the product available within a few weeks."

"I had previously spoken to the manager of the local ShopRite market about this product. I complained that it wasn't always available."

"This morning on the way to work I stopped at Lowes Foods. I noticed the manager checking over his sausage inventory. I went up to him and told him about Al Fresco. I told him about all the flavors and that I was having to shop over at Harris Teeter to purchase them. He told me that he could say some thing but that the big purchasing decisions really came from higher ups at the corporate level."

"I went to Shaw's in Revere for my first grocery shopping in two weeks. I went to the meat case where the sausages were and looked for Al Fresco. Despite the site stating that Shaw's was one of the stores carrying it they didn't have it. The meat department assistant happened to be there so I struck up a conversation. First I let her know that I had initially found them at Stop & Shop but that Shaw's was my usual store so I hated going so far to get them if I didn't have to. She said she hadn't heard about them. I let her know that they were terrific and they are a Massachusetts company. I happened to see some other Kayem products right there and pointed them out to her saying they must be able to get these Al Frescos then. I added that I really hated having to trek al the way out to Stop & Shop."

Bring It to a Party

"Arrived at Pam's party and brought along my dish, sausage and broccoli rabe, with lots of garlic. It smelled amazing! When I arrived two of the girls hosting commented on what a beautiful looking dish it was and they proceeded to take it into the kitchen. At dinner I noticed that my dish was going FAST. Meantime I took the opportunity to tell everyone about this great and healthy food and even promised to give some of the coupons that you guys so kindly provided. This stuff is awesome. I shared the recipe for my dish with some of the ladies."

"Used the product in a recipe of mine and took it to a potluck at my church. I made a teriyaki and ginger sausage with rice dish that was a huge success. I can't even count how many people stopped to ask me what was in it. When I told them, of course, the 'money off' coupons went immediately and I wound up writing down the name of the product for quite a few people."

"We had a company picnic today, so I took in a square pizza topped with the sausage and everyone raved about it and wanted to know how to make it and where to buy the sausage. I ran out of coupons but I did have copies of the recipe cards (I hope you don't mind that I made copies of your recipes)."

"There was a line at the butcher counter at Whole Foods. They had chicken sausage on sale today (they make it fresh in the store). Another woman who was waiting to be served asked me if I had tried the chicken sausage and I told her (in almost a whisper) that, yes, I had tried it and it was dry. If you want some really good juicy chicken sausage you should try Al Fresco. She asked, 'Do they sell it here?' And, I said, 'No, you have to go to Gristedes to get it.'"

"I buzzed about the sausages at a BBQ I had at my house. I cooked the sausages with the rest of my meat and served them along with the other meat. I did not tell anyone about them. After everyone was done, I asked about the food. My cousin and his wife raved about the Al Fresco sausages. They said that they were so unique in taste. They had never eaten anything like them before. I told them all about the product and how it is a healthy sausage. My cousin could not believe it and asked to see the packaging. After reading the package she swore she would pick them up the next time she went to the supermarket."

Take It to Work

"A few weeks ago I brought leftovers to work of a meal that I served at a large family party using Al Fresco sausage. Everyone raved not only because the food was great but that I actually cooked it. Anyway, today a group of us was standing around, and the subject of food came up. A coworker, who had been on vacation the time that I brought the food in, actually heard from another worker that he had missed my leftovers. Too much! A couple of other friends said that they wished they had a sausage sandwich right then and there."

"I started work a few months ago at a local attorney's office. I'm a part time legal secretary. The office staff is big on "carry-ins" for sharing at lunch. I decided to share my Chicken Sausage Caesar Salad using Al Fresco Chicken Sausage of course. All of my coworkers couldn't compliment me enough. They really enjoyed the salad. A few of them asked me for the recipe and I came prepared. I had the coupon/recipe cards in my purse and handed them out. This morning two of my coworkers thanked me again for the excellent dish and told me they were planning on making the Chicken Sausage Caesar Salad for their own families."

Talk About Dinner

"My friends and I always talk about what we had for dinner and we're all trying to eat low fat options. I thought this was the perfect opportunity to bring up the chicken sausages. I told them I had found these great new chicken sausages that were lower in fat and really high in flavor and they should try. They were actually really interested in them and asked lots of questions. By the end of the conversation I think I convinced them to try it."

"I have this customer, Dave, who is a bachelor. He eats pretty good food but he loves meat. He is always eating and he is a great cook. We always talk about what's for dinner. Today, he came and I had just picked up some Al Fresco. He asked what I was having for dinner and I told him spaghetti with sausage and I showed him the sausage. The best part is I don't have to cook them. He looked at them and asked if I picked them up from here. I told him I did and led him to the case. I also gave him some coupons. He picked up two packs and said that he'd let me know."

Notes

Chapter 1

1. Drew Griffin and Scott Bronstein, "Records: Southwest Airlines Flew Unsafe Planes," (www.cnn.com/2008/US/03/06/southwest.planes/index.html, accessed June 21, 2009).

2. Jena McGregor, "Customer Service Champs," *BusinessWeek* (March 5, 2007), pp. 52–64; "Survey: Airline Customer Service Lacking," CNN (www.businessweek.com/magazine/content/07_10/b4024001.htm, accessed June 21, 2009).

3. Kenneth E. Clow and Donald Baack, *Integrated Advertising, Promotion, and Marketing Communications* (Upper Saddle River, NJ: Prentice Hall, 2007).

4. Robert Trewatha, Gene Newport, L. Johnson, and Donald Baack (contributing editor), *Management: Embracing Change in the 21st Century* (Houston, TX: Dame, 1997).

5. Donald Baack, *Organizational Behavior* (Houston, TX: Dame, 1995).

6. Personal interview with Jessica Moreland, June 20, 2007.

7. Jena McGregor, "Customer Service Champs," *BusinessWeek* (March 5, 2007), pp. 52–64.

8. Ibid.

9. For more information visit www.advancemtg.com.

10. Arik Hesseldahl, "Not Everyone Wants an iPhone," *BusinessWeek Online* (www.msnbc.msn.com/id/19508183, accessed June 30, 2007); Peter Burrows, "How Big Will the iPhone Be?" *BusinessWeek Online* (www.msnbc.msn.com/id/19095852, accessed July 3, 2007).

Chapter 2

1. "Importance of Marketing Research," *Council of American Survey Research Organizations* (www.casro.org, accessed August 28, 2007).

2. Industry analysis based on Judie Bizzozero, "The Bottom Line: The State of the Industry Report '04," *Looking Fit* (September 2004) (www.lookingfit.com/articles/491cover1.html, accessed on June 21, 2009).

3. Michelle Nichols, "Four Reasons to Thank the Competition," *BusinessWeek Online* (February 2, 2007), p. 23.

4. Monique Reece Myron and Pamela Larson Truax, "Product's Positioning Vital to Getting Notice," *Denver Business Journal* (November 8, 1996) (http://denver.bizjournals.com/denver/stories/1996/11/11/smallb6.html, accessed August 25, 2007).

5. Kenneth E. Clow and Donald Baack, *Integrated Advertising, Promotion, and Marketing Communications* (Upper Saddle River, NJ: Prentice Hall, 2007, p. 51).

6. Ibid.

7. Matthew Lerner, "Running with Red Bull and an Arena of Specialty Drinks," *American Metal Market* (August 2007), pp. 20–22.

8. Mark Rechtin, "Mazda Seeks Improved Share of Mind from Dealers," *Automotive News,* Vol. 75 (April 16, 2007), p. 26.

9. William L. Wilkie and Edgar a Pessemier, "Issues in Marketing's Use of Multiattribute Models," *Journal of Marketing,* Vol. 10 (November 1983), pp. 428–441.

10. Aimee Rawlins, "Keepers of the Flame," *Fast Company* (September 2007), p. 53.

Chapter 3

1. *Nightline,* ABC News (April 25, 2008); Steven Greenhouse, "How Costco Became the Anti-Wal-Mart," *New York Times Online* (July 17, 2005).

2. Richard Goeke and Robert H. Faley, "Leveraging the Flexibility of Your Data Warehouse," *Communications of the ACM,* Vol. 50, No. 10 (October 2007), pp. 107–111.

3. Jennifer Marks, "Williams-Sonoma Sharpens Consumer-Direct Marketing," *Home Textiles Today,* Vol. 28, No. 12 (May 7, 2007), p. 6.

4. Arthur M. Hughes, *Strategic Database Marketing* (New York: McGraw-Hill, 2006).

5. David Raab, "Using Lifetime Value," *DM Review,* Vol. 16, No. 8 (August 2006), p. 10.

6. Steve Finlay, "Who's Ready, Willing to Buy?" *Ward's Dealer Business,* Vol. 41, No. 10 (October 2007), pp. 14–16.

7. Jordan K. Speer, "Digging Deep: Extreme Data Mining," *Apparel Magazine,* Vol. 45, No. 12 (August 2004), p. 1; Eric Cohen, "Database Marketing," *Target Marketing,* Vol. 22, No. 4 (April 1999), p. 50.

8. Michael Bartlett, "Improving Penetration, Enhance Relationships, Grow Loans," *Credit Union Journal,* Vol. 10, No. 43 (October 30, 2006), p. 28.

9. Sean Callahan, "Granular Data Lead to Precision Marketing," *B to B,* Vol. 91, No. 15 (November 13, 2006), pp. 1, 36.

Chapter 4

1. ABC News Exclusive: AFLAC CEO Dan Amos (http://abcnews.go.com/Business/story?id=2899076&page=1, accessed June 21, 2009).

2. Donald Baack and J. B. Cullen, "Decentralization in Growth and Decline: A Catastrophe Theory Approach," *Behavioral Science,* Vol. 39, No. 3 (July 1995), pp. 213–228.

3. R. White and R. Lippit, *Autocracy and Democracy: An Experimental Inquiry* (New York: Harper, 1960).

4. Peter G. Northouse, *Leadership: Theory and Practice* (Thousand Oaks, CA: Sage, 1997).

5. Donald Baack, *Organizational Behavior* (Houston, TX: Dame, 1998).

6. Steven Kerr and John M. Jermier, "Substitutes for Leadership: Their Meaning and Measurement," *Organizational Behavior and Human Performance* (December 1978), pp. 375–403.

7. Robert J. House, "A Path Goal Theory of Leader Effectiveness," *Administrative Science Quarterly,* Vol. 16 (1971), pp. 321–338; L. R. Gomez-Mejia, D. B. Balkin, and R. L. Cardy, *Management: People, Performance, Change* (New York: McGraw-Hill, 2005).

8. Donald Baack, *Organizational Behavior* (Houston, TX: Dame, 1997); R. L. Trewatha, G. Newport, J. L. Johnson, and Donald Baack, *Management* (Houston, TX: Dame, 1993, revised edition).

9. Wayne Mondy, *Human Resource Management* (Upper Saddle River, NJ: Prentice Hall, 2008, 10th edition).

10. Edwin A. Locke, "Toward a Theory of Task Motivation and Incentives," *Organizational Behavior and Human Performance* (May 1968), pp. 157–189.

11. Fred Luthans, *Organizational Behavior* (New York: McGraw-Hill, 2003, 9th edition).

12. Abraham H. Maslow, *Motivation and Personality* (New York: Harper & Row, 1954).

13. David C. McClelland, *The Achieving Society* (Princeton, NJ: Van Nostrand Reinhold, 1961).

14. B. F. Skinner, *About Behaviorism* (New York: Knopf, 1974).

15. J. Stacey Adams, "Toward an Understanding of Inequity," *Journal of Abnormal and Social Psychology* (November 1963), pp. 422–436.

16. Victor H. Vroom, *Work and Motivation* (New York: Wiley, 1964); Lyman Porter and Edward E. Lawler, *Managerial Attitudes and Performance* (Homewood, IL: Irwin, 1968).

17. Peter F. Drucker, *The Practice of Management* (New York: Harper & Row, 1954); S. J. Caroll and Henry L. Tosi, *Management by Objectives: Applications and Research* (New York: Macmillan, 1973).

18. Max H. Bazerman, *Managerial Decision-Making* (New York: Wiley, 1990); Alex F. Osborne, *Applied Imagination: Principles and Procedures of Creative Thinking* (New York: Scribner, 1941).

19. A. A. McClean, *Work Stress* (Reading, MA: AddisonWesley, 1980); J. Clifton Williams, *Human Behavior in Organizations* (Cincinnati, OH: South-Western, 1982); A. Seers, G. W. Serey, T. Timothy, G. and B. Graen, "The Interaction of Job Stress and Social Support: A Strong Inference Investigation," *Academy of Management Journal,* Vol. 26, No. 2 (1973), pp. 273–284.

20. Edward A. Charlesworth and Ronald G. Nathan, *Stress Management: A Comprehensive Guide to Wellness* (New York: Random House, 2004, 3rd edition); Julie Morgenstern, *Time Management From the Inside Out* (New York: Henry Holt, 2004).

Chapter 5

1. www.sony.com.
2. *Nightline,* ABC News, May 29, 2008.
3. Edward C. Baig, "Reading E-Books Is Fundamental," *USA Today* (November 2007), p. 5B.
4. Jean Halliday, "More Jeep Models May Mean Less Brand Equity," *Advertising Age,* Vol. 78, No. 40 (October 8, 2007), p. 6.
5. James Covert, "J.C. Penney is Stocking Up on More Private Label Styles," *Wall Street Journal* (http://online.wsj.com/ad/article/rbs_related3_1.html, accessed February 27, 2007).
6. Jeff Swystun, "Seven Habits of Highly Effective Brands," *Marketing Magazine,* Vol. 111, No. 33 (October 9, 2006), p. 37.
7. Based on Margaret C. Campbell, "Building Brand Equity," *International Journal of Medical Marketing,* Vol. 2, No. 3 (May 2002), pp. 208–218.
8. Mark Ritson, "Brand Equity Can Taint Perceptions," *Marketing* (June 21, 2006), p. 21.
9. Ibid.
10. Rajesh Iyer and James A. Muncy, "The Role of Brand Parity in Developing Loyal Customers," *Journal of Advertising Research,* Vol. 45, No. 2 (June 2005), pp. 222–228.
11. Ibid.
12. www.insurancejournal.com/news/southeast/2006/11/27/74572.htm, accessed December 7, 2007; www.chicagotribune.com/business/chi-ap-katrina-statefarm,0,5681256.story, accessed December 7, 2007.
13. Katherine Khalife, "10 Reasons Why You Should be Marketing to Grandparents" (www .museummarketingtips.com/articles/grandparents.html, accessed August 25, 2007).
14. Aaron Baar, "LensCrafters Focuses on Fashion" (www.adweek.com, accessed September 24, 2007).

Chapter 6

1. Michael V. Mann, Eric V. Roegner, and Craig C. Zawada, "Pricing New Products," *McKinsey Quarterly,* No. 3 (2003), pp. 40–49.
2. Ibid.
3. Timothy Sexton, "Weber's Law and Why Big Business Believes You Won't Notice a Price Increase Under 10%," *Associated Content* (www.associatedcontent.com/pop_print.shtml, accessed April 10, 2009).

Chapter 7

1. www.smuckers.com, accessed June 8, 2008.
2. Bozell Agency (www.bozell.com, accessed November 18, 2007).
3. Jack Myers, "Nontraditional, Internet to Lead 7% Jump in Advertising," *Jack Myers Media Business Report* (www.marketingvox.com, accessed November 16, 2007).
4. Steve White, "Guerilla Marketing: The Humorous Side," *Air Conditioning Heating & Refrigeration News,* Vol. 232, No. 15 (December 10, 2007), p. 33.
5. Beth H. Hallisy, "Taking It to the Streets: Steps to an Effective—and Ethical—Guerilla Marketing Campaign," *Public Relations Tactics,* Vol. 13, No. 3 (March 2006), p. 13.
6. Angelo Fernando, "Transparency Under Attack," *Communication World,* Vol. 24, No. 2 (March/April 2007), pp. 9–11.
7. Richard H. Levey, "Prospects Look Good," *Direct,* Vol. 16, No. 6 (December 1, 2004), pp. 1–5.
8. "Direct Results," *PROMO,* Vol. 19, No. 9 (October 2007), pp. 54–55.
9. Jim Turner, "Is Your Direct Mail Inviting 'No Reply'?" *Bank Marketing,* Vol. 39, No. 9 (November 2007), p. 38.
10. Cara Beardi, "E-Commerce Still Favors Traditional Techniques," *Advertising Age,* Vol. 71, No. 43 (October 16, 2000), pp. 2–3.
11. Carol Krol, "USPS Magazine Touts Direct Mail," *B to B,* Vol. 90, No. 3 (March 14, 2005), p. 20.
12. Megan Ouellet and Ross Kramer, "Measure Your Message," *Marketing News,* Vol. 41, No. 18 (November 1, 2007), p. 26.
13. Grant A. Johnson, "Why a Microsite?" *Direct,* Vol. 19, No. 7 (July 2007), p. 12.

14. Clare Goff, "Fruitful Alliance," *New Media Age* (May 12, 2005), pp. 21–22.

15. Based on Jay Kiltsch, "Making Your Message Hit Home: Some Basics to Consider When . . . ," *Direct Marketing,* Vol. 61, No. 2 (June 1998), pp. 32–34.

Chapter 8

1. See www.kraftfoodscompany.com

2. "Clippings Slow," *Promo* (www.promomagazine.com/mag/marketing_clipping_slows/index.html, accessed January 2, 2008).

3. Noreen O'Leary, "Dealing With Coupons," *Adweek,* Vol. 46, No. 8 (February 21, 2005), p. 29.

4. "Upward Bound," *PROMO,* Vol. 17, No. 5 (April 2004), pp. AR3–5.

5. "Industry Trends Report 2007," *Promo* (www.promomagazine.com, accessed September 2007), pp. AR1–AR27.

6. "Eight Ways to Win," *Promo Sourcebook,* Vol. 20, No. 11 (November 2007), pp. 44–52.

7. Kathleen Joyce, "Not Just a Novelty," *PROMO,* Vol. 17, No. 12 (November 2004), pp. 52–56.

8. Sandra Block, "Rattled About Rebate Hassles? Regulators Starting to Step In," *USA Today* (March 22, 2005), p. 3b.

9. Jennifer Hiscock, "The Two Faces of Sampling," *Event* (April 2004), pp. 25–26.

10. David R. Bell, Ganesh Iyer, and V. Padmanabhan, "Price Competition Under Stockpiling and Flexible Consumption," *Journal of Marketing Research,* Vol. 39, No. 3 (August 2002), pp. 292–304.

11. Miguel Gomez, Vithala Rao and Edward McLaughlin, "Empirical Analysis of Budget and Allocation of Trade Promotions in the U.S. Supermarket Industry," *Journal of Marketing Research,* Vol. 44, No. 3 (August 2007), pp. 410–424.

12. Ibid.

13. K. Sudhir and Vithala Rao, "Do Slotting Allowances Enhance Efficiency or Hinder Competition?" *Journal of Marketing Research,* Vol. 43, No. 2 (May 2006), pp. 137–155.

14. Paula Bone, Karen France, and Richard Riley, "A Multifirm Analysis of Slotting Fees," *Journal of Public Policy & Marketing,* Vol. 25, No. 2 (Fall 2006), pp. 224–237.

15. "Study: Trade Dollars Up," *Frozen Food Age,* Vol. 50, No. 2 (September 2001), p. 14.

16. Walter Heller, "Promotion Pullback," *Progressive Grocer,* Vol. 81, No. 4 (March 1, 2002), p. 19.

Chapter 9

1. John A. Fugel, "Trade Show Know-How: Turning Prospects Into Sales," *Rural Telecommunications,* Vol. 22, No. 3 (May/June 2003), pp. 48–49.

2. Roger P. Levin, "Strategic Selling," *Proofs,* Vol. 87, No. 5 (November 2004), p. 54.

3. Ken Le Meunier-FitsHugh and Nigel F. Piercy, "Does Collaboration Between Sales and Marketing Affect Business Performance," *Journal of Personal Selling & Sales Management,* Vol. 27, No. 3 (Summer 2007), pp. 207–220.

4. Patricia R. Lysak, "Changing Times Demand Front-End Model," *Marketing News,* Vol. 28, No. 9 (April 25, 1994), p. 9.

5. Ron Marks, *Personal Selling: A Relationship Approach* (Cincinnati, OH: Atomic Dog, 2006, 7th edition).

6. James C. Anderson, "Relationships in Business Markets: Exchange Episodes, Value Creation, and the Empirical Assessment," *Journal of the Academy of Marketing Science,* Vol. 23 (1996), pp. 346–350.

7. J. J. Cruden and A. W. Sherman, *Personnel Management: The Utilization of Human Resources* (Cincinnati, OH: Southwestern, 1980).

8. Mark W. Johnston and Greg W. Marshall, *Sales Force Management* (New York: McGraw-Hill, 2009).

9. Robert L. Trewatha, M. Gene Newport, J. Lynn Johnson, and Donald Baack, *Management: Embracing Change in the 21st Century* (Houston, TX: Dame, 1997).

10. Mike McCue, "Forget Cash, Show Me the Goods!" *Sales & Marketing Management,* Vol. 160, No. 3 (May/June 2008), pp. 24–27.

11. Eleanor Beaton, "Pay for Profit," *Profit,* Vol. 27, No. 2 (May 2008), pp. 39–41.

12. www.kretschmar.com, accessed June 25, 2008.

Chapter 10

1. ABC News, Nightline (www.zappos.com, accessed July 8, 2008); Sidra Durst, "Shoe In," *Business 2.0, CNNMoney.com* (http://money.cnn.com/magazines/business2/business2_archive/2006/12/01/8394993/index.htm, accessed July 8, 2008).

2. John A. Murphy, *The Lifebelt: The Definitive Guide to Managing Customer Retention* (New York: Wiley, 2001).

3. Donald Baack, *Organizational Behavior* (Houston, TX: Dame, 1998), pp. 313–337.

4. Tamar L. Gillis, "Employee Communication Is No Small Wonder," *Communication World,* Vol. 24, No. 5 (September/October 2007), pp. 28–29.

5. Michael S. Mitchell and Clifford M. Koen Jr., "Write and Wrong: Improving Employee Communication," *Supervision,* Vol. 68, No. 12 (December 2007), pp. 5–11.

6. Doug Beizer, "Email is Dead . . ." *Fast Company,* Vol. 117 (July/August 2007), p. 46.

7. Ibid.

8. C. L. McKenzie and C. J. Quazi, "Communication Barriers in the Work Place," *Business Horizons,* Vol. 26, No. 1 (1983), pp. 70–72.

9. J. F. Kikoski, "Communication: Understanding It, Improving It," *Personnel Journal* (February 1980), pp. 126–131.

10. Gerald M. Goldhaber and Donald P. Rogers, *Auditing Organizational Communication Systems: The ICA Communication Audit* (Dubuque, IA: Kendall-Hunt, 1979).

11. Xueming Luo and Christian Homburg, "Neglected Outcomes of Customer Satisfaction," *Journal of Marketing,* Vol. 71 (April 2007), pp. 133–148.

12. Anne Houlihan, "Empower Your Employees to Make Smart Decisions," *Supervision,* Vol. 68, No. 7 (July 2007), pp. 3–5.

13. James R. Detert and Amy C. Edmondson, "Why Employees Are Afraid to Speak," *Harvard Business Review,* Vol. 85, No. 5 (May 2007), pp. 23–25.

14. Special thanks to Carol Young, a Zen Master in her own right, for her thoughts on this topic.

Chapter 11

1. Interview with Reid Ryan and Jay Miller, March 9, 2008 (www.roundrockexpress.com, accessed August 13, 2008).

2. Marielle E. H. Creusen, "The Different Roles of Product Appearance in Consumer Choice," *Journal of Product Innovation Management,* Vol. 22, No. 1 (January 2005), pp. 63–81.

3. Kris Perry, "Do You Help Your Customers Sell or Market?" *Paperboard Packaging,* Vol. 89, No. 11 (November 2004), p. 8.

4. "Packaging Affects Brand Loyalty," *Supermarket News,* Vol. 53, No. 45 (November 7, 2005), p. 36.

5. "A Sleek Look for Nescafé," *Food Manufacture,* Vol. 76, No. 11 (November 2001), p. 21.

6. Lori Seidler, "Get Creative," *Private Label Buyer,* Vol. 22, No. 5 (May 2008), p. 14.

7. Scott Hume, "Reinventing the Wheel," *Restaurants & Institutions,* Vol. 114, No. 8 (April 1, 2004), pp. 89–92.

8. John A. Murphy, *The Lifebelt: The Definitive Guide to Managing Customer Retention* (New York: Wiley, 2001).

9. Amy Johannes, "Snap Decisions," *Promo,* Vol. 18, No. 11 (October 2005), p. 16.

10. "The Power of POP," *AdMedia,* Vol. 23, No. 2 (March 2008), pp. 34–38.

11. John Spomar Jr., "Keeping Up Appearances," *American Drycleaner,* Vol. 74, No. 3 (June 2007), pp. 64–66.

12. Telisha Bryan, "Windows 101," *Dance Retailer,* Vol. 6, No. 1 (January 2007), pp. 22–23.

13. Ibid.

14. Samantha Murphy, "Store Planning & Design: New Design Concepts Highlighted," *Chain Store Age,* Vol. 84, No. 5 (May 2008), pp. 172–174.

15. Tim Dreyer, "In-Store Technology Trends," *Display & Design Ideas,* Vol. 19, No. 9 (September 2007), p. 92.

16. Ibid.

17. "POP Sharpness in Focus," *Brandweek,* Vol. 44, No. 24 (June 6, 2003), pp. 31–36; David Tossman, "The Final Push—POP Boom," *New Zealand Marketing Magazine,* Vol. 18, No. 8 (September 1999), pp. 45–51.

18. Betsy Spethmann, "Retail Details," *Promo SourceBook 2005,* Vol. 17 (April 1, 2004), pp. 27–28.

19. "Events & Sponsorships," *2007 Marketing Fact Book, Marketing News,* Vol. 41, No. 12 (July 15, 2007), p. 31.

20. Gail Schiller, "Idol Sponsors Coke, Ford, AT&T Paying More," *Brandweek.com* (http://brandweek.com, accessed January 15, 2008).

21. Kenneth Hein, "Study: Purchase Intent Grows With Each Event," *Brandweek,* Vol. 49, No. 4 (January 28, 2008), p. 4.

22. Larry Chiagouris and Ipshita Ray, "Saving the World With Cause-Related Marketing," *Marketing Management,* Vol. 16, No. 4 (July/August 2007), pp. 48–51.

23. Jill Meredith Ginsberg and Paul N. Bloom, "Choosing the Right Green Marketing Strategy," *MIT Sloan Management Review,* Vol. 46, No. 1 (Fall 2004), pp. 79–84.

24. Ibid.

25. Examples based on Jill Meredith Ginsberg and Paul N. Bloom, "Choosing the Right Green Marketing Strategy," *MIT Sloan Management Review,* Vol. 46, No. 1 (Fall 2004), pp. 79–84.

26. Valerie Seckler, "Causes and Effect," *Women's Wear Daily,* Vol. 194, No. 93 (October 31, 2007), p. 9.

27. www.maybelline.com, accessed August 14, 2008.

Chapter 12

1. www.insight-mss.com, accessed July 26, 2008.

2. Hallie Mummert, "Lessons in Multichannel Marketing," *Target Marketing,* Vol. 27, No. 12 (December 2004), pp. 39–41.

3. "Japanese Trading Companies: The Giants That Refused to Die," *The Economist,* Vol. 319, No. 7709 (1991), pp. 72–73.

4. "Business Floating on Air," *The Economist,* Vol. 359, No. 8222 (May 19, 2001), p. 8.

5. Prabir K. Bagchi and Helge Virum, "Logistical Alliances: Trends and Prospects in Integrated Europe," *Journal of Business Logistics,* Vol. 19, No. 1 (1998), pp. 191–213.

6. James A. Cooke, "Costs Under Pressure," *Logistics Management,* Vol. 45, No. 7 (2006), pp. 34–38.

7. Bob Trebilcock, "Distribution Redesign at Urban Outfitters," *Modern Materials Handling,* Vol. 63, No. 4 (April 2008), pp. 37–38.

8. Sue Abdinnour-Helm, "Network Design in Supply Chain Management," *International Journal of Agile Management Systems,* Vol. 1, No. 2 (1999), pp. 99–106.

9. Henry A. Lipson and John R. Darling, *Marketing Fundamentals* (New York: Wiley, 1974).

10. "Inventory Investment: Inventory Levels Drop 10 Percent or More with Optimization Software," *Controller's Report,* Vol. 2008, No. 8 (August 2008), pp. 9–12.

11. Curt Barry, "Keeping DC Costs at Bay," *Multichannel Merchant,* Vol. 4, No. 4 (April 2008), pp. 1, 45.

12. "Transportation Services Overview," *U.S. Industry Quarterly Review: Transportation & Logistics* (2006), pp. 135–137.

13. "Air Express Surges," *Traffic World,* Vol. 271, No. 2 (January 15, 2007), p. 29.

14. DHL, www.dhl.com, accessed August 6, 2008.

15. "Transportation Services Overview," *U.S. Industry Quarterly Review: Transportation & Logistics* (2006), pp. 135–137.

16. DHL, www.dhl.com (accessed August 6, 2008).

17. Curt Barry, "Keeping DC Costs at Bay," *Multichannel Merchant,* Vol. 4, No. 4 (April 2008), pp. 1, 45.

Chapter 13

1. www.vonage.com/corporate, accessed July 27, 2008; Steven Levy, "Ma Bell's Kids Will Live on the Net," *Newsweek* (February 28, 2008) (www.newsweek.com/id/48856, accessed June 10, 2009).

2. Marshall Lager, "E-Commerce Best Practices Make Perfect," *CRM Magazine,* Vol. 10, No. 6 (June 2006), pp. 22–27.

3. Gary Evans, "La-Z-Boy Starts E-Commerce," *Furniture Today,* Vol. 32, No. 41 (June 23, 2008), p. 2.

4. Beth Viveiros, "Doing Right, in Style," *Direct,* Vol. 20, No. 7 (July 2008), p. 13.

5. Christine Dugas, "E-Retailers Increase Alternate Pay Options," *USA Today* (November 13, 2007), p. 03B.

6. Linda Abu-Shalback Zid, "More Ways to Pay," *Marketing Management,* Vol. 13, No. 6 (November/December 2004), p. 7.

7. Suzzane Bearne, "Majority of Online Shoppers Bypass E-Commerce Sites' Home Page," *New Media Age* (August 5, 2008), p. 11.

8. Marshall Lager, "E-Commerce Best Practices Make Perfect," *CRM Magazine,* Vol. 10, No. 6 (June 2006), pp. 22-27.

9. Kim Hart, "Online Networking Goes Small, and Sponsors Follow," *Washington Post* (December 29, 2007), p. D01.

10. Claire Cain Miller, "Woman to Woman, Online," *The New York Times* (www.nytimes.com/2008/08/14/technology/14women.html, accessed August 15, 2008).

11. Lisa Lockwood, "Talking to a Generation: Brands Turn to YouTube to Spread the Message," *Women's Daily Wear,* Vol. 193, No. 114 (May 29, 2007), pp. 1, 9–10.

12. Bryant Shea, "User Generated Content," *AIIM E-Doc,* Vol. 22, No. 4 (July/August 2008), pp. 16–17.

13. Emily Evans, "Simple Boosts Site's Interactive Element," *Marketing* (July 23, 2008), p. 12.

14. Andreas Eisingerich and Tobias Kretschmer, "In E-Commerce, More Is More," *Harvard Business Review,* Vol. 86, No. 3 (March 2008), pp. 20–21.

15. Rory J. Thompson, "Can't Skip This: Consumers Acclimating to Internet Ads," *Brandweek,* Vol. 48, No. 7 (December 31, 2007), p. 5; "Word of Mouse," *Economist,* Vol. 385, No. 8554 (November 10, 2007), pp. 77–78.

16. "Problem Solved," *B to B,* Vol. 92, No. 15 (November 12, 2007), p. 21.

17. Ibid.

18. Josh Quittner, Jessi Hempel, and Lindsay Blakely, "The Battle for Your Social Circle," *Fortune,* Vol. 156, No. 10 (November 26, 2007), pp. 11–13.

19. "Revlon Pushes Charlie Brand to Teen Girls Across Platforms," *New Media Age* (May 8, 2008), p. 3.

20. Catherine Holahan, "So I Married an Avatar" (February 14, 2008) (www.businessweek.com/technology/content/feb2008/tc20080214_131079.htm?chan=search, accessed July 30, 2008).

21. Catherine Arnst, "Better Loving through Chemistry" (October 24, 2005) (www.businessweek.com/magazine/content/05_43/b3956062.htm?chan=search, accessed July 30, 2008).

22. Mark Brooks, filed in (www.dating-Weblog.com/50226711/chemistrycom_in_spat_with_eharmonycom.php, accessed July 30, 2008).

23. Douglas Quenqua, "Little Love Among Matchmakers" (www.find-a-sweetheart.com/blog/item/chemistrycom_takes_on_eharmony, accessed July 30, 2008).

Chapter 14

1. www.jetblue.com, accessed January 16, 2009; Tara Weiss, "Crisis Management: Jet Blue's Survival School" (February 20, 2007) (www.forbes.com, accessed January 16, 2009); "Jet Blue Apologizes after Passengers Stranded" (February 16, 2007) (msnbc.com, accessed January 16, 2009).

2. Jill Griffin, *Customer Loyalty* (San Francisco: Jossey-Bass, 2002) pp. 22–23.

3. Roger J. Best, *Marketing-Based Management* (Upper Saddle River, NJ: Pearson, 2005) pp. 8–12.

4. Seminar presented by Kenneth E. Clow to employees of J.P. Morgan Chase, March 22, 2007.

5. Steve Trollinger, "Building Retention With Knowledge," *Multichannel Merchant,* Vol. 4, No. 3 (March 2008), p. 28.

6. Jordan K. Speer, "Women's Secret Drives Loyalty With CRM," *Apparel Magazine,* Vol. 48, No. 12 (August 2007), pp. 15–16.

7. Walfred M. Lassar, "Developing a CRM Strategy in Your Firm," *Journal of Accountancy,* Vol. 206, No. 2 (August 2008), pp. 68–73.

8. Eileen Feretic, "The Missing Piece of the CRM Puzzle," *Baseline,* No. 86 (July 2008), p. 12.

9. Jill Griffin, *Customer Loyalty* (San Francisco: Jossey-Bass, 2002) p. 179.

10. Frederick F. Reichheld and W. Earl Sasser, "Zero Defections: Quality Comes to Services," *Harvard Business Review,* Vol. 68, No. 5 (September/October 1990), pp. 105–111.

11. Elisabeth A. Sullivan, "Churning Waters," *Marketing News,* Vol. 42, No. 8 (May 1, 2008), p. 22.

12. Marc R. Okrant, "How to Convert 3's and 4's Into 5's," *Marketing News,* Vol. 36 (October 14, 2002), pp. 14–15.

Chapter 15

1. Katzenbach Partners, "Anatomy of a Turnaround," (August 2006) (www.katzenbach.com/Work/Publications/PublicationInstance/tabid/73/Default.aspx?Entity_ID=383, accessed July 30, 2008).

2. Donald Baack, *Organizational Behavior* (Houston, TX: Dame, 1995).

3. www.investorwords.com/3883/profit_center.html.

4. Arthur A. Thompson Jr., A. J. Strickland III, and John E. Gamble, *Crafting and Executing Strategy: The Quest for Competitive Advantage* (New York: McGraw-Hill, 2008, 16th edition).

5. www.bain.com/management_tools/tools_competencies, accessed September 10, 2008; Birger Wernerfelt, "A Resource-Based View of the Firm," *Strategic Management Journal* (September/October 1984), pp. 171–180.

6. Michael E. Porter, *Competitive Strategy: Techniques for Analyzing Industries and Competitors* (New York: Free Press, 1980) pp. 25–40.

7. www.pamperedpassions.com, accessed April 11, 2009.

Glossary

Administered channel arrangement   A distribution system with a dominant member that guides the channel.   319

Advertising management   The process of developing and overseeing a company's advertising program.   167

Aesthetic value   Value created by anything in a product or package that is pleasing or that a person likes.   286

Antecedents of stress   The causes or predecessors of stress.   99

Application interface   A system that connects the product database to the payment system, shopping system, internal search engine, and other features of a Web site.   348

Aptitude   A person's natural abilities, including verbal intelligence, mathematical ability, and reasoning skills.   233

Arbitrary allocation   An advertising budget that is a figure chosen based on what company leaders think should be spent or believe the firm can afford.   167

Attention-drawing value   Value created by anything that makes a product or package stand out from competing brands so that consumers notice the item.   287

Basic authentication   A customer-tracking method that involves the person signing into a Web site using a login and password.   348

Best-cost provider strategy   Giving customers the most value for their money. It combines some uniqueness with lower costs and lower prices.   410

Bonus pack   The offer of additional or extra items in a special package at a reduced or special price.   205

Bonuses   Payments for the completion of a single project or given out on an annual basis based on overall company performance.   235

Brainstorming   A verbal creativity technique.   98

Brand   The name given to a product or, in some instances, the company name.   122

Brand equity   A situation in which a company's goods and services are perceived to be different and better.   33

Brand extension   The use of a firm's current brand name on new products and new versions of current products.   123

Brand-loyal consumers   Individuals with high levels of emotional attachment to a brand combined with high levels of purchases.   208

Brand loyalty   A situation in which a consumer makes a concerted effort to find and purchase a specific brand due to an affinity with that brand.   127

Brand market share   A brand's percentage of total industry sales.   399

Brand parity   A situation in which consumers believe there are few tangible distinctions between brands.   33

Brand repositioning   Creating a new perception of the brand in the mind of a typical consumer.   412

Brand spiraling   The process of using traditional media to promote and attract consumers to a Web site.   355

Broad differentiation strategy   Seeking to make the organization's products and services unique when compared with those of competitors, therefore being able to compete based on those differences.   410

Buzz marketing (or word of mouth)   Reaching new customers by emphasizing consumers passing along information about a product.   179

Calendar promotions   Promotional campaigns the retailer plans for customers through manufacturer trade incentives.   211

Carrying costs   Monies spent on holding inventory.   324

Cause-related marketing   A program in which a firm ties a marketing program to a charity in order to generate goodwill.   299

Channel arrangement   A system that guides the administration of the marketing functions that must be performed as part of the distribution program.   319

Channel captain   The leader of an administered channel arrangement, who takes on the role based on the size, expertise, or influence of the company.   319

Channels of distribution   The paths goods and services take from the producer to the end user.   312

Churn   Customer defections from a company or brand.   383

Climate   The prevailing atmosphere or environment within a company.   271

Coaching   Teaching and training others.   273

Cobranding   The name used when two firms work together in marketing a good or a service.   125

Coercive power   Channel power based on the ability of a channel member to remove privileges or punish channel members for noncompliance.   321

Commission sales   Jobs in which employees sell bigger ticket items and receive a percentage of the sale as compensation.   225

Commissions   Payments for sales by the unit or over a period of time, typically 1 month.   235

Communication   The process of transmitting, receiving, and processing information.   257

Company culture   The symbols, rituals, language, myths, stories, and jargon present in an organization.   271

Company market share   A company's percentage of the total industry sales.   399

Competitive superiority   A form of brand equity.   410

Consideration or evoked parity set   The set of brands a customer views as being approximately equal.   146

Consumer and business-to-business segments   Types of markets.   7

Consumer promotions   Incentives directed toward end users with the goal of pulling a product through the channel.   194

Contests   Events that normally require the participant to perform some type of activity to compete for a prize.   200

Contractual channel arrangement   A binding contract that identifies all the tasks to be performed by each channel member with regard to production, delivery, sorting, pricing, and promotional support.   319

Control   The managerial process of comparing performance to standards, making corrections when needed, and rewarding success.   397

Cookies   A customer-tracking method in which personal information stored on the customer's computer is retrieved when the individual accesses a Web site.   348

Cooperative advertising promotion   A type of promotion in which the manufacturer agrees to reimburse the retailer a certain percentage of the costs associated with advertising the manufacturer's products in the retailer's ad.   212

Cooperative merchandising agreement (CMA)   A formal agreement between the retailer and manufacturer to undertake a two-way marketing effort.   211

Core competence   A firm's most proficiently performed internal activity that is central to the firm's strategy and competitiveness.   409

Corporate name   The term used to identify an entire company.   122

Cost-plus pricing   Setting the price of a product based on both the variable and fixed costs associated with producing the product and a desired contribution margin.   142

Coupon   A price reduction offer to a consumer or end user.   196

Creative brief   An outline of the major elements of an advertising campaign.   171

Cross-ruffing coupons   The placement of a coupon on one product for another product.   197

Cross-selling   The attempt to sell a second or additional product to a customer who has already purchased a product.   377

Customer contact points   The places where interactions occur between a company and its customers or prospective customers.   283

Customization   The ability to modify marketing programs or offers to different groups of individuals within a database.   71

Cyber bait   Any lure or attraction on a Web site that attracts visitors and entices them to make a purchase.   344

Data mining   A data analysis program that includes building profiles of customer segments and preparing models that predict future behaviors based on past purchases.   68

Data warehouse   The system that holds all customer data and that can be accessed by any employee who deals with customers in any capacity.   58

Decentralization   Organization-wide delegation of authority.   85

Deceptive pricing   A pricing practice that misleads consumers.   155

Decoding   What occurs when a receiver attempts to understand the message through the use of the five senses.   258

Direct channel   A channel in which the producer sends the product directly to the customer or end user.   313

Direct marketing   A marketing program in which a company sells directly to end-users.   70

Directing (or actuating)   Seeking to achieve the highest levels of performance.   11

Distinctive competence   An activity a company performs at a level that is superior to all rivals.   409

Diversion   A tactic in which a retailer purchases a product on-deal in one location and ships it to another location where it is off-deal.   210

Dual channels (or multichannel distribution or hybrid marketing system)   The use of more than one channel of distribution for a company's goods or services.   314

Economic forces   The economic trends, such as inflation, employment or unemployment levels, and the price and availability of raw materials, that have an influence on a company's marketing program.   27

Encoding   The process of forming verbal and nonverbal cues.   258

Enhancement   Increasing the value of a favorable event in the eyes of the public.   296

Entitling   Making sure the company is given credit when favorable events occur.   296

Ethnocentrism   The belief that one's culture is inherently superior to that of others.   274

Event marketing   A form of marketing in which a company pays money to support a specific event.   296

Exclusive distribution   A system that limits the number of distributors of a product to only one or two in each geographic area.   311

Expert power   Channel power based on the experience and knowledge a channel member possesses.   320

Extinction   Behaviors that are not associated with any kind of consequence, favorable or unfavorable.   94

Family brand   Is the name used when a company offers a series or a group of products under one brand.   122

Feedback   The message the sender receives in return from the receiver.   258

Field salespeople   Those who make sales calls on businesses.   225

Flanker brand   A term that is used when a company offers a series or group of products under a different brand name.   123

Focus group   A set of individuals who are prompted to discuss an item or topic.   120

Focused (market niche) strategy   The approach of concentrating on a market segment and outcompeting rivals based on price or some form of differentiation.   410

Formal communication   A communication system in which messages travel through channels that are chosen or designated by the organization.   262

Formal leader   A person who has been authorized to direct activities in an organization.   86

Forward buying   A tactic in which a retailer purchases extra amounts of a product while it is on-deal from the manufacturer   210

Freestanding inserts (FSIs)   Sheets of coupons placed in newspapers or sent by mail.   196

Frequency or customer loyalty programs   Programs designed to retain customers by giving rewards to those who make additional purchases.   377

Functional value   In a product or package, the impression created that the item will work properly.   286

Geocoding   The process of adding geographic codes to each customer record so that customer addresses can be plotted on a map.   63

Green marketing   The development and promotion of products that are environmentally safe.   299

Greenwashing   Sending out information in corporate documents via the Internet in chat rooms and on a firm's Web site, in public relations press releases, and through advertisements that suggests that a company seeks to become a friend of the environment while in fact it is engaging in exactly the opposite activities.   300

Guerrilla marketing   A method to obtain instant results with limited resources using tactics that rely on creativity, quality relationships with customers, and the willingness to try unusual approaches.   177

Horizontal integration   An acquisition or merger at the same level in the distribution channel.   318

House mark   A term used when a corporate name is attached to every company product.   122

Human resource management   The process of attaining and preparing quality workers to serve in an organization.   90

Inclusive/exclusive language   What occurs when an "in-crowd" develops its own lingo and patterns of conversation, thereby excluding others.   273

Incremental approach   Pricing a new product based on the incremental costs of producing the new product over the costs of producing a similar existing product.   148

Indirect channels   Channels in which goods and services go through one or more intermediaries before reaching customers or end users.   313

Inertia loyalty   A situation in which customers have high levels of purchases but low emotional attachment.   371

Informal communication   A communication system in which messages emerge in the form of gossip, rumors, and what travels by the grapevine.   262

Informal leader (or emergent leader)   Someone who moves into the role of leader due to circumstances or because of a personal trait or characteristic.   86

Ingredient branding   The name used when a product is featured as a key ingredient or component of another product.   125

Intensive distribution   A system that makes the product available to consumers in as many different places as possible.   311

Internal marketing   An ongoing process through which company leaders can align, motivate, and empower employees of all functions and levels to consistently deliver a positive customer experience.   261

Just-in-time (JIT)   An inventory control system that focuses on items being received just when they are needed rather than being stored in a warehouse.   326

Latent loyalty   A situation in which customers have high levels of attachment to a brand but for some reason the purchase volume is low.   370

Legitimate power   Channel power based on a contractual arrangement.   320

Lifestyle marketing   Reaching customers by tapping into a target audience's core lifestyle, music, culture, and fashion.   178

Lifetime value   A monetary figure that represents the profit stream that individual customers generate over their lifetime with a firm or product.   64

Logistics   All the activities associated with the physical movement and storage of goods from the producer to the consumer.   321

Low-cost provider strategy   Seeking to achieve the lowest overall costs as compared with competitors and therefore being able to compete with price.   410

Management   The process of getting things done through other people.   10

Management by objectives   A participative goal-setting program.   409

Management information system   The people and computer system used to collect and process organizational information.   266

Market analysis   Studying a company's customers and its competitors along with the overall industry and environment.   26

Market segmentation   Categorizing customers into groups and identifying the characteristics of each of the groups.   36

Marketing   Discovering consumer needs and wants, creating the goods and services that meet those needs and wants, pricing, promoting, and delivering the goods and services.   6

Marketing control   The assessment of all marketing activities individually and collectively.   397

Marketing management (1)   A common name for a capstone course presented to students with either a major or a concentration in marketing. The course should be designed to help the student integrate business and marketing concepts to better prepare that individual to join the workforce.   5

Marketing management (2)   The process of managing the marketing activities in a profit-seeking or nonprofit organization, at the supervisory, midlevel management, and executive levels.   6

Marketing strategies   The broad sweeping plans that are based on a company's mission.   12

Marketing tactics   The midrange or medium-term (1–3 years) efforts designed to support marketing strategies.   12

Markets   People or businesses with wants and needs, financial resources, and the willingness to use those resources to satisfy those wants and needs.   7

Markup   The difference between the selling price of an item and what it costs to produce that item.   143

Meet the competition   An advertising budget that matches estimates of competitor spending.   167

Metrics   Performance measures that serve as standards set during the planning process and that are used in the control process.   398

Mission statement   A statement of the overall, most general purpose that an organization serves.   269

Missionary salespeople   Those who make contact with businesses to deliver samples, leave information, check up to make sure things are in order, and build relationships.   225

Mission-sharing   A form of sales presentation in which two organizations develop a common mission.   229

Need-satisfaction   A form of sales presentation in which the approach is to discover a customer's needs and then provide solutions to those needs.   228

Negative reinforcement   A behavior that is used to help a person escape or end an aversive situation.   94

No loyalty   A situation in which customers have no emotional attachment to a brand and purchase the item infrequently.   370

Noise (or barriers to communication)   Anything that blocks the message in an individual communication process.   258

Nominal groups (or nominal group technique)   A written creativity technique.   99

Obfuscation   What occurs when someone tries to obscure, disguise, or confuse a message.   272

Objective and task   An advertising budget that is based on estimates of how much should be spent to achieve each advertising objective.   167

Operational audit   An audit designed to examine the procedures and processes used in operating the warehouse or distribution center, layout and usage of the facility, staff productivity, and freight analysis.   329

Operational plans (or short-term plans)   Plans created to carry out marketing strategies and tactics.   12

Opportunity costs   Monies not received from one activity because they were spent or forgone on another.   200

Order taker A sales job where the person works primarily near the cash register and may also stock shelves, answer questions, and process sales. 225

Organizing Combining people and resources to make goods and services. 10

Partnership channel arrangement A system in which the members of the channel work together for the benefit of all the members involved in distribution. 319

Penetration pricing Setting the price low to discourage competitors from entering the market and to build primary demand. 148

People A critical component of effective marketing. 9

Percentage of sales An advertising budget that allocates funds based on either a percentage of the previous year's revenues or a projection of the upcoming year's sales. 167

Permission marketing Sending marketing offers to individuals who have given the company permission to so do. 70

Personal characteristics The traits that make an individual unique. 233

Personalization A program in which a consumer receives distinct marketing offers and other advantages that are tailored to his or her individual identity. 59

Place (or distribution) Deciding where, how, and when products will be available to potential customers. 8

Planning Outlining a course of action for the future. 10

Point-of-purchase display Any form of special display that promotes merchandise. 293

Political forces The influence of governments, courts, taxes, subsidies, and laws on a company's marketing program. 27

Positive reinforcement A pleasant or pleasing consequence of a behavior. 93

Predatory pricing Pricing designed to eliminate competition. 156

Preferred-brand consumers Persons who have certain brands they prefer but who are not completely loyal to any one brand. 208

Premiums The prizes, gifts, and special offers that consumers receive when purchasing products, or trade incentives offered to members of a channel. 199

Price The amount charged for a good or a service. 8

Price discrimination Selling merchandise to different buyers at different prices. 155

Price elasticity of demand Change in demand relative to a change in price. 144

Price fixing An agreement between businesses to charge the same price for a good or service. 155

Price-off A temporary reduction in the price of a product. 206

Price perceptual map A visual tool used to examine brand image or quality and brand market position relative to the competition. 139

Price-sensitive consumers Persons who see price as the primary, if not the only, criterion to be used in making purchase decisions. 208

Pricing strategy The basic direction the company's marketing and management teams take when setting prices. 141

Problem-solution A form of sales presentation that requires employees from the selling organization to analyze the buyer's operations and then offer feasible solutions. 228

Product development A marketing strategy of adding new goods and services to current lines for existing customers. 120

Product differentiation   Attempting to create brand equity based on (1) an actual difference or (2) by creating the perception that there is a difference.   36

Product diversification   A marketing strategy of adding new goods and services targeted to a new market segment currently not being served.   120

Product life cycle   A model of how sales of an item or industry move over its lifetime.   115

Product market share   A product's percentage of total industry sales.   399

Product positioning   The place a good or service occupies (1) in the minds of consumers and (2) relative to the competition.   34

Products   The physical goods sold to consumers and other organizations as well as the services that are offered to individual consumers, other businesses, and the government.   7

Profit center   A business unit or department that is treated as a distinct entity, enabling revenues and expenses to be determined so that profitability can be measured.   398

Promotion   Advertising programs and consumer and trade promotion programs, personal selling tactics, and public relations efforts.   8

Promotion-prone consumers   Persons who regularly respond to coupons, premiums, or other promotional programs.   208

Pull strategy   A program in which the manufacturer focuses on stimulating consumer demand through extensive advertising and consumer promotions.   316

Punishment   A negative consequence that follows an act and is related to the behavior.   94

Push strategy   A program in which the manufacturer focuses on providing intermediaries with the kinds of incentives that will lead them to cooperate in marketing products.   316

Quick response   An inventory control system for retailers that creates an efficient supply flow of goods that approximates consumer purchase patterns.   326

Rebate   A cash return on hard goods, such as automobiles and appliances.   202

Receiver   The person for whom a message was intended in individual communication.   258

Reference price   The price customers initially identify with a new product.   148

Referent power   Channel power based on the channel member being liked or respected.   320

Refund   A cash return on soft goods, such as food or clothing.   202

Relationship selling   The process of turning initial transactions into stronger partnerships over time.   231

Reward power   Channel power based on the ability to provide special privileges, such as financial rewards for engaging in desirable behavior.   320

RFM   Abbreviation that stands for recency, frequency, and monetary (value).   67

Role model   Someone who presents a visible example to others.   273

Salary   A fixed amount of pay for a given time period.   234

Sampling   The delivery of a good or service for a trial use.   204

Search engine optimization   The process of increasing the probability that a particular company's Web site will emerge from an Internet search.   354

Selective distribution   A system in which only carefully chosen outlets will carry a product in a geographic area.   311

Selective filtering   A barrier to a formal communication in which the message is altered by an intermediary.   265

Semicontrollable forces The influence of various individuals and groups that create an impact on a company and that are in turn influenced by the company's leaders' responses. 28

Sender The person sending a message or idea in an individual communication. 258

Service salesperson An employee who sells the services offered by a company. 225

Share of heart The attitudes or feelings toward a company's brands and the consumer's willingness to purchase the brand. 41

Share of mind Consumer brand recall based on whether or not the brand is typically located in customers' minds. 41

Skill level A person's learned proficiencies, such as product knowledge, interpersonal communication skills, and presentation skills. 233

Skimming price strategy Setting the price high in order to recover research and development costs as quickly as possible. 147

Slotting fees Funds charged by retailers to stock new products. 211

Social forces The influence of society, culture, demographic trends, and changes in the levels of education on a company's marketing program. 27

Sponsorship marketing The company pays money to sponsor a person, group, or activity. 296

Staffing Attaining and preparing quality employees. 11

Stimulus-response A form of sales presentation using specific statements (stimuli) to elicit specific responses from customers. 228

Stock turnover The number of times per year that a firm's average inventory on hand is sold. 324

Strategic business units Clusters of activities that are typically held together by a common thread, such as a product type or type of customer served. 398

Strategic controls Performance measures that apply to the CEO and top-level management team that direct the portfolios of businesses or activities held by a single company or corporation. 398

Stress outcomes The outcomes associated with stress. 99

Supply chain management The process of managing the actual physical movement of products from the producer to the consumer or end user. 311

Sweepstakes Events with prizes that are given to people who enter, with no purchase or activity required. 200

Symbolic value In a product or package, the appearance matches a person's self-image or is emblematic of something else the individual desires or values. 286

System overload A barrier to formal communication in which the formal channel is so swamped that messages become lost. 265

Technological forces The influence of new products, product improvements, changes in production methods, and other technological trends on a company's marketing program. 28

Telemarketers Salespersons who take in-bound or make out-bound sales calls. 225

Trade allowances Financial incentives offered to other channel members to motivate them to purchase products for sale. 210

Credits

Chapter 1

Chapter opening photo: © tulcarion/iStockphoto.com.

Photo spread: © 2009 Jupiterimages Corporation.

Photo on p. 6 © 2009 Jupiterimages Corporation.

Photo on p. 9 © Juanmonino/iStockphoto.com.

Photo on p. 11 © Marcus Clackson/iStockphoto.com.

Photo on p. 13 © 2009 Jupiterimages Corporation.

Table 1.2 Adapted from Jena McGregor, "Customer Service Champs," *BusinessWeek* (March 5, 2007), pp. 52–64.

Figure 1.7 Adapted from Jena McGregor, "Customer Service Champs," *BusinessWeek* (March 5, 2007), pp. 52–64.

Ad 1.1 Newcomer, Morris, and Young Advertising Agency.

Photo on p. 19 Used with permission of Tarah Wilson.

Photo on p. 21 © 2009 Jupiterimages Corporation.

Photo on p. 22 © Yoshikazu Tsuno/Getty Images.

Chapter 2

Chapter opening photo: © Brandon Laufenberg/iStockphoto .com.

Photo spread: © 2009 Jupiterimages Corporation; © Bill Manning/iStockphoto.com; © 2009 Jupiterimages Corporation.

Photo on p. 28 © 2009 Jupiterimages Corporation.

Photo on p. 29 © © David H. Lewis/iStockphoto.com.

Photo on p. 31 © Josef Kubicek/iStockphoto.com.

Photo on p. 33 © Sean Locke/iStockphoto.com.

Figure 2.4 Adapted from "Starbucks: The Non-Coffee Treat," Report by A5 Consulting Group (September 2007), p. 13.

Photo on p. 37 © Dragan Trifunovic/iStockphoto.com.

Photo on p. 40 © 2009 Jupiterimages Corporation.

Photo on p. 43 © Zlatko Kostic/iStockphoto.com.

Photo on p. 44 © 2009 Jupiterimages Corporation.

Photo on p. 46 © tiburonstudios/iStockphoto.com.

Photo on p. 51 © 2009 Jupiterimages Corporation.

Photo on p. 54 © Gene Chutka/iStockphoto.com.

Chapter 3

Chapter opening photo: © Tom Hahn/iStockphoto.com.

Photo spread: © 2009 Jupiterimages Corporation; © Tom Hahn/ iStockphoto.com; © 2009 Jupiterimages Corporation.

Photo on p. 60 © Michael DeLeon/iStockphoto.com.

Photo on p. 62 © Matt Trommer /iStockphoto.com.

Photo on p. 63 © 2009 Jupiterimages Corporation.

Photo on p. 66 © Sean Locke/iStockphoto.com.

Photo on p. 69 © kreicher/iStockphoto.com.

Photo on p. 70 © merrymoonmary/iStockphoto.com.

Photo on p. 74 Used with permission of Jennifer Banando.

Photo on p. 79 © Ben Blankenburg/iStockphoto.com.

Chapter 4

Chapter opening photo: © 2009 Jupiterimages Corporation.

Photo spread: © 2009 Jupiterimages Corporation; © 2009 Jupiterimages Corporation; © Rob Friedman/iStockphoto.com.

Photo on p. 84 © Marcus Clackson/iStockphoto.com.

Photo on p. 85 © Arne Trautmann/iStockphoto.com

Photo on p. 88 © Chris Schmidt/iStockphoto.com.

Photo on p. 91 © dra_schwartz/iStockphoto.com.

Photo on p. 95 © 2009 Jupiterimages Corporation.

Photo on p. 96 © 2009 Jupiterimages Corporation.

Photo on p. 98 © Chris Schmidt/iStockphoto.com.

Photo on p. 106 © 2009 Jupiterimages Corporation.

Photo on p. 108 © Marcus Clackson/iStockphoto.com.

Chapter 5

Chapter opening photo: © Suprijono Suharjoto/iStockphoto.com.

Photo spread: © 2009 Jupiterimages Corporation; © 2009 Jupiterimages Corporation; © Renee Lee/iStockphoto.com.

Photo on p. 116 © iofoto/iStockphoto.com.

Photo on p. 119 © George Cairns/iStockphoto.com.

Figure 5.5 Donald Baack, *International Business* (Los Angeles: Glencoe/McGraw-Hill, 2008).

Photo on p. 123 © William Howell/iStockphoto.com.

Photo on p. 125 © Josef Philipp/iStockphoto.com.

Figure 5.7 Adapted from Mark Ritson, "Don't Catch Brand Extension Disease," *Marketing* (August 29, 2007), p. 21.

Figure 5.8 Adapted from Jeff Swystun, "Seven Habits of Highly Effective Brands," *Marketing Magazine,* Vol. 111, No. 33 (October 9, 2006), p. 37.

Figure 5.10 Adapted from "CPG Win for Brand Equity," *Marketing News,* Vol. 42, No. 13 (August 15, 2008), p. 5.

Photo on p. 131 Used with permission of Jerry Ross.

Photo on p. 133 © 2009 Jupiterimages Corporation.

Photo on p. 135 © David H. Lewis/iStockphoto.com.

Chapter 6

Chapter opening photo: © Brian Raisbeck/iStockphoto.com.

Photo spread: © 2009 Jupiterimages Corporation; © 2009 Jupiterimages Corporation; © Ceneri/iStockphoto.com.

Photo on p. 140 © 1001nights/iStockphoto.com.

Photo on p. 152 © Simone van den Berg/iStockphoto.com.

Photo on p. 159 © 2009 Jupiterimages Corporation.

Photo on p. 161 © Lisa F. Young/iStockphoto.com.

Photo on p. 162 © Floortje/iStockphoto.com.

Chapter 7

Chapter opening photo: © Thomas Perkins/iStockphoto.com.

Photo spread: © 2009 Jupiterimages Corporation; © 2009 Jupiterimages Corporation; © Leonid Nyshko/iStockphoto.com.

Table 7.1 Adapted from Schonfield & Associates Inc, Ratios and Budgets (June 2005) (http://company.news-record.com/advertising/advertising/ratio.html, accessed on June 5, 2009).

Ad 7.1 Skyjacker Suspensions.

Figure 7.5 Adapted from Jack Myers, "Nontraditional, Internet to Lead 7% Jump in Advertising," *Jack Myers Media Business Report* (www.marketingvox.com, accessed on November 16, 2007).

Figure 7.6 Adapted from Jack Myers, "Nontraditional, Internet to Lead 7% Jump in Advertising," *Jack Myers Media BusinessReport* (www.marketingvox.com, accessed on November 16, 2007).

Ad 7.2 Newcomer, Morris, and Young Agency.

Photo on p. 178 © Leah Marshall/iStockphoto.com.

Photo on p. 179 © 2009 Jupiterimages Corporation.

Photo on p. 180 © 2009 Jupiterimages Corporation.

Figure 7.9 Adapted from Richard H. Levey, "Prospects Look Good," *Direct,* Vol. 16 (December 1, 2004), pp. 1–5.

Figure 7.10 Adapted from "Direct Results," *PROMO,* Vol. 19, No. 9 (October 2007), pp. 54–55.

Figure 7.11 Adapted from Megan Ouellet and Ross Kramer, "Measure Your Results," *Marketing News,* Vol. 41, No. 18 (November 1, 2007) p. 26.

Figure 7.12 Adapted from Grant A. Johnson, "Why a Microsite?" *Direct,* Vol. 19, No. 7 (July 1, 2007), p. 12.

Photo on p. 184 © LajosRepasi/iStockphoto.com.

Photo on p. 186 Used with permission of Lee McGuire.

Photo on p. 190 © Hedda Gjerpen/iStockphoto.com.

Photo on p. 191 © Nathan McClunie/iStockphoto.com.

Chapter 8

Chapter opening photo: © Jerry Horbert/iStockphoto.com.

Photo spread:© Liza McCorkle/iStockphoto.com; © Sean Locke/iStockphoto.com; © TommL/iStockphoto.com.

Photo on p. 197 © Sean Locke/iStockphoto.com.

Photo on p. 201 © Nikada/iStockphoto.com.

Photo on p. 202 © 2009 Jupiterimages Corporation.

Photo on p. 205 © 2009 Jupiterimages Corporation.

Photo on p. 207 © Suprijono Suharjoto/iStockphoto.com.

Photo on p. 208 © Josef Philipp/iStockphoto.com.

Photo on p. 210 Photograph by Anna Giannoble.

Photo on p. 212 © Sean Locke/iStockphoto.com.

Photo on p. 214 © Ben Blankenburg/iStockphoto.com.

Photo on p. 218 © Catherine Yeulet/iStockphoto.com.

Photo on p. 220 © Krzysztof Kwiatkowski/iStockphoto.com.

Chapter 9

Chapter opening photo: © Sami Suni/iStockphoto.com.

Photo spread: © 2009 Jupiterimages Corporation; © 2009 Jupiterimages Corporation; © Joris van Caspel/iStockphoto.com.

Photo on p. 225 © iofoto/iStockphoto.com.

Photo on p. 226 © John Prescott/iStockphoto.com.

Photo on p. 228 © Sami Suni/iStockphoto.com.

Figure 9.5 Adapted from Ron Marks, *Personal Selling: A Relationship Approach* (Cincinnati, OH: Atomic Dog, 2006, 7th edition).

Figure 9.6 Adapted from Ron Marks, *Personal Selling: A Relationship Approach* (Cincinnati, OH: Atomic Dog, 2006, 7th edition).

Photo on p. 231 © Duard van der Westhuizen/iStockphoto.com.

Photo on p. 233 © Jeffrey Smith/iStockphoto.com.

Photo on p. 235 © Marcus Clackson/iStockphoto.com.

Photo on p. 238 © Sean Locke/iStockphoto.com.

Photo on p. 239 © Amanda Rohde/iStockphoto.com.

Photo on p. 245 Used with permission of Tim Clow.

Photo on p. 247 © Rafael Ramirez Lee/iStockphoto.com.

Photo on p. 251 © Sean Locke/iStockphoto.com.

Chapter 10

Chapter opening photo: © Neustockimages/iStockphoto.com.

Photo spread: © 2009 Jupiterimages Corporation.

Photo on p. 258 © zhang bo/iStockphoto.com.

Photo on p. 261 © Justin Horrocks/iStockphoto.com.

Photo on p. 264 © Marilyn Nieves/iStockphoto.com.

Photo on p. 265 © Tom England/iStockphoto.com.

Photo on p. 267 Photograph by Anna Giannoble.

Photo on p. 268 © Oleg Prikhodko/iStockphoto.com.

Photo on p. 269 © 2009 Jupiterimages Corporation.

Photo on p. 272 © Marcus Clackson/iStockphoto.com.

Photo on p. 273 © Sean Locke/iStockphoto.com.

Photo on p. 279 © Lise Gagne/iStockphoto.com.

Chapter 11

Chapter opening photo: Used with permission of Heather Tantimonaco and Taylor Jones Images.

Photo spread: © 2009 Jupiterimages Corporation; © Keith Reicher/iStockphoto.com; © Pamela Moore/iStockphoto.com.

Photo on p. 282 Used with permission of Heather Tantimonaco and Taylor Jones Images.

Photo on p. 284 © Gene Chutka/iStockphoto.com.

Figure 11.2 Adapted from Marielle E. H. Creuson and Jan P. L. Schoormans, "The Different Roles of Product Appearance in Consumer Choice," *Journal of Product Innovation Management,* Vol. 22, No. 1 (January 2005), pp. 63–81.

Photo on p. 286 © luoman/iStockphoto.com.

Photo on p. 290 © Sean Locke/iStockphoto.com.

Figure 11.7 Adapted from Amy Johannes, "Snap Decisions," *Promo,* Vol. 18, No. 11 (October 2005), p. 16.

Photo on p. 295 © Sergiy Zavgorodny/iStockphoto.com.

Ad 11.1 Sartor Associates, Inc.

Figure 11.10 Adapted from "Events & Sponsorships," *2007 Marketing Fact Book* (July 15, 2007, p. 31).

Photo on p. 300 © 2009 Jupiterimages Corporation.

Photo on p. 302 Used with permission of Lisa M. Winter.

Photo on p. 307 © Andy Green—AGMIT/iStockphoto.com.

Chapter 12

Chapter opening photo: © 2009 Jupiterimages Corporation.

Photo spread: © 2009 Jupiterimages Corporation; © Youssouf Cader/iStockphoto.com; © Steve Cole/iStockphoto.com.

Photo on p. 311 Photograph by Anna Giannoble.

Ad 12.1 Newcomer, Morris, and Young Advertising Agency.

Photo on p. 318 © Dmitriy Shironosov/iStockphoto.com.

Figure 12.6 Adapted from "Use of Logistics Information by Department," *2002 Report on Trends and Issues in Logistics and Transportation* (Cap Gemini Ernst & Young, Georgia Southern University, 2002).

Photo on p. 323 © Baloncici/iStockphoto.com.

Table 12.4 Adapted from "Inventory Investment: Inventory Levels Drop 10 Percent or More with Optimization Software," *Controller's Report,* Vol. 2008, No. 8 (August 2008), pp. 9–12.

Figure 12.7 Adapted from "Transportation Services Overview," *U.S. Industry Quarterly Review: Transportation and Logistics* (2006), pp. 135–137.

Photo on p. 327 © Wendell Franks/iStockphoto.com.

Photo on p. 329 © Tony Tremblay/iStockphoto.com.

Figure 12.8 Adapted from Curt Barry, "Keeping DC Costs at Bay," *Multichannel Merchant,* Vol. 4, No. 4 (April 2008), pp. 1, 45.

Table 12.5 Adapted from Curt Barry, "Keeping DC Costs at Bay," *Multichannel Merchant,* Vol. 4, No. 4 (April 2008), pp. 1, 45.

Photo on p. 335 © 2009 Jupiterimages Corporation.

Photo on p. 337 © fotoIE/iStockphoto.com.

Chapter 13

Chapter opening photo: © Andy Dean/iStockphoto.com.

Photo spread: © 2009 Jupiterimages Corporation; © 2009 Jupiterimages Corporation; © Tom Gufler/iStockphoto.com.

Photo on p. 341 © Rebecca Ellis/iStockphoto.com.

Photo on p. 345 © Daniel Timiraos/iStockphoto.com.

Photo on p. 351 © Renee Lee/iStockphoto.com.

Photo on p. 352 © Lise Gagne/iStockphoto.com.

Figure 13.9 Adapted from "2008 Marketing Fact Book," *Marketing News,* Vol. 42, No. 12 (July 15, 2008), p. 22.

Photo on p. 354 © Chris Bernard/iStockphoto.com.

Photo on p. 357 Used with permission of Vijay Shankar.

Photo on p. 359 © starfotograf/iStockphoto.com.

Photo on p. 361 © Kevin Russ/iStockphoto.com.

Chapter 14

Chapter opening photo: © Sieto Verver/iStockphoto.com.

Photo spread:© Christoph Ermel/iStockphoto.com; © György Hepka/iStockphoto.com; © 2009 Jupiterimages Corporation.

Photo on p. 371 © Damir Spanic/iStockphoto.com.

Photo on p. 372 © Lisa F. Young/iStockphoto.com.

Table 14.1 Adapted from Roger E. Best, *Marketing Management* (Upper Saddle River, NJ: Pearson, 2005), pp. 8–12.

Photo on p. 378 © Juanmonino/iStockphoto.com.

Photo on p. 379 © Edward Bock/iStockphoto.com.

Photo on p. 381 © Donald Gruener/iStockphoto.com.

Figure 14.11 Adapted from John Goodman, "Quantifying the Impact of Customer Service on Profitability," *Best Practices in Customer Service* (New York: HRD Press, 1998), pp. 17–29.

Figure 14.12 Adapted from John Goodman, "Quantifying the Impact of Customer Service on Profitability," *Best Practices in Customer Service* (New York: HRD Press, 1998), pp. 17–29.

Figure 14.13 Adapted from Ron Zemke, "Service Recovery," *Best Practices in Customer Service* (New York: HRD Press, 1998), pp. 279–288.

Figure 14.14 Adapted from Frederick F. Reichheld and W. Earl Sasser, "Zero Defections: Quality Comes to Services," *Harvard Business Review,* Vol. 68, No. 5 (September/October 1990), pp. 105–111.

Figure 14.15 Adapted from Marc. R. Okrant, "How to Convert 3's and 4"s into 5's," *Marketing News,* Vol. 36 (October 14, 2002), pp. 14–15.

Photo on p. 389 © Lisa F. Young/iStockphoto.com.

Photo on p. 391 © digitalskillet/iStockphoto.com.

Chapter 15

Chapter opening photo: © Jeffrey Smith/iStockphoto.com.

Photo spread: © 2009 Jupiterimages Corporation.

Figure 15.3 Adapted from "Top 10 Liquid Refreshment Beverages," Advertising Age Data Center (New York: TNS Media Intelligence, 2007).

Figure 15.4 Adapted from "Top Beverage Segments," Advertising Age Data Center (New York: TNS Media Intelligence, 2007).

Photo on p. 403 © Lise Gagne/iStockphoto.com.

Photo on p. 405 © Ben Blankenburg/iStockphoto.com.

Table 15.2 Adapted from "Ad to Sales Ratios," The Seattle Times Company (www.seattletimescompany, accessed on March 14, 2007; "U.S. Company Revenue Per 2005 Dollar," Advertising Age Data Center (www.advertisingage.com, accessed on June 13, 2007).

Photo on p. 407 Photograph by Anna Giannoble.

Photo on p. 410 Photograph by Anna Giannoble.

Photo on p. 413 © Quavondo Nguyen/iStockphoto.com.

Photo on p. 415 Photograph by Anna Giannoble.

Photo on p. 419 © 2009 Jupiterimages Corporation.

Photo on p. 421 © 2009 Jupiterimages Corporation.

Appendix B

Case 1 Reprinted with permission from the *Case Research Journal.* Copyright 2006 by Umit Akinc, Jack Meredith, Kirk Nelson, and the North American Case Research Association. All rights reserved.

Case 2 Reprinted with permission from the *Case Research Journal.* Copyright 2002 by John J. Lawrence, Linda J. Morris, Joseph J. Geiger, and the North American Case Research Association. All rights reserved.

Case 3 Reprinted with permission from the *Case Research Journal.* Copyright 2002 by Gordan H. G. McDougall and the North American Case Research Association. All rights reserved.

Case 4 Reprinted with permission from the *Case Research Journal.* Copyright 2006 by John W. O'Neill, Qu Xiao, Anna S. Mattila, and the North American Case Research Association. All rights reserved.

Case 5 Reprinted with permission from the *Case Research Journal.* Copyright 2006 by Kay M. Palan and the North American Case Research Association. All rights reserved.

Case 6 Reprinted with permission from the *Case Research Journal.* Copyright 2006 by David W. Rosenthal and the North American Case Research Association. All rights reserved.

Case 7 Reprinted with permission from the *Case Research Journal.* Copyright 2006 by Susan F. Sieloff, Raymond M. Kinnunen, and the North American Case Research Association. All rights reserved.

Case 8 Reprinted with permission from the *Case Research Journal.* Copyright 2007 by Robert F. Young, Raymond Kinnunen, and the North American Case Research Association. All rights reserved.

Name/Organization Index

Numbers followed by an n refer to a note, which is found at the back of the book.

Subject Index

Supporting researchers for more than 40 years

Research methods have always been at the core of SAGE's publishing program. Founder Sara Miller McCune published SAGE's first methods book, *Public Policy Evaluation*, in 1970. Soon after, she launched the *Quantitative Applications in the Social Sciences* series—affectionately known as the "little green books."

Always at the forefront of developing and supporting new approaches in methods, SAGE published early groundbreaking texts and journals in the fields of qualitative methods and evaluation.

Today, more than 40 years and two million little green books later, SAGE continues to push the boundaries with a growing list of more than 1,200 research methods books, journals, and reference works across the social, behavioral, and health sciences. Its imprints—Pine Forge Press, home of innovative textbooks in sociology, and Corwin, publisher of PreK–12 resources for teachers and administrators—broaden SAGE's range of offerings in methods. SAGE further extended its impact in 2008 when it acquired CQ Press and its best-selling and highly respected political science research methods list.

From qualitative, quantitative, and mixed methods to evaluation, SAGE is the essential resource for academics and practitioners looking for the latest methods by leading scholars.

For more information, visit **www.sagepub.com**.

Marketing Plan

Where theory and knowledge meet application

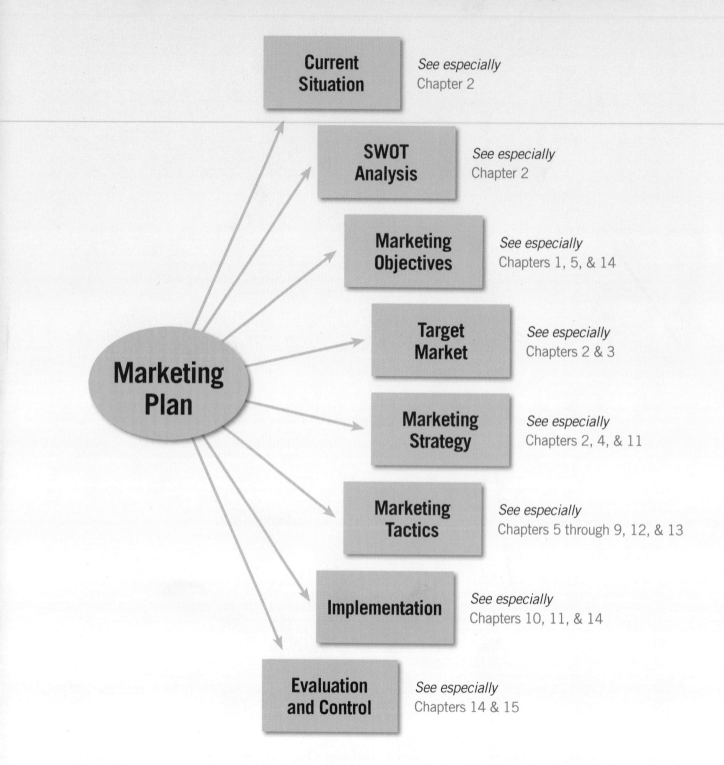

Current Situation — *See especially* Chapter 2

SWOT Analysis — *See especially* Chapter 2

Marketing Objectives — *See especially* Chapters 1, 5, & 14

Marketing Plan

Target Market — *See especially* Chapters 2 & 3

Marketing Strategy — *See especially* Chapters 2, 4, & 11

Marketing Tactics — *See especially* Chapters 5 through 9, 12, & 13

Implementation — *See especially* Chapters 10, 11, & 14

Evaluation and Control — *See especially* Chapters 14 & 15

For information on how to write a marketing plan, see www.sagepub.com/clow.